Human Language Technology Conference

Proceedings of HLT 2001

First International Conference on Human Language Technology Research

http://hlt2001.org

March 18-21, 2001

San Diego, California

Edited by James Allan

Sponsored in part by

 Defense Advanced Research Project Agency

 National Science Foundation

Production and Manufacturing by
Omipress, Inc.
Post Office Box 7214
Madison, WI 53707-7314

Order copies of this and other DARPA publications from:

Morgan Kaufmann Publishers
San Francisco

http://www.mkp.com
orders@mkp.com
800-745-7323 (407-345-3800 for international calls)
(fax) 800-874-6418 (407-345-4060 for international calls)

HLT 2001: Human Language Technology Conference
ISBN: 1-55860-786-2

Preface from the Conference and Program Chair

Human Language Technology 2001 brought together researchers in a broad spectrum of fields, all of whom are working toward enabling computers to better process and use natural language. The HLT Conference was a forum for researchers in those fields to present high-quality, cutting-edge work, and to exchange ideas and explore directions for further research.

In contrast to many conferences that address human language technology, HLT 2001 did not arise out of a single research community or nationality, but was intended to foster communication between areas and across national boundaries. To that end, the program committee and reviewers were selected to span many countries, and to include researchers within information retrieval, natural language processing, linguistics, speech recognition, dialogue processing, human computer interaction, and so on. The interesting mix of submissions and accepted papers indicates that this goal of the conference was accomplished.

HLT 2001 received 176 submissions. The overall quality of submissions was very high and it was difficult for the program committee to choose between the submissions. The final selection was intended to include the highest quality work, to represent a broad spectrum of HLT research, and to prefer work that spanned multiple HLT areas. Of the 176 submissions, 21 were demonstration requests, and 18 were accepted. Of the remaining 155 submissions, 26 (17%) were accepted for presentation in plenary session, and 31 (20%) were accepted for presentation as a poster.

I would like to thank all of the people who helped make this conference successful, but especially the Program Committee for an excellent job of high-speed reviewing, and the Executive Program Committee for working to put together an outstanding set of presentations. I am indebted to Bob Younger, Sally Parker, and Sue Ellen Moore for hosting the reviewing software and for their tireless work setting up the infrastructure at the conference itself. Thanks is also due to DARPA which provided substantial sponsorship of the conference, underwriting the cost of these proceedings as well as logistical support at the conference itself. The NSF also provided support through conference support staff time. The quality of the conference was enhanced by the keynote presentation delivered by Fernando Pereira of Whizbang! Labs, and two guest speakers, Samuel Gustman from the Survivors of the Shoah Visual History Foundation, and Gary Strong of the National Science Foundation.

The idea of HLT 2001 was germinated by Gary Strong and fleshed out by what turned into the HLT Advisory Board. The concepts behind the conference owe a great deal to their valuable insight and advice. I feel a special level of gratitude to one of that group, Eva Kingsbury, who provided incredible logistic support throughout the conference and without whom the conference would probably have collapsed.

Of course, the conference would not have been successful without attendees. 245 people attended this first HLT conference. Of the half who completed surveys about the conference, more than 75% of those thought that the various presentations were "great!", over 97% said that would come to a similar HLT 2002 conference, and all but one person loved the location in San Diego.

Thank you once again to everyone who participated in HLT 2001. It was an exciting event and a successful mingling of human language technology research areas. I hope to see you at a future HLT conference.

James Allan
HLT 2001 Conference and Program Chair
Center for Intelligent Information Retrieval
Department of Computer Science
University of Massachusetts, Amherst

HLT 2001 Conference Organization

Conference and Program Chair
James Allan, Univ. of Massachusetts (USA)

Conference co-Chair
Mitch Marcus, Univ. of Pennsylvania (USA)

Advisory Board
Donna Harman, NIST (USA)
Lynette Hirschman, MITRE (USA)
Eva Kingsbury, CNRI (USA)
Mark Liberman, Univ. of Pennsylvania (USA)
Joseph Mariani, LIMSI-CNRS (France)
Martha Palmer, Univ. of Pennsylvania (USA)
John Prange, ARDA (USA)
Allen Sears, CNRI (USA)
Karen Sparck-Jones, Cambridge Univ. (UK)
Gary Strong, DARPA and NSF (USA)
Charles Wayne, DARPA (USA)

Demonstrations Chairs
Clifford Weinstein, MIT Lincoln Laboratory (USA)
Bob Younger, SPAWAR Systems Center (USA)

Conference Administration
Alvaro Bolivar, Univ. of Massachusetts (USA)
André Gauthier, Univ. of Massachusetts (USA)
Eva Kingsbury, CNRI (USA)
Gino Orezzoli, DSIC (USA)

Local Arrangements
Bob Younger, SPAWAR Systems Center (USA)
Sue Ellen Moore, SPAWAR Systems Center (USA)
Sally Parker, SPAWAR Systems Center (USA)

HLT 2001 Executive Program Committee

Rob Gaizauskas, Sheffield Univ. (UK)
Jean-Luc Gauvain, LIMSI-CNRS (France)
Marti Hearst, U. California, Berkeley (USA)
Eduard Hovy, ISI (USA)
David D. Lewis, Independent Consultant (USA)
Kathleen McKeown, Columbia Univ. (USA)

Mari Ostendorf, Univ. of Washington (USA)
Junichi Tsujii, Univ. of Tokyo (Japan)
and UMIST (UK)
Alex Waibel, Carnegie Mellon Univ. (USA)
Ross Wilkinson, CSIRO (Australia)

HLT 2001 Program Committee

Chris Atkeson, CMU (USA)
Roberto Basili, Univ. of Roma Tor Vergata
(Italy)
Rik Belew, UC San Diego (USA)
Lou Boves, Univ. of Nijmegen (Netherlands)
Peter Bruza, Distributed Systems Technology
Centre (Australia)
Rolf Carlson, KTH (Sweden)
Yves Chiaramella, Federation IMAG (France)
Key-Sun Choi, KAIST (Korea)
Bruce Croft, Univ. of Massachusetts (USA)
Mary Czerwinski, Microsoft (USA)
Walter Daelemans, Univ. of Antwerp (Belgium)
and Tilburg Univ. (Netherlands)
Morena Danieli, Loquendo - Telecom Italia Lab
(Italy)
Sadaoki Furui, Tokyo Inst. of Tech. (Japan)
James R. Glass, MIT Lab. for Comp. Science
(USA)
Ralph Grishman, New York Univ. (USA)
Sanda Harabagiu, SMU (USA)
Vasilis Hatzivassiloglou, Columbia Univ. (USA)
Hitoshi Iida, Sony (Japan)
Pierre Isabelle, Xerox Research Centre Europe
(France)
Hiroyuki Kaji, Hitachi (Japan)
Katrin Kirchhoff, Univ. of Washington (USA)
Alon Lavie, Carnegie Mellon Univ. (USA)
Lori Lamel, LIMSI-CNRS (France)
Gianni Lazzari, IRST (Italy)
Esther Levin, AT&T Labs Research (USA)
Lori Levin, Carnegie Mellon Univ. (USA)
Mike Macon, OGI (USA)
Inderjeet Mani, MITRE (USA)
Andrew McCallum, WhizBang! Laboratories
(USA)
Marc Moens, Univ. of Edinburgh (UK)

Sung Hyon Myaeng, Chungnam National Univ.
(Korea)
Herman Ney, Aachen Univ. of Technology
(Germany)
Douglas W. Oard, Univ. of Maryland (USA)
Wanda Pratt, Univ. of California, Irvine (USA)
Dragomir Radev, Univ. of Michigan (USA)
Steve Renals, Sheffield Univ. (UK)
Owen Rambow, AT&T Labs Research (USA)
Jan van Santen, OGI (USA)
Tanja Schultz, Carnegie Mellon Univ. (USA)
Donia Scott
Amy Steier, Independent consultant (USA)
Andreas Stolcke, SRI International (USA)
Keh-Yih Su, Behavior Design Corp. (Taiwan)
Takenobu Tokunaga, Tokyo Inst. of Tech.
(Japan)
Ellen Voorhees, NIST (USA)
Marilyn Walker AT&T Labs Research (USA)
Steve Whittaker, AT&T Labs Research (USA)
Jie Yang, Carnegie Mellon Univ. (USA)
David Yarowsky, Johns Hopkins Univ. (USA)

Additional reviewers

Enrico Bocchieri AT&T Labs Research (USA)
Jamie Callan, Carnegie Mellon Univ. (USA)
Marcello Federico, IRST (Italy)
Robert McArthur, Distributed Systems
Technology Centre (Australia)
Franz-Josef Och, Aachen Univ. of Technology
(Germany)
Fabio Pianesi, IRST (Italy)
Ananth Sankar, Nuance Communications (USA)
Dawei Song, Distributed Systems Technology
Centre (Australia)
Jianqiang Wang, Univ. of Maryland (USA)

TABLE OF CONTENTS

Activity detection for information access to oral communication

Klaus Ries and Alex Waibel*
{ries|ahw}@cs.cmu.edu
Interactive Systems Labs, Carnegie Mellon University, Pittsburgh, PA, 15213, USA
Interactive Systems Labs, Universität Karlsruhe, Fakultät für Informatik, 76128 Karlsruhe, Germany
http://www.is.cs.cmu.edu/   http://werner.ira.uka.de

ABSTRACT

Oral communication is ubiquitous and carries important information yet it is also time consuming to document. Given the development of storage media and networks one could just record and store a conversation for documentation. The question is, however, how an interesting information piece would be found in a large database. Traditional information retrieval techniques use a histogram of keywords as the document representation but oral communication may offer additional indices such as the time and place of the rejoinder and the attendance. An alternative index could be the activity such as discussing, planning, informing, story-telling, etc. This paper addresses the problem of the automatic detection of those activities in meeting situation and everyday rejoinders. Several extensions of this basic idea are being discussed and/or evaluated: Similar to activities one can define subsets of larger database and detect those automatically which is shown on a large database of TV shows. Emotions and other indices such as the dominance distribution of speakers might be available on the surface and could be used directly. Despite the small size of the databases used some results about the effectiveness of these indices can be obtained.

Keywords

activity, dialogue processing, oral communication, speech, information access

*We would like to thank our lab, especially Klaus Zechner, Alon Lavie and Lori Levin for their discussions and support. We would also like to thank our sponsors at DARPA. Any opinions, findings and conclusions expressed in this material are those of the authors and may not reflect the views of DARPA, or any other party.

Proceedings of HLT 2001, First International Conference on Human Language Technology Research, J. Allan, ed., Morgan Kaufmann, San Francisco, 2001.

1. INTRODUCTION

Information access to oral communication is becoming an interesting research area since recording, storing and transmitting large amounts of audio (and video) data is feasible today. While written information is often available electronically (especially since it is typically entered on computers) oral communication is usually only documented by constructing a new document in written form such as a transcript (court proceedings) or minutes (meetings). Oral communications are therefore a large untapped resource, especially if no corresponding written documents are available and the cost of documentation using traditional techniques is considered high: Tutorial introductions by a senior staff member might be worthwhile to attend by many newcomers, office meetings may contain informations relevant for others and should be reproducable, informal and formal group meetings may be interesting but not fully documented. In essence the written form is already a reinterpretation of the original rejoinder. Such a reinterpretation are used to

- extract and condense information
- add or delete information
- change the meaning
- cite the rejoinder
- relate rejoinders to each other

Reinterpretation is a time consuming, expensive and optional step and written documentation is combining reinterpretation and documentation step in one [1]. If however reinterpretation is not necessary or unwanted a system which is producing audiovisual records is superior. If reinterpretation is wanted or needed a system using audiovisual records may be used to improve the reinterpretation by adding all audiovisual data and the option to go back to the unaltered original. Whether reinterpretation is done or not it is crucial to be able to navigate effectively within an audiovisual document and to find a specific document.

[1] The most important exception is the literal courtroom transcript, however one could argue that even transcripts are reinterpretations since they do not contain a number of informations present in the audio channel such as emotions, hesitations, the use of slang and certain types of heteroglossia, accents and so forth. This is specifically true if transcription machines are used which restrict the transcriber to standard orthography.

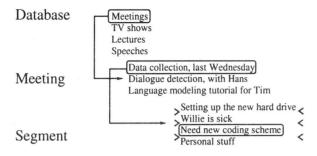

Figure 1: Information access hierarchy: Oral communications take place in very different formats and the first step in the search is to determine the database (or sub-database) of the rejoinder. The next step is to find the specific rejoinder. Since rejoinders can be very long the rejoinder has to segmented and a segment has to be selected.

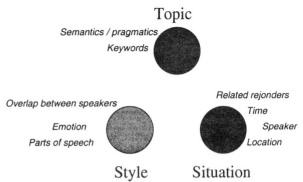

Figure 2: Bahktin's characterization of dialogue: Bahktin (1986) describes a discourse along the three major properties style, situation and topic. Current information retrieval systems focus on the topical aspect which might be crucial in written documents. Furthermore, since throughout text analysis is still a hard problem, information retrieval has mostly used keywords to characterize topic. Many features that could be extracted are therefore ignored in a traditional keyword based approach.

While keywords are commonly used in information access to written information the use of other indices such as style is still uncommon (but see Kessler et al. (1997); van Bretan et al. (1998)). Oral communication is richer than written communication since it is an interactive real time accomplishment between participants, may involve speech gestures such as the display of emotion and is situated in space and time. Bahktin (1986) characterizes a conversation by topic, situation and style. Information access to oral communication can therefore make use of indices that pertain to the oral nature of the discourse (Fig. 2). Indices other than topic (represented by keywords) increase in importance since browsing audio documents is cumbersome which makes the common interactive retrieval strategy "query, browse, reformulate" less effective. Finally the topic may not be known at all or may not be that relevant for the query formulation, for example if one just wants to be reminded what was being discussed last time a person was met. Activities are suggested as an alternative index and are a description of the type of interaction. It is common to use "action-verbs" such as story-telling, discussing, planning, informing, etc. to describe activities [2]. Items similar to activities have been shown to be directly retrievable from autobiographic memory (Herrmann, 1993) and are therefore indices that are available to participants of the conversation. Other indices may be very effective but not available: The frequency of the word "I" in the conversation, the histogram of word lengths or the histogram of pitch per participant.

In Fig. 1 the information access hierarchy is being introduced which allows to understand the problem of information access to oral communication at different levels. In Ries (1999) we have shown that the detection of general di-

alogue genre (database level in Fig. 1) can be done with high accuracy if a number of different example types have been annotated; in Ries et al. (2000) we have shown that it is hard but not impossible to distinguish activities in personal phone calls (segment level in Fig. 1) . In this paper we will address activities in meetings and other types of dialogues and show that these activities can be distinguished using certain features and a neural network based classifier (Sec. 2, segment level in Fig. 1). The concept of information retrieval assessment using information theoretic measures is applied to this task (Sec. 3). Additionally we will introduce a level somewhat below the database level in Fig. 1 that we call "sub-genre" and we have collected a large database of TV-shows that are automatically classified for their show-type (Sec. 4). We also explore whether there are other indices similar to activities that could be used and we are presenting results on emotions in meetings (Sec. 5).

2. ACTIVITY DETECTION

We are interested in the detection of activities that are described by action verbs and have annotated those in two databases:

meetings have been collected at Interactive Systems Labs at CMU (Waibel et al., 1998) and a subset of 8 meetings has been annotated. Most of the meetings are by the data annotation group itself and are fairly informal in style. The participants are often well acquainted and meet each other a lot besides their meetings.

Santa Barbara (SBC) is a corpus released by the LDC and 7 out of 12 rejoinders have been annotated.

The annotator has been instructed to segment the rejoinders into units that are coherent with respect to their topic

---

[2] The definition of activities such as planning may vary vastly across general dialogue genres, for example compare a military combat situation with a mother child interaction. However it is often possible to develop activities and dialogue typologies for a specific dialogue genre. The related problem of general typologies of dialogues is still far from being settled and action-verbs are just one potential categorization (Fritz and Hundschnur, 1994).

Activity	SBC	Meeting
Discussion	35	58
Information	25	23
Story-telling	24	10
Planning	7	19
Undetermined	5	8
Advising	5	17
Not meeting	3	2
Interrogation	2	1
Evaluation	1	0
Introduction	0	1
Closing	0	1

Table 1: Distribution of activity types: Both databases contain a lot of discussing, informing and story-telling activities however the meeting data contains a lot more planning and advising.

Feature	all		interactive	
	SBC	meet	SBC	meet
baseline	32.7	41.1	50.5	54.6
dialogue acts per channel	28.1	37.6	47.7	56.7
dialogue acts	28.0	36.2	46.7	65.3
words	38.3	39.7	53.3	54.6
dominance	32.7	44.7	64.5	58.2
style	24.3	35.5	53.3	58.9
style + words	42.1	38.3	52.3	57.5
dominance + words	41.1	41.1	52.3	58.9
dominance + style + words	42.1	39.7	53.3	60.3
dialogue acts + words	42.1	37.6	57.0	61.0
dialogue acts + style + words	39.3	40.4	57.9	61.0
Wordnet	37.4	37.6	46.7	52.5
Wordnet + words	49.5	39.0	53.3	57.5
first author	59.8	57.9	73.8	72.7

Table 3: Activity detection: Activities are detected on the Santa Barbara Corpus (SBC) and the meeting database (meet) either without clustering the activities (all) or clustering them according to their interactivity (interactive) (see Sec. 2 for details).

and activity and annotate them with an activity which follows the intuitive definition of the action-verb such as discussing, planning, etc. Additionally an activity annotation manual containing more specific instructions has been available (Ries et al., 2000; Thymé-Gobbel et al., 2001) [3]. The list of tags and the distribution can be seen in Tab. 1. The set of activities can be clustered into "interactive" activities of equal contribution rights (discussion,planning), one person being active (advising, information giving, story-telling), interrogations and all others.

Measure	Meeting		SBC		CallHome
	all	inter	all	inter	Spanish
κ	0.41	0.51	0.49	0.56	0.59
Mutual inf.	0.35	0.25	0.65	0.32	0.61

Table 2: Intercoder agreement for activities: The meeting dialogues and Santa Barbara corpus have been annotated by a semi-naive coder and the first author of the paper. The κ-coefficient is determined as in Carletta et al. (1997) and mutual information measures how much one label "informs" the other (see Sec. 3). For CallHome Spanish 3 dialogues were coded for activities by two coders and the result seems to indicate that the task was easier.

Both datasets have been annotated not only by a semi-naive annotator but also by the first author of the paper. The results for κ-statistics (Carletta et al., 1997) and mutual information between the coders can be seen in Tab. 2. The intercoder agreement would be considered moderate but compares approximately to Carletta et al. (1997) agreement on transactions ($\kappa = 0.59$), especially for the interactive activities and CallHome Spanish.

For classification a neural network was trained that uses the softmax function as its output and KL-divergence as the error function. The network connects the input directly to the output units. Hidden units have not been used since they did not yield improvements on this task. The network was trained using RPROP with momentum (Riedmiller and Braun, 1993) and corresponds to an exponential model (Nigam et al., 1999). The momentum term can be interpreted as a Gaussian prior with zero mean on the network weights. It is the same architecture that we used previously (Ries et al., 2000) for the detection of activities on CallHome Spanish. Although some feature sets could be trained using the iterative scaling algorithm if no hidden units are being used the training times weren't high enough to justify the use of the less flexible iterative scaling algorithm. The features used for classification are

words the 50 most frequent words / part of speech pairs are used directly, all other pairs are replaced by their part of speech [4].

stylistic features adapted from Biber (1988) and contain mostly syntactic constructions and some word classes.

Wordnet a total of 40 verb and noun classes (so called lexicographers classes (Fellbaum, 1998)) are defined and a word is replaced by the most frequent class over all possible meanings of the word.

dialogue acts such as statements, questions, backchannels, ... are detected using a language model based detector trained on Switchboard similar to Stolcke et al. (2000) [5]

---

[3] In contrast to (Ries et al., 2000; Thymé-Gobbel et al., 2001) the "consoling" activity has been eliminated and an "informing" activity has been introduced for segments where one or more than one member of the rejoinder give information to the others. Additionally an "introducing" activity was added to account for a introduction of people or topics at the beginning of meetings.

[4] Klaus Zechner trained an English part of speech tagger tagger on Switchboard that has been used. The tagger uses the code by Brill (1994).
[5] The model was trained to be very portable and therefore the following choices were taken: (a) the dialogue model is context-independent and (b) only the part of speech are taken as the input to the model plus the 50 most likely word/part of speech types.

dominance is described as the distribution of the speaker dominance in a conversation. The distribution is represented as a histogram and speaker dominance is measured as the average dominance of the dialogue acts (Linell et al., 1988) of each speaker. The dialogue acts are detected and the dominance is a numeric value assigned for each dialogue act type. Dialogue act types that restrict the options of the conversation partners have high dominance (questions), dialogue acts that signal understanding (backchannels) carry low dominance.

First author The activities used for classification are those of the semi-naive coder. The "first author" column describes the "accuracy" of the first author with respect to the naive coder.

The detection of interactive activities works fairly well using the dominance feature on SBC which is also natural since the relative dominance of speakers should describe what kind of interaction is exhibited. The dialogue act distribution on the other hand works fairly well on the more homogeneous meeting database were there is a better chance to see generalizations from more specific dialogue based information. Overall the combination of more than one feature is really important since word level, Wordnet and stylistic information, while sometimes successful, seem to be able to improve the result while they don't provide good features by themselves. The meeting data is also more difficult which might be due to its informal style.

3. INFORMATION ACCESS ASSESSMENT

Assuming a probabilistic information retrieval model a query r – in our example an activity – predicts a document d with the probability $q(d|r) = \frac{q(r|d)q(d)}{q(r)}$. Let $p(d,r)$ be the real probability mass distribution of these quantities. The probability mass function $q(r|d)$ is estimated on a separate training set by a neural network based classifier [6]. The quantity we are interested in is the reduction in expected coding length of the document using the neural network based detector [7]:

$$-E_p \log \frac{q(D)}{q(D|R)} \approx H(R) - E_p \log \frac{1}{q(R|D)}$$

The two expectations correspond exactly to the measures in Tab. 5, the first represents the baseline, the second the one for the respective classifier. In more standard information theoretic notation this quantity may be written as:

$$H(R) - (H_p(R|D) + D(p(r|d)||q(r|d)))$$

This equivalence is not extremely useful though since the quantities in parenthesis can't be estimated separately. For the small meeting database and SBC however no entropy reductions could be obtained. On the larger databases, on the other hand, entropy reductions could be obtained ($\approx$ 0.5bit on the CallHome Spanish database Ries et al. (2000), $\approx$ 1bit for the sub-database detection problem in Sec. 4).

---

[6]All quantities involving the neural net $q(r|d)$ have been determined using a round robin approach such that network is trained on a separate training set.

[7]Since estimating $q(d)$ is simple we may assume that $q(d) \approx \sum_r p(d,r)$.

Another option is to assume that the labels of one coder are part of D. If the query by the other coder is R we are interested in the reduction of the document entropy given the query. If we furthermore assume that $H(R|D) = H(R|R')$ where R' is the activity label embedded in D:

$$H(D) - H(D|R) = H(R) - H(R|D) = MI(R, R')$$

Tab. 2 shows that the labels of the semi-naive coder and the first author only inform each other by $0.25 - 0.65$ bits. However, since all constraints are important to apply, it might be important to include manual annotations to be matched by a query or in a graphical presentation of the output results.

Another interesting question to consider is whether the activity is correlated with the rejoinder or not. This question is important since a correlation of the activity with the rejoinder would mean that the indexing performance of activities needs to be compared to other indices that apply to rejoinders such as attendance, time and place (for results on the correlation with rejoinders see Waibel et al. (2001)). The correlation can be measured using the mutual information between the activity and the meeting identity. The mutual information is moderate for SBC (≈ 0.67 bit) and much lower for the meetings (≈ 0.20 bit). This also corresponds to our intuition since some of the rejoinders in SBC belong to very distinct dialogue genre while the meeting database is homogeneous. The conclusion is that activities are useful for navigation in a rejoinder if the database is homogeneous and they might be useful for finding conversations in a more heterogeneous database.

	#		#		#
Talk	344	Edu	25	Finance	8
News	217	Scifi	24	Religious	5
Sitcom	97	Series	24	Series-Old	3
Soap	87	Cartoon	23	Infotain	3
Game	46	Movies	22	Music	2
Law	32	Crafts	17	Horror	1
Sports	32	Specials	15		
Drama	31	Comedy	9		

Table 4: TV show types: The distribution of show types in a large database of TV shows (1067 shows) that has been recorded over the period of a couple of months until April 2000 in Pittsburgh, PA

4. DETECTION OF SUB-DATABASES

We set up an environment for TV shows that records the subtitles with timestamps continuously from one TV channel and the channel was switched every other day. At the same time the TV program was downloaded from http://tv.yahoo.com/ to obtain programming information including the genre of the show. Yahoo assigns primary and secondary show types and unless the combination of primary/secondary show-type is frequent enough the primary showtype is used (Tab. 4). The TV show database has the advantage that we were able to collect a large and varied database with little effort. The same classifier as in Sec. 2 has been used however dialogue acts have not been detected since the data contains a lot of noise, is not necessarily conversational and speaker identities can't be determined easily. Detection results for TV shows can be seen in Tab. 5. It may be noted that adding a lot of keywords does improve the detection result but not so much the entropy. It may therefore be assume that there is a limited dependence between topic and genre which isn't really a surprise since there are many shows with weekly sequels and there may be some true repeats.

Feature			accuracy	entropy
Wordnet	stylistic	words		
baseline			32.2	3.31
	•		50.9	2.73
	•	50	62.2	2.33
•	•	50	60.0	2.29
•	•		61.2	2.28
•			56.9	2.41
•		50	61.5	2.25
		50	61.3	2.35
		250	62.7	2.17
		500	66.0	2.14
•	•	500	64.9	2.13
		5000	67.2	2.08

Table 5: Show type detection: Using the neural network described in Sec. 2 the show type was detected. If there is a number in the word column the word feature is being used. The number indicates how many word/part of speech pairs are in the vocabulary additionally to the parts of speech.

5. EMOTION AND DOMINANCE

Emotions are displayed in a variety of gestures, some of which are oral and may be detected via automated methods from the audio channel (Polzin, 1999). Using only verbal information the emotions happy, excited and neutral can be detected on the meeting database with 88.1% accuracy while always picking neutral yields 83.6%. This result can be improved to 88.6% by adding pitch and power information.

While these experiments were conducted at the utterance level emotions can be extended to topical segments. For that purpose the emotions of the individual utterances are entered in a histogram over the segment and the vectors are clustered automatically. The resulting clusters roughly correspond to a "neutral", "a little happy" and "somewhat excited" segment. Using the classifier for emotions on the word level the segment can be classified automatically into categories with a 83.3% accuracy while the baseline is 68.9%. The entropy reduction by automatically detected emotional activities is ≈ 0.3bit [8]. A similar attempt can be made for dominance (Linell et al., 1988) distributions: Dominance is easy to understand for the user of an information access system and it can be determined automatically with high accuracy.

---
[8] A similar classification result for emotions on the utterance level has been obtained by just using the laughter vs. non-laughter tokens of the transcript as the input. This may indicate that (a) the index should really be the amount of laughter in the conversational segment and that (b) emotions might not be displayed very overtly in meetings. These results however would require a wider sampling of meeting types to be generally acceptable.

6. CONCLUSION AND FUTURE WORK

It has been shown that activities can be detected and that they may be efficient indices for access to oral communication. Overall it is easy to make high level distinctions with automated methods while fine-grained distinctions are even hard to make for humans – on the other hand automatic methods are still able to model some aspect of it (Fig. 3). To obtain an reduction in entropy a relatively large database such as CallHome Spanish is required (120 dialogues). Alternatives to activities might be emotional and dominance distributions that are easier to detect and that may be natural to understand for users. If activities are only used for local navigation support within a rejoinder one could also visualize by displaying the dialogue act patterns for each channel on a time line.

The author has also observed that topic clusters and activities are largely independent in the meeting domain resulting in orthogonal indices. Since activities have intuitions for naive users and they may be remembered it can be assumed that users would be able to make use of these constraints. Ongoing work includes the use of speaker activity for dialogue segmentation and further assessment of features for information access. Overall the methods presented here and the ongoing work are improving the ability to index oral communication. It should be noted that some of the techniques presented lend themselves to implementations that don't require (full) speech recognition: Speaker identification and dialogue act identification may be done without an LVCSR system which would allow to lower the computational requirements as well as to a more robust system.

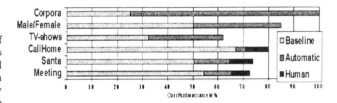

Figure 3: Detection accuracy summary: The detection of high-level genre as exemplified by the differentiation of corpora can be done with high accuracy using simple features (Ries, 1999). Similar it was fairly easy to discriminate between male and female speakers on Switchboard (Ries, 1999). Discriminating between sub-genre such as TV-show types (Sec. 4) can be done with reasonable accuracy. However it is a lot harder to discriminate between activities within one conversation for personal phone calls (CallHome) (Ries et al., 2000) or for general rejoinders (Santa) and meetings (Sec. 2).

References

M. M. Bahktin. *Speech Genres and other late Essays*, chapter Speech Genres. University of Texas Press, Austin, 1986.

D. Biber. *Variation across speech and writing*. Cambridge University Press, 1988.

E. Brill. A report on recent progress in transformation based error-driven learning. In *DARPA Workshop*, 1994.

J. Carletta, A. Isard, S. Isard, J. C. Kowtko, G. Doherty-Sneddon, and A. H. Anderson. The reliability of a dialogue structure coding scheme. *Computational Linguistics*, 23(1):13–31, March 1997.

C. Fellbaum, editor. *WordNet – An Electronic Lexical Database*. MIT press, 1998.

G. Fritz and F. Hundschnur. *Handbuch der Dialoganalyse*. Niemeyer, Tuebingen, 1994.

D. J. Herrmann. *Autobiographical memory and the validity of retrospective reports*, chapter The validity of retrospective reports as a function of the directness of retrieval processes, pages 21–31. Springer, 1993.

B. Kessler, G. Nunberg, and H. Schütze. Automatic detection of genre. In *Proceedings of the 35th Annual Meeting of the Association for Computational Linguistics and the 8th Meeting of the European Chapter of the Association for Computational Linguistics*, pages 32–38. Morgan Kaufmann Publishers, San Francisco CA, 1997. URL http://xxx.lanl.gov/abs/cmp-lg/9707002.

P. Linell, L. Gustavsson, and P. Juvonen. Interactional dominance in dyadic communication: a presentation of initiative-response analysis. *Linguistics*, 26:415–442, 1988.

K. Nigam, J. Lafferty, and A. McCallum. Using maximum entropy for text classification. In *Proceedings of the IJCAI-99 Workshop on Machine Learning for Information Filtering*, 1999. URL http://www.cs.cmu.edu/~lafferty/.

T. Polzin. *Detecting Verbal and Non-Verbal Cues in the Communication of Emotion*. PhD thesis, Carnegie Mellon University, November 1999.

M. Riedmiller and H. Braun. A direct adaptive method for faster backpropagation learning: The RPROP algorithm. In *Proc. of the IEEE Int. Conf. on Neural Networks*, pages 586–591, 1993.

K. Ries. Towards the detection and description of textual meaning indicators in spontaneous conversations. In *Proceedings of the Eurospeech*, volume 3, pages 1415–1418, Budapest, Hungary, September 1999.

K. Ries, L. Levin, L. Valle, A. Lavie, and A. Waibel. Shallow discourse genre annotation in callhome spanish. In *Proceecings of the International Conference on Language Ressources and Evaluation (LREC-2000)*, Athens, Greece, May 2000.

A. Stolcke, K. Ries, N. Coccaro, E. Shriberg, R. Bates, D. Jurafsky, P. Taylor, R. Martin, C. V. Ess-Dykema, and M. Meteer. Dialogue act modeling for automatic tagging and recognition of conversational speech. *Computational Linguistics*, 26(3), September 2000.

A. Thymé-Gobbel, L. Levin, K. Ries, and L. Valle. Dialogue act, dialogue game, and activity tagging manual for spanish conversational speech. Technical report, Carnegie Mellon University, 2001. in preperation.

van Bretan, J. Dewe, A. Hallberg, J. Karlgren, and N. Wolkert. Genres defined for a purpose, fast clustering, and an iterative information retrieval interface. In *Eighth DELOS Workshop on User Interfaces in Digital Libraries Långholmen*, pages 60–66, October 1998.

A. Waibel, M. Bett, and M. Finke. Meeting browser: Tracking and summarising meetings. In *Proceedings of the DARPA Broadcast News Workshop*, 1998.

A. Waibel, M. Bett, F. Metze, K. Ries, T. Schaaf, T. Schultz, H. Soltau, H. Yu, and K. Zechner. Advances in automatic meeting record creation and access. In *ICASSP*, Salt Lake City, Utah, USA, 2001. to appear.

Adapting an Example-Based Translation System to Chinese

Ying Zhang, Ralf D. Brown, and Robert E. Frederking
Language Technologies Institute, Carnegie Mellon University
5000 Forbes Avenue
Pittsburgh, PA 15213-3890 USA
{joy,ralf,ref}@cs.cmu.edu

ABSTRACT

We describe an Example-Based Machine Translation (EBMT) system and the adaptations and enhancements made to create a Chinese-English translation system from the Hong Kong legal code and various other bilingual resources available from the Linguistic Data Consortium (LDC).

1. BACKGROUND

We describe an Example-Based Machine Translation (EBMT) system and the adaptations and enhancements made to create a Chinese-English translation system from the Hong Kong legal code and various other bilingual resources available from the Linguistic Data Consortium (LDC).

The EBMT software [1, 3] used for the experiments described here is a shallow system which can function using nothing more than sentence-aligned plaintext and a bilingual dictionary; and given sufficient parallel text, the dictionary can be extracted statistically from the corpus [2]. To perform a translation, the program looks up all matching phrases in the source-language half of the parallel corpus and performs a word-level alignment on the entries containing matches to determine a (usually partial) translation. Portions of the input for which there are no matches in the corpus do not generate a translation.

Because the EBMT system does not generate translations for 100% of the text it is given as input, a bilingual dictionary and phrasal glossary are used to fill any gaps. Selection of a "best" translation is guided by a trigram model of the target language [6].

Supporting Chinese required a number of changes to the program and training procedures; those changes are discussed in the next section.

2. ENHANCEMENTS

The first change required of the translation software was support for the two-byte encoding used for the Chinese text (GB-2312, "GB" for short). Further, the EBMT (as well as dictionary and glossary) approaches are word-based, but Chinese is ordinarily written without breaks between words. Thus, Chinese input must be segmented into individual words. The initial baseline system used the segmenter made available by the LDC. This segmenter uses a word-frequency list to make segmentation decisions, but although the list provided by the LDC is large, it did not completely cover the vocabulary of the EBMT training corpus (described below). As a result, many sentences had incorrect segmentations or included long sequences which were not segmented at all or were broken into single characters. Almost every Chinese character has at least one meaning, and its meaning may be entirely different from the meaning of the word containing it. The mis-segmenting of Chinese words due to the inadequate dictionary makes it very hard to build a statistical dictionary and properly index the EBMT corpus.

To improve the performance of the Chinese segmenter, we augmented its word list by finding sequences of characters in the training corpus that belong together, based on their frequency and high mutual information. We developed a form of term extraction to find English phrases which should be treated as atomic units for translation, thus increasing the average length of "words" in both source and target languages. Finally, we also created an augmented bilingual dictionary for use in word-level alignment for EBMT by applying statistical dictionary extraction techniques to the training corpus.

As the improved segmenter and the term finder may be producing excessively long phrases or phrases which are impossible to match in the other language, we repeat the procedure of segmenting/bracketing/dictionary-building several times. On each successive iteration, the segmenter and bracketer are limited to words and phrases for which the statistical dictionary from the previous iteration contains translations. Through this iteration, we increased the size of the statistical dictionary from each step and guaranteed that all Chinese words generated by the segmenter have translations in the dictionary. This helps ensure that the EBMT engine can perform word-level alignments.

3. EXPERIMENTAL DESIGN

The primary purpose of this experiment was to determine the effect of each enhancement by operating with various subsets of the enhancements. Since it rapidly becomes impractical to test all possible combinations, we opted for the following test conditions:

1. baseline: parallel corpus segmented with the LDC segmenter and LDC dictionary/glossary
2. baseline plus improved segmenter
3. baseline plus improved segmenter and term finder
4. baseline plus improved segmenter and statistical dictionary
5. baseline plus improved segmenter, term finder, and statistical dictionary

Proceedings of HLT 2001, First International Conference on Human Language Technology Research, J. Allan, ed., Morgan Kaufmann, San Francisco, 2001.

7

For training, we had available two parallel Chinese-English corpora distributed by the LDC: the complete Hong Kong legal code (after cleaning: 47.86 megabytes, 5.5 million English words, 9 million Chinese characters) where 85% of the content (by sentence) is unique, and a collection of Hong Kong news articles (after cleaning: 24.58 megabytes, 2.67 million English words, 4.5 million Chinese characters). In addition, LDC distributes a bilingual dictionary/phrasebook, which we also used.

To determine the effects of varying amounts of training data on overall performance, we divided the bilingual training corpus into ten nearly equal slices. Each test condition was then run ten times, each time increasing the number of slices used for training the system. After each training pass, the test sentences were translated and the system's performance evaluated automatically; selected points were then manually evaluated for translation quality.

The automatic performance evaluation measured coverage of the input and average phrase length. Coverage is the percentage of the input text for which a translation is produced by a particular translation method (since the EBMT engine does not generally produce hypotheses that cover every word of input), while average phrase length is a crude indication of translation quality – the longer the phrase that is translated, the more context is incorporated and the less likely it is that the wrong sense will be used in the translation or that (for EBMT) the alignment will be incorrect. Since the dictionary and glossary remain constant for a given test condition, only the EBMT coverage will be presented.

Manual grading of the output was performed using a web-based system with which the graders could assign one of three scores ("Good", "OK", "Bad") in each of two dimensions: grammatical correctness and meaning preservation. This type of quality scoring is commonly used in assessing translation quality, and is used by other TIDES participants. Fifty-two test sentences were translated for each of four points from the automated evaluation and these sets of four alternatives presented to the graders. The four points chosen were the baseline system with 100% of the training corpus, the full system with 20% and 100% training, and the full system trained on a corpus of Hong Kong news text (cross-domain); only four points were selected due to the difficulty and expense of obtaining large numbers of manual quality judgements.

To assess the performance of the system in a different domain, as well as the effect of the trigram language model on the selection of translated fragments for the final translation, we obtained manual judgements for 44 sentences on an additional four test conditions, each trained with the entire available parallel text and tested on Hong Kong news text rather than legal sentences. These points were the cross-domain case (trained on the legal corpus) and three different language models for within-domain training: an English language model derived from the legal corpus, one derived from the news corpus, and a pre-existing model generated from two gigabytes of newswire and broadcast news transcriptions.

4. RESULTS

We discovered that there is a certain amount of synergy between some of the improvements, particularly the term finder and statistical dictionary extraction. Applying the term finder modifies the parallel corpus in such a way that it becomes more difficult for the EBMT engine to find matches which it can align, while adding dictionary entries derived from the modified corpus eliminates that effect. As a result, we will not present the performance results for Test Condition 3 (improved segmenter plus term finder); further, the data for Test Conditions 2 (improved segmenter only) and 4 (improved segmenter plus statistical dictionary) may not accurately reflect the contribution of those two components to the full system

Translating Legal Code

System Training	Baseline 100%	Full 20%	Full 100%	X-Dom 100%
Syntactic	42.31%	54.81%	61.06%	39.42%
Semantic	43.75%	61.54%	64.42%	34.62%

Translating Hong Kong News

Training LangModel	News Legal	News News	News Prior	Legal Legal
Syntactic	45.67%	44.71%	47.60%	34.62%
Semantic	50.00%	50.96%	51.92%	47.12%

Figure 1: Judgements – Acceptable Translations

used for Test Condition 5.

Figure 2 shows the proportion of the words in the test sentences for which the EBMT engine was able to produce a translation, while Figure 3 shows the average number of source-language words per translated fragment. These curves do not increase monotonically because, for performance reasons, the EBMT engine does not attempt to align every occurrence of a phrase, only the N (currently 12) most-recently added ones; as a result, adding more text to the corpus can cause EBMT to ignore matches that successfully align in favor of newer occurrences which it is unable to align.

Examining Figure 3, it is clear that the fifth slice (from 40 to 50%) is much more like the test data than other slices, resulting in longer matches. In general, the closer training and test text are to each other, the longer the phrases they have in common.

Figure 1 summarizes the results of human quality assessments. The "Good" and "OK" judgements were combined into "Acceptable" and the the percentage of "Acceptable" judgements was averaged across sentences and graders. As hoped and expected, the improvements do in fact result not only in better coverage by EBMT, but also in better quality assessments by the human graders. Further, the results on Hong Kong news text show that the choice of language model does have a definite effect on quality. These results also confirm the adage that there is no such thing as too much training text for language modeling, since the model generated from the EBMT corpus was unable to match the performance of the pre-existing model generated from two orders of magnitude more text.

5. CONCLUSIONS AND FUTURE WORK

As seen in Figure 2, the enhancements described here cumulatively provide a 12% absolute improvement in coverage for EBMT translations without requiring any additional knowledge resources. Further, the enhanced coverage does, in fact, result in improved translations, as verified by human judgements. We can also conclude that when we combine words into larger chunks on both sides of the corpus, the possibility of finding larger matches between the source language and the target language increases, which leads to the improvement of the translation quality for EBMT.

We will do further research on the interaction between the improved segmenter, term finder and statistical dictionary builder, utilizing the information provided by the statistical dictionary as feedback for the segmenter and term finder to modify their results. We are also investigating the effects of splitting the EBMT training into multiple sets of topic-specific sentences, automatically separated using clustering techniques.

The relatively low slope of the coverage curve also indicates that the training corpus is sufficiently large. Our prior experience with Spanish (using the UN Multilingual Corpus [5]) and French (using

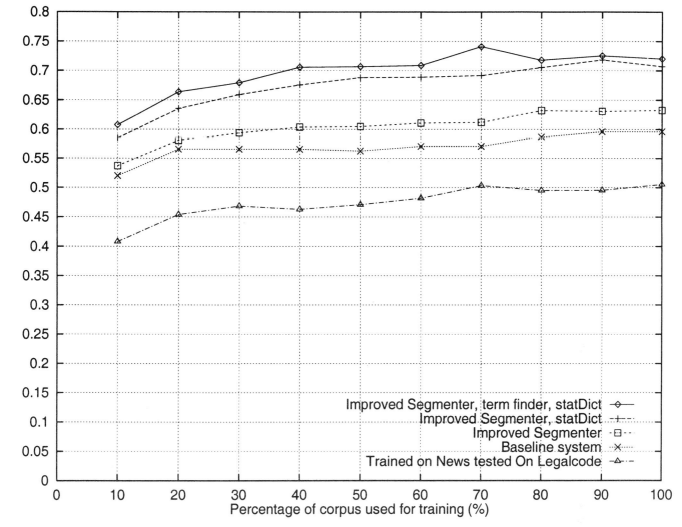

Figure 2: EBMT Coverage with Varying Training

the Hansard corpus [7]) was that the curve flattens out at between two and three million words of training text, which appears also to be the case for Chinese (each training slice contains approximately one million words of total text).

We have not yet taken full advantage of the features of the EBMT software. In particular, it supports equivalence classes that permit generalization of the training text into templates for improved coverage. We intend to test automatic creation of equivalence classes from the training corpus [4] in conjunction with the other improvements reported herein.

6. ACKNOWLEDGEMENTS

We would like to thank Alon Lavie and Lori Levin for their comments on drafts of this paper.

7. REFERENCES

[1] R. D. Brown. Example-Based Machine Translation in the PANGLOSS System. In *Proceedings of the Sixteenth International Conference on Computational Linguistics*, pages 169–174, Copenhagen, Denmark, 1996.
`http://www.cs.cmu.edu/~ralf/papers.html`.

[2] R. D. Brown. Automated Dictionary Extraction for "Knowledge-Free" Example-Based Translation. In *Proceedings of the Seventh International Conference on Theoretical and Methodological Issues in Machine Translation (TMI-97)*, pages 111–118, Santa Fe, New Mexico, July 1997.
`http://www.cs.cmu.edu/~ralf/papers.html`.

[3] R. D. Brown. Adding Linguistic Knowledge to a Lexical Example-Based Translation System. In *Proceedings of the Eighth International Conference on Theoretical and Methodological Issues in Machine Translation (TMI-99)*, pages 22–32, Chester, England, August 1999.
`http://www.cs.cmu.edu/~ralf/papers.html`.

[4] R. D. Brown. Automated Generalization of Translation Examples. In *Proceedings of the Eighteenth International Conference on Computational Linguistics (COLING-2000)*, pages 125–131, 2000.

[5] D. Graff and R. Finch. Multilingual Text Resources at the Linguistic Data Consortium. In *Proceedings of the 1994 ARPA Human Language Technology Workshop*. Morgan Kaufmann, 1994.

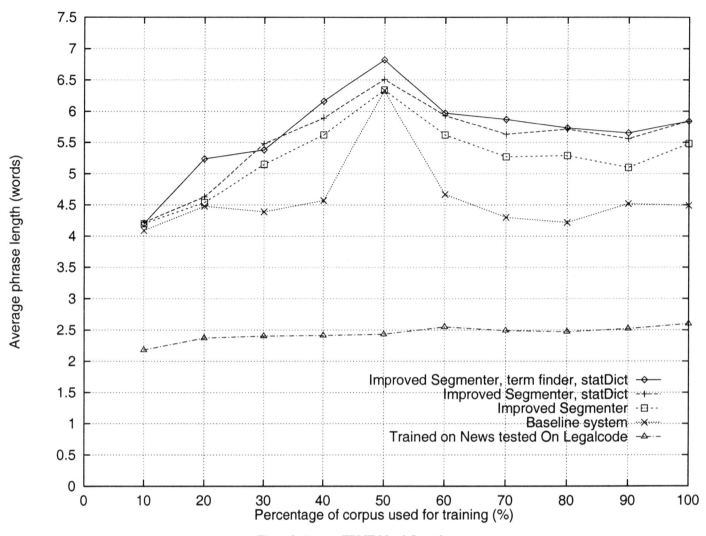

Figure 3: Average EBMT Match Lengths

[6] C. Hogan and R. E. Frederking. An Evaluation of the
Multi-engine MT Architecture. In *Machine Translation and
the Information Soup: Proceedings of the Third Conference of
the Association for Machine Translation in the Americas
(AMTA '98)*, volume 1529 of *Lecture Notes in Artificial
Intelligence*, pages 113–123. Springer-Verlag, Berlin, October
1998.

[7] Linguistic Data Consortium. *Hansard Corpus of Parallel
English and French*. Linguistic Data Consortium, December
1997. http://www.ldc.upenn.edu/.

Advances in Meeting Recognition

Alex Waibel[c,k], Hua Yu[c], Martin Westphal[k], Hagen Soltau[k],
Tanja Schultz[c,k], Thomas Schaaf[k], Yue Pan[c], Florian Metze[k], Michael Bett[c]
Interactive Systems Laboratories
[c]Carnegie Mellon University, Pittsburgh, PA, USA
[k]Universität Karlsruhe, Fakultät für Informatik, Karlsruhe, Germany
http://www.is.cs.cmu.edu/
tanja@cs.cmu.edu

1. INTRODUCTION

Speech recognition has advanced considerably, but has been limited almost entirely either to situations in which close speaking microphones are natural and acceptable (telephone, dictation, command&control, etc.) or in which high-quality recordings are ensured. Furthermore, most recognition applications involve controlled recording environments, in which the user turns the recognition event on and off and speaks cooperatively for the purpose of being recognized.

Unfortunately, the majority of situations in which humans speak with each other fall outside of these limitations. When we meet with others, we speak without turning on or off equipment, or we don't require precise positioning vis a vis the listener. Recognition of speech during human encounters, or "meeting recognition", therefore represents the ultimate frontier for speech recognition, as it forces robustness, knowledge of context, and integration in an environment and/or human experience.

2. CHALLENGES

Over the last three years we have explored meeting recognition at the Interactive Systems Laboratories [5, 6, 7]. Meeting recognition is performed as one of the components of a "meeting browser"; a search retrieval and summarization tool that provides information access to unrestricted human interactions and encounters. The system is capable of automatically constructing a searchable and browsable audiovisual database of meetings. The meetings can be described and indexed in somewhat unorthodox ways, including by what has been said (speech), but also by who said it (speaker&face ID), where (face, pose, gaze, and sound source tracking), how (emotion tracking), and why, and other meta-level descriptions such as the purpose and style of the interaction, the focus of attention, the relationships between the participants, to name a few (see [1, 2, 3, 4]).

The problem of speech recognition in unrestricted human meetings is formidable. Error rates for standard recognizers are 5-10 times higher than for dictation tasks. Our explorations based on LVCSR systems trained on BN, reveal that several types of mis-matches are to blame [6]:

- Mismatched and/or degraded recording conditions (remote, different microphone types),

- Mismatched dictionaries and language models (typically ideosynchratic discussions highly specialized on a topic of interest for a small group and therefore very different from other existing tasks),

- Mismatched speaking-style (informal, sloppy, multiple speakers talking in a conversational style instead of single speakers reading prepared text).

In the following sections, we describe experiments and improvements based on our Janus Speech Recognition Toolkit JRTk [8] applied to transcribing meeting speech robustly.

3. EXPERIMENTAL SETUP

As a first step towards unrestricted human meetings each speaker is equipped with a clip-on lapel microphone for recording. By this choice interferences can be reduced but are not ruled out completely. Compared to a close-talking headset, there is significant channel cross-talk. Quite often one can hear multiple speakers on a single channel. Since meetings consist of highly specialized topics, we face the problem of a lack of training data. Large databases are hard to collect and can not be provided on demand. As a consequence we have focused on building LVCSR systems that are robust against mismatched conditions as described above. For the purpose of building a speech recognition engine on the meeting task, we combined a limited set of meeting data with English speech and text data from various sources, namely Wall Street Journal (WSJ), English Spontaneous Scheduling Task (ESST), Broadcast News (BN), Crossfire and Newshour TV news shows. The meeting data consists of a number of internal group meeting recordings (about one hour long each), of which fourteen are used for experiments in this paper. A subset of three meetings were chosen as the test set.

4. SPEECH RECOGNITION ENGINE

To achieve robust performance over a range of different tasks, we trained our baseline system on Broadcast News (BN). The system deploys a quinphone model with 6000 distributions sharing 2000 codebooks. There are about 105K Gaussians in the system. Vocal Tract Length Normalization and cluster-based Cepstral Mean Normalization are used to compensate for speaker and channel variations. Linear Discriminant Analysis is applied to reduce feature dimensionality to 42, followed by a diagonalization transform (Maximum Likelihood Linear Transform). A 40k vocabulary and trigram

Proceedings of HLT 2001, First International Conference on Human Language Technology Research, J. Allan, ed., Morgan Kaufmann, San Francisco, 2001.

System WER on Different Tasks [%]	
BN (h4e98_1) F0-condition	9.6
BN (h4e98_1) all F-conditions	18.5
BN+ESST (h4e98_1) all F-conditions	18.4
Newshour	20.8
Crossfire	25.6
Improvements on Meeting Recognition	
Baseline ESST system	54.1
Baseline BN system	44.2
+ acoustic training BN+ESST	42.2
+ language model interpolation (14 meetings)	39.0
Baseline BN system	
+ acoustic MAP Adaptation (10h meeting data)	40.4
+ language model interpolation (14 meetings)	38.7

Table 1: Recognition Results on BN and Meeting Task

language model are used. The baseline language model is trained on the BN corpus.

Our baseline system has been evaluated across the above mentioned tasks resulting in the word error rates shown in Table 1. While we achieve a first pass WER of 18.5% on all F-conditions and 9.6% on the F0-conditions in the Broadcast News task, the word error rate of 44.2% on meeting data is quite high, reflecting the challenges of this task. Results on the ESST system [9] are even worse with a WER of 54.1% which results from the fact that ESST is a highly specialized system trained on noise-free but spontaneous speech in the travel domain.

4.1 Acoustic and Language Model Adaptation

The BN acoustic models have been adapted to the meeting data thru Viterbi training, MLLR (Maximum Likelihood Linear Regression), and MAP (Maximum A Posteriori) adaptation. To improve the robustness towards the unseen channel conditions, speaking mode and training/test mismatch, we trained a system "BN+ESST" using a mixed training corpus. The comparison of the results indicate that the mixed system is more robust (44.2% → 42.2%), without loosing the good performance on the original BN test set (18.5% vs. 18.4%).

To tackle the lack of training corpus, we investigated linear interpolation of the BN and the meeting (MT) language model. Based on a cross-validation test we calculated the optimal interpolation weight and achieved a perplexity reduction of 21.5% relative compared to the MT-LM and more than 50% relative compared to the BN-LM. The new language model gave a significant improvement decreasing the word error rate to 38.7%. Overall the error rate was reduced by 12.4% relative (44.2% → 38.7%) compared to the BN baseline system.

4.2 Model Combination based Acoustic Mapping (MAM)

For the experiments on meeting data reported above we have used comparable recording conditions as each speaker in the meeting has been wearing his or her own lapel microphone. Frequently however this assumption does not apply. We have also carried out experiments aimed at producing robust recognition when microphones are positioned at varying distances from the speaker. In this case data, specific for the microphone distance and SNR found in the test condition is unavailable. We therefore apply a new method, Model Combination based Acoustic Mapping (MAM) to the recognition of speech at different distances. MAM was originally proposed for recognition in different car noise environments, please refer to [10, 11] for details.

MAM estimates an acoustic mapping on the log-spectral domain in order to compensate for noise condition mismatches between training and test. During training, the generic acoustic models λ_k ($k = 1, 2, ..., n$) and a variable noise model N are estimated. Then, model combination is applied to get new generic models $\hat{\lambda}_k = \lambda_k + N$, which correspond to noisy speech. During decoding of a given input x, the mapping process requires a classification as a first step. The score for each $class(model)$ is computed as $g_k(x) = P(k|x, \hat{\lambda}_k)$. In the second step x is reconstructed according to the calculated score, where μ refers to the mean vector: $\hat{x} = x + \sum_{k=1}^{n} g_k(x)(\mu_k - \hat{\mu}_k)$.

System	Test Set	WER [%]
Baseline	Close	22.4
Baseline	Distant	52.9
MLLR	Distant	48.3
MAM	Distant	47.2

Table 2: Recognition results on Model Combination based Acoustic Mapping (MAM)

We applied MAM to data that was recorded simultaneously by an array of microphones positions at different distances from the speaker. Each speaker read several paragraphs of text from the Broadcast News corpus. The results of experiments with nine speakers (5 male, 4 female) are summarized in Table 2. Experiments suggest that MAM effectively models the signal condition found in the test resulting in substantial performance improvements. It outperforms unsupervised MLLR adaptation while requiring less computational effort.

5. CONCLUSIONS

In this paper we have reviewed work on speech recognition systems applied to data from human-to-human interaction as encountered in meetings. The task is very challenging with error rates of 5-10 times higher than read speech (BN F0-condition) which basically results from degraded recording conditions, highly topic dependent dictionary and language models, as well as from the informal, conversational multi-party scenario. Our experiments using different training data, language modeling interpolation, adaptation and signal mapping yield more than 20% relative improvements in error rate.

6. ACKNOWLEDGMENTS

We would like to thank Susanne Burger, Christian Fügen, Ralph Gross, Qin Jin, Victoria Maclaren, Robert Malkin, Laura Mayfield-Tomokiyo, John McDonough, Thomas Polzin, Klaus Ries, Ivica Rogina, and Klaus Zechner for their support.

7. REFERENCES

[1] Klaus Ries, "Towards the Detection and Description of Textual Meaning Indicators in Spontaneous Conversations," in *Proceedings of the Eurospeech*, Budapest, Hungary, September 1999, vol. 3, pp. 1415–1418.

[2] Michael Bett, Ralph Gross, Hua Yu, Xiaojin Zhu, Yue Pan, Jie Yang, and Alex Waibel, "Multimodal Meeting Tracker," in *Proceedings of RIAO2000*, Paris, France, April 2000.

[3] Rainer Stiefelhagen, Jie Yang, and Alex Waibel, "Simultaneous Tracking of Head Poses in a Panoramic View," in *International Conference on Pattern Recognition (ICPR)*, Barcelona, Spain, September 2000.

[4] Thomas S. Polzin and Alex Waibel, "Detecting Emotions in Speech," in *Proceedings of the CMC*, 1998.

[5] Hua Yu, Cortis Clark, Robert Malkin, Alex Waibel, "Experiments in Automatic Meeting Transcription using JRTk", in *Proceedings of the ICASSP'98*, Seattle, USA, 1998.

[6] Hua Yu, Michael Finke, and Alex Waibel, "Progress in Automatic Meeting Transcription," in *Proceedings of the EUROSPEECH*, September 1999.

[7] Hua Yu, Takashi Tomokiyo, Zhirong Wang, and Alex Waibel, "New developments in automatic meeting transcription," in *Proceedings of the ICSLP*, Beijing, China, October 2000.

[8] Michael Finke, Petra Geutner, Hermann Hild, Thomas Kemp, Klaus Ries, and Martin Westphal, "The Karlsruhe-Verbmobil Speech Recognition Engine," in *Proceedings of the ICASSP'97*, München, Germany, 1997.

[9] Alex Waibel, Hagen Soltau, Tanja Schultz, Thomas Schaaf, and Florian Metze, "Multilingual Speech Recognition," in *Verbmobil: Foundations of Speech-to-Speech Translation*, Springer-Verlag, 2000.

[10] Martin Westphal "Robust Continuous Speech Recognition in Changing Environments", University of Karlsruhe, Ph.D. thesis, 2000.

[11] Martin Westphal "Model-Combination-Based Acoustic Mapping", in *Proceedings of the ICASSP'01*, Salt Lake City, USA, May 2001.

Amount of Information Presented in a Complex List: Effects on User Performance

Dawn Dutton
AT&T Labs - Research
180 Park Avenue
D103, Bldg. 103
Florham Park, NJ 07932
+1.973.236.6522

dldutton@att.com

Selina Chu
Information and Computer Science
444 Computer Sci. Bldg.
UC Irvine
Irvine, CA 92697
+1.949.509.9762

selina@ics.uci.edu

James Hubbell
12 Lawrence Avenue
West Long Branch, NJ 07932
+1.732.728.9351

jameshubbell@hotmail.com

Marilyn Walker
AT&T Labs - Research
180 Park Avenue
E103, Bldg. 103
Florham Park, NJ 07932
+1.973.360.8956

walker@research.att.com

Shrikanth Narayanan
Speech and Image Proc. Institute
Department of EE-Systems
EEB 430, USC
Los Angeles, CA 90089
+1.213.740.6432

shri@sipi.usc.edu

ABSTRACT

AT&T Communicator is a state-of-the-art speech-enabled telephony-based application that allows the end-user to, among other things, select and reserve airline itineraries. This experiment explores how the amount and structure of information presented in complex lists influences the user experience and the ability of subjects to successfully complete a selection task. Presenting all the relevant information needed for a decision at once was the factor that most positively influenced successful task completion and the user experience. Subjects preferred hearing all of the relevant information about each flight, without initiating additional dialog with the system. Additionally, successful task completion rates improved when all of the flights were presented at once, without any intervening questions from the system.

Keywords

dialogue, user interface, human factors, spoken language, lists, selection

1. INTRODUCTION

AT&T Communicator is a state-of-the-art spoken dialogue system that allows the end-user to select and reserve various travel related resources, in particular, airfare, hotel, and rental cars [2]. One of its most challenging dialog modules is that for presenting

Proceedings of HLT 2001, First International Conference on Human Language Technology Research, J. Allan, ed., Morgan Kaufmann, San Francisco, 2001.

information that allows the user to select a desired air travel itinerary. While selecting between multiple possible itineraries in a visual domain is a relatively simple task because most of the selection criteria are listed in a single scrollable page, the same task is likely to have a much higher cognitive load in an audio-only domain [1, 3]. The selection criteria for each candidate flight must be presented to the user serially, leading to higher cognitive demands that could result in errors in itinerary selection.

A sample AT&T Communicator dialog with the prototype used in this experiment, showing the outbound flight only, follows.

System: Hello, this is AT&T Communicator. How may I help with your travel plans?

User: Yeah, I'd like to fly from Newark to San Francisco.

System: OK, a flight from Newark, New Jersey to San Francisco, California. And will this be a round trip?

User: Yes, and I need to arrive in San Francisco by 4 PM on November 22nd.

System: I found five outbound United Airlines flights.

Option 1 is flight number 635. It has one stop; it departs at 10:15 A.M. and arrives at 2:42 P.M. <pause>

Option 2 is flight number 7535. It has one stop; It departs at 12:20 P.M., and arrives at 4:37 P.M. <pause>

Option 3 is flight number 837. It' s a nonstop flight; it departs at 2:00 P.M. and arrives at 5:01 P.M. <pause>

Would you like to hold any of these flights?

User: I guess I'll take option one.

System: Got it.

Note that the second to the last system utterance, in which a set of itineraries are presented to the user for selection, is by far the longest system utterance in the dialog. This utterance includes a complex list of information. Unlike a more simple list, each list item (option) contains a number of sub-items, for example flight number, number of stops, etc. In early dialog evaluations of the Communicator system, the selection of a single itinerary from such a complex list of flights was a source of substantial usability problems; users frequently became frustrated. In fact, many users dropped out of the dialog before successfully selecting an itinerary.

This paper describes an experiment in which we vary the amount and structure of information presented about available itineraries. We predict that the amount and structure of information presented affects the ability of users to successfully select the optimal itinerary within a set, and influences subjective measures such as user satisfaction.

2. METHODS AND PROCEDURES

2.1 Subjects

Sixty-four subjects were run at a local shopping mall over a five day period. Subjects were recruited from the shoppers frequenting the mall.

2.2 Wizard of Oz

A Wizard of Oz (WOZ) experiment was run to determine the optimal way for the end-user to select a desired itinerary in the Communicator project.

A Wizard of Oz experiment is one in which no real automatic speech recognition (ASR) or natural language understanding (NLU) is used. Instead, the user interface is prototyped and a 'wizard,' or experimenter, acts in place of the ASR and NLU. Consequently, subjects believe that ASR/NLU is being used. The WOZ methodology allows competing user interface strategies to be prototyped and tested with end users in a shorter period of time than would be required to implement multiple fully-functioning systems with competing user interfaces.

2.3 Apparatus & Materials

Relevant aspects of the AT&T Communicator user interface were prototyped using the Unisys Natural Language Speech Assistant (NLSA) software. NLSA runs on a PC using the Windows NT operating system. Subjects called into the Communicator prototype using an analog telephone and interacted with the system by voice. The wizard categorized the subject's speech using the NLSA Wizard graphical user interface (GUI). Each subject completed 5 surveys in pen and paper format. During the course of the experiment, subjects also had access to a pad of paper.

2.4 Experimental Design

All itineraries presented to the subjects were round-trip.

2.4.1 Independent Variables

This was a factorial experiment with two factors, one factor between subjects and the other within subject (see Table 1).

Selection Itinerary Content. There were two levels of this between subjects factor:

--*Terse*. The presented itineraries included: airline, number of stops, and departure time[1]. In order to get additional information, the user could ask the system questions (e.g. "*When does that flight arrive?*").

--*Verbose*. The presented itineraries included: airline, flight number, number of stops, departure time, and arrival time. All the information relevant to the tasks specified in the experiment are presented about each flight; the user did not need to ask questions to get additional information.

Number of Flights Before Question. Each level is actually a combination of two separate, but related, factors.

--*Combined vs. Separate*. Whether outbound and return flights are presented separately or in combination.

--*Number of flights*. The number of flights that are presented before asking the subject to make a decision.

Four levels of this factor were chosen. In all cases (1) the total number of flights 'found' was 5, and, (2) the question was, "Would you like to hold [that flight/any of those flights]?".

--*Separate 1*. The outbound and return flights of the trip are presented separately and after each flight the subject is asked the question.

--*Separate 3*. The outbound and return flights of the trip are presented separately and after the third flight the subject is asked the question.

--*Separate 5*. The outbound and return flights of the trip are presented separately and after the last flight the subject is asked the question.

--*Combined*. The outbound and return flights of the trip are presented at the same time and after each set of two flights the subject is asked the question.

Table 1: Factors used in this experiment.

Selection Itinerary Content (Between)			
Terse		**Verbose**	
Outbound / Return	**# of Flights Before Question**	**Outbound / Return**	**# of Flights Before Question**
(Within)		(Within)	
Separate	1	Separate	1
Separate	3	Separate	3
Separate	5	Separate	5
Combined	2	Combined	2

Example. The following example could have been used in the Separate 3 condition. Text that is unformatted is common to both the terse and verbose conditions. Text in *italics is found only in the verbose condition*.

"I found 5 outbound Delta flights. Option 1 is *flight number 323.* It's a non-stop leaving at 9:10 *and arriving at 2:01.* Option 2 *is flight number 798.* It has one stop; it departs at 11:13 *and arrives at 5:07.* Option 3 is *flight number 295.* It

---

[1] All times in this experiment were presented to the minute, with either AM or PM, e.g. "...departs at 6:01 AM."

has two stops; it departs at 1:52 *and arrives at 6:57.* Would you like to hold any of those flights?"

2.4.2 *Mixed Initiative and Flow of Control*
The dialog strategy was mixed initiative. The first prompt was open-ended, e.g. "How may I help you with your travel plans?" All subsequent prompts requested specific information from the user (e.g. "What date did you want to depart?") The prototypes were built to allow the user to provide multiple informational elements (e.g. departure city and departure date) to either open-ended or specific requests. Subsequent steps in the flow of control could be skipped if multiple pieces of information were presented at a single dialog point.

2.4.3 *Tasks*
Each subject was asked to complete four tasks in the course of this experiment. In each task the subject was given a set of criteria that the subject had to meet in selecting both an outbound and a return flight. The tasks used in this experiment exercise selection criteria that are representative of selection criteria typically used by individuals actually purchasing airline tickets. The four tasks given to subjects follow:

Departure Only. The task criteria for both the outbound and return flights require the subject to choose flights based on departure time only.

Arrival Only. The task criteria for both the outbound and return flights require the subject to choose flights based on arrival time only.

Departure & Arrival. The task criteria require the subject to choose the outbound flight based on departure time and the return flight based on arrival time.

Specific Flight. The task requires the subject to book a particular flight for both the outbound and return flights.

Example. The following example was used for the Departure & Arrival task (it has been edited for presentation here).

> *You want a round trip ticket from Boston to Charleston. You want to leave Boston about 5 in the evening of Friday November 10th. You want to arrive in Boston no later than 8 PM on Tuesday November 14th.*

An important selection criterion for many purchasers of airline tickets is price. The price of the ticket was not a selection criterion used in this experiment because it would introduce possible confounds. Many users are willing to trade-off other important selection criteria, e.g. arrival time and departure time, in order to minimize price. Therefore, it was decided, *a priori*, to postpone the use of price as a selection criterion to a later experiment.

2.4.4 *Counterbalancing*
A Balanced Greco-Latin Square was used to counterbalance the orders of the conditions and tasks.

2.4.5 *Dependent Measures*
A rich set of dependent measures were gathered in this experiment:
- -- After each system prompt was played, NLSA recorded what subjects said.
- -- At the end of each task, the wizard determined whether that task was successfully completed.
- -- At the end of each task, subjects completed paper and pen surveys rating the overall dialog for that task.
- -- After experiencing all four tasks, subjects told the experimenter which of the flight selection criteria were important to them.

Objective measure. Successful task completion was the one objective measure used in determining the optimal method for presenting complex lists in an audio-only domain. For each task the subject was given a set of required criteria for selecting both the outbound and a return flight. Task completion was binary, successful or unsuccessful, and was determined by the experimenter (wizard) at the time the subject completed each task. In order for a subject to successfully complete a task, the subject had to select both the outbound and return flight that best fit the clear criteria given to subjects in the task description.

Subjective measures. Other data gathered in this experiment included a number of subjective measures. After each task, subjects were asked:

Overall, how satisfied were you with AT&T Communicator while booking this flight?
> [1] Very Satisfied
> [2] Somewhat Satisfied
> [3] Neither Satisfied, Nor Dissatisfied
> [4] Somewhat Dissatisfied
> [5] Very Dissatisfied

Overall, how easy was it to use AT&T Communicator while booking this flight?
> [1] Very Easy
> [2] Somewhat Easy
> [3] Neither Easy, Nor Difficult
> [4] Somewhat Difficult
> [5] Very Difficult

Overall, how quickly did AT&T Communicator respond to your speech?
> [1] Much Too Fast
> [2] A Little Too Fast
> [3] Just the Right Speed
> [4] A Little Too Slow
> [5] Much Too Slow

After you told Communicator the date and time to book your flight, Communicator responded with possible flights to choose from. For EACH of the possible flights, did Communicator present the right amount of information?
> [1] Too Much Information about Each Flight
> [2] Just the Right Amount of Information About Each Flight
> [3] Too Little Information about Each Flight

After completing all four tasks, subjects were asked to (1) rank order the criteria they personally use when selecting between multiple itineraries, and (2) specify the information that Communicator should present about every flight for selection purposes in the future.

3. RESULTS AND CONCLUSIONS
3.1 Terse or Verbose?
A two-way, 2x4, Analysis of Variance (ANOVA) was run for each of 5 dependent measures: successful task completion, amount of information presented about each flight, satisfaction,

ease of use, and speed of interaction. For each dependent measure, no significant interactions were found[2]. A significant main effect for Terse/Verbose was found for the subjective measure of the amount of information presented about each flight (p=.001), see Fig. 1.

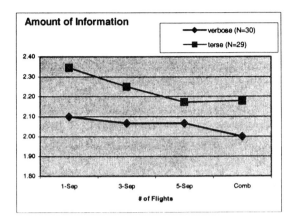

Figure 1: Verbose and Terse subject ratings to the Amount of Information question (2=Just the Right Amount of Information about each flight).

No other significant main effects were found for any of the dependent measures. The optimum value for the dependent measure amount of information is '2' (Just the right amount of information about each flight). The average value for the Verbose condition (across the 4 levels of # of Flights) was 2.06, while the equivalent average for the Terse condition was 2.24.

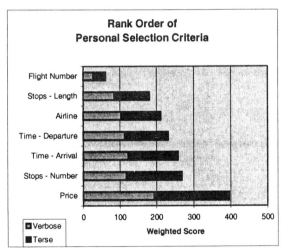

Figure 2: Summed *Weighted Scores* of subjects' rank ordering of their personal selection criteria.

Related to these results is a question that was asked of all subjects at the end of the experiment. Figure 2 shows the weighted scores based on the rank ordering of the selection

criteria subjects personally use when selecting among multiple flights. A rank order of 1 was given a score 7 points, a rank order of 7 was given a score of 1 point, etc. The Weighted Score for each selection criteria shown in Figure 2 is the sum of the Weighted Scores for all subjects.

Similarly, a second question was asked of all subjects at the end of the experiment: "In the future, what information should AT&T Communicator present about each flight when you are choosing between multiple flights?" Figure 3 shows the compiled responses to this question.

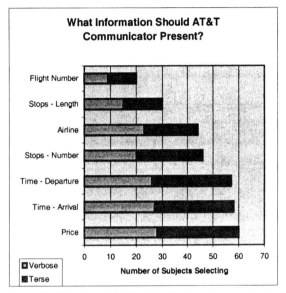

Figure 3: Number of subjects indicating that each selection criterion should, by default, be presented by AT&T Communicator.

Information that should definitely be presented to subjects when selecting between multiple flights includes: price, arrival time, departure time, number of stops and airline. The value to users of the length of stops is ambiguous. It probably should not be presented by default, although it might be useful to present the length of stops if they will be inordinately long, e.g. greater than 2 hours, or inordinately short, e.g. less than 45 minutes. Flight number was judged to be least valuable and should not be presented.

3.2 Number of Flights?

The above analyses indicate that the amount of information presented in the Verbose condition better met the expectations of subjects. The next question then was, *within* the verbose condition, which level of the number of flights before the question factor showed the best performance. A one-way, 1x4, ANOVA was run for the verbose condition for each of five dependent measures: successful task completion, amount of information about each flight, satisfaction, ease of use, and speed of interaction[3]. A significant main effect was found for successful

---

[2] Throughout the experiment, the alpha level used to determine significance of an effect was p<.05.

[3] As noted at the beginning of the Results section, subject responses to the satisfaction, ease of use, and speed of the interaction questions may be attributable to the subject's reactions to the novel user-system

task completion (p=.005). Figure 4 shows the percentage of successful task completions in the Verbose condition only. No significant effects were found for the other four dependent measures.

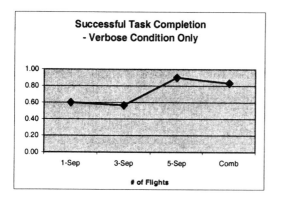

Figure 4: Successful task completion (in percent) across the four levels of the # of Flights Before Question condition (Verbose only).

The significant main effect was probed using the Tukey test[4]. Separate 5 was the condition with the highest successful task completion rate. Only one pairwise comparison was significant (p<.05). Tasks attempted in the Separate 5 condition were significantly more likely to be completed successfully than tasks attempted in the Separate 3 condition.

Table 2: Results of Tukey test for successful task completion across the four levels of # of Flights Before Question condition (Verbose only).

	Sep. 3 =.567	Sep. 1 =.600	Comb. =.833	Sep. 5 =.900
Sep. 3 =.567		p>=.05	p>=.05	p<.05*
Sep. 1 =.600			p>=.05	p>=.05
Comb. =.833				p>=.05
Sep. 5 =.900				

Among the three Separate conditions (Separate 1, Separate 3, and Separate 5), subjects were much more likely to successfully complete a task in Separate 5. That is, when all the flights for a given flight (outbound or return) were presented at once, without any intervening questions. Also, based on subject comments, it appeared that at least some subjects in the Separate 3 condition were confused about the number of flights they had available to select between. These subjects didn't realize that there were more flights available after the system presented them with the first

---

interaction style, rather than to the experimentally varied presentation of the flight selection criteria.

[4] The Tukey is a test of significance for pairwise comparisons of treatment means that controls for familywise error.

three in a total set of five flights. This is in spite of the fact that in all tasks, including the Separate 3 condition, the subjects heard a sentence like "I found five outbound Northwest Airlines flights," before the options were presented for selection.

It not possible, on the basis of the experimental data gathered in this study, to unambiguously choose one of the # of flights before question conditions over the others. It may be that a more difficult set of tasks would elicit stronger differences in both the objective and subjective measures for the levels of this factor. However, in absolute terms, the task completion rates with Separate 5 and Combined were both high (90% and 83%, respectively), relative to the Separate 1 and Separate 3 conditions (60% and 57%, respectively).

Anecdotal evidence sheds some additional light on the issue of which condition (Separate 5 or Combined) is preferred by subjects. In the Verbose condition, the last 17 subjects run in the experiment were asked a few questions that provide evidence concerning their subjective impressions of the four levels of the number of flights before question factor. The first question was "Did you notice any difference between the different versions of the system?" Twelve of seventeen subjects stated that they had noticed a difference between the four versions. Those 12 subjects were then asked to choose the version they liked the best, and then the version they considered to be the worst.

Best?
    3-Did not specify a 'best' version
    2-Combined only
    2-Separate 1 only
    1-Separate 3 only
    1-Separate 5 only
    2-Any of the Separate versions
    1-Either Separate 3 or Separate 5
Worst?
    7-Did not specify a 'worst' version
    5-Combined only
    0-Separate 1 only
    0-Separate 3 only
    0-Separate 5 only

In response to the question of which version of the system was best, the subjects stated no consistent preference for any of the versions of the system. On the other hand, the responses to the question concerning which version of the system was 'worst' resulted in a more consistent set of responses; the Combined version was selected by 5 of 12 of the subjects as the version they considered to be the 'worst.' From subject comments, it appeared that subjects didn't like it when they heard one flight that matched their constraints (e.g. outbound), while the other flight did not match their constraints (e.g. return). Some subjects found this to be frustrating, confusing, and/or tedious.

4. DISCUSSION

Presenting all the relevant information about a given flight *at once* seemed to be the single overarching factor that most positively influenced successful task completion and the user experience. Subjects wanted to hear *all of the relevant information* about a flight needed to make the best choice.

Within the Separate conditions (Separate 1, Separate 3 and Separate 5), the task completion rate was highest for the Separate 5 condition. That is, when *all of the flights* were presented at once, without any intervening system questions. The Separate 5 and Combined conditions had similar task completion rates and were not significantly different. However, the Combined condition was the only condition considered 'worst' by subjects. Thus, the condition that maximized both successful task completion and user experience was the Verbose Separate 5 condition.

A major concern in the design of this experiment was that the audio presentation of lists of complex information, in this case lists of multiple airline flights each containing multiple pieces of information, would result in cognitive overload. These findings argue that, for this task, our concern about the increased cognitive load in an audio-only domain was unfounded. There are a couple of possible reasons that cognitive load did not appear to have the influence that we anticipated. First, users knew their constraints when listening to the flights. Some users may have used a strategy of only remembering the options that potentially matched their constraints. Second, many subjects apparently dealt with the increased cognitive load by taking notes, with flight times, etc., while completing the experimental tasks. Such behaviour is certainly common when making airline reservations with a human travel agent over the telephone. Further, it is anticipated that users would generally book flights in a hands-free environment, and would be able to take notes, when it is desirable. Although less ecologically valid, future experiments primarily concerned with the issue of cognitive load should explicitly preclude subjects from taking notes.

From the above data, it appears that the standard user interface practices for Prompt & Collect (in which the system 'prompts' the user for a specific piece of information and then 'collects' their response) should be different than the standard practice for Selecting from a List. For Prompt & Collect, the standard UI practice is for the system to be as terse as possible when prompting the user. The user generally knows the information the system is asking for, they just need to be prompted so that they know what piece of information the system is currently ready to accept. When Selecting from a List, however, the level of knowledge of the system and user are very different. The system knows the possible items that can be selected. The user begins the interaction only knowing their own constraints (and their relative priority). The system must present all the relevant information so that the user can select the optimal item from the list based on their constraints and priorities. Consequently, when the user must select an item from a list, the system should be as verbose as necessary and present all the information relevant to their decision at once.

For the task of selecting between multiple airline flights, the following information should definitely be presented to users about each flight: price, arrival time, departure time, number of stops and airline. While there was agreement between subjects on the important selection criteria for flights, there are also some individual differences. For example, some users like to fly only a particular airline or have strong preferences concerning the

locations of layovers. This experiment indicates that users like to hear all of the information relevant to their decision at once. Therefore, if a user asks a question concerning information that is not by default presented by the system about each flight, the information presented to that user for each subsequent flight on that call, should include the information they have requested. For example, if after the first flight the user asks "Where does that flight stop?", the information for all subsequent flights in that call should include the location of any stops.

It thus appears likely that subjects in this experiment were using AT&T Communicator as a tool, rather than as a conversational or negotiating partner. That is, their goal was to use Communicator to quickly and efficiently select the single flight that best matched the criteria given to them in each task. Asking the system questions in order to get information relevant to this selection process, would decrease the speed and efficiency with which they were able to accomplish this task. So, subjects preferred the most verbose presentation of information in order to increase the speed and efficiency of the overall task.

Nevertheless, eighty percent of the subjects stated that the most important criterion when personally selecting a flight was price. A number of subjects commented that they were willing to trade off other important criterion, e.g. airline, number of stops, in order to get a better price. In a more complex selection task, where the user is choosing a set of flights based on multiple, *competing* selection criteria, the user may wish to use AT&T Communicator as a negotiating partner in order to get the best flight available. Such a negotiation might lend itself well to exploring machine-user dialog in a natural language telephony-based system.

5. ACKNOWLEDGMENTS
We would like to thank the AT&T Communicator team for their assistance on this project.

6. REFERENCES
[1] Blanchard, H.E. & Lewis, S.H. (1999), The Voice messaging user interface, *in* D. Gardner-Bonneau (ed.), *Human factors and voice interactive systems*, Kluwer Academic Publishers, pp.257-284.

[2] Levin, E., Narayanan, S., Pieraccini, R., Biatov, K., Bocchieri, E., Di Fabbrizio, G., Eckert, W., Lee, S., Pokrovsky, A., Rahim, M., Ruscitti, P., and Walker, M. (2000), *The AT&T-DARPA Communicator mixed-initiative spoken dialog system*, Proc. of the International Conference of Spoken Langurage Processing, (Beijing, China), pp. 122-125.

[3] Schneiderman, B. (1992). *Designing the user interface* (2nd ed.). Reading MA: Addison Wesley.

The Annotation Graph Toolkit: Software Components for Building Linguistic Annotation Tools

Kazuaki Maeda, Steven Bird, Xiaoyi Ma and Haejoong Lee
Linguistic Data Consortium, University of Pennsylvania
3615 Market St., Philadelphia, PA 19104-2608 USA
{maeda, sb, xma, haejoong}@ldc.upenn.edu

ABSTRACT

Annotation graphs provide an efficient and expressive data model for linguistic annotations of time-series data. This paper reports progress on a complete software infrastructure supporting the rapid development of tools for transcribing and annotating time-series data. This general-purpose infrastructure uses annotation graphs as the underlying model, and allows developers to quickly create special-purpose annotation tools using common components. An application programming interface, an I/O library, and graphical user interfaces are described. Our experience has shown us that it is a straightforward task to create new special-purpose annotation tools based on this general-purpose infrastructure.

Keywords

transcription, coding, annotation graph, interlinear text, dialogue annotation

1. INTRODUCTION

Annotation graphs (AGs) provide an efficient and expressive data model for linguistic annotations of time-series data [2]. This paper reports progress on a complete software infrastructure supporting the rapid development of tools for transcribing and annotating time-series data. This general-purpose infrastructure uses annotation graphs as the underlying model, and allows developers to quickly create special-purpose annotation tools using common components. This work is being done in cooperation with the developers of other widely used annotation systems, Transcriber and Emu [1, 3].

The infrastructure is being used in the development of a series of annotation tools at the Linguistic Data Consortium. Several such tools are shown in the paper: one for dialogue annotation, one for telephone conversation transcription, and one for interlinear transcription aligned to speech.

This paper will cover the following points: the application programming interfaces for manipulating annotation graph data and importing data from other formats; the model of inter-component

Proceedings of HLT 2001, First International Conference on Human Language Technology Research, J. Allan, ed., Morgan Kaufmann, San Francisco, 2001.

communication which permits easy reuse of software components; and the design of the graphical user interfaces, which have been tailored to be maximally ergonomic for the tasks.

The project homepage is: [http://www.ldc.upenn.edu/AG/]. The software tools and software components described in this paper are available through a CVS repository linked from this homepage.

2. ARCHITECTURE

2.1 General Architecture

Existing annotation tools are based on a two level model (Figure 1 Top). The systems we demonstrate are based around a three level model, in which annotation graphs provide a logical level independent of application and physical levels (Figure 1 Bottom). The application level represents special-purpose tools built on top of the general-purpose infrastructure at the logical level.

The system is built from several components which instantiate this model. Figure 2 shows the architecture of the tools currently being developed. Annotation tools, such as the ones discussed below, must provide graphical user interface components for signal visualization and annotation. The communication between components is handled through an extensible event language. An application programming interface for annotation graphs (AG-API) has been developed to support well-formed operations on annotation graphs. This permits applications to abstract away from file format issues, and deal with annotations purely at the logical level.

2.2 The Annotation Graph API

The complete IDL definition of the AG-API is provided in the appendix (also online). Here we describe a few salient features of the API.

The API provides access to internal objects (signals, anchors, annotations etc) using identifiers. Identifiers are strings which contain internal structure. For example, an AG identifier is qualified with an AGSet identifier: `AGSetId:AGId`. Annotations and anchors are doubly qualified: `AGSetId:AGId:AnnotationId`, `AGSetId:AGId:AnchorId`. Thus, it is possible to determine from any given identifiers, its membership in the overall data structure.

The functioning of the API will now be illustrated with a series of examples. Suppose we have already constructed an AG and now wish to create a new anchor. We might have the following API call:

```
CreateAnchor( "agSet12:ag5", 15.234, "sec" );
```

This call would construct a new anchor object and return its identifier: `agSet12:ag5:anchor34`. Alternatively, if we already

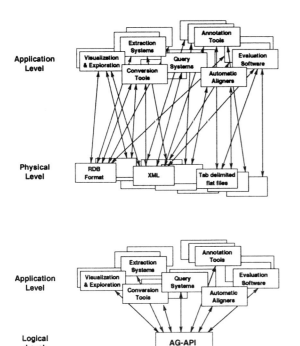

Figure 1: The Two and Three-Level Architectures for Speech Annotation

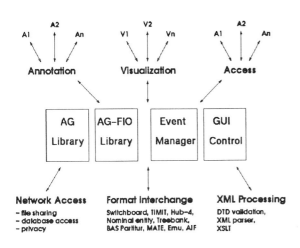

Figure 2: Architecture for Annotation Systems

have an anchor identifier that we wish to use for this new anchor (e.g. because we are reading previously created annotation data from a file and do not wish to assign new identifiers), then we could have the following API call:

```
CreateAnchor( "agset12:ag5:anchor34", 15.234, "sec" );
```

This call will return `agset12:ag5:anchor34`.

Once a pair of anchors have been created it is possible to create an annotation which spans them:

```
CreateAnnotation( "agSet12:ag5",
                  "agSet12:ag5:anchor34",
                  "agSet12:ag5:anchor35",
                  "phonetic" );
```

This call will construct an annotation object and return an identifier for it, e.g. `agSet12:ag5:annotation41`. We can now add features to this annotation:

```
SetFeature( "agSet12:ag5:annotation41",
            "date", "1999-07-02" );
```

The implementation maintains indexes on all the features, and also on the temporal information and graph structure, permitting efficient search using a family of functions such as:

```
GetAnnotationSetByFeature( "agSet12:ag5",
                           "date", "1999-07-02" );
```

2.3 A File I/O Library

A file I/O library (AG-FIO) to support creation and export of AG data has been developed. This will eventually handle all widely used annotation formats. Formats currently supported by the AG-FIO library include the TIMIT, BU, Treebank, AIF (ATLAS Interchange Format), Switchboard and BAS Partitur formats.

2.4 Inter-component Communication

Figure 3 shows the structure of an annotation tool in terms of components and their inter-communications.

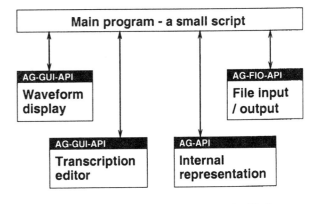

Figure 3: The Structure of an Annotation Tool

The main program is typically a small script which sets up the widgets and provides callback functions to handle widget events. In this example there are four other components which are reused by several annotation tools. The AG and AG-FIO components have already been described. The waveform display component (of which there may be multiple instances) receives instructions to pan and zoom, to play a segment of audio data, and so on. The transcription editor is an annotation component which is specialized for a particular coding task. Most tool customization is accomplished by substituting for this component.

Both GUI components and the main program support a common API for transmitting and receiving events. For example, GUI components have a notion of a "current region" — the timespan which is currently in focus. A waveform component can change an annotation component's idea of the current region by sending a `SetRegion` event (Figure 4). The same event can also be used in the reverse direction. The main program routes the events between GUI components, calling the AG-API to update the internal representation as needed. With this communication mechanism, it is a straightforward task to add new commands, specific to the annotation task.

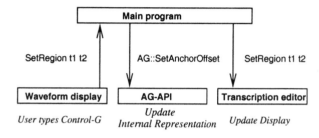

Figure 4: Inter-component Communication

2.5   Reuse of Software Components

The architecture described in this paper allows rapid development of special-purpose annotation tools using common components. In particular, our model of inter-component communication facilitates reuse of software components. The annotation tools described in the next section are not intended for general purpose annotation/transcription tasks; the goal is not to create an "emacs for linguistic annotation". Instead, they are special-purpose tools based on the general purpose infrastructure. These GUI components can be modified or replaced when building new special-purpose tools.

3.   GRAPHICAL USER INTERFACES

3.1   A Spreadsheet Component

The first of the annotation/transcription editor components we describe is a spreadsheet component. In this section, we show two tools that use the spreadsheet component: a dialogue annotation tool and a telephone conversation transcription tool.

Dialogue annotation consists of assigning a field-structured record to each utterance in each speaker turn. A key challenge is to handle overlapping speaker turns and back-channel cues without disrupting the structure of individual speaker contributions. The tool solves these problems and permits annotations to be aligned to a (multi-channel) recording. The records are displayed in a spreadsheet. Clicking on a row of the spreadsheet causes the corresponding extent of audio signal to be highlighted. As an extended recording is played back, annotated sections are highlighted (both waveform and spreadsheet displays).

Figure 5 shows the tool with a section of the TRAINS/DAMSL corpus [4]. Figure 6 shows another tool designed for transcribing telephone conversations. This latter tool is a version of the dialogue annotation tool, with the columns changed to accommodate the needed fields: in this case, speaker turns and transcriptions. Both

of these tools are for two-channel audio files. The audio channel corresponding to the highlighted annotation in the spreadsheet is also highlighted.

3.2   An Interlinear Transcription Component

Interlinear text is a kind of text in which each word is annotated with phonological, morphological and syntactic information (displayed under the word) and each sentence is annotated with a free translation. Our tool permits interlinear transcription aligned to a primary audio signal, for greater accuracy and accountability. Whole words and sub-parts of words can be easily aligned with the audio. Clicking on a piece of the annotation causes the corresponding extent of audio signal to be highlighted. As an extended recording is played back, annotated sections are highlighted (both waveform and interlinear text displays).

The following screenshot shows the tool with some interlinear text from Mawu (a Manding language of the Ivory Coast, West Africa).

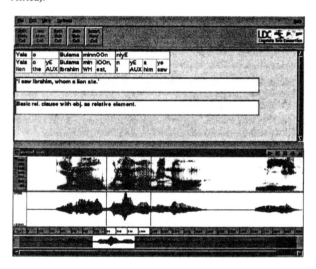

Figure 7: Interlinear Transcription Tool

3.3   A Waveform Display Component

The tools described above utilize WaveSurfer and Snack developed by Kåre Sjölander and Jonas Beskow [7, 8]. WaveSurfer allows developers to specify event callbacks through a plug-in architecture. We have developed a plug-in for WaveSurfer that enables the inter-component communication described in this paper. In addition to waveforms, it is also possible to show spectrograms and pitch contours of a speech file if the given annotation task requires phonetic analysis of the speech data.

4.   FUTURE WORK

4.1   More GUI Components

In addition to the software components discussed in this paper, we plan to develop more components to support various annotation tasks. For example, a video component is being developed, and it will have an associated editor for gestural coding. GUI components for Conversation Analysis (CA) [6] and CHAT [5] are also planned.

4.2   An Annotation Graph Server

We are presently designing a client-side component which presents the same AG-API to the annotation tool, but translates all calls

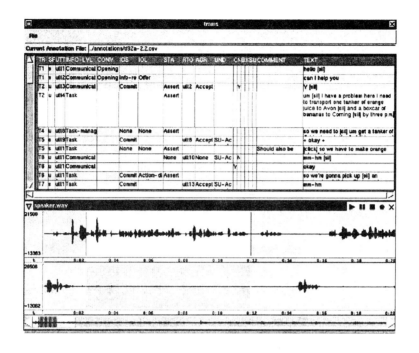

Figure 5: Dialogue Annotation Tool for the TRAINS/DAMSL Corpus

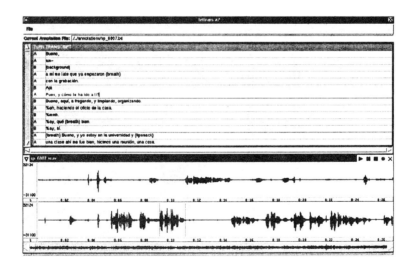

Figure 6: Telephone Conversation Transcription Tool for the CALLFRIEND Spanish Corpus

into SQL and then transmits them to a remote SQL server (see Figure 8). A centralized server could house a potentially large quantity of annotation data, permitting multiple clients to collaboratively construct annotations of shared data. Existing methods for authentication and transaction processing will be be used to ensure the integrity of the data.

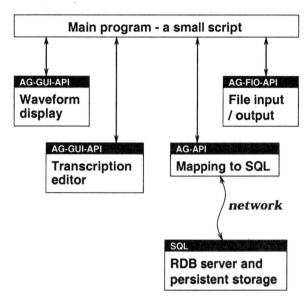

Figure 8: Annotation Tool Connecting to Annotation Server

4.3 Timeline for Development

A general distribution (Version 1.0) of the tools is planned for the early summer, 2001. Additional components and various improvements will be added to future releases. Source code will be available through a source code distribution service, SourceForge ([http://sourceforge.net/projects/agtk/]). Further schedule for updates will be posted on our web site: [http://www.ldc.upenn.edu/AG/].

5. CONCLUSION

This paper has described a comprehensive infrastructure for developing annotation tools based on annotation graphs. Our experience has shown us that it is a simple matter to construct new special-purpose annotation tools using high-level software components. The tools can be quickly created and deployed, and replaced by new versions as annotation tasks evolve. The components and tools reported here are all being made available under an open source license.

6. ACKNOWLEDGMENT

This material is based upon work supported by the National Science Foundation under Grant No. 9978056 and 9983258.

7. REFERENCES

[1] C. Barras, E. Geoffrois, Z. Wu, and M. Liberman. Transcriber: development and use of a tool for assisting speech corpora production. *Speech Communication*, 33:5–22, 2001.

[2] S. Bird and M. Liberman. A formal framework for linguistic annotation. *Speech Communication*, 33:23–60, 2001.

[3] S. Cassidy and J. Harrington. Multi-level annotation of speech: An overview of the emu speech database management system. *Speech Communication*, 33:61–77, 2001.

[4] D. Jurafsky, E. Shriberg, and D. Biasca. Switchboard SWBD-DAMSL Labeling Project Coder's Manual, Draft 13. Technical Report 97-02, University of Colorado Institute of Cognitive Science, 1997. [http://stripe.colorado.edu/~jurafsky/manual.august1.html].

[5] B. MacWhinney. *The CHILDES Project: Tools for Analyzing Talk.* Mahwah, NJ: Lawrence Erlbaum., second edition, 1995. [http://childes.psy.cmu.edu/].

[6] E. Schegloff. Reflections on studying prosody in talk-in-interaction. *Language and Speech*, 41:235–60, 1998. [http://www.sscnet.ucla.edu/soc/faculty/schegloff/prosody/].

[7] K. Sjölander. The Snack sound toolkit, 2000. [http://www.speech.kth.se/snack/].

[8] K. Sjölander and J. Beskow. WaveSurfer – an open source speech tool. In *Proceedings of the 6th International Conference on Spoken Language Processing*, 2000. [http://www.speech.kth.se/wavesurfer/].

APPENDIX

A. IDL DEFINITION FOR FLAT AG API

```
interface AG {

typedef string Id;        // generic identifier
typedef string AGSetId; // AGSet identifier
typedef string AGId;      // AG identifier
typedef string AGIds;
    // AG identifiers (space separated list)
typedef string AnnotationId;
    // Annotation identifier
typedef string AnnotationType; // Annotation type
typedef string AnnotationIds;
    // Annotation identifiers (list)
typedef string AnchorId;     // Anchor identifier
typedef string AnchorIds;
    // Anchor identifiers (list)
typedef string TimelineId; // Timeline identifier
typedef string SignalId;     // Signal identifier
typedef string SignalIds;
    // Signal identifiers (list)
typedef string FeatureName;  // feature name
typedef string FeatureNames; // feature name (list)
typedef string FeatureValue; // feature value
typedef string Features;
    // feature=value pairs (list)
typedef string URI;
    // a uniform resource identifier
typedef string MimeClass; // the MIME class
typedef string MimeType; // the MIME type
typedef string Encoding; // the signal encoding
typedef string Unit;      // the unit for offsets
typedef string AnnotationRef;
    // an annotation reference
typedef float  Offset; // the offset into a signal

//// AGSet ////
// Id is AGSetId or AGId
AGId       CreateAG( in Id          id
                     in TimelineId timelineId );
boolean    ExistsAG( in AGId         agId );
void       DeleteAG( in AGId         agId );
AGIds      GetAGIds( in AGSetId     agSetId );

//// Signals ////
```

```
TimelineId CreateTimeline( in URI        uri,
                           in MimeClass mimeClass,
                           in MimeType  mimeType,
                           in Encoding  encoding,
                           in Unit      unit,
                           in Track     track );
TimelineId CreateTimeline( in TimelineId timelineId,
                           in URI        uri,
                           in MimeClass mimeClass,
                           in MimeType  mimeType,
                           in Encoding  encoding,
                           in Unit      unit,
                           in Track     track);
boolean ExistsTimeline( in TimelineId timelineId );
void DeleteTimeline( in TimelineId timelineId );

// Id may be TimelineId or SignalId
SignalId CreateSignal( in Id         id,
                       in URI        uri,
                       in MimeClass mimeClass,
                       in MimeType  mimeType,
                       in Encoding  encoding,
                       in Unit      unit,
                       in Track     track );
boolean ExistsSignal( in SignalId signalId );
void    DeleteSignal( in SignalId signalId );
SignalIds GetSignals( in TimelineId timelineId );

MimeClass
   GetSignalMimeClass( in SignalId signalId );
MimeType
   GetSignalMimeType( in SignalId signalId );
Encoding GetSignalEncoding( in SignalId signalId );
string GetSignalXlinkType( in SignalId signalId );
string GetSignalXlinkHref( in SignalId signalId );
string GetSignalUnit(      in SignalId signalId );
Track  GetSignalTrack(     in SignalId signalId );

//// Annotation ////
// Id may be AGId or AnnotationId
AnnotationId CreateAnnotation( in Id id,
             in AnchorId anchorId1,
             in AnchorId anchorId2,
             in AnnotationType annotationType );
boolean ExistsAnnotation
             (in AnnotationId annotationId );
void    DeleteAnnotation
             (in AnnotationId annotationId );
AnnotationId CopyAnnotation
             (in AnnotationId annotationId );
AnnotationIds SplitAnnotation
             (in AnnotationId annotationId );
AnnotationIds NSplitAnnotation(
   in AnnotationId annotationId, in short N );
AnchorId
   GetStartAnchor( in AnnotationId annotationId);
AnchorId GetEndAnchor(
             in AnnotationId annotationId);
void SetStartAnchor( in AnnotationId annotationId,
             in AnchorId       anchorId );
void SetEndAnchor( in AnnotationId  annotationId,
             in AnchorId       anchorId );

Offset
   GetStartOffset( in AnnotationId annotationId );
Offset GetEndOffset(
             in AnnotationId annotationId );
void SetStartOffset( in AnnotationId annotationId,
             in Offset         offset );
void   SetEndOffset( in AnnotationId annotationId,
             in Offset         offset );
// this might be necessary to package up an id
// into a durable reference

AnnotationRef GetRef( in Id id );

//// Features ////
// this is for both the content of an annotation,
// and for the metadata associated with AGSets,
// AGs, Timelines and Signals.
void SetFeature( in Id id,
             in FeatureName  featureName,
             in FeatureValue featureValue );
boolean ExistsFeature( in Id id,
             in FeatureName featureName );
void DeleteFeature( in Id id,
             in FeatureName featureName );
string GetFeature( in Id id,
             in FeatureName featureName );
void UnsetFeature( in Id id,
             in FeatureName featureName );
FeatureNames GetFeatureNames( in Id id );
void         SetFeatures( in Id id,
             in Features features );
Features     GetFeatures( in Id id );
void         UnsetFeatures( in Id id );

//// Anchor ////
// Id may be AGId or AnchorId
AnchorId CreateAnchor( in Id id,
             in Offset offset,
             in Unit   unit,
             in SignalIds signalIds );
AnchorId CreateAnchor( in Id          id,
             in SignalIds signalIds );
AnchorId CreateAnchor( in Id        id );
boolean  ExistsAnchor( in AnchorId   anchorId );
void     DeleteAnchor( in AnchorId   anchorId );
void     SetAnchorOffset( in AnchorId anchorId,
             in Offset offset );
Offset   GetAnchorOffset( in AnchorId anchorId );
void    UnsetAnchorOffset( in AnchorId anchorId );
AnchorId SplitAnchor( in AnchorId anchorId );
AnnotationIds GetIncomingAnnotationSet(
             in AnchorId anchorId );
AnnotationIds GetOutgoingAnnotationSet(
             in AnchorId anchorId );
//// Index ////
AnchorIds GetAnchorSet( in AGId agId );
AnchorIds GetAnchorSetByOffset( in AGId agId,
             in Offset offset,
             in float  epsilon );
AnchorIds GetAnchorSetNearestOffset(
             in AGId   agId,
             in Offset offset );
AnnotationIds
   GetAnnotationSetByFeature( in AGId agId,
             in FeatureName featureName );
AnnotationIds
   GetAnnotationSetByOffset( in AGId agId,
             in Offset offset );
AnnotationIds
   GetAnnotationSetByType( in AGId agId,
             in AnnotationType annotationType );

//// Ids ////
// Id may be AGId, AnnotationId, AnchorId
AGSetId        GetAGSetId( in Id id );
// Id may be AnnotationId or AnchorId
AGId           GetAGId( in Id id );
// Id may be AGId or SignalId
TimelineId     GetTimelineId( in Id id );
};
```

Answering What-Is Questions by Virtual Annotation

John Prager
IBM T.J. Watson Research Center
Yorktown Heights, N.Y. 10598
(914) 784-6809
jprager@us.ibm.com

Dragomir Radev
University of Michigan
Ann Arbor, MI 48109
(734) 615-5225
radev@umich.edu

Krzysztof Czuba
Carnegie-Mellon University
Pittsburgh, PA 15213
(412) 268 6521
kczuba@cs.cmu.edu

ABSTRACT

We present the technique of Virtual Annotation as a specialization of Predictive Annotation for answering definitional **What is** questions. These questions generally have the property that the type of the answer is not given away by the question, which poses problems for a system which has to select answer strings from suggested passages. Virtual Annotation uses a combination of knowledge-based techniques using an ontology, and statistical techniques using a large corpus to achieve high precision.

Keywords

Question-Answering, Information Retrieval, Ontologies

1. INTRODUCTION

Question Answering is gaining increased attention in both the commercial and academic arenas. While algorithms for general question answering have already been proposed, we find that such algorithms fail to capture certain subtleties of particular types of questions. We propose an approach in which different types of questions are processed using different algorithms. We introduce a technique named Virtual Annotation (VA) for answering one such type of question, namely the **What is** question.

We have previously presented the technique of Predictive Annotation (PA) [Prager, 2000], which has proven to be an effective approach to the problem of Question Answering. The essence of PA is to index the semantic types of all entities in the corpus, identify the desired answer type from the question, search for passages that contain entities with the desired answer type as well as the other query terms, and to extract the answer term or phrase. One of the weaknesses of PA, though, has been in dealing with questions for which the system cannot determine the correct answer type required. We introduce here an extension to PA which we call Virtual Annotation and show it to be effective for those "What is/are (a/an) X" questions that are seeking hypernyms of X. These are a type of definition question, which other QA systems attempt to answer by searching in the document collection for textual clues similar to those proposed by [Hearst, 1998], that

are characteristic of definitions. Such an approach does not use the strengths of PA and is not successful in the cases in which a deeper understanding of the text is needed in order to identify the defining term in question.

We first give a brief description of PA. We look at a certain class of **What is** questions and describe our basic algorithm. Using this algorithm we develop the Virtual Annotation technique, and evaluate its performance with respect to both the standard TREC and our own benchmark. We demonstrate on two question sets that the precision improves from .15 and .33 to .78 and .83 with the addition of VA.

2. BACKGROUND

For our purposes, a question-answering (QA) system is one which takes a well-formed user question and returns an appropriate answer phrase found in a body of text. This generally excludes **How** and **Why** questions from consideration, except in the relatively rare cases when they can be answered by simple phrases, such as "by fermenting grapes" or "because of the scattering of light". In general, the response of a QA system will be a named entity such as a person, place, time, numerical measure or a noun phrase, optionally within the context of a sentence or short paragraph.

The core of most QA systems participating in TREC [TREC8, 2000 & TREC9, 2001] is the identification of the answer type desired by analyzing the question. For example, **Who** questions seek people or organizations, **Where** questions seek places, **When** questions seek times, and so on. The goal, then, is to find an entity of the right type in the text corpus in a context that justifies it as the answer to the question. To achieve this goal, we have been using the technique of PA to annotate the text corpus with semantic categories (QA-Tokens) prior to indexing.

Each QA-Token is identified by a set of terms, patterns, or finite-state machines defining matching text sequences. Thus "Shakespeare" is annotated with "PERSON$", and the text string "PERSON$" is indexed at the same text location as "Shakespeare". Similarly, "$123.45" is annotated with "MONEY$". When a question is processed, the desired QA-Token is identified and it replaces the Wh-words and their auxiliaries. Thus, "Who" is replaced by "PERSON$", and "How much" + "cost" are replaced by "MONEY$". The resulting query is then input to the search engine as a bag of words. The expectation here is that if the initial question were "Who wrote Hamlet", for example, then the modified query of "PERSON$ write Hamlet" (after lemmatization) would be a

Proceedings of HLT 2001, First International Conference on Human Language Technology Research, J. Allan, ed., Morgan Kaufmann, San Francisco, 2001.

perfect match to text that states "Shakespeare wrote Hamlet" or "Hamlet was written by Shakespeare".

The modified query is matched by the search engine against passages of 1-2 sentences, rather than documents. The top 10 passages returned are processed by our Answer Selection module which re-annotates the text, identifies all potential answer phrases, ranks them using a learned evaluation function and selects the top 5 answers (see [Radev et al., 2000]).

The problem with "What is/are (a/an) X" questions is that the question usually does not betray the desired answer type. All the system can deduce is that it must find a noun phrase (the QA-Token THING$). The trouble with THING$ is that it is too general and labels a large percentage of the nouns in the corpus, and so does not help much in narrowing down the possibilities. A second problem is that for many such questions the desired answer type is not one of the approximately 50 high-level classes (i.e. QA-Tokens) that we can anticipate at indexing; this phenomenon is seen in TREC9, whose 24 definitional **What is** questions are listed in the Appendix. These all appear to be calling out for a hypernym. To handle such questions we developed the technique of *Virtual Annotation* which is like PA and shares much of the same machinery, but does not rely on the appropriate class being known at indexing time. We will illustrate with examples from the animal kingdom, including a few from TREC9.

3. VIRTUAL ANNOTATION

If we look up a word in a thesaurus such as WordNet [Miller et al., 1993]), we can discover its hypernym tree, but there is no indication which hypernym is the most appropriate to answer a **What is** question. For example, the hypernym hierarchy for "nematode" is shown in Table 1. The level numbering counts levels up from the starting term. The numbers in parentheses will be explained later.

Table 1. Parentage of "nematode" according to WordNet.

Level	Synset
0	{nematode, roundworm}
1	{worm(13)}
2	{invertebrate}
3	{animal(2), animate being, beast, brute, creature, fauna}
4	{life form(2), organism(3), being, living thing}
5	{entity, something}

At first sight, the desirability of the hypernyms seems to decrease with increasing level number. However, if we examine "meerkat" we find the hierarchy in Table 2.

We are leaving much unsaid here about the context of the question and what is known of the questioner, but it is not unreasonable to assert that the "best" answer to "What is a meerkat" is either "a mammal" (level 4) or "an animal" (level 7). How do we get an automatic system to pick the right candidate?

Table 2. Parentage of "meerkat" according to WordNet

Level	Synset
0	{meerkat, mierkat}
1	{viverrine, viverrine mammal}
2	{carnivore}
3	{placental, placental mammal, eutherian, eutherian mammal}
4	{mammal}
5	{vertebrate, craniate}
6	{chordate}
7	{animal(2), animate being, beast, brute, creature, fauna}
8	{life form, organism, being, living thing}
9	{entity, something}

It seems very much that what we would choose intuitively as the best answer corresponds to Rosch et al.'s *basic categories* [Rosch et al., 1976]. According to psychological testing, these are categorization levels of intermediate specificity that people tend to use in unconstrained settings. If that is indeed true, then we can use online text as a source of evidence for this tendency. For example, we might find sentences such as "… meerkats and other Y …", where Y is one of its hypernyms, indicating that Y is in some sense the preferred descriptor.

We count the co-occurrences of the target search term (e.g. "meerkat" or "nematode") with each of its hypernyms (e.g. "animal") in 2-sentence passages, in the TREC9 corpus. These counts are the parenthetical numbers in Tables 1 and 2. The absence of a numerical label there indicates zero co-occurrences. Intuitively, the larger the count, the better the corresponding term is as a descriptor.

3.1 Hypernym Scoring and Selection
Since our ultimate goal is to find passages describing the target term, discovering zero co-occurrences allows elimination of useless candidates. Of those remaining, we are drawn to those with the highest counts, but we would like to bias our system away from the higher levels. Calling a nematode a life-form is correct, but hardly helpful.

The top levels of WordNet (or any ontology) are by definition very general, and therefore are unlikely to be of much use for purposes of definition. However, if none of the immediate parents of a term we are looking up co-occur in our text corpus, we clearly will be forced to use a more general term that does. We want to go further, though, in those cases where the immediate parents do occur, but in small numbers, and the very general parents occur with such high frequencies that our algorithm would select them. In those cases we introduce a tentative level ceiling to prevent higher-level terms from being chosen if there are suitable lower-level alternatives.

We would like to use a weighting function that decreases monotonically with level distance. Mihalcea and Moldovan [1999], in an analogous context, use the logarithm of the number of terms in a given term's subtree to calculate weights, and they claim to have shown that this function is optimal. Since it is approximately true that the level population increases exponentially in an ontology, this suggests that a linear function of level number will perform just as well.

Our first step is to generate a *level-adapted count* (LAC) by dividing the co-occurrence counts by the level number (we are only interested in levels 1 and greater). We then select the best hypernym(s) by using a fuzzy maximum calculation. We locate the one or more hypernyms with greatest LAC, and then also select any others with a LAC within a predefined threshold of it; in our experimentation we have found that a threshold value of 20% works well. Thus if, for example, a term has one hypernym at level 1 with a count of 30, and another at level 2 with a count of 50, and all other entries have much smaller counts, then since the LAC 25 is within 20% of the LAC 30, both of these hypernyms will be proposed.

To prevent the highest levels from being selected if there is any alternative, we tentatively exclude them from consideration according to the following scheme:

If the top of the tree is at level N, where N <= 3, we set a tentative ceiling at N-1, otherwise if N<=5, we set the ceiling at N-2, otherwise we set the ceiling at N-3. If no co-occurrences are found at or below this ceiling, then it is raised until a positive value is found, and the corresponding term is selected.

If no hypernym at all co-occurs with the target term, then this approach is abandoned: the "What" in the question is replaced by "THING$" and normal procedures of Predictive Annotation are followed.

When successful, the algorithm described above discovers one or more candidate hypernyms that are known to co-occur with the target term. There is a question, though, of what to do when the question term has more than one sense, and hence more than one ancestral line in WordNet. We face a choice of either selecting the hypernym(s) with the highest overall score as calculated by the algorithm described above, or collecting together the best hypernyms in each parental branch. After some experimentation we made the latter choice. One of the questions that benefitted from this was "What is sake". WordNet has three senses for sake: good (in the sense of welfare), wine (the Japanese drink) and aim/end, with computed scores of 122, 29 and 87/99 respectively. It seems likely (from the phrasing of the question) that the "wine" sense is the desired one, but this would be missed entirely if only the top-scoring hypernyms were chosen.

We now describe how we arrange for our Predictive Annotation system to find these answers. We do this by using these descriptors as *virtual QA-Tokens*; they are not part of the search engine index, but are tagged in the passages that the search engine returns at run time.

3.2 Integration

Let us use H to represent either the single hypernym or a disjunction of the several hypernyms found through the WordNet analysis. The original question Q =

"What is (a/an) X"

is converted to Q' =

"DEFINE$ X H"

where DEFINE$ is a *virtual* QA-Token that was never seen at indexing time, does not annotate any text and does not occur in the

index. The processed query Q' then will find passages that contain occurrences of both X and H; the token DEFINE$ will be ignored by the search engine. The top passages returned by the search engine are then passed to Answer Selection, which re-annotates the text. However, this time the virtual QA-Token DEFINE$ is introduced and the patterns it matches are defined to be the disjuncts in H. In this way, all occurrences of the proposed hypernyms of X in the search engine passages are found, and are scored and ranked in the regular fashion. The end result is that the top passages contain the target term and one of its most frequently co-occurring hypernyms in close proximity, and these hypernyms are selected as answers.

When we use this technique of Virtual Annotation on the aforementioned questions, we get answer passages such as

> *"Such genes have been found in nematode worms but not yet in higher animals."*

and

> *"South African golfer Butch Kruger had a good round going in the central Orange Free State trials, until a mongoose-like animal grabbed his ball with its mouth and dropped down its hole. Kruger wrote on his card: "Meerkat.""*

4 RESULTS
4.1 Evaluation
We evaluated Virtual Annotation on two sets of questions – the definitional questions from TREC9 and similar kinds of questions from the Excite query log (see http://www.excite.com). In both cases we were looking for definitional text in the TREC corpus. The TREC questions had been previously verified (by NIST) to have answers there; the Excite questions had no such guarantee. We started with 174 Excite questions of the form "What is X", where X was a 1- or 2-word phrase. We removed those questions that we felt would not have been acceptable as TREC9 questions. These were questions where:

- o The query terms did not appear in the TREC corpus, and some may not even have been real words (e.g. "What is a gigapop").[1] 37 questions.
- o The query terms were in the corpus, but there was no definition present (e.g "What is a computer monitor").[2] 18 questions.
- o The question was not asking about the class of the term but how to distinguish it from other members of the class (e.g. "What is a star fruit"). 17 questions.
- o The question was about computer technology that emerged after the articles in the TREC corpus were written (e.g. "What is a pci slot"). 19 questions.
- o The question was very likely seeking an example, not a definition (e.g. "What is a powerful adhesive"). 1 question plus maybe some others – see the Discussion

---

[1] That is, after automatic spelling correction was attempted.
[2] The TREC10 evaluation in August 2001 is expected to contain questions for which there is no answer in the corpus (deliberately). While it is important for a system to be able to make this distinction, we kept within the TREC9 framework for this evaluation.

section later. How to automatically distinguish these cases is a matter for further research.

Of the remaining 82 Excite questions, 13 did not have entries in WordNet. We did not disqualify those questions.

For both the TREC and Excite question sets we report two evaluation measures. In the TREC QA track, 5 answers are submitted per question, and the score for the question is the reciprocal of the rank of the first correct answer in these 5 candidates, or 0 if the correct answer is not present at all. A submission's overall score is the mean reciprocal rank (MRR) over all questions. We calculate MRR as well as mean binary score (MBS) over the top 5 candidates; the binary score for a question is 1 if a correct answer was present in the top 5 candidates, 0 otherwise. The first sets of MBS and MRR figures are for our base system, the second set the system with VA.

Table 3. Comparison of base system and system with VA on both TREC9 and Excite definitional questions.

Source	No. of Questions	MBS w/o VA	MRR w/o VA	MBS with VA	MRR with VA
TREC9 (in WN)	20	.3	.2	.9	.9
TREC9 (not in WN)	4	.5	.375	.5	.5
TREC9 Overall	24	.333	.229	.833	.833
Excite (in WN)	69	.101	.085	.855	.824
Excite (not in WN)	13	.384	.295	.384	.295
Excite Overall	82	.146	.118	.780	.740

We see that for the 24 TREC9 definitional questions, our MRR score with VA was the same as the MBS score. This was because for each of the 20 questions where the system found a correct answer, it was in the top position.

By comparison, our base system achieved an overall MRR score of .315 across the 693 questions of TREC9. Thus we see that with VA, the average score of definitional questions improves from below our TREC average to considerably higher. While the percentage of definitional questions in TREC9 was quite small, we shall explain in a later section how we plan to extend our techniques to other question types.

4.2 Errors
The VA process is not flawless, for a variety of reasons. One is that the hierarchy in WordNet does not always exactly correspond to the way people classify the world. For example, in WordNet a dog is not a pet, so "pet" will never even be a candidate answer to "What is a dog".

When the question term is in WordNet, VA succeeds most of the time. One of the error sources is due to the lack of uniformity of the semantic distance between levels. For example, the parents of "architect" are "creator" and "human", the latter being what our system answers to "What is an architect". This is technically correct, but not very useful.

Another error source is polysemy. This does not seem to cause problems with VA very often – indeed the co occurrence calculations that we perform are similar to those done by [Mihalcea and Moldovan, 1999] to perform word sense disambiguation – but it can give rise to amusing results. For example, when asked "What is an ass" the system responded with "Congress". *Ass* has four senses, the last of which in WordNet is a slang term for sex. The parent synset contains the archaic synonym *congress* (uncapitalized!). In the TREC corpus there are several passages containing the words *ass* and *Congress*, which lead to *congress* being the hypernym with the greatest score. Clearly this particular problem can be avoided by using orthography to indicate word-sense, but the general problem remains.

5 DISCUSSION AND FURTHER WORK
5.1 Discussion
While we chose not to use Hearst's approach of key-phrase identification as the primary mechanism for answering **What is** questions, we don't reject the utility of the approach. Indeed, a combination of VA as described here with a key-phrase analysis to further filter candidate answer passages might well reduce the incidence of errors such as the one with *ass* mentioned in the previous section. Such an investigation remains to be done.

We have seen that VA gives very high performance scores at answering **What is** questions – and we suggest it can be extended to other types – but we have not fully addressed the issue of automatically selecting the questions to which to apply it. We have used the heuristic of only looking at questions of the form "What is (a/an) X" where X is a phrase of one or two words. By inspection of the Excite questions, almost all of those that pass this test are looking for definitions, but some - such as "What is a powerful adhesive" - very probably do not. There are also a few questions that are inherently ambiguous (understanding that the questioners are not all perfect grammarians): is "What is an antacid" asking for a definition or a brand name? Even if it is known or assumed that a definition is required, there remains the ambiguity of the state of knowledge of the questioner. If the person has no clue what the term means, then a parent class, which is what VA finds, is the right answer. If the person knows the class but needs to know how to distinguish the object from others in the class, for example "What is a star fruit", then a very different approach is required. If the question seems very specific, but uses common words entirely, such as the Excite question "What is a yellow spotted lizard", then the only reasonable interpretation seems to be a request for a subclass of the head noun that has the given property. Finally, questions such as "What is a nanometer" and "What is rubella" are looking for a value or more common synonym.

5.2 Other Question Types

The preceding discussion has centered upon **What is** questions and the use of WordNet, but the same principles can be applied to other question types and other ontologies. Consider the question "Where is Chicago", from the training set NIST supplied for TREC8. Let us assume we can use statistical arguments to decide that, in a vanilla context, the question is about the city as opposed to the rock group, any of the city's sports teams or the University. There is still considerable ambiguity regarding the granularity of the desired answer. Is it: Cook County? Illinois? The Mid-West? The United States? North America? The Western Hemisphere? ...

There are a number of geographical databases available, which either alone or with some data massaging can be viewed as ontologies with "located within" as the primary relationship. Then by applying Virtual Annotation to **Where** questions we can find the enclosing region that is most commonly referred to in the context of the question term. By manually applying our algorithm to "Chicago" and the list of geographic regions in the previous paragraph we find that "Illinois" wins, as expected, just beating out "The United States". However, it should be mentioned that a more extensive investigation might find a different weighting scheme more appropriate for geographic hierarchies.

The aforementioned answer of "Illinois" to the question "Where is Chicago?" might be the best answer for an American user, but for anyone else, an answer providing the country might be preferred. How can we expect Virtual Annotation to take this into account? The "hidden variable" in the operation of VA is the corpus. It is assumed that the user belongs to the intended readership of the articles in the corpus, and to the extent that this is true, the results of VA will be useful to the user.

Virtual Annotation can also be used to answer questions that are seeking examples or instances of a class. We can use WordNet again, but this time look to hyponyms. These questions are more varied in syntax than the **What is** kind; they include, for example from TREC9 again:

> "Name a flying mammal."
> "What flower did Vincent Van Gogh paint?"

and

> "What type of bridge is the Golden Gate Bridge?"

6. SUMMARY

We presented Virtual Annotation, a technique to extend the capabilities of PA to a class of definition questions in which the answer type is not easily identifiable. Moreover, VA can find text snippets that do not contain the regular textual clues for presence of definitions. We have shown that VA can considerably improve the performance of answering **What is** questions, and we indicate how other kinds of questions can be tackled by similar techniques.

7. REFERENCES

[1] Hearst, M.A. "Automated Discovery of WordNet Relations" in *WordNet: an Electronic Lexical Database*, Christiane Fellbaum Ed, MIT Press, Cambridge MA, 1998.

[2] Mihalcea, R. and Moldovan, D. "A Method for Word Sense Disambiguation of Unrestricted Text". *Proceedings of the 37th Annual Meeting of the Association for Computational Linguistics (ACL-99)*, pp. 152-158, College Park, MD, 1999.

[3] Miller, G. "WordNet: A Lexical Database for English", *Communications of the ACM* 38(11) pp. 39-41, 1995.

[4] Moldovan, D.I. and Mihalcea, R. "Using WordNet and Lexical Operators to Improve Internet Searches", *IEEE Internet Computing*, pp. 34-43, Jan-Feb 2000.

[5] Prager, J.M., Radev, D.R., Brown, E.W. and Coden, A.R. "The Use of Predictive Annotation for Question-Answering in TREC8", *Proceedings of TREC8*, Gaithersburg, MD, 2000.

[6] Prager, J.M., Brown, E.W., Coden, A.R., and Radev, D.R. "Question-Answering by Predictive Annotation", *Proceedings of SIGIR 2000*, pp. 184-191, Athens, Greece, 2000.

[7] Radev, D.R., Prager, J.M. and Samn, V. "Ranking Suspected Answers to Natural Language Questions using Predictive Annotation", *Proceedings of ANLP'00*, Seattle, WA, 2000.

[8] Rosch, E. et al. "Basic Objects in Natural Categories", *Cognitive Psychology* 8, pp. 382-439, 1976.

[9] TREC8 - "The Eighth Text Retrieval Conference", E.M. Voorhees and D.K. Harman Eds., NIST, Gaithersburg, MD, 2000.

[10] TREC9 - "The Ninth Text Retrieval Conference", E.M. Voorhees and D.K. Harman Eds., NIST, Gaithersburg, MD, to appear.

APPENDIX
What-is questions from TREC9

617: What are chloroplasts? (X)
528: What are geckos?
544: What are pomegranates?
241: What is a caldera? (X)
358: What is a meerkat?
434: What is a nanometer? (X)
354: What is a nematode?
463: What is a stratocaster?
447: What is anise?
386: What is anorexia nervosa?
635: What is cribbage?
300: What is leukemia?
305: What is molybdenum?
644: What is ouzo?
420: What is pandoro? (X)
228: What is platinum?
374: What is porphyria?
483: What is sake?
395: What is saltpeter?
421: What is thalassemia?
438: What is titanium?
600: What is typhoid fever?
468: What is tyvek?
539: What is witch hazel?

Our system did not correctly answer the questions marked with an "X". For all of the others the correct answer was the first of the 5 attempts returned.

Architecture and Design Considerations in NESPOLE!: a Speech Translation System for E-commerce Applications

Alon Lavie,
Chad Langley,
Alex Waibel
Carnegie Mellon University
Pittsburgh, PA, USA

alavie@cs.cmu.edu

Fabio Pianesi,
Gianni Lazzari,
Paolo Coletti
ITC-irst
Trento, Italy

Loredana Taddei,
Franco Balducci
AETHRA
Ancona, Italy

1. INTRODUCTION

NESPOLE! [1] is a speech-to-speech machine translation research project funded jointly by the European Commission and the US NSF. The main goal of the NESPOLE! project is to advance the state-of-the-art of speech-to-speech translation in a real-world setting of common users involved in e-commerce applications. The project is a collaboration between three European research labs (IRST in Trento Italy, ISL at University of Karlsruhe in Germany, CLIPS at UJF in Grenoble France), a US research group (ISL at Carnegie Mellon in Pittsburgh) and two industrial partners (APT - the Trentino provincial tourism bureau, and Aethra - an Italian tele-communications commercial company). The speech-to-speech translation approach taken by the project builds upon previous work that the research partners conducted within the context of the C-STAR consortium (see http://www.c-star.org). The prototype system developed in NESPOLE! is intended to provide effective multi-lingual speech-to-speech communication between all pairs of four languages (Italian, German, French and English) within broad, but yet restricted domains. The first showcase currently under development is in the domain of tourism and travel information.

The NESPOLE! speech translation system is designed to be an integral part of advanced e-commerce technology of the next generation. We envision a technological scenario in which multi-modal (speech, video and gesture) interaction plays a significant role, in addition to the passive browsing of pre-designed web pages as is common in e-commerce today. The interaction between client and provider will need to support online communication with agents (both real and artificial) on the provider side. The language barrier then becomes a significant obstacle for such online communication between the two parties, when they do not speak a common language. Within the tourism and travel domain, one can imagine a scenario in which users (the clients) are planning a recreational trip and are searching for specific detailed information about the

---

[1] NESPOLE! - NEgotiating through SPOken Language in E-commerce. See the project website at http://nespole.itc.it/

Proceedings of HLT 2001, First International Conference on Human Language Technology Research, J. Allan, ed., Morgan Kaufmann, San Francisco, 2001.

regions they wish to visit. Initial general information is obtained from a web site of a tourism information provider. When more detailed or special information is required, the customer has the option of opening an online video-conferencing connection with a human agent of the tourism information provider. Speech translation is integrated within the video-conference connection; the two parties each speak in their native language and hear the synthesized translation of the speech of the other participant. Text translation (in the form of subtitles) can also be provided. Some multi-modal communication between the parties is also available. The provider agent can send web pages to the display of the customer, and both sides can annotate and refer to pictures and diagrams presented on a shared whiteboard application.

In this paper we describe the design considerations behind the architecture that we have developed for the NESPOLE! speech translation system in the scenario described above. In order to make the developed prototype as realistic as possible for use by a common user, we assume only minimal hardware and software is available on the customer side. This does include a PC-type video camera, commercially available internet video-conferencing software (such as Microsoft Netmeeting), standard audio and video hardware and a standard web browser. However, no speech recognition and/or translation software is assumed to reside locally on the PC of the customer. This implies a server-type architecture in which speech recognition and translation are accomplished via interaction with a dedicated server. The extent to which this server is centralized or distributed is one of the major design considerations taken into account in our system.

2. NESPOLE! INTERLINGUA-BASED TRANSLATION APPROACH

Our translation approach builds upon previous work that we have conducted within the context of the C-STAR consortium. We use an interlingua-based approach with a relatively shallow task-oriented interlingua representation [2] [1], that was initially designed for the C-STAR consortium and has been significantly extended for the NESPOLE! project. Interlingual machine translation is convenient when more than two languages are involved because it does not require each language to be connected by a set of transfer rules to each other language in each direction [3]. Adding a new language that has all-ways translation with existing languages requires only writing one analyzer that maps utterances into the interlingua and one generator that maps interlingua representations into sentences. The interlingua approach also allows each partner group to implement an analyzer and generator for its home language only. A fur-

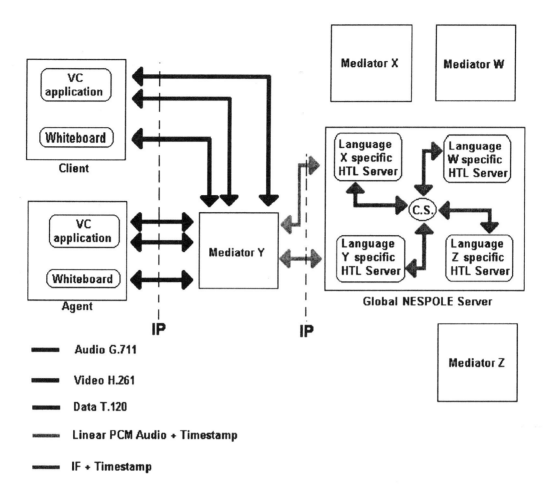

Figure 1: General Architecture of NESPOLE! System

ther advantage is that it supports a paraphrase generation back into the language of the speaker. This provides the user with some control in case the analysis of an utterance failed to produce a correct interlingua. The following are three examples of utterances tagged with their corresponding interlingua representation:

```
Thank you very much
c:thank

And we'll see you on February twelfth.
a:closing (time=(february, md12))

On the twelfth we have a single and a double
available.
a:give-information+availability+room
    (room-type=(single & double),time=(md12))
```

3. NESPOLE! SYSTEM ARCHITECTURE DESIGN

Several main considerations were taken into account in the design of the NESPOLE! Human Language Technology (HLT) server architecture: (1) The desire to cleanly separate the actual HLT system from the communication channel between the two parties, which makes use of the speech translation capabilities provided by

the HLT system; (2) The desire to allow each research site to independently develop its language specific analysis and generation modules, and to allow each site to easily integrate new and improved components into the global NESPOLE! HLT system; and (3) The desire of the research partners to build to whatever extent possible upon software components previously developed in the context of the C-STAR consortium. We will discuss the extent to which the designed architecture achieves these goals after presenting an overview of the architecture itself.

Figure 1 shows the general architecture of the current NESPOLE! system. Communication between the client and agent is facilitated by a dedicated module - the *Mediator*. This module is designed to control the video-conferencing connection between the client and the agent, and to integrate the speech translation services into the communication. The mediator handles audio and video data associated with the video-conferencing application and binary data associated with a shared whiteboard application. Standard H.323 data formats are used for these three types of data transfer. Speech-to-speech translation of the utterances captured by the mediator is accomplished through communication with the NESPOLE! global HLT server. This is accomplished via socket connections with language-specific HLT servers. The communication between the mediator and each HLT server consists mainly of linear PCM audio packets (some text and control messages are also supported and are described later in this section).

32

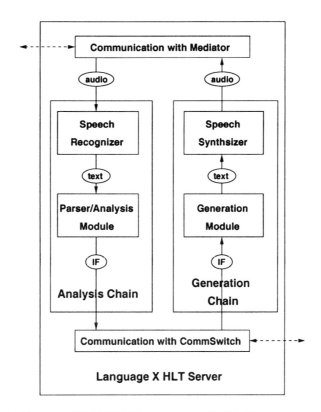

Figure 2: Architecture of NESPOLE! Language-specific HLT Servers

The global NESPOLE! HLT server comprises four separate language-specific servers. Additional language-specific HLT servers can easily be integrated in the future. The internal architecture of each language-specific HLT server is shown in figure 2. Each language-specific HLT server consists of an *analysis chain* and a *generation chain*. The analysis chain receives an audio stream corresponding to a single utterance and performs speech recognition followed by parsing and analysis of the input utterance into the interlingua representation (IF). The interlingua is then transmitted to a central HLT communication switch (the CS), that forwards it to the HLT servers for the other languages as appropriate. IF messages received from the central communication switch are processed by the generation chain. A generation module first generates text in the target language from the IF. The text utterance is then sent to a speech synthesis module that produces an audio stream for the utterance. The audio is then communicated externally to the mediator, in order to be integrated back into the video-conferencing stream between the two parties.

The mediator can, in principle, support multiple one-to-one communication sessions between client and agent. However, the design supports multiple mediators, which, for example, could each be dedicated to a different provider application. Communication with the mediator is initiated by the client by an explicit action via the web browser. This opens a communication channel to the mediator, which contacts the agent station, establishes the video-conferencing connection between client and agent, and starts the whiteboard application. The specific pair of languages for a dialogue is determined in advance from the web page from which the client initiates the communication. The mediator then establishes a socket communication channel with the two appropriate language specific HLT servers. Communication between the two language

specific HLT servers, in the form of IF messages, is facilitated by the NESPOLE! global communication switch (the CS). The language specific HLT servers may in fact be physically distributed over the internet. Each language specific HLT server is set to service analysis requests coming from the mediator side, and generation requests arriving from the CS.

Some further functionality beyond that described above is also supported. As described earlier, the ability to produce a textual paraphrase of an input utterance and to display it back to the original speaker provides useful user control in the case of translation failures. This is supported in our system in the following way. In addition to the translated audio, each HLT server also forwards the generated text in the output language to the mediator, which then displays the text on a dedicated application window on the PC of the target user. Additionally, at the end of the processing of an input utterance by the analysis chain of an HLT server, the resulting IF is passed internally to the generation chain, which produces a text generation from the IF. The result is a textual paraphrase of the input utterance in the source language. This text is then sent back to the mediator, which forwards it to the party from which the utterance originated. The paraphrase is then displayed to the original speaker in the dedicated application window. If the paraphrase is wrong, it is likely that the produced IF was incorrect, and thus the translation would also be wrong. The user may then use a button on the application interface to signal that the last displayed paraphrase was wrong. This action triggers a message that is forwarded by the mediator to the other party, indicating that the last displayed translation should be ignored. Further functionality is planned to support synchronization between multi-modal events on the whiteboard and their corresponding speech actions. As these are in very preliminary stages of planning we do not describe them here.

4. DISCUSSION AND CONCLUSIONS

We believe that the architectural design described above has several strengths and advantages. The clean separation of the HLT server dedicated to the speech translation services from the external communication modules between the two parties allows the research partners to develop the HLT modules with a large degree of independence. Furthermore, this separation will allow us in the future to explore other types of mediators for different types of applications. One such application being proposed for development within the C-STAR consortium is a speech-to-speech translation service over mobile phones. The HLT server architecture described here would be able to generally support such alternative external communication modalities as well.

The physical distribution of the individual language specific HLT servers allows each site to independently develop, integrate and test its own analysis and generation modules. The organization of each language specific HLT server as an independent module allows each of the research sites to develop its unique approaches to analysis and generation, while adhering to a simple communication protocol between the HLT servers and externally with the mediator. This allowed the research partners to "jump-start" the project with analysis and generation modules previously developed for the C-STAR consortium, and incrementally develop these modules over time. Furthermore, the global NESPOLE! communication switch (the CS) supports testing of analysis and generation among the four languages in isolation from the external parts of the system. Currently, requests for analysis of a textual utterance can be transmitted to the HLT servers via the CS, with the resulting IF sent (via the CS) to all HLT servers for generation. This gives us great flexibility in developing and testing our translation system. The functionality of the CS was originally developed for our previous C-STAR project, and was reused with little modification.

Support for additional languages is also very easy to incorporate into the system by adding new language-specific HLT servers. Any new language specific HLT server needs only to adhere to the communication protocols with both the global NESPOLE! communication switch (the CS) and the external mediator. The C-STAR consortium plans to use the general architecture described here for its next phase of collaboration, with support for at least three asian languages (Japanese, Korean and Chinese) in addition to the languages currently covered by the NESPOLE! project.

The first prototype of the NESPOLE! speech translation system is currently in advanced stages of full integration. A showcase demonstration of the prototype system to the European Commission is currently scheduled for late April 2001.

5. ACKNOWLEDGMENTS

The research work reported here was supported in part by the National Science Foundation under Grant number 9982227. Any opinions, findings and conclusions or recomendations expressed in this material are those of the author(s) and do not necessarily reflect the views of the National Science Foundation (NSF).

6. REFERENCES

[1] L. Levin, D. Gates, A. Lavie, F. Pianesi, D. Wallace, T. Watanabe, and M. Woszczyna. Evaluation of a Practical Interlingua for Task-Oriented Dialogue. In *Workshop on Applied Interlinguas: Practical Applications of Interlingual Approaches to NLP*, Seattle, 2000.

[2] L. Levin, D. Gates, A. Lavie, and A. Waibel. An Interlingua Based on Domain Actions for Machine Translation of Task-Oriented Dialogues. In *Proceedings of the International Conference on Spoken Language Processing (ICSLP'98)*, pages Vol. 4, 1155–1158, Sydney, Australia, 1998.

[3] S. Nirenburg, J. Carbonell, M. Tomita, and K. Goodman. *Machine Translation: A Knowledge-Based Approach*. Morgan Kaufmann, San Mateo, California, 1992.

Assigning Belief Scores to Names in Queries

Christopher Dozier

Research and Development
Thomson Legal and Regulatory
610 Opperman Drive
Eagan, MN 55123,USA
chris.dozier@westgroup.com

ABSTRACT

Assuming that the goal of a person name query is to find references to a particular person, we argue that one can derive better relevance scores using probabilities derived from a language model of personal names than one can using corpus based occurrence frequencies such as inverse document frequency (idf). We present here a method of calculating person name match probability using a language model derived from a directory of legal professionals. We compare how well name match probability and idf predict search precision of word proximity queries derived from names of legal professionals and major league baseball players. Our results show that name match probability is a better predictor of relevance than idf. We also indicate how rare names with high match probability can be used as virtual tags within a corpus to identify effective collocation features for person names within a professional class.

1. INTRODUCTION

Some of the most common types of queries submitted to search engines both on the internet and on proprietary text search systems consist simply of a person's name. To improve the way such queries are handled, it would be useful if search engines could estimate the likelihood or belief that a name contained in a document pertains to the name in the query. Traditionally, relevance likelihood for name phrases has been based on inverse document frequency or idf, [3][4]. The idea behind this relevance estimate is that names which rarely occur in the corpus are thought to be more indicative of relevance than names that commonly occur.

Assuming that the goal of a person name query is to find references to a particular person, we argue that one can derive better relevance scores using probabilities derived from a language model of personal names than one can using corpus based occurrence frequencies. The reason for this is that finding references to a particular person in text is more dependent upon the relative rarity of the name with respect to the human population than it is on the rarity of the name within a corpus.

To get an intuitive idea of this point, consider that, within a corpus of 27,000 Wall Street Journal articles published between January and August of the year 2000, the name "Trent Lott" occurred in 80 documents while the name "John Smith" occurred in 24. All 80 references to "Trent Lott" referred to the majority leader of the U.S. Senate, while "John Smith" references mapped to 5 different people. This is not surprising. From our experience, we know that "Trent Lott" is an uncommon name and "John Smith" is a common one.

We present here evidence that name match probability based on a language model predicts relevance for name queries far better than idf. It may be argued that idf was never intended to be used to measure the relative ambiguity of a name query. However, idf is the standard measure used in probabilistic search engines to measure the degree of relevance terms and phrases within a collection have to the terms and phrases in queries, [1] [5]. For this reason, we take idf to be the standard against which to compare name match probability.

Being able to predict relevance through name match probabilities enables us to do three things. First, it tells us when we need to add information to the query to improve precision either by prompting the user for it or automatically expanding the query. Second, and perhaps more importantly, it enables us to use names with high match probabilities as virtual tags that can help us find useful collocation features to disambiguate names within a given class of names, such as the names of attorneys and judges. For purposes of this paper, we define an ambiguous name as one likely to be shared by many people and an unambiguous name as one likely to apply to a single person or to only a few people. And third, match probability can be used as a feature within a name search operator to improve search precision.

2. DESCRIPTION OF MATCH PROBABILITY CALCULATION FOR PERSON NAMES

The motivation for our work is an effort to develop a name search operator to find attorneys and judges in the news. In our particular application, we wish to allow users to search for newspaper references to attorneys and judges listed in a directory of U.S. legal professionals. This directory contains the curriculum vitae of approximately one million people. In this section, we show how we calculate person name match probability.

To compute the probability of relevance or match probability for a name, we perform three steps. First, we compute a probability distribution for the first and last names in our name directory. This is our language model. Second, we compute a name's probability by multiplying its first name probability with its last

Proceedings of HLT 2001, First International Conference on Human Language Technology Research, J. Allan, ed., Morgan Kaufmann, San Francisco, 2001.

name probability. Third, we compute its match probability by taking the reciprocal of the product of the name probability and the size of the human population likely to be referenced in the corpus. For our Wall Street Journal test corpus, we estimated this size to be approximately the size of the U.S. population or 300 million. Formulas for the three steps are shown below.

$$(1) \quad P(\,first\_name\,) = \frac{F}{N}$$

$$P(\,last\_name\,) = \frac{L}{N}$$

where F = number of occurrences of first name, L = number of occurrences of last name, and N = number of names in the directory.

$$(2) \quad P(\,name\,) = P(\,first\_name\,) \cdot P(\,last\_name\,)$$

$$(3) \quad P(\,name\_match\,) = \frac{1}{\big(H \cdot P(\,name\,)\big) + 1}$$

where H = size of human population likely to be referenced by the collection.

Example calculations for Trent Lott and John Smith are shown below in Table 1.

In this example, the match probability for Trent Lott is approximately four orders of magnitude higher than the match probability for John Smith, while idf or document frequency suggests the likelihood of relevance for documents retrieved for John Smith is higher than for documents retrieved for Trent Lott. Both empirically and intuitively, match probability is a better predictor of relevance here than idf.

3. EVALUATION OF NAME MATCH PROBABILITY VERSUS IDF

To test our hypothesis that name match probability predicts relevance better than idf, we compared how well name queries with high match probabilities performed against name queries with high idf. We performed two experiments. In the first, we

selected names of individuals in our legal directory. In the second, we used the names of currently active major league baseball players.

To conduct the first experiment, we labeled person names in a collection of 27,000 WSJ documents with a commercially available name tagging program. We then extracted these names and created a merged list of names specified by first and last name and pulled from this list names that occurred within our legal directory. We then sorted this list by name match probability and by document occurrence frequency (which is equivalent to idf) to create two lists. We then binned the names in the name match probability list into sets that fell between the following probability ranges: 1.0-0.9, 0.9-0.8 ,0.8-0.7, 0.7-0.6, 0.6-0.5, 0.5-0.4, 0.4-0.3, 0.3-0.2, 0.2-0.1, and 0.1-0.0. We binned the names in the document frequency list into sets that fell into the following document occurrence frequencies: 1, 2, 3, 4, 5, 6, 7, 8, 9, and >=10.

We then selected 50 names at random from each of these bins (except for bins associated with 0.8-0.7 and 0.7-0.6 probabilities which contained 42 and 31 names respectively). For each name selected, we identified the legal directory entry that was compatible with the name. In most cases, only one legal directory entry was compatible with the name. In some cases, multiple entries were compatible. For example, the name "Paul Brown" is compatible with 71 legal directory entries since there are 71 people in the directory with the first name "Paul" and the last name "Brown". In these cases, we selected one of the entries at random.

For each name in each bin, we found the set of documents in the WSJ collection that would be returned by the word proximity query "First_name +2 Last_name". That is, the documents that contained the first name followed within two words by the last name.

The search precision results for match probability and document frequency bins are shown in tables 2 and 3 below. The search precision of each bin was the number of relevant documents returned by the names in the bin divided by the total number of documents returned. The row labeled "Number Unique Names in Each Category" is a count of the number of unique first and last name pairs found within the WSJ collection for the probability and document frequency ranges indicated. It was from these sets of names that we selected our queries.

The results in tables 2 and 3 show that match probability does a better job of estimating relevance than idf. Table 2 shows that search precision goes up as match probability rises. Table 3 shows no apparent correspondence between document frequency and search precision.

Table 1: Example Calculation of Match Probability

Name	P(first name)	P(last name)	P(name)	P(name match)	Doc Freq
Trent Lott	0.000084	0.000048	0.00000000408	0.449371705	80
John Smith	0.036409	0.006552	0.00023857	0.00001397	24

Table 2: Search Precision At Different Match Probabilities for Names Compatible with Judge and Attorney Names for WSJ Collection

Match Prob Range	1.0 - 0.9	0.9 – 0.8	0.8 – 0.7	0.7 – 0.6	0.6 – 0.5	0.5 – 0.4	0.4 – 0.3	0.3 – 0.2	0.2 – 0.1	0.1 – 0.0
Search Precision	0.835	0.754	0.595	0.677	0.596	0.708	0.628	0.544	0.520	0.12
Number Unique Names in Each Category	80	61	42	31	57	72	113	135	292	10758

Table 3: Search Precision At Different Document Occurrence Frequencies for Names Compatible with Judge and Attorney Names for WSJ Collection

Doc Freq	1	2	3	4	5	6	7	8	9	>=10
Search Precision	0.18	0.10	0.10	0.20	0.06	0.10	0.08	0.18	0.14	0.24
Number Unique Names in Each Category	7702	1946	703	374	224	145	95	75	55	322

Table 4: Search Precision At Different Match Probabilities for Names Compatible with Names of Major League Baseball Players for WSJ Collection

Match Prob Range	1.0 - 0.9	0.9 – 0.8	0.8 – 0.7	0.7 – 0.6	0.6 – 0.5	0.5 – 0.4	0.4 – 0.3	0.3 – 0.2	0.2 – 0.1	0.1 – 0.0
Search Precision	1.0	1.0	1.0	1.0	1.0	1.0	1.0	1.0	0.939	0.633
Number Unique Names in Each Category	15	5	2	2	2	3	2	7	7	48

Table 5: Search Precision At Different Document Occurrence Frequencies for Names Compatible with Names of Major League Baseball Players for WSJ Collection

Doc Freq	1	2	3	4	5	6	7	8	9	>=10
Search Precision	0.888	0.882	0.952	1.0	0.75	0.666	1.0	NA	1.0	0.74
Number Unique Names in Each Category	45	17	7	3	4	6	2	0	1	8

In the second experiment, we performed basically the same steps described above on the names of the 286 baseball players currently playing in the major leagues. We assigned name match probabilities to these names using the language model we derived from the legal directory. Of the 286 names, we found 82 that were compatible with one or more name instances in the WSJ collection. For all 82, we found the set of documents in the WSJ collection that would be returned by the word proximity query "First_name +2 Last_name". We then measured how frequently the documents returned for a particular word proximity query actually referenced the player with which the name query was paired. As in the attorney and judge name experiment, name match probability predicted relevance more accurately than idf. The results for baseball player names are shown in tables 4 and 5 above.

Note that on average the search precision for baseball players was higher than for attorneys and judges. This is due to the combined effects of there being far fewer baseball player names than attorney and judge names and the fact that the average probability of a baseball player being mentioned in the news is higher than the average probability for a judge or attorney being mentioned.

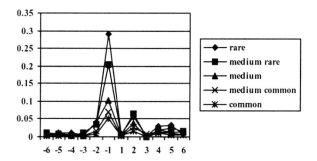

Figure1: Conditional probability of attorney terms by word position relative to name

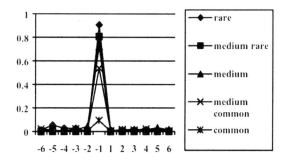

Figure2: Conditional probability of judge terms by word position relative to name

4. USING RARE NAMES TO IDENTIFY SEARCH FEATURES

An important use of name match probabilities is the identification of co-occurrence features in text that can serve to disambiguate name references. If we know certain names in the corpora very probably refer to certain individuals listed in a professional directory, we can look for words that co-occur frequently with these names but infrequently with names in general. These words are likely to work well at disambiguating references to names of low match probability.

As an example of feature identification, consider the figures 1 and 2 above. In these figures, the word "rare" stands for the 20% of names in the legal directory that have the highest match

probability. The phrase "medium rare" stands for the next 20% and so on. The word "common" then stands for the 20% of names with the lowest match probability. For each of the five categories of name rarity, the graphs in the figures show the probability of an appositive term occurring at a given word position relative to the position of a name.

Figure 1 shows the probability of attorney appositive nouns such as "attorney", "lawyer", "counsel", or "partner" occurring at 12 different word positions around attorney names of varying degrees of rarity. Position –1 stands for the word position directly before the name. Position +1 stands for the position directly after. Position –2 stands for the word position two words in front of the name and so on. Figure 2 shows the probability of judge appositive nouns such as "judge" or "justice" occurring around judge names.

The graphs in figures 1 and 2 show that the probability of appositive terms occurring at particular word positions grows steadily as the name rarity increases. This demonstrates that appositive terms are good indicators for judge and attorney names within the WSJ collection. The figures also shows the word positions in which we should look for appositive terms.

Figure 1 shows that we should look for attorney appositives in word positions –2, -1, +2, +4, and +5. This makes intuitive sense because it accounts for sentence constructs such as those shown in table 6.

Table 6: Examples of Use of Attorney Term Near Attorney Name

Relative Word Position	Example sentence
-2	**Attorney** General Janet Reno said today .....
-1	**Attorney** Jack Smith defended his client vigorously.
+2	said Vicki Patton, senior **attorney** for Environmental Defense
+4	said Jim Hahn, Los Angeles City **Attorney**
+5	says Buck Chapoton, a prominent Washington tax **attorney**

The sudden drop off in appositive term probability at word position +1 also makes sense since an article, adjective, or other part of speech often occurs between a trailing appositive head noun and the proper noun it modifies. The drop off at word position +3 is still something of a mystery and is not something we can explain at this time. Since +3 behavior seems to have no linguistic basis that we can perceive, we do not rely on it in constructing our search operator.

Figure 2 shows that we should look for judge appositives in word position -1. This makes perfect sense since it accounts for constructs such as " Judge William Rehnquist" and "Justice Antonin Scalia". Figure 2 also suggests that using the -1 appositive test should yield good search recall since the conditional probability for rare names is about 0.9.

5. PRELIMINARY SEARCH OPERATOR EXPERIMENTS

We are currently investigating what levels of search precision and recall we can achieve with special attorney and judge name search operators using name rarity together with co-occurrence features such as appositive, city, state, firm, and court terms. Our preliminary results are encouraging. Initial experiments with the attorney search operator indicate we can achieve a nine fold improvement in search precision over simple word proximity searches over the WSJ collection while sacrificing 18% recall. Preliminary results are shown in table 7 below. We produced these results by selecting 677 attorney names at random from the legal directory that existed within the WSJ collection. For each name, we ran word proximity searches using the first and last name of the lawyers and scored the results. Using the scored results from 377 of the names, we then trained a special Bayesian based name operator that used first name, last name, city, state, firm, and name rarity information as sources of name match evidence. Finally we tested the word proximity operator performance against the special name operator using the remaining 300 names.

Note that we have assumed above that word proximity searches yield 100% recall. This is not wholly accurate since it does not account for nicknames, use of first name initials, and so on. We plan to revise this recall estimate in the future, but for now we assume that a word proximity search on first and last name provides close to 100% recall in a collection such as the WSJ.

Table 7: Comparison of Performance of Word Proximity Search and Special Name Operator Searches for Attorney Names

Search Method	Precision	Recall	F-measure
Word proximity	0.09	1.00	0.17
Attorney Name Search Operator	0.85	0.82	0.83

6. FUTURE WORK

We plan to complete development of search operators for attorney and judges that make use of the combined features of name rarity, appositives, city, state, firm, and court terms. We plan to compare the performance of these operators against searches based on name indexes derived from combining MUC style extraction techniques and record linking techniques. [2] Our hope is that the search operators will perform at levels close to the indexed based searches so that we can avoid the operational costs of creating special name indexes.

We plan to mine names from text using name rarity and seed appositive phrases. For example, using a seed appositive phrase for a profession such as "expert witness", we plan to identify and extract a set of expert witness names. From this initial set of names, we will identify rare names and use these to identify more appositive phrases. Once the appositive phrases are identified, we plan to extract more names, then more appositive phrases, and so on until a stopping condition is reached. In this manner, we hope to develop a technique to automatically extract name lists from text collections.

Finally we plan to assess whether it is possible to develop similar name match probability calculations for other types of names such as company names, organization names, and product names.

7. CONCLUSION

Assuming that the goal of a person name query is to find references to a particular person, we have shown that one can derive better relevance scores using probabilities derived from a language model of personal names than one can using corpus based occurrence frequencies. We presented here a method of calculating person name match probability using a language model derived from a directory of legal professionals. We compared how well name match probability and idf predict search precision of word proximity queries derived from names of legal professionals and major league baseball players. Our results showed that name match probability is a better predictor of relevance than idf. We also indicated how rare names with high match probability can be used as virtual tags within a corpus to identify effective collocation features for person names within a professional class.

8. REFERENCES

[1] Baeza-Yates, R. and Ribeiro-Neto, B., Modern Information Retrieval. ACM Press, New York, 1999.

[2] Dozier, C. and Haschart, R., "Automatic Extraction and Linking of Person Names in Legal Text" in Proceedings of RIAO '2000; Content Based Multimedia Information Access. Paris, France. pp.1305-1321. 2000

[3] de Lima, F. and Pedersen, J., Phrase Recognition and Expansion for Short, Precision-biased Queries based on a Query Log. In Proc.of the 22nd Annual Int. ACM SIGIR Conference on Research and Development in Information Retrieval, pp. 145 – 152, Berkeley, California, USA, 1999.

[4] Thompson, P. and Dozier, C., Name Searching and Information Retrieval. In Proc.of the 2nd Conference on Empirical Methods in NLP, pp. 134 –140, Providence, Rhode Island, 1997.

[5] Turtle, H. and Croft, W., Inference Networks for Document Retrieval. In Proc.of the 13th Annual Int. ACM SIGIR Conference on Research and Development in Information Retrieval, pp. 1 – 24, Brussels, Belgium, 1990.

Automatic Pattern Acquisition
for Japanese Information Extraction

Kiyoshi Sudo
Computer Science
Department
New York University
715 Broadway, 7th floor,
New York, NY 10003 USA

sudo@cs.nyu.edu

Satoshi Sekine
Computer Science
Department
New York University
715 Broadway, 7th floor,
New York, NY 10003 USA

sekine@cs.nyu.edu

Ralph Grishman
Computer Science
Department
New York University
715 Broadway, 7th floor,
New York, NY 10003 USA

grishman@cs.nyu.edu

ABSTRACT

One of the central issues for information extraction is the cost of customization from one scenario to another. Research on the automated acquisition of patterns is important for portability and scalability. In this paper, we introduce Tree-Based Pattern representation where a pattern is denoted as a path in the dependency tree of a sentence. We outline the procedure to acquire Tree-Based Patterns in Japanese from un-annotated text. The system extracts the relevant sentences from the training data based on TF/IDF scoring and the common paths in the parse tree of relevant sentences are taken as extracted patterns.

Keywords

Information Extraction, Pattern Acquisition

1. INTRODUCTION

Information Extraction (IE) systems today are commonly based on pattern matching. New patterns need to be written when we customize an IE system for a new scenario (extraction task); this is costly if done by hand. This has led to recent research on automated acquisition of patterns from text with minimal pre-annotation. Riloff [4] reported a successful result for her procedure that needs only a pre-classified corpus. Yangarber [6] developed a procedure for unannotated natural language texts.

One of their common assumption is that the relevant documents include good patterns. Riloff implemented this idea by applying the pre-defined heuristic rules to pre-classified (relevant) documents and Yangarber advanced further so that the system can classify the documents by itself given *seed patterns* specific to a scenario and then find the best patterns from the relevant document set.

Considering how they represent the patterns, we can see that, in general, Riloff and Yangarber relied on the sentence structure of English. Riloff's predefined heuristic rules are based on syntactic structures, such as "<subj> active-verb" and "active-verb

<dobj>". Yangarber used triples of a predicate and some of its arguments, such as "<pred> <subj> <obj>".

The Challenges

Our careful examination of Japanese revealed some of the challenges for automated acquisition of patterns and information extraction on Japanese(-like) language and other challenges which arise regardless of the languages.

Free Word-ordering

Free word order is one of the most significant problems in analyzing Japanese. To capture all the possible patterns given a predicate and its arguments, we need to permute the arguments and list all the patterns separately. For example, for "<subj> <dobj> <iobj> <predicate>" with the constraint that the predicate comes last in the sentence, there would be six possible patterns (permutations of three arguments). The number of patterns to cover even simple facts would rise unacceptably high.

Flexible case marking system

There is also a difficulty in a language with a flexible case marking system, like Japanese. In particular, we found that, in Japanese, some of the arguments that are usually marked as object in English were variously marked by different post-positions, and some case markers (postpositions) are used for marking more than one grammatical category in different situations. For example, the topic marker in Japanese, "wa", can mark almost any entity that would have been variously marked in English. It is difficult to deal with this variety by simply fixing the number of arguments of a predicate for creating patterns in Japanese.

Relationships beyond direct predicate-argument

Furthermore, we may want to capture the relationship between a predicate and a modifier of one of its arguments. In previous approaches, one had to introduce an ad hoc frame for such a relationship, such as "verb obj [PP <head-noun>]", to extract the relationship between "to assume" and "<organization>" in the sentence "<person> will assume the <post> of <organization>".

Relationships beyond clausal boundaries

Another problem lies in relationships beyond clause boundaries, especially if the event is described in a subordinate clause. For example, for a sentence like "<organization> announced that <person> retired from <post>," it is hard to find a relationship between <organization> and the event of retiring without the global view

Proceedings of HLT 2001, First International Conference on Human Language Technology Research, J. Allan, ed., Morgan Kaufmann, San Francisco, 2001.

from the predicate "announce".

These problems lead IE systems to fail to capture some of the arguments needed for filling the template. Overcoming the problems above makes the system capable of finding more patterns from the training data, and therefore, more slot-fillers in the template.

In this paper, we introduce Tree-based pattern representation and consider how it can be acquired automatically.

2. TREE-BASED PATTERN REPRESENTATION (TBP)

Definition

Tree-based representation of patterns (TBP) is a representation of patterns based on the dependency tree of a sentence. A pattern is defined as a path in the dependency tree passing through zero or more intermediate nodes within the tree. The dependency tree is a directed tree whose nodes are *bunsetsu*s or phrasal units, and whose directed arcs denote the dependency between two *bunsetsu*s: A→B denotes A's dependency on B (e.g. A is a subject and B is a predicate.) Here dependency relationships are not limited to just those between a case-marked element and a predicate, but also include those between a modifier and its head element, which covers most relationships within sentences. [1]

TBP for Information Extraction

Figure 2 shows how TBP is used in comparison with the word-order based pattern, where A...F in the left part of the figure is a sequence of the phrasal units in a sentence appearing in this order and the tree in the right part is its dependency tree. To find the relationship between B→F, a word-order based pattern needs a dummy expression to hold C, D and E, while TBF can denote the direct relationship as B→F. TBP can also represent a complicated pattern for a node which is far from the root node in the dependency tree, like C→D→E, which is hard to represent without the sentence structure.

For matching with TBP, the target sentence should be parsed into a dependency tree. Then all the predicates are detected and the subtrees which have a predicate node as a root are traversed to find a match with a pattern.

Benefit of TBP

TBP has some advantages for pattern matching over the surface word-order based patterns in addressing the problems mentioned in the previous section:

- Free word-order problem

  TBP can offer a direct representation of the dependency relationship even if the word-order is different.

- Free case-marking problem

  TBP can freely traverse the whole dependency tree and find any significant path as a pattern. It does not depend on predefined case-patterns as Riloff [4] and Yangarber [6] did.

- Indirect relationships

  TBP can find indirect relationships, such as the relationship between a predicate and the modifier of the argument of the

[1] In this paper, we used the Japanese parser KNP [1] to obtain the dependency tree of a sentence.

predicate. For example, the pattern "<organization>$\overset{of}{\to}$<post>$\overset{to}{\to}$appoint" can capture the relationship between "<organization>" and "to be appointed" in the sentence
"<person> was appointed to <post> of <organization>."

- Relationships beyond clausal boundaries

  TBP can capture relationships beyond clausal boundaries. The pattern "<post>$\overset{to}{\to}$appoint$\overset{COMP}{\to}$announce" can find the relationship between "<post>" and "to announce". This relationship, later on, can be combined with the relationship "<organization>" and "to announce" and merged into one event.

3. ALGORITHM

In this section, we outline our procedure for automatic acquisition of patterns. We employ a cascading procedure, as is shown in Figure 3. First, the original documents are processed by a morphological analyzer and NE-tagger. Then the system retrieves the relevant documents for the scenario as a *relevant document set*. The system, further, selects a set of relevant sentences as a *relevant sentence set* from those in the *relevant document set*. Finally, all the sentences in the *relevant sentence set* are parsed and the paths in the dependency tree are taken as patterns.

3.1 Document Preprocessing

Morphological analysis and Named Entity (NE) tagging is performed on the training data at this stage. We used JUMAN [2] for the former and a NE-system which is based on a decision tree algorithm [5] for the latter. Also the part-of-speech information given by JUMAN is used in the later stages.

3.2 Document Retrieval

The system first retrieves the documents that describe the events of the scenario of interest, called the *relevant document set*. A set of narrative sentences describing the scenario is selected to create a query for the retrieval. For this experiment, we set the size of the *relevant document set* to 300 and retrieved the documents using CRL's stochastic-model-based IR system [3], which performed well in the IR task in IREX, Information Retrieval and Extraction evaluation project in Japan [2]. All the sentences used to create the patterns are retrieved from this *relevant document set*.

3.3 Sentence Retrieval

The system then calculates the TF/IDF-based score of relevance to the scenario for each sentence in the *relevant document set* and retrieves the n most relevant sentences as the source of the patterns, where n is set to 300 for this experiment. The retrieved sentences will be the source for pattern extraction in the next subsection.

First, the TF/IDF-based score for every word in the *relevant document set* is calculated. TF/IDF score of word w is:

$$score(w) = \begin{cases} TF(w) \cdot \frac{\log\frac{N+0.5}{DF(w)}}{\log(N+1)} & \text{if } w \text{ is Noun, Verb or Named Entity} \\ 0 & \text{otherwise} \end{cases}$$

where N is the number of documents in the collection, $TF(w)$ is the term frequency of w in the relevant document set and $DF(w)$ is the document frequency of w in the collection.

Second, the system calculates the score of each sentence based on the score of its words. However, unusually short sentences and

[2] IREX Homepage: http://cs.nyu.edu/cs/projects/proteus/irex

Dependency Tree   *Tree-Based Pattern*

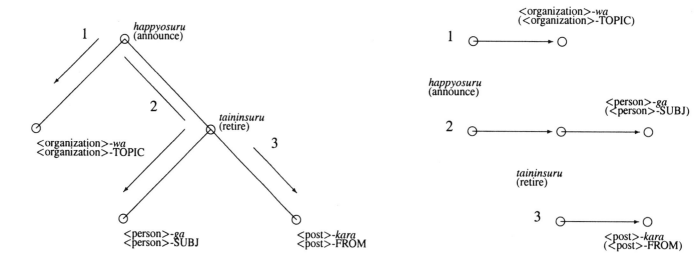

Figure 1: Tree-Based Pattern Representation

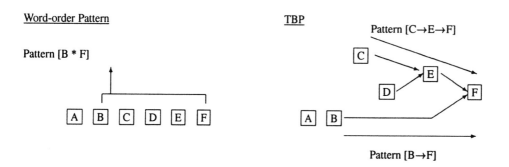

Figure 2: Extraction using Tree-Based Pattern Representation

unusually long sentences will be penalized. The TF/IDF score of sentence s is:

$$score(s) = \frac{\sum_{w \in s} score(w)}{length(s) + |length(s) - AVE|}$$

where $length(s)$ is the number of words in s, and AVE is the average number of words in a sentence.

3.4 Pattern Extraction

Based on the dependency tree of the sentences, patterns are extracted from the relevant sentences retrieved in the previous subsection. Figure 4 shows the procedure. First, the retrieved sentence is parsed into a dependency tree by KNP [1] (Stage 1). This stage also finds the predicates in the tree. Second, the system takes all the predicates in the tree as the roots of their own subtrees, as is shown in (Stage 2). Then each path from the root to a node is extracted, and these paths are collected and counted across all the relevant sentences. Finally, the system takes those paths with fre-

quency higher than some threshold as extracted patterns. Figure 5 shows examples of the acquired patterns.

4. EXPERIMENT

It is not a simple task to evaluate how good the acquired patterns are without incorporating them into a complete extraction system with appropriate template generation, etc. However, finding a match of the patterns and a portion of the test sentences can be a good measure of the performance of patterns.

The task for this experiment is to find a *bunsetsu*, a phrasal unit, that includes slot-fillers by matching the pattern to the test sentence. The performance is measured by recall and precision in terms of the number of slot-fillers that the matched patterns can find; these are calculated as follows.

$$Recall = \frac{\# \ of \ Matched \ Relevant \ SlotFillers}{\# \ of \ All \ Relevant \ SlotFillers}$$

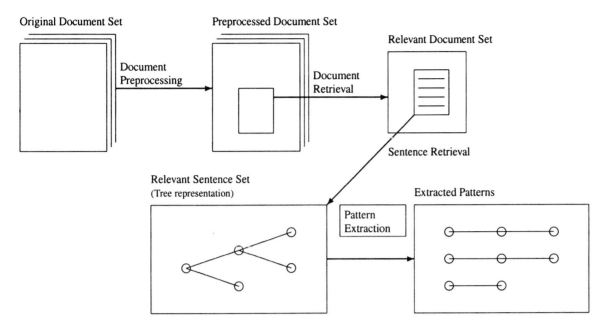

Figure 3: Pattern Acquisition Procedure Overall Process

$$Precision = \frac{\#\ of\ Matched\ Relevant\ SlotFillers}{\#\ of\ All\ Matched\ SlotFillers}$$

The procedure proposed in this paper is based on *bunsetsu*s, and an individual *bunsetsu* may contain more than one slot filler. In such cases the procedure is given credit for each slot filler.

Strictly speaking, we don't know how many entities in a matched pattern *might* be slot-fillers when, actually, the pattern does *not* contain any slot-fillers (in the case of over-generating). We approximate the potential number of slot-fillers by assigning 1 if the (falsely) matched pattern does not contain any Named-Entities, or assigning the number of Named-Entities in the (falsely) matched pattern. For example, if we have a pattern "go to dinner" for a management succession scenario and it matches falsely in some part of the test sentences, this match will gain one at the number of All Matched Slot-fillers (the denominator of the precision). On the other hand, if the pattern is "<post> <person> *laugh*" and it falsely matches "President Clinton laughed", this will gain two, the number of the Named Entities in the pattern.

For the sake of comparison, we defined the baseline system with the patterns acquired by the same procedure but only from the direct relationships between a predicate and its arguments (PA in Figure 6 and 7).

We chose the following two scenarios.

- Executive Management Succession: events in which corporate managers left their positions or assumed new ones regardless of whether it was a present (time of the report) or past event.

  Items to extract: Date, person, organization, title.

- Robbery Arrest: events in which robbery suspects were arrested.

  Items to extract: Date, suspect, suspicion.

4.1 Data

	Management Succession
Documents	15
Sentences	79
DATE	43
PERSON	41
ORGANIZATION	22
OLD-ORGANIZATION	2
NEW-POST	30
OLD-POST	39

Table 1: Test Set for Management Succession scenario

	Robbery Arrest
Documents	28
Sentences	182
DATE	26
SUSPICION	34
SUSPECT	50

Table 2: Test Set for Robbery Arrest scenario

For all the experiments, we used the Mainichi-Newspaper-95 corpus for training. As described in the previous section, the system retrieved 300 articles for each scenario as the *relevant document set* from the training data and it further retrieved 300 sentences as the *relevant sentence set* from which all the patterns were extracted.

Test data was taken from Mainichi-Newspaper-94 by manually reviewing the data for one month. The statistics of the test data are shown in Table 1 and 2.

4.2 Results

Figure 6 and Figure 7 illustrates the precision-recall curve of this

Japanese sentence :	\<organization\>-wa	\<person\>-ga	\<post\>-ni	shuninsuru-to	happyoshita.
English Translation :	\<organization\>-TOPIC	\<person\>-SBJ	\<post\>-TO	start-COMP	announced.

(\<organization\> announced that \<person\> was appointed to \<post\>.)

Stage 1 (Dependency Tree)　　　　　Stage 2 (Separated Trees)

\<org\>-wa
\<psn\>-ga　　　happyoshita(*p*)
shuninsuru(*p*)-to
\<post\>-ni

(*p* indicates the node is a predicate.)

\<org\>-wa
\<psn\>-ga　　1　happyoshita(*p*)
2　　4
3
\<post\>-ni

\<psn\>-ga　5
　　shuninsuru(*p*)
\<post\>-ni　6

Extracted Patterns

1 \<organization\>-wa → happyosuru

2 \<person\>-ga → shuninsuru-to → happyosuru

3 \<post\>-ni → shuninsuru-to → happyosuru

4 shuninsuru-to → happyosuru

5 \<person\>-ga → shuninsuru

6 \<post\>-ni → shuninsuru

Figure 4: Pattern Acquisition from "\<org\>-wa \<psn\>-ga \<pst\>-ni shuninsuru-to happyoshita."

experiment for the executive management succession scenario and robbery arrest scenario, respectively. We ranked all the acquired patterns by calculating the sum of the TF/IDF-based score (same as for sentence retrieval in Section 3.3) for each word in the pattern and sorting them on this basis. Then we obtained the precision-recall curve by changing the number of the top-ranked patterns in the list.

Figure 6 shows that TBP is superior to the baseline system both in recall and precision. The highest recall for TBP is 34% while the baseline gets 29% at the same precision level. On the other hand, at the same level of recall, TBP got higher precision (75%) than the baseline (70%).

We can also see from Figure 6 that the curve has a slightly anomalous shape where at lower recall (below 20%) the precision is also low for both TBP and the baseline. This is due to the fact that the pattern lists for both TBP and the baseline contains some non-reliable patterns which get a high score because each word in the patterns gets higher score than others.

Figure 7 shows the result of this experiment on the Robbery Arrest scenario. Although the overall recall is low, TBP achieved higher precision and recall (as high as 30% recall at 40% of precision) than the baseline except at the anomalous point where both TBP and the baseline got a small number of perfect slot-fillers by a highly ranked pattern, namely "*gotoyogi-de* → *taihosuru* (to arrest

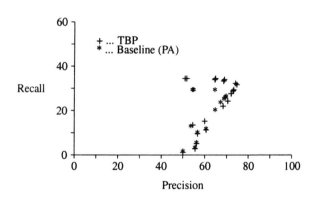

Figure 6: Result on Management Succession Scenario

44

Scenario	Patterns	
Executive Succession :	\<post>-ni → shokakusuru	(to be promoted to \<post>)
	\<post>-ni → shuninsuru	(to assume \<post>)
	\<post>-ni → shokakusuru →	(to announce an informal decision of promoting
	\<jinji>-o → happyosuru	somebody to \<post>)
Robbery Arrest :	satsujin-yogi-de → taihosuru	(to arrest in suspicion of murder)
	\<date> → taihosuru	(to arrest on \<date>)
	satsujin-yogi-de → taihosuru	(to arrest in suspicion of murder)
	\<person>-yogisha → #-o → taihosuru	(to arrest the suspect, \<person>, age #)

Figure 5: Acquired Patterns

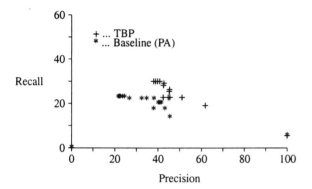

Figure 7: Result on Robbery Arrest Scenario

on suspicion of robbery)" for the baseline and "\<person> yogisha → \<number>-o → taihosuru (to arrest the suspect, \<person>, age \<number>)".

5. DISCUSSION

Low Recall

It is mostly because we have not made a class of types of crimes that the recall on the robbery arrest scenario is low. Once we have a classifier as reliable as Named-Entity tagger, we can make a significant gain in the recall of the system. And in turn, once we have a class name for crimes in the training data (automatically annotated by the classifier) instead of a separate name for each crime, it becomes a good indicator to see if a sentence should be used to acquire patterns. And also, incorporating the classes in patterns can reduce the noisy patterns which do not carry any slot-fillers of the template.

For example on the management succession scenario, all the slot-fillers defined there were able to be tagged by the Named-Entity tagger [5] we used for this experiment, including the *title*. Since we knew all the slot-fillers were in one of the classes, we also knew those patterns whose argument was not classified any of the classes would not likely capture slot-fillers. So we could put more weight on those patterns which contained \<person>, \<organization>, \<post> and \<date> to collect the patterns with higher performance, and therefore we could achieve high precision.

Erroneous Case Analysis

We also investigated other scenarios, namely train accident and airplane accident scenario, which we will not report in this paper. However, some of the problems which arose may be worth mentioning since they will arise in other, similar scenarios.

- Results or Effects of the Target Event

  Especially for the airplane accident scenario, most errors were identified as matching the effect or result of the incident. A typical example is "Because of the accident, the airport had been closed for an hour." In the airplane accident scenario, the performance of the document retrieval and the sentence retrieval is not as good as the other two scenarios, and therefore, the frequency of relevant acquired patterns is rather low because of the noise. Further improvement in retrieval and a more robust approach is necessary.

- Related but Not-Desired Sentences

  If the scenario is specific enough to make it difficult as an IR task, the result of the document retrieval stage may include many documents related to the scenario in a broader sense but not specific enough for IE tasks. In this experiment, this was the case for the airplane accident scenario. The result of document retrieval included documents about other accidents in general, such as traffic accidents. Therefore, the sentence retrieval and pattern acquisition for these scenarios were affected by the results of the document retrievals.

6. FUTURE WORK

Information Extraction

To apply the acquired patterns to an information extraction task, further steps are required besides those mentioned above. Since the patterns are a set of the binary relationships of a predicate and another element, it is necessary to merge the matched elements into a whole event structure.

Necessity for Generalization

We have not yet attempted any (lexical) generalization of pattern candidates. The patterns can be expanded by using a thesaurus and/or introducing a new (lexical) class suitable for a particular domain. For example, the class of expressions of flight number clearly helps the performance on the airplane accident scenario. Especially, the generalized patterns will help improve recall.

Robust Pattern Extraction

As is discussed in the previous section, the performance of our system relies on each component. If the scenario is difficult for the IR task, for example, the whole result is affected. The investigation of a more conservative approach would be necessary.

Translingualism

The presented results show that our procedure of automatic pattern acquisition is promising. The procedure is quite general and addresses problems which are not specific to Japanese. With an appropriate morphological analyzer, a parser that produces a dependency tree and an NE-tagger, our procedure should be applicable to almost any language.

7. ACKNOWLEDGMENTS

This research is supported by the Defense Advanced Research Projects Agency as part of the Translingual Information Detection, Extraction and Summarization (TIDES) program, under Grant N66001-00-1-8917 from the Space and Naval Warfare Systems Center San Diego. This paper does not necessarily reflect the position or the policy of the U.S. Government.

8. REFERENCES

[1] S. Kurohashi and M. Nagao. Kn parser : Japanese dependency/case structure analyzer. In *the Proceedings of the Workshop on Sharable Natural Language Resources*, 1994.

[2] Y. Matsumoto, S. Kurohashi, O. Yamaji, Y. Taeki, and M. Nagano. Japanese morphological analyzing system: Juman. *Kyoto University and Nara Institute of Science and Technology*, 1997.

[3] M. Murata, K. Uchimoto, H. Ozaku, and Q. Ma. Information retrieval based on stochastic models in irex. In *the Proceedings of the IREX Workshop*, 1994.

[4] E. Riloff. Automatically generating extraction patterns from untagged text. In *the Proceedings of Thirteenth National Conference on Artificial Intelligence (AAAI-96)*, 1996.

[5] S. Sekine, R. Grishman, and H. Shinnou. A decision tree method for finding and classifying names in japanese texts. In *the Proceedings of the Sixth Workshop on Very Large Corpora*, 1998.

[6] R. Yangarber, R. Grishman, P. Tapanainen, and S. Huttunen. Unsupervised discovery of scnario-level patterns for information extraction. In *the Proceedings of the Sixth Applied Natural Language Processing Conference*, 2000.

Automatic Predicate Argument Analysis of the Penn TreeBank

Martha Palmer, Joseph Rosenzweig and Scott Cotton
CIS Department, University of Pennsylvania
{mpalmer,josephr,cotton}@linc.cis.upenn.edu

1. INTRODUCTION

One of the primary tasks of Information Extraction is recognizing all of the different guises in which a particular type of event can appear. For instance, a meeting between two dignitaries can be referred to as *A meets B* or *A and B meet*, or *a meeting between A and B took place/was held/opened/convened/finished/dragged on* or *A had/presided over a meeting/conference with B*

There are several different lexical items that can be used to refer to the same type of event, and several different predicate argument patterns that can be used to specify the participants. Correctly identifying the type of the event and the roles of the participants is a critical factor in accurate information extraction. In this paper we refer to the specific subtask of participant role identification as predicate argument tagging. The type of syntactic and semantic information associated with verbs in Levin's Preliminary Classification of English verbs, [Levin,93] can be a useful resource for an automatic predicate argument tagging system. For instance, the *'meet'* class includes the following members, *meet, consult, debate* and *visit,* which can all be used to refer to the meeting event type described above. In addition, the following types of syntactic frames are associated with these verbs:

A *met/visited/debated/consulted* B
A *met/visited/debated/consulted* with B.
A and B *met/visited/debated/consulted*
    (with each other).

This type of frame information can be specified at the class level, but there is always a certain amount of verb-specific information that must still be associated with the individual lexical items, such as sense distinctions. For the purposes of this paper we will only be considering sense distinctions based on different predicate argument structures. We begin by giving more information about the Levin classes and then describe the system that automatically labels the arguments in a predicate argument structure. We end by giving the results of evaluating this system versus human annotators performing the same task. Our input to the tagger is the Penn TreeBank [Marcus, 94], so the sentences already have accurate syntactic parses associated with them.

2. LEXICON GUIDELINES

As mentioned above, Levin classes provide the theoretical underpinnings for many of our choices for basic predicate-argument structures [Levin, 93]. Levin verb classes are based on the ability of a verb to occur or not occur in pairs of syntactic frames that are in some sense meaning preserving (diathesis alternations). The distribution of syntactic frames in which a verb can appear determines its class membership. The sets of syntactic frames associated with a particular Levin class are not intended to be arbitrary, and they are supposed to reflect underlying semantic components that constrain allowable arguments. For example, *break* verbs and *cut* verbs are similar in that they can all occur as transitives and in the middle construction, *John broke the window, Glass breaks easily, John cut the bread, This loaf cuts easily.* However, only break verbs can also occur in the simple intransitive, *The window broke, *The bread cut.* Notice that for all of these verbs, the subject of the intransitive, *The window*

Proceedings of HLT 2001, First International Conference on Human Language Technology Research, J. Allan, ed., Morgan Kaufmann, San Francisco, 2001.

broke, plays the same role as the object of the transitive, *John broke the window*. Our goal is to capture this by using consistent argument labels, in this case Arg1 for the *window* in both sentences. So, for example, *shake* and *rock* would get the following annotation:

The earthquake   shook   the building.
Arg0   REL   Arg1

The walls   shook;
Arg1   REL

the building   rocked.
Arg1   REL

VerbNet In a related project funded by NSF, NSF-IIS98-00658, we are currently constructing a lexicon, VerbNet, that is intended to overcome some of the limitations of WordNet, an on-line lexical database of English, [Miller, 90], by addressing specifically the needs of natural language processing applications. This lexicon exploits the systematic link between syntax and semantics that motivates the Levin classes, and thus provides a clear and regular association between syntactic and semantic properties of verbs and verb classes, [Dang, et al, 98, 00, Kipper, et al. 00]. Specific sets of syntactic configurations and appropriate selectional restrictions on arguments are associated with individual senses. This lexicon gives us a first approximation of sense distinctions that are reflected in varying predicate argument structures. As such these entries provide a suitable foundation for directing consistent predicate-argument labeling of training data.

The senses in VerbNet are in turn linked to one or more WordNet senses. Since our focus is predicate-argument structure, we can rely on rigorous and objective sense distinction criteria based on syntax. Purely semantic distinctions, such as those made in WordNet, are subjective and potentially unlimited. Our senses are therefore much more coarse-grained than WordNet, since WordNet senses are purely semantically motivated and often cannot be distinguished syntactically. However, some

senses that share syntactic properties can still be distinguished clearly by virtue of different selectional restrictions, which we will also be exploring in the NSF project.

3. AUTOMATIC EXTRACTION OF PREDICATE-ARGUMENT RELATIONS FROM PARSED CORPORA

The predicate-argument analysis of a parse tree from a corpus such as the Treebank corpus is performed in three main phases. First, root forms of inflected words are identified using a morphological analyzer derived from the WordNet stemmer and from inflectional information in machine-readable dictionaries such as the Project Gutenberg version of Webster. Also in this phase, phrasal items such as verb-particle constructions, idioms and compound nominals are identified. An efficient matching algorithm is used which is capable of recognizing both continuous and discontinuous phrases, and phrases where the order of words is not fixed. The matching algorithm makes use of hierarchical declarative constraints on the possible realizations of phrases in the lexicon, and can exploit syntactic contextual cues if a syntactic analysis of the input, such as the parse tree structure of the Treebank, is present. In the next phase, the explicit antecedents of empty constituents are read off from the Treebank annotation, and gaps are filled where implicit linkages have been left unmarked. This is done by heuristic examination of the local syntactic context of traces and relative clause heads. If no explicit markings are present (for automatically generated parses or old-style Treebank parses), they are inferred. Estimated accuracy of this phase of the algorithm is upwards of 90 percent.

Finally, an efficient tree-template pattern matcher is run on the Treebank parse trees, to identify syntactic relations that signal a predicate-argument relationship between lexical items. The patterns used are fragmentary tree templates similar to the elementary and auxiliary trees of a Tree Adjoining Grammar [XTAG, 95]. Each template typically corresponds to a predication over one or more arguments. There are approximately 200 templates for: transitive, intransitive and ditransitive verbs operating on their subjects, objects and indirect objects; prenominal and predicate adjectives, operating on the nouns they modify; subordinating conjunctions operating on the two clauses that they link; prepositions; determiners; and so on. The templates are organized into a compact network in which shared substructures need to be listed only once, even when they are present in many templates.

Templates are matched even if they are not contiguous in the tree, as long as the intervening material is well-formed. This allows a transitive template for example to match a sentence where there is an intervening auxiliary verb between the subject and the main transitive verb, as in *He was dropping it*. The mechanism for handling such cases resembles the adjunction mechanism in Tree Adjoining Grammar.

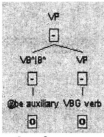

Tree grammar template for progressive auxiliary verb, licensing discontinuity in main verb tree

When a template has been identified, it is instantiated with the lexical items that occur in its predicate and argument positions. Each template is associated with one or more annotated template sets, by means of which it is linked to a bundle of thematic or semantic features, and to a class of lexical items that license the template's occurrence with those features. For instance, if the template is an intransitive verb tree, it will be associated both with an unergative feature bundle, indicating that its subject should have the label Arg0, and also with an unaccusative bundle where the subject is marked as

Arg1. Which of the feature bundles gets used depends on the semantic class of the word that

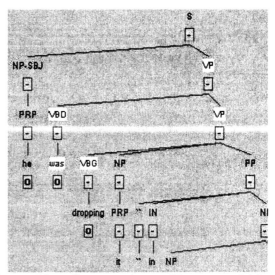

Recognition of progressive auxiliary tree which modifies and splits transitive-verb tree for drop in Treebank corpus

appears in the predicate position of the template. If the predicate is a causative verb that takes the unaccusative alternation, the subject will be assigned the Arg1 label. If however it is a verb of creation, for example, the subject will be an Arg0. The verb semantics that inform the predicate-argument extractor are theoretically motivated by the Levin classes [Levin, 93], but the actual lexical information it uses is not derived from Levin's work. Rather, it draws on information available in the WordNet 1.6 database [Miller, 90] and on frame codes are derived from the annotation scheme used in the Susanne corpus [Sampson, 95].

For example, one entry for the verb *develop* specifies its WordNet synset membership, and indicates its participation in the unaccusative alternation with the code **o_can_become_s**

develop **SF:so_N_N+W:svJ3W_W:svlM2+o_can_become_s**

The prefix **SF:** signifies that this is a frame code derived from the Susanne corpus. Each frame code picks out a lexical class of the words that take it, and the frame codes are organized into an inheritance network as well. The frame codes in turn are linked to annotated template sets, which describe how these frames can actually appear in the syntactic bracketing format of the TreeBank. In the case of the above frame code for an alternating transitive verb, two template sets are linked: **TG:V_so_N_N** for the frame with a subject and an object (here notated with **s** and **o**); and **TG:V_s_N+causative**, for the unaccusative frame. Each of the template sets lists tree-grammar templates for all the variations of syntactic structure that its corresponding frame may take on. A template for the canonical structure of a simple declarative sentence involving that frame will be present in the set, but additional templates will be added for the forms the frame takes in relative clauses, questions, or passive constructions.

The features for each set are listed separately from the templates, with indications of where they should be interpreted within the various template structures. Hence the template set **TG:V_s_N+causative** includes the feature **TGC:subject+print_as=TGPL:arg1** as part of its feature bundle. This serves to associate the label Arg1 with the **subject** node in each template in the set. When the predicate-argument extractor is able to instantiate such a template, thereby connecting its **subject** node with a piece of a TreeBank tree, it knows to print that piece of the tree as Arg1 of the predicate for that template. If another annotated feature set were active instead, for instance in a case where the predicate of the template does not belong to a verb class which licenses the unaccusative frame code and its associated annotated template set (**TG:V_s_N+causative**), the label of the subject might be different.

4. EVALUATION

The current implementation of the tagger assigns predicate argument structures to all of the 6500 verbs that occur in the Penn Treebank. However, our evaluation of its accuracy is not yet so comprehensive. Our first preliminary evaluation of the performance of the tagger was based on a 5000 word section of the Penn TreeBank. The tagger was

run on this, and the argument labeling was subsequently hand corrected by a linguistics graduate student, giving an accuracy rate of 81% out of 160 predicate argument structures. We have since automatically tagged and hand corrected an additional 660 predicate argument structures, with an accuracy rate of 86%, (556 structures), giving us a combined accuracy rate of 83.7%. There are over 100 verbs involved in the evaluation. The number of possible frames for the verbs in the second test ranges from 13 frames to 30, with the typical number being in the teens. Not all of these frames actually appear in the TreeBank data.

These results compare favorably with the results reported by Gildea and Jurafsky of 80.7% on their development set, (76.9% on the test set.) Their data comes from the Framenet project, [Lowe, et al., 97], which has been in existence for several years, and consisted of over 900 verbs out of 1500 words and almost 50,000 sentences. The Framenet project also uses more fine-grained semantic role labels, although it should be possible to map from our Arg0, Arg1 labels to their labels. They used machine learning techniques applied to human annotated data, whereas our tagger does not currently use statistics at all, and is primarily rule-based. Once we have sufficient amounts of data annotated we plan to experiment with hybrid approaches.

5. ACKNOWLEDGEMENTS

We would like to thank Paul Kingsbury and Chris Walker for their annotation efforts, and Aravind Joshi, Mitch Marcus, Hoa Dang and Christiane Fellbaum for their comments on predicate-argument tagging as a task. This work has been funded by DARPA N66001-00-1-8915 and NSF 9800658.

6. REFERENCES

[1] Hoa Trang Dang, Karin Kipper, and Martha Palmer. Integrating compositional semantics into a verb lexicon. In Proceedings of the Eighteenth International Conference on Computational

Linguistics (COLING-2000), Saarbr"ucken,
Germany, July-August 2000.

[2] Hoa Trang Dang, Karin Kipper, Martha Palmer,
and Joseph Rosenzweig. Investigating regular sense
extensions based on intersective levin classes. In
Proceedings of Coling-ACL98, Montreal, CA,
August 1998.

[3] Daniel Gildea and Daniel Jurafsky, Automatic
Labeling of Semantic Roles, In Proceedings of the
Association for Computational Linguistics
Conference, Hong Kong, October, 2000.

[4] Karin Kipper, Hoa Trang Dang, and Martha
Palmer. Class-based construction of a verb lexicon.
In Proceedings of the Seventh National Conference
on Artificial Intelligence (AAAI-2000), Austin, TX,
July-August 2000.

[5] Beth Levin. English Verb Classes and
Alternations A Preliminary Investigation. 1993.

[6] J.B. Lowe, C.F. Baker, and C.J. Fillmore. A
frame-semantic approach to semantic annotation. In
Proceedings 1997 Siglex Workshop/ANLP97,
Washington, D.C., 1997.

[7] Mitch Marcus. The penn treebank: A revised
corpus design for extracting predicate argument
structure. In Proceedings of the ARPA Human
Language Technology Workshop, Princeton, NJ,
March 1994.

[8] G. Miller, R. Beckwith, C. Fellbaum, D. Gross,
and K. Miller. Five papers on wordnet. Technical
Report 43, Cognitive Science Laboratory, Princeton
University, July 1990.

[9] Martha Palmer, Hoa Trang Dang, and Joseph
Rosenzweig. Sense tagging the penn treebank. In
Proceedings of the Second Language Resources and
Evaluation Conference, Athens, Greece.

[10] The XTAG-Group. A Lexicalized Tree
Adjoining Grammar for English. Technical Report
IRCS 95-03, University of Pennsylvania, 1995.

Automatic Title Generation for Spoken Broadcast News

Rong Jin
Language Technology Institute
Carnegie Mellon University
Pittsburgh, PA 15213
412-268-7003

rong+@cs.cmu.edu

Alexander G. Hauptmann
School of Computer Science
Carnegie Mellon University
Pittsburgh, PA 15213
412-268-1448

alex+@cs.cmu.edu

ABSTRACT

In this paper, we implemented a set of title generation methods using training set of 21190 news stories and evaluated them on an independent test corpus of 1006 broadcast news documents, comparing the results over manual transcription to the results over automatically recognized speech. We use both F1 and the average number of correct title words in the correct order as metric. Overall, the results show that title generation for speech recognized news documents is possible at a level approaching the accuracy of titles generated for perfect text transcriptions.

Keywords

Machine learning, title generation

1. INTRODUCTION

To create a title for a document is a complex task. To generate a title for a spoken document becomes even more challenging because we have to deal with word errors generated by speech recognition.

Historically, the title generation task is strongly connected to traditional summarization because it can be thought of extremely short summarization. Traditional summarization has emphasized the extractive approach, using selected sentences or paragraphs from the document to provide a summary. The weaknesses of this approach are inability of taking advantage of the training corpus and producing summarization with small ratio. Thus, it will not be suitable for title generation tasks.

More recently, some researchers have moved toward "learning approaches" that take advantage of training data. Witbrock and Mittal [1] have used Naïve Bayesian approach for learning the document word and title word correlation. However they limited their statistics to the case that the document word and the title word are same surface string. Hauptmann and Jin [2] extended this approach by relaxing the restriction. Treating title generation problem as a variant of Machine translation problem, Kennedy and Hauptmann [3] tried the iterative Expectation-Maximization algorithm. To avoid struggling with organizing selected title words into human readable sentence, Hauptmann [2] used K

nearest neighbour method for generating titles. In this paper, we put all those methods together and compare their performance over 1000 speech recognition documents.

We decompose the title generation problem into two parts: learning and analysis from the training corpus and generating a sequence of title words to form the title.

For learning and analysis of training corpus, we present five different learning methods for comparison: Naïve Bayesian approach with limited vocabulary, Naïve Bayesian approach with full vocabulary, K nearest neighbors, Iterative Expectation-Maximization approach, Term frequency and inverse document frequency method. More details of each approach will be presented in Section 2.

For the generating part, we decompose the issues involved as follows: choosing appropriate title words, deciding how many title words are appropriate for this document title, and finding the correct sequence of title words that forms a readable title 'sentence'.

The outline of this paper is as follows: Section 1 gave an introduction to the title generation problem. The details of the experiment and analysis of results are presented in Section 2. Section 3 discusses our conclusions drawn from the experiment and suggests possible improvements.

2. THE CONTRASTIVE TITLE GENERATION EXPERIMENT

In this section we describe the experiment and present the results. Section 2.1 describes the data. Section 2.2 discusses the evaluation method. Section 2.3 gives a detailed description of all the methods, which were compared. Results and analysis are presented in section 2.4.

2.1 Data Description

In our experiment, the training set, consisting of 21190 perfectly transcribed documents, are obtain from CNN web site during 1999. Included with each training document text was a human assigned title. The test set, consisting of 1006 CNN TV news story documents for the same year (1999), are randomly selected from the Informedia Digital Video Library. Each document has a closed captioned transcript, an alternative transcript generated with CMU Sphinx speech recognition system with a 64000-word broadcast news language model and a human assigned title.

2.2 Evaluation

First, we evaluate title generation by different approaches using the F1 metric. For an automatically generated title Tauto, F1 is

Proceedings of HLT 2001, First International Conference on Human Language Technology Research, J. Allan, ed., Morgan Kaufmann, San Francisco, 2001.

measured against corresponding human assigned title Thuman as follows:

$$F1 = 2 \times precision \times recall / (precision + recall)$$

Here, precision and recall is measured respectively as the number of identical words in Tauto and Thuman over the number of words in Tauto and the number of words in Thuman. Obviously the sequential word order of the generated title words is ignored by this metric.

To measure how well a generated title compared to the original human generated title in terms of word order, we also measured the number of correct title words in the hypothesis titles that were in the same order as in the reference titles.

We restrict all approaches to generate only 6 title words, which is the average number of title words in the training corpus. Stop words were removed throughout the training and testing documents and also removed from the titles.

2.3 Description of the Compared Title Generation Approaches

The five different title generation methods are:

1. **Naïve Bayesian approach with limited vocabulary (NBL).** It tries to capture the correlation between the words in the document and the words in the title. For each document word DW, it counts the occurrence of title word same as DW and apply the statistics to the test documents for generating titles.

2. **Naïve Bayesian approach with full vocabulary (NBF).** It relaxes the constraint in the previous approach and counts all the document-word-title-word pairs. Then this full statistics will be applied on generating titles for the test documents.

3. **Term frequency and inverse document frequency approach (TF.IDF).** TF is the frequency of words occurring in the document and IDF is logarithm of the total number of documents divided by the number of documents containing this word. The document words with highest TF.IDF were chosen for the title word candidates.

4. **K nearest neighbor approach (KNN).** This algorithm is similar to the KNN algorithm applied to topic classification. It searches the training document set for the closest related document and assign the training document title to the new document as title.

5. **Iterative Expectation-Maximization approach (EM).** It views documents as written in a 'verbal' language and their titles as written a 'concise' language. It builds the translation model between the 'verbal' language and the 'concise' language from the documents and titles in the training corpus and 'translate' each testing document into title.

2.4 The sequentializing process for title word candidates

To generate an ordered set of candidates, equivalent to what we would expect to read from left to right, we built a statistical trigram language model using the SLM tool-kit (Clarkson, 1997) and the 40,000 titles in the training set. This language model was used to determine the most likely order of the title word candidates generated by the NBL, NBF, EM and TF.IDF methods.

3. RESULTS AND OBSERVATIONS

The experiment was conducted both on the closed caption transcripts and automatic speech recognized transcripts. The F1

results and the average number of correct title word in correct order are shown in Figure 1 and 2 respectively.

KNN works surprisingly well. KNN generates titles for a new document by choosing from the titles in the training corpus. This works fairly well because both the training set and test set come from CNN news of the same year. Compared to other methods, KNN degrades much less with speech-recognized transcripts. Meanwhile, even though KNN performance not as well as TF.IDF and NBL in terms of F1 metric, it performances best in terms of the average number of correct title words in the correct order. If consideration of human readability matters, we would expect KNN to outperform considerably all the other approaches since it is guaranteed to generate human readable title.

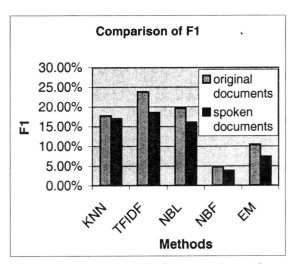

Figure 1: Comparison of Title Generation Approaches on a test corpus of 1006 documents with either perfect transcript or speech recognized transcripts using the F1 score.

NBF performs much worse than NBL. NBF performances much worse than NBL in both metrics. The difference between NBF and NBL is that NBL assumes a document word can only generate a title word with the same surface string. Though it appears that NBL loses information with this very strong assumption, the results tell us that some information can safely be ignored. In NBF, nothing distinguishes between important words and trivial words. This lets frequent, but unimportant words dominate the document-word-title-word correlation.

Light learning approach TF.IDF performances considerably well compared with heavy learning approaches. Surprisingly, heavy learning approaches, NBL, NBF and EM algorithm didn't out performance the light learning approach TF.IDF. We think learning the association between document words and title words by inspecting directly the document and its title is very problematic since many words in the document don't reflect its content. The better strategy should be distilling the document first before learning the correlation between document words and title words.

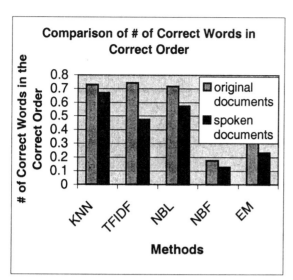

Figure 1: Comparison of Title Generation Approaches on a test corpus of 1006 documents with either perfect transcript or speech recognized transcripts using the average number of correct words in the correct order.

4. CONCLUSION

From the analysis discussed in previous section, we draw the following conclusions:

1. The KNN approach works well for title generation especially when overlap in content between training dataset and test collection is large.

2. The fact that NBL out performances NBF and TF.IDF out performance NBL and suggests that we need to distinguish important document words from those trivial words.

5. ACKNOWLEDGMENTS

This material is based in part on work supported by National Science Foundation under Cooperative Agreement No. IRI-9817496. Partial support for this work was provided by the National Science Foundation's National Science, Mathematics, Engineering, and Technology Education Digital Library Program under grant DUE-0085834. This work was also supported in part by the Advanced Research and Development Activity (ARDA) under contract number MDA908-00-C-0037. Any opinions, findings, and conclusions or recommendations expressed in this material are those of the authors and do not necessarily reflect the views of the National Science Foundation or ARDA.

6. REFERENCES

[1] Michael Witbrock and Vibhu Mittal. Ultra-Summarization: A Statistical Approach to Generating Highly Condensed Non-Extractive Summaries. Proceedings of SIGIR 99, Berkeley, CA, August 1999.

[2] R. Jin and A.G. Hauptmann. Title Generation for Spoken Broadcast News using a Training Corpus. Proceedings of 6th Internal Conference on Language Processing (ICSLP 2000), Beijing China. 2000.

[3] P. Kennedy and A.G. Hauptmann. Automatic Title Generation for the Informedia Multimedia Digital Library. ACM Digital Libraries, DL-2000, San Antonio Texas, May 2000.

A Conversational Interface for Online Shopping

Joyce Chai, Veronika Horvath, Nanda Kambhatla, Nicolas Nicolov & Margo Stys-Budzikowska

Conversational Dialog Systems

IBM T. J. Watson Research Center

30 Saw Mill River Rd, Hawthorne, NY 10532, USA

{jchai, veronika, nanda, nicolas, sm1}@us.ibm.com

ABSTRACT

We present a deployed, conversational dialog system that assists users in finding computers based on their usage patterns and constraints on specifications. We discuss findings from a market survey and two user studies. We compared our system to a directed dialog system and a menu driven navigation system. We found that the conversational interface reduced the average number of clicks by 63% and the average interaction time by 33% over a menu driven search system. The focus of our continuing work includes developing a dynamic, adaptive dialog management strategy, robustly handling user input and improving the user interface.

1. INTRODUCTION

Conversational interfaces allow users to interact with automated systems using speech or typed in text via "conversational dialog". For the purposes of this paper, a conversational dialog consists of a sequence of interactions between a user and a system. The user input is interpreted in the context of previous user inputs in the current session and from previous sessions.

Conversational interfaces offer greater flexibility to users than menu-driven (i.e., directed-dialog) interfaces, where users navigate menus that have a rigid structure [5,4]. Conversational interfaces permit users to ask queries directly in their own words. Thus, users do not have to understand the terminology used by system designers to label hyperlinks on a website or internalize the hierarchical menus of a telephone system [3] or websites.

Recently, conversational interfaces for executing simple transactions and for finding information are proliferating [7,6]. In this paper, we present a conversational dialog system, Natural Language Assistant (or **NLA**), that helps users shop for notebook computers and discuss the results of user studies that we conducted with this system.

2. NATURAL LANGUAGE ASSISTANT

NLA assists users in finding notebooks that satisfy their needs by engaging them in a dialog. At each turn of the dialog, NLA provides incremental feedback about its understanding of the user's constraints and shows products that match these constraints. By encouraging iterative refinement of the user's query, the system finds more user constraints and, ultimately, recommends a product that best matches the user's criteria.

The system consists of three major modules (cf. Figure 1): Presentation Manager, Dialog Manager, and Action Manager. The Presentation Manager interprets user input and generates system responses. It embodies the user interface and contains a shallow semantic parser and a response generator. The semantic parser

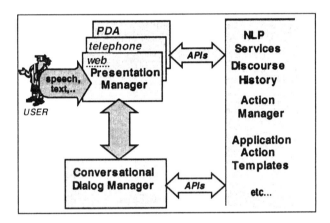

Figure 1. Architecture of the NLA conversational system.

identifies concepts (e.g., MULTIMEDIA) and constraints on product attributes (e.g., *hard disk size more than 20GB*) from the textual user input. The concepts mediate the mapping between user input and available products through product specifications. They implement the business logic.

The Dialog Manager uses the current requirements and formulates action plans for the Action Manager to perform back-end operations (e.g., database access[1]). The Dialog Manager constructs a response to the user based on the results from the Action Manager and the discourse history and sends the system response to the Presentation Manager that displays it to the user. The system prompts for features relevant in the current context. In our mixed initiative dialog system, the user can always answer the specific question put to him/her or provide any constraints.

The system has been recently deployed on an external website. Figure 2 shows the start of a dialog.[2]

Proceedings of HLT 2001, First International Conference on Human Language Technology Research, J. Allan, ed., Morgan Kaufmann, San Francisco, 2001.

---

[1] See [1] for a survey of natural language interfaces to databases.

[2] We are demonstrating the system at HLT'2001 [2].

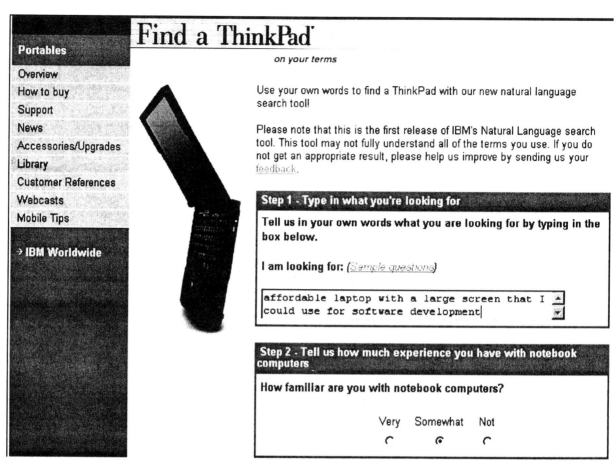

Figure 2. The start of the dialog.

3. USER STUDIES

We conducted a preliminary market survey and two user studies described in subsections 3.1 and 3.2 respectively.

3.1 Market Survey

For understanding specific user needs and user vocabulary, we conducted a user survey. Users were given three sets of questions. The first set, in turn, contained three questions: "What kind of notebook computer are you looking for?", "What features are important to you?", and "What do you plan to use this notebook computer for?". By applying statistical n-gram models and a shallow noun phrase grammar to the user responses, we extracted keywords and phrases expressing user's needs and interests. In the second set of questions, users were asked to rank 10 randomly selected terms from 90 notebook related terms in order of familiarity to them. The third set of questions asked for demographical information about users such as their gender, years of experience with notebook computers, native language, etc. We computed correlations between vocabulary/terms and user demographic information. Over a 30-day period, we received 705 survey responses. From these responses, we learned 195 keywords and phrases that were included in NLA.

3.2 Usability Testing

3.2.1 Experimental Setup

We conducted two user studies to evaluate usability of the system, focusing on: dialog flow, ease of use, system responses, and user vocabulary. The first user study focused on the functionality of NLA and the second user study compared the functionality of NLA with that of a directed dialog system and a menu driven navigation system.

The moderators interviewed 52 users in the user studies: 18 and 34 in the two studies, respectively. All participants were consumers or small business users with "beginner" or "intermediate" computer skills. Each participant was asked to find laptops for a variety of scenarios using three different systems (the NLA, a directed dialog system and a menu driven navigation system). Participants were asked to rate each system for each task on a 1 to 10 scale (10 – easiest) with respect to the *ease of navigation*, *clarity of terminology* and their *confidence in the system responses*. The test subjects were also asked whether the system had found relevant products and were prompted to share their impressions as to how well the system understood them and responded to their requests.

3.2.2 Results

In both studies, participants were very receptive to using natural language dialog-based search. The users clearly preferred dialog-based searches to non-dialog based searches[3] (79% to 21% users). Furthermore, they liked the narrowing down of a product list based on identified constraints as the interaction proceeded. In the first user study, comparing NLA with a menu driven system, we found that using NLA reduced the average number of clicks by 63% and the average interaction time by 33%.

In the second user study, we compared NLA with a directed dialog system and a menu driven search system for finding computers. One goal of the comparative study was to find out if there were any statistical differences in *confidence*, *terminology* and *navigation* ratings across the three systems and whether they were correlated with different categories of users. The ANOVA analysis reveals statistical differences in terminology ratings among the three systems for the category of beginner users only. There were no statistical differences found in the other ratings of *navigation* and *confidence* across the three sites for different categories of users. Sandler's A test confirmed that the terminology rating was significantly different for the categories of *consumers*, *small business owners*, *beginners* and *intermediates*. These comparative results suggest that asking questions relative to the right level of end user experience is crucial. Asking users questions about their lifestyle and how they were going to use a computer accounted for a slight preference of the directed dialog system over the NLA that uses questions presented on the basis of understanding features and functions of computer terms.

3.2.3 Lessons from the user studies

Both user studies revealed several dimensions along which NLA can be improved. The first user study highlighted a definite need for system *acknowledgement* and *feedback*. The users wanted to know whether the system had understood them. User comments also revealed that a *comparison* of features across the whole pool of products was important for them.

The focus of the second study, incorporating 34 subjects, was to compare systems of similar functionality and to draw conclusions about the functionality of NLA. Both the ANOVA and the Sandler's test point out that terminology was a statistically significant factor differentiating among the systems. We believe that using terminology that is not overly technical would contribute to the success of the dialog search. While the questions asked by NLA were based on features and functionality of notebook computers, the users preferred describing usage patterns and life style issues rather than technical details of computers.

We also found that users' confidence in NLA decreased when the system responses were inconsistent i.e., were not relevant to their input. Lack of consistent visual focus on the dialog box was also a serious drawback since it forced users to scroll in search of the dialog box on each interaction page.

3.2.4 Future work

Based on the results of the user studies, we are currently focused on: developing a dynamic and adaptive dialog management strategy, improving the robustness of the natural language processing (NLP), and improving the user interface. Some of issues mentioned here have been implemented in the next version of NLA.

We are currently re-designing the questions that NLA asks users to be simpler, and to focus on usage patterns rather than technical features. We are also implementing a new dialog management strategy in NLA that is more adaptive to the user's input, and implements a mapping from high-level usage patterns to constraints on low-level technical features.

We are integrating a statistical parser with NLA to more robustly handle varied user input. The statistical parser should enable NLA to scale to multiple languages and multiple domains in a more robust and reliable fashion. We are aiming at an architecture that separates the NLP processing from the business logic that will make maintenance of the system easier.[4]

Improvements to the GUI include better acknowledgement and feedback mechanisms as well as graphical UI issues. We now reiterate the user's last query at the beginning of each interaction page and also convey to the user an explanation of features incrementally accumulated in the course of the interaction. We have designed a more uniform, more compact and consistent UI. In the welcome page, we have abandoned a three-step initiation (typed input, experience level and preferences for major specifications) keeping the emphasis on the dialog box. The user preferences contributed to creating confusion as to the main means of interaction (many users just clicked on the radial buttons and did not use the full dialog functionality). We now infer the technical specifications based the user's stated needs and usage patterns. Our UI now has a no scrolling policy and we allow for larger matching set of products to be visualized over a number of pages.

4. DISCUSSION

In this paper, we have presented a conversational dialog system for helping users shop for notebook computers. User studies comparing our conversational dialog system with a menu driven system have found that the conversational interface reduced the average number of clicks by 63% and the average interaction time by 33%. Based on our findings, it appears that for conversational systems like ours, the sophistication of dialog management and the actual human computer interface are more important than the complexity of the natural language processing technique used. This is especially true for web-based systems where user queries are often brief and shallow linguistic processing seems to be adequate. For web-based systems, integrating the conversational interface with other interfaces (like menu-driven and search-driven interfaces) for providing a complete and consistent user experience assumes greater importance.

---

[3] We define a dialog-based search as one comprising of a sequence of interactions with a system where the system keeps track of contextual (discourse) information.

[4] Many systems' fate has been decided not because they cannot handle complex linguistic constructions but because of the difficulties in porting such systems out of the research environments.

The user studies we conducted have highlighted several directions for further improvements for our system. We plan to modify our interface to integrate different styles of interaction (e.g., menus, search, browsing, etc.). We also intend to dynamically classify each user as belonging to one or more categories of computer shoppers (e.g., gamers, student users, home business users, etc.) based on all the user interactions so far. We can then tailor the whole interface to the perceived category including but not limited to the actual questions asked, the technical knowledge assumed by the system and the whole style of interaction.

Another area of potential improvement for the NLA is its inability to handle any meta-level queries about itself or any deeper questions about its domain (e.g., NLA currently can not properly handle the queries, "*How can I add memory to this model?*" or "*What is DVD?*"). Our long-term goal is to integrate different sources of back-end information (databases, text documents, etc.) and present users with an integrated, consistent conversational interface to it.

We believe that conversational interfaces offer the ultimate kind of personalization. Personalization can be defined as the process of presenting each user of an automated system with an interface uniquely tailored to his/her preference of content and style of interaction. Thus, mixed initiative conversational interfaces are highly personalized since they allow users to interact with systems using the words they want, to fetch the content they want in the style they want. Users can converse with such systems by phrasing their initial queries at a right level of comfort to them (e.g., "*I am looking for a gift for my wife*" or "*I am looking for a fast computer with DVD under 1500 dollars*").

5. CONCLUSIONS

Based on our results, we conclude that conversational natural language dialog interfaces offer powerful personalized alternatives to traditional menu-driven or search-based interfaces to websites. For such systems, it is especially important to present users with a consistent interface integrating different styles of interaction and to have robust dialog management strategies. The system feedback and the follow up questions should strike a delicate balance between exposing the system limitations to users, and making users aware of the flexibility of the system. In current work we are focusing on developing dynamic, adaptive dialog management, robust multi-lingual NLP and improving the user interface.

6. REFERENCES

[1] Androutsopoulos, Ion, and Ritchie, Graeme. Natural Language Interfaces to Databases – An Introduction, *Natural Language Engineering* 1.1:29-81, 1995.

[2] Budzikowska, M., Chai, J., Govindappa, S., Horvath, V., Kambhatla, N., Nicolov, N., and Zadrozny, W. Conversational Sales Assistant for Online Shopping, Demonstration at *Human Language Technologies Conference (HLT'2001)*, San Diego, Calif., 2001.

[3] Carpenter, Bob, and Chu-Carroll, J. Natural Language Call Routing: A Robust, Self-organizing Approach, *Proceedings of the 5th Int. Conf. on Spoken Language Processing.* 1998

[4] Chai, J., Lin, J., Zadrozny, W., Ye, Y., Budzikowska, M., Horvath, V., Kambhatla, N., and Wolf, C. Comparative Evaluation of a Natural Language Dialog Based System and a Menu-Driven System for Information Access: A Case Study, *Proceedings of RIAO 2000*, Paris.

[5] Saito, M., and Ohmura, K. A Cognitive Model for Searching for Ill-defined Targets on the Web - The Relationship between Search Strategies and User Satisfaction, *21st Int. Conference on Research and Development in Information Retrieval*, Australia, 1998.

[6] Walker, M., Fromer, J., and Narayanan, S. Learning Optimal Dialogue Strategies: A Case Study of a Spoken Dialogue Agent for Email, *36th Annual Meeting of the ACL*, Montreal, Canada, 1998.

[7] Zadrozny, W., Wolf, C., Kambhatla, N. & Ye, Y. Conversation Machines for Transaction Processing, *Proceedings of AAAI / IAAI - 1998*, Madison, Wisconsin, U.S.A. 1998.

Conversational Sales Assistant for Online Shopping

Margo Budzikowska, Joyce Chai, Sunil Govindappa, Veronika Horvath, Nanda Kambhatla,

Nicolas Nicolov & Wlodek Zadrozny

Conversational Machines Group
IBM T. J. Watson Research Center
30 Saw Mill River Rd, Hawthorne, NY 10532, U.S.A.
{*sm1, jchai, govindap, veronika, nanda, nicolas, wlodz*}@*us.ibm.com*

ABSTRACT

Websites of businesses should accommodate both customer needs and business requirements. Traditional menu-driven navigation and key word search do not allow users to describe their intentions precisely. We have developed a *conversational interface to online shopping* that provides convenient, personalized access to information using natural language dialog. User studies show significantly reduced length of interactions in terms of time and number of clicks in finding products. The core dialog engine is easily adaptable to other domains.

1. INTRODUCTION

Natural language dialog has been used in many areas, such as for call-center/routing application (Carpenter & Chu-Carroll 1998), email routing (Walker, Fromer & Narayanan 1998), information retrieval and database access (Androutsopoulos & Ritchie 1995), and for telephony banking (Zadrozny et al. 1998). In this demonstration, we present a natural language dialog interface to online shopping. Our user studies show natural language dialog to be a very effective means for negotiating user's requests and intentions in this domain.

2. SYSTEM ARCHITECTURE

In our system, a *presentation manager* captures queries from users, employs a parser to transform the user's query into a logical form, and sends the logical form to a *dialog manager*. The presentation manager is also responsible for obtaining the system's response from the dialog manager and presenting it to the user using template-based generation. The dialog manager formulates action plans for an *action manager* to perform back-end tasks such as database access, business transactions, etc. The dialog manager applies information state-based dialog strategies to formulate responses depending on the current state, discourse history and the action results from the action manager.

The **Data Management Subsystem** maintains a "concept" repository with common sense "concepts" and a phrasal lexicon that lists possible ways for referring to the concepts. Business Rules map concepts to business specifications by defining concepts using a propositional logic formula of constraints over product specifications. Thus, the Business Rules reflect business goals and decisions. The Extended Database combines product specifications and precompiled evaluations of the concept definitions for each product to provide a representation that guides the natural language dialog. We are investigating automated tools for helping developers and maintainers extract relevant concepts and terms on the basis of user descriptions and queries about products.

3. EVALUATION

We conducted several user studies to evaluate the usability of NLA (Chai et al. 2000). In one study, seventeen test subjects preferred the dialog-driven navigation of NLA two to one over menu-driven navigation. Moreover, with NLA, the average number of clicks was reduced by 63.2% and the average time was reduced by 33.3%. Analysis of the user queries (average length = 5.31 words long; standard deviation = 2.62; 85% of inputs are noun phrases) revealed the brevity and relative linguistic simplicity of user input. Hence, shallow parsing techniques were adequate for processing user input. In general, sophisticated dialog management appears to be more important than the ability to handle complex natural language sentences. The user studies also highlighted the need to combine multiple modalities and styles of interaction.

4. REFERENCES

[1] Androutsopoulos, Ion & Ritchie, Graeme. Natural Language Interfaces to Databases – An Introduction, *Natural Language Engineering* 1.1:29-81, 1995.

[2] Carpenter, Bob & Chu-Carroll, Jeniffer. Natural Language Call Routing: A Robust, Self-organizing Approach, *Proceedings of the 5th International Conference on Spoken Language Processing*, 1998.

[3] Chai, J., Lin, J., Zadrozny, W., Ye, Y., Budzikowska, M., Horvath, V., Kambhatla, N. & Wolf, C. Comparative Evaluation of a Natural Language Dialog Based System and a Menu-Driven System for Information Access: A Case Study, *Proceedings of RIAO 2000*, Paris, 2000.

Proceedings of HLT 2001, First International Conference on Human Language Technology Research, J. Allan, ed., Morgan Kaufmann, San Francisco, 2001.

Find a ThinkPad®

on your terms

Portables

Overview
How to buy
Support
News
Accessories/Upgrades
Library
Customer References
Webcasts
Mobile Tips

→ **IBM Worldwide**

Use your own words to find a ThinkPad with our new natural language search tool!

Please note that this is the first release of IBM's Natural Language search tool. This tool may not fully understand all of the terms you use. If you do not get an appropriate result, please help us improve by sending us your feedback.

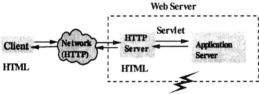

Step 1 - Type in what you're looking for

Tell us in your own words what you are looking for by typing in the box below.

I am looking for: *(Sample questions)*

```
affordable laptop with a large screen that I
could use for software development
```

Step 2 - Tell us how much experience you have with notebook computers

How familiar are you with notebook computers?

Very   Somewhat   Not
○   ⊙   ○

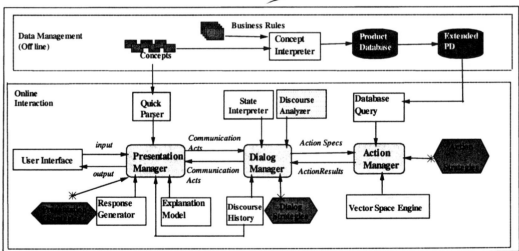

[4] Saito, M. & Ohmura, K. A Cognitive Model for Searching for Ill-defined Targets on the Web – The Relationship between Search Strategies and User Satisfaction. *21st Int. Conf. on Research and Development in Information Retrieval*, Australia, 1998.

[5] Walker, M., Fromer, J. & Narayanan, S. Learning Optimal Dialogue Strategies: A Case Study of a Spoken Dialogue Agent for Email, *36th Annual Meeting of the ACL*, Montreal, Canada, 1998.

[6] Zadrozny, W., Wolf, C., Kambhatla, N. & Ye, Y. Conversation Machines for Transaction Processing, *Proceedings of AAAI / IAAI - 1998*, Madison, Wisconsin, U.S.A., 1998.

Converting Dependency Structures to Phrase Structures

Fei Xia and Martha Palmer
University of Pennsylvania
Philadelphia, PA 19104, USA
{fxia,mpalmer}@linc.cis.upenn.edu

1. INTRODUCTION

Treebanks are of two types according to their annotation schemata: phrase-structure Treebanks such as the English Penn Treebank [8] and dependency Treebanks such as the Czech dependency Treebank [6]. Long before Treebanks were developed and widely used for natural language processing, there had been much discussion of comparison between dependency grammars and context-free phrase-structure grammars [5]. In this paper, we address the relationship between dependency structures and phrase structures from a practical perspective; namely, the exploration of different algorithms that convert dependency structures to phrase structures and the evaluation of their performance against an existing Treebank. This work not only provides ways to convert Treebanks from one type of representation to the other, but also clarifies the differences in representational coverage of the two approaches.

2. CONVERTING PHRASE STRUCTURES TO DEPENDENCY STRUCTURES

The notion of *head* is important in both phrase structures and dependency structures. In many linguistic theories such as X-bar theory and GB theory, each phrase structure has a head that determines the main properties of the phrase and a head has several levels of projections; whereas in a dependency structure the head is linked to its dependents. In practice, the head information is explicitly marked in a dependency Treebank, but not always so in a phrase-structure Treebank. A common way to find the head in a phrase structure is to use a head percolation table, as discussed in [7, 1] among others. For example, the entry (S right S/VP) in the head percolation table says that the head child[1] of an S node is the first child from the right with the label S or VP.

Once the heads in phrase structures are found, the conversion from phrase structures to dependency structures is straightforward, as shown below:

(a) Mark the head child of each node in a phrase structure, using the head percolation table.

---

[1] The *head-child* of a node XP is the child of the node XP that is the ancestor of the head of the XP in the phrase structure.

(b) In the dependency structure, make the head of each non-head-child depend on the head of the head-child.

Figure 1 shows a phrase structure in the English Penn Treebank [8]. In addition to the syntactic labels (such as NP for a noun phrase), the Treebank also uses function tags (such as SBJ for the subject) for grammatical functions. In this phrase structure, the root node has two children: the NP and the VP. The algorithm would choose the VP as the head-child and the NP as a non-head-child, and make the head *Vinkin* of the NP depend on the head *join* of the VP in the dependency structure. The dependency structure of the sentence is shown in Figure 2. A more sophisticated version of the algorithm (as discussed in [10]) takes two additional tables (namely, the argument table and the tagset table) as input and produces dependency structures with the argument/adjunct distinction (i.e., each dependent is marked in the dependency structure as either an argument or an adjunct of the head).

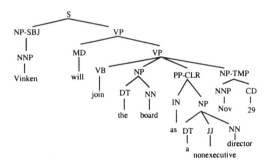

Figure 1: A phrase structure in the Penn Treebank

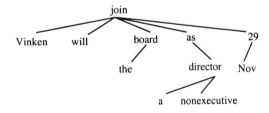

Figure 2: A dependency tree for the sentence in Figure 1. Heads are marked as parents of their dependents in an ordered tree.

It is worth noting that quite often there is no consensus on what the *correct* dependency structure for a particular sentence should be. To build a dependency Treebank, the Treebank annotators must decide which word depends on which word; for example, they have to decide whether the subject *Vinken* in Figure 1 depends on the

Proceedings of HLT 2001, First International Conference on Human Language Technology Research, J. Allan, ed., Morgan Kaufmann, San Francisco, 2001.

modal verb *will* or the main verb *join*. In contrast, the annotators for phrase-structure Treebanks do not have to make such decisions. The users of phrase-structure Treebanks can modify the head percolation tables to get different dependency structures from the same phrase structure. In other words, phrase structures offer more flexibility than dependency structures with respect to the choices of heads.

The feasibility of using the head percolation table to identify the heads in phrase structures depends on the characteristics of the language, the Treebank schema, and the definition of the correct dependency structure. For instance, the head percolation table for a strictly head-final (or head-initial) language is very easy to build, and the conversion algorithm works very well. For the English Penn Treebank, which we used in this paper, the conversion algorithm works very well except for the noun phrases with the appositive construction. For example, the conversion algorithm would choose the appositive *the CEO of FNX* as the head child of the phrase *John Smith, the CEO of FNX*, whereas the correct head child should be *John Smith*.

3. CONVERTING DEPENDENCY STRUCTURES TO PHRASE STRUCTURES

The main information that is present in phrase structures but not in dependency structures is the type of syntactic category (e.g., NP, VP, and S); therefore, to recover syntactic categories, any algorithm that converts dependency structures to phrase structures needs to address the following questions:

Projections for each category: for a category X, what kind of projections can X have?

Projection levels for dependents: Given a category Y depends on a category X in a dependency structure, how far should Y project before it attaches to X's projection?

Attachment positions: Given a category Y depends on a category X in a dependency structure, to what position on X's projection chain should Y's projection attach?

In this section, we discuss three conversion algorithms, each of which gives different answers to these three questions. To make the comparison easy, we shall apply each algorithm to the dependency structure (*d-tree*) in Figure 2 and compare the output of the algorithm with the phrase structure for that sentence in the English Penn Treebank, as in Figure 1.

Evaluating these algorithms is tricky because just like dependency structures there is often no consensus on what the *correct* phrase structure for a sentence should be. In this paper, we measure the performance of the algorithms by comparing their output with an existing phrase-structure Treebank (namely, the English Penn Treebank) because of the following reasons: first, the Treebank is available to the public, and provides an objective although imperfect standard; second, one goal of the conversion algorithms is to make it possible to compare the performance of parsers that produce dependency structures with the ones that produce phrase structures. Since most state-of-the-art phrase-structure parsers are evaluated against an existing Treebank, we want to evaluate the conversion algorithms in the same way; third, a potential application of the conversion algorithms is to help construct a phrase-structure Treebank for one language, given parallel corpora and the phrase structures in the other language. One way to evaluate the quality of the resulting Treebank is to compare it with an existing Treebank.

3.1 Algorithm 1

According to X-bar theory, a category X projects to X', which

further projects to XP. There are three types of rules, as shown in Figure 3(a). Algorithm 1, as adopted in [4, 3], strictly follows X-bar theory and uses the following heuristic rules to build phrase structures:

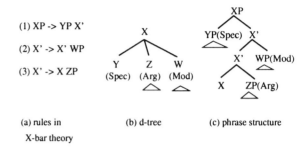

(1) XP -> YP X'

(2) X' -> X' WP

(3) X' -> X ZP

(a) rules in X-bar theory

(b) d-tree

(c) phrase structure

Figure 3: Rules in X-bar theory and Algorithm 1 (which is based on it)

Two levels of projections for any category: any category X has two levels of projection: X' and XP.

Maximal projections for dependents: a dependent Y always projects to Y' then YP, and the YP attaches to the head's projection.

Fixed positions of attachment: Dependents are divided into three types: specifiers, modifiers, and arguments. Each type of dependent attaches to a fixed position, as shown in Figure 3(c).

The algorithm would convert the d-tree in Figure 3(b) to the phrase structure in Figure 3(c). If a head has multiple modifiers, the algorithm could use either a single X' or stacked X' [3]. Figure 4 shows the phrase structure for the d-tree in Figure 2, where the algorithm uses a single X' for multiple modifiers of the same head.[2]

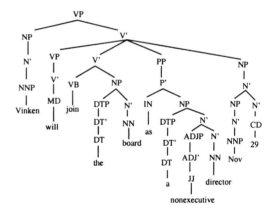

Figure 4: The phrase structure built by algorithm 1 for the d-tree in Figure 2

3.2 Algorithm 2

Algorithm 2, as adopted by Collins and his colleagues [2] when they converted the Czech dependency Treebank [6] into a phrase-structure Treebank, produces phrase structures that are as flat as possible. It uses the following heuristic rules to build phrase structures:

One level of projection for any category: X has only one level of projection: XP.

---

[2]To make the phrase structure more readable, we use N' and NP as the X' and XP for all kinds of POS tags for nouns (e.g., NNP, NN, and CD). Verbs and adjectives are treated similarly.

Minimal projections for dependents: A dependent Y does not project to YP unless it has its own dependents.

Fixed position of attachment: A dependent is a sister of its head in the phrase structure.[3]

The algorithm treats all kinds of dependents equally. It converts the pattern in Figure 5(a) to the phrase structure in Figure 5(b). Notice that in Figure 5(b), Y does not project to YP because it does not have its own dependents. The resulting phrase structure for the d-tree in Figure 2 is in Figure 6, which is much flatter than the one produced by Algorithm 1.

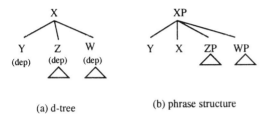

| (a) d-tree | (b) phrase structure |

Figure 5: The scheme for Algorithm 2

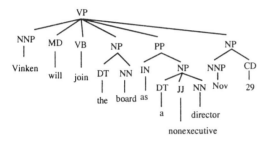

Figure 6: The phrase structure built by Algorithm 2 for the d-tree in Figure 2

3.3 Algorithm 3

The previous two algorithms are linguistically sound. They do not use any language-specific information, and as a result there are several major differences between the output of the algorithms and the phrase structures in an existing Treebank, such as the Penn English Treebank (PTB).

Projections for each category: Both algorithms assume that the numbers of projections for all the categories are the same, whereas in the PTB the number of projections varies from head to head. For example, in the PTB, determiners do not project, adverbs project only one level to adverbial phrases, whereas verbs project to VP, then to S, then to SBAR.[4]

Projection levels for dependents: Algorithm 1 assumes the maximal projections for all the dependents, while Algorithm 2 assumes minimal projections; but in the PTB, the level of projection of a dependent may depend on several factors such as the categories of the dependent and the head, the position of the dependent with respect to the head, and the dependency type. For example, when a

noun modifies a verb (or VP) such as *yesterday* in *he came yesterday*, the noun always projects to NP, but when a noun N_1 modifies another noun N_2, N_1 projects to NP if N_1 is to the right of N_2 (e.g., in an appositive construction) and it does not project to NP if N_1 is to the left of N_2.

Attachment positions: Both algorithms assume that all the dependents of the same dependency type attach at the same level (e.g., in Algorithm 1, modifiers are sisters of X', while in Algorithm 2, modifiers are sisters of X); but in the PTB, that is not always true. For example, an ADVP, which depends on a verb, may attach to either an S or a VP in the phrase structure according to the position of the ADVP with respect to the verb and the subject of the verb. Also, in noun phrases, left modifiers (e.g., JJ) are sisters of the head noun, while the right modifiers (e.g., PP) are sisters of NP.

For some applications, these differences between the Treebank and the output of the conversion algorithms may not matter much, and by no means are we implying that an existing Treebank provides the gold standard for what the phrase structures should be. Nevertheless, because the goal of this work is to provide an algorithm that has the flexibility to produce phrase structures that are as close to the ones in an existing Treebank as possible, we propose a new algorithm with such flexibility. The algorithm distinguishes two types of dependents: arguments and modifiers. The algorithm also makes use of language-specific information in the form of three tables: the projection table, the argument table, and the modification table. The projection table specifies the projections for each category. The argument table (the modification table, resp.) lists the types of arguments (modifiers, resp) that a head can take and their positions with respect to the head. For example, the entry $V \rightarrow VP \rightarrow S$ in the projection table says that a verb can project to a verb phrase, which in turn projects to a sentence; the entry (P 0 1 NP/S) in the argument table indicates that a preposition can take an argument that is either an NP or an S, and the argument is to the right of the preposition; the entry (NP DT/JJ PP/S) in the modification table says that an NP can be modified by a determiner and/or an adjective from the left, and by a preposition phrase or a sentence from the right.

Given these tables, we use the following heuristic rules to build phrase structures:[5]

One projection chain per category: Each category has a unique projection chain, as specified in the projection table.

Minimal projection for dependents: A category projects to a higher level only when necessary.

Lowest attachment position: The projection of a dependent attaches to a projection of its head as lowly as possible.

The last two rules require further explanation, as illustrated in Figure 7. In the figure, the node X has three dependents: Y and Z are arguments, and W is a modifier of X. Let's assume that the algorithm has built the phrase structure for each dependent. To form the phrase structure for the whole d-tree, the algorithm needs to attach the phrase structures for dependents to the projection chain $X^0, X^1, ...X^k$ of the head X. For an argument such as Z, suppose its projection chain is $Z^0, Z^1, ...Z^u$ and the root of the phrase structure headed by Z is Z^s. The algorithm would find the lowest position X^h on the head projection chain, such that Z has a projection Z^t that can be an argument of X^{h-1} according to the argument table and Z^t is no lower than Z^s on the projection chain for Z. The algorithm then makes Z^t a child of X^h in the phrase structure. Notice that based on the second heuristic rule (i.e., minimal projection for dependents), Z^t does not further project to Z^u in

---

[3]If a dependent Y has its own dependents, it projects to YP and YP is a sister of the head X; otherwise, Y is a sister of the head X.

[4]S is similar to IP (IP is the maximal projection of INFL) in GB theory, so is SBAR to CP (CP is the maximal projection of Comp); therefore, it could be argued that only VP is a projection of verbs in the PTB. Nevertheless, because PTB does not mark INFL and Comp, we treat S and SBAR as projections of verbs.

[5]In theory, the last two heuristic rules may conflict each other in some cases. In those cases, we prefer the third rule over the second. In practice, such conflicting cases are very rare, if exist.

this case although Z^u is a valid projection of Z. The attachment for modifiers is similar except that the algorithm uses the modification table instead of the argument table.[6]

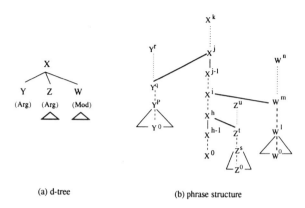

(a) d-tree   (b) phrase structure

Figure 7: The scheme for Algorithm 3

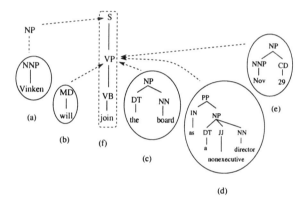

Figure 8: The phrase structure produced by Algorithm 3

The phrase structure produced by Algorithm 3 for the d-tree in Figure 2 is in Figure 8. In Figure 8, (a)-(e) are the phrase structures for five dependents of the head *join*; (f) is the projection chain for the head. The arrows indicate the positions of the attachment. Notice that to attach (a) to (f), the NNP *Vinken* needs to further project to NP because according to the argument table, a VP can take an NP, but not an NNP, as its argument.

In the PTB, a modifier either sister-adjoins or Chomsky-adjoins to the modifiee. For example, in Figure 1, the MD *will* Chomsky-adjoins whereas the NP *Nov. 29* sister-adjoins to the VP node. To account for that, we distinguish these two types of modifiers in the modification table and Algorithm 3 is extended so that it would attach Chomsky-adjoining modifiers higher by inserting extra nodes. To convert the d-tree in Figure 2, the algorithm inserts an extra VP node in the phrase structure in Figure 8 and attaches the MD *will* to the new VP node; the final phrase structure produced by the algorithm is identical to the one in Figure 1.

3.4 Algorithm 1 and 2 as special cases of Algorithm 3

Although the three algorithms adopt different heuristic rules to build phrase structures, the first two algorithms are special cases of the last algorithm; that is, we can design a distinct set of projection/argument/modification tables for each of the first two algorithms so that running Algorithm 3 with the associated set of tables for Algorithm 1 (Algorithm 2, respectively) would produce the same results as running Algorithm 1 (Algorithm 2, respectively).

For example, to produce the results of Algorithm 2 with the code for Algorithm 3, the three tables should be created as follows:

(a) In the projection table, each head X has only one projection XP;

(b) In the argument table, if a category Y can be an argument of a category X in a d-tree, then include both Y and YP as arguments of X;

(c) In the modification table, if a category Y can be a modifier of a category X in a d-tree, then include both Y and YP as sister-modifiers of XP.

4. EXPERIMENTS

So far, we have described two existing algorithms and proposed a new algorithm for converting d-trees into phrase structures. As explained at the beginning of Section 3, we evaluated the performance of the algorithms by comparing their output with an existing Treebank. Because there are no English dependency Treebanks available, we first ran the algorithm in Section 2 to produce d-trees from the PTB, then applied these three algorithms to the d-trees and compared the output with the original phrase structures in the PTB.[7] The process is shown in Figure 9.

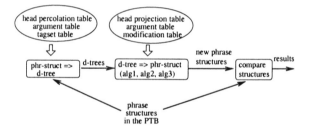

Figure 9: The flow chart of the experiment

The results are shown in Table 1, which use Section 0 of the PTB. The precision and recall rates are for unlabelled brackets. The last column shows the ratio of the number of brackets produced by the algorithms and the number of brackets in the original Treebank. From the table (especially the last column), it is clear that Algorithm 1 produces many more brackets than the original Treebank, resulting in a high recall rate but low precision rate. Algorithm 2 produces very flat structures, resulting in a low recall rate and high precision rate. Algorithm 3 produces roughly the same number of brackets as the Treebank and has the best recall rate, and its precision rate is almost as good as that of Algorithm 2.

The differences between the output of the algorithms and the phrase structures in the PTB come from four sources:

(S1) Annotation errors in the PTB

(S2) Errors in the Treebank-specific tables used by the algorithms in Sections 2 and 3 (e.g., the head percolation table, the projection table, the argument table, and the modification table)

---

[6]Note that once Z^t becomes a child of X^h, other dependents of X (such as W) that are on the same side as Z but are further away from X can attach only to X^h or higher on the projection chain of X.

[7]Punctuation marks are not part of the d-trees produced by Lex-Tract. We wrote a simple program to attach them as high as possible to the phrase structures produced by the conversion algorithms.

	recall (%)	prec (%)	no-cross (%)	ave cross	test/ gold
Alg1	81.34	32.81	50.81	0.90	2.48
Alg2	54.24	91.50	94.90	0.10	0.59
Alg3	86.24	88.72	84.33	0.27	0.98

Table 1: Performance of three conversion algorithms on the Section 0 of the PTB

(S3) The imperfection of the conversion algorithm in Section 2 (which converts phrase structures to d-trees)

(S4) Mismatches between the heuristic rules used by the algorithms in Section 3 and the annotation schemata adopted by the PTB

To estimate the contribution of (S1)–(S4) to the differences between the output of Algorithm 3 and the phrase structures in the PTB, we manually examined the first twenty sentences in Section 0. Out of thirty-one differences in bracketing, seven are due to (S1), three are due to (S2), seven are due to (S3), and the remaining fourteen mismatches are due to (S4).

While correcting annotation errors to eliminate (S1) requires more human effort, it is quite straightforward to correct the errors in the Treebank-specific tables and therefore eliminate the mismatches caused by (S2). For (S3), we mentioned in Section 2 that the algorithm chose the wrong heads for the noun phrases with the appositive construction. As for (S4), we found several exceptions (as shown in Table 2) to the one-projection-chain-per-category assumption (i.e., for each POS tag, there is a unique projection chain), an assumption which was used by all three algorithms in Section 3. The performance of the conversion algorithms in Section 2 and 3 could be improved by using additional heuristic rules or statistical information. For instance, Algorithm 3 in Section 3 could use a heuristic rule that says that an adjective (JJ) projects to an NP if the JJ follows the determiner *the* and the JJ is not followed by a noun as in *the rich are getting richer*, and it projects to an ADJP in other cases. Notice that such heuristic rules are Treebank-dependent.

most likely projection	other projection(s)
JJ → ADJP	JJ → NP
CD → NP	CD → QP → NP
VBN → VP → S	VBN → VP → RRC
NN → NP	NN → NX → NP
VBG → VP → S	VBG → PP

Table 2: Some examples of heads with more than one projection chain

Empty categories are often explicitly marked in phrase-structures, but they are not always included in dependency structures. We believe that including empty categories in dependency structures has many benefits. First, empty categories are useful for NLP applications such as machine translation. To translate a sentence from one language to another, many machine translation systems first create the dependency structure for the sentence in the source language, then produce the dependency structure for the target language, and finally generate a sentence in the target language. If the source language (e.g., Chinese and Korean) allows argument deletion and the target language (e.g., English) does not, it is crucial that the dropped argument (which is a type of empty category) is explicitly marked in the source dependency structure, so that the machine translation systems are aware of the existence of the dropped argument and can handle the situation accordingly. The second benefit of including empty categories in dependency structures is that it can

improve the performance of the conversion algorithms in Section 3, because the phrase structures produced by the algorithms would then have empty categories as well, just like the phrase structures in the PTB. Third, if a sentence includes a non-projective construction such as wh-movement in English, and if the dependency tree did not include an empty category to show the movement, traversing the dependency tree would yield the wrong word order.[8]

5. CONCLUSION

We have proposed a new algorithm for converting dependency structures to phrase structures and compared it with two existing ones. We have shown that our algorithm subsumes the two existing ones. By using simple heuristic rules and taking as input certain kinds of Treebank-specific information such as the types of arguments and modifiers that a head can take, our algorithm produces phrase structures that are very close to the ones in an annotated phrase-structure Treebank; moreover, the quality of the phrase structures produced by our algorithm can be further improved when more Treebank-specific information is used. We also argue for including empty categories in the dependency structures.

6. ACKNOWLEDGMENTS

This research reported here was made possible by NSF under Grant NSF-89-20230-15 and by DARPA as part of the Translingual Information Detection, Extraction and Summarization (TIDES) program under Grant N66001-00-1-8915.

7. REFERENCES

[1] M. Collins. Three Generative, Lexicalised Models for Statistical Parsing. In *Proc. of the 35th ACL*, 1997.

[2] M. Collins, J. Hajič, L. Ramshaw, and C. Tillmann. A Statistical Parser for Czech. In *Proc. of ACL-1999*, pages 505–512, 1999.

[3] M. Covington. An Empirically Motivated Reinterpretation of Dependency Grammar, 1994. Research Report AI-1994-01.

[4] M. Covington. GB Theory as Dependency Grammar, 1994. Research Report AI-1992-03.

[5] H. Gaifman. Dependency Systems and Phrase-Structure Systems. *Information and Control*, pages 304–337, 1965.

[6] J. Hajič. Building a Syntactically Annotated Corpus: The Prague Dependency Treebank, 1998. Issues of Valency and Meaning (Festschrift for Jarmila Panevová).

[7] D. M. Magerman. Statistical Decision-Tree Models for Parsing. In *Proc. of the 33rd ACL*, 1995.

[8] M. Marcus, B. Santorini, and M. A. Marcinkiewicz. Building a Large Annotated Corpus of English: the Penn Treebank. *Computational Linguistics*, 1993.

[9] O. Rambow and A. K. Joshi. A formal look at dependency grammars and phrase structure grammars with special considertaion of word-order phenomena. In L. Wenner, editor, *Recent Trends in Meaning-Text Theory*. John Benjamin, Amsterdam, Philadelphia, 1997.

[10] F. Xia, M. Palmer, and A. Joshi. A Uniform Method of Grammar Extraction and its Applications. In *Proc. of Joint SIGDAT Conference on Empirical Methods in Natural Language Processing and Very Large Corpora (EMNLP/VLC)*, 2000.

---

[8]For more discussion of non-projective constructions, see [9].

DATE: A Dialogue Act Tagging Scheme for Evaluation of Spoken Dialogue Systems

Marilyn Walker and Rebecca Passonneau
AT&T Shannon Labs
180 Park Ave.
Florham Park, N.J. 07932 {walker,becky}@research.att.com

ABSTRACT

This paper describes a dialogue act tagging scheme developed for the purpose of providing finer-grained quantitative dialogue metrics for comparing and evaluating DARPA COMMUNICATOR spoken dialogue systems. We show that these dialogue act metrics can be used to quantify the amount of effort spent in a dialogue maintaining the channel of communication or, establishing the frame for communication, as opposed to actually carrying out the travel planning task that the system is designed to support. We show that the use of these metrics results in a 7% improvement in the fit in models of user satisfaction. We suggest that dialogue act metrics can ultimately support more focused qualitative analysis of the role of various dialogue strategy parameters, e.g. initiative, across dialogue systems, thus clarifying what development paths might be feasible for enhancing user satisfaction in future versions of these systems.

1. INTRODUCTION

Recent research on dialogue is based on the assumption that dialogue acts provide a useful way of characterizing dialogue behaviors in human-human dialogue, and potentially in human-computer dialogue as well [16, 27, 11, 7, 1]. Several research efforts have explored the use of dialogue act tagging schemes for tasks such as improving recognition performance [27], identifying important parts of a dialogue [12], and as a constraint on nominal expression generation [17]. This paper reports on the development and use of a dialogue act tagging scheme for a rather different task: the evaluation and comparison of spoken dialogue systems in the travel domain. We call this scheme DATE: Dialogue Act Tagging for Evaluation.

Our research on the use of dialogue act tagging for evaluation focuses on the corpus of DARPA COMMUNICATOR dialogues collected in the June 2000 data collection [28]. This corpus consists of 662 dialogues from 72 users calling the nine different COMMUNICATOR travel planning systems. Each system implemented a logfile standard for logging system behaviors and calculating a set of core metrics. Each system utterance and each recognizer result was logged, and user utterances were transcribed and incorporated into the logfiles. The logfile standard supported the calculation of metrics that were hypothesized to potentially affect the user's perception of the system; these included task duration, per turn measures, response latency measures and ASR performance measures. Each dialogue was also hand labelled for task completion.

The hypothesis underlying our approach is that a system's dialogue behaviors have a strong effect on the user's perception of the system. Yet the core metrics that were collected via the logfile standard represent very little about dialogue behaviors. For example, the logging counts system turns and tallies their average length, but doesn't distinguish turns that reprompt the user, or give instructions, from those that present flight information. Furthermore, each COMMUNICATOR system had a unique dialogue strategy and a unique way of achieving particular communicative goals. Thus, in order to explore our hypothesis about the differential effect of these strategies, we needed a way to characterize system dialogue behaviors that would capture such differences yet be applied uniformly to all nine systems. While some sites logged system dialogue behaviors using site-specific dialogue act naming schemes, there existed no scheme that could be applied across sites.

Our goal was thus to develop a dialogue act tagging scheme that would capture important distinctions in this set of dialogues; these distinctions must be useful for testing particular hypotheses about differences among dialogue systems. We also believed that it was important for our tagging scheme to allow for multiple views of each dialogue act. This would allow us, for example, to investigate what part of the task an utterance contributes to separately from what speech act function it serves. A central claim of the paper is that these goals require a tagging scheme that makes distinctions within three orthogonal dimensions of utterance classification: (1) a SPEECH-ACT dimension; (2) a TASK-SUBTASK dimension; and (3) a CONVERSATIONAL-DOMAIN dimension. Figure 1 shows a COMMUNICATOR dialogue with each system utterance classified on these three dimensions. The labels on each utterance are fully described in the remainder of the paper.

Sections 2, 3, and 4, describe the three dimensions of DATE. In these sections, we describe two aspects of our annotation scheme that are not captured in existing tagging schemes, which we believe are important for characterizing how much effort in a dialogue is devoted to the task versus different kinds of dialogue maintenance. Section 5 describes how the dialogue act labels are assigned to system utterances and section 6 discusses results showing that the DATE dialogue act metrics improve models of user satisfaction by an absolute 7% (an increase from 38% to 45%). The dialogueue act metrics that are important predictors of user satisfaction are various kinds of meta-dialogue, apologies and acts that may be landmarks for achieving particular dialogueue subtasks. In section 7 we summarize the paper, discuss our claim that a dialogue annotation

Proceedings of HLT 2001, First International Conference on Human Language Technology Research, J. Allan, ed., Morgan Kaufmann, San Francisco, 2001.

scheme is a partial model of a natural class of dialogues, and discuss the ways in which the DATE scheme may be generalizable to other dialogue corpora.

2. CONVERSATIONAL DOMAINS

The CONVERSATIONAL-DOMAIN dimension characterizes each utterance as primarily belonging to one of three arenas of conversational action. The first arena is the domain task, which in this case is air travel booking, and which we refer to below as ABOUT-TASK. The second domain of conversational action is the management of the communication channel, which we refer to as ABOUT-COMMUNICATION. This distinction has been widely adopted [19, 2, 9]. In addition, we identify a third domain of talk that we refer to as ABOUT-SITUATION-FRAME. This domain is particularly relevant for distinguishing human-computer from human-human dialogues, and for distinguishing dialogue strategies across the 9 COMMUNICATOR systems. Each domain is described in this section.

2.1 About-Task

The ABOUT-TASK domain reflects the fact that many utterances in a task-oriented dialogue originate because the goal of the dialogue is to complete a particular task to the satisfaction of both participants. Typically an about-task utterance directly asks for or presents task-related information, or offers a solution to a task goal.

As Figure 1 shows, most utterances are in the ABOUT-TASK dimension, reflecting the fact that the primary goal of the dialogue is to collaborate on the task of making travel arrangements. The task column of Figure 1 specifies the subtask that each task-related utterance contributes to. DATE includes a large inventory of subtasks in the task/subtask dimension in order to make fine-grained distinctions regarding the dialogue effort devoted to the task or its subcomponents. Section 4 will describe the task model in more detail.

2.2 About-Communication

The ABOUT-COMMUNICATION domain reflects the system goal of managing the verbal channel and providing evidence of what has been understood [29, 8, 25]. Although utterances of this type occur in human-human dialogue, they are more frequent in human-computer dialogue, where they are motivated by the need to avoid potentially costly errors arising from imperfect speech recognition. In the COMMUNICATOR corpus, many systems use a conservative strategy of providing feedback indicating the system's understanding of the information provided by the user after each user turn. A typical example is the repetition of the origin and destination cities in Figures 1 and 6. This type of repetition is the IMPLICIT-CONFIRMATION speech-act (see Section 3 below). Some systems used a variable confirmation strategy where some information items may be confirmed as they are understood, but the system requests explicit confirmation of all task parameters before searching the database for matching flights. An example is in Figure 2. Here the system asks for explicit confirmation in SYS3 before going to the database. This is the first opportunity that the user has for making a correction, which he does in USER3. The system then again asks for explicit confirmation of its new understanding, which the user provides in USER4. After the user informs the system that it is a one-way flight in USER6, the system accesses the database. These explicit confirmations have the goal of avoiding a costly database lookup, where the retrieval is conditioned on the wrong parameters.

All implicit and explicit confirmation speech-acts are categorized as ABOUT-COMMUNICATION because they are motivated by the potential errors that the system might make in understanding

Speaker	Utterance
SYS1	....What are your travel plans? ?
USER1	I WISH TO FLY FROM LEXICON KENTUCKY TO SPRINGFIELD MISSOURI THE MORNING OF OCTOBER FIFTH
SYS2	do you have a preferred airline?
USER2	NO
SYS3	I have you going from Kentucky to Gainesville Missouri on October fifth . Is that correct?
USER3	IT'S LEXINGTON KENTUCKY TO SPRINGFIELD MISSOURI
SYS4	I have you going from Lexington to Springfield Missouri on October fifth, Is that correct?
USER4	YES
SYS5	Will you return to Lexington from Springfield?
USER5	NO
SYS6	Is Springfield your final destination?
USER6	YES
SYS7	Hold on while I check availability..... Three options were returned. Option one has a fare of four hundred and thirty three dollars.....

Figure 2: Dialogue Illustrating Variable Confirmation Strategy

the caller, or in diagnosing the causes of misunderstandings. In general, any utterance that reflects the system's understanding of something the user said is classified as ABOUT-COMMUNICATION.

A second set of ABOUT-COMMUNICATION utterances are APOLOGIES that the system makes for misunderstandings (see Section 3 below), i.e. utterances such as *I'm sorry. I'm having trouble understanding you.*, or *My mistake again. I didn't catch that.* or *I can see you are having some problems.*

The last category of ABOUT-COMMUNICATION utterances are the OPENINGS/CLOSINGS by which the system greets or says goodbye to the caller. (Again, see Section 3 below.)

2.3 About Situation-Frame

The SITUATION-FRAME domain pertains to the goal of managing the culturally relevant framing expectations. The term is inspired by Goffman's work on the organization and maintenance of social interaction [13, 14]. An obvious example of a framing assumption is that the language of the interaction will be English [13, 14]. Another is that there is an asymmetry between the knowledge and/or agency of the system (or human travel agent) and that of the user (or caller): the user cannot issue an airline ticket.

In developing the DATE tagging scheme, we compared human-human travel planning dialogues collected by CMU with the human-machine dialogues of the June 2000 data collection and noticed a striking difference in the ABOUT-FRAME dimension. Namely, very few ABOUT-FRAME utterances occur in the human-human dialogues, whereas they occur frequently enough in human-computer dialogues that to ignore them is to risk obscuring significant differences in habitability of different systems. In other words, certain differences in dialogue strategies across sites could not be fully represented without such a distinction. Figure 3 provides examples motivating this dimension.

Dialogue acts that are ABOUT-FRAME are cross-classified as one of three types of speech-acts, PRESENT-INFO, INSTRUCTION or APOLOGY. They are not classified as having a value on the TASK-SUBTASK dimension. Most of the ABOUT-FRAME dialogue acts fall into the speech-act category of INSTRUCTIONS, utterances directed at shaping the user's behavior and expectations about how to interact with a machine. Sites differ regarding how much instruction is provided up-front versus within the dialogue; most sites have different utterance strategies for dialogue-initial versus dialogue-

67

Speech-Act	Example
PRESENT-INFO	*You are logged in as a guest user of A T and T Communicator.*
PRESENT-INFO	*I'll enroll you temporarily as a guest user.*
PRESENT-INFO	*I know about the top 150 cities worldwide.*
PRESENT-INFO	*This call is being recorded for development purposes, and may be shared with other researchers.*
PRESENT-INFO	*I cannot handle rental cars or hotels yet. Please restrict your requests to air travel.*
PRESENT-INFO	*I heard you ask about fares. I can only price an itinerary. I cannot provide information on published fares for individual flights.*
INSTRUCTION	*First, always wait to hear the beep before you say anything*
INSTRUCTION	*You can always start over again completely just by saying: start over.*
INSTRUCTION	*Before we begin, let's go over a few simple instructions.*
INSTRUCTION	*Please remember to speak after the tone. If you get confused at any point you can say start over to cancel your current itinerary.*
APOLOGY	*Sorry, an error has occurred. We'll have to start over.*
APOLOGY	*I am sorry I got confused. Thanks for your patience. Let us try again.*
APOLOGY	*Something is wrong with the flight retrieval.*
APOLOGY	*I have trouble with my script.*

Figure 3: Example About-Frame Utterances

medial instructions. One site gives minimal up-front framing information; further, the same utterances that can occur up-front also occur dialogue-medially. A second site gives no up-front framing information, but it does provide framing information dialogue-medially. Yet a third site gives framing information dialogue-initially, but not dialogue-medially. The remaining sites provide different kinds of general instructions dialogue-initially, e.g. (*Welcome. ...You may say repeat, help me out, start over, or, that's wrong, you can also correct and interrupt the system at any time.*) versus dialogue-medially: (*Try changing your departure dates or times or a nearby city with a larger airport.*) This category also includes statements to the user about the system's capabilities. These occur in response to a specific question or task that the system cannot handle: *I cannot handle rental cars or hotels yet. Please restrict your requests to air travel.* See Figure 3.

Another type of ABOUT-FRAME utterance is the system's attempt to disambiguate the user's utterance; in response to the user specifying *Springfield* as a flight destination, the system indicates that this city name is ambiguous (*I know of three Springfields, in Missouri, Illinois and Ohio. Which one do you want?*). The system's utterance communicates to the user that *Springfield* is ambiguous, and goes further than a human would to clarify that there are only three known options. It is important for evaluation purposes to distinguish the question and the user's response from a simple question-answer sequence establishing a destination. A direct question, such as *What city are you flying to?*, functions as a REQUEST-INFO speech act and solicits information about the task. The context here contrasts with a direct question in that the system has already asked for and understood a response from the caller about the destination city. Here, the function of the system turn is to remediate the caller's assumptions about the frame by indicating the system's confusion about the destination. Note that the question within this pattern could easily be reformulated as a more typical instruction statement, such as *Please specify which Springfield you mean*, or *Please say Missouri, Illinois or Ohio.*.

3. THE SPEECH-ACT DIMENSION

The SPEECH-ACT dimension characterizes the utterance's communicative goal, and is motivated by the need to distinguish the communicative goal of an utterance from its form. As an example, consider the functional category of a REQUEST for information, found in many tagging schemes that annotate speech-acts [24, 18, 6]. Keeping the functional category of a REQUEST separate from the sentence modality distinction between question and statement makes it possible to capture the functional similarity between question and statement forms of requests, e.g., *Can you tell me what time you would like to arrive?* versus *Please tell me what time you would like to arrive.*

In DATE, the speech-act dimension has ten categories. We use familiar speech-act labels, such as OFFER, REQUEST-INFO, PRESENT-INFO, ACKNOWLEDGMENT, and introduce new ones designed to help us capture generalizations about communicative behavior in this domain, on this task, given the range of system and human behavior we see in the data. One new one, for example, is STATUS-REPORT, whose speech-act function and operational definition are discussed below. Examples of each speech-act type are in Figure 4.

Speech-Act	Example
REQUEST-INFO	*And, what city are you flying to?*
PRESENT-INFO	*The airfare for this trip is 390 dollars.*
OFFER	*Would you like me to hold this option?*
ACKNOWLEDGMENT	*I will book this leg.*
STATUS-REPORT	*Accessing the database; this might take a few seconds.*
EXPLICIT-CONFIRM	*You will depart on September 1st. Is that correct?*
IMPLICIT-CONFIRM	*Leaving from Dallas.*
INSTRUCTION	*Try saying a short sentence.*
APOLOGY	*Sorry, I didn't understand that.*
OPENINGS/CLOSINGS	*Hello. Welcome to the C M U Communicator.*

Figure 4: Example Speech Acts

In this domain, the REQUEST-INFO speech-acts are designed to solicit information about the trip the caller wants to book, such as the destination city (*And what city are you flying to?*), the desired dates and times of travel (*What date would you like to travel on*), or information about ground arrangements, such as hotel or car rental (*Will you need a hotel in Chicago?*).

The PRESENT-INFO speech-acts also often pertain directly to the domain task of making travel arrangements: the system presents the user with a choice of itinerary (*There are several flights from Dallas Fort Worth to Salisbury Maryland which depart between eight in the morning and noon on October fifth. You can fly on American departing at eight in the morning or ten thirty two in the morning, or on US Air departing at ten thirty five in the morning.*), as well as a ticket price (*Ticket price is 495 dollars*), or hotel or car options.

OFFERS involve requests by the caller for a system action, such as to pick a flight (*I need you to tell me whether you would like to take this particular flight*) or to confirm a booking (*If this itinerary meets your needs, please press one; otherwise, press zero.*) They typically occur after the prerequisite travel information has been obtained, and choices have been retrieved from the database.

The ACKNOWLEDGMENT speech act characterizes system utterances that follow a caller's acceptance of an OFFER, e.g. *I will book this leg* or *I am making the reservation.*

The STATUS-REPORT speech-act is used to inform the user about the status of the part of the domain task pertaining to the database retrieval, and can include apologies, mollification, requests to be patient, and so on. Their function is to let the user know what is happening with the database lookup, whether there are problems with it, and what types of problems. While the form of these acts are typically statements, their communication function is different than typical presentations of information; they typically function to keep the user apprised of progress on aspects of the task that the user has no direct information about, e.g. *Accessing the database; this might take a few seconds.* There is also a politeness function to utterances like *Sorry this is taking so long, please hold.*, and they often provide the user with error diagnostics: *The date you specified is too far in advance.*; or *Please be aware that the return date must be later than the departure date.*; or *No records satisfy your request.*; or *There don't seem to be any flights from Boston.*

The speech-act inventory also includes two types of speech acts whose function is to confirm information that has already been provided by the caller. In order to identify and confirm the parameters of the trip, systems may ask the caller direct questions, as in SYS3 and SYS4 in Figure 2. These EXPLICIT-CONFIRM speech acts are sometimes triggered by the system's belief that a misunderstanding may have occurred. A typical example is *Are you traveling to Dallas?*. An alternative form of the same EXPLICIT-CONFIRM speech-act type asserts the information the system has understood and asks for confirmation in an immediately following question: *I have you arriving in Dallas. Is that correct?* In both cases, the caller is intended to provide a response.

A less intrusive form of confirmation, which we tag as IMPLICIT-CONFIRM, typically presents the user with the system's understanding of one travel parameter immediately before asking about the next parameter. Depending on the site, implicit information can either precede the new request for information, as in *Flying to Tokyo. What day are you leaving?*, or can occur within the same utterance, as in *What day do you want to leave London?* More rarely, an implicit confirmation is followed by PRESENT-INFO: *a flight on Monday September 25. Delta has a flight departing Atlanta at nine thirty.* One question about the use of implicit confirmation strategy is whether the caller realizes they can correct the system when necessary [10]. Although IMPLICIT-CONFIRMS typically occur as part of a successful sequence of extracting trip information from the caller, they can also occur in situations where the system is having trouble understanding the caller. In this case, the system may attempt to instruct the user on what it is doing to remediate the problem in between an IMPLICIT-CONFIRM and a REQUEST-INFO: *So far, I have you going from Tokyo. I am trying to assemble enough information to pick a flight. Right now I need you to tell me your destination.*

We have observed that INSTRUCTIONS are a speech-act type that distinguishes these human-computer travel planning dialogues from corresponding human-human travel planning dialogues. Instructions sometimes take the form of a statement or an imperative, and are characterized by their functional goal of clarifying the system's own actions, correcting the user's expectations, or changing the user's future manner of interacting with the system. Dialogue systems are less able to diagnose a communication problem than human travel agents, and callers are less familiar with the capabilities of such systems. As noted above, some systems resort to explicit instructions about what the system is doing or is able to do, or about what the user should try in order to assist the system: *Try asking for flights between two major cities*; or *You can cancel the San Antonio, Texas, to Tampa, Florida flight request or change it. To change it, you can simply give new information such as a new departure time.* Note that INSTRUCTIONS, unlike the preceding dialogue act types, do not directly involve a domain task.

Like the INSTRUCTION speech-acts, APOLOGIES do not address

a domain task. They typically occur when the system encounters problems, for example, in understanding the caller (*I'm sorry, I'm having trouble understanding you*), in accessing the database (*Something is wrong with the flight retrieval*), or with the connection (*Sorry, we seem to have a bad connection. Can you please call me back later?*).

The OPENING/CLOSING speech act category characterizes utterances that open and close the dialogue, such as greetings or goodbyes [26]. Most of the dialogue systems open the interactions with some sort of greeting—*Hello, welcome to our Communicator flight travel system*, and end with a sign-off or salutation—*Thank you very much for calling. This session is now over.* We distinguish these utterances from other dialogue acts, but we do not tag openings separate from closings because they have a similar function, and can be distinguished by their position in the discourse. We also include in this category utterances in which the systems survey the caller as to whether s/he got the information s/he needed or was happy with the system.

4. THE TASK-SUBTASK DIMENSION

The TASK-SUBTASK dimension refers to a task model of the domain task that the system is designed to support and captures distinctions among dialogue acts that reflect the task structure.[1] Our domain is air travel reservations, thus the main communicative task is to specify information pertaining to an air travel reservation, such as the destination city. Once a flight has been booked, ancillary tasks such as arranging for lodging or a rental car become relevant. The fundamental motivation for the TASK-SUBTASK dimension in the DATE scheme is to derive metrics related to subtasks in order to quantify how much effort a system expends on particular subtasks.[2]

This dimension distinguishes among 13 subtasks, some of which can also be grouped at a level below the top level task. The subtasks and examples are in Figure 5. The TOP-LEVEL-TRIP task describes the task which contains as its subtasks the ORIGIN, DESTINATION, DATE, TIME, AIRLINE, TRIP-TYPE, RETRIEVAL and ITINERARY tasks. The GROUND task includes both the HOTEL and CAR subtasks.

Typically each COMMUNICATOR dialogue system acts as though it utilizes a task model, in that it has a particular sequence in which it will ask for task information if the user doesn't take the initiative to volunteer this information. For example, most systems ask first for the origin and destination cities, then for the date and time. Some systems ask about airline preference and others leave it to the caller to volunteer this information. A typical sequence of tasks for the flight planning portion of the dialogue is illustrated in Figure 6.

As Figure 6 illustrates, any subtask can involve multiple speech acts. For example, the DATE subtask can consist of acts requesting, or implicitly or explicitly confirming the date. A similar example is provided by the subtasks of CAR (rental) and HOTEL, which include dialogue acts requesting, confirming or acknowledging arrangements to rent a car or book a hotel room on the same trip.

---

[1] This dimension is used as an elaboration of each speech-act type in other tagging schemes [24].

[2] It is tempting to also consider this dimension as a means of inferring discourse structure on the basis of utterance level labels, since it is widely believed that models of task structure drive the behavior of dialogue systems [23, 3, 22], and the relationship between discourse structure and task structure has been a core topic of research since Grosz's thesis [15]. However, we leave the inference of discourse structure as a topic for future work because the multifunctionality of many utterances suggests that the correspondence between task structure and dialogue structure may not be as straightforward as has been proposed in Grosz's work [30].

Task	Example
TOP-LEVEL-TRIP	*What are your travel plans?*
ORIGIN	*And, what city are you leaving from?*
DESTINATION	*And, where are you flying to?*
DATE	*What day would you like to leave?*
TIME	*Departing at what time?.*
AIRLINE	*Did you have an airline preference?*
TRIP-TYPE	*Will you return to Boston from San Jose?*
RETRIEVAL	*Accessing the database; this might take a few seconds.*
ITINERARY	*The airfare for this trip is 390 dollars.*
GROUND	*Did you need to make any ground arrangements?.*
HOTEL	*Would you like a hotel near downtown or near the airport?.*
CAR	*Do you need a car in San Jose?*

Figure 5: Example Utterances for each Subtask

Speaker	Utterance	Task
SYS	Welcome .... What trip would you like to take?	TOP-LEVEL-TRIP
USER	STARTING FROM ATLANTA GEORGIA TO LONDON ENGLAND	
SYS	flying from atlanta to london.	ORIGIN, DESTINATION
SYS	What day are you leaving Atlanta?	DATE
USER	MONDAY SEPTEMBER TWENTY FIVE	
SYS	on monday, september twenty fifth.	DATE
SYS	About what time do you want to leave?	TIME
USER	[UH] DAYTIME	
SYS	Leaving in the daytime.	TIME
SYS	Please stand by while I look up the flight schedules on the web.	RETRIEVAL
SYS	OK, got them. I have 13 flights. The first flight is on American at six fifty nine eh M, arriving at ten forty five PM, with a connection in Chicago. . Is that OK?	ITINERARY
USER	[UH] YES OKAY	
SYS	Do you want a return flight from London to Atlanta?	TRIP-TYPE
USER	[UH] YES	
SYS	Returning from london to atlanta.	TRIP-TYPE
SYS	What day are you leaving London?	DATE
USER	[UH] LEAVING [UM] MONDAY OCTOBER THE SECOND	
SYS	on monday, october second.	DATE
SYS	About what time do you want to leave?	TIME
USER	ANY TIME'S OKAY	
SYS	Please stand by while I look up the flight schedules on the web... OK, got them.	RETRIEVAL, ITINERARY

Figure 6: Dialogue Illustrating a Typical Task Sequence

There are also differences in how each site's dialogue strategy reflects it conceptualization of the travel planning task. For example, some systems ask the user explicitly for their airline preferences whereas others do not (the systems illustrated in Figures 1 and 6 do not, wherase the one in Figure 2 does). Another difference is whether the system asks the user explicitly whether s/he wants a round-trip ticket. Some systems ask this information early on, and search for both the outbound and the return flights at the same time. Other systems do not separately model round-trip and multi-leg trips. Instead they ask the user for information leg by leg, and after requesting the user to select an itinerary for one leg of the flight, they ask whether the user has an additional destination.

A final difference was that, in the June 2000 data collection, some systems such as the one illustrated in Figure 1 included the ground arrangements subtasks, and others did not.

5. IMPLEMENTATION

Our focus in this work is in labelling the system side of the dialogue; our goal was to develop a fully automatic 100% correct dialogue parser for the limited range of utterances produced by the 9 COMMUNICATOR systems. While we believe that it would be useful to be able to assign dialogue acts to both sides of the conversation, we expect that to require hand-labelling [1]. We also believe that in many cases the system behaviors are highly correlated with the user behaviors of interest; for example when a user has to repeat himself because of a misunderstanding, the system has probably prompted the user multiple times for the same item of information and has probably apologized for doing so. Thus this aspect of the dialogue would also be likely to be captured by the APOLOGY dialogue act and by counts of effort expended on the particular subtask.

We implemented a pattern matcher that labels the system side of each dialogue. An utterance or utterance sequence is identifed automatically from a database of patterns that correspond to the dialogue act classification we arrived at in cooperation with the site developers. Where it simplifies the structure of the dialogue parser, we assign two adjacent utterances that are directed at the same goal the same DATE label, thus ignoring the utterance level segmentation, but we count the number of characters used in each act. Since some utterances are generated via recursive or iterative routines, some patterns involve wildcards.

The current implementation labels the utterances with tags that are independent of any particular markup-language or representation format. We have written a transducer that takes the labelled dialogues and produces HTML output for the purpose of visualizing the distribution of dialogue acts and meta-categories in the dialogues. An additional summarizer program is used to produce a summary of the percentages and counts of each dialogue act as well as counts of meta-level groupings of the acts related to the different dimensions of the tagging scheme. We intend to use our current representation to generate ATLAS compliant representations [4].

6. RESULTS

Our primary goal was to achieve a better understanding of the qualitative aspects of each system's dialogue behavior. We can quantify the extent to which the dialogue act metrics have the potential to improve our understanding by applying the PARADISE framework to develop a model of user satisfaction and then examining the extent to which the dialogue act metrics improve these models [31]. In other work, we show that given the standard metrics collected for the COMMUNICATOR dialogue systems, the best model accounts for 38% of the variance in user satisfaction [28].

When we retrain these models with the dialogue act metrics extracted by our dialogue parser, we find that many metrics are significant predictors of user satisfaction, and that the model fit increases from 38% to 45%. When we examine which dialogue metrics are significant, we find that they include several types of meta-dialogue such as explicit and implicit confirmations of what the user said, and acknowledgments that the system is going to go ahead and do the action that the user has requested. Significant negative predictors include apologies. On interpretation of many of the significant predictors is that they are landmarks in the dialogue for achievement of particular subtasks. However the predictors based on the core metrics included a ternary task completion metric that captures

70

succinctly whether any task was achieved or not, and whether the exact task that the user was attempting to accomplish was achieved. A plausible explanation for the increase in the model fits is that user satisfaction is sensitive to exactly how far through the task the user got, even when the user did not in fact complete the task. The role of the other significant dialogue metrics are plausibly interpreted as acts important for error minimization. As with the task-related dialogue metrics, there were already metrics related to ASR performance in the core set of metrics. However, several of the important metrics count explicit confirmations, one of the desired date of travel, and the other of all information before searching the database, as in utterances SYS3 and SYS4 in Figure 2.

7. DISCUSSION

This paper has presented DATE, a dialogue act tagging scheme developed explicitly for the purpose of comparing and evaluating spoken dialogue systems. We have argued that such a scheme needs to make three important distinctions in system dialogue behaviors and we are investigating the degree to which any given type of dialogue act belongs in a single category or in multiple categories.

We also propose the view that a tagging scheme be viewed as a partial model of a natural class of dialogues. It is a model to the degree that it represents claims about what features of the dialogue are important and are sufficiently well understood to be operationally defined. It is partial in that the distributions of the features and their relationship to one another, i.e., their possible manifestations in dialogues within the class, are an empirical question.

The view that a dialogue tagging scheme is a partial model of a class of dialogues implies that a pre-existing tagging scheme can be re-used on a different research project, or by different researchers, only to the degree that it models the same natural class with respect to similar research questions, is sufficient for expressing observations about what actually occurs within the current dialogues of interest, and is sufficiently well-defined that high reliability within and across research sites can be achieved. Thus, our need to modify existing schemes was motivated precisely to the degree that existing schemes fall short of these requirements. Other researchers who began with the goal of re-utilizing existing tagging schemes have also found it necessary to modify these schemes for their research purposes [11, 18, 7].

The most substantial difference between our dialogue act tagging scheme and others that have been proposed is in our expansion of the two-way distinction between dialogue *tout simple* vs. meta-dialogue, into a three-way distinction among the immediate dialogue goals, meta-dialogue utterances, and meta-situation utterances. Depending on further investigation, we might decide these three dimensions have equal status within the overall tagging scheme (or within the overall dialogue-modeling enterprise), or that there are two types of meta-dialogue: utterances devoted to maintaining the channel, versus utterances devoted to establishing/maintaining the frame. Further, in accord with our view that a tagging scheme is a partial model, and that it is therefore necessarily evolving as our understanding of dialogue evolves, we also believe that our formulation of any one dimension, such as the speech-act dimension, will necessarily differ from other schemes that model a speech-act dimension.

Furthermore, because human-computer dialogue is at an early stage of development, any such tagging scheme must be a moving target, i.e., the more progress is made, the more likely it is we may need to modify along the way the exact features used in an annotation scheme to characterize what is going on. In particular, as system capabilities become more advanced in the travel domain, it will probably be necessary to elaborate the task model to capture differ-

ent aspects of the system's problem solving activities. For example, our task model does not currently distinguish between different aspects of information about an itinerary, e.g. between presentation of price information and presentation of schedule information.

We also expect that some domain-independent modifications are likely to be necessary as dialogue systems become more successful, for example to address the dimension of "face", i.e. the positive politeness that a system shows to the user [5]. As an example, consider the difference between the interpretation of the utterance, *There are no flights from Boston to Boston*, when produced by a system vs. when produced by a human travel agent. If a human said this, it would be be interpretable by the recipient as an insult to their intelligence. However when produced by a system, it functions to identify the source of the misunderstanding. Another distinction that we don't currently make which might be useful is between the initial presentation of an item of information and its re-presentation in a summary. Summaries arguably have a different communicative function [29, 7]. Another aspect of function our representation doesn't capture is rhetorical relations between speech acts [20, 21].

While we developed DATE to answer particular research questions in the COMMUNICATOR dialogues, there are likely to be aspects of DATE that can be applied elsewhere. The task dimension tagset reflects our model of the domain task. The utility of a task model may be general across domains and for this particular domain, the categories we employ are presumably typical of travel tasks and so, may be relatively portable.

The speech act dimension includes categories typically found in other classifications of speech acts, such as REQUEST-INFO, OFFER, and PRESENT-INFO. We distinguish information presented to the user about the task, PRESENT-INFO, from information provided to change the user's behavior, INSTRUCTION, and from information presented in explanation or apology for an apparent interruption in the dialogue, STATUS-REPORT. The latter has some of the flavor of APOLOGIES, which have an inter-personal function, along with OPENINGS/CLOSINGS. We group GREETINGS and SIGN-OFFS into the single category of OPENINGS/CLOSINGS on the assumption that politeness forms make less contribution to perceived system success than the system's ability to carry out the task, to correct misunderstandings, and to coach the user.

Our third dimension, conversational-domain, adds a new category, ABOUT-SITUATION-FRAME, to the more familiar distinction between utterances directed at a task goal vs. utterances directed at a maintaining the communication. This distinction supports the separate classification of utterances directed at managing the user's assumptions about how to interact with the system on the air travel task. As we mention above, the ABOUT-SITUATION-FRAME utterances that we find in the human-computer dialogues typically did not occur in human-human air travel dialogues. In addition, as we note above, one obvious difference in the dialogue strategies implemented at different sites had to do with whether these utterances occurred upfront, within the dialogue, or both.

In order to demonstrate the utility of dialogue act tags as metrics for spoken dialogue systems, we show that the use of these metrics in the application of PARADISE [31] improves our model of user satisfaction by an absolute 7%, from 38% to 45%. This is a large increase, and the fit of these models are very good for models of human behavior. We believe that we have only begun to discover the ways in which the output of the dialogue parser can be used. In future work we will examine whether other representations derived from the metrics we have applied, such as sequences or structural relations between various types of acts might improve our performance model further. We are also collaborating with other members of the COMMUNICATOR community who are investigating the use of dialogue act and initiative tagging schemes for the purpose of comparing human-human to human-computer dialogues [1].

8. ACKNOWLEDGMENTS

This work was supported under DARPA GRANT MDA 972 99 3 0003 to AT&T Labs Research. Thanks to Payal Prabhu and Sungbok Lee for their assistance with the implementation of the dialogue parser. We also appreciate the contribution of J. Aberdeen, E. Bratt, S. Narayanan, K. Papineni, B. Pellom, J. Polifroni, A. Potamianos, A. Rudnicky, S. Seneff, and D. Stallard who helped us understand how the DATE classification scheme applied to their COMMUNICATOR systems' dialogues.

9. REFERENCES

[1] J. Aberdeen and C. Doran. Human-computer and human-human dialogues. DARPA Communicator Principle Investigators Meeting (Philadelphia, PA USA). http://www.dsic-web.net/ito/meetings/communicator sep2000/, September, 2000.

[2] J. Allen and M. Core. Draft of DAMSL: Dialog act markup in several layers. Coding scheme developed by the MultiParty group, 1st Discourse Tagging Workshop, University of Pennsylvania, March 1996, 1997.

[3] J. F. Allen. Recognizing intentions from natural language utterances. In M. Brady and R. Berwick, editors, *Computational Models of Discourse*. MIT Press, 1983.

[4] S. Bird and M. Liberman. A formal framework for linguistic annotation. *Speech Communication*, 33(1,2):23–60, 2001.

[5] P. Brown and S. Levinson. *Politeness: Some universals in language usage*. Cambridge University Press, 1987.

[6] J. C. Carletta, A. Isard, S. Isard, J. C. Kowtko, G. Dowerty-Sneddon, and A. H. Anderson. The reliability of a dialogue structure coding scheme. *Computational Linguistics*, 23-1:13–33, 1997.

[7] R. Cattoni, M. Danieli, A. Panizza, V. Sandrini, and C. Soria. Building a corpus of annotated dialogues: the ADAM experience. In *Proc. of the Conference Corpus-Linguistics-2001, Lancaster, U.K.*, 2001.

[8] H. H. Clark and E. F. Schaefer. Contributing to discourse. *Cognitive Science*, 13:259–294, 1989.

[9] S. L. Condon and C. G. Cech. Functional comparison of face-to-face and computer-mediated decision-making interactions. In S. Herring, editor, *Computer-Mediated Converstaion*. John Benjamins, 1995.

[10] M. Danieli and E. Gerbino. Metrics for evaluating dialogue strategies in a spoken language system. In *Proceedings of the 1995 AAAI Spring Symposium on Empirical Methods in Discourse Interpretation and Generation*, pages 34–39, 1995.

[11] B. Di Eugenio, P. W. Jordan, J. D. Moore, and R. H. Thomason. An empirical investigation of collaborative dialogues. In *ACL-COLING98, Proceedings of the Thirty-sixth Conference of the Association for Computational Linguistics*, 1998.

[12] M. Finke, M. Lapata, A. Lavie, L. Levin, L. M. Tomokiyo, T. Polzin, K. Ries, A. Waibel, and K. Zechner. Clarity: Inferring discourse structure from speech. In *American Association for Artificial Intelligence (AAAI) Symposium on Applying Machine Learning to Discourse Processing Proceedings, Stanford, California*, March 1998.

[13] E. Goffman. *Frame Analysis: An Essay on the Organization of Experience*. Harper and Row, New York, 1974.

[14] E. Goffman. *Forms of Talk*. University of Pennsylvania Press, Philadelphia, Pennsylvania, USA, 1981.

[15] B. J. Grosz. The representation and use of focus in dialogue understanding. Technical Report 151, SRI International, 333 Ravenswood Ave, Menlo Park, Ca. 94025, 1977.

[16] A. Isard and J. C. Carletta. Replicability of transaction and action coding in the map task corpus. In M. Walker and J. Moore, editors, *AAAI Spring Symposium: Empirical Methods in Discourse Interpretation and Generation*, pages 60–67, 1995.

[17] P. W. Jordan. *Intentional Influences on Object Redescriptions in Dialogue: Evidence from an Empirical Study*. PhD thesis, Intelligent Systems Program, University of Pittsburgh, 2000.

[18] D. Jurafsky, E. Shriberg, and D. Biasca. Swbd-damsl labeling project coder's manual. Technical report, University of Colorado, 1997. available as http://stripe.colorado.edu/ jurafsky/manual.august1.html.

[19] D. Litman. Plan recognition and discourse analysis: An integrated approach for understanding dialogues. Technical Report 170, University of Rochester, 1985.

[20] D. Marcu. Perlocutions: The achilles' heel of speech act theory. *Journal of Pragmatics*, 1999.

[21] M. G. Moser, J. Moore, and E. Glendening. Instructions for coding explanations: Identifying segments, relations and minimal units. Technical Report 96-17, University of Pittsburgh, Department of Computer Science, 1996.

[22] R. Perrault and J. Allen. A plan-based analysis of indirect speech acts. *American Journal of Computational Linguistics*, 6:167–182, 1980.

[23] R. Power. *A Computer Model of Conversation*. PhD thesis, University of Edinburgh, 1974.

[24] N. Reithinger and E. Maier. Utilizing statistical speech act processing in verbmobil. In *ACL 95*, 1995.

[25] D. R.Traum and E. A. Hinkelman. Conversation acts in task-oriented spoken dialogue. *Computational Intelligence*, 8(3):575–599, 1992.

[26] E. A. Schegloff and H. Sacks. Opening up closings. *Semiotica*, 8:289–327, 1977.

[27] E. Shriberg, P. Taylor, R. Bates, A. Stolcke, K. Ries, D. Jurafsky, N. Coccaro, R. Martin, M. Meteer, and C. V. Ess-Dykema. Can prosody aid the automatic classification of dialog acts in conversational speech. *Language and Speech: Special Issue on Prosody and Conversation*, 2000.

[28] M. Walker, J. Aberdeen, J. Boland, E. Bratt, J. Garofolo, L. Hirschman, A. Le, S. Lee, S. Narayanan, K. Papineni, B. Pellom, J. Polifroni, A. Potamianos, P. Prabhu, A. Rudnicky, G. Sanders, S. Seneff, D. Stallard, and S. Whittaker. Darpa communicator dialog travel planning systems: The june 2000 data collection. In *Submitted to EUROSPEECH 2001*, 2001.

[29] M. A. Walker. Redundancy in collaborative dialogue. In *Fourteenth International Conference on Computational Linguistics*, pages 345–351, 1992.

[30] M. A. Walker. Limited attention and discourse structure. *Computational Linguistics*, 22-2:255–264, 1996.

[31] M. A. Walker, C. A. Kamm, and D. J. Litman. Towards developing general models of usability with PARADISE. *Natural Language Engineering: Special Issue on Best Practice in Spoken Dialogue Systems*, 2000.

Speaker	Utterance	Speech Act	Task	C-Domain
SYS	Welcome.	opening/closing	nil	task
	You are logged in as a guest user.	instruct	nil	frame
	You may say repeat, help me out, start over, or, that's wrong,	instruct	nil	frame
	you can also correct and interrupt the system at any time.	instruct	nil	frame
	What airport woodja like to fly out of?	request-info	origin	task
USER	MIAMI FLORIDA			
SYS	Leaving from Miami,	implicit-conf	origin	communication
	And, what city are you flying to?	request-info	dest	task
USER	MINNEAPOLIS MINNESOTA			
SYS	Flying from Miami to Minneapolis,	implicit-conf	origin, dest	communication
	What date would you like to fly?	request-info	date	task
USER	UH MONDAY OCTOBER TWENTY THIRD			
SYS	Leaving on the 23rd of October,	implicit-conf	date	communication
	And what time didja wanna leave?	request-info	time	task
USER	UH LATE MORNING			
SYS	From Minneapolis.	implicit-conf	origin	communication
	Are you returning to Miami?	request-info	trip-type	task
USER	UM			
SYS	Are you going back to Miami?	request-info	trip-type	task
	Please say yes or no.	instruct	nil	frame
USER	NO			
SYS	Okay, it will just take a moment while I look.	status-report	retrieval	task
SYS	I found 3 flights from Miami to Minneapolis on October 23rd . For option one I have a	present-info	itinerary	task
	flight with United departing at 10 A M and arriving at 3 P M with one stopover and			
	Ticket price is 390 dollars.	present-info	price	task
	Please say next option, or, flight details, or, I'll take it.	offer	itinerary	task
USER	NEXT OPTION			
SYS	For option two I have a flight with Delta departing at 12 and arriving at 4 P M non-stop.	present-info	itinerary	task
	Ticket price is 450 dollars.	present-info	itinerary	task
	Would you like me to hold this option?	offer	itinerary	task
USER	NEXT OPTION			
SYS	For the last option I have a flight with Northwest departing at 2 P M and arriving at 7 P M	present-info	itinerary	task
	with 1 stopover and			
	Ticket price is 470 dollars.	present-info	itinerary	task
	say next option, or, flight details, or, I'll take it.	offer	itinerary	task
USER	NEXT OPTION			
SYS	Here is your third option again. a flight with Northwest departing at 2 P M and arriving at	present-info	itinerary	task
	7 P M with 1 stopover and			
	Ticket price is 470 dollars.	present-info	itinerary	task
	say next option, or, flight details, or, I'll take it.	offer	itinerary	task
USER	I'LL TAKE IT			
SYS	Great! I am adding this flight to your itinerary.	acknowledge	booking	task
	Okay, Is Minneapolis your final destination?	request-info	trip-type	task
USER	YES IT IS			
SYS	Would you like to make any ground arrangements?	offer	ground	task
USER	NO			
SYS	Now, would you like to hear a summary of your itinerary?	offer	itinerary	task
USER	YES PLEASE			
SYS	Okay, Here's your itinerary. On October 23rd Northwest Flight 123 departs Miami at 2 P	present-info	itinerary	task
	M, arrives Pittsburgh at 4 30 P M connecting to Northwest Flight 146 that departs Pittsburgh			
	at 5 P M and arrives Minneapolis at 7 P M.			

Figure 1: Dialogue Illustrating the Speech Act, Task-Subtask and Conversational Domain Dimensions of DATE

Development of the HRL Route Navigation Dialogue System

Robert Belvin
HRL Laboatories, LLC
3011 Malibu Canyon Road
Malibu, CA 90265
310-317-5799

rsBelvin@hrl.com

Ron Burns
HRL Laboatories, LLC
3011 Malibu Canyon Road
Malibu, CA 90265
310-317-5445

rBurns@hrl.com

Cheryl Hein
HRL Laboatories, LLC
3011 Malibu Canyon Road
Malibu, CA 90265
310-317-5489

cheryl@hrl.com

ABSTRACT

In this paper we report on our work on a prototype route navigation dialogue system for use in a vehicle. The system delivers spoken turn-by-turn directions, and has been developed to accept naturally phrased navigation queries, as part of our overall effort to create an in-vehicle information system which delivers information as requested while placing minimal cognitive load on the driver.

Keywords

Dialogue Systems, Discourse, Navigation, NLP, Pragmatics, Dialogue Manager

1. INTRODUCTION

In this paper we report on our work on a spoken language navigation system which runs in real-time on a high-end laptop or PC, for use in a vehicle. We focus on issues in developing a system which can understand natural conversational queries and respond in such a way as to maximize ease of use for the driver. Because today's technology has the potential to deliver massive amounts of information to automobiles, it is crucial to deliver this information in such way that the driver's attention is not diverted from the primary task of safe driving. Our assumption has been that a dialogue system with a near-human conversational ability would place less of a cognitive load on the driver than one which behaves very differently than a human.

We have implemented a testbed on which to develop and evaluate driver interfaces to navigation systems. Our approach is multimodal and the interface will include a head-up display, steering hub controls, and spoken language, though it is only the latter modality that we report on here. We first discuss our development phases, and after this we provide an overview of our implementation, emphasizing the natural language processing aspects and application interface to the map databases. Next we provide results of our initial evaluation of the system, and finally we draw conclusions and summarize plans for future work.

2. DEVELOPMENT PHASES

One can identify four distinct subproblems which must be solved for a navigation system: 1) the natural language navigation interface, 2) street name recognition, 3) the natural language destination entry interface given street name recognition, and 4) the map database interface. We have partitioned the problem and

Proceedings of HLT 2001, First International Conference on Human Language Technology Research, J. Allan, ed., Morgan Kaufmann, San Francisco, 2001.

have phased our development to progressively implement solutions with increasing complexity.

Navigation system implementation is complicated by the potential of having a very large street name vocabulary with many unusual and uncommon pronunciations with significant variations across speakers. The appropriate name space is dynamic since it depends on the location of the vehicle.

Our initial system does not accept queries with proper street names. In addition, we assume separate destination entry and route planning systems, and that one or more routes have been loaded into the navigation system. The system relies on open dialogue to resolve the directions at any stage of the journey and may or may not use the Global Positioning System (GPS) to determine the progress along the route. By implementing this system first we could concentrate on the dialogue aspects of the navigation problem and also establish a baseline with which to compare our other implementations.

In the second phase we include a limited set of street names as part of the language model and lexicons. Initially we are using a predefined set of names with hand tuning of the pronunciations. Additional research is required to solve the street name recognition problem generally and automatically. We assume in-vehicle GPS and use a map matching system to determine the vehicle's position and if it is on-route. This phase includes development of the natural language components for destination entry and also broadens the scope of the navigation queries to include questions with and about street names. More distant plans include on-road route replanning, providing information to requests for specific street names or points of interest along the route, and traffic information and workarounds.

3. IMPLEMENTATION

Our implementation is based on the Galaxy-II system [6] from the Massachusetts Institute of Technology (MIT), which is the baseline for the Communicator program of the Defense Advance Research Projects Agency (DARPA). The architecture consists of a hub client that communicates, using a standard protocol, with a number of servers as shown in Figure 1. Each server generally implements a key system function including Speech Recognition, Frame Construction (language parsing), Context Tracking, Dialogue Management, Application Interface, Language Generation, and Text-to-speech.

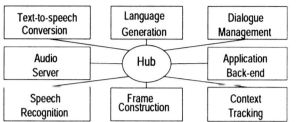

Figure 1. The client-server architecture of the MIT Galaxy-II is used to implement our navigation system testbed.

3.1 Speech Recognition

We use the latest MIT SUMMIT recognizer [8] using weighted finite-state transducers for the lexical access search. We have also "plugged in" alternate recognizers such as the Microsoft Speech SDK recognizer and the Sphinx [3] speech recognizer available as open source code from Carnegie Mellon University.

We are in the process of developing a large database of in-vehicle utterances collected in various car models under a wide range of road and other background noise conditions. This data collection will be carried out in two phases, the first of which is completed; phase two is underway. Limited speech data will result from the first phase and subtantial speech data (appropriate for training acoustic models to represent in-vehicle noise conditions and testing of recognition engines) will come out of the second phase, and will become available through our partners in this collection effort, CSLR at University of Colorado, Boulder [4]. In the meantime we are using the MIT JUPITER acoustic models. The performance is acceptable for our language and dialogue model development, but we refrain from presenting any detailed recognizer results here since they would not reflect fairly on optimized recognizer performance.

Our vocabulary consists of about 400 words without street names. We have an additional 600 street names gleaned from the Los Angeles area where we do much of our system evaluation. Baseforms for the vocabulary are derived from the PRONLEX dictionary from the Linguistic Data Consortium at the University of Pennsylvania. Extensive hand editing is needed especially for the street names. The MIT rule set is used for production of word graphs for the alternate pronunciation forms. We have derived a language model from a set of utterances that were initially generated based our best guess of the query space. As evaluation evolves, we modify the utterance list and retrain the language model. The language model uses classes and includes both bigram and trigram models.

3.2 Application Interface

We are building the application interface in several phases. Initially we are only answering queries about turns and distances during navigation. We obtain the database in two steps. First, we access a commercial map database using standard text I/O for destination entry and route planning. This produces a detailed set of instruction that includes many short segments such as on- and off-ramps. We filter this and rewrite the data to provide a set of natural driving instructions suitable for verbal communication.

The result is a flat database, such as the one shown in Figure 2. This is loaded into to the system and used to formulate answers to the route queries. In the example in Figure 2 the estimated driving time is 45 minutes. Each row is a segment of the trip. The first and second columns code right, left, straight, and compass direction information. The third column is the segment length in miles and the last is the segment name.

```
HRL,                  Airport           45
0  0   1.0   Malibu Canyon Road
0  2  13.3   PCH
1  1   3.4   East I-10 freeway
0  1   4.5   South I-405 freeway
3  0   0.3   Howard Hughes Parkway
0  1   1.7   Sepulveda Boulevard
0  4   0.4   Los Angeles International Airport
```

Figure 2: Example database used as source data to generate guidance instructions for the route between HRL Laboratories and the Los Angeles airport

A sample dialogue is shown in Figure 3 which illustrates the kind of responses the system can generate from a database such as that shown above, given navigation queries of the sort shown; this sample was drawn from our phase I user-system data logs:

S	Welcome to Navigator
U	*What routes are loaded?*
S	I have one set of directions loaded. It is for the route to the airport from HRL
U	*What's my first turn?*
S	From Malibu Canyon Road turn left onto Pacific Coast Highway
U	*And after that?*
S	From Pacific Coast Highway go straight onto East I-10 freeway
U	*How far is that turn?*
S	The distance is 14.3 miles
U	*My odometer reads fifteen point one miles.*
S	Your odometer reading is fifteen point one
U	*What is my next turn?*
S	From East I-10 freeway turn right onto South I-405 freeway
U	*How far is it from here?*
S	The distance is 2.6 miles
U	*How far is the airport from there?*
S	The distance is 6.7 miles
U	*Bye Bye.*
S	Goodbye. Have a nice day.

Figure 3. A navigation system dialog illustrating some sample queries and showing the responses derived by the dialogue manager based on the database of Figure 2.

Off-line construction of the global navigation database is not unrealistic since it could be done, at least in the near term, by a service organization such as OnStar from General Motors (GM). However as navigation systems become widely deployed, users will expect destination entry including real time route re-planning to be an integral part of system. We are developing a direct voice interface to the commercial map database that includes destination entry, route planning, and map matching using GPS data to determine if the vehicle is on-route or not.

During the destination entry phase street names need to be robustly recognized. We are currently working with a subset of street names in the Los Angeles area preloaded in the recognizer and language models. It is untenable to keep all of the street names in Los Angeles loaded in the recognizer simultaneously (there are around 16,000, including 8,000 base names), thus we are developing a method for dynamic loading of map names local to the vehicle position which we will report on in the near future.

We have experimented with using a subset of street names as a filter list, and as a lookup list based on spelling the first few letters, to try to resolve the destination requested. If this fails, or if the trip is outside of the area from which names are loaded, we rely on more complete spelling to determine the destination. The origin for the route plan is generally implied since it is determined by the GPS position of the vehicle most of the time. Once the destination is determined it is straightforward to continuously re-plan the route based on the current vehicle position and thereby be able to provide remedial instruction if the driver departs from the route plan.

3.3 NL Analysis and Generation

The core NLP components in our system are a TINA [5] grammar, context tracking mechanisms, and the GENESIS language generation module. The TINA grammar includes both syntactic and semantic elements and we try to extract as much information as possible from the parse. The information is coded in a hierarchical frame (Figure 4a) as well as a flat key-value pair (Figure 4b). In addition to handcrafting this grammar, a set of rules was also developed for the TINA inheritance mechanism. These rules are applied during context tracking, after the parse, to incorporate information from the dialog history into phrases such as "and after that" and "how about my second turn," and are also used to incorporate modifications that are a result of dialogue management.

a) Parse frame
```
{c locate
 :domain "Nav"
 :pred {p locate_object
       :topic {q turn
               :quantifier "poss_pro"
               :pred {p ord
                     :topic 2 }}}}
```

b) Key-values Pairs
```
:clause "locate" :locate_object "turn" :ORD 2
```

c) Reply Frame
```
{c speak_turn
  :topic {q turn
       :turn_direction "straight"
       :current_roadway "PCH"
             :new_roadway "East I-10 freeway"
  :domain :Nav" }
```

Figure 4. Example frames produced for the simple query "What's my second turn?"

As noted, we use the MIT GENESIS server for language generation. Again this module is rule driven and we developed the lexicon, templates and rewrite rules needed for the three ways we use GENESIS. We extract the key-value pairs (e.g. Figure 4b) from the TINA parse frame. The key values are used to help

control the dialogue management as well as provide easy access to the variable values. We use GENESIS to produce the English reply string that is spoken by the synthesizer. The example frame in Figure 4c in conjunction with our rules generates the sentence "From Pacific Coast Highway turn straight onto East I-10 freeway" Lastly GENESIS is used to produce an SQL query string for database access. Templates and rewrite rules determine which form the output from GENESIS will take. Technically these three uses (key-value, reply string, and SQL) are just generation of different languages.

3.4 Dialogue Management

We have developed servers for dialog management and to control the application interface for database query. The hub architecture supports use of a control table to direct which server function is called. This is especially useful for dialogue management. The control table is specified by a set of rules using logic and arithmetic operations on the key-value pairs. A well-designed set of rules makes it far easier to visualize the flow and debug the dialogue logic. For example, when a control rule such as:

```
Clause "locate" !:from --> turn_from_here
```
fires on the key-value pairs (Figure 4b), the hub calls the turn manager function "turn_from_here". In this simplified case, we are assuming if there is no ":from" key, the request is to locate an object (i.e. "turn") relative to the vehicle's current position. In this case the function needs only to extract the value of the key ":ORD" and look up the data for the second turn of Figure 2. This data is then written into the response frame, here called "speak_turn" and shown in Figure 4c. GENESIS uses this frame to generate the English language reply that is spoken by the synthesizer as described above.

In the examples shown here we communicate with the database from the dialogue manager by downloading a flat database such as that of Figure 2, perhaps via a data link to an off-board service organization such as OnStar. In cases where we access databases directly, we use a separate server for this function. Generally, communications between the dialogue manager and database servers are routed via the Hub.

Our dialogue manager has been designed to use GPS data when available (in which case GPS coordinates would also be a part of the database) or to use location information based on current odometer readings provided as input by drivers when GPS is not available. We use this latter method for demonstrating the system in a desktop setting, though we have also recently completed a utility for employing maps generated by our commercial navigation database, graphically displaying a driver's progress along an imaginary route. We are now employing this tool as part of our current iteration of system testing and revision.

3.4.1 Referential amiguities in driver queries

The driver can query to determine turn or distance information relative to current vehicle position, relative to another turn or reference point in the database, or as an absolute reference into the route plan stored in the database. We have devoted considerable effort to dealing with ambiguities which may arise as a result of different ways users may be conceptualizing the route (that is, in absolute or relative terms), as well as the driver being at different points in the route, and at different points in the progression of a discourse segment. Queries such as "what's next?" can be ambiguous. Determining the correct interpretation requires consideration of the discourse history and the user's circumstances. For example, in the following dialog sequence (drawn from our data), there are at least two possible interpretations for "what is next?" in the third turn (U:user, S:system):[1]

```
---------------
U:  what's my next turn
S:  From Malibu Canyon Road turn left
    onto Pacific Coast Highway.
---------------
U:  and after that
S:  From Pacific Coast Highway go
    straight onto East I-10 freeway
---------------
→ U:  what's next
```
Figure 5. Sample dialog containing ambiguous "What is next".

Notice that this query could be requesting information about the next turn from the driver's current position (i.e. the immediately approaching turn), or it could be requesting information about the *third* turn from the driver's current position, that is, the next turn from the most recently referred to turn. We will henceforth refer to these two interpretations as *next-from-here* and *next-after-that*, respectively.

The factor which *appears* to have the most influence on which interpretation is given to this utterance originates neither in the utterance itself nor in the preceding dialog, but is purely circumstantial, namely, how much time has passed since the last utterance. Our assumption has been that there is a kind of time-dependency factor in coherent discourses: while "what is next" is still within the scope of the preceding discourse context, it may (most likely will) be given the *next-after-that* interpretation. But after a certain length of time has elapsed, "what is next" cannot be interpreted as referring to some previously uttered instruction, but only as referring to the driver's current position. If we think of this in terms of the user's frame of reference for talking about their real or imagined location (we'll refer to this as the FROM value), then we could characterize this phenomenon as the value of FROM being reset to HERE in the absence of immediate discourse context.

Interpretations of *numbered* turn references (e.g. "what's my *second* turn") can also vary depending on another purely circumstantial factor, namely whether the driver is querying the system while preparing to begin the trip, or after she has begun driving. Some drivers will want to preview trip information before beginning to drive, and in this situation, interpretation of certain query types may differ from interpretation done during the trip. When the driver is querying the system before beginning to drive, she is more likely to conceive of and speak of the route in an absolute sense (cf. [7]). That is, the driver may conceive of the route as a fixed plan, wherein each turn and segment have a unique and constant order in a sequence. When conceiving of the

route in this way, one may refer to turns by *number in the route*, rather than by *number relative to current position*. Although we have yet to gather real user data bearing on this question, our intuition is that once the trip is underway, especially once any significant distance has been traveled, if users do use numbered turn references at all, they will be much more likely to use them relative to their current position.

Queries of this type are, for practical purposes, only ambiguous once the user has begun the trip, but prior to the absolute numbered turn. Drivers are very unlikely to be asking about the second turn in the route once they have passed the second turn. Moreover, since people will generally only keep track of turn numbers in the range of 1-3, (give or take 1), numbered turn references will only be ambiguous prior to the third or fourth turn in the route (nobody is likely to be asking "what is the eighth turn in the route"). What is more, if the user asks a numbered turn query before beginning the trip, the system response will be the same, since the relative and absolute turn numbers will at that point coincide. Thus, the only time a true ambiguity must be handled by the system is the time after the trip is underway, and before the fourth turn. It is perhaps worth noting that if one looks at the overall query interpretation problem as entailing a determination of whether the user is asking a question relative to their current position, or some other position, then the absolute/relative distinction is just a special case that.

We have gone on the assumption that there are a substantial number of these ambiguous queries, not only for those of the "what's next" type, but also for some numbered turn requests, and for a class of distance query [1]. However, we have now carried out an experiment in which subjects interpreted such queries in a controlled setting, and the results indicate there is far less ambiguity in truly felicitous driver utterances than we originally hypothesized [2]. There probably will be some genuinely ambiguous queries, especially for a system which is not capable of detecting prosodic cues, however, we now are of the opinion that they will *not* comprise a significant percentage of driver queries. For the system which we describe herein, however, the control logic for queries of the type under discussion includes consideration of the temporal "reset" threshold discussed above, as indicated in the following table:

Table 1. Decision matrix showing some determining factors for interpreting "next" and numbered turn queries.

n-route	--	--	√	--	--	--	--
eset threshold eached	--	--	--	--	--		√
ext turn		√			√	√	√
umbered turn	n		n	n			
From here"	√	√					
After that"				√	√		
QL Turn number	c+n	c+1	n	r+n	r+1	r+1	c+1

√ = set   **c** = current position
blank = not set   **r** = most recently mentioned turn
n = number value   -- = irrelevant

---

[1] There is at least one further possible interpretation to "what is next?" here, at least if the proper prosodic features are present. If heavy emphasis is placed on "what," the query has a quasi *echo-question* interpretation, indicating either that the user did not hear, or else is surprised at the prior instruction and is asking for clarification or repetition.

The table is to be read column-by-column. Thus, the first column tells us that if we have a query with a numbered turn reference and a phrase which is semantically equivalent to "from here" (which is also the default), then the instruction number which will be requested (via SQL query) from the database is **current+number**.

4. EVALUATION

We are have implemented an initial system and are conducting ongoing evaluations and iterative enhancements as part of a second phase of effort. We are in advanced development on the second phase. We report here on some results of the first phase of our project.

Evaluation of a route guidance system is difficult because the majority of time is spent driving with only a periodic need for instructions. Therefore, for the purposes of developing the language and dialogue models we tried to expedite data collection by having dialogues in which the user simulated a trip by means of a more or less continuous conversation with the system. The position of the vehicle along the route was determined by the user providing odometer readings relative to the start of the trip. At each point the user would query the system and input a new odometer location along the route and continue the dialogue. While certainly not as meaningful as queries under normal driving condition, we did obtain good data for our recognizer language model and grammar coverage. In addition we could debug and tune our turn manager functions to make sure we were properly accessing the database and providing correct responses.

Each query essentially represents a single task and the most meaningful metric for this type of system seems to be the number of dialogue turns per correct response. By correct response we mean that the system provides the final answer versus providing a request to repeat or disambiguate the user query. We have accumulated several thousand utterances during dialogues that run around fifteen to twenty turns per session for a simple route like the one in Figure 2. About a third of the utterances are used to set the vehicle position via inputting odometer data.

We can also divide the dialogues into task oriented dialogues, where the user is trying to get helpful answers, and dialogues where the user is exploring the limits of the system. We find with the task oriented dialogues that the number of dialogue turns are about 15-20% greater that the number of correct responses and that the inital implementations even without street name recognition is a useful system.

5. SUMMARY AND FUTURE PLANS

We have reported on our initial implementation and results for an in-vehicle navigation system through the first phase of our system development effort and into the second phase. Full exploitation of the natural language interface is not fully completed in the first phase because we are still developing an operational in-vehicle navigation system to integrate with our dialogue system. The full interface, including destination entry, route planning, position tracking, and map matching will be available later this year. We have, however, developed most of the NL components needed for accessing the database functionality as it comes on-line. We plan to add other important functionality such as points-of-interest and traffic conditions as the project progresses.

Two other major elements need to be further explored to gain full system functionality. The first is recognizer robustness in the presence of in-vehicle noise during normal everyday use; the second is the street name recognition and pronunciation synthesis problem. Recognizer performance is being addressed by means of a full-scale data collection and corpora development project, in collaboration with GM and the Center for Spoken Language Research at the University of Colorado at Boulder. This work will provide the in-vehicle acoustic data needed to re-train the recognizer models as well as provide a database for developing noise-mitigation and speaker adaptation algorithms for improving recognizer performance. We are developing a method for dynamic loading of street names which we will report on in the near future.

Acknowledgments. This work was supported in part by a research contract from General Motors.

6. REFERENCES

[1] R. Belvin, R. Burns and C Hein "*What's next*: A Case Study in the Multidimensionality of a Dialogue System," *Proceedings of ICSLP 2000*, Beijing, China, October 2000.

[2] A. Kessell and R. Belvin "Unambiguous Amiguous Questions: Pronominal Resolution in Human-to-Human Navigation," unpublished ms., HRL Laboratories, 2001.

[3] K-F. Lee, *Automatic Speech Recognition: The Development of the Sphinx System*, Kluwer, Boston, 1989.

[4] B. Pellom, W. Ward, J. Hansen, K. Hacioglu, J. Zhang, X. Yu, and S. Pradhan, "University of Colorado Dialog Systems for Travel and Navigation," these proceedings, 2001.

[5] S. Seneff. "TINA: A Natural Language System for Spoken Language Applications," *Computational Linguistics*, Vol. 18, No. 1, pp. 61-86, 1992.

[6] S. Seneff, E. Hurley, R. Lau, C. Pao, P. Schmidt and V. Zue, "Galaxy-II: A Reference Architecture For Conversational System Development," *Proc. ICSLP '98*, pp. 931-934, Sydney, Australia, November 1998.

[7] L. Suchman. *Plans and situated actions*. Cambridge University Press, Cambridge, 1987.

[8] V. Zue, S. Seneff, J. Glass, J. Polifroni, C. Pao, T. Hazen & L. Heatherington, "Jupiter: A Telephone-Based Conversational Interface for Weather Information," *IEEE:Transactions on Speech and Audio Processing*, Vol. 8, No. 1, pp. 85-96, 2000.

Dialogue Interaction with the DARPA Communicator Infrastructure: The Development of Useful Software

Samuel Bayer
The MITRE Corporation
202 Burlington Rd.
Bedford, MA 01730

sam@mitre.org

Christine Doran
The MITRE Corporation
202 Burlington Rd.
Bedford, MA 01730

cdoran@mitre.org

Bryan George
The MITRE Corporation
11493 Sunset Hills Rd.
Reston, VA 20190

bgeorge@mitre.org

ABSTRACT

To support engaging human users in robust, mixed-initiative speech dialogue interactions which reach beyond current capabilities in dialogue systems, the DARPA Communicator program [1] is funding the development of a distributed message-passing infrastructure for dialogue systems which all Communicator participants are using. In this presentation, we describe the features of and requirements for a genuinely useful software infrastructure for this purpose.

Keywords

Spoken dialogue, speech interfaces

1. INTRODUCTION

Over the last five years, three technological advances have cooperated to push speech-enabled dialogue systems back into the limelight: the availability of robust real-time speech recognition tools, the explosion of Internet-accessible information sources, and the proliferation of mobile information access devices such as cell phones. However, the systems being fielded, and the standards arising from these efforts, represent only a limited set of capabilities for robust voice-enabled interaction with knowledge sources. The most prominent indication of these limitations is the fact that these systems are overwhelmingly system-directed; the system asks a question, and the user responds. While this type of interactions sidesteps a number of problems in speech recognition and dialogue tracking, it is overwhelmingly likely that these restrictions are not manageable in the long term.

The DARPA Communicator program [1] is exploring how to engage human users in robust, mixed-initiative speech dialogue interactions which reach beyond current capabilities in dialogue systems. To support this exploration, the Communicator program has funded the development of a distributed message-passing infrastructure for dialogue systems which all Communicator participants are using. In this presentation, we describe the features of and requirements for a genuinely useful software infrastructure for this purpose.

2. BUILDING USEFUL SOFTWARE

The Galaxy Communicator software infrastructure (GCSI) is an elaboration and extension of MIT's Galaxy-II distributed infrastructure for dialogue interaction [3]. The fact that all program participants are required to use the GCSI imposes a somewhat more severe set of requirements on the infrastructure than usual, and these requirements range far beyond the straightforward considerations of functionality.

- **Flexibility**: the infrastructure should be flexible enough to encompass the range of interaction strategies that the various Communicator sites might experiment with

- **Obtainability**: the infrastructure should be easy to get and to install

- **Learnability**: the infrastructure should be easy to learn to use

- **Embeddability**: the infrastructure should be easy to embed into other software programs

- **Maintenance**: the infrastructure should be supported and maintained for the Communicator program

- **Leverage**: the infrastructure should support longer-term program and research goals for distributed dialogue systems

3. FLEXIBILITY

The GCSI is a distributed hub-and-spoke architecture based on message-passing. The hub of the GCSI incorporates a scripting mechanism that allows the programmer to take control of the message traffic by implementing "hub programs" in a simple scripting language. The benefits of this sort of infrastructure are considerable in the context of exploring different interaction and control strategies for dialogue. For example:

- Because the infrastructure is based on message-passing instead of APIs, there's no need for the hub to have any compile-time knowledge of the functional properties of the servers it communicates with (in contrast to, for instance, a CORBA infrastructure).

Proceedings of HLT 2001, First International Conference on Human Language Technology Research, J. Allan, ed., Morgan Kaufmann, San Francisco, 2001.

- Because the hub scripting allows the programmer to alter the flow of control of messages, it's possible to integrate servers with a variety of implicit interaction paradigms (e.g., synchronous vs. asynchronous) without modifying the servers themselves

- Because the hub scripting allows the programmer to alter the flow of control of messages, it's possible to insert simple tools and filters to convert data among formats without modifying the servers themselves.

- Because the hub scripting language fires rules based on aspects of the hub state, it's easy to write programs which modify the message flow of control in real time.

4. OBTAINABILITY

We believe that the simplest licensing and distribution model for software like the GCSI is an open source model. With the appropriate open source licensing properties, there are no barriers to freely distributing and redistributing the GCSI, or to distributing dialogue systems created using the GCSI, or to building commercial products based on it. The GCSI is distributed under a modified version of the MIT X Consortium license, and we are reasonably certain that the license simplifies all these tasks. In particular, two Communicator sites are planning to distribute their entire dialogue systems as open source, which would not be possible without appropriate licensing of the GCSI.

It's also important to address the level of complexity of installing the software once it's obtained. Research software is notoriously hard to install, and it's far more useful to ensure that the software can be used straightforwardly on a small number of common platforms and operating systems than to try to make it run on as many platforms as possible. We've targeted the three platforms which the program participants were developing on: Windows NT, Intel Linux, and Sparc Solaris. The GCSI is known to work or to have worked on other configurations (HP-UX and SGI IRIX, for instance), but these configurations are not supported in any meaningful way. The open source model can help here, too: if someone wants to port the infrastructure to a BSD OS, for instance, they have all the source (and will hopefully contribute their modifications to the open source code base).

5. LEARNABILITY

Once the software is installed, it's important to know where to start and how to proceed. We have offered a series of two-day intensive training courses on the Communicator infrastructure which have been attended by the majority of Communicator participants. In addition, the GCSI comes with extensive documentation and examples, including a toy end-to-end dialogue system example which illustrates one possible configuration of Communicator-compliant servers. Our goal is to ensure that it's possible to learn to use the Communicator infrastructure from the documentation alone, and at least two sites have succeeded in creating dialogue systems using the GCSI in a short period of time without attending our training course.

6. EMBEDDABILITY

The GCSI includes libraries and templates to create Communicator-compliant servers in C, Java, Python, and Allegro Common Lisp. However, it's not enough to provide a software library; this library has to be well-behaved in a number of ways. In particular, if the GCSI is to be used in conjunction with CORBA or various windowing systems, it must be possible to embed the GCSI server libraries into other main loops, and to control all the features of the GCSI without controlling the toplevel flow of control. To enable this goal, the GCSI is based on a straightforward event-based programming model, which is used to implement the default Communicator server main loop, as well as the implementation of the Python and Allegro server libraries. The GCSI is distributed with a number of examples illustrating this embedding.

7. MAINTENANCE

Finally, GCSI consumers must be able to rely on getting help when something goes wrong, and expect that design and implementation problems will be rectified and that desired complex behaviors will be supported. The importance of responsiveness and flexibility in maintenance is one of the reasons we prefer the GCSI for Communicator instead of a third-party tool such as SRI's Open Agent Architecture [2], which the Communicator program does not control the development of.

In addition to maintaining a bug queue for the GCSI, we have addressed successively more complicated infrastructure requirements in successive releases of the GCSI. For instance, in the most recent release (3.0), we addressed infrastructure support for asynchronous delegation strategies being explored by the Communicator effort at MIT and issues relating to consumption of audio input by multiple recognizers.

8. LEVERAGE

Ultimately, we hope that the GCSI, together with open-source servers such as recognizers, parsers, synthesizers and dialogue modules provided by application developers, will foster a vigorous explosion of work in speech-enabled dialogue systems. For example:

- The programming-language-independent nature of the GCSI message-passing paradigm allows the Communicator program to develop implementation-independent service standards for recognition, synthesis, and other better-understood resources.

- The freely available nature of the GCSI allows application developers to contribute dialogue system modules which are already configured to work with other components.

- The availability of an "environment" for dialogue system development will support the development of an open source "toolkit" of state-of-the art, freely available modules. A number of Communicator sites are already releasing such modules.

- A common infrastructure will contribute to the elaboration of "best practice" in dialogue system development.

There are certainly a number of emerging and existing alternatives to the GCSI for dialogue system development (SRI's Open Agent Architecture, for instance). However, we believe that the combination of a software package like the GCSI and the critical mass generated by its use in the DARPA Communicator program presents a unique opportunity for progress in this area.

The GCSI is available under an open source license at http://fofoca.mitre.org/download.

9. ACKNOWLEDGMENTS

This work was funded by the DARPA Communicator program under contract number DAAB07-99-C201. © 2001 The MITRE Corporation. All rights reserved.

10. REFERENCES

[1] http://www.darpa.mil/ito/research/com/index.html.

[2] D. L. Martin, A. J. Cheyer, and D. B. Moran. The open agent architecture: A framework for building distributed software systems. Applied Artificial Intelligence, vol. 13, pp. 91--128, January-March 1999.

[3] S. Seneff, E. Hurley, R. Lau, C. Pao, P. Schmid, and V. Zue. Galaxy-II: A Reference Architecture for Conversational System Development. Proc. ICSLP 98, Sydney, Australia, November 1998.

Domain Portability in Speech-to-Speech Translation

Alon Lavie, Lori Levin, Tanja Schultz, Chad Langley, Benjamin Han
Alicia Tribble, Donna Gates, Dorcas Wallace and Kay Peterson
Language Technologies Institute
Carnegie Mellon University
Pittsburgh, PA, USA

alavie@cs.cmu.edu

1. INTRODUCTION

Speech-to-speech translation has made significant advances over the past decade, with several high-visibility projects (C-STAR, Verbmobil, the Spoken Language Translator, and others) significantly advancing the state-of-the-art. While speech recognition can currently effectively deal with very large vocabularies and is fairly speaker independent, speech translation is currently still effective only in limited, albeit large, domains. The issue of domain portability is thus of significant importance, with several current research efforts designed to develop speech-translation systems that can be ported to new domains with significantly less time and effort than is currently possible.

This paper reports on three experiments on portability of a speech-to-speech translation system between semantic domains.[1] The experiments were conducted with the JANUS system [5, 8, 12], initially developed for a narrow travel planning domain, and ported to the doctor-patient domain and an extended tourism domain. The experiments cover both rule-based and statistical methods, and hand-written as well as automatically learned rules. For rule-based systems, we have investigated the re-usability of rules and other knowledge sources from other domains. For statistical methods, we have investigated how much additional training data is needed for each new domain. We are also experimenting with combinations of hand-written and automatically learned components. For speech recognition, we have conducted studies of what parameters change when a recognizer is ported from one domain to another, and how these changes affect recognition performance.

2. DESCRIPTION OF THE INTERLINGUA

The first two experiments concern the analysis component of our interlingua-based MT system. The analysis component takes a sentence as input and produces an interlingua representation as output. We use a task-oriented interlingua [4, 3] based on domain actions. Examples of domain actions are giving information about the onset of a symptom (e.g., *I have a headache*) or asking a patient

---

[1] We have also worked on the issue of portability across languages via our interlingua approach to translation [3] and on portability of speech recognition across languages [10].

to perform some action (e.g., *wiggle your fingers*). The interlingua, shown in the example below, has five main components: (1) a speaker tag such as a: for doctor (agent) and c: for a patient (customer), (2) a speech act, in this case, `give-information` (3) some concepts (`+body-state` and `+existence`), and (4) some arguments (`body-state-spec=` and `body-location=`), and (5) some sub-arguments (`identifiability=no` and `inside=head`).

```
I have a pain in my head.
c:give-information+existence+body-state
  (body-state-spec=(pain,identifiability=no),
  body-location=(inside=head))
```

3. EXPERIMENT 1: EXTENSION OF SEMANTIC GRAMMAR RULES BY HAND AND BY AUTOMATIC LEARNING

Experiment 1 concerns extension of the coverage of semantic grammars in the medical domain. Semantic grammars are based on semantic constituents such as request information phrases (e.g., *I was wondering . . .*) and location phrases (e.g., *in my right arm*) rather than syntactic constituents such as noun phrases and verb phrases. In other papers [12, 5], we have described how our modular grammar design enhances portability across domains. The portable grammar modules are the cross-domain module, containing rules for things like greetings, and the shared module, containing rules for things like times, dates, and locations. Figure 1 shows a parse tree for the sentence *How long have you had this pain?* XDM indicates nodes that were produced by cross-domain rules. MED indicates nodes that were produced by rules from the new medical domain grammar.

The preliminary doctor-patient grammar focuses on three medical situations: `give-information+existence` — giving information about the existence of a symptom (*I have been getting headaches*); `give-information+onset` – giving information about the onset of a symptom (*The headaches started three months ago*); and `give-information+occurrence` — giving information about the onset of an instance of the symptoms (*The headaches start behind my ears*). Symptoms are expressed as `body-state` (e.g., pain), `body-object` (e.g., rash), and `body-event` (e.g., bleeding).

Our experiment on extendibility was based on a hand written seed grammar that was extended by hand and by automatic learning. The seed grammar covered the domain actions mentioned above, but did not cover very many ways to phrase each domain action. For example, it might have covered *The headaches started*

Proceedings of HLT 2001, First International Conference on Human Language Technology Research, J. Allan, ed., Morgan Kaufmann, San Francisco, 2001.

```
[request-information+existence+body-state]::MED
(  WH-PHRASES::XDM
    ( [q:duration=]::XDM ( [dur:question]::XDM ( how long ) ) )
  HAVE-GET-FEEL::MED ( GET ( have ) ) you
  HAVE-GET-FEEL::MED ( HAS ( had ) )
  [super_body-state-spec=]::MED
  ( [body-state-spec=]::MED
      ( ID-WHOSE::MED
          ( [identifiability=]
              ( [id:non-distant] ( this ) ) )
          BODY-STATE::MED ( [pain]::MED ( pain ) ) ) ) ) )
```

Figure 1: Parser output with nodes produced by medical and cross-domain grammars.

	Seed	Extended	Learned
IF	37.2	37.2	31.3
Domain Action	37.2	37.2	31.3
Speech Act			
Recall	43.3	48.2	49.3
Precision	71.0	75.0	45.8
Concept List			
Recall	2.2	10.1	32.5
Precision	12.5	42.2	25.1
Top-Level Arguments			
Recall	0.0	7.2	29.6
Precision	0.0	42.2	34.4
Top-Level Values			
Recall	0.0	8.3	29.8
Precision	0.0	50.0	39.2
Sub-Level Arguments			
Recall	0.0	28.3	14.1
Precision	0.0	48.2	12.6
Sub-level Values			
Recall	1.2	28.3	14.1
Precision	6.2	48.2	12.9

Table 1: Comparison of seed grammar, human-extended grammar, and machine-learned grammar on unseen data

three months ago but not *I started getting the headaches three months ago.* The seed grammar was extended by hand and by automatic learning to cover a development set of 133 utterances. The result was two new grammars, a human-extended grammar and a machine-learned grammar, referred to as the extended and learned grammars in Table 1. The two new grammars were then tested on 132 unseen sentences in order to compare generality of the rules. Results are reported only for 83 of the 132 sentences which were covered by the current interlingua design. The remaining 49 sentences were not covered by the current interlingua design and were not scored. Results are shown in Table 1.

The parsed test sentences were scored in comparison to a hand-coded correct interlingua representation. Table 1 separates results for six components of the interlingua: speech act, concepts, top-level arguments, top-level values, sub-level arguments, and sub-level values, in addition to the total interlingua, and the domain action (speech act and concepts combined). The components of the interlingua were described in Section 2.

The scores for the total interlingua and domain action are reported as percent correct. The scores for the six components of the interlingua are reported as average percent precision and recall. For example, if the correct interlingua for a sentence has two concepts, and the parser produces three, two of which are correct and one of which is incorrect, the precision is 66% and the recall is 100%.

Several trends are reflected in the results. Both the human-extended grammar and the machine-learned grammar show improved performance over the seed grammar. However, the human extended grammar tended to outperform the automatically learned grammar in precision, whereas the automatically learned grammar tended to outperform the human extended grammar in recall. This result is to be expected: humans are capable of formulating correct rules, but may not have time to analyze the amount of data that a machine can analyze. (The time spent on the human extended grammar after the seed grammar was complete was only five days.)

Grammar Induction: Our work on automatic grammar induction for Experiment 1 is still in preliminary stages. At this point, we have experimented with completely automatic induction (no interaction with a user)[2] of new grammar rules starting from a core grammar and using a development set of sentences that are not parsable according to the core grammar. The development sentences are tagged with the correct interlingua, and they do not stray from the concepts covered by the core grammar — they only correspond to alternative (previously unseen) ways of expressing the same set of covered concepts. The automatic induction is based on performing tree matching between a skeletal tree representation obtained from the interlingua, and a collection of parse fragments

---

[2]Previous work on our project [2] investigated learning of grammar rules with user interaction.

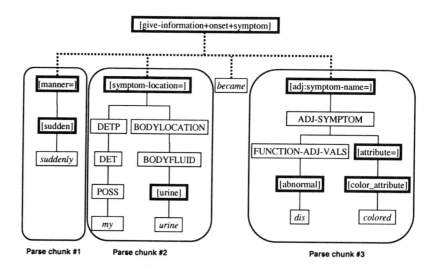

Original interlingua:
```
give-information+onset+symptom
(symptom-name=(abnormal,attribute=color_attribute),symptom-location=urine,
manner=sudden)
```

Learned Grammar Rule:
```
s[give-information+onset+symptom]
( [manner=] [symptom-location=] *+became [adj:symptom-name=] )
```

Figure 2: A reconstructed parse tree from the Interlingua

that is derived from parsing the new sentence with the core grammar. Extensions to the existing rules are hypothesized in a way that would produce the correct interlingua representation for the input utterance.

Figure 2 shows a tree corresponding to an automatically learned rule. The input to the learning algorithm is the interlingua (shown in bold boxes in the figure) and three parse chunks (circled in the figure). The dashed edges are augmented by the learning algorithm.

4. EXPERIMENT 2: PORTING TO A NEW DOMAIN USING A HYBRID RULE-BASED AND STATISTICAL ANALYSIS APPROACH

We are in the process of developing a new alternative analysis approach for our interlingua-based speech-translation systems that combines rule-based and statistical methods and we believe inherently supports faster porting into new domains. The main aspects of the approach are the following. Rather than developing complete semantic grammars for analyzing utterances into our interlingua (either completely manually, or using grammar induction techniques), we separate the task into two main levels. We continue to develop and maintain rule-based grammars for phrases that correspond to argument-level concepts of our interlingua representation (e.g., time expressions, locations, symptom-names, etc.). However, instead of developing grammar rules for assembling the argument-level phrases into appropriate domain actions, we apply machine learning and classification techniques [1] to learn these mappings from a corpus of interlingua tagged utterances. (Earlier work on this task is reported in [6].)

We believe this approach should prove to be more suitable for fast porting into new domains for the following reasons. Many of the required argument-level phrase grammars for a new domain are likely to be covered by already existing grammar modules, as can be seen by examining the XDM (cross-domain) nodes in Figure 1. The remaining new phrase grammars are fairly fast and straightforward to develop. The central questions, however, are whether the statistical methods used for classifying strings of arguments into domain actions are accurate enough, and what amounts of tagged data are required to obtain reasonable levels of performance. To assess this last question, we tested the performance of the current speech-act and concept classifiers for the expanded travel-domain when trained with increasing amounts of training data. The results of these experiments are shown in Figure 3. We also report the performance of the domain-action classification derived from the combined speech-act and concepts. As can be seen, performance reaches a relative plateau at around 4000-5000 utterances. We see these results as indicative that this approach should indeed prove to be significantly easier to port to new domains. Creating a tagged database of this order of magnitude can be done in a few weeks, rather than the months required for complete manual grammar development time.

5. EXPERIMENT 3: PORTING THE SPEECH RECOGNIZER TO NEW DOMAINS

When the speech recognition components (acoustic models, pronunciation dictionary, vocabulary, and language model) are ported across domains and languages mainly three types of mismatches

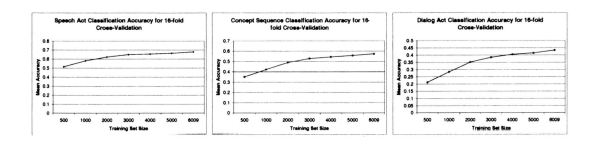

Figure 3: Performance of Speech-Act, Concept, and Domain-Action Classifiers Using Increasing Amounts of Training Data

Baseline Systems WER on Different Tasks [%]	
BN (Broadcast News) h4e98_1, all F-conditions	18.5
ESST (scheduling and travel planning domain)	24.3
BN+ESST	18.4
C-STAR (travel planning domain)	20.2
Adaptation → Meeting Recognition	
ESST on meeting data	54.1
BN on meeting data	44.2
+ acoustic MAP Adaptation (10h meeting data)	40.4
+ language model interpolation (16 meetings)	38.7
BN+ESST on meeting data	42.2
+ language model interpolation (16 meetings)	39.0
Adaptation → Doctor-Patient Domain	
C-STAR on doctor-patient data	34.1
+ language model interpolation ($\approx$ 34 dialogs)	25.1

Table 2: Recognition Results

occur: (1) mismatches in recording condition; (2) speaking style mismatches; as well as (3) vocabulary and language model mismatches. In the past these problems have mostly been solved by collecting large amounts of acoustic data for training the acoustic models and development of the pronunciation dictionary, as well as large text data for vocabulary coverage and language model calculation. However, especially for highly specialized domains and conversational speaking styles, large databases cannot always be provided. Therefore, our research has focused on the problem of how to build LVCSR systems for new tasks and languages [7, 9] using only a limited amount of data. In this third experiment we investigate the results of porting the speech recognition component of our MT system to different new domains. The experiments and improvements were conducted with the Janus Speech Recognition Toolkit JRTk [13].

Table 2 shows the results of porting four baseline speech recognition systems to the doctor-patient domain, and to the meeting domain. The four baseline systems are trained on Broadcast News (BN), English Spontaneous Scheduling Task (ESST), combined BN and ESST, and the travel planning domain of the C-STAR consortium (http://www.c-star.org). The given tasks illustrate a variety of domain size, speaking styles and recording conditions ranging from clean spontaneous speech in a very limited domain (ESST, C-STAR) to highly conversational multi-party speech in an extremely broad domain (Meeting). As a consequence the error rates on the meeting data are quite high but using MAP (Maximum A Posteriori) acoustic model adaptation and language model adaptation the error rate can be reduced by about 10.2% relative over the BN baseline system. With the doctor-patient data the drop in error

rate was less severe which can be explained by the similar speaking style and recording conditions for C-STAR and doctor-patient data. Details about the applied recognition engine can be found in [10] for ESST and [11] for the BN system.

6. ACKNOWLEDGMENTS

The research work reported here was funded in part by the DARPA TIDES Program and supported in part by the National Science Foundation under Grant number 9982227. Any opinions, findings and conclusions or recomendations expressed in this material are those of the author(s) and do not necessarily reflect the views of the National Science Foundation (NSF) or DARPA.

7. REFERENCES

[1] W. Daelemans, J. Zavrel, K. van der Sloot, and A. van den Bosch. TiMBL: Tilburg Memory Based Learner, version 3.0 Reference Guide. Technical Report Technical Report 00-01, ILK, 2000. Avaliable at http://ilk.kub.nl/ ilk/papers/ilk0001.ps.gz.

[2] M. Gavaldà. Epiphenomenal Grammar Acquisition with GSG. In *Proceedings of the Workshop on Conversational Systems of the 6th Conference on Applied Natural Language Processing and the 1st Conference of the North American Chapter of the Association for Computational Linguistics (ANLP/NAACL-2000)*, Seattle, U.S.A, May 2000.

[3] L. Levin, D. Gates, A. Lavie, F. Pianesi, D. Wallace, T. Watanabe, and M. Woszczyna. Evaluation of a Practical Interlingua for Task-Oriented Dialogue. In *Workshop on*

Applied Interlinguas: Practical Applications of Interlingual Approaches to NLP, Seattle, 2000.

[4] L. Levin, D. Gates, A. Lavie, and A. Waibel. An Interlingua Based on Domain Actions for Machine Translation of Task-Oriented Dialogues. In *Proceedings of the International Conference on Spoken Language Processing (ICSLP'98)*, pages Vol. 4, 1155–1158, Sydney, Australia, 1998.

[5] L. Levin, A. Lavie, M. Woszczyna, D. Gates, M. Gavaldà, D. Koll, and A. Waibel. The Janus-III Translation System. *Machine Translation*. To appear.

[6] M. Munk. Shallow statistical parsing for machine translation. Master's thesis, University of Karlsruhe, Karlsruhe, Germany, 1999. `http://www.is.cs.cmu.edu/papers/ speech/masters-thesis/MS99.munk.ps.gz`.

[7] T. Schultz and A. Waibel. Polyphone Decision Tree Specialization for Language Adaptation. In *Proceedings of the ICASSP*, Istanbul, Turkey, 2000.

[8] A. Waibel. Interactive Translation of Conversational Speech. *Computer*, 19(7):41–48, 1996.

[9] A. Waibel, P. Geutner, L. Mayfield-Tomokiyo, T. Schultz, and M. Woszczyna. Multilinguality in Speech and Spoken Language Systems. *Proceedings of the IEEE, Special Issue on Spoken Language Processing*, 88(8):1297–1313, 2000.

[10] A. Waibel, H. Soltau, T. Schultz, T. Schaaf, and F. Metze. *Multilingual Speech Recognition*, chapter From Speech Input to Augmented Word Lattices, pages 33–45. Springer Verlag, Berlin, Heidelberg, New York, artificial Intelligence edition, 2000.

[11] A. Waibel, H. Yu, H. Soltau, T. Schultz, T. Schaaf, Y. Pan, F. Metze, and M. Bett. Advances in Meeting Recognition. Submitted to HLT 2001, January 2001.

[12] M. Woszczyna, M. Broadhead, D. Gates, M. Gavaldà, A. Lavie, L. Levin, and A. Waibel. A Modular Approach to Spoken Language Translation for Large Domains. In *Proceedings of Conference of the Association for Machine Translation in the Americas (AMTA'98)*, Langhorn, PA, October 1998.

[13] T. Zeppenfeld, M. Finke, K. Ries, and A. Waibel. Recognition of Conversational Telephone Speech using the Janus Speech Engine. In *Proceedings of the ICASSP'97*, München, Germany, 1997.

English-Chinese CLIR using a Simplified PIRCS System

K.L. Kwok, N. Dinstl and P. Deng
Computer Science Department, Queens College, CUNY
65-30 Kissena Blvd.
Flushing, N.Y. 11367

kwok@ir.cs.qc.edu

ABSTRACT
A GUI is presented with our PIRCS retrieval system for supporting English-Chinese cross language information retrieval. The query translation approach is employed using the LDC bilingual wordlist. Given an English query, different translation methods and their retrieval results can be demonstrated.

1. INTRODUCTION
The purpose of cross language information retrieval (CLIR) is to allow a user to search, retrieve, and gain some content understanding of documents written in a language different from the one that the user is familiar with. This is to be accomplished automatically without expert linguist assistance. CLIR is of growing importance because it can literally open up a whole world of information for the user, especially with the ease and convenience of access and delivery of foreign documents provided by Internet logistics nowadays. Searching and retrieving Chinese documents via English is a major sub-problem within CLIR because many people in the world use these two languages. For example, one would expect trade between China and the U.S. (and other countries) to grow significantly in the near future because of the impending WTO membership for China. Monitoring trends and status information from Chinese sources may be an essential operation for organizations interested in these affairs. Chinese is a language completely different from English, and it is conceived to be difficult for foreigners to learn. This paper describes some of the methods that we employ to deal with this problem, and presents a demonstrable system to illustrate the workings of cross language document retrieval. In Section 2, techniques for the query translation approach to CLIR are discussed. Section 3 contains a description of our simplified PIRCS retrieval system that is the basis for monolingual retrieval. Section 4 describes the GUI supporting interactive query input, document output and other implementation issues, and Section 5 contains our conclusion and future work.

Proceedings of HLT 2001, First International Conference on Human Language Technology Research, J. Allan, ed., Morgan Kaufmann, San Francisco, 2001.

2. STRATEGY FOR CROSS LANGUAGE INFORMATION RETRIEVAL
When faced with the situation of a language mismatch between the target documents and the query (information need statement) of a user, one could reduce them to a common representation language for retrieval purposes by automatically translating the query to the document language, by translating the documents to the query language, or by converting both to a third representation language [1]. By far the simplest and most common approach seems to be the first method, and probably as effective as the others, and we have also taken this route. The question is what tools to use for query translation.

It is well known that machine translation is generally fuzzy and inaccurate [6]. This is particularly true when translation output are judged by humans, who tend to be unforgiving. However, translation for machine consumption (such as for information retrieval (IR)) may not be so bad because IR can operate with a bag of content terms without grammar, coherence or readability. What IR needs is that important content terms are correctly covered, even at the expense of noise translations. For this purpose, we have combined two different methods of query translation to hedge for errors and improve coverage, viz. dictionary translation and MT software.

2.1 Translation Using LDC Bilingual Wordlist
One method we employ is dictionary translation using the LDC Chinese-English bilingual wordlist (www.morph.ldc.edu/Projects/Chinese) which we label as ldc2ce. It has about 120K entries. Each entry maps a Chinese character sequence (character, word or phrase) into one or more English explanation strings delimited with slashes. Sample entries are shown below:

1) 集会 /gather/assembly/meeting/convocation/
2) 部件 /parts/components/assembly/..
3) 礼堂 /assembly hall/auditorium/..
4) 议院 /legislative assembly/
5) 立法局 /legislative council/..

When an English word from a query is looked up in the ldc2ce wordlist, it will usually be mapped into many Chinese terms and reduction of the output is necessary. For this disambiguation purpose, we employ several methods in succession as tabulated below:

- Dictionary structure-based: ldc2ce format is employed to select the more correct mappings among word translations. For example, when the word to translate is 'assembly', we would pick line 1) and 2) only, rather than the additional 3) or 4) because in the latter two, 'assembly' appears in context with other words.

- Phrase-based: ld2ce can also be regarded as a phrase dictionary by matching query strings with English explanations of Chinese terms, giving much more accurate phrase translations. For example, if 'legislative assembly' appears in a query, it would match line 4) exactly and correctly, and would supersede all other single word translations such as those from lines 1), 2), 3) and 5).

- Corpus frequency-based: for single word translations with many candidates, those with higher occurrence frequency usually have higher probability of being correct.

- Weight-based: a Chinese term set translated for one English word can be considered as a synonym set, so that each individual Chinese term is weighted with the inverse of the sum of the collection frequencies, and generally gives more effective retrieval.

These dictionary disambiguation techniques have been implemented and tested with TREC collections. In general, they accumulatively lead to successively more accurate retrievals [4]. Their output can be demonstrated in our system.

2.2 Translation Using MT Software

COTS MT software for English to Chinese (or vice versa) are now quite readily available on the market. They cost from scores to about a thousand dollars for a single license. These software mostly operate on the PC Windows platform. Their codes are proprietary and usually do not come with an API. Interfacing them with a UNIX and C platform thus becomes quite difficult and perhaps impossible. However, if one runs retrieval from a Windows environment, one can 'cut and paste' from their translation results. We investigated several and found that one from Mainland China called HuaJian (www.atlan.com) performs quite well. A number of other such packages can also be demonstrated within our system.

Once an English query has been translated into Chinese, we can perform monolingual Chinese IR using our PIRCS system described in the next section. The two translation outcomes, from dictionary and MT software, can be combined for retrieval and the final result is usually more effective than single translation method alone [3].

3. A SIMPLIFIED PIRCS RETRIEVAL SYSTEM

PIRCS (Probabilistic Indexing and Retrieval – Components – System) is our in-house developed document retrieval system that has participated in all previous TREC large-scale blind retrieval experiments with consistently good results. It supports both English and Chinese languages. PIRCS retrieval approach is based on the probabilistic indexing and retrieval methods, but extended with the ability to account for the influence of term frequencies and item length of documents or queries. PIRCS can best be viewed as activation spreading in a three- layer network,

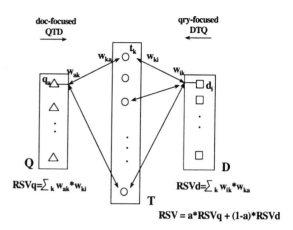

$$RSVq = \sum_k w_{ak} * w_{kl} \qquad RSVd = \sum_k w_{ik} * w_{ka}$$

$$RSV = a*RSVq + (1-a)*RSVd$$

Figure 1. 3-Layer PIRCS Network

Figure 1, that also supports learning from user-judged or pseudo-relevant documents. The details of our model are given in [4, 5]. As shown in Figure 1, PIRCS treats queries and documents as objects of the same kind. They form a Q and a D layer of nodes connecting to the middle layer of term nodes. Retrieval means spreading activation from a query node via common term nodes to a document node and summed into a retrieval status value RSVd for ranking. This operation is gated by intervening edges with weights that are set according to the PIRCS model. An analogous operation is to spread activation from document to query nodes, resulting in another RSVq that has been shown to have similarity to a simple language model [2, 4]. The final retrieval status value RSV is a linear combination of the two.

Documents are pre-processed to create a direct file, an inverted file and a master dictionary that contains all the content terms and their usage statistics extracted from the collection. After appropriate processing, the master dictionary helps construct the middle layer T nodes of Figure 1. The direct file facilitates obtaining the terms and statistics contained in a given document, and helps construct the D node and D-to-T edges with weights. The inverted file facilitates obtaining the posting information of a given term, and helps construct the T-to-D edges with weights. At query time, a Q layer of one node is formed and the query terms are located on the T layer and linked in to define the Q-to-T and T-to-Q edges with weights.

Once the 3-layer network is defined, ranking of documents for the query is achieved by activation spreading Q-T-D realizing the document-focused retrieval status value RSVd, and vice versa for the query-focused RSVq. They are then linearly combined. This crosslingual PIRCS demonstration runs either on a SUN Solaris or Linux platform. The current implementation is a simplification of our batch PIRCS system and does not support automatic two-stage retrieval for pseudo-relevance feedback. However, users can interactively modify their queries to perform manual feedback.

4. GUI FOR INTERACTIVE CLIR

A simplified PIRCS system with first stage retrieval will be used for demonstrating English-Chinese CLIR. This system is based on an applet-servlet model that runs on a UNIX operating system (such as Solaris or Linux). User's interaction with PIRCS is supported via a GUI based on the Netscape browser (Internet Explorer is a better browser for this GUI, but UNIX has Netscape only). The applet or HTML forms in the browser communicate with the servlet on the Apache server. The servlet works as a bridge between the front-end program (in HTML and applet) and the background programs that do the translation or retrieval. Based on the input from the user, it can dispatch calls to the retrieval system and then format the output and send results back to the applet or directly into user's browser through a customized applet-servlet channel via HTTP protocol.

A GUI software that is modeled on that of ZPRISE (www.itl.nist.gov/iaui/894.02/works/papers/zp2/zp2.html) but enhanced for CLIR will be demonstrated. The GUI supports five windows: one for English query input and editing, a translation window for displaying the Chinese terms mapped from the English query via the ldc2ce wordlist, a search-result window for displaying the fifty top-ranked document identities after retrieval, a document box for displaying the content of the current selected document in Chinese, and another index box showing the index terms used for retrieval together with their frequency statistics. This allows a user to do CLIR interactively.

If run in a Windows environment, the translation box also allows input and editing for those users who know some Chinese. In this test system, all Chinese are GB-encoded. A query of a few words currently takes a few seconds for translation and about 20 seconds or more for retrieval depending on the number of unique terms. This response time can be improved in the future.

A typical screen of the GUI is shown in Figure 2. A user starts by typing in an English query in free text. When the 'Convert to Chinese GB' button is clicked, translation via the LDC dictionary look-up based on a default (best) option will be displayed. Other options for translation such as using dictionary-structure only, add phrase matching, or include target collection frequency disambiguation, etc. (Section 2.1) can be chosen. If the user finds too many English words left un-translated, s/he can re-phrase the English query wordings and repeat the process. Otherwise, the retrieval button can be clicked and the top 50 document ID's will be displayed in the search-result box (below the translation) sorted by the retrieval status value shown next to each ID. Content of the top document is also displayed automatically in the large window with index terms high-lighted. Additional documents following the one displayed can also be brought in for browsing purposes.

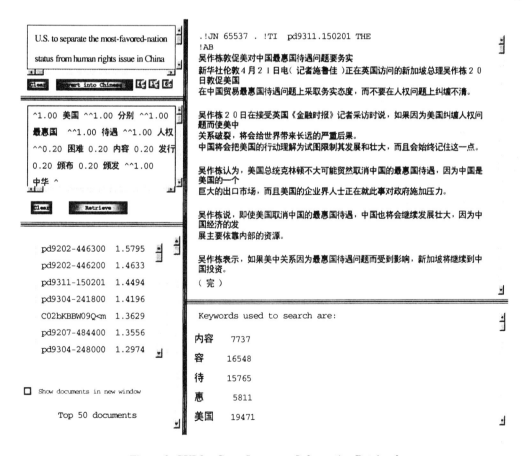

Figure 2. GUI for Cross Language Information Retrieval

If the user knows some Chinese, s/he can have more options for interaction. For example, the user can 'cut and paste' terms that s/he likes during perusal of the retrieved documents to do relevance feedback manually. In addition, the query index terms (in Chinese) and their document frequencies are also displayed at the right hand bottom of the screen. They can provide useful information about the query and can help the user make changes to it.

As discussed before, we also make use of COTS MT software for query translation. These can also be demonstrated separately. However, these packages are proprietary, run under Windows platform, and are not interfaced with our retrieval system that is Linux based. Another set-up that we can demonstrate is to use a Windows platform to run Internet Explorer that is also compatible with our GUI. Internet connection will have to be made to our home computers at Queens College. In this case, an MT software can be running in the background for query translation. The translation result can then be 'cut and paste' to the translation window of our GUI. Users can compare retrieval results based on our dictionary approach and the MT software. Alternatively, both translations can be combined to improve retrieval.

5. CONCLUSION AND FUTURE WORK
English-Chinese CLIR is an important topic in Human Language Technology and has great utility. This project demonstration combines simple translation with IR to provide a workable solution to CLIR. It is an ongoing project and eventually can help non-Chinese speaking users access Chinese text in a reasonable fashion. Our next step is to add capability to show gistings of a retrieved Chinese document in English to assist the user in understanding the document content. Faster machines and upgrading of the programs would also provide speedier response time.

6. ACKNOWLEDGMENTS
This work was partially supported by the Space and Naval Warfare Systems Center San Diego, under grant No. N66001-1-8912.

7. REFERENCES
[1] Grefenstette, G. *Cross Language Information Retrieval*. Kluwer, 1998.

[2] Hiemstra, D & Kraaj, W. Twenty-One at TREC-7:ad-hoc and cross language track. In: *Information Technology: The Seventh Text Retrieval Conference (TREC-7)*. E.M.Voorhees & D.K. Harman, (eds.), NIST Special Publication 500-242, GPO: Washington, D.C, 227-238, 1999.

[3] Kwok, K.L, Grunfeld, L., Dinstl, N & Chan, M. TREC-9 cross-lingual, web and question-answering track experiments using PIRCS (Draft). Preliminary paper at TREC-9 Conference, Gaithersburg, MD, Nov, 2000.

[4] Kwok, K.L. Improving English and Chinese ad-hoc retrieval: a Tipster Text Phase 3 project report. Information Retrieval, 3(4):313-338, 2000.

[5] Kwok, K.L. A network approach to probabilistic information retrieval. ACM Transactions on Office Information System, 13:324-353, July 1995.

[6] Nirenburg, S, Carbonell, J, Tomita, M & Goodman, K. (Eds.) *MT: A Knowledge-Based Approach*. Morgan Kaufmann, 1994.

Entry Vocabulary – a Technology to Enhance Digital Search

Fredric Gey, Michael Buckland, Aitao Chen and Ray Larson
University of California
Berkeley, CA 94720

gey@ucdata.berkeley.edu, {aitao,buckland,ray}@sims.berkeley.edu

ABSTRACT

This paper describes a search technology which enables improved search across diverse genres of digital objects – documents, patents, cross-language retrieval, numeric data and images. The technology leverages human indexing of objects in specialized domains to provide increased accessibility to non-expert searchers. Our approach is the reverse-engineer text categorization to supply mappings from ordinary language vocabulary to specialist vocabulary by constructing maximum likelihood mappings between words and phrases and classification schemes. This forms the training data or 'entry vocabulary'; subsequently user queries are matched against the entry vocabulary to expand the search universe. The technology has been applied to search of patent databases, numeric economic statistics, and foreign language document collections.

1. INTRODUCTION

The internet has provided a vast and growing amount of searchable information. In the "deep web" (that part of the internet which is not directly searchable using ordinary search engines) we find information deriving from multiple and quite distinct genres, such as images and numeric statistical data as well as textual information in unfamiliar languages. For example United States Foreign Trade Imports and Exports are available at
http://govinfo.kerr.orst.edu/impexp.html.
Data are classified by commodity being shipped, so one can find out, for example, how many purebred Arabian horses were imported to Louisville, Kentucky from Saudi Arabia in any particular month. A commodity search mechanism is provided at this sites to search commodity descriptions associated with the 8,000 commodity codes. However, the search term 'automobile' retrieves nothing, even though we know billions of U.S. dollars of automobile imports enter the United States each year. In order to retrieve automobile imports with using the string search one needs to know that the description is actually "Pass Mtr Veh" an abbreviation

Proceedings of HLT 2001, First International Conference on Human Language Technology Research, J. Allan, ed., Morgan Kaufmann, San Francisco, 2001.

for "Passenger Motor Vehicle" and obtain the data shown in Figure 1.

In another case, suppose a searcher from Germany is interested in articles on economic policy and wishes to search in his/her native language. The search term "Wirtschaftspolitik" will likely retrieve documents in German but not English. We need an automatic way to take familiar search terms and map them to unfamiliar terms or classifications without necessarily even knowing what language they were originally expressed in.

We consider vocabulary to be central to search. The vocabulary used by a searcher may not be the same as contained in a document or as the metadata used to classify the document. In order to provide vocabulary mappings, we need to find resources which we can mine for those mappings. Such resources are available in the form of the world's existing electronic library catalogs. If we undertake to mine these resources and we have a technology which can create statistical mappings between vocabularies, we can create *Entry Vocabulary Indexes (EVI)*. **EVIs** are software modules which enhance search by mapping from the users ordinary language to the (sometimes arcane) metadata of the digital resource.

2. ENTRY VOCABULARY TECHNOLOGY

Entry vocabulary technology to create Entry Vocabulary Indexes rests upon four basic components:

- a sufficiently large training set of documents
- a part of speech tagger to identify noun phrases in documents
- software and algorithms to develop probabilistic mappings between words/phrases and metadata classifications
- software to accept search words/phrases and return classifications

In our system we have utilized the Z39.50 protocol to query textual databases located in electronic libraries and download the MARC records which are the results of such queries. Typically, these records are then processed and converted into an XML representation which can be used for further processing and display. The text representation is then (usually, but not always in developing prototypes) processed using a POS tagger such as the Brill tagger [2] and a list of nouns and noun phrases are extracted from each document

```
         - - -   U.  S.    I m p o r t s   o f   M e r c h a n d i s e     - - -

                      General Imports                  Imports for Comsumption
          Year        Quantity   Customs Value          Quantity   Customs Value

PASS MTR VEH,NESOI, SPARK IGN,4 CYL, 1500-3000CC
(HS: 8703230044)  (SIC: 3711)
Unit of Quantity -- Number
1994           361,535   4,606,893,087          1,169,719   6,474,810,449
1995           314,175   3,963,197,536          1,125,534   5,396,909,612
1996           322,248   4,381,403,774          1,295,532   5,630,167,625
1997           488,692   6,661,333,393          1,184,855   7,458,690,130
1998           474,633   6,091,373,316            912,740   6,573,997,869
```

Figure 1: Import Data for Automobiles

along with the classifications which have been manually assigned to the document.

The final stage to creation of an Entry Vocabulary Index is to develop a maximum likelihood weighting associated with each term (word or phrase) and each classification. One constructs a two-way contingency table for each pair of word/phrase terms t and classifications C as shown in table 1. where a is the number of document titles/abstracts

	C	$\neg C$
t	a	b
$\neg t$	c	d

Table 1: Contingency table from words/phrases to classification

containing the word or phrase and classified by the classification; b is the number of document titles/abstracts containing the word or phrase but not the classified by the classification; c is the number of titles/abstracts not containing the word or phrase but is classified by the classification; and d is the number of document titles/abstracts neither containing the word or phrase nor being classified by the classification.

The association score between a word/phrase t and an classification C is computed following Dunning [4]

$$W(C,t) = 2[logL(p_1, a, a+b) + logL(p_2, c, c+d) - (1)$$
$$= logL(p, a, a+b) - logL(p, c, c+d)] \quad (2)$$

where

$$logL(p,n,k) = klog(p) + (n-k)log(1-p) \quad (3)$$

and $p_1 = \frac{a}{a+b}$, $p_2 = \frac{c}{c+d}$, and $p = \frac{a+c}{a+b+c+d}$.

3. APPLICATIONS

3.1 Cross-language search

A very interesting application of Entry Vocabulary Indexes is to multilingual information access. Because large university electronic catalogs contain bibliographic references for thousands of documents in foreign languages (the Library of Congress language list contains 400 languages), one can build EVIs which map to the (English) Library of Congress

Subject Headings (LCSH). Library catalogers typically manually index and assign multiple LCSH entries to each book or other item being cataloged. Our training set for construction of a multilingual EVI for LCSH is the six million record set of the University of California MELVYL online catalog (http://www.melvyl.ucop.edu). As the following figure demonstrates, one can enter foreign language words and be pointed to the

subject headings which most closely match on a maximum likelihood basis. This subject heading can be used as a reliable search query in online library catalogs, since LCSH is an industry standard. In the example, the German query word "Wirtschaftspolitik" presents the subject heading "Economic Policy" as its top ranked metadata item. This happens to be an exact translation of Wirtschaftspolitik.

Our initial use of EVIs has been applied to cross-language search of the NTCIR collection of Japanese-English scientific documents [5] and more recently to English-German retrieval for the domain specific task of the CLEF European language evaluation [7] on the GIRT collection of German documents in the social science domain.

3.2 Numeric data

The example of import data in the introduction demonstrates an important genre of digital objects for which search is difficult. Numeric statistical databases, their classifications and descriptions could be called 'evidence poor' because they lack the rich and abundant textual clues so important in information discovery. Neither string search (as provided by the sites) nor inverted word indexing will properly search the data. Yet the humanly indexed categories within each classification scheme contain a precise description of that category, useable if you are expertly knowledgeable about the details of foreign trade. To provide search support for novice or non-expert searching, we must somehow expand the search possibilities.

We can do this by mining the textual resources of electronic libraries in much the same way as above for cross-language search. A large selection of trade magazine abstracts in these libraries have been indexed manually by the assignment of the very same category codes used to classify the numeric statistical information. For example a magazine article about the new management directions of Apple

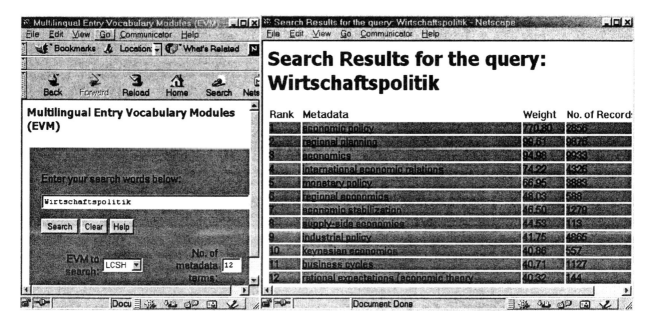

Figure 2: EVI Multilingual Search against Library of Congress Subject Headings

Computer will be assigned (by a human indexer) the industrial classification code 3571 for 'Electronic Computers'. By mining the textual descriptions found in the documents (either titles or abstracts), one can build an Entry Vocabulary Indexes which map ordinary words and phrases to the classification codes. Examples of such entry vocabulary modules can be found at the site
http://www.sims.berkeley.edu/research/metadata
under the 'prototypes' section. The one for 'SIC' will demonstrate entry vocabulary search for U.S. Imports and Exports. The process by which this numeric classification EVI was constructed has been described in [6, 8].

More recently we have taken the 1997 Economic Census for which the Census Bureau provides a selection and display mechanism http://www.census.gov/epcd/www/econ97.html for data summarized to the North American Industrial Classification (NAICS) coding system [10]. The census system lacks the specificity to address particular instances of companies associated with NAICS codes. However, our NAICS EVI prototype (at the url above) will take the query 'IBM' and return a selection of NAICS codes (by entry vocabulary mapping from textual documents indexed by these codes) of industries closely associated with IBM's corporate activities (see Figure 3).

3.3 Patents and Other Specialty Areas

Multiple Entry Vocabulary Indexes have been built for the U.S. Patent Databases. The documents in the U.S. Patent office system have been indexed by both the U.S. patent classification system and the international Patent classification system of the World Intellectual Patent Organization (WIPO). Other EVIs were constructed for the INSPEC service (science and engineering abstracts) and MEDLINE (medical specialties).

4. EVALUATION STRATEGIES

Since EVI technology and prototypes have only been available for the past year or so, formal evaluation has yet to be undertaken. The DARPA Information Management program is funding an in-depth evaluation of this technology with one or more of the following evaluation strategies:

- TREC-like recall precision improvement for specific tasks
- Hands-on interactive search with/without EVI
- Web session log analysis

Each of these strategies could be used to test search with or without the use of an entry vocabulary module as if they were two different systems. We have performed preliminary TREC-style evaluations for cross-language conferences and they show promising improvements over retrieval without EVIs.

5. CONCLUSIONS AND FUTURE WORK

5.1 Summary

Entry vocabulary technology, in the form of Entry Vocabulary Indexes, offers a new approach to digital object search. The approach capitalizes and leverages the worldwide investment in human indexing and development of manual classification schemes, subject indexes and thesauri. Its central feature incorporates a probabilistic mapping between ordinary language and technical vocabulary or classifications. The technology may be applied to digital genres not normally associated with textual search, such as numeric statistical databases. A more detailed discussion of vocabulary, metadata and search may be found in [3].

5.2 Search with non-Roman Scripts

For the future, we are interested in dealing with languages with other than a latin or Roman alphabet. Consider, for

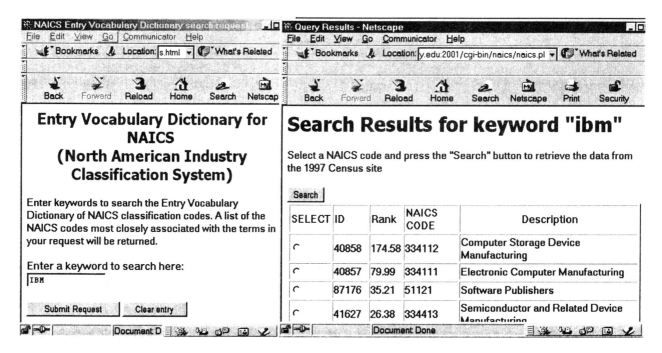

Figure 3: NAICS Search Example

example the Russian phrase економическаиа политика. The electronic libraries of the United States follow a cataloging standard [1] for transformation (called 'transliteration' or 'Romanization') from non-Roman scripts into their Romanized equivalents. For example, the Cyrillic letter щ is expressed as 'shch'. Such transformations are one-to-one and reversible. If we prepared a transliteration front end to the above Cyrillic input, it would obtain the phrase "ekonomicheskaia politika." Submitting this phrase to the Entry Vocabulary Index for the Library of Congress subject headings, it should return the same subject heading "economic policy" as the previous German term "Wirtschaftspolitik." We are in the process of developing such transliteration and EVI search for the Cyrillic alphabet.

5.3 Images

Image data provides an interesting challenge for EVI technology. In work conducted in conjunction with the NSF/ NASA/DARPA-sponsored Digital Library Initiative project [9], "blob" representations (each "blob" is a coherent region of color and texture within an image) were derived from a collection of 35000 images and indexes were created for probabilistic matching of images, based on representations of the blobs. Since each of the images in the "BlobWorld" database have associated keywords in their metadata records, we are able to apply the same basic EVI concept to these image records.

In this case the metadata keywords describing the images are associated with the individual blobs extracted from the images. Thus we are building a probabilistic association between certain keywords and patterns of color and texture in the image database. For example blobs with orange and black stripes might be associated with the keyword "TIGER".

6. ACKNOWLEDGMENTS

Entry Vocabulary Technology has been developed under support by Defense Advanced Research Projects Agency (DARPA) Information Management program through DARPA Contract N66001-97-8541; AO# F477: Search Support for Unfamiliar Metadata Vocabularies. Application of the EVI technology to cross-language retrieval was supported by research grant number N66001-00-1-8911 (Mar 2000-Feb 2003) from the DARPA Translingual Information Detection Extraction and Summarization (TIDES) program. Application of EVI technology to numeric data search was supported by a National Library Leadership award from the Institute of Museum and Library Services entitled "Seamless Searching of Numeric and Textual Resources."

Many graduate students have been associated with the development of various phases of the entry vocabulary technology, chief among them Barbara Norgard and Youngin Kim. Other contributions were made by Hui-Min Chen, Michael Gebbie, Natalia Perelman, Vivien Petras, and Jacek Purat.

7. REFERENCES

[1] Randall K. Barry. *ALA-LC romanization tables : transliteration schemes for non-Roman scripts.* Washington : Cataloging Distribution Service, Library of Congress, 1997.

[2] Eric Brill. A simple rule-based part of speech tagger. In *Proceedings of the Third Conference on Applied Natural Language Processing*, 1992.

[3] Michael Buckland et al. Mapping entry vocabulary to unfamiliar metadata vocabularies. In *D-Lib Magazine*. http://www.dlib.org/dlib/january99/buckland/01buckland.html January 1999.

[4] Ted Dunning. Accurate methods for the statistics of surprise and coincidence. *Computational Linguistics*,

19:61–74, March 1993.

[5] Fredric Gey, Aitao Chen, and Hailing Jiang. Applying text categorization to vocabulary enhancement for japanese-english cross-language information retrieval. In S. Annandiou, editor, *The Seventh Machine Translation Summit, Workshop on MT for Cross-language Information Retrieval, Singapore,* pages 35–40, September 1999.

[6] Fredric Gey et al. Advanced search technologies for unfamiliar metadata. In *Proceedings of the Third IEEE Metadata Conference.* IEEE, 1999.

[7] Fredric Gey, Hailing Jiang, Vivien Petras, and Aitao Chen. Cross-language retrieval for the clef collections - comparing multiple methods of retrieval. In Carol Peters, editor, *Proceedings of the CLEF 2000 Cross-Language Text Retreival System Evaluation Campaign.* Springer, to appear 2001.

[8] Youngin Kim, Barbara Norgard, Aitao Chen, and Fredric Gey. Using ordinary language to access metadata of diverse types of information resources: Trade classification and numeric data. In *Proceedings of the 62nd Annual Meeting of the American Society for Information Science,* pages 172–180. ASIS, 1999.

[9] Ray R. Larson and Chad Carson. Information access for a digital library: Cheshire ii and the berkeley environmental digital library. In *Proceedings of the 62nd Annual Meeting of the American Society for Information Science,* pages 515–535, November 1999.

[10] U.S. Office of Management and Budget. *North American Industry Classification System.* Maryland: Berman Press, ISBN 0-89059-09704, 1997.

Evaluating Question-Answering Techniques in Chinese

Xiaoyan Li and W. Bruce Croft

Computer Science Department

University of Massachusetts, Amherst, MA

{xiaoyan, croft}@cs.umass.edu

ABSTRACT

An important first step in developing a cross-lingual question answering system is to understand whether techniques developed with English text will also work with other languages, such as Chinese. The Marsha Chinese question answering system described in this paper uses techniques similar to those used in the English systems developed for TREC. Marsha consists of three main components: the query processing module, the Hanquery search engine, and the answer extraction module. It also contains some specific techniques dealing with Chinese language characteristics, such as word segmentation and ordinals processing. Evaluation of the system is done using a method based on the TREC question-answering track. The results of the evaluation show that the performance of Marsha is comparable to some English question answering systems in TREC 8 track. An English language version of Marsha further indicates that the heuristics used are applicable to the English question answering task.

Keywords

Question-Answering (QA); Search engine; multilingual retrieval, Chinese QA.

Proceedings of HLT 2001, First International Conference on Human Language Technology Research, J. Allan, ed., Morgan Kaufmann, San Francisco, 2001.

1. Introduction

A number of techniques for "question answering" have recently been evaluated both in the TREC environment (Voorhees and Harman, 1999) and in the DARPA TIDES program. In the standard approach to information retrieval, relevant text documents are retrieved in response to a query. The parts of those documents that may contain the most useful information or even the actual answer to the query are typically indicated by highlighting occurrences of query words in the text. In contrast, the task of a question-answering system is to identify text passages containing the relevant information and, if possible, extract the actual answer to the query. Question answering has a long history in natural language processing, and Salton's first book (Salton, 1968) contains a detailed discussion of the relationship between information retrieval and question-answering systems. The focus in recent research has been on extracting answers from very large text databases and many of the techniques use search technology as a major component. A significant number of the queries used in information retrieval experiments are questions, for example, TREC topic 338 "What adverse effects have people experienced while taking aspirin repeatedly?" and topic 308 "What are the advantages and/or disadvantages of tooth implants?" In question-answering experiments, the queries tend to be more restricted questions, where answers are likely to be found in a single text passage, for example, TREC question-answering question 11 "Who was President Cleveland's wife?" and question 14 "What country is the biggest producer of Tungsten?"

The TREC question-answering experiments have, to date, used only English text. As the first step towards our goal of cross-lingual question answering, we investigated whether the general approaches to question answering that have been used in English will also be effective for Chinese. Although it is now well known that statistical information retrieval techniques are effective in many languages, earlier research, such as Fujii and Croft (1993, 1999), was helpful in pointing out which techniques were particularly useful for languages like Japanese. This research was designed to provide similar information for question answering. In the next section, we describe the components of the Chinese question answering system (Marsha) and the algorithm used to determine answers. In section 3, we describe an evaluation of the system using queries obtained from Chinese students and the TREC-9 Chinese cross-lingual database (164,779 documents from the Peoples Daily and the Xing-Hua news agencies in the period 1991-1995).

2. Overview of the Marsha Question Answering System

The Chinese question-answering system consists of three main components. These are the query processing module, the Hanquery search engine, and the answer extraction module. The query processing module recognizes known question types and formulates queries for the search engine. The search engine retrieves candidate texts from a large database. The answer extraction module identifies text passages that are likely to contain answers and extracts answers, if possible, from these passages. This system architecture is very similar to other question-answering systems described in the literature.

More specifically, the query processing module carries out the following steps:

(1) The query is matched with templates to decide the question type and the "question words" in the query. We define 9 question types. Most of these correspond to typical named entity classes used in information extraction systems. For each question type, there are one or more templates. Currently there are 170 templates. If more than one template matches the question, we pick the longest match. For example, a question may include "多少元" (how many dollars). Then both 多少元 (how many dollars) and 多少 (how many) will match the question. In this case, we will pick 多少元 and assign "MONEY" to the question type.

The following table gives examples for each question type:

TEMPLATE	QUESTION TYPE	TRANSLATION
哪个人	PERSON	which person
哪个城市	LOCATION	which city
什么组织	ORGANIZATION	what organization
哪一年哪一月哪一天	DATE	what date
什么时间	TIME	what time
多少元	MONEY	how many dollars
百分比是什么	PERCENTAGE	what is the percentage
多少	NUMBER	how many
什么意思	OTHER	what is the meaning of

(2) Question words are removed from the query. This is a form of "stop word" removal. Words like "哪个人" (which person) are removed from the query since they are unlikely to occur in relevant text.

(3) Named entities in the query are marked up using BBN's IdentiFinder system. A named entity is kept as a word after segmentation.

(5) The query is segmented to identify Chinese words.

(6) Stop words are removed.

(7) The query is formulated for the Hanquery search engine. Hanquery is the Chinese version of Inquery (Broglio, Callan and Croft, 1996) and uses the Inquery query language that supports the specification of a variety of evidence combination methods. To support question answering, documents containing most of the query words were strongly preferred. If the number of query words left after the previous steps is greater than 4, then the operator #and (a probabilistic AND) is used. Otherwise, the probabilistic passage operator #UWn (unordered window) is used. The parameter n is set to twice the number of words in the query.

Hanquery is used to retrieve the top 10 ranked documents. The answer extraction module then goes through the following steps:

(8) IdentiFinder is used to mark up named entities in the documents.

(9) Passages are constructed from document sentences. We used passages based on sentence pairs, with a 1-sentence overlap.

(10) Scores are calculated for each passage. The score is based on five heuristics:

· *First Rule:*

Assign 0 to a passage if no expected name entity is present.

· *Second Rule:*

Calculate the number of match words in a passage.

Assign 0 to the passage if the number of matching words is less than the threshold. Otherwise, the score of this passage is equal to the number of matching words (*count_m*).

The threshold is defined as follows:

threshold = *count_q*   if *count_q*<4

threshold = *count_q*/2.0+1.0 if 4<=*count_q*<=8

threshold = *count_q*/3.0+2.0 if *count_q*>8

count_q is the number of words in the query.

· *Third Rule:*

Add 0.5 to score if all matching words are within one sentence.

· *Fourth Rule:*

Add 0.5 to score if all matching words are in the same order as they are in the original question.

· *Fifth Rule:*

score = score + *count_m*/(size of matching window)

(11) Pick the best passage for each document and rank them.

(12) Extract the answer from the top passage:

Find all candidates according to the question type. For example, if the question type is LOCATION, then each location marked by IdentiFinder is an answer candidate. An answer candidate is removed if it appears in the original question. If no candidate answer is found, no answer is returned.

Calculate the average distance between an answer candidate and the location of each matching word in the passage.

Pick the answer candidate that has the smallest average distance as the final answer.

3. Evaluating the System

We used 51 queries to do the initial evaluation of the question-answering system. We selected 26 queries from 240 questions collected from Chinese students in our department, because only these had answers in the test collection. The other 25 queries were constructed by either reformulating a question or asking a slightly different question. For example, given the question "which city is the biggest city in China?" we also generated the questions "where is the biggest city in China?" and "which city is the biggest city in the world?".

The results for these queries were evaluated in a similar, but not identical way to the TREC question-answering track. An "answer" in this system corresponds to the 50 byte responses in TREC and passages are approximately equivalent to the 250 byte TREC responses.

For 33 of 51 queries, the system suggested answers. 24 of the 33 were correct. For these 24, the "reciprocal rank" is 1, since only the top ranked passage is used to extract answers. Restricting the answer extraction to the top ranked passage also means that the other 27 queries have reciprocal rank values of 0. In TREC, the reciprocal ranks are calculated using the highest rank of the correct answer (up to 5). In our case, using only the top passage means that the mean reciprocal rank of 0.47 is a lower bound for the result of the 50 byte task.

 As an example, the question "哪个城市是中国最大的城市" (Which city is the biggest city in China?), the answer returned is 上海 (Shanghai). In the top ranked passage, "China" and "Shanghai" are the two answer candidates that have the smallest distances. "Shanghai" is chosen as the final answer since "China" appears in the original question.

As an example of an incorrect response, the question "谢军在哪一年战胜了前苏联选手第一次获得国际象棋世界冠军" (In which year did Jun Xie defeat a Russian player and win the world chess championship for the first time?) produced an answer of 今天 (today). There were two candidate answers in the top passage, "October 18" and "today". Both were marked as DATE by Identifinder, but "today" was closer to the matching words. This indicates the need for more date normalization and better entity classification in the system.

For 44 queries, the correct answer was found in the top-ranked passage. Even if the other queries are given a reciprocal rank of 0, this gives a mean reciprocal rank of 0.86 for a task similar to the 250 byte TREC task. In fact, the correct answer for 4 other queries was found in the top 5 passages, so the mean reciprocal rank would be somewhat higher. For 2 of the remaining 3 queries, Hanquery did not retrieve a document in the top 10 that contained an answer, so answer extraction could not work.

4. Further Improvements

These results, although preliminary, are promising. We have made a number of improvements in the new version (v2) of the system. Some of these are described in this section.

One of the changes is designed to improve the system's ability to extract answers for the questions that ask for a number. A number recognizer was developed to recognize numbers in Chinese documents. The numbers here are numbers other than DATE, MONEY and PERCENTAGE that are recognized by IdentiFinder. The version of IdentiFinder used in our system can only mark up seven types of name entities and this limits the system's ability to answer other types of questions. The number recognizer is the first example of the type of refinement to named entity recognition that must be done for better performance.

An example of a question requiring a numeric answer is:

"克林顿是第几任美国总统？ (What is the number of Clinton's presidency?)". This question could be answered in Marsha v2 by extracting the marked up number from the best passage in the answer extraction part, while Marsha v1 could only return the top 5 passages that were likely to have the answer to this question.

Another improvement relates to the best matching window of a passage. The size of the matching window in each passage is an important part of calculating the belief score for the passage. Locating the best matching window is also important in the answer-extraction processing because the final answer picked is the candidate that has the smallest average distance from the matching window. The best matching window of a passage here is the window that has the most query words in it and has the smallest window size. In the previous version of our system, we only consider the first occurrence of each query word in a passage and index the position accordingly. The matching window is thus from the word of the smallest index to the word of the largest index in the passage. It is only a rough approximation of the best matching window though it works well for many of the passages. In the second version of Marsha, we developed a more accurate algorithm to locate the best matching window of each passage. This

change helped Marsha v2 find correct answers for some questions that previously failed. The following is an example of such a question.

For the question "美国贫困线以下的人口总数是多少？ (How many people in the United States are below the poverty line?)"

The best passage is as follows:

"本报华盛顿９月２８日电记者张启昕报道：由于经济衰退，人民收入下降，*美国*穷人去年一年增加<u>２００多万</u>，使*美国*生活在政府规定的*贫困线以下的人口总数*达<u>３３５８．５万</u>，比１９８９年增加６．７％，这个数字还不包括大批流落街头的无家可归者"

This passage has two occurrences of query word "美国". In v1, the first occurrence of "美国" is treated as the start of the matching window, whereas the second occurrence is actually the start of the best matching window. There are two numbers "<u>２００多万</u>" (more than 2 million) and "<u>３３５８．５万</u>" (33.585 million) in the passage. The right answer "<u>３３５８．５万</u>" (33.585 million) is nearer to the best matching window and "<u>２００多万</u>" (more than 2 million) is nearer to the estimated matching window. Therefore, the right answer can be extracted after correctly locating the best matching window.

The third improvement is with the scoring strategies of passages. Based on the observation that the size of the best matching window of a passage plays a more important role than the order of the query words in a passage, we adjusted the score bonus for same order satisfaction from 0.5 to 0.05. This adjustment makes a passage with a smaller matching window get a higher belief score than a passage that satisfies the same order of query words but has a bigger matching window. As an example, consider the question:

"谁是第一个美国总统？ (Who was the first president in the United States?)".

Passage 1 is the passage that has the right answer "乔治华盛顿".

Passage 1.

"１９９２年１２月２６日 星期六#pn:第七版#pm:国际副刊#xh:5#lm:世界一角#ti:美国总统的就职典礼#au:允文#rw:美国第一任总统乔治华盛顿#rw:比尔克林顿#rw:托马斯杰弗逊"

Passage 2.

"德国总理科尔二十五日下午离开波恩前往华盛顿进行
为期一天的访问, 这将是他第一次会见美国总统克林顿"

Passage 1 and Passage 2 both have all query words. The
size of the best matching window in Passage 1 is smaller
than that in Passage 2 while query words in Passage 2 have
the same order as that in the question. The scoring strategy
in Marsha v2 selects Passage 1 and extracts the correct
answer while Marsha v1 selected Passage 2.

Special processing of ordinals has also been considered in
Marsha v2. Ordinals in Chinese usually start with the
Chinese character "第" and are followed by a cardinal. It is
better to retain ordinals as single words during the query
generation in order to retrieve better relevant documents.
However, the cardinals (part of the ordinals in Chinese) in a
passage are marked up by the number recognizer for they
might be answer candidates for questions asking for a
number. Thus ordinals in Chinese need special care in a QA
system. In Marsha v2, ordinals appearing in a question are
first retained as single words for the purpose of generating a
good query and then separated in the post processing after
relevant documents are retrieved to avoid answer
candidates being ignored.

5. Comparison with English Question Answering Systems

Some techniques used in Marsha are similar to the
techniques in English question answering systems
developed by other researchers. The template matching in
Marsha for deciding the type of expected answer for a
question is basically the same as the one used in the
GuruQA (Prager et al., 2000) except that the templates
consist of Chinese word patterns instead of English word
patterns. Marsha has the ability of providing answers to
eight types of questions: PERSON, LOCATION,
ORGANIZATION, DATE, TIME, MONEY,
PERCENTAGE, and NUMBER. The first seven types
correspond to the named entities from IdentiFinder
developed by BBN. We developed a Chinese number-
recognizer ourselves which marks up numbers in the
passages as answer candidates for questions asking for a
number. The number could be represented as a digit
number or Chinese characters. David A. Hull used a proper
name tagger ThingFinder developed at Xerox in his
question answering system. Five of the answer types
correspond to the types of proper names from ThingFinder
(Hull, 1999). The scoring strategy in Marsha is similar to
the computation of score for an answer window in the
LASSO QA system (Moldovan et al., 1999) in terms of the
factors considered in the computation. Factors such as the
number of matching words in the passage, whether all

matching words in the same sentence, and whether the
matching words in the passage have the same order as they
are in the question are common to LASSO and Marsha.

We have also implemented an English language version of
Marsha. The system implements the answer classes
PERSON, ORGANIZATION, LOCATION, and DATE.
Queries are generated in the same fashion as Marsha. If
there are any phrases in the input query (named entities
from IdentiFinder, quoted strings) these are added to an
Inquery query in a #N operator all inside a #sum operator.
For example:

Question: "Who is the author of "Bad Bad Leroy
Brown"

Inquery query: #sum(#uw8(author Bad Bad Leroy
Brown) #6(Bad Bad Leroy Brown))

Where N is number of terms + 1 for named entities, and
number of terms + 2 for quoted phrases. If a query retrieves
no documents, a "back off" query uses #sum over the query
terms, with phrases dropped. The above would become
#sum(author Bad Bad Leroy Brown).

The system was tested against the TREC9 question
answering evaluation questions. The mean reciprocal rank
over 682/693 questions was 0.300 with 396 questions going
unanswered. The U.Mass. TREC9 (250 byte) run had a
score of 0.367. Considering only the document retrieval, we
find a document containing an answer for 471 of the
questions, compared to 477 for the official TREC9 run
which used expanded queries. This indicates that the
Marsha heuristics have applicability to the English question
answering task and are not limited to the Chinese question
answering task.

6. Summary and Future Work

The evaluations on Marsha, although preliminary, indicate
that techniques developed for question answering in English
are also effective in Chinese. In future research, we plan to
continue to improve these techniques and carry out more
careful evaluations to establish whether there are any
significant differences in the question-answering task
between these two languages.

The evaluation of the English version of Marsha indicates
that the Marsha heuristics work well in English as well as in
Chinese. We now plan to incorporate these techniques in a
cross-lingual question-answering system for English and
Chinese. By using two systems with similar question
processing strategies, we hope to exploit the query
templates to produce accurate question translations.

We have also started to develop a probabilistic model of question answering using the language model approach (Ponte and Croft, 1998). This type of model will be essential for extending the capability of QA systems beyond a few common query forms.

Acknowledgements

This material is based on work supported in part by the Library of Congress and Department of Commerce under cooperative agreement number EEC-9209623 and in part by SPAWARSYSCEN-SD grant number N66001-99-1-8912.

Any opinions, findings and conclusions or recommendations expressed in this material are the author(s) and do not necessarily reflect those of the sponsor.

We also want to express out thanks to people at CIIR for their help. Special thanks to David Fisher who implemented the English language version of Marsha, and Fangfang Feng for his valuable discussions on Chinese related research issues.

7. References

Broglio, J., Callan, J.P. and Croft, W.B. "Technical Issues in Building an Information Retrieval System for Chinese," CIIR Technical Report IR-86, Computer Science Department, University of Massachusetts, Amherst, (1996).

H. Fujii and W.B. Croft, "A Comparison of Indexing Techniques for Japanese Text Retrieval," Proceedings of SIGIR 93, 237-246, (1993).

H. Fujii and W.B. Croft, "Comparing the performance of English and Japanese text databases", in S. Armstrong et al (eds.), *Natural Language Processing using Very Large Corpora*, 269-282, Kluwer, (1999). (This paper first appeared in a 1994 workshop)

G. Salton, Automatic Information Organization and Retrieval, McGraw-Hill, (1968).

E. Voorhees and D. Harman (eds.), *The 7th Text Retrieval Conference (TREC-7)*, NIST Special Publication 500-242, (1999).

Ponte, J. and Croft, W.B. "A Language Modeling Approach to Information Retrieval," in the Proceedings of SIGIR 98, pp. 275-281(1998).

Moldovan, Dan et al, "LASSO: A Tool for Surfing the Answer Net," in the proceedings of TREC-8, pp 175-183. (1999).

Hull, David A., "Xerox TREC-8 Questio Answering Track Report," in the proceedings of TREC-8, pp743.

Prager, John, Brown, Eric, and Coden, Anni, "Question_Answering by Predictive Annotation," in the proceedings of SIGIR 2000.

An Evaluation Corpus For Temporal Summarization

Vikash Khandelwal, Rahul Gupta, and James Allan
Center for Intelligent Information Retrieval
Department of Computer Science
University of Massachusetts
Amherst, MA 01003
{vikas,rgupta,allan}@cs.umass.edu

ABSTRACT

In recent years, a lot of work has been done in the field of Topic Tracking. The focus of this work has been on identifying stories belonging to the same topic. This might result in a very large number of stories being reported to the user. It might be more useful to a user if a summary of the main events in the topic rather than the entire collection of stories related to the topic were presented. Though work on such a fine-grained level has been started, there is currently no standard evaluation testbed available to measure the accuracy of such techniques. We describe a scheme for developing a testbed of user judgments which can be used to evaluate the above mentioned techniques. The corpus that we have created can also be used to evaluate single or multi-document summaries.

1. THE PROBLEM

In recent years, a lot of progress has been made in the field of Topic Tracking ([2], [3], [8], etc). The focus of this work has been on identifying news stories belonging to the same topic. This might result in a very large number of stories being reported to the user. It would be more useful to a user if a summary of the main events/developments in the topic rather than the entire collection of stories related to the topic were presented. We can formulate the problem as follows.

We are given a stream of chronologically ordered and topically related stories. We strive to identify the shifts in the topic which represent the developments within the topic. For example, consider the topic "*2000 Presidential Elections*". On the night of November 7, there were reports of Gore conceding defeat to Bush. The next morning, there were reports claiming his retraction of the previous concession. Most of the stories on the next day would also contain old information including details of Gore's first phone call to Bush. We want to present only the new development (i.e., Gore's retraction) on the next day.

We assume that sentence extracts can identify such topic shifts. At the very least, they can convey enough information to a user to keep track of the developments within that topic. For example, in Figure 1, the mappings indicate how the sentences in a story correspond to events.

Human judgments are required to evaluate accuracy of extracts. The approach usually taken is to have each such extract evaluated by human beings but such a process is expensive and time consuming. We need an evaluation corpus similar to the TDT or TREC corpora that can be used over and over again to do such evaluations automatically. We propose a new scheme for building such a corpus.

Summarization evaluation is difficult because summaries can be created for a range of purposes. The Tipster SUMMAC evaluation [7] required human assessors to evaluate each summary, and most other evaluations have also required human checking of every summary [6]. There are others who have attempted automatic evaluations ([5], [9]) but none of these evaluation schemes captures all the desirable properties in a summary.

The particular problem of summarizing shifts in a news topic was attacked slightly differently at a Summer 1999 workshop on Novelty Detection [4]. Those efforts towards "*new information detection*" were a dead end because the granularity of new information was too small, e.g., a mention of a person's age might count as new information even when it is not the focus of the story. Swan and Allan also created an event-level summary "timeline" ([10], [11]) but they did not develop any evaluation corpus for their work.

This paper is organised as follows. In Section 2, we discuss the desirable properties of such an evaluation corpus. Section 3 discusses the entire annotation process, as well as the interesting practical issues, the problems faced and then the statistics of the corpus that we have built. Finally, in Section 4, we discuss one possible way of utilising this corpus.

2. DESIRABLE PROPERTIES OF THE EVALUATION CORPUS

Any evaluation corpus of sentence extracts and events which is to be used for the purpose of evaluating summaries of topic shifts in a news stream should have the following properties:

- It should be possible to identify all new events on a periodic basis. This would be required to estimate the recall of a system.

Proceedings of HLT 2001, First International Conference on Human Language Technology Research, J. Allan, ed., Morgan Kaufmann, San Francisco, 2001.

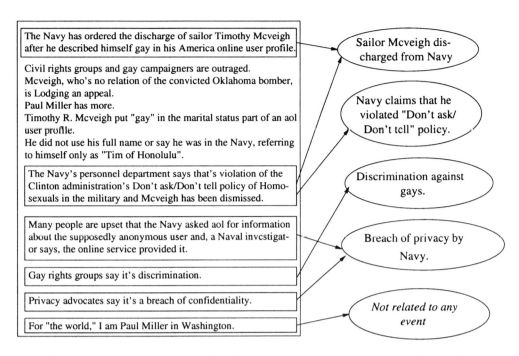

Figure 1: An example showing how sentence extracts can indicate events

- It should be possible to quantify the precision of a summary, i.e., it should be possible to find the proportion of relevant sentences in the summary,

- It should be possible to identify redundancy in the system output being evaluated. There should be some way of assigning a marginal utility to sentences containing relevant but redundant information

- It should be possible to quantify the "usefulness" of a summary taking recall, precision as well as redundancy into account.

- Sentence boundaries should be uniquely identified (though they need not be perfect) because the aim of the system is to identify the relevant portions in the summary.

3. BUILDING AN EVALUATION CORPUS

3.1 The annotation process

We collect a stream of stories related to a certain topic from the TDT-2 corpus of stories from January 1 to June 30 1998. We used stories that were judged "on-topic" by annotators from LDC. The topics were selected from the TDT 1998 and 1999 evaluations. The stories are parsed to obtain sentence boundaries and all the sentences are given unique identifiers. We proceed with collecting the human judgments in the following four steps.

1. Each judge reads all the stories and identifies the important events.

2. The judges sit together to merge the events identified by them, to form a single list of events for that topic. All the events are given unique identifiers.

3. Each judge goes through the stories again, connecting sentences to the relevant events. Obviously, not all sentences need to be related to any event. However, if some sentence is relevant to more than one event, it is linked to all those events.

4. Another judge now verifies the mapping between the sentences and the events. This gives us the final mapping from sentences to events.

This way we obtain all the events mentioned within a story and we can also find out the events which find their first mention within this story. The advantage of building the evaluation corpus in this way is that these judgments can be used both for summarizing topic shifts as well as summarizing any given story by itself.

We have built a user interface in Java to allow judges to do the above work systematically. Figure 2 shows a snapshot of the interface used by the judges.

3.2 Statistics of the judgments obtained

We have obtained judgments for 22 topics. Three judges worked on each topic. We summarize the results of the annotation process for a subset of the topics in Table 1. We define the interjudge agreement for an event to be the ratio of the number of sentences linked to that event, as agreed upon by the third judge, to the number of sentences in the union of the sentences individually marked by the first two judges for that event. For a topic, the interjudge agreement is defined to be the average of the agreement for all the events in that topic. It is to be noted that the Kappa statistic is not applicable here in any standard form.

We found a large variance in the number of sentences linked to different events. As an example, in Table 2, we show the statistics for a group of news stories describing

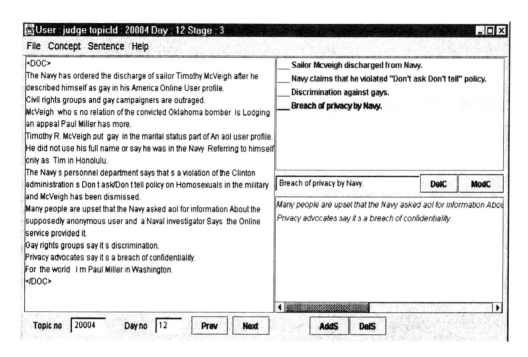

Figure 2: A snapshot of the user interface used for annotating the topics

Table 1: Annotation statistics for some of the topics

Topic id	# of stories	# of events	Time taken (in hours)	Inter-judge Agreement
20008	49	10	4.5	0.91
20020	34	23	4.5	0.98
20021	48	9	2.5	0.97
20022	27	10	3.5	0.85
20024	38	12	2.75	0.98
20026	68	11	2.5	0.87
20031	34	15	2.5	0.62
20041	24	11	2	0.94
20042	28	14	2.5	0.66
20057	19	9	2	0.66
20065	57	16	2.33	0.94
20074	51	13	3	0.96
Average	39.75	12.75	2.88	0.86

Table 2: Variance in the number of sentences linked to different events for topic 20021

Event id	# of sentences	Inter-judge Agreement
1	43	1.0
2	9	1.0
3	33	0.97
4	8	1.0
5	4	0.8
6	5	1.0
7	14	1.0
8	19	1.0
9	9	1.0

the damage due to tornados in Florida. We see that event 5 ("Relief agencies needed more than $300,000 to provide relief") is linked to 4 sentences while event 1 ("At least 40 people died in Florida due to 10-15 tornados.") is linked to 43 sentences. We may be able to use the number of sentences linked to a event as an indicator of the weight/importance of the event.

We have divided our corpus into two parts - one each for training and testing respectively. Each part consists of 11 topics. Care was taken to ensure that both the parts had topics of roughly the same size and time of occurrence. The statistics of both parts of the corpus are given in Table 3.

3.3 Problems faced

- Sometimes our sentence parser broke up a valid sentence into multiple parts. One judge linked only the relevant part of the sentence to the corresponding event while another linked all the parts to that event. This happened in the case of three of the topics (topics 20031, 20042 and 20057) before we detected the problem.

- Sometimes when similar sentences occur in different stories, one of the judges neglected the later occurrences of the sentence.

3.4 Interesting issues/judges' comments

We asked the judges for feedback on the annotation process and the difficulties faced. Here are some of the interesting issues which cropped up :

- Some ideas/events cannot be covered by any single sentence but only by a group of sentences. By themselves, none of the sentences might be relevant to the event. For example, Suppose, the event is *The Navy and AOL contradict each other* and we have two sentences - *"the navy has said in sworn testimony that*

104

	Training	Test	All
Number of topics	11	11	22
Number of stories	474	470	944
per topic	43.1	42.7	42.9
Number of events	162	181	343
per topic	14.7	16.5	15.6
Number of sentences	8043	9006	17049
per topic	731.2	818.7	775.0
per story	17.0	19.2	18.1
Off-event sentences	72%	70%	71%
Single-event sentences	24%	26%	25%
Multi-event sentences	4%	4%	4%

Table 3: Characteristics of the corpus. All numbers except for the number of topics are averaged over all topics included in that column.

this did happen." and "america online is saying this never happened." Clearly, any one sentence does not adequately represent the event. This can be easily taken care of by considering groups of sentences rather than single sentences.

- Abstract ideas : Sometimes the meaning of individual sentences is totally different from overall idea they convey. Satirical articles are an example of this. These kind of ideas cannot be represented by sentence extracts. We omitted such events.

- Sometimes different stories totally contradict each other. For example, some stories (on the same day) claim a lead for Bush while others claim Gore to be far ahead. This is more of a summarization issue though and need not be dealt with while building the evaluation corpus.

4. USING THE EVALUATION CORPUS

We have used the corpus for evaluating our system which produces temporal summaries in news stream ([1]). The problem of temporal summarization can be formalized as follows. A news topic is made up of a set of events and is discussed in a sequence of news stories. Most sentences of the news stories discuss one or more of the events in the topic. Some sentences are not germane to any of the events. Those sentences are called "off-event" sentences and contrast with "on-event" sentences. The task of the system is to assign a score to every sentence that indicates the importance of the sentence in the summary. This scoring yields a ranking on all sentences in the topic, including off- and on-event sentences.

We will use measures that are analogues of recall and precision. We are interested in multiple properties:

- *Useful* sentences are those that have the potential to be a meaningful part of the summary. Off-event sentences are not useful, but all other sentences are.

- *Novel* sentences are those that are not redundant—i.e., are new in the presentation. The first sentence about an event is clearly novel, but all following sentences discussing the same event are not.

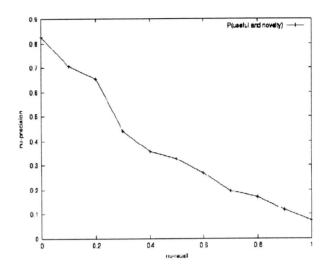

Figure 3: nu-recall vs nu-precision plot for the task of summarizing topic shifts in a news stream

- *Size* of the summary is a typical measure used in summarization research and we include it here.

Based on those properties, we could define the following measure to capture the combination of usefulness and novelty:

$$nu - recall = \frac{\sum I(r(e_i) > 0)}{E}$$
$$nu - precision = \frac{\sum I(r(e_i) > 0)}{S_r}$$

where S_r is the number of sentences retrieved, E is the number of events in the topic, e_i is event number i ($1 \leq i \leq E$), $r(e_i)$ is the number of sentences retrieved for event e_i, $I(exp)$ is 1 if exp is true and 0 if not. All summations are as i ranges over the set of events. Note that $S_r \neq \sum r(e_i)$ since completely off-topic sentences might be retrieved.

The nu-recall measure is the proportion of the events that have been mentioned in the summary, and nu-precision is the proportion of sentences retrieved that are the first mentions of an event.

We used this measure to evaluate the performance of our system over the entire training corpus. The results for the training corpus are shown in the nu-recall/nu-precision graph in figure 3. This work is described in detail elsewhere([1]).

This is just one of the possible ways of using the corpus. We can define a number of other similar measures which could be easily computed using the data provided by such a corpus. These same measures can also be used to evaluate a system producing single or multi-document summaries too.

5. FUTURE WORK

We intend to complete collecting user judgments for more topics soon. After analyzing the reliablity of these judgments and correcting the few mistakes that we had made initially, we will collect annotations for more topics. Initially, we had used a simple barebones sentence parser, since that is mostly sufficient for the work such a corpus would be put to. Nevertheless, in future annotations, we will need to improve the sentence parser. We intend to continue using these judgments to evaluate the performance of the systems that we are currently building to identify and summarize topic shifts in news streams.

Acknowledgements

This material is based on work supported in part by the Library of Congress and Department of Commerce under cooperative agreement number EEC-9209623 and in part by SPAWARSYSCEN-SD grant number N66001-99-1-8912. Any opinions, findings and conclusions or recommendations expressed in this material are the author(s) and do not necessarily reflect those of the sponsor.

6. REFERENCES

[1] J. Allan, R. Gupta, and V. Khandelwal. Temporal Summaries of News Topics. *Proceedings of SIGIR 2001 Conference, New Orleans, LA.*, 2001.

[2] J. Allan, V. Lavrenko, D. Frey, and V. Khandelwal. UMASS at TDT2000. *TDT 2000 Workshop notebook*, 2000.

[3] J. Allan, R. Papka, and V. Lavrenko. On-line New Event Detection and Tracking. *Proceedings of SIGIR 1998, pp. 37-45*, 1998.

[4] J. Allan et al. Topic-based novelty detection. *1999 Summer Workshop at CLSP Final Report. Available at http://www.clsp.jhu.edu/ws99/tdt*, 1999.

[5] J. Goldstein, M. Kantrowitz, V. Mittal, and J. Carbonell. Summarizing text documents: Sentence Selection and Evaluation Metrics. *Proceedings of SIGIR 1999*, August 1999.

[6] H. Jing, R. Barzilay, K. McKeown, and M. Elhadad. Summarization Evaluation Methods: Experiments and Analysis. *Working notes, AAAI Spring Symposium on Intelligent Text Summarization, Stanford, CA*, April, 1998.

[7] Inderjeet Mani and et al. The TIPSTER SUMMAC Text Summarization Evaluation Final Report. 1998.

[8] R. Papka, J. Allan, and V. Lavrenko. UMASS Approaches to Detection and Tracking at TDT2. *Proceedings of the DARPA Broadcast News Workshop, Herndon, VA, pp. 111-125*, 1999.

[9] D. R. Radev, H. Jing, and M. Budzikowska. Summarization of multiple documents: clustering, sentence extraction, and evaluation. *ANLP/NAACL Workshop on Summarization, Seattle, WA*, 2000.

[10] R. Swan and J. Allan. Extracting Significant Time Varying Features from Text. *Proceedings of the Eighth International Conference on Information and Knowledge Management, pp.38-45*, 1999.

[11] R. Swan and J. Allan. Automatic Generation of Overview Timelines. *Proceedings of SIGIR 2000 Conference, Athens, pp.49-56*, 2000.

Evaluation Results for the Talk'n'Travel System

David Stallard

BBN Technologies, Verizon

70 Fawcett. St.

Cambridge, MA, 02140

Stallard@bbn.com

ABSTRACT

We describe and present evaluation results for Talk'n'Travel, a spoken dialogue language system for making air travel plans over the telephone. Talk'n'Travel is a fully conversational, mixed-initiative system that allows the user to specify the constraints on his travel plan in arbitrary order, ask questions, etc., in general spoken English. The system was independently evaluated as part of the DARPA Communicator program and achieved a high success rate.

1. INTRODUCTION

This paper describes and presents evaluation results for Talk'n'Travel, a spoken language dialogue system for making complex air travel plans over the telephone. Talk'n'Travel is a research prototype system sponsored under the DARPA Communicator program (MITRE, 1999). Some other systems in the program are Ward and Pellom (1999), Seneff and Polifroni (2000) and Rudnicky et al (1999). The common task of this program is a mixed-initiative dialogue over the telephone, in which the user plans a multi-city trip by air, including all flights, hotels, and rental cars, all in conversational English over the telephone. A similar research program is the European ARISE project (Den Os et al, 1999).

An earlier version of Talk'n'Travel was presented in (Stallard, 2000). The present paper presents and discusses results of an independent evaluation of Talk'n'Travel, recently conducted as part of the DARPA Communicator program.

The next section gives a brief overview of the system.

2. SYSTEM OVERVIEW

The figure shows a block diagram of Talk'n'Travel. Spoken language understanding is provided by statistical N-gram speech recognition and a robust language understanding component. A plan-based dialogue manager coordinates interaction with the user, handling unexpected user input more flexibly than conventional finite-state dialogue control networks. It works in tandem with a state management component that adjusts the current model of user intention based on the user's last utterance

Proceedings of HLT 2001, First International Conference on Human Language Technology Research, J. Allan, ed., Morgan Kaufmann, San Francisco, 2001.

in context.

Meaning and task state are represented by the path constraint representation (Stallard, 2000). An inference component is included which allows the system to deduce implicit requirements from explicit statements by the user, and to retract them if the premises change.

The system is interfaced to the Yahoo/Travelocity flight schedule website, for access to live flight schedule information. Queries to the website are spawned off in a separate thread, which the dialogue manager monitors ands reports on to the user.

Figure 1 : System Architecture

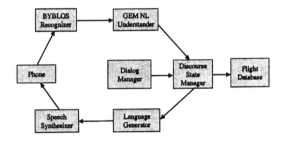

3. DIALOGUE STRATEGY

Talk'n'Travel employs both open-ended and directed prompts. Sessions begin with open prompts like "What trip would you to take?". The system then goes to directed prompts to get any information the user did not provide ("What day are you leaving?", etc). The user may give arbitrary information at any prompt, however. The system provides implicit confirmation of the change in task state caused by the user's last utterance ("Flying from Boston to Denver tomorrow ") to ensure mutual understanding.

The system seeks explicit confirmation in certain cases, for example where the user appears to be making a change in date of travel. Once sufficient information is obtained, the system offers a set of candidate flights, one at a time, for the user to accept or reject.

4. EVALUATION

4.1 Evaluation Design

The 9 groups funded by the Communicator program (ATT, BBN, CMU, Lucent, MIT, MITRE, SRI, and University of Colorado) took part in an experimental common evaluation conducted by the National Institute of Standards and Technology (NIST) in June and July of 2000. A pool of approximately 80 subjects was recruited from around the United States. The only requirements were that the subjects be native speakers of American English and have Internet access. Only wireline or home cordless phones were allowed.

The subjects were given a set of travel planning scenarios to attempt. There were 7 such prescribed scenarios and 2 open ones, in which the subject was allowed to propose his own task. Prescribed scenarios were given in a tabular format. An example scenario would be a round-trip flight between two cities, departing and returning on given dates, with specific arrival or departure time preferences.

Each subject called each system once and attempted to work through a single scenario; the design of the experiment attempted to balance the distributions of scenarios and users across the systems.

Following each scenario attempt, subjects filled out a Web-based questionnaire to determine whether subjects thought they had completed their task, how satisfied they were with using the system, and so forth. The overall form of this evaluation was thus similar to that conducted under the ARISE program (Den Os, et al 1999).

4.2 Results

Table 1 shows the result of these user surveys for Talk'n'Travel. The columns represent specific questions on the user survey. The first column represents the user's judgement as to whether or not he completed his task. The remaining columns, labeled Q1-Q5, are Likert scale items, for which a value of 1 signifies complete agreement, and 5 signifies complete disagreement. Lower numbers for these columns are thus better scores. The legend below the table identifies the questions.

Table 1 : Survey Results

	Task Comp%	Q1	Q2	Q3	Q4	Q5
BBN	80.5%	2.23	2.09	2.10	2.36	2.84
Mean	62.0%	2.88	2.23	2.54	2.95	3.36

Scale: 1 = strongly agree, 5 = strongly disagree

Q1 It was easy to get the information I wanted
Q2 I found it easy to understand what the system said
Q3 I knew what I could do or say at each point in the dialog
Q4 The system worked the way I expected it to
Q5 I would use this system regularly to get travel information

The first row gives the mean value for the measurements over all 78 sessions with Talk'n'Travel. The second row gives the mean value of the same measurements for all 9 systems participating.

Talk'n'Travel's task completion score of 80.5% was the highest for all 9 participating systems. Its score on question Q5, representing user satisfaction, was the second highest.

An independent analysis of task completion was also performed by comparing the logs of the session with the scenario given.

Table 2 shows Talk'n'Travel's results for this metric, which are close to that seen for the user questionnaire.

Table 2: Objective Analysis

Completion of required scenario	70.5%
Completion of different scenario	11.5%
Total completed scenarios	82.0%

Besides task completion, other measurements were made of system operation. These included time to completion, word error rate, and interpretation accuracy. The values of these measurements are given in Table 3.

Table 3: Other Metrics

Average time to completion	246 secs
Average word error rate	21%
Semantic error rate/utterance	10%

4.3 Analysis and Discussion

We analyzed the log files of the 29.5% of the sessions that did not result in the completion of the required scenario. Table 4 gives a breakdown of the causes.

Table 4: Causes of Failure

City not in lexicon	39% (9)
Unrepaired recognition error	22% (5)
User error	17% (4)
System diversion	13% (3)
Other	9% (2)

The largest cause (39%) was the inability of the system to recognize a city referred to by the user, simply because that city was absent from the recognizer language model or language understander's lexicon. These cases were generally trivial to fix.

The second, and most serious, cause (22%) was recognition errors that the user either did not attempt to repair or did not succeed in repairing. Dates proved troublesome in this regard, in which one date would be misrecognized for another, e.g. "October twenty third" for "October twenty first

Another class of errors were caused by the user, in that he either gave the system different information than was prescribed by the scenario, or failed to supply the information he was supposed to. A handful of sessions failed because of additional causes, including system crashes and backend failure.

Both time to completion and semantic error rate were affected by scenarios that failed because because of a missing city. In such scenarios, users would frequently repeat themselves many times in a vain attempt to be understood, thus increasing total utterance count and utterance error.

An interesting result is that task success did not depend too strongly on word error rate. Even successful scenarios had an average WER of 18%, while failed scenarios had average WER of only 22%.

A key issue in this experiment was whether users would actually interact with the system conversationally, or would respond only to directive prompts. For the first three sessions, we experimented with a highly general open prompt ("How can I help you?'), but quickly found that it tended to elicit overly general and uninformative responses (e.g. "I want to plan a trip"). We therefore switched to the more purposeful "What trip would you like to take?" for the remainder of the evaluation. Fully 70% of the time, users replied informatively to this prompt, supplying utterances "I would like an American flight from Miami to Sydney" that moved the dialogue forward.

In spite of the generally high rate of success with open prompts, there was a pronounced reluctance by some users to take the initiative, leading them to not state all the constraints they had in mind. Examples included requirements on airline or arrival time. In fully 20% of all sessions, users refused multiple flights in a row, holding out for one that met a particular unstated requirement. The user could have stated this requirement explicitly, but chose not to, perhaps underestimating what the system could do. This had the effect of lengthening total interaction time with the system.

4.4 Possible Improvements
Several possible reasons for this behavior on the part of users come to mind, and point the way to future improvements. The synthesized speech was fairly robotic in quality, which naturally tended to make the system sound less capable. The prompts themselves were not sufficiently variable, and were often repeated verbatim when a reprompt was necessary. Finally, the system's dialogue strategy needs be modified to detect when more initiative is needed from the user, and cajole him with open prompts accordingly.

5. ACKNOWLEDGMENTS
This work was sponsored by DARPA and monitored by SPAWAR Systems Center under Contract No. N66001-99-D-8615.

6. REFERENCES
[1] MITRE (1999) DARPA Communicator homepage http://fofoca.mitre.org/

[2] Ward W., and Pellom, B. (1999) The CU Communicator System. In *1999 IEEE Workshop on Automatic Speech Recognition and Understanding*, Keystone, Colorado.

[3] Den Os, E, Boves, L., Lamel, L, and Baggia, P. (1999) Overview of the ARISE Project. *Proceedings of Eurospeech, 1999*, Vol 4, pp. 1527-1530.

[4] Miller S. (1998) The Generative Extraction Model. Unpublished manuscript.

[5] Constantinides P., Hansma S., Tchou C. and Rudnicky, A. (1999) A schema-based approach to dialog control. *Proceedings of ICSLP*, Paper 637.

[6] Rudnicky A., Thayer, E., Constantinides P., Tchou C., Shern, R., Lenzo K., Xu W., Oh A. (1999) Creating natural dialogs in the Carnegie Mellon Communicator system. *Proceedings of Eurospeech, 1999*, Vol 4, pp. 1531-1534

[7] Rudnicky A., and Xu W. (1999) An agenda-based dialog management architecture for soken language systems. In *1999 IEEE Workshop on Automatic Speech Recognition and Understanding*, Keystone, Colorado.

[8] Seneff S., and Polifroni, J. (2000) Dialogue Management in the Mercury Flight Reservation System. *ANLP Conversational Systems Workshop*.

Experiments in Multi-Modal Automatic Content Extraction

Lance Ramshaw, Elizabeth Boschee, Sergey Bratus, Scott Miller,
Rebecca Stone, Ralph Weischedel, and Alex Zamanian

BBN Technologies
70 Fawcett St.
Cambridge, MA 02138 USA
1-617-873-2236

{lramshaw, eboschee, sbratus, szmiller, rwstone, weischedel, azamania}@bbn.com

ABSTRACT

Unlike earlier information extraction research programs, the new ACE (Automatic Content Extraction) program calls for entity extraction by identifying and linking all of the mentions of an entity in the source text, including names, descriptions, and pronouns. Coreference is therefore a key component. BBN has developed statistical co-reference models for this task, including one for pronoun co-reference that we describe here in some detail. In addition, ACE calls for extraction not just from clean text, but also from noisy speech and OCR input. Since speech recognizer output includes neither case nor punctuation, we have extended our statistical parser to perform sentence breaking integrated with parsing in a probabilistic model.

1. INTRODUCTION

The Automatic Content Extraction (ACE) program, a new effort to stimulate and benchmark research in information extraction, presents two challenges:

1. *Recognition of entities is paramount.* In named entity evaluations, recognizing and classifying name strings is the focus; in the MUC Template Element (TE) task, all names for an entity but only one description were to be collected. In the ACE entity detection and tracking (EDT) task, all mentions of an entity, whether a name, a description, or a pronoun, are to be found and collected into equivalence classes based on reference to the same entity. Therefore, practical co-reference resolution is fundamental.

2. *Extraction is measured not merely on text, but also on speech and on OCR input.* Named entity recognition had previously been benchmarked on text, speech, and OCR, but extraction above the level of names had rarely been attempted. Moving beyond name finding is a crucial leap for

modalities other than text, since the ability to relate two strings (as in ACE) in very noisy input may degrade much more than finding strings in isolation (as in named entity recognition.) Furthermore, the lack of case and punctuation, including the lack of sentence boundary markers, poses a challenge to full parsing of speech.

To address challenge 1 above, BBN developed statistical learning algorithms for pronoun resolution and name co-reference and is developing a statistical learning algorithm for co-reference of definite noun phrases (beyond names and pronouns). The pronoun co-reference algorithm is described here.

Challenge 2 did not require abandoning our statistical approach to full parsing, even though there is no punctuation in automatic speech recognition (ASR) output, which removes many of the clues that help to determine sentence boundaries in printed text. Rather, we developed a technique to parse a window of words, successively sliding the window a word at a time over a whole speaker turn. A non-overlapping sequence of trees that covers the speaker turn is chosen to obtain full parses of ASR output. As a side effect of selecting full parses for a speaker turn, sentence boundaries are predicted. This new algorithm is described here.

In addition to describing these two algorithms, this paper overviews the task briefly, describes the system, and reports results from two evaluations performed under the auspices of NIST.

2. TASK

The ACE program uses the term "mention" for any text span that refers to an entity of one of the ACE target types. For example, in the phrase "Lincoln was 51 when he became president of the US", "Lincoln" is a name mention, "he" is a pronoun mention, and "president of the US" is a nominal (other noun phrase) mention. In the current specification for the ACE Entity Detection and Tracking (EDT) task, all mentions of an entity are to be collected within a document. The entity must be classified by type, i.e., person, organization, location, facility, or GPE (geo-political entity: country, state, province, or city). In addition to the "type" attribute, all names, if any, are reported as "name" attributes for the entity. Future versions of the task specification may include both additional types of entities and additional attributes for each entity, and will include tracking entities across documents, rather than merely within documents.

Proceedings of HLT 2001, First International Conference on Human Language Technology Research, J. Allan, ed., Morgan Kaufmann, San Francisco, 2001.

BAGHDAD, ███ (AP) _ ███'s deputy foreign minister attacked ███ National Security Advisor Sandy Berger Friday, accusing him of "lies and deception."

Riyadh al-Qaysi picked his way through Berger's press conference in Washington hours earlier, criticizing the security advisor's assertion that Iraq had been repeatedly in "material breach" of U.N. Security Council resolutions.

PERSON
• Iraq's deputy foreign minister Riyadh • al-Qaysi • his
• U.S. National Security Advisor Sandy Berger • him • Berger • the security advisor
ORGANIZATION
• AP
• U.N. Security Council
GEO-POLITICAL ENTITY
• BAGHDAD, Iraq
• Iraq • Iraq • Iraq
• U.S.
• Washington

Figure 1: Sample Text with EDT Entities and Mentions

Figure 1 shows a sample of text with the mentions of EDT entities highlighted, and a table showing the types of EDT entities and listing the different mentions for each.

3. BRIEF SYSTEM OVERVIEW

BBN's ACE system for the EDT task involves three primary components: name finding, parsing, and co-reference. The name finding component [1] provides some of the strongest clues for entity detection and tracking. The parsing component [2] determines the extent and head word of each mention, which is particularly useful for those noun phrases not headed by proper names. Both components are implemented as trained statistical models. The parsing model considers only parses that are consistent with the name boundaries already predicted by the name finding model.

There are co-reference components for names, for pronouns, and for other noun phrases. For names, the model decides for each name mention encountered whether it is more likely to be the first mention of a new entity or if it should be linked to a previous name mention of some existing entity. For pronouns, the model determines similarly for each pronoun mention which earlier mention (whether pronoun, name, or nominal) it should be linked to, or whether it should be left unlinked. The nominal co-

reference component performs two tasks for every noun phrase in the parse:

1. Determine what ACE class, if any, the noun phrase has.

2. Determine which previous entity the noun phrase refers to or that this is an entity not previously seen in the document.

BBN has statistical models for all of these tasks, though the nominal co-reference model was not ready in time for the formal evaluation in early November. The following section describes the pronoun co-reference model in more detail.

4. PRONOUN CO-REFERENCE MODEL

A statistical model is used to predict pronoun co-reference. Although the algorithm is designed to produce antecedents for all pronouns except expletives and those with implicit antecedents, our focus was on cases when the antecedent was an ACE mention. We could therefore focus on connecting the parse constituent corresponding to a pronoun either to an NP in a parse tree or else declaring the pronoun "unresolvable" when no such constituent node could be found. The pronoun resolution algorithm takes as input a parse tree where each constituent corresponding to a mention has been labeled with one of the EDT types (*Person, Organization, GPE, Location,* or *Facility*) and with the mention type (*Name* or *Descriptor*). Further, if the mention has already been found to be a member of a co-reference chain by the name or nominal co-reference components, the constituent node was also labeled with the ID of this chain.

Pronouns are processed in a depth-first traversal of the parse tree. For each pronoun, all earlier NP nodes in the document are considered as possible antecedents. Candidates are processed by walking backwards through the parse trees from the pronoun towards the beginning of the document (as proposed by Hobbs [3]). Each of these NPs and the "unresolvable" case are then scored using the following model, and the choice with the highest probability is selected.

The goal of the probabilistic model is choose the antecedent (*ant*) so as to maximize its probability given the pronoun (*pro*) and its surrounding environment (*env*). Using Bayes Rule to invert the probabilities and an independence assumption to separate the pronoun from its environment, this is approximately equivalent to the following expression:

$$P(ant \mid pro, env) \approx \frac{P(ant)P(pro \mid ant)P(env \mid ant)}{P(pro, env)}$$

Since the denominator is constant regardless of the choice of antecedent, we only need to maximize the following expression:

$$P(ant)P(pro \mid ant)P(env \mid ant)$$

As features to predict the probability of the possible antecedents, we use their *Type* (either one of the EDT types or *Undetermined* for non-mention candidates), their *Number* and *Gender*, and their *Distance*. The distance for an antecedent is computed by searching through the parse trees of the current and previous sentences in the order suggested by Hobbs [3], and counting the number of NP constituents between the pronoun and the antecedent. Making another independence assumption, the distance is also modeled separately from the type, number, and gender.

For example, in the following case:

… Mrs. Brown … < 7 other constituents > … She said …

the probability of the "Mrs. Brown" phrase being the antecedent is computed as follows:

$$P(ant) \approx P(person, singular, female) \, P(dist=7)$$

The probability of the pronoun itself is estimated as the probability of that particular word, conditioned on the type, number, and gender of the antecedent, in this case:

$$P(pro \mid ant) \approx P(\text{"she"} \mid person, singular, female)$$

As a feature for estimating the probability of the pronoun's environment, we used just the head word of the constituent that was the parent of the pronoun in the parse tree, conditioned on the type of the antecedent. In this example, that means:

$$P(env \mid ant) \approx P(\text{"said"} \mid person)$$

When the parent head word in the actual parse tree was an auxiliary verb, it was augmented by the main verb.

The training counts for each part of the model were taken from 300K words of Penn Treebank data that had been annotated for pronoun co-reference. The lexical model for the parent head word was smoothed by using the uniform distribution as a back-off.

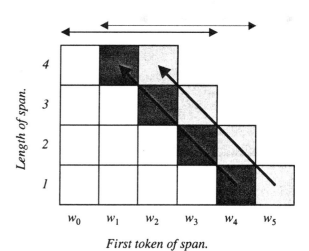

First token of span.

Figure 2: Windowing Parser, window_size=4

5. PARSING AUTOMATICALLY TRANSCRIBED SPEECH

For speech, in order to apply our system to ASR output, we modified the parser component to combine syntactic parsing and sentence-breaking functionality into a single module. Our primary goal in integrating these two processes was to avoid the serious parsing errors that could be caused by relying on a potentially errorful independent sentence-breaking mechanism. At the same time, we wanted as much as possible to maintain optimal parser accuracy.

For each speaker turn, we begin by providing the parser with a window of the first N words of text. The bottom-up, statistical parser is then called to construct a chart for that initial portion of the text, showing the syntactic constituents that can cover each span of words, along with their estimated probabilities. Some of those chart cells will typically contain "TOP" entries, the symbol used for separate utterances in the training data (which syntactically are often sentences, but can also be isolated noun phrases or the like).

The algorithm then shifts the chart window one word to the right, giving the parser words 2 through N+1, computing any new constituents that include the new word. The process of sliding the window over proceeds until the parser has processed the last N words of the speaker turn. The window size N defines the maximum number of tokens per constituent (and thus the maximum sentence length). This value is set at 30 in the current system. The final parse of the speaker turn is then formed by finding the sequence of sentence parses that exactly covers the full text with the best overall probability.

At the lowest levels, the windowing chart algorithm runs much the same as the original, updating chart entries from the same subordinate entries and according to identical statistical formulas. The differences lie in the "outer loops" of the algorithm.

1. First, rather than filling in the chart in the usual left-to-right, bottom-to-top order, we iterate over tokens, proceeding upward along the diagonal for each [see Figure 2].

112

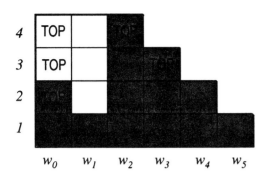

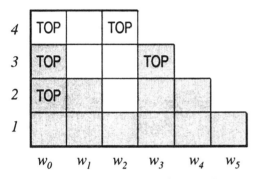

Figure 3: Alternate Possible Sentence Sequences

At each position, there are at most window_size possibilities to consider, working up the diagonal. If a TOP element is found along that diagonal in column k, the cost of the best path through that element is the cost of the element itself combined with the known cost of the best path up to column $k-1$. Once the optimal cost for a path through the entire speaker turn has been computed, the final constituent pointers can be traced back right-to-left to output the complete best path.

6. PERFORMANCE

Two ACE EDT evaluations were performed in 2000, with four participating sites submitting systems. Extensive graphs analyzing the combined results are available through the NIST Web site[1]. Table 1 shows the entity error rates from the second of these evaluations for BBN's system when run both on newswire texts and on the ASR output from broadcast news programs.

The scoring program searched for the mapping between the entities found by the system and those in the answer key that best aligned their mentions. Based on that mapping, answer key entities not found by the system were counted as misses, and system entities not in the answer key were counted as false alarms. Mapped entities to which the system had assigned the wrong type were counted as errors. The final column sums the three kinds of error.

These scores were state-of-the-art as of the November evaluation. Human performance based on limited studies of inter-annotator agreement is estimated at roughly 20% sum of errors.

2. We cap our chart at window_size rows, thereby constraining the sentence length and the required parse computation. Only window_size columns are active at a time, making it simple to visualize shifting the chart by one column per token iteration.

3. Unlike the standard parser, which at the end of each sentence only has to choose the best sentence (TOP) constituent from the upper-left-most chart entry, this algorithm needs to select a sequence of high probability sentence (TOP) constituents that together cover the entire speaker turn. We use a Viterbi search to determine the best path through this space of sentences.

At the end of processing a speaker turn, the algorithm must search back to identify the most likely sequence of TOP constituents that together cover all the words in the turn. For example, given the TOP constituents found in Figure 3, that six-word turn could be parsed as shown either as a two-word sentence followed by a four-word sentence, or as two three-word sentences. The four-word TOP constituent beginning at word 0 does not form an alternative path because no TOP constituent covers words 4 and 5. (In the actual system, there is a fall-back provision allowing any individual words to be treated as a TOP constituent. This ensures that some path can always be found, although an artificial probability cost is added for each word so treated that is high enough to force the system to prefer linking normal TOP constituents whenever possible.)

Using the Viterbi algorithm to efficiently search for the most likely sequence involves storing for each column the cost of the best path up to that point and a pointer to the final constituent along that best path. The search proceeds first from left to right.

Table 1: BBN Entity Detection Results

Entity Scores	Miss	False Alarm	Error	Sum of Errors
Newswire	28.2	24.9	8.3	61.4
Broadcast News ASR	38.9	28.6	6.4	73.9

7. REFERENCES

[1] Bikel, D., Schwartz, R., and Weischedel, R., "An Algorithm that Learns What's in a Name," Machine Learning 34 (1999), 211-231,

[2] Miller, S., Ramshaw, L., Fox, H., and Weischedel, R. "A Novel Use of Statistical Parsing to Extract Information from Text", In Proceedings of 1st Meeting of the North American Chapter of the ACL, (Seattle, WA, 2000), 226-233.

[3] Hobbs, J. R., "Resolving Pronoun References", reprinted in 1986 in Readings in Natural Language Processing, B. Grosz, K. Jones, and B. Webber, eds., Morgan Kaufmann, (1977)

---

[1]   http://www.itl.nist.gov/iad/894.01/tests/ace/phase1/work-shop.htm and ftp://jaguar.ncsl.nist.gov/ace/phase1/acekick/nist-2000-11-edt-results.pdf

Exploring Speech-Enabled Dialogue with the Galaxy Communicator Infrastructure

Samuel Bayer
The MITRE Corporation
202 Burlington Rd.
Bedford, MA 01730
sam@mitre.org

Christine Doran
The MITRE Corporation
202 Burlington Rd.
Bedford, MA 01730
cdoran@mitre.org

Bryan George
The MITRE Corporation
11493 Sunset Hills Rd.
Reston, VA 20190
bgeorge@mitre.org

ABSTRACT
This demonstration will motivate some of the significant properties of the Galaxy Communicator Software Infrastructure and show how they support the goals of the DARPA Communicator program.

Keywords
Spoken dialogue, speech interfaces

1. INTRODUCTION
The DARPA Communicator program [1], now in its second fiscal year, is intended to push the boundaries of speech-enabled dialogue systems by enabling a freer interchange between human and machine. A crucial enabling technology for the DARPA Communicator program is the Galaxy Communicator software infrastructure (GCSI), which provides a common software platform for dialogue system development. This infrastructure was initially designed and constructed by MIT [2], and is now maintained and enhanced by the MITRE Corporation. This demonstration will motivate some of the significant properties of this infrastructure and show how they support the goals of the DARPA Communicator program.

2. HIGHLIGHTED PROPERTIES
The GCSI is a distributed hub-and-spoke infrastructure which allows the programmer to develop Communicator-compliant servers in C, C++, Java, Python, or Allegro Common Lisp. This system is based on message passing rather than CORBA- or RPC-style APIs. The hub in this infrastructure supports routing of messages consisting of key-value pairs, but also supports logging and rule-based scripting. Such an infrastructure has the following desirable properties:

- The scripting capabilities of the hub allow the programmer to weave together servers which may not otherwise have been intended to work together, by rerouting messages and their responses and transforming their keys.

- The scripting capabilities of the hub allow the programmer to insert simple tools and filters to convert data among formats.

- The scripting capabilities of the hub make it easy to modify the message flow of control in real time.

- The scripting capabilities of the hub and the simplicity of message passing make it simple to build up systems bit by bit.

- The standard infrastructure allows the Communicator program to develop platform- and programming-language-independent service standards for recognition, synthesis, and other better-understood resources.

- The standard infrastructure allows members of the Communicator program to contribute generally useful tools to other program participants.

This demonstration will illustrate a number of these properties.

3. DEMO CONFIGURATION AND CONTENT
By way of illustration, this demo will simulate a process of assembling a Communicator-compliant system, while at the same time exemplifying some of the more powerful aspects of the infrastructure. The demonstration has three phases, representing three successively more complex configuration steps. We use a graphical display of the Communicator hub to make it easy to see the behavior of this system.

As you can see in Figure 1, the hub is connected to eight servers:

- MITRE's Java Desktop Audio Server (JDAS)
- MIT SUMMIT recognizer, using MIT's Mercury travel domain language model
- CMU Sphinx recognizer, with a Communicator-compliant wrapper written by the University of Colorado Center for Spoken Language Research (CSLR), using CSLR's travel domain language model
- A string conversion server, for managing incompatibilities between recognizer output and synthesizer input
- CSLR's concatenative Phrase TTS synthesizer, using their travel domain voice

Proceedings of HLT 2001, First International Conference on Human Language Technology Research, J. Allan, ed., Morgan Kaufmann, San Francisco, 2001.

- CMU/Edinburgh Festival synthesizer, with a Communicator-compliant wrapper written by CSLR, using CMU's travel domain language model for Festival's concatenative voice

- MIT TINA parser, using MIT's Mercury travel domain language model

- MIT Genesis paraphraser, using MIT's Mercury travel domain language model

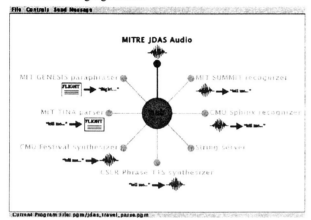

Figure 1: Initial demo configuration

We will use the flexibility of the GCSI, and the hub scripting language in particular, to change the path that messages follow among these servers.

3.1 Phase 1

In phase 1, we establish audio connectivity. JDAS is MITRE's contribution to the problem of reliable access to audio resources. It is based on JavaSound 1.0 (distributed with JDK 1.3), and supports barge-in. We show the capabilities of JDAS by having the system echo the speaker's input; we also demonstrate the barge-in capabilities of JDAS bye showing that the speaker can interrupt the playback with a new utterance/input. The goal in building JDAS is that anyone who has a desktop microphone and the Communicator infrastructure will be able to use this audio server to establish connectivity with any Communicator-compliant recognizer or synthesizer.

3.2 Changing the message path

The hub maintains a number of information states. The Communicator hub script which the developer writes can both access and update these information states, and we can invoke "programs" in the Communicator hub script by sending messages to the hub. This demonstration exploits this capability by using messages sent from the graphical display to change the path that messages follow, as illustrated in Figure 2. In phase 1, the hub script routed messages from JDAS back to JDAS (enabled by the message named "Echo"). In the next phase, we will change the path of messages from JDAS and send them to a speech recognizer.

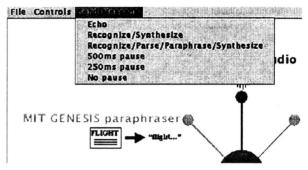

Figure 2: Modifying the hub information state

3.3 Phase 2

Now that we've established audio connectivity, we can add recognition and synthesis. In this configuration, we will route the output of the preferred recognizer to the preferred synthesizer. When we change the path through the hub script using the graphical display, the preferred servers are highlighted. Figure 3 shows that the initial configuration of phase 2 prefers SUMMIT and Festival.

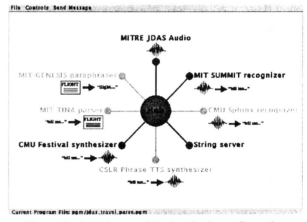

Figure 3: Initial recognition/synthesis configuration

The SUMMIT recognizer and the Festival synthesizer were not intended to work together; in fact, while there is a good deal of activity in the area of establishing data standards for various aspects of dialogue systems (cf. [3]), there are no programming-language-independent service definitions for speech. The hub scripting capability, however, allows these tools to be incorporated into the same configuration and to interact with each other. The remaining incompatibilities (for instance, the differences in markup between the recognizer output and the input the synthesizer expects) are addressed by the string server, which can intervene between the recognizer and synthesizer. So the GCSI makes it easy both to connect a variety of tools to the hub and make them interoperate, as well as to insert simple filters and processors to facilitate the interoperation.

In addition to being able to send general messages to the hub, the user can use the graphical display to send messages associated with particular servers. So we can change the preferred recognizer or synthesizer. (as shown in Figure 4), or change the Festival voice (as shown in Figure 5). All these messages are configurable from the hub script.

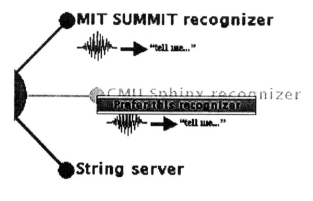

Figure 4: Preferring a recognizer

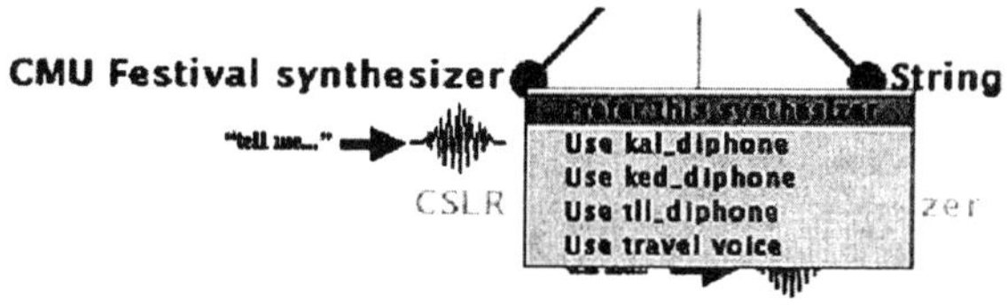

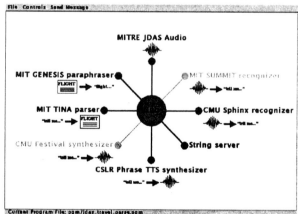

Figure 5: Changing the Festival voice

3.4 Phase 3

Now that we've established connectivity with recognition and synthesis, we can add parsing and generation (or, in this case, input paraphrase). Figure 6 illustrates the final configuration, after changing recognizer and synthesizer preferences. In this phase, the output of the recognizer is routed to the parser, which produces a structure which is then paraphrased and then sent to the synthesizer. So for instance, the user might say "I'd like to fly to Tacoma", and after parsing and paraphrase, the output from the synthesizer might be "A trip to Tacoma".

Figure 6: Adding parsing and paraphrase

4. CONCLUSION

The configuration at the end of phase 3 is obviously not a complete dialogue system; this configuration is missing context management and dialogue control, as well as an application backend, as illustrated by the remaining components in white in Figure 7. However, the purpose of the demonstration is to illustrate the ease of plug-and-play experiments within the GCSI, and the role of these capabilities to assemble and debug a complex Communicator interface. The GCSI is available under an open source license at http://fofoca.mitre.org/download.

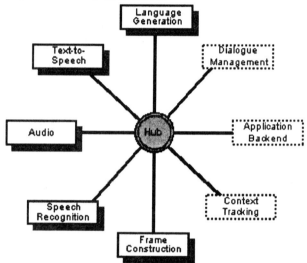

Figure 7: A sample full dialogue system configuration

5. ACKNOWLEDGMENTS

This work was funded by the DARPA Communicator program under contract number DAAB07-99-C201. © 2001 The MITRE Corporation. All rights reserved.

6. REFERENCES

[1] http://www.darpa.mil/ito/research/com/index.html.

[2] S. Seneff, E. Hurley, R. Lau, C. Pao, P. Schmid, and V. Zue. Galaxy-II: A Reference Architecture for Conversational System Development. Proc. ICSLP 98, Sydney, Australia, November 1998.

[3] "'Voice Browser' Activity." http://www.w3.org/Voice.

Facilitating Treebank Annotation Using a Statistical Parser

Fu-Dong Chiou, David Chiang, and Martha Palmer
Dept of Computer and Information Science
University of Pennsylvania
200 S 33rd Street, Philadelphia, PA 19104-6389
{chioufd,dchiang,mpalmer}@linc.cis.upenn.edu

1. INTRODUCTION

Corpora of phrase-structure-annotated text, or treebanks, are useful for supervised training of statistical models for natural language processing, as well as for corpus linguistics. Their primary drawback, however, is that they are very time-consuming to produce. To alleviate this problem, the standard approach is to make two passes over the text: first, parse the text automatically, then correct the parser output by hand.

In this paper we explore three questions:

- How much does an automatic first pass speed up annotation?

- Does this automatic first pass affect the reliability of the final product?

- What kind of parser is best suited for such an automatic first pass?

We investigate these questions by an experiment to augment the Penn Chinese Treebank [15] using a statistical parser developed by Chiang [3] for English. This experiment differs from previous efforts in two ways: first, we quantify the increase in annotation speed provided by the automatic first pass (70–100%); second, we use a parser developed on one language to augment a corpus in an unrelated language.

2. THE PARSER

The parsing model described by Chiang [3] is based on stochastic TAG [13, 14]. In this model a parse tree is built up out of tree fragments (called *elementary trees*), each of which contains exactly one lexical item (its *anchor*).

In the variant of TAG used here, there are three kinds of elementary trees: initial, (predicative) auxiliary, and modifier, and three corresponding composition operations: substitution, adjunction, and sister-adjunction. Figure 1 illustrates all three of these operations. The first two come from standard TAG [8]; the third is borrowed from D-tree grammar [11].

In a stochastic TAG derivation, each elementary tree is generated with a certain probability which depends on the elementary tree itself as well as the node it gets attached to. Since every tree is lexicalized, each of these probabilities involves a bilexical dependency, as in many recent statistical parsing models [9, 2, 4].

Since the number of parameters of a stochastic TAG is quite high, we do two things to make parameter estimation easier. First, we generate an elementary tree in two steps: the unlexicalized tree, then a lexical anchor. Second, we smooth the probability estimates of these two steps by backing off to reduced contexts.

When trained on about 80,000 words of the Penn Chinese Treebank and tested on about 10,000 words of unseen text, this model obtains 73.9% labeled precision and 72.2% labeled recall [1].

3. METHODOLOGY

For the present experiment the parsing model was trained on the entire treebank (99,720 words). We then prepared a new set of 20,202 segmented, POS-tagged words of Xinhua newswire text, which was blindly divided into 3 sets of equal size (±10 words).

Each set was then annotated in two or three passes, as summarized by the following table:

Set	Pass 1	Pass 2	Pass 3
1	—	Annotator A	Annotators A&B
2	parser	Annotator A	Annotators A&B
3	revised parser	Annotator A	Annotators A&B

Here "Annotators A&B" means that Annotator B checked the work of Annotator A, then for each point of disagreement, both annotators worked together to arrive at a consensus structure. "Parser" is Chiang's parser, adapted to parse Chinese text as described by Bikel and Chiang [1].

"Revised parser" is the same parser with additional modifications suggested by Annotator A after correcting Set 2. These revisions primarily resulted from a difference between the artificial evaluation metric used by Bikel and Chiang [1] and this real-world task. The metric used earlier, following common practice, did not take punctuation or empty elements into account, whereas the present task ideally requires that they be present and correctly placed. Thus following changes were made:

- The parser was originally trained on data with the punctuation marks moved, and did not bother to move the punctuation marks back. For Set 3 we simply removed the preprocessing phase which moved the punctuation marks.

- Similarly, the parser was trained on data which had all empty elements removed. In this case we simply applied a rule-based postprocessor which inserted null relative pronouns.

- Finally, the parser often produced an NP (or VP) which dominated only a single NP (respectively, VP), whereas such a

Proceedings of HLT 2001, First International Conference on Human Language Technology Research, J. Allan, ed., Morgan Kaufmann, San Francisco, 2001.

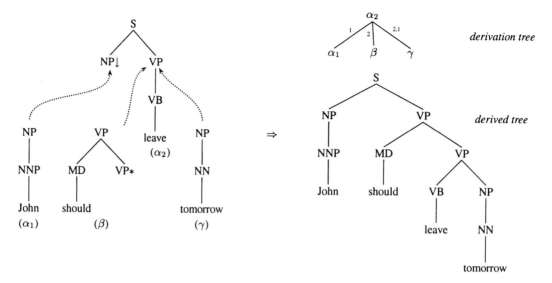

Figure 1: Grammar and derivation for "John should leave tomorrow." α_1 and α_2 **are initial trees,** β **is a (predicative) auxiliary tree,** γ **is a modifier tree.**

structure is not specified by the bracketing guidelines. Therefore we applied another rule-based postprocessor to remove these nodes. (This modification would have helped the original evaluation as well.)

In short, none of the modifications required major changes to the parser, but they did improve annotation speed significantly, as we will see below.

4. RESULTS

The annotation times and rates for Pass 2 are as follows:

Set	Pass 1	Time (Pass 2) (hours:min)	Rate (Pass 2) (words/hour)
1	—	28:01	240
2	parser	16:21	412
3	revised parser	14:06	478

The rate increase for Set 2 over Set 1 was about 70%; for Set 3 over Set 1, about double. Thus the time saved by the use of an automatic first pass is substantial.

Assessing the reliability of the final product is somewhat trickier.

Set	Pass 1	Accuracy (Pass 1) LP	LR	Accuracy (Pass 2) LP	LR
1	—	—	—	99.84	99.76
2	parser	76.73	75.36	99.76	99.65
3	revised parser	82.87	81.42	99.81	99.26

where LP stands for labeled precision and LR stands for labeled recall. The third column reports the accuracy of Pass 1 (the parser) using the results of Pass 2 (Annotator A) as a gold standard. The fourth column reports the accuracy of Pass 2 (Annotator A) using the results of Pass 3 (Annotators A&B) as a gold standard.

We note several points:

- There is no indication that the addition of an automatic first pass affected the accuracy of Pass 2. On the other hand, the near-perfect reported accuracy of Pass 2 suggests that in fact each pass biased subsequent passes substantially. We need a more objective measure of reliability, which we leave for future experiments.

- The parser revisions significantly improved the accuracy of the parser with respect to the present metric (which is sensitive to punctuation and empty elements). On Set 2 the revised parser obtained 78.98/77.39% labeled precision/recall, an error reduction of about 9%.

- Not surprisingly, errors due to large-scale structural ambiguities were the most time-consuming to correct by hand. To take an extreme example, one parse produced by the parser is shown in Figure 2. It often matches the correct parse (shown in Figure 3) at the lowest levels but the large-scale errors require the annotator to make many corrections.

5. DISCUSSION

In summary, although Chiang's parser was not specifically designed for Chinese, and trained on a moderate amount of data (less than 100,000 words), the parses it provided were reliable enough that the annotation rate was effectively doubled.

Now we turn to our third question: what kind of parser is most suitable for an automatic first pass? Marcus et al. [10] describe the use of the deterministic parser Fidditch [6] as an automatic first pass for the Penn (English) Treebank. They cite two features of this parser as strengths:

1. It only produces a single parse per sentence, so that the annotator does not have to search through many parses.

2. It produces reliable partial parses, and leaves uncertain structures unspecified.

The Penn-Helsinki Parsed Corpus of Middle English was constructed using a statistical parser developed by Collins [4] as an automatic first pass. This parser, as well as Chiang's, retains the first advantage but not the second. However, we suggest two ways a statistical parser might be used to speed annotation further:

First, the parser can be made more useful to the annotator. A statistical parser typically produces a single parse, but can also (with little additional computation) produce multiple parses. Ratnaparkhi [12] has found that choosing (by oracle) the best parse out of the 20 highest-ranked parses boosts labeled recall and precision

118

```
(IP (NP (DP (DT 这些))                                              these
        (NP (NN 企业)))                                            businesses
    (VP (VP (ADVP (AD 还))                                         also
            (VP (BA 把)                                            BA
                (IP (NP (QP (CD 三点六万)                           36,000
                            (CLP (M 项)))                          item
                        (CP (WHNP (-NONE- *OP*))
                            (CP (IP (VP (VV 拥有)                   possess
                                        (NP (NN 自主)              to be one's own master
                                            (NN 知识)              knowledge
                                            (NN 产权))))           property rights
                                (DEC 的)))                         DE
                        (NP (NN 技术)))                            technologies
                    (VP (PP (P 向)                                 toward
                            (NP (DP (DT 其它))                     other
                                (NP (NN 企业)                      businesses
                                    (PU 、)
                                    (NN 机构))))                   organizations
                        (VP (VV 转移))))))                         transfer
        (CC 和)                                                    and
        (VP (VV 扩散)                                              spread
            (IP (VP (PU ，)
                    (VP (VV 创造)                                  create
                        (NP (NN 收入))                             income
                        (QP (CD 四十四点三亿)                       4.43 billion
                            (CLP (M 元)))))))))                    RMB
    (PU 。))
```

Figure 2: Parser output. Translation: "These businesses also transfer and spread the intellectual property rights of 36,000 technologies to other businesses and organizations, creating an income of 4.43 billion RMB."

```
(IP (NP-SBJ (DP (DT 这些))                                         these
            (NP (NN 企业)))                                        businesses
    (VP (ADVP (AD 还))                                             also
        (VP (VP (BA 把)                                            BA
                (IP-OBJ (NP-SBJ (QP (CD 三点六万)                   36,000
                                    (CLP (M 项)))                  item
                        (CP (WHNP-1 (-NONE- *OP*))
                            (CP (IP (NP-SBJ (-NONE- *T*-1))
                                    (VP (VV 拥有)                  possess
                                        (NP-OBJ (NN 自主)          to be one's own master
                                                (NN 知识)          knowledge
                                                (NN 产权)))        property rights
                                (DEC 的)))                         DE
                        (NP (NN 技术)))                            technologies
                    (VP (PP-DIR (P 向)                             toward
                            (NP (DP (DT 其它))                     other
                                (NP (NN 企业)                      businesses
                                    (PU 、)
                                    (NN 机构))))                   organizations
                        (VP (VP (VV 转移))                         transfer
                            (CC 和)                                and
                            (VP (VV 扩散))))))                     spread
            (PU ，)
            (VP (VV 创造)                                          create
                (NP-OBJ (NN 收入))                                 income
                (QP-EXT (CD 四十四点三亿)                           4.43 billion
                        (CLP (M 元)))))))                          RMB
    (PU 。))
```

Figure 3: Corrected parse for sentence of Figure 2.

119

from about 87% to about 93%. This suggests that if the annotator had access to several of the highest-ranked parses, he or she could save time by choosing the parse with the best gross structure and making small-scale corrections.

Would such a change defeat the first advantage above by forcing the annotator to search through multiple parses? No, because the parses produced by a statistical parser are ranked. The additional lower-ranked parses can only be of benefit to the annotator. Indeed, because the chart contains information about the certainty of each subparse, a statistical parser might regain the second advantage as well, provided this information can be suitably presented.

Second, the annotator can be made more useful to the parser by means of *active learning* or *sample selection* [5, 7]. (We are assuming now that the parser and annotator will take turns in a train-parse-correct cycle, as opposed to a simple two-pass scheme.) The idea behind sample selection is that some sentences are more informative for training a statistical model than others; therefore, if we have some way of automatically guessing which sentences are more informative, these sentences are the ones we should hand-correct first. Thus the parser's accuracy will increase more quickly, potentially requiring the annotator to make fewer corrections overall.

6. ACKNOWLEDGMENTS

We would like to thank Fei Xia, Mitch Marcus, Aravind Joshi, Mary Ellen Okurowski and John Kovarik for their helpful comments on the design of the evaluation, Beth Randall for her postprocessing and error-checking code, and Nianwen Xue for serving as "Annotator B." This research was funded by DARPA N66001-00-1-8915, DOD MDA904-97-C-0307, and NSF SBR-89-20230-15.

7. REFERENCES

[1] Daniel M. Bikel and David Chiang. Two statistical parsing models applied to the Chinese Treebank. In *Proceedings of the Second Chinese Language Processing Workshop*, pages 1–6, 2000.

[2] Eugene Charniak. Statistical parsing with a context-free grammar and word statistics. In *Proceedings of the Fourteenth National Conference on Artificial Intelligence (AAAI-97)*, pages 598–603. AAAI Press/MIT Press, 1997.

[3] David Chiang. Statistical parsing with an automatically-extracted tree adjoining grammar. In *Proceedings of the 38th Annual Meeting of the Assocation for Computational Linguistics*, pages 456–463, Hong Kong, 2000.

[4] Michael Collins. Three generative lexicalised models for statistical parsing. In *Proceedings of the 35th Annual Meeting of the Assocation for Computational Linguistics (ACL-EACL '97)*, pages 16–23, Madrid, 1997.

[5] Ido Dagan and Sean P. Engelson. Committee-based sampling for training probabilistic classifiers. In *Proceedings of the Twelfth International Conference on Machine Learning*, pages 150–157. Morgan Kaufmann, 1995.

[6] Donald Hindle. Acquiring disambiguation rules from text. In *Proceedings of the 27th Annual Meeting of the Association for Computational Linguistics*, 1989.

[7] Rebecca Hwa. Sample selection for statistical grammar induction. In *Proceedings of EMNLP/VLC-2000*, pages 45–52, Hong Kong, 2000.

[8] Aravind K. Joshi and Yves Schabes. Tree-adjoining grammars. In Grzegorz Rosenberg and Arto Salomaa, editors, *Handbook of Formal Languages and Automata*, volume 3, pages 69–124. Springer-Verlag, Heidelberg, 1997.

[9] David M. Magerman. Statistical decision-tree models for parsing. In *Proceedings of the 33rd Annual Meeting of the Assocation for Computational Linguistics*, pages 276–283, Cambridge, MA, 1995.

[10] Mitchell P. Marcus, Beatrice Santorini, and Mary Ann Marcinkiewicz. Building a large annotated corpus of English: the Penn Treebank. *Computational Linguistics*, 19:313–330, 1993.

[11] Owen Rambow, K. Vijay-Shanker, and David Weir. D-tree grammars. In *Proceedings of the 33rd Annual Meeting of the Association for Computational Linguistics*, pages 151–158, Cambridge, MA, 1995.

[12] Adwait Ratnaparkhi. *Maximum entropy models for natural language ambiguity resolution*. PhD thesis, University of Pennsylvania, 1998.

[13] Philip Resnik. Probabilistic tree-adjoining grammar as a framework for statistical natural language processing. In *Proceedings of the Fourteenth International Conference on Computational Linguistics (COLING-92)*, pages 418–424, Nantes, 1992.

[14] Yves Schabes. Stochastic lexicalized tree-adjoining grammars. In *Proceedings of the Fourteenth International Conference on Computational Linguistics (COLING-92)*, pages 426–432, Nantes, 1992.

[15] Fei Xia, Martha Palmer, Nianwen Xue, Mary Ellen Okurowski, John Kovarik, Fu-Dong Chiou, Shizhe Huang, Tony Kroch, and Mitch Marcus. Developing guidelines and ensuring consistency for Chinese text annotation. In *Proceedings of the Second International Conference on Language Resources and Evaluation (LREC-2000)*, Athens, Greece, 2000.

FactBrowser Demonstration

Scott Miller, Sergey Bratus, Lance Ramshaw, Ralph Weischedel, and Alex Zamanian
BBN Technologies
70 Fawcett St
Cambridge, MA 02138
1-617-873-2078

{szmiller, sbratus, lramshaw, weischedel, azamanian}@bbn.com

ABSTRACT

The FactBrowser demonstration illustrates automatic database update from live feeds based on information extraction from text and the ability to browse the resulting database for unexpected connections. The technology used has four interesting features:

1. The demonstration employs a **light architecture** based on the Web; using an XML-based client-server architecture, the graphical user interface requires only Internet Explorer 5.0 or higher. No application code resides on the client.

2. A **permanent database** grows based on cross-document entity tracking and accumulating facts.

3. The database is **updated daily** based on automatic processing of documents distributed by the Foreign Broadcasting Information Service (FBIS). Document capture and database update are fully automatic, requiring no human intervention.

4. The following key components: name finding, parsing, and pronoun resolution are all based on the trained, language-independent **statistical modeling techniques**.

The strategic focus throughout the design of FactBrowser has been on producing high precision output so as to maintain quality in the data base.

1. INTRODUCTION

FactBrowser analyzes a daily stream of world news documents, extracting information about entities and relations between them. Extracted information is stored in a database and viewable through tables that list all entities and all the relations found in the collection. The types of entities currently extracted are *Person*, *Organization*, and *Location*. For each entity, the table lists both

Proceedings of HLT 2001, First International Conference on Human Language Technology Research, J. Allan, ed., Morgan Kaufmann, San Francisco, 2001.

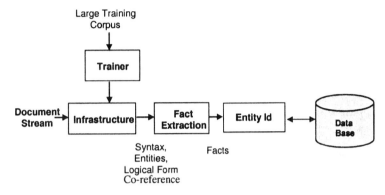

Figure 1: Information Extraction System Structure

the type and the different names and descriptions of that entity, allowing the user also to display every mention of an entity in their source document context. The system currently tracks three relations:

OfficeHolder, i.e., who plays what role in what organization

OrganizationAt, i.e., where an organization is located

Attribution, i.e., who is quoted as saying what.

In addition to automatic updating of the database daily, a browser interface enables exploring the database. By following threads across the fact and entity tables, the user can determine, for example, other people who work at the same organization as a given speaker. FactBrowser produces versions of the documents annotated with the results of the analysis, including a full syntactic parse of the text with additional semantic information like name types and descriptor co-reference links attached to the appropriate parse tree nodes.

The extraction system consists of three subsystems, as illustrated in Figure 1.

2. DOCUMENT LEVEL ENTITY EXTRACTION

The bulk of the analysis for each document can be done independently of other documents in the collection and so can be easily parallelized. The path of a document through this stage of processing is as follows:

Loading: A document is loaded, sentence-broken, and tokenized (in the style of the UPenn Treebank). If the input document contains section, paragraph, or topic markup, this markup is preserved.

Name finding: BBN's IdentiFinder™ (Bikel et al., 1999), a statistical name finder, is used to mark name mentions of the three semantic types. These mentions, marked as spans of tokens, are called *base name mentions.*

Parsing: Constrained syntactic parsing is performed, using a lexicalized probabilistic context free grammar (Miller, et al., 2000). BBN's statistical parser is trained on the UPenn Treebank and run in a constrained mode that ensures that the constituent brackets that it identifies will not conflict with the base name mentions previously found by IdentiFinder.

Parse merging: The name information from IdentiFinder is merged into the syntactic parses, which sometimes involves inserting additional nodes into the parse tree. Since the parser follows Treebank style, it produces relatively flat parses for NPs. For example, a name with premodifiers like "small town America" would parse as a single, three-element node. In such cases, the system introduces a new node covering just the name portion. Futhermore, if the name is that of a *Person* and the premodifiers include what appears to be a title, as in "Microsoft President Bill Gates", the system also introduces an NP node over the title, making it available for descriptor finding in the next stage.

Descriptor finding: A statistical model classifies the NP-type nodes in the parse trees, in order to identify those that are probable descriptors of persons or organizations. The model is based on the head word of the NP, the head word of its parent constituent, and any left modifier. The model is trained on newswire data in which the descriptor types were marked by hand. The resulting descriptors are referred to as *base descriptor mentions* and are appropriately labeled in the parse.

Structured mention analysis: Some local co-references between the base name and a description can be recognized with high reliability. For example, NPs that contain appositives or that contain a base name mention with a post-modifying clause are marked at this stage as *structured mentions*, and the name co-referenced with the description.

Document-level name co-reference: The system finds non-local co-reference relations between the name mentions in the document. Rules specific to the name's type are used to generate a list of possible alternate or abbreviated forms for each name. For example, the person name "John Smith" would generate the alternate forms "Smith" and "Mr. Smith", while the company name "Smith Enterprises" would generate "Smith Enterprises, Inc." and "SE". Any of those alternate forms that occur elsewhere in the document are then linked together with the source name.

Pronoun resolution: A generative statistical model resolves pronouns. The estimated probability of a link between the pronoun and its antecedent relies on features like number, gender (determined by heuristics), and a distance measure based on the Hobbs [1977] tree search that outlines the order in which NP-type nodes are considered as possible antecedents for a pronoun.

Entity creation: Sets of co-referring mentions (names, locally-linked descriptors, and pronouns) are *entities*, and the corresponding metadata for each entity is added to the document.

3. FACT/RELATIONSHIP EXTRACTION

The FactBrowser demonstration system extracts three types of relations: 1) person has role in organization, 2) organization is located in place, and 3) statement is attributed to person. To maintain database integrity, the system is intentionally biased toward high precision, at the cost of some recall.

Relations are identified by recognizing syntactic patterns in parse trees produced by the statistical parsing component. The entities mentioned in the relations are resolved to underlying database entries by the name co-reference and pronoun resolution components. Thus, pronominal mentions and shortened versions of names are resolved to the most descriptive known strings for those entities.

Fact/relationship extraction is the final stage in document level processing. Once complete, the system has marked the entities that the document is about, the places in the document where each entity is mentioned, and the relations in which they are said to participate.

4. COLLECTION LEVEL PROCESSING (CROSSDOC)

The third component connects the entities found in document-level processing with entities previously encountered in other documents. This stage is less amenable to parallelization, and requires growing resources as the collection size grows.

In the current system, only the simplest heuristic is implemented. The connection between a document-level entity and a *global entity* is established on the basis of *canonical name mentions*. For each document-level entity, a *canonical name mention* is constructed from the tokens of the mentions in its mention set. This process includes removal of all punctuation, case normalization, and removal of any parenthesized groups of tokens. After such processing, the longest base name mention is chosen as the canonical one to represent the document-level entity. A database query using this canonical name as a key then returns all records from the global database that may match the entity. Finally, a decision is made as to whether the document-level entity matches one of these records, in which case its mentions join that record, and that database record is updated. If none of the existing database records match, a new record is created and introduced, based solely on the mentions of the document-level entity.

After the cross-document stage, each mention in the processed document text is marked with its global co-reference information, which can then be used for generating cross-linked views.

5. VISUAL DISPLAY

The FactBrowser interface displays tables of entities (people or organizations) and of facts. The entry for each entity points to all of the locations in each of the documents where that entity was mentioned, and the system can display the source text surrounding any of the mentions.

FactBrowser thus enables database level, rather than sentence level, analysis. In Figure 2, for example, although the sentence identifies Bangaru Laxman as the chief of "BJP", the spreadsheet view correctly shows Laxman as head of the Bharatiya Janata Party. (The longest name, or the longest description, if the entity has no name in the data base, is used for display in the spreadsheet browser.)

6. CONCLUSIONS

This effort is still in its early stages. Much has been learned from transitioning from processing a file of data as an experiment to processing documents as a continuous stream, from assimilating information across documents, from updating an existing data base of entities, and from the challenge of maintaining a 24 by 7 portal into the data. Yet there is much to be done. The fundamental challenges still remain: significantly reducing the error in extracted data (reducing both missed data and incorrectly extracted data), improving cross-document correlation of both entities and facts, and massively reducing the amount of training data required to achieve high performance.

7. ACKNOWLEDGEMENTS

The work reported here was supported in part by the Defense Advanced Research Projects Agency under contract numbers N66001-99-D-8615 and N66001-00-C8008. The views and conclusions contained in this document are those of the authors and should not be interpreted as necessarily representing the official policies, either expressed or implied, of the Defense Advanced Research Projects Agency or the United States Government.

8. REFERENCES

[1] Bikel, D., Schwartz, R., and Weischedel, R. "An Algorithm that Learns What's in a Name," Machine Learning 34 (1999), 211-231.

[2] Miller, S., Ramshaw, L., Fox, H., and Weischedel, R. "A Novel Use of Statistical Parsing to Extract Information from Text", In Proceedings of 1st Meeting of the North American Chapter of the ACL, (Seattle, WA, 2000), 226-233.

[3] Hobbs, J. R., "Resolving Pronoun References", reprinted in 1986 in Readings in Natural Language Processing, B. Grosz, K. Jones, and B. Webber, eds., Morgan Kaufmann, (1977).

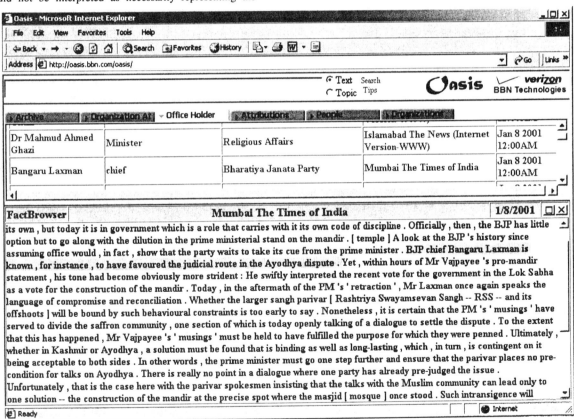

Figure 2: Screen shot illustrating demonstration

Finding Errors Automatically in Semantically Tagged Dialogues

John Aberdeen, Christine Doran, Laurie Damianos,
Samuel Bayer and Lynette Hirschman
The MITRE Corporation
202 Burlington Road
Bedford, MA 01730 USA
+1.781.271.2000

{aberdeen,cdoran,laurie,sam,lynette}@mitre.org

ABSTRACT

We describe a novel method for detecting errors in task-based human-computer (HC) dialogues by automatically deriving them from semantic tags. We examined 27 HC dialogues from the DARPA Communicator air travel domain, comparing user inputs to system responses to look for slot value discrepancies, both automatically and manually. For the automatic method, we labeled the dialogues with semantic tags corresponding to "slots" that would be filled in "frames" in the course of the travel task. We then applied an automatic algorithm to detect errors in the dialogues. The same dialogues were also manually tagged (by a different annotator) to label errors directly. An analysis of the results of the two tagging methods indicates that it may be possible to detect errors automatically in this way, but our method needs further work to reduce the number of false errors detected. Finally, we present a discussion of the differing results from the two tagging methods.

Keywords

Dialogue, Error detection, DARPA Communicator.

1. INTRODUCTION

In studying the contrasts between human-computer (HC) and human-human (HH) dialogues [1] it is clear that many HC dialogues are plagued by disruptive errors that are rarely seen in HH dialogues. A comparison of HC and HH dialogues may help us understand such errors. Conversely, the ability to detect errors in dialogues is critical to understanding the differences between HC and HH communication. Understanding HC errors is also crucial to improving HC interaction, making it more robust, trustworthy and efficient.

The goal of the work described in this paper is to provide an annotation scheme that allows automatic calculation of misunderstandings and repairs, based on semantic information presented at each turn. If we represent a dialogue as a sequence of pairs of partially-filled semantic frames (one for the user's

utterances, and one for the user's view of the system state), we can annotate the accumulation and revision of information in the paired frames. We hypothesized that, with such a representation, it would be straightforward to detect when the two views of the dialogue differ (a misunderstanding), where the difference originated (source of error), and when the two views reconverge (correction). This would be beneficial because semantic annotation often is used for independent reasons, such as measurements of concepts per turn [8], information bit rate [9], and currently active concepts [10]. Given this, if our hypothesis is correct, then by viewing semantic annotation as a representation of filling slots in user and system frames, it should be possible to detect errors automatically with little or no additional annotation.

2. SEMANTIC TAGGING

We tagged 27 dialogues from 4 different systems that participated in a data collection conducted by the DARPA Communicator program in the summer of 2000. These are dialogues between paid subjects and spoken language dialogue systems operating in the air travel domain. Each dialogue was labeled with semantic tags by one annotator. We focused on just the surface information available in the dialogues, to minimize inferences made by the annotator.

The semantic tags may be described along two basic dimensions: slot and type. The slot dimension describes the items in a semantic frame that are filled over the course of a dialogue, such as DEPART_CITY and AIRLINE (see Table 1 for the complete list).

The type dimension describes whether the tag is a PROMPT, a FILL, or an OFFER. This type dimension is critical to semantic analysis since it allows one to describe the effect a tag has on slots in the frame. PROMPTs are attempts to gather values to fill slots, e.g., "what city do you want to fly to". FILLs are actual slot fills, e.g., "I'd like to fly to San Francisco". OFFERs represent actual flight information based on previous slot FILLs, e.g., "there is a 9:45 flight to San Francisco on Delta". However, OFFERs often do not exactly match slot FILLs (e.g., the user requests a flight at 9:30, but the closest match flight is at 9:45), and thus must be distinguished from FILLs.

In addition to the two basic dimensions of slot and type, each tag takes a leg attribute to indicate which leg of a trip is being discussed. There is also an initial USER_ID slot which has two types (PROMPT_USER_ID and FILL_USER_ID), but no leg attribute.

Proceedings of HLT 2001, First International Conference on Human Language Technology Research, J. Allan, ed., Morgan Kaufmann, San Francisco, 2001.

124

Figure 1. Portion of a Sample Dialogue Labeled with Semantic Tags

S0: System said: Welcome to our travel planning system.

    <prompt_user_id>Please say your PIN number**</prompt_user_id>**.

U1: User said: My PIN is **<fill_user_id>**four four four four**</fill_user_id>**.

S2: System said: What are your travel plans?

U3: User said: I want to go to **<fill_arrive_city leg="1">**San Francisco**</fill_arrive_city>**.

S4: System said: Traveling to **<fill_arrive_city leg="1">**San Francisco**</fill_arrive_city>**.

    <prompt_depart_city leg="1">Where are you departing from?**</prompt_depart_city>**

U5: User said: **<fill_depart_city leg="1">**Boston**</fill_depart_city>**.

S6: System said: **<prompt_date leg="1">**When would you like to leave**</prompt_date>**

    <fill_depart_city leg="1">Boston**</fill_depart_city>**?

U7: User said: **<fill_date leg="1">**July twenty-fifth**</fill_date>** at

    <fill_depart_time leg="1">12 noon**</fill_depart_time>**.

S8: System said: I have a **<offer_airline leg="1">**Delta**</offer_airline>** flight that leaves

    <offer_depart_city leg="1">Boston**</offer_depart_city>** at

    <offer_depart_time leg="1">11:10AM**</offer_depart_time>** on

    <offer_date leg="1">July twenty-fifth**</offer_date>** and arrives in

    <offer_arrive_city leg="1">San Francisco**</offer_arrive_city>** at

    <offer_arrive_time>5:19PM**</offer_arrive_time>**. Is that OK?

Our semantic tag set also includes two special tags, YES and NO, for annotating responses to offers and yes/no questions. Finally, we have two tags, PROMPT_ERASE_ FRAMES and FILL_ERASE_FRAMES, for annotating situations where the frames are erased and the dialogue is restarted (e.g., the user says "start over"). Figure 1 shows part of a sample dialogue with semantic tags. Our semantic tagset is summarized in Table 1.

Table 1. Semantic Tagset

	PROMPT	FILL	OFFER
DEPART_CITY	X	X	X
ARRIVE_CITY	X	X	X
DEPART_AIRPORT	X	X	X
ARRIVE_AIRPORT	X	X	X
DATE	X	X	X
DEPART_TIME	X	X	X
ARRIVE_TIME	X	X	X
AIRLINE	X	X	X
USER_ID	X	X	
ERASE_FRAMES	X	X	
YES	(single bare tag)		
NO	(single bare tag)		

3. ERROR DETECTION

To provide a baseline for comparison to an algorithm that detects errors automatically, we had an annotator (not the same person who did the semantic tagging described above) manually tag the problem areas. This annotator marked four items:

(1) occurrence: where the problem first occurs in the dialogue (e.g. where the user says the item which the system later incorporates incorrectly)

(2) detection: where the user could first be aware that there is a problem (e.g. where the system reveals its mistake)

(3) correction attempt: where the user attempts to repair the error

(4) correction detection: where the user is first able to detect that the repair has succeeded

We next developed an algorithm for automatically finding errors in our semantically tagged dialogues. In this phase of the research, we concentrated on deriving an automatic method for assigning the first two of the four error categories, occurrence and detection (in a later phase we plan to develop automatic methods for correction attempt and correction detection). First, the algorithm derives the turn-by-turn frame states for both the user's utterances and the system's utterances (i.e., what the user heard the system say), paying special attention to confirmation tags such as YES or deletion tags like FILL_ERASE_FRAMES. Then, the algorithm compares patterns of user and system events to hypothesize errors. Occurences and detections are hypothesized for three types of errors: hallucinations (system slot fill without user slot fill), mismatches (system slot fill does not match user slot fill), and prompts after fills (system prompt after user slot fill).

Figure 2 shows a sample dialogue that illustrates several error types. Utterance S12 shows a prompt after fill error – the user has already supplied (in utterance U11) the information the system is requesting. In utterance U13 the user supplies contradictory information, and the system catches this and tries to resolve it in utterances S14 and S16. Next a mismatch error is illustrated – the user specifies ARRIVE_CITY in utterance U17, and the system shows that it has misrecognized it in utterance S18. The user attempts to correct this misrecognition in utterance U21, and as can be seen from utterance S22, the system again has misrecognized the user's utterance.

Below we describe the results from running the automatic algorithm on our 27 semantically tagged dialogues.

4. RESULTS

In the 27 dialogues considered, a total of 131 items were flagged by one or both of the methods as error items (60 occur, 71 detect). A breakdown of these errors and which method found them is in Table 2.

Table 2. Unique Errors Identified

# errors found by:	Occur	Detect	Total
Both Methods	14	23	37
Automatic Only	28	38	66
Manual Only	18	10	28
Totals	60	71	131

As can be seen in Table 2 the automatic method flagged many more items as errors than the manual method.

Table 3. Error Judgements

	Occur			Detect		
	E	NE	Q	E	NE	Q
Auto	48%	40%	12%	52%	38%	10%
Man	84%	13%	3%	82%	15%	3%

We carefully examined each of the items flagged as errors by the two methods. Three judges (the semantic tagging annotator, the manual error tagging annotator, and a third person who did not participate in the annotation) determined which of the errors found by each of the two methods were real errors (E), not real errors (NE), or questionable (Q). For calculations in the present analysis, we used E as the baseline of real errors, rather than E+Q. Table 3 shows the judgements made for both the automatic and manual method, which are discussed in the next section. It is important to note that human annotators do not perform this task perfectly, with error rates of 13% and 15%. This is also shown in the precision and recall numbers for the two methods in Table 4.

Table 4. Precision & Recall

Precision & Recall	Occur		Detect	
	P	R	P	R
Automatic	0.48	0.57	0.52	0.84
Manual	0.84	0.77	0.82	0.71

5. ANALYSIS

The automatic method flagged 40 items as errors that the judges determined were not errors (17 occur, 23 detect). These 40 false errors can be classified as follows:

A. 10 were due to bugs in the algorithm or source data

B. 19 were false errors that can be eliminated with non-trivial changes to the semantic tagset and/or algorithm

C. 3 were false errors that could not be eliminated without the ability to make inferences about world knowledge

D. 8 were due to mistakes made by the semantic annotator

One example of the 19 false errors above in B is when the first user utterance in a dialogue is a bare location, it is unclear whether the user intends it to be a departure or arrival location. Our semantic tagset currently has no tags for ambiguous situations such as these. Adding underspecified tags to our tagset (and updating the automatic algorithm appropriately) would solve this problem. Another example is a situation where a system was legitimately asking for clarification about a slot fill, but the algorithm flagged it as prompting for keys that had already been filled. This could be fixed by adding a CLARIFY element to the type dimension (currently PROMPT, FILL, and OFFER). We believe that making these changes would not compromise the generality of our semantic tagset. However, as the point of our approach is to derive errors without much additional annotation, additions to the semantic tagset should only be made when there is substantial justification.

There were also 21 errors (15 occur, 6 detect) that were not detected by the automatic method, but were judged as real errors. These 21 errors may be categorized as follows:

A. 2 were due to bugs in the algorithm

B. 8 were situations where the algorithm correctly flagged the detect point of an error, but missed the associated occur point

C. 6 were situations that could be fixed by modifications to the semantic tagset

D. 1 was an error that could be fixed either by a revision to the semantic tagset or a revision to the algorithm

E. 2 were situations where the system ignored a user fill, and the automatic algorithm interpreted it as no confirmation (not an error). Human judgement is required to detect these errors

F. 2 were due to mistakes made by the semantic annotator

6. PREVIOUS WORK

In Hirschman & Pao [5], annotation was done by manual inspection of the exchanges in the dialogue. Each exchange was evaluated based on the portion of information "visible to the other party". Errors and problems were identified manually

> **Figure 2. Portion of a Sample Dialogue Illustrating Several Errors**
>
> U11: User said: I want to fly from **<fill_depart_city leg="1">**Seattle**</fill_depart_city>** to
> **<fill_arrive_city leg="1">**Tokyo**</fill_arrive_city>**
>
> S12: System said: **<prompt_arrive_city leg="1">**to which city would you like to fly**</prompt_arrive_city>**
> from **<fill_depart_city leg="1">**seattle**</fill_depart_city>**
>
> U13: User said: **<fill_arrive_city leg="1">**seattle washington**</fill_arrive_city>**
>
> S14: System said: excuse me, i didn't hear you well. I think you want to fly from
> **<fill_depart_city leg="1">**seattle**</fill_depart_city>** If this is okay, let's continue. Otherwise,
> please specify the locations again.
>
> U15: User said: **<yes>**that's okay**</yes>**
>
> S16: System said: **<prompt_arrive_city leg="1">**what city would you like to fly to?**</prompt_arrive_city>**
>
> U17: User said: **<fill_arrive_city leg="1">**tokyo japan**</fill_arrive_city>**
>
> S18: System said: flying to **<fill_arrive_city leg="1">**togiak**</fill_arrive_city>**
> **<prompt_date leg="1">**on what date?**</prompt_date>**
>
> U19: User said: **<fill_date leg="1">**monday September twenty fifth**</fill_date>**
>
> S20: System said: there don't seem to be any flights **from <fill_depart_city leg="1">**seattle**</fill_depart_city>**
> to **<fill_arrive_city leg="1">**togiak**</fill_arrive_city>** which depart
> **<fill_depart_time leg="1">**about ten PM**</fill_depart_time>** on
> **<fill_date leg="1">**september twenty fifth**</fill_date>**.
>
> U21: User said: destination **<fill_arrive_city leg="1">**tokyo japan**</fill_arrive_city>**
>
> S22: System said: did you say you want to fly to
> **<prompt_arrive_city leg="1">**san diego**</prompt_arrive_city>**?

and traced back to their point of origin. This is quite similar to our baseline manual annotation described in section 3.

There have been other approaches to detecting and characterizing errors in HC dialogues. Danieli [2] used expectations to model future user utterances, and Levow [6][7] used utterance and pause duration, as well as pitch variability to characterize errors and corrections. Dybkjær, Bernsen & Dybkjær [4] developed a set of principles of cooperative HC dialogue, as well as a taxonomy of errors typed according to which of the principles are violated. Finally, Walker et. al. [11][12] have trained an automatic classifier that identifies and predicts problems in HC dialogues.

7. DISCUSSION

It is clear that our algorithm and semantic tagset, as they stand now, need improvements to reduce the number of false errors detected. However, even now the automatic method offers some advantages over tagging errors manually, the most important of which is that many researchers already annotate their dialogues with semantic tags for other purposes and thus many errors can be detected with no additional annotation. Also, the automatic method associates errors with particular slots, enabling researchers to pinpoint aspects of their dialogue management strategy that need the most work. Finally, Day et. al. [3] have shown that correcting existing annotations is more time efficient than annotating from scratch. In this way, the automatic method may be used to "seed" an annotation effort, with later hand correction.

8. ACKNOWLEDGMENTS
This work was funded by the DARPA Communicator program under contract number DAAB07-99-C201. © 2001 The MITRE Corporation. All rights reserved.

9. REFERENCES

[1] Aberdeen, J. and Doran, C. Human-computer and human-human dialogues. *DARPA Communicator Principle Investigators Meeting* (Philadelphia, PA USA 2000). http://www.dsic-web.net/ito/meetings/communicator_sep2000/

[2] Danieli, M. On the use of expectations for detecting and repairing human-machine miscommunication. *Proceedings of AAAI Workshop on Detecting, Repairing and Preventing Human-Machine Miscommunication* (Portland OR, USA 1996).

[3] Day, D., Aberdeen, J., Hirschman, L., Kozierok, R., Robinson, P. and Vilain, M. Mixed-initiative development of language processing systems. In *Proceedings of the Fifth Conference on Applied Natural Language Processing* (Washington DC, USA 1997).

[4] Dybkjær, L., Bernsen, N.O. and Dybkjær, H. Reducing miscommunication in spoken human-machine dialogue. *Proceedings of AAAI Workshop on Detecting, Repairing and Preventing Human-Machine Miscommunication* (Portland OR, USA 1996).

[5] Hirschman, L. and Pao, C. The cost of errors in a spoken language system. *Proceedings of the Third European*

Conference on Speech Communication and Technology (Berlin, Germany 1993).

[6] Levow, G.A. Characterizing and recognizing spoken corrections in human-computer dialogue. *Proceedings of COLING-ACL* (Montreal, Canada 1998).

[7] Levow, G.A. Understanding recognition failures in spoken corrections in human-computer dialogue. *Proceedings of ECSA Workshop on Dialogue and Prosody* (Eindhoven, The Netherlands 1999).

[8] Luo, X. and Papineni, K. IBM DARPA Communicator v1.0. *DARPA Communicator Principle Investigators Meeting* (Philadelphia, PA USA 2000). http://www.dsic-web.net /ito/meetings/communicator_sep2000/

[9] Polifroni, J. and Seneff, S. Galaxy-II as an architecture for spoken dialogue evaluation. *Proceedings of the Second International Conference on Language Resources and Evaluation* (Athens, Greece 2000).

[10] Rudnicky, A. CMU Communicator. *DARPA Communicator Principle Investigators Meeting* (Philadelphia, PA USA 2000). http://www.dsic-web.net/ito/meetings /communicator_sep2000/

[11] Walker, M., Langkilde, I., Wright, J., Gorin, A. and Litman, D. Learning to predict problematic situations in a spoken dialogue system: experiments with how may I help you? *Proceedings of the Seventeenth International Conference on Machine Learning* (Stanford, CA USA 2000).

[12] Walker, M., Wright, J. and Langkilde, I. Using natural language processing and discourse features to identify understanding errors in a spoken dialogue system. *Proceedings of the North American Meeting of the Association of Computational Linguistics* (Seattle, WA USA 2000).

Fine-Grained Hidden Markov Modeling for Broadcast-News Story Segmentation

Warren Greiff, Alex Morgan, Randall Fish, Marc Richards, Amlan Kundu,
MITRE Corporation
202 Burlington Road
Bedford, MA 01730-1420

(greiff, amorgan, fishr, marc, akundu)@mitre.org

ABSTRACT

We present the design and development of a Hidden Markov Model for the division of news broadcasts into story segments. Model topology, and the textual features used, are discussed, together with the non-parametric estimation techniques that were employed for obtaining estimates for both transition and observation probabilities. Visualization methods developed for the analysis of system performance are also presented.

1. INTRODUCTION

Current technology makes the automated capture, storage, indexing, and categorization of broadcast news feasible allowing for the development of computational systems that provide for the intelligent browsing and retrieval of news stories [Maybury, Merlino & Morey '97; Kubula, et al., '00]. To be effective, such systems must be able to partition the undifferentiated input signal into the appropriate sequence of news-story segments.

In this paper we discuss an approach to segmentation based on the use of a fine-grained Hidden Markov Model [Rabiner, '89] to model the generation of the words produced during a news program. We present the model topology, and the textual features used. Critical to this approach is the application of non-parametric estimation techniques, employed to obtain robust estimates for both transition and observation probabilities. Visualization methods developed for the analysis of system performance are also presented.

Typically, approaches to news-story segmentation have been based on extracting features of the input stream that are likely to be different at boundaries between stories from what is observed within the span of individual stories. In [Beeferman, Berger, & Lafferty '99], boundary decisions are based on how well predictions made by a long-range exponential language model compare to those made by a short range trigram model. [Ponte and Croft, '97] utilize Local Context Analysis [Xu, J. and Croft, '96]

to enrich each sentence with related words, and then use dynamic programming to find an optimal boundary sequence based on a measure of word-occurrence similarity between pairs of enriched sentences. In [Greiff, Hurwitz & Merlino, '99], a naïve Bayes classifier is used to make a boundary decision at each word of the transcript. In [Yamron, et al., '98], a fully connected Hidden Markov Model is based on automatically induced topic clusters, with one node for each topic. Observation probabilities for each node are estimated using smoothed unigram statistics.

The approach reported in this paper goes further along the lines of find-grained modeling in two respects: 1) differences in feature patterns likely to be observed at different points in the development of a news story are exploited, in contrast to approaches that focus on boudary/no-boundary differences; and 2) a more detailed modeling of the story-length distribution profile, unique to each news source (for example, see the histogram of story lengths for ABC World News Tonight shown in the top graph of Figure 3, below).

2. GENERATIVE MODEL

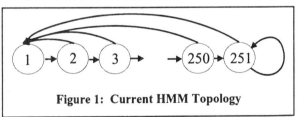

Figure 1: Current HMM Topology

We model the generation of news stories as a 251 state Hidden Markov Model, with the topology shown in Figure 1. States labeled, 1 to 250, correspond to each of the first 250 words of a story. One extra state, labeled 251, is included to model the production of all words at the end of stories exceeding 250 words in length.

Several other models were considered, but this model is particularly suited to the features used, as it allows one to model features that vary with depth into the story (Section 3.1), while simultaneously, by delaying certain features. It also allows one to model features that occur in specific regions the boundaries (Section 3.3). This is possible because all states can feed into the initial state, i.e. all stories end by going into the first word of a new story.

Proceedings of HLT 2001, First International Conference on Human Language Technology Research, J. Allan, ed., Morgan Kaufmann, San Francisco, 2001.

For example, the original model involved a series of beginning and then end states, with a single middle state that could be cycled through (Figure 2). This proved to be a problem because the ends of long stories were being mixed with the ends of short stories which led to problems with our spaced coherence feature (Section 3.1). Another possibility involved splitting the model into two main paths, one to model the shorter stories, and one to model the longer as there is something of a bimodal distribution in story lengths (Figure 4). However, the fine-grained nature of our model would suffer from splitting the data in this manner, and a choice about at which length to fork the model would be somewhat artificial.

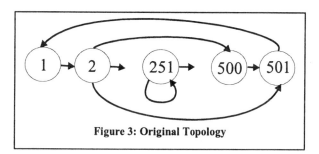

Figure 3: Original Topology

3. FEATURES

Associated with the model is a set of features. For each state, the model assigns a probability distribution over all possible combinations of values the features may take on. The probability assigned to value combinations is assumed to be independent of the state/observation history, conditioned on the state. We further assume that the value of any one feature is independent of all others, once the current state is known. Features have been explicitly designed with this assumption in mind. Three categories of features have been used, which we refer to as *coherence* features, *x-duration* feature, and the *trigger* features.

3.1. Coherence

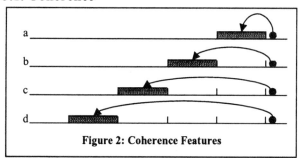

Figure 2: Coherence Features

We have used four coherence features. The COHER-1 feature, shown schematically in Figure 2a, is based on a buffer of 50 words immediately prior to the current word. If the current word does not appear in the buffer, the value of COHER-1 is 0. If it does appear in the buffer, the value is -log(s_w/s), where s_w is the number of stories in which the word appears, and s is the total number of stories, in the training data. Words that did not appear in the training data, are treated as having appeared once. In this way, rare words get high feature values, and common words get low feature values. Three other features: COHER-2, COHER-3, and

COHER-4 (Figures 3b, c & d) correspond to similar features; for these, however, the buffer is separated by 50, 100, and 150 words, respectively, from the current word. Interestingly, the COHER-4 feature actually caused a reduction in performance, and was not used in the final evaluation.

3.2. X-duration

This feature is based on indications given by the speech recognizer that it was unable to transcribe a portion of the audio signal. The existence of an untranscribable section prior to the word gives a non-zero X-DURATION value based on the extent of the section. Empirically this is an excellent predictor of boundaries in that an untranscribable event has uniform likelihood of occurring anywhere in a news story, except prior to the first word of a story, where it is extremely likely to occur.

3.3. Triggers

Trigger features correspond to small regions at the beginning and end of stories, and exploit the fact that some words are far more likely to occur in these positions than in other parts of a news segment. One region, for example, is restricted to the first word of the story. In ABC's World News Tonight, for example, the word "finally" is far more likely to occur in the first word of a story than would be expected by its general rate of occurrence in the training data. For a word, w, appearing in the input stream, the value of the feature is an estimate of how likely it is for w to appear in the region of interest. The estimate used is given by:

$$\hat{p}(w \in R) = \frac{n_{w \in R} + 1}{n_w + (1/f_R)}$$

where $n_{w \in R}$ is the number of times w appeared in R in the training data; n_w is the total number of occurrences of w; and f_R is the fraction of all tokens of w that occurred in the region. This estimate can be viewed as Bayesian estimate with a beta prior. The beta prior is equivalent to a uniform prior and the observation of one occurrence of the word in the region out of $(1/f_R)$ total occurrences. This estimate was chosen so that: 1) the prior probability would not be greatly affected for words observed only a few times in the training data; 2) it would be pushed strongly towards the empirical probability of the word appearing in the region for words that were encountered in R; 3) it has a prior probability, f_R, equal to the expectation for a randomly selected word. The regions used for the submission were restricted to the one-word regions for: first word, second word, last word, and next-to-last word. Limited experimentation with multi-state regions, was not fruitful. For example, including the regions, {3,4,…,10} and {-10,-9,…,-3}, where $-i$ is interpreted as i words prior to the end of the story, did not improve segmentation performance.

Since, as described, the current HMM topology does not model end-of-story words (earlier versions of the topology did model these states directly), trigger features for end-of-story regions are delayed. That means that a trigger related to the last word in a story would be delayed by a one word buffer. In this way, it is linked to the first word in the next story. For example, the word "Jennings" (the name of the main anchorperson) is strongly correlated with the last word in news stories in the ABC World News Tonight corpus. The estimated probability of it being the last word of the story in which it appears is .235 (obtained by the aforementioned method). The trained model associates a high likelihood of seeing the value .235 at state = 1; the intuitive interpretation being, "a word highly likely to appear at the last word of a story, occurred 1-word ago".

4. PARAMETER ESTIMATION

The Hidden Markov Model requires the estimation of transition and conditional observation probabilities. There are 251 transition probabilities to be estimated. Much more of a problem are the observation probabilities, there being 9 features in the model, for each of which a probability distribution over as many as 100 values must be estimated, for each of 251 states. With the goal of developing methods for robust estimation in the context of story segmentation, we have applied non-parametric kernel estimation techniques, using the LOCFIT library [Loader, '99] of the R open-source statistical analysis package, which is based on the S-plus system [Venables & Ripley,

'99; Chambers & Hastie, '92, Becker, Chambers & Wilks, '88]. For the transition probabilities, it is assumed that the underlying probability distribution over story length is smooth, allowing the empirical histogram, shown at the top of Figure 4, to be transformed to the probability density estimate shown at the bottom. From this probability distribution over story lengths, the conditional transition probabilities can be estimated directly.

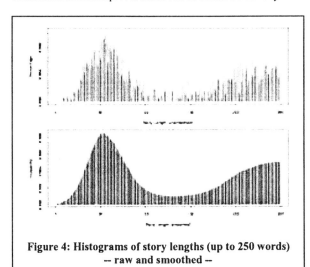

Figure 4: Histograms of story lengths (up to 250 words)
-- raw and smoothed --

Conditional observation probabilities are also deduced from an estimate of the joint probability distribution. First, observation values were binned. Binning limits were set in an attempt to 1) be large enough to obtain sufficient counts for the production of robust probability estimates, and yet, 2) be constrained enough so that important distinctions in the probabilities for different feature values will be reflected in the model. For each bin, the observation counts are smoothed by performing a non-parametric regression of the observation counts as a function of state. The smoothed observations counts corresponding to the regression are then normalized so as to sum to the total observation count for the

bin. The result is a conditional probability distribution over states for a given binned feature value, $p(State=s|Feature=fv)$. Once this is done for all bin values, each conditional probability is multiplied by the marginal probability, $p(State=s)$, of being in a given state, resulting in a joint distribution, $p(fv,s)$, over the entire space of *(Feature,State)* values. From this joint distribution, the necessary conditional probabilities, $p(Feature=fv|State=s)$, can be deduced directly.

Figure 5 shows the conditional probability estimates, $p(fv \mid s)$, for the feature value COHER-3=20, across all states, confirming the intuition that, while the probability of seeing a value of 20 is small for all states, the likelihood of seeing it is much higher in latter parts of a story than it is in early-story states.

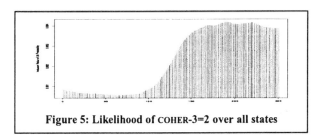

Figure 5: Likelihood of COHER-3=2 over all states

5. SEGMENTATION

Once parameters for the HMM have been determined, segmentation is straightforward. The Viterbi algorithm [Rabiner, '89], is employed to determine the sequence of states most likely to have produced the observation sequence associated with the broadcast. A boundary is then associated with each word produced from State 1 for the maximum likelihood state sequence.

The version of the Viterbi algorithm we have implemented provides for the specification of "state-penalty" parameters, which we have used for the "boundary state", state 1. In effect, the probability for each path in consideration is multiplied by the value of this parameter (which can be less than, equal to, or greater than, 1) for each time the path passes through the boundary state. Variation of the parameter effectively controls the "aggressiveness" of segmentation, allowing for tuning system behavior in the context of the evaluation metric.

6. RESULTS

Preliminary test results of this approach are encouraging. After training on all but 15 of the ABC World News Tonight programs from the TDT-2 corpus [Nist, '00], a test on the remaining 15 produced a false-alarm (boundary predicted incorrectly) probability of .11, with a corresponding miss (true boundary not predicted) probability of .14, equal to the best performance reported to date, for this news source.

A more intuitive appreciation for the quality of performance can be garnered from the graphs in Figure 6, which contrast the segmentation produced by the system (middle) with ground truth (the top graph), for a typical member of the ABC test set. The x-axis corresponds to time (in units of word tokens); i.e., the index of the word produced by the speech recognizer, and the y-axis

131

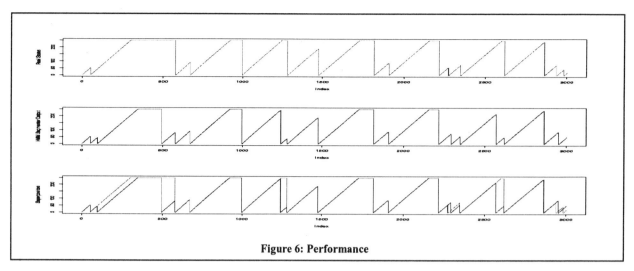

Figure 6: Performance

corresponds to the state of the HMM model. A path passing through the point (301, 65), for example, corresponds to a path through the network that produced the 65th word from state 301. Returns to state=1 correspond to boundaries between stories. The bottom graph shows the superposition of the two to help illustrate the agreement between the path chosen by the system and the path corresponding to perfect segmentation..

7. VISUALIZATION

The evolution of the segmentation algorithm was driven by analysis of the behavior of the system, which was supported by visualization routines developed using the graphing capability of the R package. Figure 7 gives an example of the kind of graphical displays that were used for analysis of the segmentation of a specific broadcast news program; in this case, analysis of the role of the X-DURATION feature. This graphical display allows for the comparison of the maximum likelihood path produced by the HMM to the path through the HMM that would be produced by a perfect system – one privy to ground-truth.

The top graph corresponds to the bottom graph of Figure 6, showing the states traversed by the two systems. The second graph shows the value of the X-DURATION feature corresponding to each word of the broadcast. So, the plotting of a point at (301, 3) corresponds to an X-DURATION value of 3 having been observed at time, 301. One thing that can be seen from this graph is that being at a story boundary (low-points on the thicker-darker line of the top graph) is more frequent when higher values of the X-DURATION cue are observed, than when lower values are observed, as could be expected.

The third graph shows, on a log scale, how many times more likely it is that the observed X-DURATION value would be generated from the true state than from the state predicted by the system. Most points are close to 0, indicating that the X-DURATION value observed was as likely to have come from the true state as it is to have come from the state predicted by the Viterbi algorithm. Of course, this is the case wherever the true state has been correctly predicted. Negative points indicate that the X-DURATION value observed is less likely to be produced from

the true state than from the predicted state. Strongly negative points are a major component of the probability calculation that resulted in the system preferring the path it chose over the true path. These points suggest potential deficiencies in the modeling. Their identification directs the focus of analysis so that system performance can be improved by correcting weaknesses of the existing model.

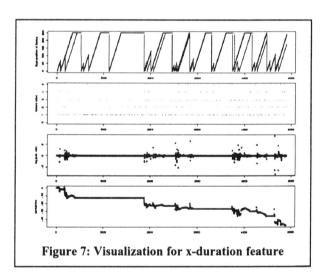

Figure 7: Visualization for x-duration feature

The final graph shows the cumulative sum of the values from the graph above it. (Note that the sum of the logs of the probabilities is equivalent to the cumulative product of probabilities on a log scale.) The graphing of the cumulative sum can be very useful when the system is performing poorly due to a small but consistent preference for the observations having been produced by the state sequence chosen by the system. This phenomenon is made evident by a steady downward trend in the graph of the cumulative sum. This is in contrast to an overall level trend with occasional downward dips. Note, that a similar graph for the total probability (equal to the product of all the individual feature value probabilities) will always have an overall downward trend, since the maximum likelihood path will always have a likelihood greater than the likelihood of any other path.

Aside from supporting the detailed analysis of specific features, the productions of these graphs for each of the features, together with the corresponding graph for the total observation probability, allowed us to quickly asses which of the features was most problematic at any given stage of model development.

8. FURTHER WORK

It should be kept in mind that experimentation with this approach has been based on relatively primitive features – our focus, to this point, having been on the development of the core segmentation mechanism. Features based on more sophisticated extraction techniques, which have been reported in the literature – for example, the use of exponential models for determining trigger cues used in [Beeferman, Berger, & Lafferty '99] – can easily be incorporated into this general framework. Integration of such techniques can be expected to result in significant further improvement in segmentation quality.

To date, the binning method described has given much better results than two dimensional kernel density estimation techniques which we also attempted to employ. One of the main difficulties with using traditional kernel density estimation techniques is that they tend to inaccurately estimate the density at areas of discontinuity, such as state=1 in our model and our trigger features. Preliminary work with boundary kernels [Scott, '92] is very promising. It is certainly an area worthy of more in-depth investigation.

Work done by another group [Liu, '00] to segment documentaries based on video cues alone has been moderately successful in the past. We engineered a neural network in an attempt to identify video frames containing an anchorperson, a logo, and blank frames, with a belief that these are all features that would contain information about story boundaries. Preliminary work was also done to extract features directly from the audio signal, such as trying to identify speaker change. Initial work with the audio and video has been unable to aid in segmentation, but we feel this is also an area worth continuing to pursue.

9. REFERENCES

1. [Becker, Chambers & Wilks, '88] Becker, Richard A., Chambers, John M., and Wilks, Allan R. *The New S Language.* Wadsworth & Brooks/Cole, Pacific Grove, Cal.

2. [Beeferman, Berger, & Lafferty '99] D. Beeferman, D., A. Berger, A. and Lafferty, J. Statistical models for text segmentation. *Machine Learning*, vol. 34, pp. 1-34, 1999.

3. [Chambers & Hastie, '88] Chambers, John M. and Hastie, Trevor, J. *Statistical Models in S.* Wadsworth & Brooks/Cole, Pacific Grove, Cal., 1988.

4. [Greiff, Hurwitz & Merlino, '99] Greiff, Warren, Hurwitz, Laurie, and Merlino, Andrew. MITRE TDT-3 segmentation system. *TDT-3 Topic Detection and Tracking Conference*, Gathersburg, Md, February, 2000.

5. [Kubula, et al., '00] Kubula, F., Colbath, S., Liu, D., Srivastava, A. and Makhoul, J. Integrated technologies for indexing spoken language, *Communication of the ACM*, vol.

43, no. 2, Feb., 2000.

6. [Liu, '00] Liu, Tiecheng and Kender, John R. A hidden Markov model approach to the structure of documentaries. *Proceedings of the IEEE Workshop on Content-based Access of Image and Video Libraries, 2000.*

7. [Loader, '99] Loader, C. *Local Regression and Likelihood.* Springer, Murray Hill, N.J., 1999.

8. [Maybury, Merlino & Morey '97] Maybury, M., Merlino, A. Morey, D. Broadcast news navigation using story segments. *Proceedings of the ACM International Multimedia Conference*, Seattle, WA, Nov., 1997.

9. [Nist, '00] Topic Detection and Tracking (TDT-3) Evaluation Project. http://www.nist.gov/speech/tests/tdt/tdt99/.

10. [Ponte and Croft, '97] Ponte, J.M. and Croft, W.B. Text segmentation by topic, *Proceedings of the First European Conference on Research and Advanced Technology for Digital Libraries*, pp. 120--129, 1997.

11. [Rabiner, '89] L. R. Rabiner, A tutorial on hidden Markov models and selected applications in speech recognition. *Proceedings of the IEEE*, vol. 37, no. 2, pp. 257-86, February, 1989.

12. [Scott, '92] David W. Scorr, Boundary kernels, *Multivariate Density Estimation: Theory and Practice*, pp 146-149, 1992.

13. [Venables & Ripley, '99] Venables, W. N. and Ripley, B. D. *Modern Applied Statistics with S-PLUS.* Springer, Murray Hill, N.J., 1999.

14. [Xu, J. and Croft, '96] Xu, J. and Croft, W.B., Query expansion using local and global document analysis, *Proceedings of the Nineteenth Annual International ACM SIGIR Conference on Research and Development in Information Retrieval*, pp. 4--11, 1996

15. [Yamron, et al., '98] Yamron, J. P., Carp, I., Gillick, L., Lowe, S. and van Mulbregt, P. A Hidden Markov Model approach to text segmentation and event tracking. *Proceedings ICASSP-98*, Seattle, WA. May, 1998.

First Story Detection using a Composite Document Representation.

Nicola Stokes, Joe Carthy,
Department of Computer Science,
University College Dublin,
Ireland.

{nicola.stokes,joe.carthy}@ucd.ie

ABSTRACT

In this paper, we explore the effects of data fusion on First Story Detection [1] in a broadcast news domain. The data fusion element of this experiment involves the combination of evidence derived from two distinct representations of document content in a single cluster run. Our composite document representation consists of a concept representation (based on the lexical chains derived from a text) and free text representation (using traditional keyword index terms). Using the TDT1 evaluation methodology we evaluate a number of document representation strategies and propose reasons why our data fusion experiment shows performance improvements in the TDT domain.

Keywords

Lexical Chaining, Data Fusion, First Story Detection.

1. INTRODUCTION

The goal of TDT is to monitor and reorganize a stream of broadcast news stories in such a way as to help a user recognize and explore different news events that have occurred in the data set. First story detection (or online new event detection [1]) is one aspect of the detection problem which constitutes one of the three technical tasks defined by the TDT initiative (the other two being segmentation and tracking). Given a stream of news stories arriving in chronological order, a detection system must group or cluster articles that discuss distinct news events in the data stream. The TDT initiative has further clarified the notion of topic detection by differentiating between classification in a retrospective (Event Clustering) and an online environment (First Story Detection). In FSD the system must identify all stories in the data stream that discuss novel news events. This classification decision is made by considering only those documents that have arrived prior to the current document being evaluated, forcing the system to adhere to the temporal constraints of a real-time news stream.

Proceedings of HLT 2001, First International Conference on Human Language Technology Research, J. Allan, ed., Morgan Kaufmann, San Francisco, 2001.

In other words the system must make an irrevocable classification decision (i.e. either the document discusses a *new event* or *previously detected event*) as soon as the document arrives on the input stream. The goal of event clustering on the other hand is to partition the data stream into clusters of related documents that discuss distinct events. This decision can be made after the system has considered all the stories in the input stream.

In addition to defining three research problems associated with broadcast news, the TDT initiative also attempted to formally define an event with respect to how it differs from the traditional IR notion of a subject or a topic as defined by the TREC community. An *event* is defined as 'something that happens at some specific time and place (e.g. an assassination attempt, or a volcanic eruption in Greece)'. A *topic* on the other hand is a 'seminal event or activity along with all directly related events and activities (e.g. an investigation or a political campaign)' [1]. Initial TDT research into event tracking and detection focused on developing a classification algorithm to address this subtle distinction between an event and a topic. For example successful attempts were made to address the temporal nature of news stories[1] by exploiting the time between stories when determining their similarity in the detection process [1]. However current research is now focusing on the use of NLP techniques such as language modeling [2, 3], or other forms of feature selection like the identification of events based on the domain dependencies between words [4], or the extraction of certain word classes from stories i.e. noun phrases, noun phrases heads [5]. All these techniques offer a means of determining the most informative features about an event as opposed to classifying documents based on all the words in the document. The aim of our research is also based on this notion of feature selection. In this paper we investigate if the use of lexical chains to classify documents can better encapsulate this notion of an event. In particular we look at the effect on FSD when a composite document representation (using a lexical chain representation and free text representation) is used to represent events in the TDT domain.

---

[1] Stories closer together on the input stream are more likely to discuss the same event than stories further apart on this stream.

In sections 2 and 3 we describe the first component of our composite document representation derived from lexical chains, with a subsequent description of FSD classification based on our data fusion strategy in Section 4. The remaining sections of this paper give a detailed account of our experimental results, concluding with a discussion of their significance in terms of two general criteria for successful data fusion.

2. LEXICAL CHAINING

A lexical chain is a set of semantically related words in a text. For example in a document concerning cars a typical chain might consist of the following words {vehicle, engine, wheel, car, automobile, steering wheel}, where each word in the chain is directly or indirectly related to another word by a semantic relationship such as *holonymy, hyponymy, meronymy* and *hypernymy*.

When reading any text it is obvious that it is not merely made up of a set of unrelated sentences, but that these sentences are in fact connected to each other in one of two ways cohesion and coherence. As Morris and Hirst [6] point out cohesion relates to the fact that the elements of a text 'tend to hang together'. Whilst coherence refers to the fact that 'there is sense in the text'. Obviously coherence is a semantic relationship and needs computationally expensive processing for identification, however cohesion is a surface relationship and is hence more accessible. As indicated by Halliday and Hasan [7] cohesion can be roughly classified into three distinct classes, *reference, conjunction* and *lexical cohesion*. Conjunction is the only class, which explicitly shows the relationship between two sentences, *'I have a cat and his name is Felix'*. Reference and lexical cohesion on the other hand indicate sentence relationships in terms of two semantically same or related words. In the case of reference, pronouns are the most likely means of conveying referential meaning. For example in the following sentences, ' *"Get inside now!" shouted the teacher. When nobody moved, he was furious'*. In order for the reader to understand that 'the teacher' is being referred to by the pronoun 'he' in the second sentence, they must refer back to the first sentence. Lexical cohesion on the other hand arises from the selection of vocabulary items and the semantic relationships between them. For example, *'I parked outside the* library*, and then went inside the building to return my books'*, where cohesion is represented by the semantic relationship between the lexical items 'library', 'building' and 'books'. For automatic identification of these relationships it is far easier to work with lexical cohesion than reference because less underlying implicit information is needed to discover the relationship between the above pronoun and the word it references. Hence lexical cohesion is used as a linguistic device for investigating the discourse structure of texts and lexical chains have been found to be an adequate means of

exposing this discourse structure. These lexical chains have many practical applications in IR and computational linguistics such as hypertext construction [8], automatic document summarization [9], the detection of malapropisms within text [10], as a term weighting technique capturing the lexical cohesion in a text [11], as a means of segmenting text into distinct blocks of self contained text [12]. For the purpose of this project we exploit three such applications:

1. We use lexical chains as a means of exploring and presenting the most prevalent topics discussed in news stories.
2. A valuable side effect of lexical chain creation is that the words of a text are automatically disambiguated.
3. Because lexical chains disambiguate words based on the context in which they occur, lexical chains also address two linguistic problems *synonymy* and *polysemy*, which hinder the effectiveness of traditional IR systems such as the vector space model.

3. CHAIN FORMATION ALGORITHM

In general the first task of an IR system is to execute a set of text operations (e.g. stemming, removal of stopwords) to reduce the complexity of a full text representation of a document into a more manageable set of index terms. Although these index terms are a subset of the original representation, their purpose is to adequately represent the semantic content of the original document in a more concise manner. This is a difficult NLP task, as natural language frequently does not obey the principle of compositionality where the meaning of the whole can be strictly determined from its parts. So in order to derive the correct representation of a text, we need to determine the interpretation of a word or phase in the context in which it occurs i.e. before the original text is manipulated into a set of index terms. The creation of lexical chains which is described below, aims to capture this additional textual information while still maintaining a manageable representation size.

Firstly each term contained in a particular document is dealt with in chronological order. Then each subsequent word is added to an existing lexical chain or becomes the seed of a new chain, in much the same manner as the clustering of documents. A stronger criterion than simple semantic similarity is imposed on the addition of a term to a chain, where terms must be added to the most recently updated (semantically related) chain. This favors the creation of lexical chains containing words that are in close proximity within the text, prompting the correct disambiguation of a word based on the context in which it was used. We use WordNet to determine the semantic relatedness between a candidate word and the words of a chain. If we view WordNet as a large semantic network of nodes (meanings) inter-related by semantic relations (meronymy, hyponymy, etc.), then finding a relationship between two words in the chaining process involves activating the network of one node and observing the activity of the other in this activated network.

CAR

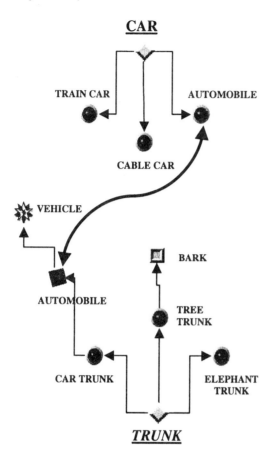

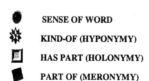

Figure 1: Shows expanded document terms 'car' and 'trunk' and their semantic relatedness.

So far we have talked abstractly about how to determine if a word is semantically related to a chain. To explain this fully it is first necessary to discuss the structure of the WordNet thesaurus, which is used to determine this semantic connection or closeness between words in a text. In WordNet, nouns, verbs, adjectives, and adverbs are arranged into synsets (group of synonymous words e.g. cat, feline, tabby), which are further organized into a set of lexical source files by syntactic category. In our case we

are only interested in the noun index and data files, because the verb file in WordNet has no relation with the three other files (noun, adverb and adjective files), and the adverb file has only unidirectional relations with the adjective file. So each word in a particular document is searched for in the noun index file, if it is not found then we make the assumption that this word is not a noun and hence will play no further part in the chaining process. If the word is found then it will be represented by a unique set of synset numbers, where each synset number represents a particular sense associated with that word. Each synset number points to the position in the noun data file where words related to this sense of the word are stored with a gloss, and sample sentence using this word. Words related to a particular sense are associated with it by several different semantic relations, such as *hyponymy* (kind-of, lorry/vehicle), *hypernymy* (is-a, vehicle/car), *holonymy* (has-part, tree/branch) and *meronymy* (part-of, engine/car). As shown in Figure 1, each sense associated with a word is expanded using WordNet (in reality these senses and senses related to them are represented by synset numbers). This example of the chain formation process shows us that the word 'car' is related to the word 'trunk' by the fact that 'car trunk', one of the senses of 'trunk', is a meronymy of 'automobile' which is a possible sense of 'car'. In this way both words have been successfully disambiguated so all redundant senses belonging to each word are eliminated and 'car' is added to the chain containing 'trunk'. This chain may also contain other semantically related words pertaining to the topic of an automobile e.g. {car, trunk, engine, vehicle…}. The chain formation process is continued in this way until all the words in a particular document (in our case nouns) have been chained. Any words that remain unchained or ambiguous after this chaining process are eliminated from our chain word representation based on the following hypothesis:

'The occurrence of words in a text which fail to participate in the overall cohesive structure of a text (i.e. remain unchained) is purely coincidental. Consequently these words are considered irrelevant in describing the general topic of a document.'

This implies that our lexical chaining strategy also provides us with an automatic means of selecting the most salient features of a particular news story. So when all redundant words have been removed in this manner, all remaining chains are then merged into a single chain containing all the synset numbers from each individual chain involved in this process. This representation is a semantic representation as opposed to a syntactic representation (in the case of a 'bag of words' representation) because it contains concepts (i.e. synset numbers) rather than simple terms to represent the content of a document.

The final stage of our combined document representation strategy involves collecting all free text words for each document and storing them in a set of index files. So effectively our composite document representation used in the detection process (described in the next section) consists of two weighted vectors, a chain vector and an ordinary term vector, where both chain words and free text words are weighted simply in terms of the frequency in which they occur in a document.

4. DETECTION ALGORITHM USING THE FUSION METHOD

Online Detection or First Story Detection is in essence a classification problem where documents arriving in chronological order on the input stream are tagged with a 'YES' flag if they discuss a previously unseen news event, or a 'NO' flag when they discuss an old news topic. However unlike detection in a retrospective environment a story must be identified as novel before subsequent stories can be considered. The single-pass clustering algorithm bases its clustering methodology on the same assumption, the general structure of which is summarised as follows.

1. Convert the current document into a weighted chain word vector and a weighted free text vector.

2. The first document on the input stream will become the first cluster.

3. All subsequent incoming documents are compared with all previously created clusters up to the current point in time. A comparison strategy is used here to determine the extent of the similarity between a document and a cluster. In our IR model we use sub-vectors to describe our two distinct document representations. This involves calculating the closeness or similarity between the chain word vectors and free text vectors for each document/cluster comparison using the standard cosine similarity measure (used in this variation of the vector space model to compute the cosine of the angle between two weighted vectors). The data fusion element of this experiment involves the combination of two distinct representations of document content in a single cluster run i.e. j equals 2 in equation (1). So the overall similarity between a document D and a cluster C is a linear combination of the similarities for each sub-vector formally defined as:

$$Sim\,(D,\,C) \;=\; \sum_{j=1}^{k} w_j \cdot Sim\,(D_j,\,C_j) \qquad (1)$$

where $Sim(X,\,Y)$ is the cosine similarity measure for two vectors X and Y, and w is a coefficient that biases the weight of evidence each document representation j, contributes to the similarity measure.

4. When the most similar cluster is found a thresholding strategy [13] is used to discover if this similarity measure is high enough to warrant the addition of that document to the cluster and the classification of the current document as an old event. If this document does not satisfy the similarity condition set out by the thresholding methodology then the document is declared as discussing a new event, and this document will form the seed of a new cluster.

5. This clustering process will continue until all documents in the input stream have been classified.

5. EXPERIMENTAL RESULTS

A number of experiments were conducted on the TDT-1 broadcast news collection [1]. The results of these experiments were used to observe the effects on first story detection when lexical chains are used in conjunction with free text as a combined document classifier. The main aim of the experiments was to determine if lexical chains are a suitable document representation when classifying news stories in the TDT domain. The official TDT evaluation requires that the system output is a declaration (a YES or NO flag) for each story processed. These declarations are then used to calculate two system errors percentage *misses* and *false alarms*. Misses occur when the system fails to detect the first story discussing a new event and false alarms occur when a document discussing a previously detected event is classified as a new event.

5.1 System Descriptions

Three distinct detection systems TRAD, CHAIN and LexDetect are examined in the following set of experiments. The TRAD system [13], our benchmark system in these experiments is a basic FSD system that classifies news stories based on the syntactic similarity between documents and clusters. The design of this system is based on a traditional vector space model which represents documents as a vector, each component of which corresponds to a particular word and who's value reflects the frequency of that word in the document. Classification of a new event occurs in a similar manner to that described in Section 4, the most important difference between the two methods is that a single free text representation is used to express document content, rather than a combined representation. A *Time Window* [13] of length 30 is employed in the TRAD, CHAIN and LexDetect systems.

The design of our second system LexDetect has been described in detail in sections 3 and 4. The dimensionality of LexDetect (80 words) remains static through out these experiments. Using the current method of lexical chain creation, just under 72% of documents contained greater than or equal to 30 chained words. We therefore normalized the length of chain word representations by imposing a chain dimensionality value of 30 on all LexDetect schemes[2]. In theory it is possible to vary the length of the free text representation in our combined representation however in these experiments all schemes contain free text representations of length 50, since optimal performance is achieved for TRAD when dimensionality 50 is used. The final system parameter to be varied in these experiments is the weighting coefficient w_j used in equation (1). The design of our third system CHAIN like TRAD, involves the use of a singular document representation. However this document representation contains chain words only rather than free text terms, and so the dimensionality of the system must be 30.

5.2 The Data Fusion Experiment

From the results shown in Figure 2 (a Detection Error Tradeoff Graph where points closer to the origin indicate better overall performance), we deduce that a marginal increase in system effectiveness can be achieved when lexical chain representations are used in conjunction with free text representations in the detection process. In particular, we see that the miss rate of our FSD system LexDetect decreased with little or no impact to the false alarm rate of the system.

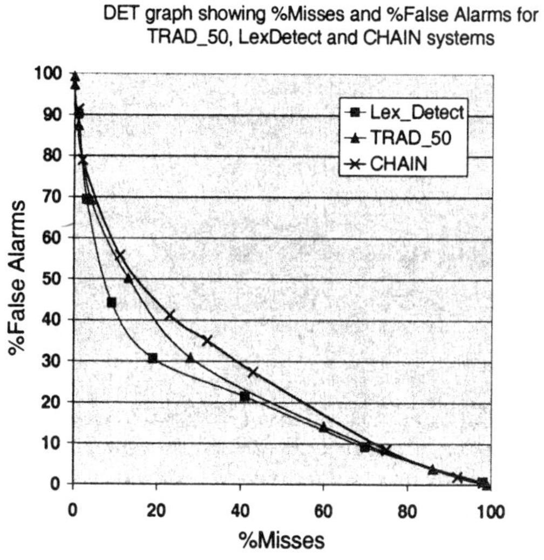

Optimal performance for the LexDetect system (as shown in Figure 2) was found when a weighted combination of evidence was used. This involved treating our free text representation as weaker evidence during the detection process. Results shown in Figure 3 contrast the effect on LexDetect performance when both the chain and free text representations are given equal weight (Lex) and when the weight of the free text representation is halved (LexDetect). This is an interesting result as similar experiments using composite document representations to improve search system performance based on ranking, only experienced optimal effectiveness when they allowed free text evidence to bias the retrieval process [14, 15]. This prompted us to question the necessity of the free text component of our composite representation, however results show that system performance degrades when this element of document content is excluded. This is due to the inability of WordNet to correlate the relationship between proper nouns and other semantically related concepts i.e. {Bill Clinton, US president}, which are often crucial in representing journalistic event identity because they reflect the *who, what, where, when and how* of a news story.

Our final experiment involves plotting TRAD_80 against LexDetect shown in Figure 4. The aim of this experiment is to prove that the increase in system effectiveness observed when a composite document representation is used can be attributed solely to the combination of evidence derived from our free text and chain representations rather than as a consequence of increasing the dimensionality of the system to 80 features. As the DET graph in Figure 4 shows, our LexDetect system still outperforms our TRAD system under conditions of equal dimensionality.

DET graph showing %Misses and %False Alarms for TRAD_50, LexDetect and CHAIN systems

Figure 2: The effect on performance when a weighted combined document representation is used.

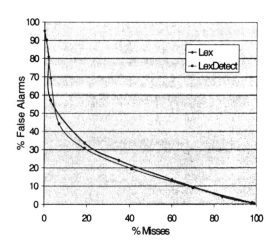

DET graph showing % Misses and %False Alarms for LexDetect and Lex

Figure 3: The effect on performance when equal weight is given to both representations (Lex) in contrast to a weighted combined document representation (LexDetect).

---

[2] An IR 'system' and an IR 'scheme' are used in this context to describe two different concepts. An IR system refers to the physical implementation of an IR algorithm, which can have various operational modes or various parameter settings. The same IR system may be used to execute different IR schemes by adjusting these parameters [20].

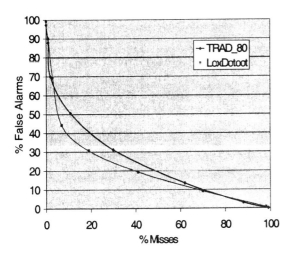

DET graph showing % Misses and %False Alarms for LexDetect and TRAD_80

Figure 4: The effect on performance when equal dimensionality of 80 is given to both the LexDetect and TRAD systems.

6. CRITERIA FOR SUCCESSFUL DATA FUSION

In the previous section our results showed that when a chain word representation is used in conjunction with a free text representation of a document, improvements in FSD effectiveness are observed. However these results fail to provide any concrete reasoning as to why data fusion under these particular conditions work. There are many papers in the data fusion literature, which attempt to explain why certain data fusion experiments succeed where others have failed. Many of these papers look at the effects of combining specific sources of evidence such as the combination of rank retrieval lists, multiple searches or multiple queries. However Ng and Kantor [16] have tried to formulate some general preconditions for successful data fusion involving non-specific sources of evidence.

The first of these criteria is based on the *dissimilarity* between two sources of evidence.

1. *Dissimilarity*: Data fusion between operationally very similar IR systems may not give better performance.

To calculate the level of dissimilarity between our FSD systems described in Section 5, we now define two ratios based on the number of common relevant and common non-relevant tagged documents between two distinct systems. The number of relevant tagged documents, $|r_1 \cap r_2|$ is defined as the number of documents that were correctly classified (as a new or old event) by both systems. The total number of relevant documents, r_1+r_2 is the sum of the number of correctly classified documents for each

system. $|n_1 \cap n_2|$ and n_1+n_2 are similarly defined in terms of the number of incorrectly classified documents returned by both systems (i.e. missed events or wrongly detected new events) as shown in equation 3.

$$R_{overlap} = \frac{|r_1 \cap r_2| \cdot 2}{r_1 + r_2} \qquad (2)$$

$$N_{overlap} = \frac{|n_1 \cap n_2| \cdot 2}{n_1 + n_2} \qquad (3)$$

The results for this experiment are shown in tables 1 and 2 below. We can see that in general the relevant document overlap $R_{overlap}$ between the pair-wise similarities of all four systems is between 85% and 92%, the most similar systems being not surprisingly our two TRAD schema which differ only in the length of their classifiers. The pair-wise similarities $N_{overlap}$ of all four systems regarding non-relevant document classifications exhibit a similar trend of high similarity between the TRAD and LexDetect systems. However the most important point to be taken from these sets of results regards the fact that our CHAIN and TRAD systems exhibit the lowest relevant and non-relevant document overlap of all our pair-wise comparisons. This is an important and encouraging result as it shows that our chain word representations (used in CHAIN) is sufficiently dissimilar to our simple 'bag of words' representation (used in TRAD) to contribute additional evidence to a combination experiment involving both these representations. In particular this satisfaction of Ng and Kantor's dissimilarity criteria explains why marginal improvements in system performance were observed in our data fusion experiment.

Table 1: Relevant document overlap between FSD systems.

$R_{OVERLAP}$	LexDetect	TRAD_50	TRAD_80	CHAIN
LexDetect	1			
TRAD_50	0.85	1		
TRAD_80	0.85	0.92	1	
CHAIN	0.56	0.52	0.53	1

Table 2: Non-relevant document overlap between FSD systems.

$N_{OVERLAP}$	LexDetect	TRAD_50	TRAD_80	CHAIN
LexDetect	1			
TRAD_50	0.67	1		
TRAD_80	0.68	0.82	1	
CHAIN	0.58	0.51	0.53	1

The second criteria defined for successful data fusion regards efficacy or the quality of the individual sources of evidence before they are combined in the data fusion process.

2. *Efficacy*: Data fusion between a capable IR system and a very incapable IR system may not give better performance.

In our data fusion experiment in Section 5 we observed that our CHAIN system was our worst performing FSD system. So as the efficacy criteria suggests a better performing chain word representation is needed before further improvements are observed in our combination system LexDetect.

7. FUTURE WORK

There are many factors which can affect the final chain word representation of a document, ranging from the greedy nature of the chaining algorithm, to the effects caused when varying degrees of freedom are used in this algorithm (i.e. system parameters such as the amount of activation used in WordNet). However the single biggest influence on the quality of the resultant lexical chains is the knowledge source used to create them. In other words the quality of our lexical chain formation is directly dependent on the comprehensiveness/complexity of the thesaurus used to create them. In the case of WordNet, there are a number of structural inadequacies that degrade the effectiveness of our chain representation:

1. Missing semantic links between related words.
2. Inconsistent semantic distances between different concepts.
3. Overloaded synsets such as 'being' which are connected to a large number of synsets. These types of synsets cause spurious chaining, where an unrelated word is added to a chain based on a weak yet semantically close relationship with one of these overloaded synsets (a special case of 2.).
4. No means of correlating the relationship between proper nouns and other noun phrases (see Section 5.2).
5. The level of sense granularity used to define word meanings in WordNet is often too fine for the chain formation process.

All of these factors play a part in reducing the effectiveness of the disambiguation process and the comprehensiveness and accuracy of the final chain representation. A number of these weaknesses are discussed in previous work on lexical chaining [8, 12]. However the last two cases are particularly important when considering the similarity between documents and clusters in the detection process. As explained in Section 6.2 lexical chains are an incomplete means of representing events in a topic detection application since they fail to contain information on the proper nouns involved in the discourse structure of the text.

The last case is more a comment on the unsuitability of WordNet as a knowledge source in this application rather than as a reference to any specific weakness in its design. For example consider two distinct documents which both contain the word 'city' in their respective chain representations. WordNet defines three distinct meanings or senses of this word:

⇒ An incorporated administrative district establish by a state charter.
⇒ A large densely populated municipality.
⇒ An urban center.

When disambiguating a word like 'city' in the chain formation process this level of sense distinction is unnecessary. In fact if our aforementioned documents have chosen two different yet closely related definitions of this word (i.e. different synset numbers) then these documents will be considered less related than they actually are. Other research efforts in the lexical chaining area have suggested 'cleaning' WordNet [8] of rare senses or using some additional knowledge source in the chaining process that could biases the suitability of certain senses in particular contexts[3]. In future work we hope to address this problem by considering the use of collocation information like noun pairs such as 'physician/hospital' or 'Gates/Microsoft' in the chain formation process. Using such information will help to smooth out the discrepancies in semantic distances between concepts and help detect missing semantic relationships between these concepts. This occurrence information could also reduce the sensitivity of the detection process to fine levels of sense granularity if such information was used when determining the similarity between two document representations. So effectively this technique would eliminate the need for a composite representation in the identification of novel events in a news stream. Instead the data fusion element of our system would involve supplementing our knowledge source WordNet with word co-occurrence information in the chain formation process.

8. CONCLUSIONS

A variety of techniques for data fusion have been proposed in IR literature. Results from data fusion research have suggested that significant improvements in system effectiveness can be obtained by combining multiple sources of evidence of relevancy such as document representations, query formulations and search strategies.

---

[3] Recent editions of WordNet now contain information on the probability of use of a word based on polysemy. WordNet researchers noted the direct relationship between the increase in the frequency of occurrence of a word and the number of distinct meanings it has. This frequency value could also be used in the 'cleaning' process.

In this paper we investigated the impact on FSD performance when a composite document representation is used in this TDT task. Our results showed that a marginal increase in system effectiveness could be achieved when lexical chain representations were used in conjunction with free text representations. In particular, we saw that the miss rate of our FSD system LexDetect, decreased with little or no impact to the false alarm rate of the system. When a weighted combination of evidence was used on the same system this improvement was even more apparent. From these results we deduced that using our chain word representation as stronger evidence in the classification process could lead to improved performance. Based on Ng and Kantor's dissimilarity criteria for successful data fusion we attributed the success of our composite document representation to the fact that a chain word classifier is sufficiently dissimilar to a simple 'bag of words' classifier to contribute additional evidence to a combination experiment involving both these representations. In future experiments, we expect an even greater improvement in FSD effectiveness as we continue to refine our lexical chain representation.

9. ACKNOWLEDGMENT

This project is funded by an Enterprise Ireland research grant [SC/1999/083].

10. REFERENCES

[1] R. Papka, J. Allan, Topic Detection and Tracking: Event Clustering as a basis for first story detection, Kluwer Academic Publishers, pp. 97-126, 2000.

[2] Y. Yang, T. Ault, T. Pierce, *Combining multiple learning strategies for effective cross validation*, the Proceedings of the 17th International Conference on Machine Learning (ICML), pp. 1167-1182, 2000.

[3] F. Walls, H. Jin, S.Sista, R. Schwartz, *Topic Detection in broadcast news*, In the proceedings of the DARPA Broadcast News Workshop, pp. 193-198, San Francisco, CA: Morgan Kaufman Publishers Inc, 1999.

[4] F. Fukumoto, Y. Suzuki, Event Tracing based on Domain Dependency, In the proceedings of the 23rd ACM SIGIR Conference, Athens, pp. 57-63, 2000.

[5] V. Hatzivassiloglou, L. Gravano, A. Maganti, *An Investigation of Linguistic Features and Clustering Algorithms for Topical Document Clustering*, In the proceedings of the 23rd ACM SIGIR Conference, Athens, pp. 224-231, 2000.

[6] J. Morris, G. Hirst, *Lexical Cohesion by Thesaural Relations as an Indicator of the Structure of Text*, Computational Linguistics 17(1), March 1991.

[7] M. Halliday, R. Hasan, *Cohesion in English*, Longman: 1976.

[8] S. J. Green, *Automatically Generating Hypertext By Comparing Semantic Similarity*, University of Toronto, Technical Report number 366, October 1997.

[9] R. Barzilay, M. Elhadad, *Using Lexical Chains for Text Summarization*, In Proceedings of the Intelligent Scalable Text Summarization Workshop (ISTS'97), ACL, Madrid, 1997.

[10] D. St-Onge, *Detection and Correcting Malapropisms with Lexical Chains*, Dept. of Computer Science, University of Toronto, M.Sc Thesis, March 1995.

[11] M. A. Stairmand, W. J. Black, *Conceptual and Contextual Indexing using WordNet-derived Lexical Chains*, In the Proceedings of BCS IRSG Colloquium, pp. 47-65, 1997.

[12] M. Okumura, T. Honda, *Word sense disambiguation and text segmentation based on lexical cohesion*, In Proceedings of the Fifteen Conference on Computational Linguistics (COLING-94), volume 2, pp. 755-761, 1994.

[13] N. Stokes, P. Hatch, J. Carthy, *Topic Detection, a new application for lexical chaining?*, In the Proceedings of the 22nd BCS IRSG Colloquium on Information Retrieval, pp. 94-103, 2000.

[14] E. Fox, G. Nunn, W. Lee, *Coefficients for combining concept classes in a collection*, In the proceedings of the 11th ACM SIGIR Conference, pp. 291-308, 1988.

[15] J. Katzer, M. McGill, J. Tessier, W. Frakes, P. DasGupta, *A study of the overlap among document representations*, Information Technology: Research and Development, 1(4):261-274, 1982.

[16] K. Ng, P. Kantor, *An Investigation of the preconditions for effective data fusion in IR: A pilot study*, In the Proceedings of the 61th Annual Meeting of the American Society for Information Science 1998.

Guidelines for Annotating Temporal Information

Inderjeet Mani, George Wilson
The MITRE Corporation, W640
11493 Sunset Hills Road
Reston, Virginia 20190-5214, USA
+1-703-883-6149
imani@mitre.org

Lisa Ferro
The MITRE Corporation, K329
202 Burlington Road, Rte. 62
Bedford, MA 01730-1420, USA
+1-781-271-5875
lferro@mitre.org

Beth Sundheim
SPAWAR Systems Center, D44208
53140 Gatchell Road, Room 424B
Sand Diego, CA 92152-7420, USA
+1-619-553-4195
sundheim@spawar.navy.mil

ABSTRACT

This paper introduces a set of guidelines for annotating time expressions with a canonicalized representation of the times they refer to. Applications that can benefit from such an annotated corpus include information extraction (e.g., normalizing temporal references for database entry), question answering (answering "when" questions), summarization (temporally ordering information), machine translation (translating and normalizing temporal references), and information visualization (viewing event chronologies).

Keywords

Annotation, temporal information, semantics, ISO-8601.

1. INTRODUCTION

The processing of temporal information poses numerous challenges for NLP. Progress on these challenges may be accelerated through the use of corpus-based methods. This paper introduces a set of guidelines for annotating time expressions with a canonicalized representation of the times they refer to. Applications that can benefit from such an annotated corpus include information extraction (e.g., normalizing temporal references for database entry), question answering (answering "when" questions), summarization (temporally ordering information), machine translation (translating and normalizing temporal references), and information visualization (viewing event chronologies).

Our annotation scheme, described in detail in [Ferro et al. 2000], has several novel features:

- It goes well beyond the one used in the Message Understanding Conference [MUC7 1998], not only in terms of the range of expressions that are flagged, but, also, more importantly, in terms of representing and normalizing the

time *values* that are communicated by the expressions.

- In addition to handling fully-specified time expressions [e.g., *September 3rd, 1997*), it also handles *context-dependent* expressions. This is significant because of the ubiquity of context-dependent time expressions; a recent corpus study [Mani and Wilson 2000] revealed that more than two-thirds of time expressions in print and broadcast news were context-dependent ones. The context can be local (within the same sentence), e.g., *In 1995, the months of June and July were devilishly hot*, or global (outside the sentence), e.g., *The hostages were beheaded that afternoon*. A subclass of these context-dependent expressions are 'indexical' expressions, which require knowing when the speaker is speaking to determine the intended time value, e.g., *now, today, yesterday, tomorrow, next Tuesday, two weeks ago*, etc.

Our scheme differs from the recent scheme of [Setzer and Gaizauskas 2000] in terms of our in-depth focus on representations for the values of specific classes of time expressions, and in the application of our scheme to a variety of different genres, including print news, broadcast news, and meeting scheduling dialogs.

The annotation scheme has been designed to meet the following criteria:

Simplicity with precision: We have tried to keep the scheme simple enough to be executed confidently by humans, and yet precise enough for use in various natural language processing tasks.

Naturalness: We assume that the annotation scheme should reflect those distinctions that a human could be expected to reliably annotate, rather than reflecting an artificially-defined smaller set of distinctions that automated systems might be expected to make. This means that some aspects of the annotation will be well beyond the reach of current systems.

Expressiveness: The guidelines require that one specify time values as fully as possible, within the bounds of what can be confidently inferred by annotators. The use of 'parameters' and the representation of 'granularity' (described below) are tools to help ensure this.

Reproducibility: In addition to leveraging the [ISO-8601 1997] format for representing time values, we have tried to ensure consistency among annotators by providing an example-based approach, with each guideline closely tied to specific examples.

Proceedings of HLT 2001, First International Conference on Human Language Technology Research, J. Allan, ed., Morgan Kaufmann, San Francisco, 2001.

While the representation accommodates both points and intervals, the guidelines are aimed at using the point representation to the extent possible, further helping enforce consistency.

The annotation process is decomposed into two steps: flagging a temporal expression in a document, and identifying the time value that the expression designates, or that the speaker intends for it to designate. The flagging of temporal expressions is restricted to those temporal expressions which contain a reserved time word used in a temporal sense, called a 'lexical trigger', which include words like *day*, *week*, *weekend*, *now*, *Monday*, *current*, *future*, etc.

2. SEMANTIC DISTINCTIONS

Three different kinds of time values are represented: points in time (answering the question "when?"), durations (answering "how long?"), and frequencies (answering "how often?").

Points in time are calendar dates and times-of-day, or a combination of both, e.g., *Monday 3 pm, Monday next week, a Friday, early Tuesday morning, the weekend*. These are all represented with values (the tag attribute VAL) in the ISO format, which allows for representation of date of the month, month of the year, day of the week, week of the year, and time of day, e.g.,

<TIMEX2 VAL="2000-11-29-T16:30">4:30 p.m. yesterday afternoon</TIMEX2>.

Durations also use the ISO format to represent a period of time. When only the period of time is known, the value is represented as a duration, e.g.,

<TIMEX2 VAL="P3D">a three-day</TIMEX2> visit.

Frequencies reference *sets* of time points rather than particular points. SET and GRANULARITY attributes are used for such expressions, with the PERIODICITY attribute being used for regularly recurring times, e.g., *<TIMEX2 VAL="XXXX-WXX-2" SET="YES" PERIODICITY="F1W" GRANULARITY="G1D">every Tuesday</TIMEX2>*. Here "F1W" means frequency of once a week, and the granularity "G1D" means the set members are counted in day-sized units.

The annotation scheme also addresses several semantic problems characteristic of temporal expressions:

Fuzzy boundaries. Expressions like *Saturday morning* and *Fall* are fuzzy in their intended value with respect to when the time period starts and ends; *the early 60's* is fuzzy as to which part of the 1960's is included. Our format for representing time values includes parameters such as FA (for *Fall*), EARLY (for *early*, etc.), PRESENT_REF (for *today*, *current*, etc.), among others. For example, we have *<TIMEX2 VAL="1990-SU">Summer of 1990</TIMEX2>*. Fuzziness in modifiers is also represented, e.g., *<TIMEX2 VAL="1990" MOD="BEFORE">more than a*

decade ago</TIMEX2>. The intent here is that a given application may choose to assign specific values to these parameters if desired; the guidelines themselves don't dictate the specific values.

Non-Specificity. Our scheme directs the annotator to represent the values, where possible, of temporal expressions that do not indicate a specific time. These non-specific expressions include generics, which state a generalization or regularity of some kind, e.g., *<TIMEX2 VAL="XXXX-04" NON_SPECIFIC="YES">April</TIMEX2> is usually wet*, and non-specific indefinites, like *<TIMEX2 VAL="1999-06-XX" NON_SPECIFIC="YES" GRANULARITY="G1D">a sunny day in <TIMEX2 VAL="1999-06">June</TIMEX2></TIMEX2>*.

3. USEFULNESS

Based on the guidelines, we have annotated a small reference corpus, consisting of 35,000 words of newspaper text and 78,000 words of broadcast news [TDT2 1999]. Portions of this corpus were used to train and evaluate a time tagger with a reported F-measure of .83 [Mani and Wilson 2000]; the corpus has also been used to order events for summarization.

Others have used temporal annotation schemes for the much more constrained domain of meeting scheduling, e.g., [Wiebe et al. 1998], [Alexandersson et al. 1997], [Busemann et al. 1997]; our scheme has been applied to such domains as well. In particular, we have begun annotation of the 'Enthusiast' corpus of meeting scheduling dialogs used at CMU and by [Wiebe et al. 1998]. Only minor revisions to the guidelines' rules for tag extent have so far been required for these dialogs.

This annotation scheme is also being leveraged in the Automatic Content Extraction (ACE) program of the U.S. Department of Defense, whose focus is on extraction of time-dependent relations between pairs of 'entities' (persons, organizations, etc.).

Finally, initial feedback from Machine Translation system grammar writers [Levin, personal communication] indicates that the guidelines were found to be useful in extending an existing interlingua for machine translation.

4. CONCLUSION

The annotation scheme we have developed appears applicable to a wide variety of different genres of text. The semantic representation used is also highly language-independent. In Spring 2001, we will be embarking on a large-scale annotation effort using a merged corpus consisting of Enthusiast data as well as additional TDT2 data (inter-annotator agreement will also be measured then). An initial annotation exercise carried out on a sample of this merged corpus by 20 linguistics students using our guidelines has been encouraging, with 12 of the students following the guidelines in a satisfactory manner. In the future, we expect to extend this scheme to multilingual corpora.

5. ACKNOWLEDGMENTS

Our thanks to Lynn Carlson (Department of Defense), Lori Levin (Carnegie Mellon University), and Janyce Wiebe (University of Pittsburgh) for providing the Enthusiast corpus to us.

6. REFERENCES

[1] Alexandersson, J., Riethinger, N. and Maier, E. *Insights into the Dialogue Processing of VERBMOBIL.* Proceedings of the Fifth Conference on Applied Natural Language Processing, 1997, 33-40.

[2] Busemann, S., Decleck, T., Diagne, A. K., Dini, L., Klein, J. and Schmeier, S. *Natural Language Dialogue Service for Appointment Scheduling Agents.* Proceedings of the Fifth Conference on Applied Natural Language Processing, 1997, 25-32.

[3] Ferro, L., Mani, I., Sundheim, B., and Wilson, G. TIDES Temporal Annotation Guidelines. Draft Version 1.0. MITRE Technical Report MTR 00W0000094, October 2000.

[4] ISO-8601 ftp://ftp.qsl.net/pub/g1smd/8601v03.pdf 1997.

[5] Mani, I. and Wilson, G. *Robust Temporal Processing of News*, Proceedings of the ACL'2000 Conference, 3-6 October 2000, Hong Kong.

[6] MUC-7. Proceedings of the Seventh Message Understanding Conference, DARPA. 1998.

[7] Setzer, A. and Gaizauskas, R. *Annotating Events and Temporal Information in Newswire Texts.* Proceedings of the Second International Conference On Language Resources And Evaluation (LREC-2000), Athens, Greece, 31 May- 2 June 2000.

[8] TDT2 http://morph.ldc.upenn.edu/Catalog/LDC99T37.html 1999

[9] Wiebe, J. M., O'Hara, T. P., Ohrstrom-Sandgren, T. and McKeever, K. J. *An Empirical Approach to Temporal Reference Resolution.* Journal of Artificial Intelligence Research, 9, 1998, pp. 247-293.

Hypothesis Selection and Resolution
in the Mercury Flight Reservation System

Stephanie Seneff and Joseph Polifroni
Spoken Language Systems Group
Laboratory for Computer Science
Massachusetts Institute of Technology
Cambridge, Massachusetts 02139 USA
{seneff,joe}@sls.lcs.mit.edu) *

ABSTRACT

In a spoken dialogue system, the degree to which the dialogue manager informs and controls the behavior of other human language technology components is an important research topic. Although each separate server can be developed and trained on its own, it must function as part of an entire system, and do so in the context of a complex dialogue with a human user. The dialogue manager is the one component that has not only local information from each server, but also global knowledge about the task and specific knowledge about a particular user's constraints. In this paper, we describe various algorithms we have developed for exploiting the knowledge of the dialogue manager in the selection of recognition hypotheses in the context of human-machine interactions. We describe enhancements we have made to other human language technology servers for the purpose of providing useful information to the dialogue manager, as well as new capabilities in the dialogue manager itself aimed at detecting and repairing problematic spots in the dialogue. We conclude by describing some evaluation metrics and tools we have developed for monitoring system performance.

1. INTRODUCTION

In a spoken dialogue system, one of the most difficult aspects is assuring that the system understood correctly each user query, or, if not, that the system is able to recover gracefully and efficiently from the errors. A tedious though effective strategy is to prompt the user at each turn, soliciting only one piece of information, subsequently verifying through a confirmation subdialogue that it has been correctly understood. A more natural interface would allow the user much greater freedom, but at the price of signifi-

---

*This research was supported by DARPA under contract N66001-99-8904 monitored through Naval, Command, Control and Ocean Surveillance Center.

cantly higher perplexity. In such a mixed-initiative system, it becomes important to draw on as many constraints as possible to aid in the hypothesis selection task. Explicit confirmation can yield greater confidence in the validity of hypothesized utterances, but, again, at the risk of increased tediousness.

This paper discusses how the MIT MERCURY flight reservation system [8] deals with the issues of hypothesis selection and verification. It utilizes a mixed-initiative dialogue strategy supported by confirmation subdialogues that are invoked only when the system actively suspects miscommunication. The system is implemented within the Galaxy Communicator architecture [7], where a central hub mediates interactions among a distributed set of specialized servers. For hypothesis selection, relevant information is retained from prior turns, stored by the hub and distributed to the appropriate servers as requested, mediated via the hub program. The recognizer and the parser, as well as the discourse, dialogue, and generation components, all play a role in the selection process.

The MERCURY system poses interesting and challenging problems for dialogue systems in that the interaction is complex and involves multiple variables. Once these variables are specified, users can become quite confused and the dialogue can be derailed if a serious misrecognition occurs. In the remainder of this paper, we will first give a brief overview of the entire MERCURY system, and describe both the hypothesis selection process and the method that is used to control dialogue management. Next we describe the confirmation algorithm, which as a policy only confirms when it detects an unexpected response from the user. Following this is a section on our various knowledge sources and their representations. After giving a few example dialogues, we present some evaluation results, including a discussion of how we evaluate the system. We conclude with a summary and a look to the future.

2. OVERALL SYSTEM DESCRIPTION

MERCURY is a spoken dialogue system that allows users to plan air travel between over 500 cities worldwide. The system currently gets all of its flight and fare information from the Travelocity Web site (www.travelocity.com). Following log-on, the user interacts with the system to select the flights of their itinerary. When the flight plan is completed, the system takes the initiative in offering to price and email the itinerary. Finally, the system optionally asks the user a

Proceedings of HLT 2001, First International Conference on Human Language Technology Research, J. Allan, ed., Morgan Kaufmann, San Francisco, 2001.

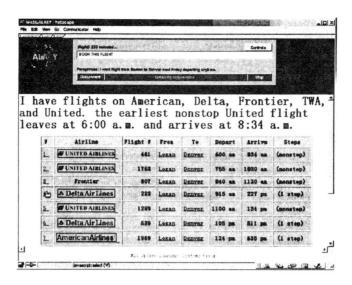

Figure 1: An illustration of the graphical interface to MERCURY. **Airline names and source and destination are linked to Web pages for the corresponding airlines and airports. Th user has clicked on the fourth flight, and is asking to add it to the itinerary.**

S:	Welcome to the MIT air travel planning system. . . . For enrolled users, please say your first and last name. Otherwise, say, new user.
U:	john doe
S:	Please speak the month and day you registered as your password, as in, 'May first'.
U:	october nineteenth
S:	Welcome John. How may I help you?
U:	i need to fly to salt lake city on may eighth in the afternoon
S:	Okay, flights from Boston to Salt Lake City departing between noon and 6:00 p.m. on Tuesday May eighth. One moment please . . . I have a nonstop Delta flight leaving at 5:55 p.m. and arriving at 9:19 p.m.? Would that work?
U:	is there an earlier flight
S:	Okay, flights from Boston to Salt Lake City departing before 5:55 p.m. on Tuesday May eighth. One moment please . . . What about a Delta flight connecting in New York's Kennedy leaving at 3:25 p.m.? Would that work? I also have a United flight connecting in Chicago O'Hare leaving at 3:30 p.m.
U:	i would like a nonstop flight leaving anytime during the day
S:	Okay, nonstop flights from Boston to Salt Lake City departing between 5:00 am and 8:00 p.m. on Tuesday May eighth. One moment please . . . I have 3 nonstop Delta flights: a flight leaving at 7:00 a.m., a flight leaving at 10:25 a.m., and a flight leaving at 5:55 p.m. Please select one of these flights or change any constraint you have already specified.
U:	i will take the ten twenty [five] flight please
S:	Delta flight 1035 has been added to your itinerary. you depart Boston at 10:25 am and arrive in Salt Lake City at 1:45 p.m. What date will you be returning on?
U:	i would like to return on friday
S:	Okay, Delta flights from Salt Lake City to Boston on Friday May eleventh. One moment please . . . I have 3 nonstop flights: a flight leaving at 9:55 a.m., a flight leaving at 2:35 p.m., and a flight leaving at 5:00 p.m. Please select one.
U:	what time does the two thirty five flight arrive in boston
S:	Delta flight 1473 arrives at 9:05 p.m. in Boston. Shall I add this flight to your itinerary?
U:	what time is [does] that flight leave
S:	I have a nonstop Delta flight leaving at 2:35 p.m. and arriving at 9:05 p.m.? Would that work?
U:	yes please
S:	Delta flight 1473 has been added to your itinerary. you depart Salt Lake City at 2:35 p.m. and arrive in Boston at 9:05 p.m. Would you like me to find out how much your trip will cost?
U:	yes please
S:	Pricing your itinerary will take a while. In the meantime I'll summarize your itinerary for you.On Tuesday May eighth on Delta flight 1035, you depart from Boston at 10:25 a.m. and arrive in Salt Lake City at 1:45 p.m., on Friday May eleventh on Delta flight 1473, you depart from Salt Lake City at 2:35 p.m. and arrive in Boston at 9:05 p.m. The cheapest price for your trip is $455.00. Shall I email your itinerary to you?
U:	yes please
S:	Your itinerary has been emailed to you. Can I help you with anything else?

Figure 2: Example dialogue between a user and the system involving a real trip. "U" denotes a user utterance, and "S" a system utterance. The name has been changed for reasons of anonymity. Words in brackets under the user's turn represent what was actually said rather than what was recognized.

:Week | :Day | :RelDate	$\longrightarrow$	ResolveRelativeDate
:ReturnDate : :Date	$\longrightarrow$	CheckInvalidDate
:HypList & :ImplausibleReturnDate | :RejectedDate	$\longrightarrow$	SelectAlternateDate
:RequestDateConfirmation	$\longrightarrow$	PromptDateConfirm
:ConfirmDate deny	$\longrightarrow$	RequestKeypadDate

Figure 3: Selected entries from MERCURY's dialogue control table concerning dates.

few questions to help determine user satisfaction. MERCURY is intended to be up at all times, and can be reached via a toll-free telephone number (877-628-8255). It is also accessible in displayful mode from a Web page, in which case the spoken interaction is augmented with a graphical display of the set of retrieved flights. A multimodal interface supports clicking on a displayed flight and referring to it verbally: "Book this one," as illustrated in Figure 1.

A telephone dialogue between a naive user and MERCURY is shown in Figure 2. It should be clear from the dialogue that the system offers specific suggestions when appropriate: "Shall I add this flight to your itinerary?" "Can you provide a departure or arrival time?" However, the user is free to say anything at any time; i.e., the full recognition vocabulary is always present. We have always been interested in building dialogue systems that were flexible in this regard, but we are fully aware that a consequence is that recognition errors, which are inevitable, may lead to incoherent dialogues, unless a great deal of attention is devoted to error recovery.

We have thus far collected over 2000 dialogues with users, mostly over the course of the last year. These dialogues were all recorded in detail in log files, and the user queries were also digitally recorded to be used later for training both the recognizer and the natural language component. Perusal of the log files has led to the design of several interrelated strategies for hypothesis resolution, where we make use of diverse sources of information to infer the most plausible solution, including, at times, an explicit request for confirmation of a suspicious hypothesis.

2.1 System Architecture

MERCURY makes use of the GALAXY architecture [6, 7], consisting of a number of specialized servers that communicate with one another via a central programmable hub. An audio server captures the user's speech via a Dialogic board, and transmits the waveform to the speech recognizer [2]. The language understanding component [9] parses a word graph produced by the recognizer and delivers a semantic frame, encoding the meaning of the utterance, to the discourse component. The output of the discourse component [5] is the frame-in-context, which is transformed into a flattened E-form (electronic form) by the generation server. This E-form is delivered to the dialogue manager, and provides the initial settings of the dialogue state.

The dialogue manager consults a *dialogue control table* to decide which operations to perform, and typically engages in a module-to-module subdialogue to retrieve tables from the database. It prepares a response frame, which may or may not include tabular entries. The response frame is sent to the generation component [1] which transforms it in parallel into both a text string and an annotated string that specifies the input controls for the speech synthesizer. Finally, the speech synthesizer [10] transmits a waveform to the audio

server which then relays the spoken response to the user over the telephone. The entire dialogue is recorded in detail in a log file for later examination.

2.2 Hypothesis Selection Process

Hypothesis selection is a complex process in MERCURY that involves several steps, including interactions among multiple servers. This process is represented schematically in Figure 4. The recognizer provides a *word graph* representing multiple sentence hypotheses, with associated confidence scores for each word in the graph. The NL component parses the graph, producing an N-best list of *semantic frames*, capturing alternative candidates for the meaning of the utterance. A selection process singles out the most promising of these frames, taking into account possible discourse context, and presents this candidate to the dialogue manager. The dialogue manager then decides whether this request is consistent with the prior dialogue. If some part of the query is problematic, it may do one of several things:

1. Ask the user for explicit confirmation,
2. Seek an alternative hypothesis from the N-best list, that may be more appropriate pragmatically,
3. Reject (delete) certain attributes that are both pragmatically inappropriate and poorly scoring,
4. Initiate a subdialogue asking for confirmation,
5. Ask the user to keypad in the information, as a redundant, but less errorful, source.

The recognizer processes the recorded user waveform and produces a word graph with associated confidence scores for each word in the graph [4]. The confidence scores are based mainly on the log likelihood probabilities of the words, obtained from the acoustic models for their component phones. The confidence scores are obtained from a set of ten features that are combined into a single score using linear discriminant techniques. In addition to the mean and minimum log likelihood score of the word in all of its possible local alignments, the combined score takes into account also the difference between the word's score and the best score obtainable over the same acoustic space, and also against the score of a "catch-all" model. The number of competitors for the acoustic region is also taken into account.

The first step in hypothesis selection is to parse the recognizer's word graph into a set of candidate semantic frames. This is done with our TINA natural language system [9], which parses from a context free grammar augmented with feature unification and a trace mechanism for movement. A stochastic grammar, trained on a large corpus of within-domain sentences, guides the Viterbi search through the word graph. Acoustic and linguistic scores are combined to give an overall sentence score. In addition to the total combined score for each hypothesis, critical content words (e.g., cities and dates) retain their confidence score associ-

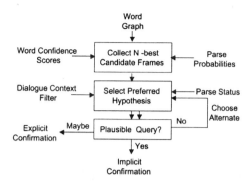

Figure 4: A block diagram of the process of hypothesis selection and verification.

ated with the corresponding element in the semantic frame, for possible later consideration by the dialogue manager.

Each candidate semantic frame is also labelled according to its parse status, with one of four possible categories: "full parse," "robust parse," "phrase spot," and "no parse." "Full parse" means that a single coherent parse tree accounted for every word in the hypothesis. "Robust parse" means that every word was accounted for, but the parse structure consists of a sequence of parsed fragments with possibly interspersed licensed "skip words." "Phrase spot" means that large parts of the hypothesis may have been totally ignored, but certain critical, high scoring, content words were singled out for parsing. Even with all of these back-off mechanism, it is still the case that some user utterances are unparseable. The dialogue manager is responsible for providing a context-dependent response for this "no parse" category (see below).

The next step is to use a simple heuristic to select the most promising candidate from the set of parsed frames. In the absence of any directives from the dialogue component, the system simply chooses the highest scoring full-parse theory, backing off to robust-parse, and finally phrase-spotting. However, it is often the case that the dialogue component has set up context conditions that will preferentially favor an otherwise sub-optimal theory. This can include a list of one or more semantic categories that are in focus, and/or, in some cases, individual words that are highlighted, or individual words that are to be selected *against*. For example, if the system has just asked the user for a return date, then all dates are given preferential treatment. Similarly, if it has just listed the cities it knows in Kentucky, those cities will be highlighted.

Once the most promising hypothesis has been singled out, it is processed through context resolution and delivered to the dialogue manager for consideration. If all goes well, the new information is interpreted and a response is prepared that moves the dialogue plan closer to a conclusion. The alternative hypotheses are retained, but utilized only when there is reason to believe the selected hypothesis is erroneous, as discussed in the following section.

2.3 Dialogue Control Mechanism

The dialogue manager is tasked with the difficult responsibility of determining how best to answer each user's query. With each turn, it processes the user's query, represented as a semantic frame, and prepares its meaning response, also

represented as a semantic frame. The generation component converts the reply *frame* into a well formed *reply string*, to be spoken back to the user.

As mentioned earlier, dialogue control is managed in MER-CURY through the use of a *dialogue control table*. This table is a simple device for managing complexity – it enforces a linear organization of the complex planning tasks of dialogue management, and provides a high-level representation of dialogue activities in an outline form. The table takes the form of a set of rules, specifying functions to be called when specified conditions are met. The conditions are tests (boolean, arithmetic, string match, etc.) on variables maintained in a dynamic *dialogue state* frame. The variables are initialized from the user's query (in context), and are augmented in the course of a dialogue turn by the various functions that are executed. Each function, which has access to the entire knowledge base (see Section 4), is allowed to return one of three possible "move" states: *continue*, *restart*, and *stop*, with the obvious meanings. *Restart* is typically used to reevaluate a query after dropping a constraint, given that no flights match against the original set of constraints. A final "exit function" is executed at the conclusion of each turn, which updates the dialogue history and finalizes the various parameters that are to be returned to the hub program.

It is up to the system developer to partition the dialogue tasks into a set of specific functions, and to choreograph the order in which, and conditions under which each function should be called. Ideally, each function has a very specific role, some having to do with verifying that the query is fully specified, others involved with retrieving the information from the database, and still others involved with preparing the reply frame. MERCURY's dialogue control table currently contains over 350 rules. Typically, up to twenty or more rules may fire in a single turn.

A selected subset of the rules concerned with managing dates is shown in Figure 3. The first rule is concerned with resolving references such as "the following Friday" or "three days later." The second rule tests whether the understood date is within the time window of MERCURY's knowledge base (ten months into the future), and whether the dates of the itinerary are causal and plausible. It sets up keys that are used by the third rule to search for a more plausible date hypothesis from the N-best list. The fourth rule sets up a prompt to confirm with the user whether the understood date is indeed what they said. The final rule initiates a request for a keypad entry of the date, after the user has rejected a confirmation.

3. CONFIRMATION

By default, the system confirms implicitly what the user said, as illustrated in figure 2, by repeating the understood constraints in the reply. The user then has the opportunity to override any incorrectly understood constraints in a follow-up utterance. However, a number of different conditions can trigger an *explicit* confirmation subdialogue, in which the system delays action pending further input from the user. The general strategy is as follows: if the system detects an unanticipated request from the user, it asks for confirmation. In some cases, it also requests redundant entry via the telephone keypad. The critical pieces of information that may invoke a confirmation subdialogue include signing on, source and destination, travel date, and signing off. The system also considers "no parse" to be a problematic condition, and a context-dependent response to this situation has been implemented.

Signing On The user signs on by providing orally their name and a password encoded as a date. If an incompatibility is detected, the system then invites the user to enter the password using the telephone keypad. At this point, if the password still appears to be incorrect, the system reexamines alternative hypotheses for the user name, applying a strict filter on the subset that are supported by the password. If this last step fails, the system defaults to a guest-user status.

Source and Destination A number of difficult situations can arise regarding cities, each of which is given special treatment. For example, whenever the user appears to change the source or destination at a point in the dialogue where this is unexpected, the system asks for confirmation. If confirmation fails, it then offers help by informing the user that they can ask what cities it knows in a particular state or country. It is essentially hypothesizing that the user may want to travel to a city that is outside of its known vocabulary.

An interesting case is when the user appears to have identified both a city and a state/country, but they are pragmatically incompatible, e.g., "to Dallas New Jersey." In such cases, it compares the confidence scores to decide which one is most likely to be trustworthy. If it is the state, it lists the cities it knows for that state. Otherwise it accepts the hypothesized city and discards the state.

Under special circumstances, when the system determines that a hypothesized source or destination is likely to be incorrect, it invites the user to enter the city using the telephone keypad. We have determined that, although MER-CURY knows over 500 cities, they are uniquely represented by the letter mappings corresponding to the keypad, despite the 3-to-1 ambiguity in spelling words using the keypad. Cities are highly ambiguous if only the first three characters are entered. Thus, the system is licensed to accept a partially spelled city only if it matches a prior hypothesis available from the dialogue history. The algorithm that triggers keypadding of the city is conservative, as this is a rather tedious process and should be avoided unless repeated spoken attempts are failing.

Dates The first time the user provides a date for the next leg of a trip, the system assumes it was correctly recognized, unless it violates pragmatic constraints. However, if the user appears to change a prespecified date, the system prompts for confirmation prior to accepting the changed date. If confirmation fails, the user is invited to key in the date using the telephone keypad. If the user appears to be repeating the same date in isolation, the system suspects a miscommunication. It then browses through any alternative candidate frames, seeking one that provides a novel date. Regardless of whether it succeeds, it prompts the user for confirmation of the selected date candidate, again invoking the telephone keypad upon failure.

We make use of a "date history" (see below) as a way of determining whether a given recognized date conforms with what we know about the dialogue so far, or if the user should be prompted for confirmation. The heuristics around this date history are an ongoing research issue, but this detailed record has proven to be a valuable source of knowledge about

```
{c city_history
 :source "BOS"   :source_status "inherited"
 :dest "GSO"  :dest_status "changed"
 :history {c city_history
          :source "BOS" :source_status "inherited"
          :dest "GSP" :dest_status "repeated"
          :history {c city_history
                   :source "BOS"
                   :source_status "first"
                   :dest "GSP"
                   :dest_status "first" } } }
```

Figure 5: Example city history frame representing the activities in the last three utterances concerning source and destination. This record shows that the source was inherited in the last two utterances, whereas the destination was apparently first repeated and then changed, a likely condition for recognition error. Note: GSO = Greensboro, GSP = Greenville, and BOS = Boston.

the dialogue.

Signing Off A surprisingly difficult aspect of mixed-initiative dialogue is deciding when the user is saying "good bye." The problem is that a false recognition is catastrophic here, because the effect is to terminate the conversation. When the user is apparently terminating, the system uses pragmatics to determine whether this is a point at which reasonable closure has been reached. If not, it asks for confirmation.

No Parse Whenever the system fails to understand the user's query, there is the potential that the user's plan and the system's plan may be in conflict. It could be that the user is trying to go to a city that is not supported, or that the system is making a false presupposition about the itinerary. Thus, for example, a "no parse" will trigger a request for keypadding the source or destination, if there is any evidence of confusion with regard to this attribute at that time.

The system asks, "where would you like to go next?" after each flight is selected for the itinerary, and if the user intends a one-way trip, they may phrase that information in a way that is not covered by the grammar. Therefore, in this context, the system always responds to a "no parse" with the reply, "Is this a one-way trip?"

A single "no parse" without any clear evidence for a dialogue disconnect yields a simple apology: "I'm sorry, I'm not sure what you said." A subsequent "no parse" is treated as a request for "help," and invokes a sophisticated dialogue-context dependent *help* mechanism, to try to dislodge the user from an ineffective communication strategy.

4. KNOWLEDGE SOURCES

In order to inform hypothesis selection at any point in the dialogue, we make use of several knowledge sources that are maintained and updated continually throughout the user's conversation with the system. The dialogue state is, of course, one of the most useful of these knowledge sources. The dialogue state encodes parts of both sides of the conversation, in that it identifies any preceding system-initiated query as well as all user-specified constraints. The dialogue state also contains information on how far the user has come in the overall travel plan, which is helpful in determining if

149

S:	Welcome . . . For enrolled users, please say your first and last name. Otherwise, say 'new user.'
U:	Jane Doe
S:	Please speak the month and day you registered as your password, as in 'May first.'
U:	September six [misrecognized]
S:	Sorry. I didn't catch that. Please enter your four digit date password using the telephone keypad. [successful enrollment]

Figure 6: A dialogue with a user involving logging on, where the keypad entry of the date was successful. The name has been altered for privacy reasons.

S:	. . . Continental flight 1662 has been added to your itinerary. You depart San Francisco at 6:30 a.m. and arrive in Houston at 12:20 p.m. What date will you be returning on?
U:	May third [misrecognized]
S:	Okay. Continental flights from Houston to San Francisco on Thursday May third. One moment please . . . Can you provide a departure or arrival time? The earliest nonstop flight leaves at 7:40 a.m. and arrives at 9:59 a.m.
U:	Nope March third
S:	Please enter the four digit month and day using the telephone keypad.
U:	0303 [keypad]
S:	Okay. Continental flights from Houston to San Francisco on Saturday, March third. One moment please . . .

Figure 7: A dialogue with a user where the system prompted for a keypad entry of the date, with subsequent success.

U:	When is the next flight from Anchorage to Seattle?
S:	Flights from Anchorage to Seattle. What airline are you interested in?
U:	Delta
S:	Okay. Delta flights from Anchorage to Seattle on Thursday February 22. One moment please . . . I couldn't find any flights on Delta. I have a nonstop Alaska Airlines flight leaving at 8:59 p.m. and arriving at 1:14 a.m. You arrive the following day. Would that work?
U:	Yes, connecting to San Diego
S:	I heard you say you want to arrive in San Diego. Is that correct? If you need help, you can say, for example, 'What cities do you know in Oregon.'
U:	[I] know Portland.
S:	Please enter the full name of the destination city using the telephone keypad.

Figure 8: A dialogue in which the system was provoked to request a keypad input on the destination city. This request was unsuccessful (the user hung up).

a particular dialogue move is likely.

The system also retains in history a *user model* which is continually augmented as the dialogue progresses through the itinerary plan. It includes any as yet unverified constraints that have been specified but are not yet enforceable, such as an early specification of the return date or the mention of a desired fare class before the itinerary is completed. It also includes the particular details of the selected partial itinerary, which are useful for applying date and source constraints to later legs. In addition, a set of frames is maintained for alternative recognizer hypotheses of dates, for possible later reselection. If the original date is pragmatically implausible, alternative dates are selected from this set. The alternates are flushed each time a new leg is selected.

We have instrumented a detailed record-keeping mechanism for tracking source and destination throughout a dialogue. We have found these two keys to be especially problematic, particularly in cases where the user may be attempting to travel to or from a city that is not in the recognizer's vocabulary. In these cases, the same misrecognition tends to occur repeatedly, as the recognizer continues to substitute the same incorrect hypothesis for the intended city, or the source/destination in question varies from query to query, as the recognizer hypothesizes different cities within its known vocabulary. By monitoring the patterns of source/destination keys from query to query, we hope to be

able to decide when to prompt for verification or to solicit keypad input.

Each source and destination city is entered into this history throughout the course of a single dialogue. This history is updated for each turn in which these values are present, either from the user utterance or from inheritance. A status is stored along with the city, indicating whether the city was newly introduced in that turn, changed, repeated, or inherited from a previous turn. The record is stored in a nested frame structure, as illustrated in Figure 5. For each query containing source or destination keys, this record is consulted to determine if the values are consistent with what has appeared before in the dialogue. The city history is flushed whenever a flight is selected for the itinerary. We are currently developing heuristics for determining how to proceed when specific patterns of activity are showing up. Options, as discussed above, are to enter a subdialogue to confirm a newly introduced destination, or to seek a redundant (but in some cases more reliable) entry using the telephone keypad.

5. EXAMPLE DIALOGUES

In this section, we present a number of real dialogues, to illustrate various situations where keypad entry was requested. Figure 6 shows a segment of a dialogue where keypad entry was successful for enrolling the password during the logging on stage. Figure 7 provides an example dialogue where successful keypad entry of a date was triggered. Fig-

To: sls-developers@sls.lcs.mit.edu
From: mercury
Subject: successful dialogue with mercury

The fourth successful dialogue with john doe has just finished. The itinerary was priced at 567.25. The following itinerary was reserved. on Wednesday April 18 on American flight 277, you depart from Boston at 9:30 am and arrive in San Diego at 12:49 pm., on Friday April 20 on American flight 2790, you depart from San Diego at 6:04 pm and arrive in San Jose California at 7:20 pm., on Monday April 23 on American flight 108, you depart from San Jose California at 8:00 am and arrive in Boston at 4:45 pm.

Figure 9: Example of the email message that is sent to system developers when a MERCURY dialogue is completed.

ure 8 shows a rather confusing dialogue in which the system was provoked to request a keypad entry of the departure city. The system did not understand how to interpret the user's rather cryptic utterance, "Yes, connecting to San Diego." One might surmise that the user was not attentive to the system's response during the third turn, and therefore *answered* the question, "What cities do you know in Oregon," rather than asking it. The user hung up at this point, so the keypad request was *not* successful.

We have seen several cases where keypadding was effective for both passwords and dates. Since we have only recently introduced the option to keypad cities into the live system, we are not yet able to say whether this is a productive strategy. At issue is whether the user can keypad an entire city name without errors. We will also probably need to refine the algorithm based on the outcomes of continued dialogue collections.

6. EVALUATION

Dialogue is a notoriously difficult aspect of human language technology to evaluate. The dialogue manager informs and affects the performance of many other parts of the system. The intelligence built into the dialogue manager, exemplified above, is essential for the correct selection and interpretation of utterances in the context of a dialogue. Word, sentence, and concept error rate, all applied on a per-utterance basis, are not sufficient by themselves to indicate that a particular dialogue strategy is more effective for a particular task.

It is not possible to compare two dialogue strategies on the same data. Furthermore, it is difficult both to implement and to interpret a re-evaluation of an enhanced version of the system, because of problems related to both dialogue incoherence and dynamic knowledge sources. We have had some success in reprocessing log files, although the results must be interpreted with care. Furthermore, it is essential to maintain detailed log files that contain representations of all knowledge sources, in order to be able to use them for reprocessing.

6.1 Dialogue Evaluation Metrics

We have recently developed two new metrics, *Query Density* and *Concept Efficiency* to attempt to measure system performance at the dialogue level [3]. These metrics are meant to quantify how effectively a user can convey new information to a system (the "query density"), and how efficiently the system can absorb information from a user ("concept efficiency").

Computing the QD and CE metrics requires reprocessing of dialogue data, after an orthographic transcription has been supplied by hand. Two parallel paths through the entire system are mediated by hub scripts. In the first, the recognizer hypothesis from the time the data were collected is processed; in the second, the orthography of what the user actually said is similarly processed. For each of these paths, a separate key-value representation is obtained and sent to the evaluation server for processing. However, the discourse and dialogue content is maintained exclusively by the branch dealing with the recognizer hypothesis. In this way, the dialogue proceeds as it did at the time of data collection, modulo changes to the data sources and the dialogue manager. Because all of our systems make use of continually updated, dynamic data sources, it is virtually impossible to guarantee that the dialogue interactions which occur during a subsequent evaluation will be coherent.

In typical evaluations on these measures, the system obtains around 1.5 for QD, i.e., on average, one and a half successfully communicated attributes per query, and .92 on CE, i.e., 8% of the attributes had to be repeated.

6.2 "Living" Evaluation

We have found that one of the most important assessment procedures is to manually examine log files of interactions with users, and to guide system development based on interactions where it is clear that alternative approaches would have benefited. This is an iterative procedure tightly coupling data collection efforts with system development. To expedite this process, we have developed mechanisms for monitoring MERCURY's performance on a daily basis, which have been instrumented both in hub programs and by automatic post-processing of session log files.

When a dialogue is completed with the MERCURY system, mail is immediately sent to system developers. This mail is triggered by a rule in a hub program, and provides a summary in English (generated by the system's generation component) of the itinerary obtained, as illustrated in Figure 9. In addition, the mail specifies who the user was and how much experience the user has had in using the MERCURY system (i.e., how many previous calls have been logged to that user). The system also sends a daily email to system developers, summarizing MERCURY's activity on that day. It includes statistics on itineraries obtained and utterances parsed per dialogue, as well as providing a to-date summary of total data collected for the MERCURY system.

Each call to the MERCURY system produces a detailed log file of the interaction, as well as digitized waveform files for each utterance spoken. We have set up a web-based interface to these data, summarizing the interactions for any given day on one page and providing links to separate web pages for each dialogue. By going to a particular dialogue page, a developer can see at a glance the entire interaction, listen to what was spoken, and examine the frames that were used by the MERCURY system in answering each query. In addition, the developer can transcribe or edit a transcript of the speech. Figure 10 shows an example of such a webpage for a recent MERCURY dialogue.

Finally, we ask the users themselves to rate the system

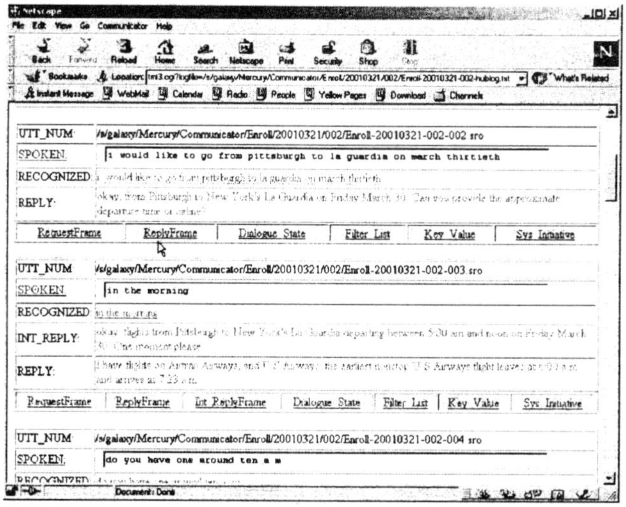

Figure 10: A web page showing a dialogue with a Mercury user. Links point to multiple knowledge sources derived from the log file, as well as enabling playing and transcribing user utterances.

at the end of every dialogue. When a user completes an itinerary or otherwise ends a session, the system asks the user to remain on the line to answer two Yes/No questions ("Was this a real trip you were planning?", "Were you satisfied with the system?") and one query to elicit any comments or suggestions the user has. By transcribing and parsing the responses to these queries, we can automatically correlate user satisfaction and system relevance to other more easily quantified measures of system performance.

7. SUMMARY

This paper has focused on the process involved in determining what the user has plausibly intended at each dialogue turn in a mixed-initiative dialogue, conditioned on a recognizer word graph with associated word confidence scores. The dialogue component directly influences the initial selection process, at least whenever it has provided a specific context. While a set of N-best semantic frames is produced, most of the attention is directed towards the primary selected candidate. After perusal, several problematic situations trigger a response that involves confirmation requests and/or help messages. Sometimes components of the frame are ignored, either because the system can find no appropriate interpretation for them, they have low confidence scores, and/or they conflict with other information present in the same frame. The general strategy is to invoke confirmation subdialogues only when the user appears to make a surprise move. Similarly, alternative hypotheses are only considered when the top hypothesis leads to pragmatically implausible outcomes.

We have found the strategy of backing off to the telephone keypad to be an effective way to ensure successful communication in the face of compromised recognition. We have had extensive experience with keypadding the login password and the dates of the itinerary. Keypadding source and destination city has only been introduced very recently, and it is too early to tell if this method will be effective for cities. Plans are underway to extend this capability to apply to the enrollment of the user name, and ultimately, as an aid in the

enrollment of unknown words (e.g., new city or user name).

8. REFERENCES

[1] L. Baptist and S. Seneff, "Genesis-II: A Versatile System for Language Generation in Conversational System Applications," *Proc. ICSLP '00*, Beijing, China, Oct. 2000.

[2] J. Glass, J. Chang, and M. McCandless. "A Probabilistic Framework for Feature-based Speech Recognition," *Proc. ICSLP '96*, pp. 2277–2280, Philadelphia, PA, 1996.

[3] J. Glass, J. Polifroni, S. Seneff, and V. Zue, "Data Collection and Performance Evaluation of Spoken Dialogue Systems: The MIT Experience," *Proc. ICSLP '00*, Vol. IV, pp. 1–4, Beijing, China, 2000, Oct. 2000.

[4] T. Hazen, T. Burianek, J. Polifroni, and S. Seneff, "Integrating Recognition and Confidence Scoring with Language Understanding and Dialogue Modelling," *Proc. ICSLP-2000*, pp. 1042–1045, Beijing, China, Oct., 2000.

[5] S. Seneff, D. Goddeau, C. Pao, and J. Polifroni, "Multimodal Discourse Modelling in a Multi-user Multi-domain Environment," *Proc. ICSLP-96*, pp 192-195, Oct., 1996.

[6] S. Seneff, E. Hurley, R. Lau, C. Pao, P. Schmid, and V. Zue, "Galaxy-II: A Reference Architecture for Conversational System Development," *Proc. ICSLP '98*, pp. 931-934, Sydney, Australia, Dec., 1998.

[7] S. Seneff, R. Lau, and J. Polifroni, "Organization, Communication, and Control in the GALAXY-II Conversational System," *Proc. Eurospeech '99*, Budapest, Hungary, pp. 1271–1274, Oct., 1999.

[8] S. Seneff and J. Polifroni, "Dialogue Management in the MERCURY Flight Reservation System," *Proc. ANLP-NAACL 2000, Satellite Workshop*, Seattle, WA, May, 2000.

[9] S. Seneff, "TINA: A Natural Language System for Spoken Language Applications," *Computational Linguistics*, Vol. 18, No. 1, pp. 61–86, 1992.

[10] J. R. Yi, and Glass, J. R., 1998. Natural-sounding Speech Synthesis using Variable-length Units. *Proc. ICSLP '98*, Sydney, Australia, pp. 1167-1170, Nov., 1998.

Improved Cross-Language Retrieval using Backoff Translation

Philip Resnik,[1,2] Douglas Oard,[2,3] and Gina Levow[2]
Department of Linguistics,[1]
Institute for Advanced Computer Studies,[2]
College of Information Studies,[3]
University of Maryland
College Park, MD 20742
{resnik,gina}@umiacs.umd.edu, oard@glue.umd.edu

ABSTRACT

The limited coverage of available translation lexicons can pose a serious challenge in some cross-language information retrieval applications. We present two techniques for combining evidence from dictionary-based and corpus-based translation lexicons, and show that backoff translation outperforms a technique based on merging lexicons.

1. INTRODUCTION

The effectiveness of a broad class of cross-language information retrieval (CLIR) techniques that are based on term-by-term translation depends on the coverage and accuracy of the available translation lexicon(s). Two types of translation lexicons are commonly used, one based on translation knowledge extracted from bilingual dictionaries [1] and the other based on translation knowledge extracted from bilingual corpora [8]. Dictionaries provide reliable evidence, but often lack translation preference information. Corpora, by contrast, are often a better source for translations of slang or newly coined terms, but the statistical analysis through which the translations are extracted sometimes produces erroneous results. In this paper we explore the question of how best to combine evidence from these two sources.

2. TRANSLATION LEXICONS

Our term-by-term translation technique (described below) requires a translation lexicon (henceforth *tralex*) in which each word f is associated with a ranked set $\{e_1, e_2, \ldots e_n\}$ of translations. We used two translation lexicons in our experiments.

2.1 WebDict Tralex

We downloaded a freely available, manually constructed English-French term list from the Web[1] and inverted it to French-English

---

[1] http://www.freedict.com

Proceedings of HLT 2001, First International Conference on Human Language Technology Research, J. Allan, ed., Morgan Kaufmann, San Francisco, 2001.

format. Since the WebDict translations appear in no particular order, we ranked the e_i based on target language unigram statistics calculated over a large comparable corpus, the English portion of the Cross-Language Evaluation Forum (CLEF) collection, smoothed with statistics from the Brown corpus, a balanced corpus covering many genres of English. All single-word translations are ordered by decreasing unigram frequency, followed by all multi-word translations, and finally by any single-word entries not found in either corpus. This ordering has the effect of minimizing the effect of infrequent words in non-standard usages or of misspellings that sometimes appear in bilingual term lists.

2.2 STRAND Tralex

Our second lexical resource is a translation lexicon obtained fully automatically via analysis of parallel French-English documents from the Web. A collection of 3,378 document pairs was obtained using STRAND, our technique for mining the Web for bilingual text [7]. These document pairs were aligned internally, using their HTML markup, to produce 63,094 aligned text "chunks" ranging in length from 2 to 30 words, ~8 words on average per chunk, for a total of ~500K words per side. Viterbi word-alignments for these paired chunks were obtained using the GIZA implementation of the IBM statistical translation models.[2] An ordered set of translation pairs was obtained by treating each alignment link between words as a co-occurrence and scoring each word pair according to the likelihood ratio [2]. We then rank the translation alternatives in order of decreasing likelihood ratio score.

3. CLIR EXPERIMENTS

Ranked tralexes are particularly well suited to a simple ranked term-by-term translation approach. In our experiments, we use top-2 balanced document translation, in which we produce exactly two English terms for each French term. For terms with no known translation, the untranslated French term is generated twice (often appropriate for proper names). For French terms with one translation, that translation is generated twice. For French terms with two or more translations, we generate the first two translations in the tralex. Thus balanced translation has the effect of introducing a uniform weighting over the top n translations for each term (here $n = 2$).

Benefits of the approach include simplicity and modularity — notice that a lexicon containing ranked translations is the only requirement, and in particular that there is no need for access to the internals of the IR system or to the document collection in order to

---

[2] http://www.clsp.jhu.edu/ws99/projects/mt/

perform computations on term frequencies or weights. In addition, the approach is an effective one: in previous experiments we have found that this balanced translation strategy significantly outperforms the usual (unbalanced) technique of including all known translations [3]. We have also investigated the relationship between balanced translation and Pirkola's structured query formulation method [6].

For our experiments we used the CLEF-2000 French document collection (approximately 21 million words from articles in *Le Monde*). Differences in use of diacritics, case, and punctuation can inhibit matching between tralex entries and document terms, so we normalize the tralex and the documents by converting characters to lowercase and removing all diacritic marks and punctuation. We then translate the documents using the process described above, index the translated documents with the Inquery information retrieval system, and perform retrieval using "long" queries formulated by grouping all terms in the title, narrative, and description fields of each English topic description using Inquery's #sum operator. We report mean average precision on the 34 topics for which relevant French documents exist, based on the relevance judgments provided by CLEF. We evaluated several strategies for using the WebDict and STRAND tralexes.

3.1 WebDict Tralex

Since a tralex may contain an eclectic mix of root forms and morphological variants, we use a four-stage backoff strategy to maximize coverage while limiting spurious translations:

1. Match the **surface form** of a document term to **surface forms** of French terms in the tralex.

2. Match the **stem** of a document term to **surface forms** of French terms in the tralex.

3. Match the **surface form** of a document term to **stems** of French terms in the tralex.

4. Match the **stem** of a document term to **stems** of French terms in the tralex.

We used unsupervised induction of stemming rules based on the French collection to build the stemmer [5]. The process terminates as soon as a match is found at any stage, and the known translations for that match are generated. The process may produce an inappropriate morphological variant for a correct English translation, so we used Inquery's English kstem stemmer at indexing time to minimize the effect of that factor on retrieval effectiveness.

3.2 STRAND Tralex

One limitation of a statistically derived tralex is that any term has *some* probability of aligning with any other term. Merely sorting translation alternatives in order of decreasing likelihood ratio will thus find *some* translation alternatives for every French term that appeared at least once in the set of parallel Web pages. In order to limit the introduction of spurious translations, we included only translation pairs with at least N co-occurrences in the set used to build the tralex. We performed runs with $N = 1, 2, 3$, using the four-stage backoff strategy described above.

3.3 WebDict Merging using STRAND

When two sources of evidence with different characteristics are available, a combination-of-evidence strategy can sometimes outperform either source alone. Our initial experiments indicated that the WebDict tralex was the better of the two (see below), so we adopted a reranking strategy in which the WebDict tralex was refined according a voting strategy to which both the original WebDict and STRAND tralex rankings contributed.

Condition	MAP
STRAND ($N = 1$)	0.2320
STRAND ($N = 2$)	0.2440
STRAND ($N = 3$)	0.2499
Merging	0.2892
WebDict	0.2919
Backoff	0.3282

Table 1: Mean Average Precision (MAP), averaged over 34 topics

For each French term that appeared in both tralexes, we gave the top-ranked translation in each tralex a score of 100, the next a score of 99, and so on. We then summed the WebDict and STRAND scores for each translation, reranked the WebDict translations based on that sum, and then appended any STRAND-only translations for that French term. Thus, although both sources of evidence were weighted equally in the voting, STRAND-only evidence received lower precedence in the merged ranking. For French terms that appeared in only one tralex, we included those entries unchanged in the merged tralex. In this experiment run we used a threshold of $N = 1$, and applied the four-stage backoff strategy described above to the merged resource.

3.4 WebDict Backoff to STRAND

A possible weakness of our merging strategy is that inflected forms are more common in our STRAND tralex, while root forms are more common in our WebDict tralex. STRAND tralex entries that were copied unchanged into the merged tralex thus often matched in step 1 of the four-stage backoff strategy, preventing WebDict contributions from being used. With the WebDict tralex outperforming the STRAND tralex, this factor could hurt our results. As an alternative to merging, therefore, we also tried a simple backoff strategy in which we used the original WebDict tralex with the four-stage backoff strategy described above, to which we added a fifth stage in the event that fewer than two WebDict tralex matches were found:

5. Match the **surface form** of a document term to **surface forms** of French terms in the STRAND tralex.

We used a threshold of $N = 2$ for this experiment run.

4. RESULTS

Table 1 summarizes our results. Increasing thresholds seem to be helpful with the STRAND tralex, although the differences were not found to be statistically significant by a paired two-tailed t-test with $p < 0.05$. Merging the tralexes provided no improvement over using the WebDict tralex alone, but our backoff strategy produced a statistically significant 12% improvement in mean average precision (at $p < 0.01$) over the next best tralex (WebDict alone). As Figure 1 shows, the improvement is remarkably consistent, with only four of the 34 topics adversely affected and only one topic showing a substantial negative impact.

Breaking down the backoff results by stage (Table 2), we find that the majority of query-to-document hits are obtained in the first stage, i.e. matches of the term's surface form in the document to a translation of the surface form in the dictionary. However, the backoff process improves by-token coverage of terms in documents by 8%, and gives a 3% relative improvement in retrieval results; it also contributed additional translations to the top-2 set in approximately 30% of the cases, leading to the statistically significant 12% relative improvement in mean average precision as compared to the baseline using WebDict alone with 4-stage backoff.

154

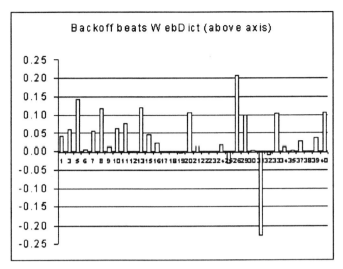

Figure 1: WebDict-to-tralex backoff vs. WebDict alone, by query

Stage (forms)	Lexicon matches
1 (surface-surface)	70.38%
2 (stem-surface)	3.18%
3 (surface-stem)	0.46%
4 (stem-stem)	0.98%
5 (STRAND)	8.34%
No match found	16.66%

Table 2: Term matches in 5-stage backoff

5. CONCLUSIONS

There are many ways of combining evidence from multiple translation lexicons. We use tralexes similar to those used by Nie et al. [4], but our work differs in our use of balanced translation and a backoff translation strategy (which produces a stronger baseline for our WebDict tralex), and in our comparison of merging and backoff translation strategies for combining resources. In future work we plan to explore other combinations of merging and backoff and other merging strategies, including post-retrieval merging of the ranked lists.

In addition, parallel corpora can be exploited for more than just the extraction of a non-contextualized translation lexicon. We are currently engaged in work on lexical selection methods that take advantage of contextual information, in the context of our research on machine translation, and we expect that CLIR results will be improved by contextually-informed scoring of term translations.

6. ACKNOWLEDGMENTS

This research was supported in part by Department of Defense contract MDA90496C1250 and TIDES DARPA/ITO Cooperative Agreement N660010028910,

7. REFERENCES

[1] L. Ballesteros and W. B. Croft. Resolving ambiguity for cross-language retrieval. In W. B. Croft, A. Moffat, and C. V. Rijsbergen, editors, *Proceedings of the 21st Annual International ACM SIGIR Conference on Research and Development in Information Retrieval*, pages 64–71. ACM Press, Aug. 1998.

[2] T. Dunning. Accurate methods for the statistics of surprise and coincidence. *Computational Linguistics*, 19(1):61–74, March 1993.

[3] G.-A. Levow and D. W. Oard. Translingual topic tracking with PRISE. In *Working Notes of the Third Topic Detection and Tracking Workshop*, Feb. 2000.

[4] J.-Y. Nie, M. Simard, P. Isabelle, and R. Durand. Cross-language information retrieval based on parallel texts and automatic mining of parallel texts from the web. In M. Hearst, F. Gey, and R. Tong, editors, *Proceedings of the 22nd Annual International ACM SIGIR Conference on Research and Development in Information Retrieval*, pages 74–81, Aug. 1999.

[5] D. W. Oard, G.-A. Levow, and C. I. Cabezas. CLEF experiments at Maryland: Statistical stemming and backoff translation. In C. Peters, editor, *Proceedings of the First Cross-Language Evaluation Forum*. 2001. To appear. http://www.glue.umd.edu/~oard/research.html.

[6] D. W. Oard and J. Wang. NTCIR-2 ECIR experiments at Maryland: Comparing structured queries and balanced translation. In *Second National Institute of Informatics (NII) Test Collection Information Retrieval (NTCIR) workshop*. forthcoming.

[7] P. Resnik. Mining the Web for bilingual text. In *37th Annual Meeting of the Association for Computational Linguistics (ACL'99)*, College Park, Maryland, June 1999.

[8] P. Sheridan and J. P. Ballerini. Experiments in multilingual information retrieval using the SPIDER system. In *Proceedings of the 19th Annual International ACM SIGIR Conference on Research and Development in Information Retrieval*, Aug. 1996.

Improving Information Extraction by Modeling Errors in Speech Recognizer Output

David D. Palmer †‡
† The MITRE Corporation
202 Burlington Road
Bedford, MA 01730
palmer@mitre.org

Mari Ostendorf ‡
‡Electrical Engineering Dept.
University of Washington
Seattle, WA 98195
mo@ee.washington.edu

ABSTRACT

In this paper we describe a technique for improving the performance of an information extraction system for speech data by explicitly modeling the errors in the recognizer output. The approach combines a statistical model of named entity states with a lattice representation of hypothesized words and errors annotated with recognition confidence scores. Additional refinements include the use of multiple error types, improved confidence estimation, and multi-pass processing. In combination, these techniques improve named entity recognition performance over a text-based baseline by 28%.

Keywords

ASR error modeling, information extraction, word confidence

1. INTRODUCTION

There has been a great deal of research on applying natural language processing (NLP) techniques to text-based sources of written language data, such as newspaper and newswire data. Most NLP approaches to spoken language data, such as broadcast news and telephone conversations, have consisted of applying text-based systems to the output of an automatic speech recognition (ASR) system; research on improving these approaches has focused on either improving the ASR accuracy or improving the text-based system (or both). However, applying text-based systems to ASR output ignores the fact that there are fundamental differences between written texts and ASR transcriptions of spoken language: the style is different between written and spoken language, the transcription conventions are different, and, most importantly, there are errors in ASR transcriptions. In this work, we focus on the third problem: handling errors by explicitly modeling uncertainty in ASR transcriptions.

Proceedings of HLT 2001, First International Conference on Human Language Technology Research, J. Allan, ed., Morgan Kaufmann, San Francisco, 2001.

The idea of explicit error handling in information extraction (IE) from spoken documents was introduced by Grishman in [1], where a channel model of word insertions and deletions was used with a deterministic pattern matching system for information extraction. While the use of an error model resulted in substantial performance improvements, the overall performance was still quite low, perhaps because the original system was designed to take advantage of orthographic features. In looking ahead, Grishman suggests that a probabilistic approach might be more successful at handling errors.

The work described here provides such an approach, but introduces an acoustically-driven word confidence score rather than the word-based channel model proposed in [1]. More specifically, we provide a unified approach to predicting and using uncertainty in processing spoken language data, focusing on the specific IE task of identifying named entities (NEs). We show that by explicitly modeling multiple types of errors in the ASR output, we can improve the performance of an IE system, which benefits further from improved error prediction using new features derived from multi-pass processing.

The rest of the paper is organized as follows. In Section 2 we describe our error modeling, including explicit modeling of multiple ASR error types. New features for word confidence estimation and the resulting performance improvement is given in Section 3. Experimental results for NE recognition are presented in Section 4 using Broadcast News speech data. Finally, in Section 5, we summarize the key findings and implications for future work.

2. APPROACH

Our approach to error handling in information extraction involves using probabilistic models for both information extraction and the ASR error process. The component models and an integrated search strategy are described in this section.

2.1 Statistical IE

We use a probabilistic IE system that relates a word sequence $W = w_1, \ldots, w_M$ to a sequence of information states $S = s_1, \ldots, s_M$ that provide a simple parse of the word sequence into phrases, such as name phrases. For the work described here, the states s_t correspond to different types of NEs. The IE model is essentially a phrase language model:

$$p(S,W) = p(s_1,\dots,s_M,w_1,\dots,w_M) \qquad (1)$$

$$= \prod_{t=1}^{M} p(w_t|w_{t-1},s_t)p(s_t|s_{t-1},w_{t-1})$$

with state-dependent bigrams $p(w_t|w_{t-1},s_t)$ that model the types of words associated with a specific type of NE, and state transition probabilities $p(s_t|s_{t-1},w_{t-1})$ that mix the Markov-like structure of an HMM with dependence on the previous word. (Note that titles, such as "President" and "Mr.", are good indicators of transition to a name state.)

This IE model, described further in [2], is similar to other statistical approaches [3, 4] in the use of state dependent bigrams, but uses a different smoothing mechanism and state topology. In addition, a key difference in our work is explicit error modeling in the "word" sequence, as described next.

2.2 Error Modeling

To explicitly model errors in the IE system, we introduce new notation for the hypothesized word sequence, $H = h_1,\dots,h_M$, which may differ from the actual word sequence W, and a sequence of error indicator variables $K = k_1,\dots,k_M$, where $k_t = 1$ when h_t is an error and $k_t = 0$ when h_t is correct. We assume that the hypothesized words from the recognizer are each annotated with confidence scores

$$\gamma_t = p(k_t = 0|H,A) = p(h_t = w_t|H,A),$$

where A represents the set of features available for initial confidence estimation from the recognizer, acoustic or otherwise.

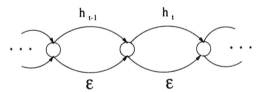

Figure 1: Lattice with correct and error paths.

We construct a simple lattice from $h_1,\dots,h_M$ with "error" arcs indicated by ϵ-tokens in parallel with each hypothesized word h_t, as illustrated in Figure 1. We then find the maximum posterior probability state sequence by summing over all paths through the lattice:

$$S^* = \underset{S}{\operatorname{argmax}}\, p(S|H,A), \qquad (2)$$

$$= \underset{S}{\operatorname{argmax}} \sum_K p(S,K|H,A) \qquad (3)$$

or, equivalently, marginalizing over the sequence K. Equation 3 thus defines the decoding of named entities via the state sequence S, which (again) provides a parse of the word sequence into phrases.

Assuming first that K and H encode all the information from A about S, and then that the specific value h_t occurring at an error does not provide additional information for the NE states[1] S, we can rewrite Equation 3 as:

$$S^* = \underset{S}{\operatorname{argmax}} \sum_K p(K|H,A)p(S|K,H,A)$$

$$= \underset{S}{\operatorname{argmax}} \sum_K p(K|H,A)p(S|K,H)$$

$$= \underset{S}{\operatorname{argmax}} \sum_K p(K|H,A)p(S|W_{(K,H)}).$$

For the error model, $p(K|H,A)$, we assume that errors are conditionally independent given the hypothesized word sequence H and the evidence A:

$$p(K|H,A) = \prod_{t=1}^{M} p(k_t|H,A). \qquad (4)$$

where $\gamma_t = p(k_t = 0|H,A)$ is the ASR word "confidence". Of course, the errors are not independent, which we take advantage of in our post-processing of confidence estimates, described in Section 3.

We can find $p(S|W)$ directly from the information extraction model, $p(S,W)$ described in Section 2.1, but there is no efficient decoding algorithm. Hence we approximate

$$p(S|W) = \frac{p(S,W)}{p(W)} \approx \bar{p}(S,W) \qquad (5)$$

assuming that the different words that could lead to an error are roughly uniform over the likely set. More specifically, $\bar{p}(S,W)$ incorporates a scaling term as follows:

$$\bar{p}(\epsilon|w_{t-1}=v,s_t) = \frac{1}{N_v}p(\epsilon|w_{t-1}=v,s_t) \qquad (6)$$

where N_v is the number of different error words observed after v in the training set and $p(\epsilon|v,s_t)$ is trained by collapsing all different errors into a single label ϵ. Training this language model requires data that contains ϵ-tokens, which can be obtained by aligning the reference data and the ASR output. In fact, we train the language model with a combination of the original reference data and a duplicate version with ϵ-tokens replacing error words.

Because of the conditional independence assumptions behind equations 1 and 4, there is an efficient algorithm for solving equation 3, which combines steps similar to the forward and Viterbi algorithms used with HMMs. The search is linear with the length M of the hypothesized word sequence and the size of the state space (the product space of NE states and error states). The forward component is over the error state (parallel branches in the lattice), and the Viterbi component is over the NE states.

If the goal is to find the words that are in error (e.g. for subsequent correction) as well as the named entities, then the objective is

$$(S,K)^* = \underset{S,K}{\operatorname{argmax}}\, p(S,K|H,A) \qquad (7)$$

$$\approx \underset{S,K}{\operatorname{argmax}}\, p(K|H,A)\bar{p}(S,W_{(K,H)}), \qquad (8)$$

---

[1]Clearly, some hypotheses do provide information about S in that a reasonably large number of errors involve simple ending differences. However, our current system has no mechanism for taking advantage of this information explicitly, which would likely add substantially to the complexity of the model.

which simply involves finding the best path K^* through the lattice in Figure 1. Again because of the conditional independence assumption, an efficient solution involves Viterbi decoding over an expanded state space (the product of the names and errors). The sequence K^* can help us define a new word sequence $\hat{W}$ that contains ϵ-tokens: $\hat{w}_t = h_t$ if $k_t^* = 0$, and $\hat{w}_t = \epsilon$ if $k_t^* = 1$. Joint error and named entity decoding results in a small degradation in named entity recognition performance, since only a single error path is used. Since errors are not used explicitly in this work, all results are based on the objective given by equation 3.

Note that, unlike work that uses confidence scores γ_t as a weight for the hypothesized word in information retrieval [5], here the confidence scores also provide weights $(1 - \gamma_t)$ for explicit (but unspecified) sets of alternative hypotheses.

2.3 Multiple Error Types

Though the model described above uses a single error token ϵ and a 2-category word confidence score (correct word vs. error), it is easily extensible to multiple classes of errors simply by expanding the error state space. More specifically, we add multiple parallel arcs in the lattice in Figure 1, labeled ϵ_1, ϵ_2, etc., and modify confidence estimation to predict multiple categories of errors.

In this work, we focus particularly on distinguishing out-of-vocabulary (OOV) errors from in-vocabulary (IV) errors, due to the large percentage of OOV words that are names (57% of OOVs occur in named entities). Looking at the data another way, the percentage of name words that are OOV is an order of magnitude larger than words in the "other" phrase category, as described in more detail in [6]. As it turns out, since OOVs are so infrequent, it is difficult to robustly estimate the probability of IV vs. OOV errors from standard acoustic features, and we simply use the relative prior probabilities to scale the single error probability.

3. CONFIDENCE PREDICTION

An essential component of our error model is the word-level confidence score, $p(k_t|H, A)$, so one would expect that better confidence scores would result in better error modeling performance. Hence, we investigated methods for improving the confidence estimates, focusing specifically on introducing new features that might complement the features used to provide the baseline confidence estimates. The baseline confidence scores used in this study were provided by Dragon Systems. As described in [7], the Dragon confidence predictor used a generalized linear model with six inputs: the word duration, the language model score, the fraction of times the word appears in the top 100 hypotheses, the average number of active HMM states in decoding for the word, a normalized acoustic score and the log of the number of recognized words in the utterance. We investigated several new features, of which the most useful are listed below.

First, we use a short window of the original confidence scores: γ_t, γ_{t-1} and γ_{t+1}. Note that the post-processing paradigm allows us to use non-causal features such as γ_{t+1}. We also define three features based on the ratios of γ_{t-1}, γ_t, and γ_{t+1} to the average confidence for the document in which h_t appears, under the assumption that a low con-

fidence score for a word is less likely to indicate a word error if the average confidence for the entire document is also low. We hypothesized that words occurring frequently in a large window would be more likely to be correct, again assuming that the ASR system would make errors randomly from a set of possibilities. Therefore, we define features based on how many times the hypothesis word h_t occurs in a window $(h_{t-n}, ..., h_t, ..., h_{t+n})$ for $n = 5, 10, 25, 50,$ and 100 words. Finally, we also use the relative frequency of words occurring as an error in the training corpus, again looking at a window of ± 1 around the current word.

Due to the close correlation between names and errors, we would expect to see improvement in the error modeling performance by including information about which words are names, as determined by the NE system. Therefore, in addition to the above set of features, we define a new feature: *whether the hypothesis word h_t is part of a location, organization, or person phrase*. We can determine the value of this feature directly from the output of the NE system. Given this additional feature, we can define a multi-pass processing cycle consisting of two steps: confidence re-estimation and information extraction. To obtain the name information for the first pass, the confidence scores are re-estimated without using the name features, and these confidences are used in a joint NE and error decoding system. The resulting name information is then used, in addition to all the features used in the previous pass, to improve the word confidence estimates. The improved confidences are in turn used to further improve the performance of the NE system.

We investigated three different methods for using the above features in confidence estimation: decision trees, generalized linear models, and linear interpolation of the outputs of the decision tree and generalized linear model. The decision trees and generalized linear models gave similar performance, and a small gain was obtained by interpolating these predictions. For simplicity, the results here use only the decision tree model.

A standard method for evaluating confidence prediction [8] is the normalized cross entropy (NCE) of the binary correct/error predictors, that is, the reduction in uncertainty in confidence prediction relative to the ASR system error rate. Using the new features in a decision tree predictor, the NCE score of the binary confidence predictor improved from 0.195 to 0.287. As shown in the next section, this had a significant impact on NE performance. (See [6] for further details on these experiments and an analysis of the relative importance of different factors.)

4. EXPERIMENTAL RESULTS

The specific information extraction task we address in this work is the identification of name phrases (names of persons, locations, and organizations), as well as identification of temporal and numeric expressions, in the ASR output. Also known as named entities (NEs), these phrases are useful in many language understanding tasks, such as coreference resolution, sentence chunking and parsing, and summarization/gisting.

4.1 Data and Evaluation Method

The data we used for the experiments described in this paper consisted of 114 news broadcasts automatically annotated with recognition confidence scores and hand labeled with NE types and locations. The data represents an intersection of the data provided by Dragon Systems for the 1998 DARPA-sponsored Hub-4 Topic, Detection and Tracking (TDT) evaluation and those stories for which named entity labels were available. Broadcast news data is particularly appropriate for our work since it contains a high density of name phrases, has a relatively high word error rate, and requires a virtually unlimited vocabulary.

We used two versions of each news broadcast: a reference transcription prepared by a human annotator and an ASR transcript prepared by Dragon Systems for the TDT evaluation [7]. The Dragon ASR system had a vocabulary size of about 57,000 words and a word error rate (WER) of about 30%. The ASR data contained the word-level confidence information, as described earlier, and the reference transcription was manually-annotated with named entity information. By aligning the reference and ASR transcriptions, we were able to determine which ASR output words corresponded to errors and to the NE phrases.

We randomly selected 98 of the 114 broadcasts as training data, 8 broadcasts as development test, and 8 broadcasts as evaluation test data, which were kept "blind" to ensure unbiased evaluation results. We used the training data to estimate all model parameters, the development test set to tune parameters during development, and the evaluation test set for all results reported here. For all experiments we used the same training and test data.

4.2 Information Extraction Results

Table 1 shows the performance of the baseline information extraction system (row 1) which does not model errors, compared to systems using one and two error types, with the baseline confidence estimates and the improved confidence estimates from the previous section. Performance figures are the standard measures used for this task: F-measure (harmonic mean of recall and precision) and slot error rate (SER), where separate type, extent and content error measures are averaged to get the reported result.

The results show that modeling errors gives a significant improvement in performance. In addition, there is a small but consistent gain from modeling OOV vs. IV errors separately. Further gain is provided by each improvement to the confidence estimator.

Since the evaluation criterion involves a weighted average of content, type and extent errors, there is an upper bound of 86.4 for the F-measure given the errors in the recognizer output. In other words, this is the best performance we can hope for without running additional processing to correct the ASR errors. Thus, the combined error modeling improvements lead to recovery of 28% of the possible performance gains from this scheme. It is also interesting to note that the improvement in identifying the extent of a named entity actually results in a decrease in performance of the content component, since words that are incorrectly recognized are introduced into the named entity regions.

5. DISCUSSION

In this paper we described our use of error modeling to improve information extraction from speech data. Our model is the first to explicitly represent the uncertainty inherent in the ASR output word sequence. Two key in-

Table 1: *Named entity (NE) recognition results using different error models and feature sets for predicting confidence scores. The baseline confidence scores are from the Dragon recognizer, the secondary processing re-estimates confidences as a function of a window of these scores, and the names are provided by a previous pass of named entity detection.*

ϵ-tokens	Confidence Scores	NE F-Measure	NE SER
none	none	68.4	50.9
1	baseline	71.4	46.1
2	baseline	71.5	45.9
1	+ secondary	71.8	44.9
2	+ secondary	72.0	44.8
1	+ secondary + names	73.1	44.3
2	+ secondary + names	73.4	43.9

novations are the use of word confidence scores to characterize the ASR outputs and alternative hypotheses, and integration of the error model with a statistical model of information extraction. In addition, improvements in performance were obtained by modeling multiple types of errors (in vocabulary vs. out of vocabulary) and adding new features to the confidence estimator obtained using multipass processing. The new features led to improved confidence estimation from a baseline NCE of 0.195 to a value of 0.287. The use of the error model with these improvements resulted in a reduction in slot error rate of 14% and an improvement in the F-measure from 68.4 to 73.4.

The integrated model can be used for recognition of NE's alone, as in this work, or in joint decoding of NEs and errors. Since ASR errors substantially degrade NE recognition rates (perfect NE labeling with the errorful outputs here would have an F-measure of 86.4), and since many names are recognized in error because they are out of the recognizer's vocabulary, an important next step in this research is explicit error detection and correction. Preliminary work in this direction is described in [6]. In addition, while this work is based on 1-best recognition outputs, it is straightforward to use the same algorithm for lattice decoding, which may also provide improved NE recognition performance.

Acknowledgments

The authors thank Steven Wegmann of Dragon Systems for making their ASR data available for these experiments and BBN for preparing and releasing additional NE training data. This material is based in part upon work supported by the National Science Foundation under Grant No. IIS0095940. Any opinions, findings, and conclusions or recommendations expressed in this material are those of the author(s) and do not necessarily reflect the views of the National Science Foundation.

6. REFERENCES

[1] R. Grishman, "Information extraction and speech recognition," *Proceedings of the Broadcast News*

Transcription and Understanding Workshop, pp. 159–165, 1998.

[2] D. Palmer, M. Ostendorf, and J. Burger 'Robust Information Extraction from Automatically Generated Speech Transcriptions," *Speech Communication,* vol. 32, pp. 95–109, 2000.

[3] D. Bikel, R. Schwartz, R. Weischedel, "An Algorithm that Learns What's in a Name," *Machine Learning,* 34(1/3):211–231, 1999.

[4] Y. Gotoh, S. Renals, "Information Extraction From Broadcast News,"*Philosophical Transactions of the Royal Society,* series A: Mathematical, Physical and Engineering Sciences, 358(1769):1295–1308, 2000.

[5] A. Hauptmann, R. Jones, K. Seymore, S. Slattery, M. Witbrock, and M. Siegler, "Experiments in information retrieval from spoken documents," *Proceedings of the Broadcast News Transcription and Understanding Workshop,* pp. 175–181, 1998.

[6] D. Palmer, *Modeling Uncertainty for Information Extraction from Speech Data,* Ph.D. dissertation, University of Washington, 2001.

[7] L. Gillick, Y. Ito, L. Manganaro, M. Newman, F. Scattone, S. Wegmann, J. Yamron, and P. Zhan, "Dragon Systems' Automatic Transcription of New TDT Corpus," *Proceedings of the Broadcast News Transcription and Understanding Workshop,* pp. 219–221, 1998.

[8] M. Siu and H. Gish, "Evaluation of word confidence for speech recognition systems," *Computer Speech & Language,* 13(4):299–319, 1999.

Inducing Multilingual Text Analysis Tools via Robust Projection across Aligned Corpora

David Yarowsky

Dept. of Computer Science
Johns Hopkins University
Baltimore, MD 21218 USA
yarowsky@cs.jhu.edu

Grace Ngai

Dept. of Computer Science
Johns Hopkins University
Baltimore, MD 21218 USA
gyn@cs.jhu.edu

Richard Wicentowski

Dept. of Computer Science
Johns Hopkins University
Baltimore, MD 21218 USA
richardw@cs.jhu.edu

ABSTRACT

This paper describes a system and set of algorithms for automatically inducing stand-alone monolingual part-of-speech taggers, base noun-phrase bracketers, named-entity taggers and morphological analyzers for an arbitrary foreign language. Case studies include French, Chinese, Czech and Spanish.

Existing text analysis tools for English are applied to bilingual text corpora and their output projected onto the second language via statistically derived word alignments. Simple direct annotation projection is quite noisy, however, even with optimal alignments. Thus this paper presents noise-robust tagger, bracketer and lemmatizer training procedures capable of accurate system bootstrapping from noisy and incomplete initial projections.

Performance of the induced stand-alone part-of-speech tagger applied to French achieves 96% core part-of-speech (POS) tag accuracy, and the corresponding induced noun-phrase bracketer exceeds 91% F-measure. The induced morphological analyzer achieves over 99% lemmatization accuracy on the complete French verbal system.

This achievement is particularly noteworthy in that it required absolutely no hand-annotated training data in the given language, and virtually no language-specific knowledge or resources beyond raw text. Performance also significantly exceeds that obtained by direct annotation projection.

Keywords

multilingual, text analysis, part-of-speech tagging, noun phrase bracketing, named entity, morphology, lemmatization, parallel corpora

1. TASK OVERVIEW

A fundamental roadblock to developing statistical taggers, bracketers and other analyzers for many of the world's 200+ major languages is the shortage or absence of annotated training data for the large majority of these languages. Ideally, one would like to lever-

Proceedings of HLT 2001, First International Conference on Human Language Technology Research, J. Allan, ed., Morgan Kaufmann, San Francisco, 2001.

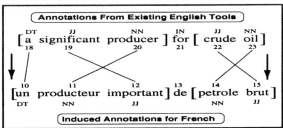

Figure 1: Projecting part-of-speech tags, named-entity tags and noun-phrase structure from English to Chinese and French.

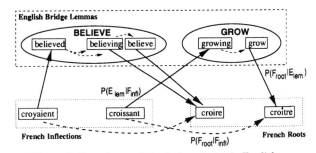

Figure 2: French morphological analysis via English

age the large existing investments in annotated data and tools for resource-rich languages (such as English and Japanese) to overcome the annotated resource shortage in other languages.

To show the broad potential of our approach and methods, this paper will investigate four fundamental language analysis tasks: POS tagging, base noun phrase (baseNP) bracketing, named entity tagging, and inflectional morphological analysis, as illustrated in Figures 1 and 2. These bedrock tools are important components of the language analysis pipelines for many applications, and their low cost extension to new languages, as described here, can serve as a broadly useful enabling resource.

2. BACKGROUND

Previous research on the word alignment of parallel corpora has tended to focus on their use in translation model training for MT rather than on monolingual applications. One exception is bilingual parsing. Wu (1995, 1997) investigated the use of concurrent parsing of parallel corpora in a transduction inversion framework, helping to resolve attachment ambiguities in one language by the coupled parsing state in the second language. Jones and Havrilla (1998) utilized similar joint parsing techniques (twisted-pair grammars) for word reordering in target language generation.

However, with these exceptions in the field of parsing, to our knowledge no one has previously used linguistic annotation projection via aligned bilingual corpora to induce traditional stand-alone monolingual text analyzers in other languages. Thus both our proposed projection and induction methods, and their application to multilingual POS tagging, named-entity classification and morphological analysis induction, appears to be highly novel.

3. DATA RESOURCES

The data sets used in these experiments included the English-French Canadian Hansards, the English-Chinese Hong Kong Hansards, and parallel Czech-English Reader's Digest collection. In addition, multiple versions of the Bible were used, including the French Douay-Rheims Bible, Spanish Reina Valera Bible, and three English Bible Versions (King James, New International and Revised Standard), automatically verse-aligned in multiple pairings. All corpora were automatically word-aligned by the now publicly available EGYPT system (Al-Onaizan et al., 1999), based on IBM's Model 3 statistical MT formalism (Brown et al., 1990). The tagging and bracketing tasks utilized approximately 2 million words in each language, with the sample sizes for morphology induction given in Table 3. All word alignments utilized strictly raw-word-based model variants for English/French/Spanish/Czech and character-based model variants for Chinese, with *no* use of morphological analysis or stemming, POS-tagging, bracketing or dictionary resources.

4. PART-OF-SPEECH TAGGER INDUCTION

Part-of-speech tagging is the first of four applications covered in this paper. The goal of this work is to project POS analysis capabilities from one language to another via word-aligned parallel bilingual corpora. To do so, we use an existing POS tagger (e.g. Brill, 1995) to annotate the English side of the parallel corpus. Then, as illustrated in Figure 1 for Chinese and French, the raw tags are transferred via the word alignments, yielding an extremely noisy initial training set for the 2nd language. The third crucial step is to generalize from these noisy projected annotations in a robust way, yielding a stand-alone POS tagger for the new language that is considerably more accurate than the initial projected tags.

Additional details of this algorithm are given in Yarowsky and Ngai (2001). Due to lack of space, the following sections will serve primarily as an overview of the algorithm and its salient issues.

4.1 Part-of-speech Projection Issues

First, because of considerable cross-language differences in fine-grained tag set inventories, this work focuses on accurately assigning core POS categories (e.g. noun, verb, adverb, adjective, etc.),

with additional distinctions in verb tense, noun number and pronoun type as captured in the English tagset inventory. Although impoverished relative to some languages, and incapable of resolving details such as grammatical gender, this Brown-corpus-based tagset granularity is sufficient for many applications. Furthermore, many finer-grained part-of-speech distinctions are resolved primarily by morphology, as handled in Section 7. Finally, if one desires to induce a finer-grained tagging capability for case, for example, one should project from a reference language such as Czech, where case is lexically marked.

Figure 3 illustrates six scenarios encountered when projecting POS tags from English to a language such as French. The first two show straightforward 1-to-1 projections, which are encountered in roughly two-thirds of English words. Phrasal (1-to-N) alignments offer greater challenges, as typically only a subset of the aligned words accept the English tag. To distinguish these cases, we initially assign position-sensitive phrasal parts-of-speech via subscripting (e.g. *Les*/NNS_a *lois*/NNS_b), and subsequently learn a probablistic mapping to core, non-phrasal parts of speech (e.g. $P(DT|NNS_a)$) that is used along with tag sequence and lexical prior models to re-tag these phrasal POS projections.

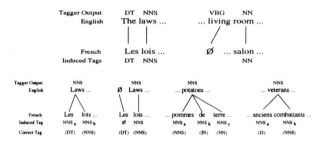

Figure 3: French POS tag projection scenarios

4.2 Noise-robust POS Tagger Training

Even at the relatively low tagset granularity of English, direct projection of core POS tags onto French achieves only 76% accuracy using EGYPT's automatic word alignments (as shown in Table 1). Part of this deficiency is due to word-alignment error; when word alignments were manually corrected, direct projection core-tag accuracy increased to 85%. Also, standard bigram taggers trained on the automatically projected data achieve only modest success at generalization (86% when reapplied to the noisy training data). More highly lexicalized learning algorithms exhibit even greater potential for overmodeling the specific projection errors of this data.

Thus our research has focused on noise-robust techniques for distilling a conservative but effective tagger from this challenging raw projection data. In particular, we modify standard n-gram modeling to separate the training of the tag sequence model $P(T)$ from the lexical prior models $P(W|T)$, and apply different confidence weighting and signal amplification techniques to both.

4.2.1 Lexical Prior Estimation

Figure 4 illustrates the process of hierarchically smoothing the lexical prior model $\hat{P}(t|w)$. One motivating empirical observation is that words in French, English and Czech have a strong tendency to exhibit only a single core POS tag (e.g. N or V), and very rarely have more than 2. In English, with relatively high $P(POS|w)$ ambiguity, only 0.37% of the tokens in the Brown Corpus are not covered by a word type's two most frequent core tags, and in French the percentage of tokens is only 0.03%. Thus we employ an ag-

162

Model	Evaluate on E-F Aligned French		Evaluate on Unseen Monolingual French	
	Core Tagset	Eng Eqv Tagset	Core Tagset	Eng Eqv Tagset
(a) Direct transfer (on auto-aligned data)	.76	.69	N/A	N/A
(b) Direct transfer (on hand-aligned data)	.85	.78	N/A	N/A
(c) Standard bigram model (on auto-aligned data)	.86	.82	.82	.68
(d) Noise-robust bigram induction (on auto-aligned data)	**.96**	.93	.94	.91
(e) Fully supervised bigram training (on goldstandard)	.97	.96	.98	.97

Table 1: Evaluation of 5 POS tagger induction models on 2 French datasets and 2 tagset granularities

gressive re-estimation in favor of this bias, amplifying the model probability of the majority POS tag, and reducing or zeroing the model probability of 2nd or lower ranked core tags proportional to their relative frequency with respect to the majority tag. This process is then applied recursively, similarly amplifying the probability of the majority subtags within each core tag. Further details, including the handling of *1-to-N* phrasal alignment projections, are given in Yarowsky and Ngai (2001).

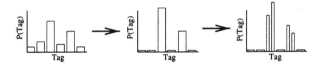

Word	Directly Projected Tag					Smoothed $\hat{P}(t|w)$					
	J	N	V	R	I	N	V	NN	NNS	VBN	VBG
achat	0	62	48	0	1	.76	.24	.73	.03	.03	.21
cadre	2	35	7	1	1	.90	.10	.86	.04	.03	.00
cadres	1	5	0	0	0	.94	.00	.04	.90	.00	.00
prévu	1	11	48	0	0	.09	.91	.08	.01	.86	.00

Figure 4: Hierarchical smoothing of $\hat{P}(t|w)$ tag probabilities

4.2.2 Tag Sequence Model Estimation

In contrast, the training of the tag sequence model $P(t_i|t_{i-1},...)$ focuses on confidence weighting and filtering of projected training subsequences. The contribution of each candidate training sentence is weighted proportionally with both its EGYPT/GIZA sentence-level alignment score and an agreement measure between the projected tags and the 1st iteration lexical priors, a rough measure of alignment reasonableness. Given the observed bursty distribution of alignment errors in the corpus, this downweighting of low-confidence alignment regions substantially improves sequence model quality with tolerable reduction in training volume.

4.3 Evaluation of POS Tagger Induction

As shown in Table 1, performance is evaluated on two evaluation data sets, including an independent 200K-word hand-tagged French dataset provided by Université de Montréal, which is used to gauge stand-alone tagger performance. Signal amplification and noise reduction techniques yield a 71% error reduction, achieving a core tagset accuracy of 96%, closely approaching the upper-bound 97% performance of an equivalent bigram model trained directly on an 80% subset of the hand-tagged evaluation set (using 5-fold cross-validation). Thus robust training on 500K words of very noisy but automatically-derived tag projections can approach the performance obtained by fully supervised learning on 80K words of hand-tagged training data.

5. NOUN PHRASE BRACKETER INDUCTION

Our empirical studies show that there is a very strong tendency for noun phrases to cohere as a unit when translated between languages, even when undergoing significant internal re-ordering. This strong noun-phrase cohesion even tends to hold for relatively free word order languages such as Czech, where both native speakers and parallel corpus data indicate that nominal modifiers tend to remain in the same contiguous chunk as the nouns they modify. This property allows collective word alignments to serve as a reliable basis for bracket projection as well.

5.1 BaseNP Projection Methodology

The projection process begins by automatically tagging and bracketing the English data, using Brill (1995) and Ramshaw & Marcus (1994), respectively.

As illustrated in Figure 5, each word within an English noun phrase is then subscripted with the number of its NP in the sentence, and this subscript is projected onto the aligned French (or Chinese) words. In the most common case, the corresponding French/Chinese noun phrase is simply the maximal span of the projected subscript.

Figure 6 shows some of the projection challenges encountered. Nearly all such cases of interwoven projected NPs are due to alignment errors, and a strong inductive bias towards NP cohesion was utilized to resolve these incompatible projections.

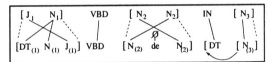

Figure 5: Standard NP projection scenarios.

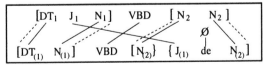

Figure 6: Problematic NP projection scenarios.

5.2 BaseNP Training Algorithm

For stand-alone tool development, the Ramshaw & Marcus IOB bracketing framework and a fast transformation-based learning system (Ngai and Florian, 2001) were applied to the noisy baseNP-projected data described above.

As with POS tagger induction, bracketer induction is improved by focusing training on the highest quality projected data and excluding regions with the strongest indications of word-alignment error. Thus sentences with the lowest 25% of model-3 alignment scores were excluded from training, as were sentences where projected bracketings overlapped and conflicted (also an indicator of

163

alignment errors). Data with lower-confidence POS tagging were not filtered, however, as this filtering reduces robustness when the stand-alone bracketers are applied to noisy tagger output. Additional details are provided in Yarowsky and Ngai (2001).

Current efforts to further improve the quality of the training data include use of iterative EM bootstrapping techniques. Separate projection of bracketings from aligned parallel data with a 3rd language also shows promise for providing independent supervision, which can further help distinguish consensus signal from noise.

5.3 BaseNP Projection Evaluation

Because no bracketed evaluation data were available to us for French or Chinese, a third party fluent in these languages hand-bracketed a small, held-out 40-sentence evaluation set in both languages, using a set of bracketing conventions that they felt were appropriate for the languages. Table 2 shows the performance relative to these evaluation sets, as measured by exact-match bracketing precision (Pr), recall (R) and F-measure (F).

	Exact Match			Acceptable Match		
Method	Pr	R	F	Pr	R	F
Chinese:						
Direct (auto)	.26	.58	.36	.48	.58	.51
Direct (hand)	.47	.61	.53	.86	.86	.86
French:						
Direct (auto)	.43	.48	.45	.60	.58	**.59**
Direct (hand)	.56	.51	.53	.74	.70	.72
FTBL (auto)	.82	.81	.81	**.91**	**.91**	**.91**

Table 2: Performance of BaseNP induction models

It is important to note, however, that many decisions regarding BaseNP bracketing conventions are essentially arbitrary, and agreement rates between additional human judges on these data were measured at 64% and 80% for French and Chinese respectively. Since the translingual projections are essentially unsupervised and have no data on which to mimic arbitrary conventions, it is also reasonable to evaluate the degree to which the induced bracketings are deemed acceptable and consistent with the arbitrary goldstandard (e.g. no crossing brackets). To this end, an additional pool of 3 judges were asked to further adjudicate the differences between the goldstandard and the projection output, annotating such situations as either *acceptable/compatible* or *unacceptable/incompatible*.

Overall, these translingual projection results are quite encouraging. For the Chinese, they are similar to Wu's 78% precision result for translingual-grammar-based NP bracketing, and especially promising given that no word segmentation (only raw characters) were used. For French, the increase from 59% to 91% F-measure for the stand-alone induced bracketer shows that the training algorithm is able to generalize successfully from the noisy raw projection data, distilling a reasonably accurate (and transferable) model of baseNP structure from this high degree of noise.

6. NAMED ENTITY TAGGER INDUCTION

Multilingual named entity tagger induction is based on the extended combination of the part-of-speech and noun-phrase bracketing frameworks. The entity class tags used for this study were FNAME, LNAME, PLACE and OTHER (other entities including organizations). They were derived from an anonymously donated MUC-6 named entity tagger applied to the English side of the French-English Canadian Hansards data.

Initial classification proceeds on a per-word basis, using an aggressively smoothed transitive projection model similar to those de-

scribed in Section 7. For a given second-language word *FW* and all English words EW_i aligned to it:

$$P(\text{NEclass}_j|\text{FW}) = \sum_i P(\text{NEclass}_j|\text{EW}_i)\, P_a(\text{EW}_i|\text{FW})$$

$$P(\text{PLACE}|\text{Corée}) = P(\text{PLACE}|\text{Korea})\, P_a(\text{Korea}|\text{Corée}) + ...$$

The co-training-based algorithm given in Cucerzan and Yarowsky (1999) was then used to train a stand-alone named entity tagger from the projected data. Seed words for this algorithm were those French words that were both POS-tagged as proper nouns and had an above-threshold entity-class confidence from the lexical projection models.

Performance was measured in terms of per-word entity-type classification accuracy on the French Hansard test data, using the 4-class inventory listed above. Classification accuracy of raw tag projections was only 64% (based on automatic word alignment). In contrast, the stand-alone co-training-based tagger trained on the projections achieved 85% classification accuracy, illustrating its effectivess at generalization in the face of projection noise. Notably, most of its observed errors can be traced to entity classification errors from the original English tagger. In fact, when evaluated on the English translation of the French test data set, the English tagger only achieved 86% classification accuracy on this directly comparable data set. It appears that the projection-induced French tagger achieves performance nearly as high as its original training source. Thus further improvements should be expected from higher quality English training sources.

7. MORPHOLOGICAL ANALYSIS INDUCTION

Bilingual corpora can also serve as a very successful bridge for aligning complex inflected word forms in a new language with their root forms, even when their surface similarity is quite different or highly irregular.

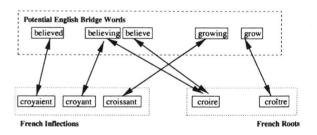

Figure 7: Direct-bridge French inflection/root alignment

As illustrated in Figure 7, the association between a French verbal inflection (*croyant*) and its correct root (*croire*), rather than a similar competitor (*croître*), can be identified by a single-step transitive association via an English bridge word (*believing*). However, in the case of morphology induction, such direct associations are relatively rare given that inflections in a second language tend to associate with similar tenses in English while the singular/infinitive forms tend to associate with analogous singular/infinitive forms, and thus *croyaient* (*believed*) and its root *croire* have no direct English link in our aligned corpus.

However, Figure 2 (first page) illustrates that an existing investment in a lemmatizer for English can help bridge this gap by joining a multi-step transitive association *croyaient→believed→believe→croire*. Figure 8 illustrates how this transitive linkage via English

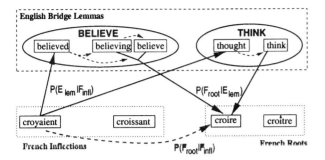

English Bridge Lemmas

BELIEVE: believed, believing, believe
THINK: thought, think

$P(E_{lem}|F_{infl})$ $P(F_{root}|E_{lem})$

croyaient   croissant   croire   croître

French Inflections $P(F_{root}|F_{infl})$ French Roots

Figure 8: Multi-bridge French inflection/root alignment

lemmatization can be potentially utilized for all other English lemmas (such as THINK) with which *croyaient* and *croire* also associate, offering greater potential coverage and robustness via multiple bridges.

Formally, these multiple transitive linkages can be modeled as shown below, by summing over all English lemmas (E_{lem_i}) with which either a candidate foreign inflection (F_{infl}) or its root (F_{root}) exhibit an alignment in the parallel corpus:

$$P_{mp}(F_{root}|F_{infl}) = \sum_i P_a(F_{root}|E_{lem_i})\, P_a(E_{lem_i}|F_{infl})$$

For example:

$$P_{mp}(\text{croire}|\text{croyaient}) =$$
$$P_a(\text{croire}|\text{BELIEVE})\, P_a(\text{BELIEVE}|\text{croyaient})+$$
$$P_a(\text{croire}|\text{THINK})\, P_a(\text{THINK}|\text{croyaient}) + ...$$

This projection/bridge-based similarity measure $P_{mp}(F_{root}|F_{infl})$ can be quite effective on its own, as shown in the *MProj only* entries in Table 3 (for multiple parallel corpora in 3 different languages), especially when restricted to the highest-confidence subset of the vocabulary (5.2% to 77.9% in these data) for which the association exceeds simple fixed probability and frequency thresholds. When estimated using a 1.2 million word subset of the French Hansards, for example, the MProj measure alone achives 98.5% precision on 32.7% of the inflected French verbs in the corpus (constituting 97.6% of the tokens in the corpus). Unlike traditional string-transduction-based morphology induction methods where irregular verbs pose the greatest challenges, these typically high-frequency words are often the *best* modelled data in the vocabulary making these multilingual projection techniques a natural complement to existing models.

7.1 Trie-based Morphology Models

The high precision on the MProj-covered subset also make these partial pairings effective training data for robust supervised algorithms that can generalize the string transformation behavior to the remaining uncovered vocabulary. While any supervised morphological analysis technique is possible here, we employ a trie-based modeling technique where the probability of a given stem-change (from the inventory observed in the MProj-paired training data) is modeled hierarchically using variable suffix context, as described in Yarowsky and Wicentowski (2000):

$$P(\text{root}|\text{inflection}) = P(\delta\beta|\delta\alpha) = P(\alpha \to \beta|\delta\alpha) =$$
$$\sum_i \lambda_i P(\alpha \to \beta|h_i) \quad \text{for } h_i = \text{suffix}(i, \delta\alpha)$$

For example:

$$P(\text{commencer}|\text{commença}) = P(\text{ça} \to \text{cer}|\text{commença}) =$$
$$\lambda_0 P(\text{ça} \to \text{cer}) + \lambda_1 P(\text{ça} \to \text{cer}|\text{a}) + \lambda_2 P(\text{ça} \to \text{cer}|\text{ça})+$$
$$+\lambda_3 P(\text{ça} \to \text{cer}|\text{nça}) + \lambda_4 P(\text{ça} \to \text{cer}|\text{ença}) + ...$$

$$P(\text{ployer}|\text{ploie}) = P(\text{ie} \to \text{yer}|\text{ploie}) =$$
$$\lambda_0 P(\text{ie} \to \text{yer}) + \lambda_1 P(\text{ie} \to \text{yer}|\text{e}) + \lambda_2 P(\text{ie} \to \text{yer}|\text{ie})+$$
$$+\lambda_3 P(\text{ie} \to \text{yer}|\text{oie}) + \lambda_4 P(\text{ie} \to \text{yer}|\text{loie}) + ...$$

An important property of the trie-based models is their effectiveness at clustering words that exhibit similar morphological behavior, both reducing model size and facilitating generalization to previously unseen examples. This property is illustrated in Figure 9, showing a sample (inflection → root) trie branch for French verbal inflections, with suffix histories $h=$'oie', $h=$'noie', $h=$'roie', etc. At each history node, the hierarchically smoothed probabilities of several $\alpha \to \beta$ (inflection→root) changes are given. Note that the relative probabilities of the competing analyses *ie→ir* and *ie→yer* differ substantially for diffent suffix histories, and that there are subexceptions that tend to cluster by affix history. This allows for the successful analysis of 8 of the 9 italicized test words that had not been seen in the bilingual projection data or where the MProj model yielded no root candidate above threshold.

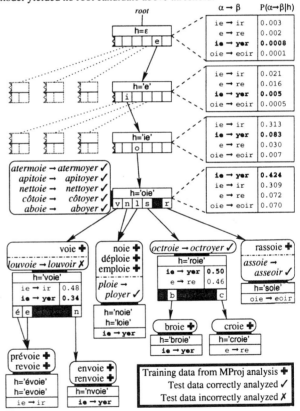

Figure 9: Example of a French MTrie branch, showing inflection → root probabilities ($P(\alpha \to \beta|h_i)$) for variable length suffix histories (h_i). MTrie analyses on test data are given in italics.

Table 3 illustrates the performance of a variety of morphology induction models. When using the projection-based MProj and trie-based MTrie models together (with the latter extending coverage to words that may not even appear in the parallel corpus), full verb lemmatization precision on the 1.2M word Hansard subset exceeds 99.5% (by type) and 99.9% (by token) with 95.8% coverage by type and 99.8% coverage by token. A backoff model based on Levenshtein-distance and distributional context similarity handles the relatively small percentage of cases where MProj and MTrie together are not sufficiently confident, bringing the system coverage to 100% coverage with a small drop in precision to 97.9% (by type) and 99.8% (by token) on the unrestricted space of inflected verbs observed in the full French Hansards. As shown in Section 7.3, performance is strongly correlated with size of the initial aligned bilingual corpus, with a larger Hansard subset of 12M words yielding 99.4% precision (by type) and 99.9% precision (by token). Performance on Czech is discussed in Section 7.3.

Model	Precision		Coverage	
	Typ	Tok	Typ	Tok

FRENCH Verbal Morphology Induction

French Hansards (12M words):

Model	Typ	Tok	Typ	Tok
MProj only	.992	.999	.779	.994
MProj+MTrie	.998	.999	.988	.999
MProj+MTrie+BKM	**.994**	**.999**	1.00	1.00

French Hansards (1.2M words):

Model	Typ	Tok	Typ	Tok
MProj only	.985	.998	.327	.976
MProj+MTrie	.995	.999	.958	.998
MProj+MTrie+BKM	**.979**	**.998**	1.00	1.00

French Hansards (120K words):

Model	Typ	Tok	Typ	Tok
MProj only	.962	.931	.095	.901
MProj+MTrie	.984	.993	.916	.994
MProj+MTrie+BKM	**.932**	**.989**	1.00	1.00

French Bible (300K words) via 1 English Bible:

Model	Typ	Tok	Typ	Tok
MProj only	1.00	1.00	.052	.747
MProj+MTrie	.991	.998	.918	.992
MProj+MTrie+BKM	**.954**	**.994**	1.00	1.00

French Bible (300K words) via 3 English Bibles:

Model	Typ	Tok	Typ	Tok
MProj only	.928	.975	.100	.820
MProj+MTrie	.981	.991	.931	.990
MProj+MTrie+BKM	**.964**	**.991**	1.00	1.00

CZECH Verbal Morphology Induction

Czech Reader's Digest (500K words):

Model	Typ	Tok	Typ	Tok
MProj only	.915	.993	.152	.805
MProj+MTrie	.916	.917	.893	.975
MProj+MTrie+BKM	**.878**	**.913**	1.00	1.00

SPANISH Verbal Morphology Induction

Spanish Bible (300K words) via 1 English Bible:

Model	Typ	Tok	Typ	Tok
MProj only	.973	.935	.264	.351
MProj+MTrie	.988	.998	.971	.967
MProj+MTrie+BKM	**.966**	**.985**	1.00	1.00

Spanish Bible (300K words) via French Bible:

Model	Typ	Tok	Typ	Tok
MProj only	.980	.935	.722	.765
MProj+MTrie	.983	.974	.986	.993
MProj+MTrie+BKM	**.974**	**.968**	1.00	1.00

Spanish Bible (300K words) via 3 English Bibles:

Model	Typ	Tok	Typ	Tok
MProj only	.964	.948	.468	.551
MProj+MTrie	.990	.998	.978	.987
MProj+MTrie+BKM	**.976**	**.987**	1.00	1.00

Table 3: Performance of full verbal morphological analysis, including precision/coverage by type/token

7.2 Morphology Induction via Aligned Bibles

Performance using even small parallel corpora (e.g. a 120K subset of the French Hansards) still yields a respectable 93.2% (type) and 98.9% (token) precision on the verb-lemmatization test set for the full Hansards. Given that the Bible is actually larger (approximately 300K words, depending on version and language) and available on-line or via OCR for virtually all languages (Resnik et al., 2000), we also conducted several experiments on Bible-based morphology induction, further detailed in Table 3.

7.2.1 Boosting Performance via Multiple Parallel Translations

Even though at most one translation of the Bible is typically available in a given foreign language, numerous English Bible versions are freely available and a performance increase can be achieved by simultaneously utilizing alignments to each English version. As illustrated in Figure 10, different aligned Bible pairs may exhibit (or be missing) different full or partial bridge links for a given word (due both to different lexical usage and poor textual parallelism in some text-regions or version pairs). However, $P_a(F_{root}|E_{lem_i})$ and $P_a(E_{lem_i}|F_{infl})$ need not be estimated from the same Bible pair. Even if one has only one Bible in a given source language, each alignment with a distinct English version gives new bridging opportunities with no additional resources needed on the source language side. The baseline approach (evaluated here) is simply to concatenate the different aligned versions together. While word-pair instances translated the same way in each version will be repeated, this rather reasonably reflects the increased confidence in this particular alignment. An alternate model would weight version pairs differently based on the otherwise-measured translation faithfulness and alignment quality between the version pairs. Doing so would help decrease noise. Increasing from 1 to 3 English versions reduces the type error rate (at full coverage) by 22% on French and 28% on Spanish with no increase in the source language resources.

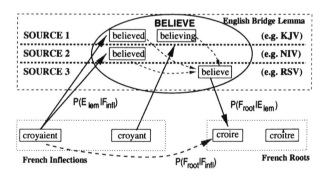

Figure 10: Use of multiple parallel Bible translations

7.2.2 Boosting Performance via Multiple Bridge Languages

Once lemmatization capabilities have been successfully projected to a new language (such as French), this language can then serve as an additional bridging source for morphology induction in a third language (such as Spanish), as illustrated in Figure 11. This can be particularly effective if the two languages are very similar (as in Spanish-French) or if their available Bible versions are a close translation of a common source (e.g. the Latin Vulgate Bible). As shown in Table 3, using the previously analyzed French Bible as a bridge for Spanish achieves performance (97.4% precision) comparable to the use of 3 parallel English Bible versions.

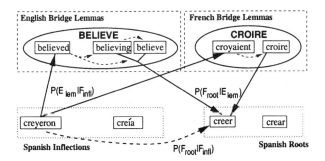

Figure 11: Use of bridges in multiple languages.

7.3 Morphology Induction: Observations

This section includes additional detail regarding the morphology induction experiments, supplementing the previous details and analyses given in Section 7 and Table 3.

- Performance induction using the French Bible as the bridge source is evaluated using the full test verb set extracted from the French Hansards. The strong performance when trained only using the Bible illustrates that even a small single text in a very different genre can provide effective transfer to modern (conversational) French. While the observed genre and topic-sensitive vocabulary differs substantially between the Bible and Hansards, the observed inventories of stem changes and suffixation actually have large overlap, as do the set of observed high-frequency irregular verbs. Thus the inventory of morphological phenomena seem to translate better across genre than do lexical choice and collocation models.

- Over 60% of errors are due to gaps in the candidate rootlists. Currently the candidate rootlists are derived automatically by applying the projected POS models and selecting any word with the probability of being an uninflected verb greater than a generous threshold and also ending in a canonical verb suffix. False positives are easily tolerated (less than 5% of errors are due to spurious non-root competitors), but with missing roots the algorithms are forced either to propose previously unseen roots or align to the closest previously observed root candidate. Thus while *no* non-English dictionary was used in the computation of these results, it would substantially improve performance to have a dictionary-based inventory of potential roots, increasing coverage and decreasing noise from competing non-roots and spelling errors.

- Performance in all languages has been significnatly hindered by low-accuracy parallel-corpus word-alignments using the original Model-3 GIZA tools. Use of Och and Ney's recently released and enhanced GIZA++ word-alignment models (Och and Ney, 2000) should improve performance for all of the applications studied in this paper, as would iterative re-alignments using richer alignment features (including lemma and part-of-speech) derived from this research.

- The current somewhat lower performance on Czech is due to several factors. They include (a) very low accuracy initial word-alignments due to often non-parallel translations of the Reader's Digest sample and the failure of the initial word-alignment models to handle the highly inflected Czech

morphology. (b) the small size of the Czech parallel corpus (less than twice the length of the Bible). (c) the common occurrence in Czech of two very similar perfective and non-perfective root variants (e.g. *odolávat* and *odolat*, both of which mean *to resist*). A simple monolingual dictionary-derived list of canonical roots would resolve ambiguity regarding which is the appropriate target.

- Many of the errors are due to all (or most) inflections of a single verb mapping to the same incorrect root. But for many applications where the function of lemmatization is to cluster equivalent words (e.g. stemming for information retrieval), the choice of label for the lemma is less important than correctly linking the members of the lemma.

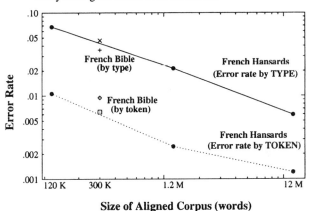

Figure 12: Learning Curves for French Morphology

- The learning curves in Figure 12 show the strong correlation between performance and size of the aligned corpus. Given that large quantities of parallel text currently exist in translation bureau archives and OCR-able books, not to mention the increasing online availability of bitext on the web, the natural growth of available bitext quantities should continue to support performance improvement.

- The system analysis examples shown in Table 4 are representative of model performance and are selected to illustrate the range of encountered phenomena. All system evaluation is based on the task of selecting the correct root for a given inflection (which has a long lexicography-based consensus regarding the "truth"). In contrast, the descriptive analysis of any such pairing is very theory dependent without standard consensus. The "TopBridge" column shows the strongest English bridge lemma utilized in mapping (typically one of many potential bridge lemmas).

These results are quite impressive in that they are based on essentially no language-specific knowledge of French, Spanish or Czech. In addition, the multilingual bridge algorithm is surface-form independent, and can just as readily handle obscure infixational or reduplicative morphological processes.

8. CONCLUSION

This paper has presented a detailed survey of original algorithms for cross-language annotation projection and noise-robust tagger induction, evaluated on four diverse applications. It shows how previous major investments in English annotated corpora and tool development can be effectively leveraged across languages, achieving accurate stand-alone tool development in other languages without comparable human annotation efforts. Collectively this work is the most comprehensive existing exploration of a very promising new paradigm for cross-language resource projection.

Acknowledgements

This research has been partially supported by NSF grant IIS-9985033 and ONR/MURI contract N00014-01-1-0685. The authors thank Silviu Cucerzan, Radu Florian, Jan Hajic, Gideon Mann and Charles Schafer for their valuable contributions and feedback.

9. REFERENCES

[1] Y. Al-Onaizan, J. Curin, M. Jahr, K. Knight, J. Lafferty, D. Melamed, FJ Och, D. Purdy, N. Smith and D. Yarowsky. 1999. *Statistical Machine Translation* (tech report). Johns Hopkins University.

[2] E. Brill. 1995. Transformation-based error-driven learning and natural language processing: A case study in part of speech tagging. *Computational Linguistics*, 24(1): 543–565.

[3] P. Brown, J. Cocke, S. DellaPietra, V. DellaPietra, F. Jelinek, J. Lafferty, R. Mercer, and P. Rossin. 1990. A statistical approach to machine translation. *Computational Linguistics*, 16(2):29–85.

[4] S. Cucerzan and D. Yarowsky. 1999. Language independent named entity recognition combining morphological and contextual evidence." In *Proceedings, 1999 Joint SIGDAT Conference on Empirical Methods in NLP and Very Large Corpora*, pp. 90-99.

[5] P. Fung and K. Church. 1994. K-vec: a new approach for aligning parallel texts. In *Proceedings of COLING-94*, pp. 1096–1102.

[6] P. Fung and K. McKeown. 1994. Aligning noisy parallel corpora across language groups: Word pair feature matching by dynamic warping. In *Proceedings of AMTA-94*, pp. 81–88.

[7] D. Jones, and R. Havrilla. 1998 Twisted pair grammar: Support for rapid development of machine translation for low density languages In *Procs. of AMTA'98*, pp. 318–332.

[8] D. Melamed. 1999. Bitext maps and alignment via pattern recognition. *Computational Linguistics*, 25(1):107–130.

[9] G. Ngai and R. Florian. 2001. Transformation-based learning in the fast lane. In *Proceedings of NAACL-2001*, pp. 40-47.

[10] F.J. Och and H. Ney. 2000. Improved statistical alignment models. In *Proceedings of ACL-2000*, pp. 440-447.

[11] L. Ramshaw and M. Marcus, 1999. Text chunking using transformation-based learning. In Armstrong et al. (Eds.), *Natural Language Processing Using Very Large Corpora*. Kluwer, pp. 157-176.

[12] P. Resnik, M. Olsen, and M. Diab. 2000. The Bible as a parallel corpus: annotating the 'Book of 2000 Tongues' *Computers and the Humanities*, 33(1-2):129-153.

[13] D. Wu. 1995. An algorithm for simultaneously bracketing parallel texts. In *Proc. of ACL-95*, pp. 244–251.

[14] D. Wu. 1997. Statistical inversion transduction grammars an bilingual parsing of parallel corpora. *Computational Linguistics*, 23(3):377-404.

[15] D. Yarowsky and G. Ngai. 2001. Inducing multilingual POS taggers and NP Bracketers via robust projection across aligned corpora. In *Proceedings of NAACL-2001*, pp. 377-404.

[16] D. Yarowsky and R. Wicentowski. 2000. Minimally supervised morphological analysis by multimodal alignment. In *Proceedings of ACL-2000*, pp. 207-216.

Induced Morphological Analyses for CZECH

Inflection	Root Out	Analysis	TopBridge
bral	brát	al→át	marry
brala	brát	ala→át	accept
brali	brát	ali→át	marry
byl	být	yl→ýt	be
byli	být	yli→ýt	be
bylo	být	ylo→ýt	be
chovala	chovat	la→t	behave
chová	chovat	á→at	behave
chováme	chovat	áme→at	behave
chodila	chodit	la→t	walk
chodí	chodit	í→it	walk
choďte	chodit	ďte→dit	swim
chránila	chránit	la→t	protect
chrání	chránit	í→it	protect
couval	couvat	l→t	back
chce	chtít	ce→tít	want
chcete	chtít	cete→tít	want
chceš	chtít	ceš→tít	want
chci	chtít	ci→tít	want
chtějí	chtít	ějí→ít	want
chtěli	chtít	ěli→ít	want
chtělo	chtít	ělo→ít	want

Induced Morphological Analyses for SPANISH

Inflection	Root Out	Analysis	TopBridge
aborreció	aborrecer	ió→er	hate
aborrecía	aborrecer	ía→er	hate
aborrezco	aborrecer	zco→cer	hate
abrace	abrazar	ce→zar	embrace
abrazado	abrazar	ado→ar	embrace
adquiere	adquirir	ere→rir	get
andamos	andar	amos→ar	walk
andando	andar	ando→ar	walk
andarán	andar	arán→ar	wander
andarás	andar	arás→ar	wander
andemos	andar	emos→ar	walk
anden	andar	en→ar	walk
anduvo	andar	uvo→ar	walk
buscáis	buscar	áis→ar	seek
buscó	buscar	ó→ar	seek
busque	buscar	que→car	seek
busqué	buscar	qué→car	seek

Induced Morphological Analyses for FRENCH

Inflection	Root Out	Analysis	TopBridge
abrège	abréger	ège→éger	shorten
abrègent	abréger	ègent→éger	shorten
abrégerai	abréger	erai→er	curtail
achète	acheter	ète→eter	buy
achètent	acheter	ètent→eter	buy
achètera	acheter	ètera→eter	buy
advenait	advenir	ait→ir	happen
advenu	advenir	u→ir	happen
adviendrait	advenir	iendrait→enir	happen
advient	advenir	ient→enir	happen
aliène	aliéner	ène→éner	alienate
aliènent	aliéner	ènent→éner	alienate
conçu	concevoir	çu→cevoir	conceive
crois	croire	s→re	believe
croyaient	croire	yaient→ire	believe

Table 4: Sample of induced morphological analyses

Information Extraction with Term Frequencies[*]

T. R. Lynam   C. L. A. Clarke   G. V. Cormack

Computer Science
University of Waterloo
Ontario, Canada
mt@plg.uwaterloo.ca

1. INTRODUCTION

Every day, millions of people use the internet to answer questions. Unfortunately, at present, there is no simple and successful means to consistently accomplish this goal. One common approach is to enter a few terms from a question into a Web search system and scan the resulting pages for the answer, a laborious process. To address this need, a question answering (QA) system was created to find and extract answers from a corpus. This system contains three parts: a parser for generating question queries and categories, a passage retrieval element, and an information extraction (IE) component. The extraction method was designed to elicit answers from passages collected by the information retrieval engine. The subject of this paper is the information extraction component. It is based on the premise that information related to the answer will be found many times in a large corpus like the Web.

The system was applied to the Question Answering Track at TREC-9 and achieved the second best results overall[3]. The information extraction and parsing components were new for TREC-9; the TREC-8 system solely used passage retrieval[4]. Each new component yielded greater than 10% improvement in mean reciprocal rank, TREC's standard evaluation measure.

In the sections that follow, the extraction component is described and evaluated according to its contribution to the system's effectiveness. In particular, this paper investigates the contribution of a voting scheme favouring terms found in many candidate passages.

2. BACKGROUND

Architecturally, the question answering system is simple. First the parser analyses the question and generates a query for the passage retrieval component. It also provides selection rules for the information extraction component. Next, the passage retrieval component executes the query over the target corpus and retrieves a ranked list of passages for the answer IE component to process. Thirdly, the information extraction component finds the answers' extracts in the passages retrieved.

The parser is a probabilistic version of Earley's algorithm. It determines all possible parses of the grammar and selects the most probable. The grammar contains only 80 production rules[3].

Proceedings of HLT 2001, First International Conference on Human Language Technology Research, J. Allan, ed., Morgan Kaufmann, San Francisco, 2001.

The passage retrieval component collects arbitrary substrings of a document in the corpus. These substrings are considered passages and given a score. Passage scores are based on the terms contained in the query and the passage length. Passages with a length of one thousand words were retrieved in the TREC-9 system.

The information extraction component locates possible answers in the top ten passages. It then selects the best answer extracts of a predetermined length.

The overall approach of question analysis followed by IR succeeded by IE is nearly universal in QA systems[1, 2, 5, 6, 7, 8, 9]. The TREC-9 question answering track required the QA system to find solutions to 693 questions. Two different runs were judged: 50- and 250-byte answer extracts. Question answering systems were evaluated by the mean reciprocal answer rank (MRR). Five passages of the desired length are evaluated in order. The score is based on the rank of the first correct passage according to the formula:

$$MRR = \frac{1}{\#questions} \sum_{i=1}^{\#questions} \frac{1}{answer_i\ rank}$$

If the answer is found at multiple ranks, the best (lowest) rank will be used. If an answer is not found in the top five, the score for that particular question is zero.

The TREC-9 results reveal the improvements of the new components added to the system. The TREC-8 system was used as a baseline. With the combination of the parse-generated queries and the information extraction components, there is a total improvement of 106% and 25% for 50- and 250-byte runs respectively. The information extraction element has a greater impact when the answer is shorter as seen in Table 1.

3. TERM FREQUENCY ALGORITHM

The algorithm requires a set of passages that are likely to contain an answer, and a category for each question. This algorithm is similar to the information extraction technique used in the GuruQA system[8]. The key to the algorithm is using term frequencies to give individual terms a score. Important information is uncovered by looking at repeated terms in a set of passages. In addition, terms are scored based on their recurrence in the corpus. The system applies very simple patterns to discover individual words or numbers, allowing the evaluation of the term's frequency. This method proceeds in the following sequence:

1. Simplify the question category from the parser output.

2. Scan the passages for patterns matching the question category.

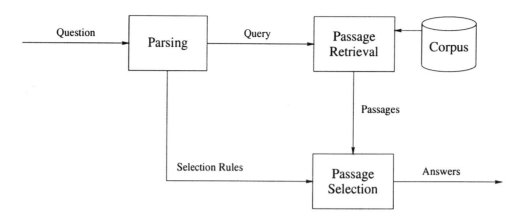

Figure 1: Overview of QA processing.

Table 1: Mean reciprocal ranks using TREC-9 evaluation

	50-byte answer MRR		250-byte answer MRR	
baseline	0.189		0.407	
parse-generated queries improvement	0.191	(+1%)	0.464	(+14%)
information extraction improvement	0.357	(+89%)	0.467	(+15%)
TREC-9 system	0.390	(+106%)	0.507	(+25%)

3. Assign each possible answer term an initial weight based on its rareness.

4. Modify each term weight depending on its distance from the centre and rank of the passage.

5. Select the (50-byte or 250-byte TREC 9 format) answer that maximizes the sum of the terms' weight found within the passage.

6. Set all terms' weight in the selected answer to zero.

7. Repeat steps 5 and 6 until five answers are selected.

The initial procedure simplifies the answer categories. The algorithm utilizes the question classification given by the parser in the following categories: *Proper* (person, name, company), *Place* (city, country, state), *Time* (date, time of day, weekday, month, duration, age), *How* (much, many, far, tall, etc.). The latter category is divided into sub-categories for monetary values, numbers, distances and other methods of measurement.

Next, the passages are scanned using the patterns for the given question classification. The purpose of the patterns is to narrow the number of possible answers which will increases the performance. It is important to note that the patterns do not contribute to the terms' weight. These simple patterns are regular expressions that have been hand-coded. For example, the pattern for *Proper* is [^A-Za-z][A-Z][A-Za-z][^A-Za-z0-9], which matches a capital letter followed by one or more letters surrounded by white space or punctuation. Each word in the passage either matches a pattern or not. Patterns do not stretch over more than one word. In the passage "Bank of America" only "Bank" and "America" would be considered possible answers. The algorithm can find the correct answer "Bank of America" by determining that "Bank" and "America" should be in the answer. When question classification is unknown, the term frequency for all words in the passages is computed. The system was evaluated using no question classification

and still achieved a MRR of 0.338. With no classification, only the term frequency equation is utilized to evaluate answers. This confirms the power of the term frequency equation (1). The patterns for each question classification are very naive so in theory, if the patterns were improved the entire system would also improve.

Thirdly, the terms are differentiated by assigning each term a weight. The term weight is related to the term's rareness. The rarer the term, the higher the term's value. The power of the information extraction component is almost entirely derived from this step. Each term's weight is calculated by the following formula:

$$w_t = c_t log(N/f_t) \qquad (1)$$

where f_t is the number of times the term is in the corpus, c_t is the number of times the term is in the set of passages, and N is the total number of terms in the corpus. Knowing the term's corpus frequency is important; however, the strength of the formula is drawn from the multiple occurrences of terms appearing in the retrieved passages. An answer extract containing "Bank of America" will most likely be selected if "Bank" and "America" have high term frequency values. Essentially, this calculation employs the corpus term frequency in conjunction with a voting scheme. The equation will reveal the rarest term in the corpus that occurs most often in the passages retrieved.

The fourth step modifies the term weight depending on its location. The centre of the passages is the centre of the query terms' locations. As a possible answer's distance from the centre increases its relation to the query, terms decrease. To utilize this information, the term weight is modified in conjunction with its distance from the centre of the passage. The farther from the centre, the more the term weight is decreased. The term value is then modified according to the passage ranking in which it was found; the lower the ranking, the more the term weight is decreased. Step four is important because it distinguishes duplicate terms depending on each term's position. This means that if there are many duplications of a possible answer each one will have a different term weight. For

Effect of Repetition on MRR

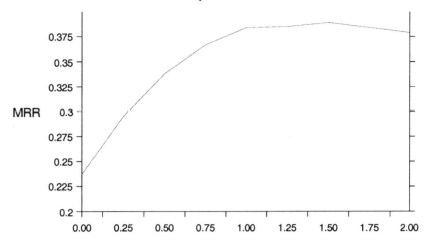

Figure 2: Significance of repetition in term frequency equation.

example, the term "Bank" found in the best passage would have a higher term weight than a "Bank" term found in a lower ranking passage.

For TREC-9, the system was required to produce 50- and 250-byte substrings. Each substring is assigned a score equal to the sum of the terms' weight within it. The best answer is the substring of the required length with the highest score. The weight of all the terms appearing in the answer substring is reduced to zero (step six). The final step is the selection of the next best substring; this process repeats until the number of desired substrings is fulfilled. Reducing the terms' weight to zero allows for distinction between each of the answers, eliminating answers that are almost the same. When a term is part of a phrase like "knowing is half the battle" the terms in the phrase will usually appear together in the retrieved passages. This means the phrase would be selected if "knowing" , "half", and "battle" scored highly.

The idea behind the algorithm is to evaluate potential answers in the passages retrieved using the term frequency equation. The question classification patterns are used to limit the number of possible answers evaluated, which heightens accuracy. The algorithm will select phrases even if all the words are not possible answers. The term frequency algorithm does not need to know the answer classification to perform proficiently. This is a very robust method to extract answers, though knowing the question classification does improve the system's mean reciprocal rank considerably.

In the future, term frequencies may be used in combination with Natural Language Processing (NLP) techniques such as a name entity tagging to further enhance the system's results.

4. RESULTS

In a large corpus there is duplicate or supporting information for almost any given question. The term frequency formula utilizes this knowledge, through two simple premises: the more a term is repeated, the more conceivable it is the correct answer, and the less likely a term appears by chance, the more probable it is also correct.

The duplication component's importance in formula (1) can be evaluated by modifying the value of α in the term frequency equation:

$$w_t = c_t^\alpha log(N/f_t) \qquad (2)$$

Figure 2 demonstrates the value that duplicate information in the passages has on the result by modifying α.

The graph reveals that as the importance of duplicate terms increases, the performance of the system strengthens. By eliminating the repetition part of the equation ($\alpha = 0$) the system only achieves a mean reciprocal rank of 0.237. As expected and demonstrated in the graph, the value of this part of the formula reaches a maximum before decreasing the overall system's accuracy.

5. CONCLUSION

Overall, the information extraction component improves the question answering system. Notably, the term frequency algorithm does not require information regarding the structure or grammar of a natural language; therefore the algorithm may be use in many natural languages. The term frequency algorithm can even extract answers when the question's meaning is completely unknown. Having an elementary and reliable way to evaluate each term in a set of passages is useful. One possibility is to add highly weighted terms to the original query.

In theory, as the corpus size expands, the performance of the system should increase as more duplicate information will become available. Finally, the initial value of the term frequency algorithm is beneficial to the overall system and future applications of question answering.

6. REFERENCES

[1] E. Breck, J. Burger, D. House, M. Light, and I. Mani. Question answering from large document collections. In *1999 AAAI Fall Symposium on Question Answering Systems*, North Falmouth, MA, 1999.

[2] C. Cardie, V. Ng, D. Pierce, and C. Buckley. Examining the role of statistical and linguistic knowledge sources in a general-knowledge question-answering system. In *Sixth Applied Natural Language Processing Conference*, pages 180–187, 2000.

171

[3] C. L. A. Clarke, G. V. Cormack, D. I. E. Kisman, and T. R. Lynam. Question answering by passage selection. In *9th Text REtrieval Conference*, Gaithersburg, MD, 2000.

[4] G. V. Cormack, C. L. A. Clarke, C. R. Palmer, and D. I. E. Kisman. Fast automatic passage ranking. In *8th Text REtrieval Conference*, Gaithersburg, MD, November 1999.

[5] S. M. Harabagiu and S. J. Maiorano. Finding answers in large collections of texts: Paragraph indexing + abductive inference. In *1999 AAAI Fall Symposium on Question Answering Systems*, pages 63–71, North Falmouth, MA, 1999.

[6] E. Hovy, U. Hermjakob, C.-Y. Lin, M. Junk, and L. Gerber. The Webclopedia. In *9th Text REtrieval Conference*, Gaithersburg, MD, 2000.

[7] A. Ittycheriah, M. Franz, W.-J. Zhu, and A. Ratnaparkhi. IBM's statistical question answering system. In *9th Text REtrieval Conference*, Gaithersburg, MD, 2000.

[8] D. R. Radev, J. Prager, and V. Samn. Ranking suspected answers to natural language questions using predictive annotation. In *6th Conference on Applied Natural Language Processing*, Seattle, May 2000.

[9] W. A. Woods, S. Green, P. Martin, and A. Houston. Halfway to question answering. In *9th Text REtrieval Conference*, Gaithersburg, MD, 2000.

The Integrated Feasibility Experiment (IFE) Process

J. Allen Sears
Corporation for National Research
Initiatives
1895 Preston White Drive
Reston, Va. 20191

asears@cnri.reston.va.us

Stephen E. Cross
Software Engineering Institute
Carnegie Mellon University
Pittsburgh, PA 15213-3890

sc@sei.cmu.edu

ABSTRACT

In this paper, we describe a process used for guiding the
evaluation and transformation process for language processing
research and development. The Integrated Feasibility Experiment
process is explained by describing the key six steps, and then
providing a specific example to help understand how to implement
the steps.

1. INTRODUCTION

The objective of this paper is to describe a reliable and repeatable
process used to guide the development of information systems
where technology teams must come together to implement a
concept. This paper describes an "IFE process" that has been
used successfully multiple times over the last eight years, and has
served as both a framework for language experimentation, and as a
vehicle for integrating and applying language technology
components.

2. DESCRIBING THE IFE SIX KEY STEPS

The IFE process consists of six steps that guide development and
experimentation. The emphasis placed on each step depends on
the maturity of the technology and the involvement of the users.
The six steps are as follows (note that the six steps are
summarized in Figure 1)

2.1 Step #1: Scenario

Describe a scenario for employing the information technology that
will allow everyone to visualize how the technology is to be used
during a real situation. This step places emphasis on making the
technology look and behave like a system. This is a critical step
for two main reasons:

a. For the technology teams that are to integrate technology, the
scenario provides a real and accessible description of how the
technology should be used. This assists the teams directly in
describing the architecture and components needed to build an
information system for the given scenario.

b. The scenario is key in describing the intent of the information
system to the operational user. Typically, operational users
become involved in this scenario building process to give early and
helpful feedback to the technology development teams.

2.2 Step #2: Architecture

Many people believe that describing the architecture is the key
step in building and information system. However, if the ideas
about components and interconnections are vague or incomplete,
then the architecture step is actually best developed using a
hypothesis and test process. In all cases the architecture must
allow plug-and-play concepts that support the inclusion and reuse
of mature processing components, plus the inclusion of new
components that will be the focus of experimentation.

2.3 Step #3: Reuse Components:

The third step is to identify and make plans to reuse components
that one will depend on during the IFE. This step is critical for
the technology teams because many of the components to be used
come from years of development and experimentation. With
mature components populating a large share of the architecture,
the development teams are then free to experiment with new
components that are considered to be necessary for end-to-end
processing. Moreover, the developers can experiment with data
flow and interconnection strategies. This experimentation step is
critical in order to transform into tomorrows' network-centric
processing models supported by communication interoperability
provide by TCP/IP processing.

2.4 Step #4: User Involvement

Obtaining operational user involvement early-on is an important
step to support a technology transformation objective. The
operational user will have insights and needs that cannot be
predicted by the technology developers. Moreover, user
involvement improves the interest, understanding and potential
commitment to the technology. If user centered final exam metrics
are stated clearly then they provide a useful objective to help

*Proceedings of HLT 2001, First International Conference
on Human Language Technology Research*, J. Allan, ed.,
Morgan Kaufmann, San Francisco, 2001.

focus technology development and implementation. This all may sound like motherhood, but it is a critical step that is missing often from technology development projects large and small.

2.5 Step #5: Rapid Prototyping

The use of a rapid prototype approach is not new. In the mid 1980s it became the key focus for specifying and building information systems. However, the rapid prototype process must be used in conjunction with other steps of the IFE, or else the development effort will end up as a simple demonstration that does not scale to real user needs. The spiral development model for development that emphasizes the "build a little, test a little" approach, should be used to keep development on track and headed toward the target needs of the user.

2.6 Step #6: Evaluation and Feedback

Metric-based evaluation is important for any development process. For an IFE the specification of usable metrics is not easy because the teams are coming together to build a "new" capability. The best approach comes by making an early commitment and following through with the measurement process and then later changing the evaluation process to better represent the emerging information processing capability. One should have measures for technology accomplishment and such measures should focus on component performance. In addition, one must have an overall "task performance" metric or metrics that reflect the needs of the operational user and the intent of the scenario.

Integrated Feasibility Experiment Steps

1. **Scenario** .. Helps to visualize the use of new technology

2. **Architecture** .. Components, interconnects, data flow, and processing model

3. **Reuse components** .. Must build on past accomplishments

4. **User** .. The user provides application pull, as opposed to technology push

5. **Rapid prototype** .. Build a little, test a little strategy to keep effort on track and on target

6. **Evaluation and feedback**: Metrics-based evaluations are key to understanding accomplishment

---

Figure 1: The six steps of an Integrated Feasibility Experiment

2.7 Historical Note

An Integrated Feasibility Development (IFD) process was first used in 1990 by Steve Cross and his team to guide development of the DARPA and Rome Labs replanning system called DART (Dynamic Adaptive Replanning Technology). DART was developed to assist logistics and transportation planners in scheduling the movement and deliver of people and materials. An operational prototype was actually used during the Persian Gulf

conflict in 1990. The IFD name has been changed to IFE by replacing "Development" with "Experimentation" in order to emphasize the experimentation and scientific exploration aspect of the effort, but the steps of the process have remained the same.

3. WHY THE IFE PROCESS WORKS

Their three good reasons the process works and a forth explanation that deals with the basics of building and implementing information technology.

3.1 Application Pull

The scenario and user involvement (steps 1 and 4) work together to provide an "application pull" on the technology. To many efforts fail because they start with a new idea which is pushed and developed and then is found to be in search of (ISO) of a meaningful application. This "application push" model fails in most cases because no user is willing or able to invest in an acquisition follow-on process. Instead, the application pull process will address new information system introduction methods that take full advantage of commercially created information technology, and blend in radically new ideas that provide for scale and success. These steps insure transformation efforts will be based on innovation and speed.

3.2 Scalable Baseline

The architecture and reuse-of-components focus (steps 2 and 3) provides a baseline capability that will enable the information technology to scale up to deal with operational needs. Moreover, this investment in the software architecture provides the infrastructure needed to explore new ideas in an affordable and repeatable fashion.

3.3 Build A Little, Test A Little

Rapid prototyping and evaluation steps (steps 5 and 6) offer a simple and understandable approach to allow for incremental progress that is informed by failure as much as by achievement. This is key. Innovation must be allowed to fail just as long as the process moves forward and is informed in a positive way by the failure. Too many projects fail to provide for the process of managing risk and failure. Such projects are doomed to incremental advancement at best.

3.4 A Managed Process That Works

Some observers of the IFE process have said the six steps are necessary and sufficient to provide guidelines for information systems development and implementation. Necessary and sufficient does not guarantee success. It does however provide a small and simple set of steps that can help the technology community to shape information technology, and give it an outstanding shot at success. In most instances the IFE methodology has addressed crisis action and crisis response scenarios that address dynamic problems in the effective use of people, resources, information, and network-centric computing.

This methodology has been used to increase cooperation between defense and intelligence groups to develop command, control, computing, and intelligence infrastructure fundamental to developing new concepts of operation, and the foundation on which future capabilities are built.

4. AN EXAMPLE IFE

The following provides an example of the Strong Angel IFE used for the "PacTIDES" exercise in June 2000. This exercise was sponsored by the US Joint Military Command known as CinCPAC and included seven other nations and the United Nations. Both the accomplishments and the lessons learned will be covered. The Strong Angel IFE provided and outstanding framework for learning more about end-to-end language processing.

4.1 Strong Angel IFE Overview

Step 1. Scenario: The primary application focus for the IFE was the spread of disease, with special emphasis given to information processing techniques. The operational user was Dr. Eric Rasmussen, MD who was the Third Fleet Surgeon for the United States Navy. Dr. Rasmussen was most concerned about providing effective support and relief to people during "Humanitarian Assistance" operations that are becoming common through out the world. Examples like Bosnia and Kosovo come to mind immediately. The story line was that refugees were caught in a border location and world organizations were coming together to provide food, shelter, and security. The spread of disease soon became one of the top security risks. The TIDES system was used by the security teams to get timely information about relevant events so they could anticipate critical situations they may face instead of simply reacting to issues.

Step 2. Technology teams outlined a plug-and-play architecture called the "TIDES Portal" that was used to guide the development and experimentation process. The architecture was built on a client – server model where components for language processing were loosely confederated over the Internet.

Step 3: Component specification: The three primary information processing components were focused on detection, extraction, and user interaction. There also was a translingual component that provided two way translations to and from Korean. The scenario was expanded to include the treat of a missile launce from North Korea that could carry a biological war-head. The translingual component was an add-on rather than a main line processing component. There were seven

different sources of news that was being processed to provide information to relief and security personnel. These sources included both text and speech information. The speech information was transformed into text and then became input to detection and extraction processing. The user interface component was the most difficult to construct because the underlying end-to-end processing model was emerging and changing each month. Moreover, the loosely coupled distributed processing model for the TIDES Portal was difficult to realize in a coherent user interface. This issue and other shortcomings are discussed in the lessons learned section of this paper.

Step 4: Operational User Involvement. The scenario definition process helped Dr Rasmussen and the other relief and security operators understand how the technology would come together to be used. The TIDES Portal and the "PacTIDES" experiments were use by representatives of several of the RIMPAC nations and also by United Nations personnel. For the first time ever the RIMPAC exercises conducted by seven nations: US, Canada, Japan, Chile, Australia, Korea, and UK, included a focus on a humanitarian assistance issues. For the first time users were able to understand in context the kinds of capability an automated information processing system such as TIDES may provide in the future. The potential for TIDES support received strong endorsement from these operators who are literally overwhelmed by data, documents, and email, but who are often starved for actionable information.

Step 5. The rapid prototype process was used to develop the IFE integrated system called the "TIDES Portal". Initial TIDES Portal implementation was tested in early 2000, and the final exam for TIDES Portal was conducted during Strong Angel was held In June 2000 on the Parker Ranch in Hawaii. The system was used by military and by UN World Food Program personnel. There was one situation where UN folks needed timely information about a situation in Africa, and the TIDES Portal came through. The UN team was impressed. However, most of the lessons learned at Strong Angel pointed to weaknesses in the TIDES Portal concept of operations. These weaknesses have become the main focus for development of IFE-Bio in 2001.

Step 6. Metric-based evaluation was used in Strong Angel with limited success. The weaknesses in the end-to-end processing capability of the TIDES Portal dominated the IFE and limited the ability of research groups to conduct full metrics-based evaluations in a meaningful way. This issue will receive more attention in during IFE-Bio final exams in June 2001.

5. LESSONS LEARNED

The Strong Angel IFE was judged to be a success even though several parts of the effort resulted in failure. The important point is that the TIDES Program learned from both the failures and the accomplishments and the lessons help guide the IFE process in 2001. The following provides an example of the Strong Angel IFE used for the "PacTIDES" exercise in June 2000. This exercise was sponsored by the US Joint Military Command known as CinCPAC and included seven other nations and the United Nations. Both the accomplishments and the lessons learned will be covered. The Strong Angel IFE provided and outstanding framework for learning more about end-to-end language processing.

5.1 Lessons Learned From Negative Examples in Strong Angel IFE

A. Process model was too uncoupled. Several groups came together integrated by only the Internet. The processing components were not synchronized and basically had little inter-dependency. Therefore, there was little in the way of information management within the infrastructure to hold the information processing model together.

B. Late-binding decisions about distributed processing burned up critical development cycles. The situation here is simple: initially the assumption was made that full Internet connectivity at T1 rates would be available, and then the assumption was changed to anticipate NO Internet connectivity outside of the camp. The change in the Internet connectivity and quality of service assumptions were made with two months to go. Most of the time was then spent on building local servers and processes that would simulate that external communications was in place. During the critical last two months critical development and testing was stopped and attention was turned to re-engineering the processing infrastructure.

C. Collection issues were not properly anticipated: The strengths of TIDES processing comes from end-to-end processing of streams of information from sources such as radio, TV, email, newswire, etc. Unfortunately the language detection and extraction communities are conditioned to processing from training and test sets provided to them in efforts such as TREC and MUC.

Strong Angel concepts of operation actually required continuous processing of streaming information from multiple sources. These capture and processing priorities were not realized soon enough in the IFE process, and were therefore sorely lacking at the Strong Angel final exam.

D. TDT processing concepts were not included: The detection, extraction, and summarization process for Strong Angel anticipated Topic Detection and Tracking (TDT) capabilities, but the algorithms were never incorporated. This means that critical front-end filtering and grouping functions were missing.

5.2 Lessons Learned From Positive Examples in Strong Angel IFE

A. The Strong Angel team never imagined how difficult the living and information processing environment could be in a refugee camp. In fact there was fine grain dust everywhere and the power was intermittent. Better understanding of these environmental factors was a positive coming from the Strong Angel effort.

B. A key positive was developing the understanding for how detection, extraction, and summarization must work together with collection and distribution to provide an end-to-end processing infrastructure.

C. An important accomplishment occurred when UN folks wanted to know more about a growing crisis in Uganda after a humanitarian incident. It turns out that TIDES processing was able to give the UN contingent information that they needed that was current and multi-source. The UN folks were thrilled and amazed. Most amazing to the TIDES folks was the capability only used 10% of what was anticipated for TIDES processing. In other words, a very small and easy product provided significant value. There is great confidence that much more can be accomplished in IFE processing in 2001.

6. LOOKING AHEAD FOR THE IFE PROCESS

For TIDES two different but concurrent IFE processes are being pursued during 2001. First a team including MITRE, UMASS, NYU, and the Navy are developing IFE-Bio concerned with gathering real time information to aid in the analysis of spread of disease. A team of BBN, UMASS, and CIA are looking at automatically extracting information in real time from a wide range of Arabic open source material. When ready and mature, technology and language processing techniques will be incorporated into Foreign Broadcast Information Service (FBIS) processing. A short abstraction of IFE processing six steps is provided in figure 2 for the 2001 effort called IFE-Bio. In addition the DARPA Communicator is using the IFE process to help in the development and transformation process for dialogue interaction. The Communicator IFE process is being continued aggressively in 2001 by a team including Lockheed, MIT, and the United States Marines Corps. For DARPA Communicator the initial LCS Marine IFE process has matured and is now being applied to a wider range of military exercises. Valuable lessons learned emerge from every exercise and aggressive concepts of operation are being investigated.

IFE - Bio: Example for TIDES

- **Scenario:** TIDES technology will be used to extract information about spread of specific diseases. Crisis response teams will pose ad hoc questions to the system.

- **Architecture:** End-to-end processing to include source capture from audio and text, TDT processing, extraction, summarization, and finally alerting & distribution.

- **Reuse components:** IFE - Bio will use language processing components from NYU, UMASS, and MITRE

- **User:** LCDR. Eric Rassmussen, former Third Fleet Surgeon, will stress test the IFE crew to see how well they respond to questions that would come up during a crisis.

- **Rapid prototype:** Initial build for 27 Feb, then mid-term in April will test second build, finally the June 2001 will test the final build of the prototype.

- **Evaluation and feedback:** Technical evaluations will cover all key components. The user evaluation will focus on ease-of-use and performance improvement

Figure 2: Overview example of IFE-Bio

Integrated Feasibility Experiment for Bio-Security: IFE-Bio A TIDES Demonstration

Lynette Hirschman, Kris Concepcion, Laurie Damianos, David Day, John Delmore, Lisa Ferro, John Griffith, John Henderson, Jeff Kurtz, Inderjeet Mani, Scott Mardis, Tom McEntee, Keith Miller, Beverly Nunan, Jay Ponte, Florence Reeder, Ben Wellner, George Wilson, Alex Yeh

The MITRE Corporation
Bedford, Massachusetts, USA and
McLean, Virginia, USA
781-271-7789

lynette@mitre.org

ABSTRACT

As part of MITRE's work under the DARPA TIDES (Translingual Information Detection, Extraction and Summarization) program, we are preparing a series of demonstrations to showcase the TIDES Integrated Feasibility Experiment on Bio-Security (IFE-Bio). The current demonstration illustrates some of the resources that can be made available to analysts tasked with monitoring infectious disease outbreaks and other biological threats.

Keywords

Translation, information extraction, summarization, topic detection and tracking, system integration.

1. INTRODUCTION

The long-term goal of TIDES is to provide delivery of information on demand in real-time from live on-line sources. For IFE-Bio, the resources made available to the analyst include e-mail, news groups, digital library resources, and eventually (in later versions), topic-specific segments from broadcast news. Because of the emphasis on global monitoring, there is a need to process incoming information in multiple languages. The system must deliver the appropriate information content in the appropriate form and in the appropriate language (taken for now to be English). This means that the IFE-Bio system will have to deliver news stories, clusters of relevant documents, threaded discussions, alerts on new events, tables, summaries (particularly over document collections), answers to questions, graphs and geo-spatial temporal displays of information.

The demonstration system for the Human Language Technology Conference in March 2001 represents an early stage of the full IFE-Bio system, with an emphasis on end-to-end processing. Future demonstrations will make use of MITRE's Catalyst architecture, providing an efficient, scalable architecture to

facilitate integration of multiple stages of linguistic processing. By June 2001, the IFE-Bio system will provide richer linguistic processing through the integration of modules contributed by other TIDES participants. By June 2002, the IFE-Bio system will include additional functionality, such as real-time broadcast news feeds, new machine translation components, support for question-answering, cross-language information retrieval, multi-document summarization, automatic extraction and normalization of temporal and spatial information, and automated geospatial and temporal displays.

2. The IFE-Bio System

The current demonstration (March 2001) highlights the basic functionality required by an analyst, including:

- **Capture** of sources, including e-mail, digital library material, news groups, and web-based resources;

- **Categorizing** of the sources into multiple orthogonal hierarchies useful to the analyst, e.g., disease, region, news source, language;

- **Processing** of the information through various stages, including "zoning" of the text to select the relevant portions for processing; named entity detection, event detection, extraction of temporal information, summarization, and translation from Spanish, Portuguese, and Chinese into English;

- **Access** to the information through use of any mail and news group reader, which allows the analyst to organize, save, and share the information in a familiar, readily accessible environment;

- **Display** of the information in alternate forms, including color-tagged documents, tables, summaries, graphs, and geospatial, map-based displays.

Figure 1 below shows the overall functionality envisioned for the IFE-Bio system, including capture, categorizing, processing, access and display.

Collection capability for the current IFE-Bio system includes email, news groups, journals, and Web resources. We have a complete copy of the ProMED mailings (a moderated source

Proceedings of HLT 2001, First International Conference on Human Language Technology Research, J. Allan, ed., Morgan Kaufmann, San Francisco, 2001.

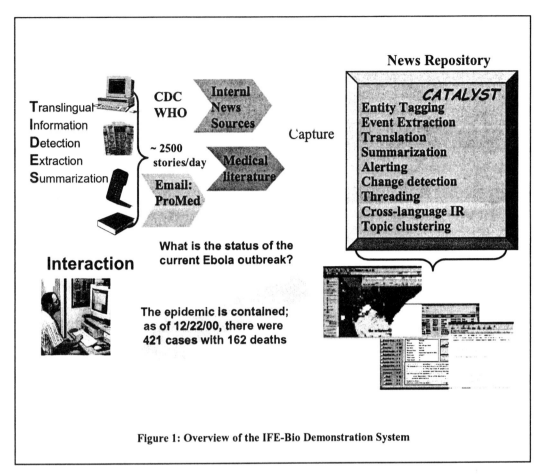

Figure 1: Overview of the IFE-Bio Demonstration System

tracking global infectious disease outbreaks), and are routinely collecting other information sources from the World Health Organization and CDC. In addition, we are collecting several general global news feeds. Current volume is around 2000 messages per day; we estimate capacity for the current system at around 4500 messages/day. Once we have integrated a filtering capability, we expect the volume of messages saved in IFE-Bio should drop significantly, since many of the global news services report on a wide range of events and not all need to be passed on to IFE-Bio analysts. The categorizing of sources is done based on the message header. The header is synthesized by extracting key information about disease name, the country, and other relevant information such as type of victim and source of information, as well as date of message receipt.

The processing for the current demonstration system uses a limited subset of the Catalyst architecture capabilities and a number of in-house linguistic modules. The linguistic modules in the current demonstration system include tokenization, sentence segmentation, part-of-speech tagging, named entity detection, temporal extraction (Mani and Wilson 2000) and source-specific event detection. In addition, we have incorporated the CyberTrans embedded machine translation system which "wraps" available machine translation engines to make them available via an e-mail or Web interface (Reeder 2000). Single document summarization is performed by the MITRE WebSumm system (Mani and Bloedorn 1999).

We carefully chose a light-weight interface mechanism for delivery of the information to the analyst. By treating the incoming streams of data as feeds to a news server, the analyst can inspect and organize the information using a familiar news and e-mail browser. The analyst can subscribe to areas of interest, flag important messages, watch specific threads, and create tailored filters for monitoring outbreaks. The stories are crossed-posted to multiple relevant news groups, based on the information in the header, e.g., a story on Ebola in Africa would be cross posted to the Africa regional newsgroup and to the Ebola disease newsgroup. Search by subject and date allow the analyst to select subsets of the messages for further processing, annotation or sharing. The news client provides notification of incoming messages. In later versions, we plan to integrate topic detection and tracking capabilities, to provide improved filtering and routing of messages, as well as detection of new topics. The use of this simple delivery mechanism provides a familiar environment with almost no learning curve, and it avoids issues of platform and operating system dependence.

Finally, the system makes use of several different devices to display the information appropriately. Figure 2 shows the layout of the Netscape news browser interface. It includes the list of newsgroups that have been subscribed to (on the left), the list of messages from the chosen newsgroup (on top), and a particular message with color-coded named entities (including disease terms displayed in red, so that they are easy to spot in the message).

179

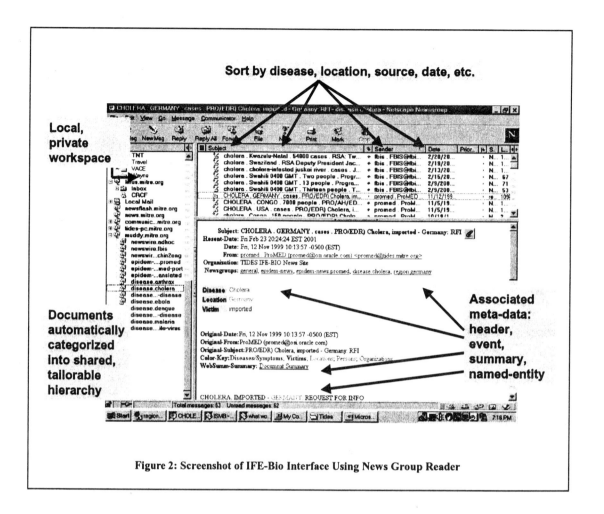

Figure 2: Screenshot of IFE-Bio Interface Using News Group Reader

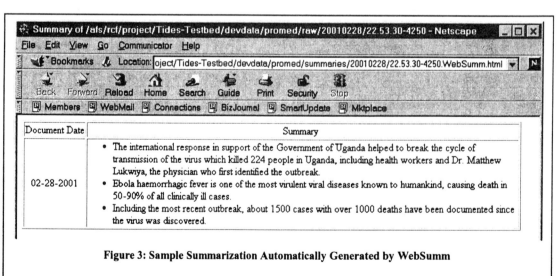

Figure 3: Sample Summarization Automatically Generated by WebSumm

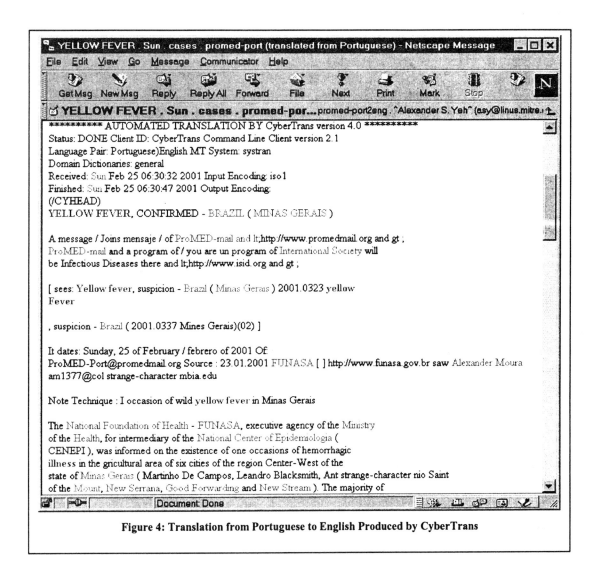

Figure 4: Translation from Portuguese to English Produced by CyberTrans

There are multiple display modalities available. The message in Figure 2 contains a short tabular display in the beginning, identifying disease, region and victim type. Below that is a URL to a document summary, created by MITRE's WebSumm system (see Figure 3 for a sample summary). If an incoming message is in a language other than English, then CyberTrans is called to run code set and language identification modules, and the language is translated into English for further processing. Figure 4 below shows a sample translated message; note that there are a number of untranslated words, but it is still possible to get the gist of the message.

In addition, we are working on a mechanism to provide geographic and eventually, temporal display of outbreak information. Figure 5 shows the stages of processing involved. Stage 1 shows onamed entity and temporal tagging to identify the items of interest. These are combined into disease events by further linguistic processing; the result is shown in the table in Stage 2. This spreadsheet of events serves as input for a map-based display, shown in Stage 3. The graph plots number of new cases and number of cumulative cases over time. In the map, the size of the outer dot represents total number of cases to date, and the inner dot represents new cases. This allows the analyst to visualize spread of the disease, as well as the stage of the outbreak (spreading or subsiding).

3. REFERENCES

[1] Mani, I. and Bloedorn, E. (1999). "Summarizing Similarities and Among Related Documents". Information Retrieval 1(1): 35-67.

[2] Mani, I. and Wilson, G. (2000). "Robust Temporal Processing of News," Proceedings of the 38th Annual Meeting of the Association for Computational Linguistics (ACL'2000), 69-76. New Brunswick, New Jersey. Association for Computational Linguistics.

[3] Reeder, F. (2000) "At Your Service: Embedded MT as a Service", NAACL Workshop on Embedded MT, March, 2000.

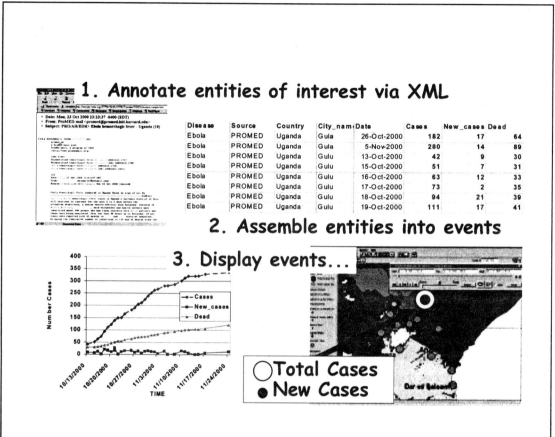

1. Annotate entities of interest via XML

Disease	Source	Country	City_nam	Date	Cases	New_cases	Dead
Ebola	PROMED	Uganda	Gula	26-Oct-2000	182	17	64
Ebola	PROMED	Uganda	Gula	5-Nov-2000	280	14	89
Ebola	PROMED	Uganda	Gulu	13-Oct-2000	42	9	30
Ebola	PROMED	Uganda	Gulu	15-Oct-2000	51	7	31
Ebola	PROMED	Uganda	Gulu	16-Oct-2000	63	12	33
Ebola	PROMED	Uganda	Gulu	17-Oct-2000	73	2	35
Ebola	PROMED	Uganda	Gulu	18-Oct-2000	94	21	39
Ebola	PROMED	Uganda	Gulu	19-Oct-2000	111	17	41

2. Assemble entities into events

3. Display events...

○ Total Cases
● New Cases

Figure 5: Steps in Extraction to Support Temporal and Geospatial Displays of Disease Outbreak

182

Integrated Information Management: An Interactive, Extensible Architecture for Information Retrieval

Eric Nyberg
Language Technologies Institute
Carnegie Mellon University
Pittsburgh, PA 15213

ehn@cs.cmu.edu

Hal Daume
Language Technologies Institute
Carnegie Mellon University
Pittsburgh, PA 15213

hcd@cs.cmu.edu

1. INTRODUCTION

Most current IR research is focused on specific technologies, such as filtering, classification, entity extraction, question answering, etc. There is relatively little research on merging multiple technologies into sophisticated applications, due in part to the high cost of integrating independently-developed text processing modules.

In this paper, we present the Integrated Information Management (IIM) architecture for component-based development of IR applications[1]. The IIM architecture is general enough to model different types of IR tasks, beyond indexing and retrieval. Rather than providing a single framework or toolkit, our goal is to create a higher-level framework which is used to build a variety of different class libraries or toolkits for different problems. Another goal is to promote the educational use of IR software, from an "exploratory programming" perspective. For this reason, it is also important to provide a graphical interface for effective task visualization and real-time control.

Prior architecture-related work has focused on toolkits or class libraries for specific types of IR or NLP problems. Examples include the SMART system for indexing and retrieval [17], the FIRE [18] and InfoGrid [15] class models for information retrieval applications, and the ATTICS [11] system for text categorization and machine learning. Some prior work has also focused on the user interface, notably FireWorks [9] and SketchTrieve [9][2]. Other systems such as GATE [4] and Corelli [20] have centered on specific approaches to NLP applications.

The Tipster II architecture working group summarized the requirements for an ideal IR architecture [6], which include:

- *Standardization.* Specify a standard set of functions and interfaces for information services.

- *Rapid Deployment.* Speed up the initial development of new applications.

- *Maintainability.* Use standardized modules to support plug-and-play updates.

- *Flexibility.* Enhance performance by allowing novel combinations of existing components.

- *Evaluation.* Isolate and test specific modules side-by-side in the same application.

One of the visions of the Tipster II team was a "marketplace of modules", supporting mix-and-match of components developed at different locations. The goals of rapid deployment and flexibility require an excellent user interface, with support for drag-and-drop task modeling, real-time task visualization and control, and uniform component instrumentation for cross-evaluation. The modules themselves should be small, downloadable files which run on a variety of hardware and software platforms. This vision is in fact a specialized form of component-based software engineering (CBSE) [14], where the re-use environment includes libraries of reusable IR components, and the integration process includes real-time configuration, control, and tuning.

Section 2 summarizes the architectural design of IIM. Section 3 provides more detail regarding the system's current implementation in Java. In Section 5 we describe three different task libraries that have been constructed using IIM's generic modules. Current instrumentation, measurement, and results are presented in Section 6. We conclude in Section 7 with some relevant comparisons of IIM to related prior work.

2. ARCHITECTURAL DESIGN

IIM uses a flow-based (pipe and filter [16]) processing model. Information processing steps are represented as nodes in a graph. Each edge in the graph represents a flow connection between a parent node and a child node; the documents produced by the parent node are passed to each child node. In IIM, the flow graph is referred to as a *node chain*. A sample node chain is shown in Figure 1. The IIM class model includes six basic node types, which can be used to model a variety of IR problems:

1. *Source.* Generates a document stream (from a static collection, web search, etc.) and passes documents one at a time to its child node(s).

2. *Filter.* Passes only documents which match the filter to its child node(s).

3. *Annotator.* Adds additional information to the document regarding a particular region in the document body.

---

[1]This work is supported by National Science Foundation (KDI) grant number 9873009.
[2]For further discussion on how these systems compare with the present work, see Section 7.

Proceedings of HLT 2001, First International Conference on Human Language Technology Research, J. Allan, ed., Morgan Kaufmann, San Francisco, 2001.

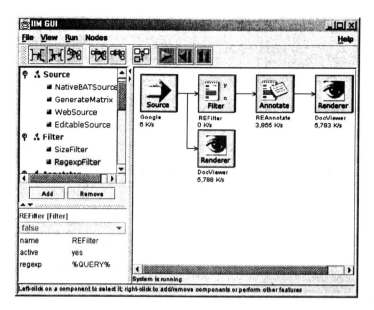

Figure 1: IIM User Interface

4. *Sink*. Creates and passes either a single document or a collection to its child node(s), after pooling the input documents it receives.

5. *Transformer*. Creates and passes on a single new document, presumably the result of processing its input document.

6. *Renderer*. Produces output for documents received (to disk, to screen, etc.).

The IIM class model is embedded in a Model-View-Controller architecture [5], which allows the system to be run with or without the graphical interface. Pre-stored node chains can be executed directly from the shell, or as a background process, completely bypassing all user interaction when optimal performance is required. The Controller subsystem and interface event dispatching subsystem must run as separate threads to support dynamic update of parameters in a running system. The View (user interface) should support: a) plug-and-play creation of new node chains; b) support for saving, loading and importing new node chains; c) dynamic visualization of a task's status; and d) direct manipulation of a node's parameters at any time.

In addition to the nodes themselves, IIM supports two other important abstractions for IR task flows:

- *Macro Nodes*. Certain sequences of nodes are useful in more than one application, so it is convenient to store them together as a single reusable unit, or *macro node*. IIM allows the user to export a portion of a node chain as a macro node to be loaded into the Node Library and inserted into a new chain as a single node. The user may specify which of the properties of the original nodes are visible in the exported macro node (see Figure 3).

- *Controllers*. Some IR tasks require iteration through multiple runs; the system's behavior on each successive trial is modified based on feedback from a previous run. For example, a system might wish to ask for more documents or perform query expansion if the original query returns an insufficient number of relevant documents. IIM includes a *Controller* interface, which specifies methods for sending feedback from

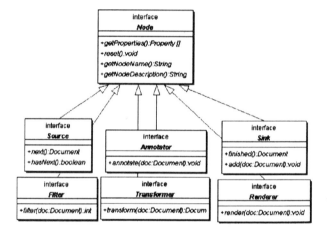

Figure 2: Node Interface and Subtypes.

one node to another. The user can implement a variety of controllers, depending on the needs of the particular application.

3. JAVA IMPLEMENTATION

In the IIM Java implementation, nodes are specified by the abstract interface Node and its six abstract subinterfaces: *Source, Filter, Annotator, Transformer, Sink* and *Renderer* (see Figure 2). Any user-defined Java class which implements one of the *Node* subinterfaces can be loaded into IIM and used in a node chain. The visualization of a node is represented by a separate Java class, Box, which handles all of the details related to drawing the node and various visual cues in the node chain display.

The graphical user interface (Figure 1) is implemented as a set of Java Swing components:

- *Node Chain Display*. The canvas to the right displays the current node chain, as described in the previous section. While

184

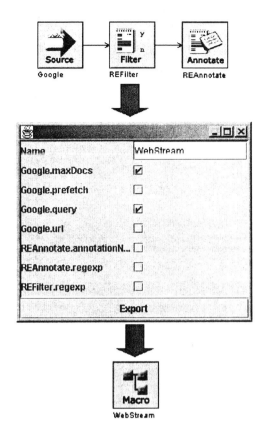

Figure 3: Exporting A Macro Node.

the node chain is running, IIM provides two types of visual feedback regarding task progress. To indicate the percentage of overall run-time that the node is active, the border color of each node varies from bright green (low) to bright red (high). To indicate the amount of output per node per unit of time spent (throughput), the system indicates bytes per second as a text label under each node. A rectangular meter at the right of each node provides a graphic visualization of relative throughput; the node with the highest throughput will have a solid red meter, while other nodes will have a meter level which shows their throughput as a percentage of maximum throughput.

- *Node Library*. The tree view to the upper left displays the library of nodes currently available on the user's machine for building and extending node chains. New nodes or node directories can be downloaded from the web and added while the system is running. The component loader examines each loaded class using Java's reflection capabilities, and places it in the appropriate place(s) in the component tree according to which of the *Node* subinterfaces it implements.

- *Node Property Editor*. The Property Editor (table view) to the lower left in Figure 1 displays the properties of a selected node, which the user can update by clicking on it and entering a new value.

- *Node Chain Editor*. IIM supports dynamic, interactive manipulation of node chains. The left side of the toolbar at the top of the IIM Window contains a set of chain editing but-

tons. These allow the user to create, modify and tune new node chains built from pre-existing components.

- *Transport Bar*. IIM uses a tape transport metaphor to model the operation of the node chain on a given data source. The "Play", "Pause" and "Rewind" buttons in the toolbar (right side) allow the user to pause the system in mid-task to adjust component parameters, or to start a task over after the node chain has been modified.

The run-time Controller subsystem is implemented as a Java class called *ChainRunner*, which can be invoked with or without a graphical interface component. *ChainRunner* is implemented as a *Thread* object separate from the Java Swing event dispatching thread, so that user actions can be processed concurrently with the ongoing operation of a node chain on a particular task.

4. IIM COMPONENTS

The current IIM system includes a variety of nodes which implement the different IIM component interfaces. These nodes are described in this section.

4.1 Source Nodes

- *EditableSource*. Prompts the user to interactively enter sample documents (used primarily for testing, or entering queries).

- *WebSource*. Generic support for access to web search engines (e.g., Google). Includes multithreading support for simultaneous retrieval of multiple result documents.

- *NativeBATSource*. Generic support for access to document collections stored on local disk. Implemented in C, with a Java wrapper that utilized the Java Native Interface (JNI).

4.2 Filter Nodes

- *SizeFilter*. Only passes documents which are above a user-defined size threshold.

- *RegexpFilter*. Only passes documents which match a user-defined regular expression; incorporates the GNU regexp package.

4.3 Annotator Nodes

- *NameAnnotator*. Locates named entities (currently, person names) in the body of the document, and adds appropriate annotations to the document.

- *IVEAnnotator*. For each named entity (person) annotation, checks a networked database for supplemental information about that individual. An interface to a database of information about individuals, publications, and organizations, created as part of the Information Validation and Evaluation project at CMU [12]. Implemented using Java Database Connectivity (JDBC).

- *BrillAnnotator*. Accepts a user-defined annotation (e.g., PASSAGE) and adds a new annotation created by calling the Brill Tagger [1] on the associated text. Implemented via a TCP/IP socket protocol which accesses a remote instance of the tagger running as a network service.

185

- *ChartAnnotator*. Accepts a user-defined annotation, and adds new annotations based on the results of bottom-up chart parsing with a user-defined grammar. The user can select which linguistic categories (e.g., NP VP, etc.) are to be annotated.

- *RegexpAnnotator*. Annotates passages which match a user-defined regular expression.

4.4 Transformer Nodes

- *BrillTransformer*. Similar to the *BrillAnnotator* (see above), but operates directly on the document body (does not create separate annotations).

- *Inquery*. Accepts a query (represented as an input document) and retrieves a set of documents from the Inquery search engine [2]. Accesses an Inquery server running as a networked service, using TCP/IP sockets.

- *WordNet*. Accepts a document, and annotates each word with a hypernym retrieved from WordNet [19]. Accesses a WordNet server running as a networked service, using TCP/IP sockets.

4.5 Sink Nodes

- *Ranker*. Collects documents and sorts them according to a user-defined comparator. The current implementation supports sorting by document size or by annotation count.

- *CooccuranceSink*. Builds a matrix of named entity associations within a given text window; uses NAME annotations created by the *NameAnnotator* (see above). The output of this node is a special subclass of *Document*, called *MatrixDocument*, which stores the association matrix created from the document collection.

- *QAnswer*. Collects a variety of annotations from documents relevant to a particular query (e.g., "What is Jupiter?"), and uses them to synthesize an answer.

4.6 Renderer Nodes

- *StreamRenderer*. Outputs any documents it receives to a user-specified file stream (or to standard output, by default).

- *DocumentViewer*. Pops up a document display window, which allows the user to browse documents as they are accepted by this node.

- *MatrixRenderer*. A two-dimensional visualization of the association matrix created by the *CoocurrenceSink* (see above). Accepts instances of *MatrixDocument*.

5. IIM APPLICATIONS

The initial set of component nodes has been used as the basis for three experimental applications:

- *Filtering and Annotation*. An interactive node chain that allows the user to annotate and collect documents matching any regular expression; the resulting collection can then be viewed interactively (with highlighted annotations) in a pop-up viewer window.

- *Named Entity Association*. A node chain which performs named-entity annotation using a phi-square measure[3], producin a *MatrixDocument* object (a user-defined *Document* subclass, which represents the association matrix). Note that the addition of a specialized *Document* subclass does not require recompilation of IIM (although the user must take care that specialized document objects are properly handled by user-defined nodes).

- *Question Answering*. A node chain which answers "What is" questions by querying the web for relevant documents, finding relevant passages [8, 10], and synthesizing answers from the results of various regular expression matches[3].

6. PERFORMANCE

In order to support accurate side-by-side evaluation of different modules, IIM implements two kinds of instrumentation for run-time performance data:

- *Per-Node Run Time*. The *ChainRunner* and *Box* classes automatically maintain run-time statistics for every node in a chain (including user-defined nodes). These statistics are printed at the end of every run.

- *Node-Specific Statistics*. For user-defined nodes, it may be useful to report task-specific statistics (e.g., for an *Annotator*, the total number of annotations, the average annotation size, etc.). IIM provides a class called *Options*, which contains a set of optional interfaces that can be implemented to customize a node's behavior. Any node that wishes to report task-specific statistical data can implement the *ReportsStatistics* interface, which is called by the *ChainRunner* when the chain finishes.

An example of the statistical data produced by the system is shown in Figure 4. The system is careful to keep track of time spent "inside" the nodes, as well as the overall clock time taken for the task. This allows the user to determine how much overhead is added by the IIM system itself.

The throughput speed of the prototype system is acceptably fast, averaging better than 50M of text per minute on a sample filtering task (530M of web documents), running on a typical Pentium III PC with 128M RAM. IIM requires about 10M of memory (including the Java run-time environment) for the core system and user interface, with additional memory requirements depending on the size of the document stream and the sophistication of the node chain[4]. Although the core system is implemented in Java, we have also implemented nodes in C++, using appropriate wrapper classes and the Java Native Interface (JNI). This technique allows us to implement critical, resource-intensive nodes using native code, without sacrificing the benefits of the Java-based core system.

7. DISCUSSION

The preliminary results of the IIM prototype are promising. IIM's drag-and-drop component library makes it possible to build and tune a new application in a matter of minutes, greatly reducing the amount of effort required to integrate and reuse existing modules.

---

[3] We are currently expanding this application to include part of speech tagging and syntactic parsing, both of which are straightforwardly modeled as examples of the *Annotator* interface.

[4] Node chains which create a high volume of annotations per document use more memory, as do node chains which create new collections, transform documents, etc.

IIM Stats	
Google[0]	110.00 sec(s)
REFilter[1]	0.06 sec(s)
regexp: %QUERY%	
REAnnotate[2]	1.30 sec(s)
regexp: [Tt]he ([^\s\.]+) %QUERY%	
docs annotated	49 doc(s)
total annotations	18 SEM(s)
avg annotations/doc	0.37 ann/doc
REAnnotate[3]	57.85 sec(s)
regexp: [^\<>]*%QUERY% is [^\<>]*	
docs annotated	49 doc(s)
total annotations	7 VERB_BE(s)
avg annotations/doc	0.14 ann/doc
QAnswer[4]	0.00 sec(s)
DocViewer[5]	0.01 sec(s)
DocViewer[6]	0.59 sec(s)
System Time	0.03 sec(s)
Total Time	169.84 sec(s)
Total Bytes from Source	1,083,941 byte(s)
Total Docs from Source	55 doc(s)
Bytes per Second	6,382.02 bytes/sec
Docs per Second	0.32 docs/sec

Figure 4: Statistics for a Node Chain.

In the future, we hope this high degree of flexibility will encourage greater experimentation and the creation of new aggregate systems from novel combinations of components, leading to a true "market-place of modules".

Building extensible architectures as "class library plus application framework" is not a new idea, and has been discussed before with respect to information retrieval systems [7, 18, 9]. One might claim that any new IR architecture should adopt a similar design pattern, given the proven benefits of separating the modules from the application framework (flexibility, extensibility, high degree of reuse, easy integration, etc.). To some extent, IIM consolidates, refines and/or reimplements ideas previously published in the literature. Specifically, the following characteristics of the IIM architecture can be directly compared with prior work:

- The IIM classes *Renderer*, *Document*, *MultiDocument*, and annotations on *Document* can be considered alternative implementations of the InfoGrid classes *Visualizer*, *Document*, *DocumentSet* and *DocumentPart* [15]. However, in IIM annotations are "lightweight", meaning that they do not require the instantiation of a separate user object, but can be modeled as simple String instances in Java when a high degree of annotation requires optimal space efficiency.

- The use of color to indicate status of a node is also used in the SketchTrieve system [18].

- IIM's visualization of the document flow as a "node chain" can be compared to the "wire and dock" approach used in other IR interfaces [9, 4, 13].

- The use of a Property Editor to customize component behavior is an alternative approach to the IrDialogs provided by the FireWorks toolkit [9] for display and update of a component's state.

Nevertheless, IIM is at once simpler and more general than systems such as InfoGrid [15] and FIRE [18]. One could claim that IIM supports a higher degree of *informality* [9] than FIRE, since it enforces no type-checking on node connectivity. Since all tasks are modeled abstractly as document flows, nodes need only implement one of the *Node* sub-interfaces, and each node chain must begin

with a *Source*. Another point of comparison is the task-specific detail present in the FIRE class hierarchy. In IIM, task-specific objects are left up to the developer (for example, representing particulars of access control on information sources, or details of indexing and retrieval, such as *Index*, *Query*, etc.).

Hendry and Harper [9] have used the *degree of user control* as a dimension of comparison for IR architectures. At one extreme are systems which allow dynamic view and access to the run-time state of components, while at the other lie systems which hide implementation detail and perform some functions automatically, for improved performance. In their comparison of SketchTrieve and InfoGrid, Hendry and Harper note that "a software architecture should provide abstractions for implementing both these". In IIM, the use of macro nodes can hide component details from the end user, especially when the component's parameter values have been tuned in advance for optimal performance.

8. ONGOING RESEARCH

While the initial results reported here show promise, we are still evaluating the usability of IIM in terms of trainability (how fast does a novice learn the system), reusability (how easily a novice can build new applications from existing node libraries) and ease of integration (effort required to integrate external components and systems). The current version of IIM lacks the explicit document management component found in systems like GATE [4] and Corelli [20]; we are in the process of adding this functionality for the official release of IIM.

The IIM system (source code, class documentation, and node libraries) will be made available via the web as one of our final project milestones later in 2001. Anyone interested in using the system or participating in ongoing research and development is invited to visit the IIM web site and join the IIM mailing list:

$$http://hakata.mt.cs.cmu.edu/IIM$$

9. ACKNOWLEDGEMENTS

The authors would like to thank Jamie Callan for his guidance on the architecture design, and Krzysztof Czuba for providing networked instances of the Brill Tagger, Inquery, and WordNet.

10. REFERENCES

[1] Brill, Eric (1992). "A simple rule-based part of speech tagger", *Proceedings of the Third Conference on Applied Natural Language Processing*.

[2] Callan, J. P., W. B. Croft, and S. M. Harding (1992). "The INQUERY Retrieval System", *Proceedings of the 3rd International Conference on Database and Expert Systems*.

[3] Conrad, J., and M. H. Utt (1994). "A System for Discovering Relationships by Feature Extraction from Text Databases", *SIGIR '94*.

[4] Gaizauskas, R. Cunningham, H. Wilks, Y. Rodgers, P. and Humphreys, K. GATE – an environment to support research and development in natural language engineering. Proceedings of the 8th IEEE International Conference on Tools with Artificial Intelligence (ICTAI96) , Toulouse, France, pp 58-66, 1996.

[5] Gamma, E., Helm, R., Johnson, R. and Vlissides, J. (1995). *Design Patterns: Elements of Reusable Object-Oriented Software*, Addison-Wesley.

[6] Grishman, R. (1996). "Building an Architecture: A CAWG Saga", in *Advances in Text Processing: Tipster Program Phase II*, sponsored by DARPA ITC.

187

[7] Harper, D.J. and A.D.M. Walker (1992). "ECLAIR: An extensible Class Library for Information Retrieval", *Computer Journal*, 35(3):256–267.

[8] Hearst, M. "Automatic acquisition of hyponyms from large text corpora." *COLING '92*.

[9] Hendry, D. G., and Harper, D. J. (1996). "An architecture for implementing extensible information-seeking environments", *SIGIR '96*.

[10] Joho, H. and M. Sanderson, "Retrieving descriptive phrases from large amounts of free text", *CIKM 2000*.

[11] Lewis, D., D. Stern and A. Singhal (1999). "ATTICS: A Software Platform for Online Text Classification", *SIGIR '99*.

[12] Mitamura, T. (2001). "Language Resources for Determining Authority", unpublished manuscript.

[13] Neuendorffer, T. (2000). "Analyst's Workbench: A CAD-like GUI for Textual Search and Filter Creation", HCII Seminar Series, Carnegie Mellon University, November 29.

[14] Pressman, R. (2000). *Software Engineering: A Practitioner's Approach*, 5th edition, McGraw-Hill.

[15] Rao, R., S.K. Card, H.D. Jellinek, J.D. MacKinlay and G. Robertson: The Information Grid: A Framework for Information Retrieval and Retrieval–Centred Applications. *UIST '92*.

[16] Shaw, M. and D. Garlan (1996). *Software Architecture: Perspectives on an Emerging Discipline*, Prentice-Hall.

[17] Salton, G. (1971). *The SMART Retrieval System - Experiments in Automatic Document Processing*, Prentice-Hall.

[18] Sonnenberger, G. and H. Frei (1995). "Design of a reusable IR framework", *SIGIR '95*.

[19] Fellbaum, C. (ed) (1998). WordNet: An electronic lexical database. Cambridge, MA: MIT Press.

[20] Zajac, R. (1997). "An Open Distributed Architecture for Reuse and Integration of Heterogenous NLP Components", In *Proceedings of the 5th conference on Applied Natural Language Processing (ANLP-97)*.

188

Intelligent Access to Text: Integrating Information Extraction Technology into Text Browsers

Robert Gaizauskas[a] Patrick Herring[a] Michael Oakes[a]
Michelline Beaulieu[b] Peter Willett[b] Helene Fowkes[b] Anna Jonsson[b]

[a]Department of Computer Science / [b]Department of Information Studies
University of Sheffield
Regent Court, Portobello Road
Sheffield S1 4DP UK
{initial.surname}@sheffield.ac.uk

ABSTRACT

In this paper we show how two standard outputs from information extraction (IE) systems – named entity annotations and scenario templates – can be used to enhance access to text collections via a standard text browser. We describe how this information is used in a prototype system designed to support information workers' access to a pharmaceutical news archive as part of their "industry watch" function. We also report results of a preliminary, qualitative user evaluation of the system, which while broadly positive indicates further work needs to be done on the interface to make users aware of the increased potential of IE-enhanced text browsers.

1. INTRODUCTION

Information extraction (IE) technology, as promoted and defined by the DARPA Message Understanding Conferences [4, 5] and the current ACE component of TIDES [1], has resulted in impressive new abilities to extract structured information from texts, and complements more traditional *information retrieval* (IR) technology which retrieves documents or passages of relevance from text collections and leaves information seekers to browse the retrieved sub-collection (e.g. [2]). However, while IR technology has been readily incorporated into end-user applications (e.g. web search engines), IE technology has not yet been as successfully deployed in end-user systems as its proponents had hoped. There are several reasons for this, including:

1. Porting cost. Moving IE systems to new domains requires considerable expenditure of time and expertise, either to create/modify domain-specific resources and rule bases, or to annotate texts for supervised machine learning approaches.

2. Sensitivity to inaccuracies in extracted data. IE holds out the promise of being able to construct structured databases from text sources automatically, but extraction results are by no means perfect. Thus, the technology is only appropriate

for applications where some error is tolerable and readily detectable by end users.

3. Complexity of integration into end-user systems. IE systems produce results (named entity tagged texts, filled templates) which must be incorporated into larger, more sophisticated application systems if end users are to gain benefit from them.

In this paper we present the approach taken in the TRESTLE project (Text Retrieval Extraction and Summarisation Technologies for Large Enterprises) which addresses the second and third of these problems; and also preliminary results from the user testing evaluation of the TRESTLE interface. The goal of the TRESTLE project is to develop an advanced text access facility to support information workers at GlaxoSmithKline (GSK), a large pharmaceutical corporation. Specifically, the project aims to provide enhanced access to *Scrip*[1], the largest circulation pharmaceutical industry newsletter, in order to increase the effectiveness of employees in their "industry watch" function, which involves both broad current awareness and tracking of people, companies and products, particularly the progress of new drugs through the clinical trial and regulatory approval process.

2. IE AND INFORMATION SEEKING IN LARGE ENTERPRISES

While TRESTLE aims to support information workers in the pharmaceutical industry, most of the functionality it embodies is required in any large enterprise. Our analysis of user requirements at GlaxoSmithKline has led us to distinguish various categories of information seeking. At the highest level we must distinguish requirements for current awareness from those for retrospective search. Current awareness requirements can be further split into general updating (what's happened in the industry news today/this week) and entity or event-based tracking (e.g. what's happened concerning a specific drug or what regulatory decisions have been made).

Retrospective search tends to break down into historical tracking of entities or events of interest (e.g. where has a specific person been reported before, what is the clinical trial history of a particular drug) and search for a specific event or a remembered context in which a specific entity played a role.

---

[1]*Scrip* is the trademark of PJB Publications Ltd. See http://www.pjbpub.co.uk.

Proceedings of HLT 2001, First International Conference on Human Language Technology Research, J. Allan, ed., Morgan Kaufmann, San Francisco, 2001.

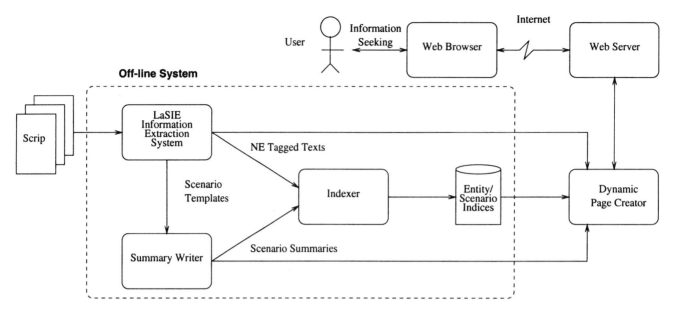

Figure 1: TRESTLE Architecture

Notice that both types of information seeking require the identification of entities and events in the news – precisely the functionality that IE systems are intended to deliver.

3. THE TRESTLE SYSTEM

The overall archictecture of the TRESTLE system is shown in Figure 1. The system comprises an on-line and an off-line component. The off-line component runs automatically whenever a new electronic delivery of *Scrip* takes place. It runs an IE System (the LaSIE system, developed for participation in the MUC evaluations [6]), which yields as output Named Entity (NE) tagged texts and Scenario Templates. To address the domain of interest, the MUC-7 NE categories of person, location and organisation have been retained and the categories of drug names and diseases have been added. The system generates three scenario templates: person tracking (a minor modification of the MUC-6 management succession scenario), clinical trials experimental results (drug, phase of trial, experimental parameters/outcomes) and regulatory announcements (drugs approved, rejected by various agencies).

After the IE system outputs the NE tagged texts and scenario templates, an indexing process is run to update indices which are keyed by entity type (person, drug, disease, etc.) and date, and by scenario type and date.

The on-line component of TRESTLE is a dynamic web page creation process which responds to the users' information seeking behaviour, expressed as clicks on hypertext links in a browser-based interface, by generating web pages from the information held in the indexed IE results and the original *Scrip* texts. A basic Information Retrieval component has also been plugged in to TRESTLE to provide users with seamless access to query *Scrip* texts, i.e., not confined to the pre-defined named entities in the index.

3.1 Interface Overview

The interface allows four ways of accessing *Scrip*: by headline, by named entity category, by scenario summary, and by freetext search. For the three first access routes the date range of *Scrip* articles accessible may be set to the current day, previous day, last week, last four weeks or full archive.

The interface is a browser whose main window is divided into three independently scrollable frames (see Figure 2). An additional frame (the "head frame") is located at the top displaying the date range options, as well as information about where the user currently is in the system. Down the full length of the left side of the window is the "access frame", in which text access options are specified. The remainder of the main window is split horizontally into two frames, the upper of which is used to display the automatically generated index information (the "index frame") and the lower of which is used to present the *Scrip* articles themselves (the "text frame").

Headline access is the traditional way GSK *Scrip* users access text, and is retained as the initial default presentation in TRESTLE. In the index frame a list of *Scrip* headlines is presented in reverse chronological order. Each headline is a clickable link to full text of the article; clicking on one displays the full text in the text frame (like Figure 2, only without the second column in the index frame).

Named entity and scenario access are the novel IE-based techniques TRESTLE supports.

3.2 NEAT: Named Entity Access to Text

From the access frame a user selects a category, for example, drugs. The index frame then displays an alphabetically ordered list of drug names extracted from the *Scrip* texts by the IE engine (Figure 2). To the right of each drug name is the title of the article from which the name was extracted (if a name occurs in multiple texts, there are multiple lines in the index frame). Once again the title is a hyperlink to the text and if followed the full text is displayed in the text frame.

When a text is displayed in the text frame, every occurrence of every name which has been identified as a named entity of any category is displayed as a clickable link; furthermore, each name category is displayed in a different colour. Clicking on a name, say a company name (e.g. Warner-Lambert in Figure 2) occurring in a text which was accessed initially via the drug index, updates the index frame with the subset of entries from the index for that name only – in our example, all entries for the selected company.

In addition to listing the full drug index alphabetically, the user may also enter a specific drug name in the Index Look-up box

190

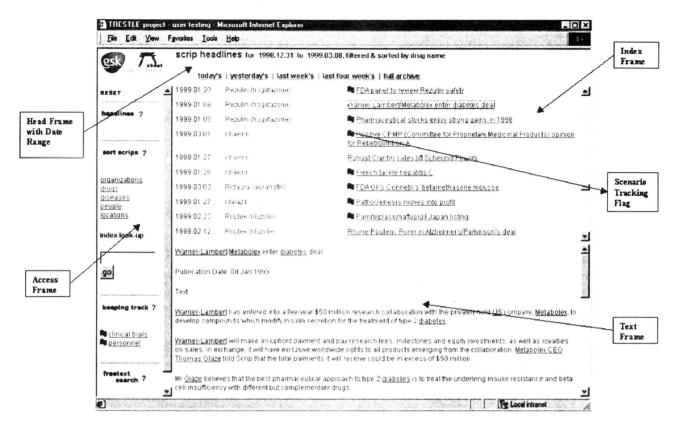

Figure 2: TRESTLE Interface: NEAT

in the access frame, and the index frame will then list the titles of all articles containing that drug name.

NEAT allows rapid text navigation by named entity. A user with a watching brief on, say diabetes, can start by reviewing recent articles mentioning diabetes, but then follow up all recent references to companies or drugs mentioned in these articles, extending the search back in time as necessary, and at any point branching off to pursue related entities.

3.3 SCAT: Scenario Access to Text

While NEAT allows navigation by named entity, the user still derives information by reading the original *Scrip* texts. Scenario access to text (SCAT) utilises summaries generated from templates extracted by the scenario template filling component of the IE system to provide access to the source texts. It is based on the observation that many scenarios of interest can be expressed via single sentence summaries. For example, regulatory announcements in the pharmaceutical industry can be captured in a template and summarised via one or more simple sentence schemas such as "Agency approves/rejects/considers Company's Drug for Disease in Jurisdiction".

To use SCAT a user selects one of the tracking options (`keeping track`) from the access frame of the interface. A list of one line summaries, one per extracted scenario, is then presented in the index frame. Along with each summary is a link to the source text, which allows the user to confirm the correctness of the summary, or to follow up for more detail/context. Clicking on this link causes the source text to appear in the text frame (see Figure 3). The presence of a summary in a *Scrip* article is also presented to the user through coloured tracking flags next to the article headline (see Figure 2). This feature can be viewed as a shortcut to the

summary facility; clicking the flag gives the generated summary in the text frame together with the link to the source. Of course sufficient information may have been gleaned from the summary alone, obviating the need to read the full text.

4. PRELIMINARY USER EVALUATION

Although input from users has informed each stage of the design process from the conceptual non-interactive mock-ups to the development of the web-based prototype, this section reports on a preliminary evaluation of user testing of the first fully functional prototype. The aim was to elicit feedback on the presentation and usability of NEAT and SCAT and the overall interface design. The objectives were two-fold. Firstly, and more broadly, to assess to what extent the interface conformed to principles of good usability design such as simplicity, consistency, predictability, and flexibility [7]. Secondly, and more importantly, to focus on the interaction issues presented by NEAT and SCAT:

- procedurally, in terms of users' ability to move between different search options in a logical and seamless fashion; and

- conceptually, in terms of users' awareness and understanding of the respective functions for exploiting current and retrospective Scrip headlines and full text.

4.1 Evaluation Methodology

A group of eight users consisting of postgraduate students and research staff were recruited from the Department of Information Studies at the University of Sheffield. The subjects had different subject backgrounds and all had experience of using web based

191

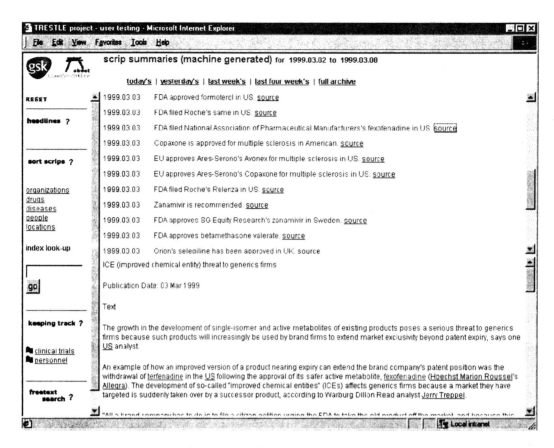

Figure 3: TRESTLE Interface: SCAT

interfaces, searching for information online and some knowledge of alerting/current awareness bulletins.

The focus of the exercise was to observe user-system interactions 'real time' to gain insight into:

- ease of use and learnability of the system;
- preferred strategies for accessing text;
- problems in interpreting the interface.

In addition, user perceptions of the interface were also elicited to provide further explanations on searcher behaviour. A combination of instruments was thus used including a usability questionnaire, verbal protocols and observational notes. Note that this evaluation was a purely quantitative exercise aimed at gaining an understanding of how the users responded to the novel functions offerred by the interface. A further evaluation will take place in an operational setting with real end users from GSK.

After a brief introduction to the purpose of the evaluation and a brief overview of the system, users were asked to explore the system in an undirected manner, asking questions and providing comments as they proceeded. Following this, they were asked to carry out a number of tasks from a set of tasks that simulated typical information needs characteristic of real end-users at GSK and were instructed to identify a 'relevant' article for each task. The tasks were designed to exploit the full functionality of the prototype; an example of the task is given below:

You've heard that one of your colleagues, Mr Garcia, has recently accepted an appointment at another phar-maceutical company. You want to find out which company he will be moving to and what post he has taken up.

The number of tasks completed by each subject varied according to the subject's thoroughness in exploring the system. The order in which the tasks were assigned was random.

4.2 Access Strategies

Access to named entities was made available in three ways:

1. by clicking directly on a list of four categories;
2. through the index look up query box;
3. through the free-text keyword search option.

The optimal strategy differed for the different assigned tasks. Most subjects tended to use the index look-up as a first attempt irrespective of its appropriateness for the task in hand. Preference for the use of the index look-up as opposed to selecting more general entity categories may be explained by the fact that users knew what they were looking for (i.e. an artefact of the assigned task). Moreover the query box for the index look-up option may have been a more familiar feature which encouraged searchers to adopt a searching strategy as opposed to browsing named entities. The preference for using the index look-up option over free text searching may have been influenced by the order of presentation as well as the prominence of the text entry box in the access frame. In addition for assigned tasks where the choice was between any of the three entity access strategies, or using the tracking options, the majority of users opted for the entity access via the index look-up. The novelty of the tracking options appeared to be a contributory factor.

4.3 User Perceptions

4.3.0.1 Colour Coding.

The colour coding of the named entities was highly noticeable, although there was some disagreement on its usefulness. Of those subjects that found the colour coding unhelpful, it was the choice of colours that they objected to rather than the function of the colour *per se*. Although subjects claimed that coloured entity links were distracting when reading full news items, the majority indicated that the linking to previous Scrip items was very useful. The distraction often had a positive effect in leading to useful and related articles. The overall integration of the current awareness and retrospective searching functions through named entities was thus widely appreciated.

4.3.0.2 Index Look-up.

All subjects except one found the index look-up function useful, once they discovered that it was a quick way of accessing predefined named entity categories. The fact that the approach only provided exact string matching was judged to be limiting.

4.3.0.3 Scenario Tracking.

The keeping track option was not as easily understood as the named entity options. The label "keeping track" was misinterpreted by some subjects as a search history function or an alerting service based on user profiles. After having used the tracking facility half of the subjects did, however, correctly understand the function. One problem that arose was the differentiation between summaries presented in SCAT and the actual Scrip headlines. Although the header informed searchers that they were viewing Scrip summaries, the display of the summaries in the same frame where the headlines were normally presented as well as the similarity in content led to confusion.

The coloured flags next to the headlines, which were meant to serve as a tracking label to allow users to move seamlessly from headlines to scenario summaries, raised another problem. Not only was the meaning of the flag symbol poorly understood, but also subjects did not realise that they could click on it. Moreover when they clicked on the flag they expected to see a full news item rather than a summary. Hence, the scenario access was both procedurally and conceptually confusing.

5. CONCLUSIONS

To date IE has largely been a "technology push" activity, with language engineers working to develop core technologies. For the technology to become usable, and for its further development to be influenced by end user requirements ("user pull"), prototype end-user application systems must be built which exploit the significant achievement of the technology to date, while acknowledging its limitations. In this paper we have described such a prototype, the TRESTLE system, which exploits named entity and scenario template IE technology to offer users novel ways to access textual information.

Our preliminary evaluation has revealed that although search options initially selected from the access frame were not always optimal for undertaking set tasks, the colour coded textual and iconic cues embedded in the headline index and full text frames on the whole enabled users to exploit the different functions seamlessly. Whilst the TRESTLE interface appeared to support interaction at a procedural level, at the conceptual level however, searchers did not necessarily gain sufficient understanding of the underlying functionality, particularly in respect to the scenario access. For exam-

ple the inability to distinguish between the original headlines and the system generated summaries for SCAT was problematic and requires further investigation. Other studies have reported similar issues in introducing more complex interactive search functions [3, 8]. More meaningful labelling may in part address some of the difficulties encountered. A more extensive evaluation in a work setting will follow to assess to what extent the integration of new and established conventions can support users with domain knowledge and greater familiarity with alerting systems to adopt new searching and awareness approaches effectively.

6. ACKNOWLEDGEMENTS

The authors would like the acknowledge the financial support of GlaxoSmithKline which has made this work possible, and in addition the helpful comments and insights of many staff at GSK, in particular Peter McMeekin, Charlie Hodgman, David Pearson and Derek Black.

7. REFERENCES

[1] ACE: Automatic Content Extraction. http://www.itl.nist.gov/iaui/894.01/tests/ace/. Site visited 08/01/01.

[2] R. Baeza-Yates and B. Ribiero-Neto. *Modern Information Retrieval*. ACM Press Books, 1999.

[3] M. Beaulieu and S. Jones. Interactive searching and interface issues in the Okapi best match probabilistic retrieval system. *Interacting with Computers*, 10:237–248, 1998.

[4] Defense Advanced Research Projects Agency. *Proceedings of the Sixth Message Understanding Conference (MUC-6)*. Morgan Kaufmann, 1995.

[5] Defense Advanced Research Projects Agency. *Proceedings of the Seventh Message Understanding Conference (MUC-7)*, 1998. Available at http://www.saic.com.

[6] K. Humphreys, R. Gaizauskas, S. Azzam, C Huyck, B. Mitchell, H. Cunningham, and Y. Wilks. Description of the LaSIE-II system as used for MUC-7. In MUC-7 [5]. Available at http://www.saic.com.

[7] J. Nielson. *Designing Web Usability: The Practice of Simplicity*. New Riders, 2000.

[8] A. Sutcliffe. Evaluating the effectiveness of visual user interfaces for information retrieval. *International Journal Human-Computer Studies*, 53:741–763, 1982.

Interlingua-Based Broad-Coverage Korean-to-English Translation in CCLINC

Young-Suk Lee

MIT Lincoln Laboratory
244 Wood Street
Lexington, MA 02420
U.S.A
1-781-981-2703
YSL@LL.MIT.EDU

Wu Sok Yi

MIT Lincoln Laboratory
244 Wood Street
Lexington, MA 02420
U.S.A
1-781-981-4609
WUYI@LL.MIT.EDU

Stephanie Seneff

MIT/LCS
77 Mass Avenue
Cambridge, MA 02673
U.S.A
1-617-254-0456
SENEFF@LCS.MIT.EDU

Clifford J. Weinstein

MIT Lincoln Laboratory
244 Wood Street
Lexington, MA 02420
U.S.A
1-781-981-7621
CJW@LL.MIT.EDU

ABSTRACT

At MIT Lincoln Laboratory, we have been developing a Korean-to-English machine translation system CCLINC (Common Coalition Language System at Lincoln Laboratory). The CCLINC Korean-to-English translation system consists of two core modules, language understanding and generation modules mediated by a language neutral meaning representation called a semantic frame. The key features of the system include: (i) Robust efficient parsing of Korean (a verb final language with overt case markers, relatively free word order, and frequent omissions of arguments). (ii) High quality translation via word sense disambiguation and accurate word order generation of the target language. (iii) Rapid system development and porting to new domains via knowledge-based automated acquisition of grammars. Having been trained on Korean newspaper articles on "missiles" and "chemical biological warfare," the system produces the translation output sufficient for content understanding of the original document.

1. SYSTEM OVERVIEW

 The CCLINC   The CCLINC Korean-to-English translation system is a component of the CCLINC Translingual Information System, the focus languages of which are English and Korean, [11,17]. Translingual Information System Structure is given in Figure 1.

Given the input text or speech, the language understanding system parses the input, and transforms the parsing output into a language neutral meaning representation called a *semantic frame*, [16,17]. The semantic frame — the key properties of which will be discussed in Section 2.3 — becomes the input to the generation system. The generation system produces the target to the generation system, the semantic frame can be utilized for other applications such as translingual information extraction and

language translation output after word order arrangement, vocabulary replacement, and the appropriate surface form realization in the target language, [6]. Besides serving as the input question-answering, [12].* In this paper, we focus on the Korean-to-English text translation component of CCLINC.[1]

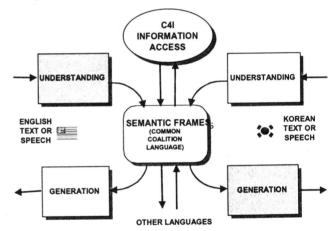

Figure 1. CCLINC Translingual Information System Structure

2. ROBUST PARSING, MEANING REPRESENTATION, AND AUTOMATED GRAMMAR ACQUISITION

* This work was sponsored by the Defense Advanced Research Project Agency under the contract number F19628-00-C-0002. Opinions, interpretations, conclusions, and recommendations are those of the authors and are not necessarily endorsed by the United States Air Force.

[1] For other approaches to Korean-to-English translation, the readers are referred to *Korean-to-English translation* by Egedi, Palmer, Park and Joshi 1994, a transfer-based approach using synchronous tree adjoining grammar, [5], and Dorr 1997, a small-scale interlingua-based approach, using Jackendoff's lexical conceptual structure as the interlingua, [4].

Proceedings of HLT 2001, First International Conference on Human Language Technology Research, J. Allan, ed., Morgan Kaufmann, San Francisco, 2001.

1.1 Robust Parsing

The CCLINC parsing module, TINA [16], implements the top-down chart parsing and the best-first search techniques, driven by context free grammars rules compiled into a recursive transition network augmented with features, [8]. The following properties of Korean induce a great degree of ambiguity in the grammar: (i) relatively free word order for arguments --- given a sentence with three arguments, subject, object, indirect object, all 6 logical word order permutations are possible in reality, (ii) frequent omissions of subjects and objects, and (iii) the strict verb finality, [10]. Due to the free word order and argument omissions, the first word of an input sentence can be many way ambiguous --- it can be a part of a subject, an object, and any other post-positional phrases.[2] The ambiguity introduced by the first input word grows rapidly as the parser processes subsequent input words. Verbs, which usually play a crucial role in reducing the ambiguity in English by the subcategorization frame information, are not available until the end, [1,3,11].

Our solution to the ambiguity problem lies in a novel grammar writing technique, which reduces the ambiguity of the first input word. We hypothesize that (i) the initial symbol in the grammar (i.e. Sentence) always starts with the single category *generic_np*, the grammatical function (subject, object) of which is undetermined. This ensures that the ambiguity of the first input word is reduced to the number of different ways the category *generic_np* can be rewritten. (ii) The grammatical function of the *generic_np* is determined after the parser processes the following case marker via a trace mechanism.[3]

Figure 2 illustrates a set of sample context free grammar rules, and Figure 3 (**on the next page**) is a sample parse tree for the input sentence "*URi Ga EoRyeoUn MunJe Reul PulEox Da* (We solved a difficult problem)."[4]

(i)	sentence → generic_np clause sentence_marker
(ii)	clause → subject generic_np object verbs
(iii)	subject → subj_marker np_trace

Figure 2. Sample context free grammar rules for Korean

The *generic_np* dominated by the initial symbol *sentence* in (i) of Figure 2 is parsed as an element moved from the position occupied by *np_trace* in (iii), and therefore corresponds to the category *np_trace* dominated by *subject* in Figure 3 (**placed on the next page for space reasons**). All of the subsequent *generic_np*'s, which are a part of a direct object, an indirect object, a post-positional phrase, etc. are unitarily handled by the same trace mechanism. By hypothesizing that all sentences start with *generic_np*, the system can parse Korean robustly and efficiently. The trace mechanism determines the grammatical function of *generic_np* by repositioning it after the appropriate case marker.

Utilization of overt case markers to improve the parsing efficiency precisely captures the commonly shared intuition for parsing relatively free word order languages with overt case markers such as Korean and Japanese, compared with parsing relatively strict word order languages with no overt case markers such as English: In languages like English, the verb of a sentence plays the crucial role in reducing the ambiguity via the verb subcategorization frame information on the co-occuring noun phrases, [1,3,11]. In languages like Korean, however, it is typically the case marker which identifies the grammatical function of the co-occuring noun phrase, assuming the role similar to that of verbs in English. The current proposal is the first explicit implementation of this intuition, instantiated by the novel idea that all noun phrases are moved out of the case marked phrases immediately following them.

2.2 Meaning Representation and Generation

The CCLINC Korean-to-English translation system achieves high quality translation by (i) robust mapping of the parsing output into the semantic frame, and (ii) word sense disambiguation on the basis of the selection preference between two grammatical relations (verb-object, subject-verb, head-modifier) easily identifiable from the semantic frame, [13]. The former facilitates the accurate word order generation of various target language sentences, and the latter, the accurate choice of the target language word given multiple translation candidates for the same source language word. Given the parsing output in Figure 3, the system produces the semantic frame in Figure 4:[5]

---

[2] Post-positional phrases in Korean correspond to pre-positional phrases in English. We use the term post-positional phrase to indicate that the function words at issue are located after the head noun.

[3] The hypothesis that all sentences start with a single category *generic_np* is clearly over simplified. We can easily find a sentence starting with other elements such as coordination markers which do not fall under *generic_np*. For the sentences which do not start with the category *generic_np*, we discard these elements for parsing purposes. And this method has proven to be quite effective in the overall design of the translation system, especially due to the fact that most of *non generic_np* sentence initial elements (e.g. coordination markers, adverbs, etc.) do not contribute to the core meaning of the input sentence.

[4] Throughout this paper, "subj_marker" stands for "subject marker", and "obj_marker", "object marker".

---

[5] Strictly speaking, the meaning representation in Figure 4 is not truly language neutral in that the terminal vocabularies are represented in Korean rather than in interlingua vocabulary. It is fairly straightforward to adapt our system to produce the meaning representation with the terminal vocabularies specified by an interlingua. However, we have made a deliberate decision to leave the Korean vocabularies in the representation largely (1) to retain the system efficiency for mapping parsing output into meaning representation, and (2) for unified execution of automation algorithms for both Korean-to-English and English-to-Korean translation. And we would like to point out that this minor compromise in meaning representation still ensures the major benefit of interlingua approach to machine translation, namely, *2 x N* sets of grammar rules for N language pairs, as opposed to 2^N.

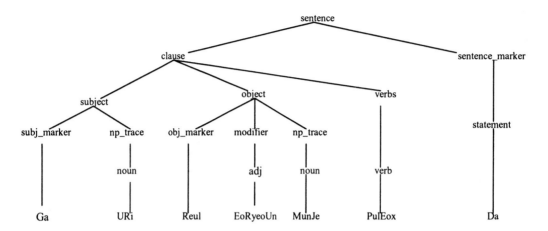

Figure 1. Parse Tree for the Sentence *URi Ga   EoRyeoUn MunJe   Reul PulEox*

```
{c statement
    :topic {q pronoun
              :name "URi" }
    :pred {p pul_v
             :topic {q problem
                       :name "MunJe"
                       :pred {p EoRyeoUn } } }
```

Figure 4. Semantic Frame for the input sentence "*URi Ga EoRyeoUn MunJe Reul PulEox Da.*"

The semantic frame captures the core predicate-argument structure of the input sentence in a hierarchical manner, [9,10] (i.e. the internal argument, typically object, is embedded under the verb, and the external argument, typically subject, is at the same hierarchy as the main predicate, i.e. verb phrase in syntactic terms). The predicate and the arguments along with their representation categories are bold-faced in Figure 4. With the semantic frame as input, the generation system generates the English translation using the grammar rules in (1), and the Korean paraphrase using the grammar rules in (2).

The semantic frame captures the core predicate-argument structure of the input sentence in a hierarchical manner, [9,10] (i.e. the internal argument, typically object, is embedded under the verb, and the external argument, typically subject, is at the same hierarchy as the main predicate, i.e. verb phrase in syntactic terms). The predicate and the arguments along with their representation categories are bold-faced in Figure 4. With the semantic frame as input, the generation system generates the English translation using the grammar rules in (1), and the Korean paraphrase using the grammar rules in (2).

(1)	a. statement	:topic :predicate
	b. pul_v	**:predicate :topic**
(2)	a. statement	:topic :predicate
	b. pul_v	**:topic :predicate**

(1b) and (2b) state that the topic category for the object follows the verb predicate in English, whereas it precedes the verb predicate in Korean.

The predicate-argument structure also provides a means for word sense disambiguation, [13,15]. The verb *pul_v* is at least two-way ambiguous between *solve* and *untie*. Word sense disambiguation is performed by applying the rules, as in (3).

(3) a .pul_v		b .pul_v
problem pul+solve_v		thread pul+untie_v

(3a) states that if the verb *pul_v* occurs with an object of type **problem**, it is disambiguated as *pul+solve_v*. (3b) states that the verb occurring with an object of type **thread** is disambiguated as *pul+untie_v*. The disambiguated verbs are translated into *solve* and *untie*, respectively, in the Korean-to-English translation lexicon.

1.2 Knowledge-Based Automated Acquisition of Grammars

To overcome the knowledge bottleneck for robust translation and efficient system porting in an interlingua-based system [7], we have developed a technique for automated acquisition of grammar rules which leads to a simultaneous acquisition of rules for (i) the parser, (ii) the mapper between the parser and the semantic frame, and (iii) the generator.

The technique **utilizes** a list of words and their corresponding parts-of-speech in the corpus as the knowledge source, **presupposes** a set of knowledge-based rules to be derived from a word and its part-of-speech pair, and gets **executed** according to the procedure given in Figure 5. The rationale behind the technique is that (i) given a word and its part-of-speech, most of the syntactic rules associated with the word can be automatically derived according to the **projection principle** (the syntactic representation must observe the subcategorization properties of each lexical item) and the **X-bar schema** (major syntactic categories such as N, V, Adj, Adv project to the same syntactic structures) in linguistic theories, [2], and (ii) the mapping from the syntactic structure to the semantic frame representation is algorithmic. The specific rules to be acquired for a language largely depend on the grammar of the language for parsing. Some example rules acquired for the verb *BaiChiHa* (arrange) in Korean — consistent with the parsing technique discussed in Section 2.1 — are given in (4) through (7).

Initialization: Create the list of words and their parts-of-speech in the corpus.

Grammar Update: For each word and its associated part-of-speech, check to see whether or not the word and the rules associated with the corresponding part-of-speech occur in each lexicon and grammar.

If they already occur, do nothing.

If not:

   (i)   Create the appropriate rules and vocabulary items for each entry.

   (ii)   Insert the newly created rules and vocabulary items into the appropriate positions of the grammar/lexicon files for the parser, the grammar file for the mapper between the parser and the semantic frame, and the grammar/lexicon files for the generator .

Figure 5. Automated Gammar Acquistion Procedure

---

(4) Rules for the parser[6]
.verbs
[negation] vBaiChiHa [negation] [aspect] [tense] [auxiliary]
[negation] [aspect] [tense] [and_verbs] [or_verbs]

.vBaiChiHa
#BaiChiHa

(5) Rules for the mapper from the parser to the semantic frame
.bachiha_v
vBaiChiHa

---

[6] The rules for the parser for the verb *tell* in English are given below, to illustrate the dependency of the rules acquired to the specific implementation of the grammar of the language for parsing:

.vp_tell
  vtell [adverb_phrase] dir_object [v_pp]
  vtell [adverb_phrase] indir_object dir_object
  vtell [adverb_phrase] dir_object v_to_pp [v_pp]
  vtell [adverb_phrase] dir_object that_clause
  vtell [and_verb] [or_verb] [adverb_phrase] dir_object wh_clause

The contrast in complexity of verb rules in (4) for Korean, and (i) for English, reflects the relative importance of the role played by verbs for parsing in each language. That is, verbs play the minimal role in Korean, and the major role in English for ambiguity reduction and efficiency improvement.

(6) Lexicon for the generation vocabulary
baichiha_v V2 "arrang"
V2   V "e" ING "ing" PP "ed" THIRD "es" ROOT "e"
PAST "ed" PASSIVE "ed"

(7) Rules for the generation grammar
baichiha_v   :predicate :conj :topic :sub_clause
np-baichiha_v :noun_phrase :predicate :conj :topic :sub_clause

The system presupposes the flat phrase structure for a sentence in Korean, as shown in Figure 3, and therefore the rules for the verbs do not require the verb subcategorization information, as in (4). The optional elements such as [negation], [tense], etc. are possible prefixes and suffixes to be attached to the verb stem, illustrating a fairly complex verb morphology in this language. The rules for the generation grammar in (7) are the subcategorization frames for the verb *arrange* in English, which is the translation of the Korean verb *baichiha_v*, as given in (6).

The current technique is quite effective in expanding the system's capability when there is no large syntatically annotated corpus available from which we can derive and train the grammar rules, [14], and applicable across languages in so far as the notion of part-of-speech, the projection principle and the X-bar schema is language independent. With this technique, manual acquisition of the knowledge database for the overall translation system is reduced to the acquisition of (i) the bilingual lexicon, and (ii) the corpus specific top-level grammar rules which constitute less than 20% of the total grammar rules in our system. And this has enabled us to produce a fairly large-scale interlingua-based translation system within a short period of time. One apparent limitation of the technique, however, is that it still requires the manual acquisition of corpus-specific rules (i.e. the patterns which do not fall under the linguistic generalization). And we are currently developing a technique for automatically deriving grammar rules and obtaining the rule production probabilities from a syntactically annotated corpus.

3. EVALUATION AND RESEARCH ISSUES

We have trained the system with about 1,600 Korean newspaper articles on *"missiles"* and *"chemical biological warfare"*, as in Table 1.

Table 1. Korean-to-English translation training data statistics

# of articles	# of sents/article	# of words/sent	# of distinct words
1,631	24	17	15,220

For quality evaluation, we have adopted a 5-point scale evaluation score, defined as follows. **Score 4:** Translation is both accurate and natural. **Score 3:** Translation is accurate with minor grammatical errors which do not affect the intended meaning of the input, e.g. morphological errors such as *"swam* vs. *swimmed."* **Score 2:** Translation is partially accurate, and sufficient for content understanding. Most errors are due to inaccurate word choice, inaccurate word order, and partial translation. **Score 1:** Translation is word-for-word, and partial content understanding is possible. **Score 0**: There is no translation output, or no content understanding is possible.

We have performed the quality evaluation on 410 clauses from the training data, and 80 clauses from the test data. We have conducted the evaluation in 3 phases. **Eval 1**: Baseline evaluation after grammar and lexicon acquisition. **Eval 2**: Evaluation after augmenting word sense disambiguation rules. **Eval 3**: Evaluation after augmenting word sense disambiguation rules and accurate word order generation rules. The purpose of the 3-phase evaluation was to examine the contribution of parsing, word sense disambiguation and accurate word order generation to the overall translation quality. Once the score had been assigned to each clause, the translation score was obtained by the formula: (Sum of the scores for each clause * 25) / Number of clauses evaluated.

Evaluation results are shown in Table 2 and Table 3 in terms of parsing coverage (**P**) and the translation score (**T**).[7]

Table 2. Translation Quality Evaluation on Training Data

Eval 1		Eval 2		Eval 3	
P	T	P	T	P	T
92	**58**	94	**69**	94	**74**

Table 3. Translation Quality Evaluation on Test Data

Eval 1		Eval 2		Eval 3	
P	T	P	T	P	T
79	**55**	89	**63**	89	**65**

For both training and test data, the baseline translation quality score is over 50, sufficient for content understanding of the documents. Word sense disambiguation (Eval 1 vs. Eval 2) increases the translation score by about 10%, indicating that effective word sense disambiguation has a great potential for improving the translation quality.

We would like to point out that the evaluations reported in this paper are performed on clauses rather than sentences (which often consist of more than one clause). In a very recent evaluation, we have found out that evaluations on sentences decrease the overall translation score about by 15. Nevertheless, the translation quality is still good enough for content understanding with some effort. The primary cause for the lower translation scores when the evaluation unit is a sentence as opposed to a clause is due to either an incorrect clause boundary identification, or some information (e.g. missing arguments in embedded clauses) which cannot be easily recovered after a sentence is fragmented into clauses. This has led to the ability to handle complex sentences as

---

[7] We would like to note that the evaluation reported here was a self-evaluation of the system by a system developer, primarily to identify the key research issues in system development. We will report evaluation results by non system developers who have no knowledge of Korean in the future. A system evaluation by a non-bilingual speaker will avoid the issue of implicitly utilizing the knowledge the evaluator has about the source language in the evaluation process.

the primary research issue, and we are working out the solution of utilizing syntactically annotated corpus for both grammar and probability acquisition, as discussed in Section 2.3.

4. SUMMARY AND ONGOING WORK

We have described the key features of the CCLINC interlingua-based Korean-to-English translation system which is capable of translating a large quantity of Korean newspaper articles on missiles and chemical biological warfare in real time. Translation quality evaluations on the training and test data indicate that the current system produces translation sufficient for content understanding of a document in the training domains. The key research issues identified from the evaluations include (i) parsing complex sentences, (ii) automated acquisition of word sense disambiguation rules from the training corpus, and (iii) development of discourse module to identify the referents of missing arguments. Our solution to the key technical challenges crucially draws upon the utilization of annotated corpora: For complex sentence parsing, we acquire both rules and rule production probabilities from syntactically annotated corpus. For automated word sense disambiguation, we utilize a sense-tagged corpus to identify various senses of a word, and obtain probabilities for word senses in various contexts. For discourse understanding, we are developing an algorithm for our 2-way speech translation work, [12], and plan to expand the module for document translations.

5. ACKNOWLEDGMENTS

We would like to acknowledge Dr. Jun-Tae Yoon, who provided us with a high-quality robust Korean morphological analyzer called *morany* during his stay at the Institute for Research in Cognitive Science, University of Pennsylvania as a postdoctoral fellow. *Morany* has served as a pre-processor of the understanding module in the CCLINC Korean-to-English translation system.

6. REFERENCES

[1] Srinivas Bangalore and Aravind Joshi. "Some Novel Applications of Explnation-Based Learning for Parsing Lexicalized Tree-Adjoining Grammars," *Proceedings of 33rd Association for Computational Linguistics*. pp. 268—275. 1995.

[2] Noam Chomsky. *Barriers*. Linguistic Inquiry Monograph 13. MIT Press, Cambridge, MA. 1986.

[3] Michael Collins. Three Generative, Lexicalized Models for Statistical Parsing. *Procceedings of the 35th Annual Meeting of ACL*. pp. 16—23. Madrid, Spain. July. 1997.

[4] Bonnie Dorr. "LCS-based Korean Parsing and Translation," Ms. Institute for Advanced Computer Studies and Department of Computer Science, University of Maryland. 1997.

[5] Diana Egedi, Martha Palmer, H-S. Park, Aravind Joshi. "Korean to English Translation Using Synchronous TAGs," *Proceedings of the First Conference of the Association for Machine Translation in the Americas*. pp. 48—55. Columbia, Maryland. October 1994.

[6] James Glass, Joe Polifroni and Stephanie Seneff. "Multilingual Language Generation across Multiple Domains,"

Proceedings of International Conference on Spoken Language Processing, pp. 983—986. Yokohama, Japan. September, 1994.

[7] W.J. Hutchins and H.L. Somers. *An Introduction to Machine Translation*. Academic Press. London. 1992.

[8] James Allen. *Natural Language Understanding*, 2nd Edition. Benjamin-Cummings Publisher. 1995

[9] Ken Hale. "Preliminary Remarks on Configurationality," *Proceedings of NELS 12*, pp. 86—96. 1982.

[10] Young-Suk Lee. *Scrambling as Case-Driven Obligatory Movement*. PhD Thesis (IRCS Report No.: 93-06). University of Pennsylvania. 1993.

[11] Young-Suk Lee, Clifford Weinstein, Stephanie Seneff, Dinesh Tummala, "Ambiguity Resolution for Machine Translation of Telegraphic Messages," *Proceedings of the 35th Annual Meeting of ACL*. pp. 120—127. Madrid, Spain. July 1997.

[12] Young-Suk Lee and Clifford Weinstein. "An Integrated Approach to English-Korean Translation and Translingual Information Access," *Proceedings of CSTAR Workshop*. Schwetzingen, Germany. September, 1999.

[13] Young-Suk Lee, Clifford Weinstein, Stephanie Seneff, Dinesh Tummala. "Word Sense Disambiguation for Machine Translation in Limited Domains," Manuscript. Information Systems Technology Group. MIT Lincoln Laboraotry. January 1999.

[14] Mitch Marcus, Beatrice Santorini, and Mary Ann Marcinkiewicz. "Building a large annotated corpus of English: the Penn Treebank," *Computational Linguistics 19 (2)*. pp. 313—330. 1993.

[15] Philip Resnik. "Semantic Similarity in a Taxonomy: An Information-Based Measure and Its Application to Problems of Ambiguity in Natural Language," *Journal of Artificial Intelligence Research (JAIR) 11*. pp. 95—130. 1999.

[16] Stephanie Seneff. "TINA: A Natural Language System for Spoken Language Applications," *Computational Linguistics 18 (1)*. pp. 61—92. 1992.

[17] Clifford Weinstein, Young-Suk Lee, Stephanie Seneff, Dinesh Tummala, Beth Carlson, John T. Lynch, Jung-Taik Hwang, Linda Kukolich. "Automated English-Korean Translation for Enhanced Coalition Communications," *The Lincoln Laboratory Journal 10 (1)*. pp. 35—60. 1997.

Is That Your Final Answer?

Florence Reeder
George Mason Univ./MITRE Corp.
1820 Dolley Madison Blvd.
McLean VA 22102

703-883-7156

freeder@mitre.org

ABSTRACT

The purpose of this research is to test the efficacy of applying automated evaluation techniques, originally devised for the evaluation of human language learners, to the output of machine translation (MT) systems. We believe that these evaluation techniques will provide information about both the human language learning process, the translation process and the development of machine translation systems. This, the first experiment in a series of experiments, looks at the intelligibility of MT output. A language learning experiment showed that assessors can differentiate native from non-native language essays in less than 100 words. Even more illuminating was the factors on which the assessors made their decisions. We tested this to see if similar criteria could be elicited from duplicating the experiment using machine translation output. Subjects were given a set of up to six extracts of translated newswire text. Some of the extracts were expert human translations, others were machine translation outputs. The subjects were given three minutes per extract to determine whether they believed the sample output to be an expert human translation or a machine translation. Additionally, they were asked to mark the word at which they made this decision. The results of this experiment, along with a preliminary analysis of the factors involved in the decision making process will be presented here.

Keywords

Machine translation, language learning, evaluation.

1. INTRODUCTION

Machine translation evaluation and language learner evaluation have been associated for many years, for example [5, 7]. One attractive aspect of language learner evaluation which recommends it to machine translation evaluation is the expectation that the produced language is not perfect, well-formed language. Language learner evaluation systems are geared towards determining the specific kinds of errors that language learners make. Additionally, language learner evaluation, more than many MT evaluations, seeks to build models of language acquisition which could parallel (but not correspond directly to) the development of MT systems. These models frequently are

Proceedings of HLT 2001, First International Conference on Human Language Technology Research, J. Allan, ed., Morgan Kaufmann, San Francisco, 2001.

feature-based and may provide informative metrics for diagnostic evaluation for system designers and users.

In a recent experiment along these lines, Jones and Rusk [2] present a reasonable idea for measuring intelligibility, that of trying to score the English output of translation systems using a wide variety of metrics. In essence, they are looking at the degree to which a given output is English and comparing this to human-produced English. Their goal was to find a scoring function for the quality of English that can enable the learning of a good translation grammar. Their method for accomplishing this is through using existing natural language processing applications on the translated data and using these to come up with a numeric value indicating degree of "Englishness". The measures they utilized included syntactic indicators such as word n-grams, number of edges in the parse (both Collins and Apple Pie parser were used), log probability of the parse, execution of the parse, overall score of the parse, etc. Semantic criteria were based primarily on WordNet and incorporated the average minimum hyponym path length, path found ratio, percent of words with sense in WordNet. Other semantic criteria utilized mutual information measures.

Two problems can be found with their approach. The first is that the data was drawn from dictionaries. Usage examples in dictionaries, while they provide great information, are not necessarily representative of typical language use. In fact, they tend to highlight unusual usage patterns or cases. Second, and more relevant to our purposes, is that they were looking at the glass as half-full instead of half-empty. We believe that our results will show that measuring intelligibility is not nearly as useful as finding a lack of intelligibility. This is not new in MT evaluation – as numerous approaches have been suggested to identify translation errors, such as [1, 6]. In this instance, however, we are not counting errors to come up with a intelligibility score as much as finding out how quickly the intelligibility can be measured. Additionally, we are looking to a field where the essence of scoring is looking at error cases, that of language learning.

2. SIMPLE LANGUAGE LEARNING EXPERIMENT

The basic part of scoring learner language (particularly second language acquisition and English as a second language) consists of identifying likely errors and understanding the cause of them. From these, diagnostic models of language learning can be built and used to effectively remediate learner errors, [3] provide an excellent example of this. Furthermore, language learner testing seeks to measure the student's ability to produce language which is fluent (intelligible) and correct (adequate or informative). These are the same criteria typically used to measure MT system capability[1]

In looking at different second language acquisition (SLA) testing paradigms, one experiment stands out as a useful starting point for our purposes. One experiment in particular serves as the model for this investigation. In their test of language teachers, Meara and Babi [3] looked at assessors making a native speaker (L1) / language learner (L2) distinction in written essays[2] They showed the assessors essays one word at a time and counted the number of words it took to make the distinction.

They found that assessors could accurately attribute L1 texts 83.9% of the time and L2 texts 87.2% of the time for 180 texts and 18 assessors. Additionally, they found that assessors could make the L1/L2 distinction in less than 100 words. They also learned that it took longer to confirm that an essay was a native speaker's than a language learner's. It took, on average, 53.9 words to recognize an L1 text and only 36.7 words to accurately distinguish an L2 text. While their purpose was to rate the language assessment process, the results are intriguing from an MT perspective.

They attribute the fact that L2 took less words to identify to the fact that L1 writing "can only be identified negatively by the absence of errors, or the absence of awkward writing." While they could not readily select features, lexical or syntactic, on which evaluators consistently made their evaluation, they hypothesize that there is a "tolerance threshold" for low quality writing. In essence, once the pain threshold had been reached through errors, missteps or inconsistencies, then the assessor could confidently make the assessment. It is this finding that we use to disagree with Jones and Rusk [2] basic premise. Instead of looking for what the MT system got right, it is more fruitful to analyze what the MT system failed to capture, from an intelligibility standpoint. This kind of diagnostic is more difficult, as we will discuss later.

We take this as the starting point for looking at assessing the intelligibility of MT output. The question to be answered is does this apply to distinguishing between expert translation and MT output? This paper reports on an experiment to answer this question. We believe that human assessors key off of specific error types and that an analysis of the results of the experiment will enable us to do a program which automatically gets these.

---

3. SHORT READING TEST

We started with publicly available data which was developed during the 1994 DARPA Machine Translation Evaluations [8], focusing on the Spanish language evaluation first. They may be obtained at: http://ursula.georgetown.edu.[3] We selected the first 50 translations from each system and from the reference translation. We extracted the first portion of each translation (from 98 to 140 words as determined by sentence boundaries). In addition, we removed headlines, as we felt these served as distracters. Participants were recruited through the author's workplace, through the author's neighborhood and a nearby daycare center. Most were computer professionals and some were familiar with MT development or use. Each subject was given a set of six extracts – a mix of different machine and human translations. The participants were told to read line by line until they were able to make a distinction between the possible authors of the text – a human translator or a machine translator. The first twenty-five test subjects were given no information about the expertise of the human translator. The second twenty-five test subjects were told that the human translator was an expert. They were given up to three minutes per text, although they frequently required much less time. Finally, they were asked to circle the word at which they made their distinction. Figure 1 shows a sample text.

```
3001GP

The general secretary of the UN, Butros
Butros-Ghali, was pronounced on Wednesday in
favor of a solution "more properly Haitian"
resulting of a "commitment" negotiated
between the parts, if the international
sanctions against Haiti continue being
ineffectual to restore the democracy in that
country.

While United States multiplied the last days
the threats of an intervention to fight to
compel to the golpistas to abandon the
power, Butros Ghali estimated in a directed
report on Wednesday to the general Assembly
of the UN that a solution of the Haitian
crisis only it will be able be obtained
"with a commitment, based on constructive
and consented grants" by the parts.
```

Figure 1: Sample Test Sheet

4. RESULTS

Our first question is does this kind of test apply to distinguishing between expert translation and MT output? The answer is yes. Subjects were able to distinguish MT output from human translations 88.4% of the time, overall. This determination is

---

more straightforward for readers than the native/non-native speaker distinction. There was a degree of variation on a per-system basis, as captured in Table 1. Additionally, as presented in Table 2, the number of words to determine that a text was human was nearly twice the closest system.[4]

Table 1: Percentage correct for each system

SYSTEM	SCORE
GLOBALINK	93.9%
LINGSTAT	95.9%
PANGLOSS	95.9%
PAHO	69.4%
SYSTRAN	87.8%
HUMAN	89.8%

Table 2: Average Number of Words to Determine

SYSTEM	AVG. # WORDS
PANGLOSS	17.6
GLOBALINK	25.9
SYSTRAN	31.7
LINGSTAT	33.8
PAHO	37.6
HUMAN	62.2

The second question is does this ability correlate with the intelligibility scores applied by human raters? One way to look at the answer to this is to view the fact that the more intelligible a system output, the harder it is to distinguish from human output. So, systems which have lower scores for human judgment should have higher intelligibility scores. Table 3 presents the scores with the fluency scores as judged by human assessors.

Table 3: Percentage Correct and Fluency Scores

SYSTEM	SCORE	FLUENCY
PANGLOSS	95.9	21.0
LINGSTAT	95.9	30.4
GLOBALINK	93.9	42.0
SYSTRAN	87.8	45.4
PAHO	69.4	56.7

Indeed, the systems with the lowest fluency scores were most easily attributed. The system with the best fluency score was also the one most confused. Individual articles in the test sample will need to be evaluated statistically before a definite correlation can be determined, but the results are encouraging.

---

[4] For those texts where the participants failed to mark a specific spot, the length of the text was included in the average.

The final question is are there characteristics of the MT output which enable the decision to be made quickly? The initial results lead us to believe that it is so. Not translated words (non proper nouns) were generally immediate clues as to the fact that a system produced the results. Other factors included: incorrect pronoun translation; incorrect preposition translation; incorrect punctuation. A more detailed breakdown of the selection criteria and the errors occurring before the selected word is currently in process.

5. ANALYSIS
An area for further analysis is that of the looking at the details of the post-test interviews. These have consistently shown that the deciders utilized error spotting, although the types and sensitivities of the errors differed from subject to subject. Some errors were serious enough to make the choice obvious where others had to occur more than once to push the decision above a threshold. Extending this to a new language pair is also desirable as a language more divergent than Spanish from English might give different (and possibly even stronger) results. Finally, we are working on constructing a program, using principles from Computer Assisted Language Learning (CALL) program design, which is aimed to duplicate the ability to assess human versus system texts.

6. ACKNOWLEDGMENTS
My thanks goes to all test subjects and Ken Samuel for review.

7. REFERENCES
[1] Flanagan, M. 1994. Error Classification for MT Evaluation. In Technology Partnerships for Crossing the Language Barrier: Proceedings of the First Conference of the Association for Machine Translation in the Americas, Columbia, MD.

[2] Jones, D. & Rusk, G. 2000. Toward a Scoring Function for Quality-Driven Machine Translation. In Proceedings of COLING-2000.

[3] Meara, P. & Babi, A. 1999. Just a few words: how assessors evaluate minimal texts. Vocabulary Acquisition Research Group Virtual Library. www.swan.ac.uk/cals/vlibrary/ab99a.html

[4] Michaud, L. & K. McCoy. 1999. Modeling User Language Proficiency in a Writing Tutor for Deaf Learners of English. In M. Olsen, ed., Computer-Mediated Language Assessment and Evaluation in Natural Language Processing, Proceedings of a Symposium by ACL/IALL. University of Maryland, p. 47-54

[5] Somers, H. & Prieto-Alvarez, N. 2000. Multiple Choice Reading Comprehension Tests for Comparative Evaluation of MT Systems. In Proceedings of the Workshop on MT Evaluation at AMTA-2000.

[6] Taylor, K. & J. White. 1998. Predicting What MT is Good for: User Judgments and Task Performance. Proceedings of AMTA-98, p. 364-373.

[7] Tomita, M., Shirai, M., Tsutsumi, J., Matsumura, M. & Yoshikawa, Y. 1993. Evaluation of MT Systems by TOEFL. In Proceedings of the Theoretical and Methodological Implications of Machine Translation (TMI-93).

[8] White, John, et al. 1992-1994. ARPA Workshops on Machine Translation. Series of 4 workshops on comparative evaluation. PRC Inc. McLean, VA.

[9] Wilks, Y. (1994) Keynote: Traditions in the Evaluation of MT. In Vasconcellos, M. (ed.) MT Evaluation: Basis for Future Directions. Proceedings of a workshop sponsored by the National Science Foundation, San Diego, California.

Japanese Case Frame Construction by Coupling the Verb and its Closest Case Component

Daisuke Kawahara
Graduate School of Informatics, Kyoto University
Yoshida-Honmachi, Sakyo-ku, Kyoto, 606-8501,
Japan

kawahara@pine.kuee.kyoto-u.ac.jp

Sadao Kurohashi
Graduate School of Informatics, Kyoto University
Yoshida-Honmachi, Sakyo-ku, Kyoto, 606-8501,
Japan

kuro@pine.kuee.kyoto-u.ac.jp

ABSTRACT

This paper describes a method to construct a case frame dictionary automatically from a raw corpus. The main problem is how to handle the diversity of verb usages. We collect predicate-argument examples, which are distinguished by the verb and its closest case component in order to deal with verb usages, from parsed results of a corpus. Since these couples multiply to millions of combinations, it is difficult to make a wide-coverage case frame dictionary from a small corpus like an analyzed corpus. We, however, use a raw corpus, so that this problem can be addressed. Furthermore, we cluster and merge predicate-argument examples which does not have different usages but belong to different case frames because of different closest case components. We also report on an experimental result of case structure analysis using the constructed case frame dictionary.

1. INTRODUCTION

Syntactic analysis or parsing has been a main objective in Natural Language Processing. In case of Japanese, however, syntactic analysis cannot clarify relations between words in sentences because of several troublesome characteristics of Japanese such as scrambling, omission of case components, and disappearance of case markers. Therefore, in Japanese sentence analysis, case structure analysis is an important issue, and a case frame dictionary is necessary for the analysis.

Some research institutes have constructed Japanese case frame dictionaries manually [2, 3]. However, it is quite expensive, or almost impossible to construct a wide-coverage case frame dictionary by hand.

Others have tried to construct a case frame dictionary automatically from analyzed corpora. However, existing syntactically analyzed corpora are too small to learn a dictionary, since case frame information consists of relations between nouns and verbs, which multiplies to millions of combinations. Based on such a consideration, we took the

unsupervised learning strategy to Japanese case frame construction[1].

To construct a case frame dictionary from a raw corpus, we parse a raw corpus first, but parse errors are problematic in this case. However, if we use only reliable modifier-head relations to construct a case frame dictionary, this problem can be addressed. Verb sense ambiguity is rather problematic. Since verbs can have different cases and case components depending on their meanings, verbs which have different meanings should have different case frames. To deal with this problem, we collect predicate-argument examples, which are distinguished by the verb and its closest case component, and cluster them. That is, examples are not distinguished by verbs such as *naru* 'make, become' and *tsumu* 'load, accumulate', but by couples such as *tomodachi ni naru* 'make a friend', *byouki ni naru* 'become sick', *nimotsu wo tsumu* 'load baggage', and *keiken wo tsumu* 'accumulate experience'. Since these couples multiply to millions of combinations, it is difficult to make a wide-coverage case frame dictionary from a small corpus like an analyzed corpus. We, however, use a raw corpus, so that this problem can be addressed. The clustering process is to merge examples which does not have different usages but belong to different case frames because of different closest case components.

2. VARIOUS METHODS FOR CASE FRAME CONSTRUCTION

We employ the following procedure of case frame construction from raw corpus (Figure 1):

1. A large raw corpus is parsed by KNP [5], and reliable modifier-head relations are extracted from the parse results. We call these modifier-head relations **examples**.

2. The extracted examples are distinguished by the verb and its closest case component. We call these data **example patterns**.

3. The example patterns are clustered based on a thesaurus. We call the output of this process **example case frames**, which is the final result of the system. We call words which compose case components **case examples**, and a group of case examples **case example group**. In Figure 1, *nimotsu* 'baggage', *busshi*

---

[1]In English, several unsupervised methods have been proposed[7, 1]. However, it is different from those that combinations of nouns and verbs must be collected in Japanese.

Proceedings of HLT 2001, First International Conference on Human Language Technology Research, J. Allan, ed., Morgan Kaufmann, San Francisco, 2001.

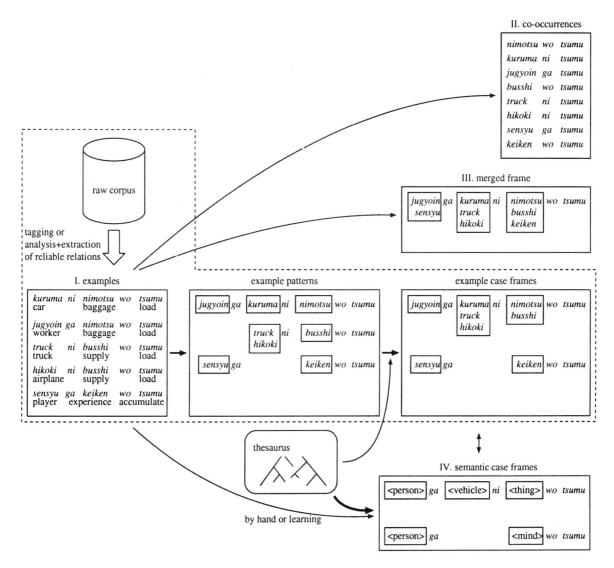

Figure 1: Several methods for case frame construction.

'supply', and *keiken* 'experience' are case examples, and {*nimotsu* 'baggage', *busshi* 'supply'} (of *wo* case marker in the first example case frame of *tsumu* 'load, accumulate') is a case example group. A **case component** therefore consists of a case example and a case marker (CM).

Let us now discuss several methods of case frame construction as shown in Figure 1.

First, examples (I of Figure 1) can be used individually, but this method cannot solve the sparse data problem. For example,

(1) *kuruma ni   nimotsu wo   tsumu*
    car dat-CM   baggage acc-CM   load
(load baggage onto the car)

(2) *truck ni   busshi wo   tsumu*
    truck dat-CM   supply acc-CM   load

(load supply onto the truck)

even if these two examples occur in a corpus, it cannot be judged whether the expression "*kuruma ni busshi wo tsumu*" (load supply onto the car) is allowed or not.

Secondly, examples can be decomposed into binomial relations (II of Figure 1). These co-occurrences are utilized by statistical parsers, and can address the sparse data problem. In this case, however, verb sense ambiguity becomes a serious problem. For example,

(3) *kuruma ni   nimotsu wo   tsumu*
    car dat-CM   baggage acc-CM   load
(load baggage onto the car)

(4) *keiken wo   tsumu*
    experience acc-CM   accumulate
(accumulate experience)

from these two examples, three co-occurrences ("*kuruma ni*

tsumu", *"nimotsu wo tsumu"*, and *"keiken wo tsumu"*) are extracted. They, however, allow the incorrect expression *"kuruma ni keiken wo tsumu"* (load experience onto the car, accumulate experience onto the car).

Thirdly, examples can be simply merged into one frame (III of Figure 1). However, information quantity of this is equivalent to that of the co-occurrences (II of Figure 1), so verb sense ambiguity becomes a problem as well.

We distinguish examples by the verb and its closest case component. Our method can address the two problems above: verb sense ambiguity and sparse data.

On the other hand, semantic markers can be used as case components instead of case examples. These we call **semantic case frames** (IV of Figure 1). Constructing semantic case frames by hand leads to the problem mentioned in Section 1. Utsuro et al. constructed semantic case frames from a corpus [8]. There are three main differences to our approach: they use an annotated corpus, depend deeply on a thesaurus, and did not resolve verb sense ambiguity.

3. COLLECTING EXAMPLES

This section explains how to collect examples shown in Figure 1. In order to improve the quality of collected examples, reliable modifier-head relations are extracted from the parsed corpus.

3.1 Conditions of case components

When examples are collected, case markers, case examples, and case components must satisfy the following conditions.

Conditions of case markers

Case components which have the following case markers (CMs) are collected: *ga* (nominative), *wo* (accusative), *ni* (dative), *to* (with, that), *de* (optional), *kara* (from), *yori* (from), *he* (to), and *made* (to). We also handle **compound case markers** such as *ni-tsuite* 'in terms of', *wo-megutte* 'concerning', and others.

In addition to these cases, we introduce **time case marker**. Case components which belong to the class <time>(see below) and contain a *ni*, *kara*, or *made* CM are merged into time CM. This is because it is important whether a verb deeply relates to time or not, but not to distinguish between surface CMs.

Generalization of case examples

Case examples which have definite meanings are generalized. We introduce the following three classes, and use these classes instead of words as case examples.

<time>

- nouns which mean time
  e.g. *asa* 'morning', *haru* 'spring', *rainen* 'next year'
- case examples which contain a unit of time
  e.g. *1999nen* 'year', *12gatsu* 'month', *9ji* 'o'clock'
- words which are followed by the suffix *mae* 'before', *tyu* 'during', or *go* 'after' and do not have the semantic marker <place> on the thesaurus
  e.g. *kaku mae* 'before ··· write', *kaigi go* 'after the meeting'

<quantity>

- numerals
  e.g. *ichi* 'one', *ni* 'two', *juu* 'ten'

- numerals followed by a numeral classifier[2] such as *tsu*, *ko*, and *nin*.

  They are expressed with pairs of the class <quantity> and a numeral classifier: <quantity>*tsu*, <quantity>*ko*, and <quantity>*nin*.

  e.g. *1tsu* → <quantity>*tsu*
  2ko → <quantity>*ko*

<clause>

- quotations ("··· *to*" 'that ···') and expressions which function as quotations ("··· *koto wo*" 'that ···').

  e.g. *kaku to* 'that ··· write', *kaita koto wo* 'that ··· wrote'

Exclusion of ambiguous case components

We do not use the following case components:

- Since case components which contain topic markers (TMs) and clausal modifiers do not have surface case markers, we do not use them. For example,

  sono giin   wa   ··· wo teian-shita.
  the assemblyman   TM   acc-CM proposed

  wa is a topic marker and *giin wa* 'assemblyman TM' depends on *teian-shita* 'proposed', but there is no case marker for *giin* 'assemblyman' in relation to *teian-shita* 'proposed'.

  ··· wo teian-shiteiru giin ga ···
  acc-CM proposing   assemblyman

  "··· *wo teian-shiteiru*" is a clausal modifier and *teian-shiteiru* 'proposing' depends on *giin* 'assemblyman', but there is no case marker for *giin* 'assemblyman' in relation to *teian-shiteiru* 'proposing'.

- Case components which contain a *ni* or *de* case marker are sometimes used adverbially. Since they have the optional relation to their verbs, we do not use them.

  e.g. *tame ni* 'because of', *mujouken ni* 'unconditionally', *ue de* 'in addition to'

For example,

30nichi ni souri daijin   ga
30th   on prime minister nom-CM

sono 2nin   ni
those two people dat-CM

syou wo   okutta
award acc-CM   gave

---

[2]Most nouns must take a numeral classifier when they are quantified in Japanese. An English equivalent to it is 'piece'.

(On 30th the prime minister gave awards to those two people.)

from this sentence, the following example is acquired.

<time>:time-CM *daijin:ga*
            minister:nom-CM

<quantity>*nin:ni syou:wo okuru*
     people:dat-CM award acc-CM give

3.2 Conditions of verbs

We collect examples not only for verbs, but also for adjectives and noun+copulas[3]. However, when a verb is followed by a causative auxiliary or a passive auxiliary, we do not collect examples, since the case pattern is changed.

3.3 Extraction of reliable examples

When examples are extracted from automatically parsed results, the problem is that the parsed results inevitably contain errors. Then, to decrease influences of such errors, we discard modifier-head relations whose parse accuracies are low and use only reliable relations.

KNP employs the following heuristic rules to determine a head of a modifier:

HR1 KNP narrows the scope of a head by finding a clear boundary of clauses in a sentence. When there is only one candidate verb in the scope, KNP determines this verb as the head of the modifier.

HR2 Among the candidate verbs, verbs which rarely take case components are excluded.

HR3 KNP determines the head according to the preference: a modifier which is not followed by a comma depends on the nearest candidate, and a modifier with a comma depends on the second nearest candidate.

Our approach trusts HR1 but not HR2 and HR3. That is, modifier-head relations which are decided in HR1 (there is only one candidate of the head in the scope) are extracted as examples, but relations which HR2 and HR3 are applied to are not extracted. The following examples illustrate the application of these rules.

(5) *kare wa kai-tai hon wo*
    he TM want to buy book acc-CM

    takusan mitsuketa node,
    a lot found because

    Tokyo he okutta.
    Tokyo to sent

(Because he found a lot of books which he wants to buy, he sent them to Tokyo.)

In this example, an example which can be extracted without ambiguity is "*Tokyo he okutta*" 'sent ϕ to Tokyo' at the end of the sentence. In addition, since *node* 'because' is analyzed as a clear boundary of clauses, the head candidate of *hon wo* 'book acc-CM' is only *mitsuketa* 'find', and this is also extracted.

Verbs excluded from head candidates by HR2 possibly become heads, so we do not use the examples which HR2 is applied to. For example, when there is a strong verb right

---

[3]In this paper, we use 'verb' instead of 'verb/adjective or noun+copula' for simplicity.

after an adjective, this adjective tends not to be a head of a case component, so it is excluded from head candidates.

(6) *Hi no mawari ga hayaku*
    fire of spread nom-CM rapidly

    sukuidase-nakatta.
    could not save

(The fire spread rapidly, so ϕ_1 could not save ϕ_2.)

In this example, the correct head of *mawari ga* 'spread' is *hayaku* 'rapidly'. However, since *hayaku* 'rapidly' is excluded from the head candidates, the head of *mawari ga* 'spread' is analyzed incorrectly.

We show an example of the process HR3:

(7) *kare ga shitsumon ni*
    he nom-CM question acc-CM

    sentou wo kitte kotaeta.
    lead acc-CM take answered

(He took the lead to answer the question.)

In this example, head candidates of *shitsumon ni* 'question acc-CM' are *kitte* 'take' and *kotaeta* 'answered'. According to the preference "modify the nearer head", KNP incorrectly decides the head is *kitte* 'take'. Like this example, when there are many head candidates, the decided head is not reliable, so we do not use examples in this case.

We extracted reliable examples from Kyoto University Corpus[6], that is a syntactically analyzed corpus, and evaluated the accuracy of them. The accuracy of all the case examples which have the target cases was 90.9%, and the accuracy of the reliable examples was 97.2%. Accordingly, this process is very effective.

4. CONSTRUCTION OF EXAMPLE CASE FRAMES

As shown in Section 2, when examples whose verbs have different meanings are merged, a case frame which allows an incorrect expression is created. So, for verbs with different meanings, different case frames should be acquired.

In most cases, an important case component which decides the sense of a verb is the closest one to the verb, that is, the verb sense ambiguity can be resolved by coupling the verb and its closest case component. Accordingly, we distinguish examples by the verb and its closest case component. We call the case marker of the closest case component **closest case marker**.

The number of example patterns which one verb has is equal to that of the closest case components. That is, example patterns which have almost the same meaning are individually handled as follows:

(8) *jugyoin:ga kuruma:ni*
    worker:nom-CM car:dat-CM

    nimotsu:wo tsumu
    baggage:acc-CM load

(9) *{truck,hikoki}:ni*
    {truck,airplane}:dat-CM

    busshi:wo tsumu
    supply:acc-CM load

In order to merge example patterns that have almost the same meaning, we cluster example patterns. The final ex-

$$\frac{1.0 \cdot (5 \cdot 3) + 0.86 \cdot (5 \cdot 2)}{(5 \cdot 3) + (5 \cdot 2)} = 0.94$$

similarity between case example groups :
$$\frac{0.94 \cdot \left((5 \cdot 3)^{1/2} + (5 \cdot 2)^{1/2} \right)^{1/2} + 0.91 \cdot (8 \cdot 10)^{1/4}}{\left((5 \cdot 3)^{1/2} + (5 \cdot 2)^{1/2} \right)^{1/2} + (8 \cdot 10)^{1/4}} = 0.92$$

ratio of common cases :
$$\left(\frac{(5+8)+(3+2+10)}{(3+5+8)+(3+2+10)} \right)^{1/2} = 0.90$$

similarity between example patterns :
$$0.92 \cdot 0.90 = 0.83$$

Figure 2: Example of calculating the similarity between example patterns (Numerals in the lower right of examples represent their frequencies.)

ample case frames consist of the example pattern clusters. The detail of the clustering is described in the following section.

4.1 Similarity between example patterns

The clustering of example patterns is performed by using the similarity between example patterns. This similarity is based on the similarities between case examples and the ratio of common cases. Figure 2 shows an example of calculating the similarity between example patterns.

First, the similarity between two examples e_1, e_2 is calculated using the NTT thesaurus as follows:

$$sim_e(e_1, e_2) = max_{x \in s_1, y \in s_2} sim(x, y)$$

$$sim(x, y) = \frac{2L}{l_x + l_y}$$

where x, y are semantic markers, and s_1, s_2 are sets of semantic markers of e_1, e_2 respectively[4]. l_x, l_y are the depths of x, y in the thesaurus, and the depth of their lowest (most specific) common node is L. If x and y are in the same node of the thesaurus, the similarity is 1.0, the maximum score based on this criterion.

Next, the similarity between the two case example groups E_1, E_2 is the normalized sum of the similarities of case examples as follows:

$$sim_E(E_1, E_2)$$
$$= \frac{\sum_{e_1 \in E_1} \sum_{e_2 \in E_2} \sqrt{|e_1||e_2|}\, sim_e(e_1, e_2)}{\sum_{e_1 \in E_1} \sum_{e_2 \in E_2} \sqrt{|e_1||e_2|}}$$

where $|e_1|, |e_2|$ represent the frequencies of e_1, e_2 respectively.

The ratio of common cases of example patterns F_1, F_2 is

---

[4]In many cases, nouns have many semantic markers in NTT thesaurus.

calculated as follows:

$$cs = \sqrt{\frac{\sum_{i=1}^{n} |E_{1cc_i}| + \sum_{i=1}^{n} |E_{2cc_i}|}{\sum_{i=1}^{l} |E_{1c1_i}| + \sum_{i=1}^{m} |E_{2c2_i}|}}$$

where the cases of example pattern F_1 are $c1_1, c1_2, \cdots, c1_l$, the cases of example pattern F_2 are $c2_1, c2_2, \cdots, c2_m$, and the common cases of F_1 and F_2 is $cc_1, cc_2, \cdots, cc_n$. E_{1cc_i} is the case example group of cc_i in F_1. E_{2cc_i}, E_{1c1_i}, and E_{2c2_i} are defined in the same way. The square root in this equation decreases influences of the frequencies.

The similarity between F_1 and F_2 is the product of the ratio of common cases and the similarities between case example groups of common cases of F_1 and F_2 as follows:

$$score = cs \cdot \frac{\sum_{i=1}^{n} \sqrt{w_i}\, sim_E(E_{1cc_i}, E_{2cc_i})}{\sum_{i=1}^{n} \sqrt{w_i}}$$

$$w_i = \sum_{e_1 \in E_{1cc_i}} \sum_{e_2 \in E_{2cc_i}} \sqrt{|e_1||e_2|}$$

where w_i is the weight of the similarities between case example groups.

4.2 Selection of semantic markers of example patterns

The similarities between example patterns are deeply influenced by semantic markers of the closest case components. So, when the closest case components have semantic ambiguities, a problem arises. For example, when clustering example patterns of *awaseru* 'join, adjust', the pair of example patterns (*te* 'hand', *kao*, 'face')[5] is created with the common semantic marker <part of an animal>, and (*te* 'method', *syouten* 'focus') is created with the common semantic marker <logic, meaning>. From these two pairs, the pair (*te* 'hand', *kao* 'face', *syouten* 'focus') is created, though <part of an animal> is not similar to <logic, meaning> at all.

To address this problem, we select one semantic marker of the closest case component of each example pattern in order of the similarity between example patterns as follows:

1. In order of the similarity of a pair, (p, q), of two example patterns, we select semantic markers of the closest case components, n_p, n_q of p, q. The selected semantic markers s_p, s_q maximize the similarity between n_p and n_q.

2. The similarities of example patterns related to p, q are recalculated.

3. These two processes are iterated while there are pairs of two example patterns, of which the similarity is higher than a threshold.

4.3 Clustering procedure

The following is the clustering procedure:

1. Elimination of example patterns which occur infrequently

   Target example patterns of the clustering are those whose closest case components occur more frequently than a threshold. We set this threshold to 5.

---

[5]Example patterns are represented by the closest case components.

2. Clustering of example patterns which have the same closest CM

   (a) Similarities between pairs of two example patterns which have the same closest CM are calculated, and semantic markers of closest case components are selected. These two processes are iterated as mentioned in 4.2.

   (b) Each example pattern pair whose similarity is higher than some threshold is merged.

3. Clustering of all the example patterns

   The example patterns which are output by 2 are clustered. In this phase, it is not considered whether the closest CMs are the same or not. The following example patterns have almost the same meaning, but they are not merged by 2 because of the different closest CM. This clustering can merge these example patterns.

   (10) {busshi,kamotsu}:wo
        {supply,cargo}:acc-CM

        truck:ni   tsumu
        truck:dat-CM   load

   (11) {truck,hikoki}:ni
        {truck,airplane}:dat-CM

        {nimotsu,busshi}:wo   tsumu
        {baggage,supply}:acc-CM load

5. SELECTION OF OBLIGATORY CASE MARKERS

If a CM whose frequency is lower than other CMs, it might be collected because of parsing errors, or has little relation to its verb. So, we set the threshold for the CM frequency as $2\sqrt{mf}$, where mf means the frequency of the most found CM. If the frequency of a CM is less than the threshold, it is discarded. For example, suppose the most frequent CM for a verb is wo, 100 times, and the frequency of ni CM for the verb is 16, ni CM is discarded (since it is less than the threshold, 20).

However, since we can say that all the verbs have ga (nominative) CMs, ga CMs are not discarded. Furthermore, if an example case frame do not have a ga CM, we supplement its ga case with semantic marker <person>.

6. CONSTRUCTED CASE FRAME DICTIONARY

We applied the above procedure to Mainichi Newspaper Corpus (9 years, 4,600,000 sentences). We set the threshold of the clustering 0.80. The criterion for setting this threshold is that case frames which have different case patterns or different meanings should not be merged into one case frame. Table1 shows examples of constructed example case frames.

From the corpus, example case frames of 71,000 verbs are constructed; the average number of example case frames of a verb is 1.9; the average number of case slots of a verb is 1.7; the average number of example nouns in a case slot is 4.3. The clustering led a decrease in the number of example case frames of 47%.

Table 1: Examples of the constructed case frames(* means the closest CM).

verb	CM	case examples
*kau*1	*ga*	person, passenger
'buy'	*wo**	stock, land, dollar, ticket
	de	shop, station, yen
*kau*2	*ga*	treatment, welfare, postcard
	wo*	anger, disgust, antipathy
⋮	⋮	⋮
*yomu*1	*ga*	student, prime minister
'read'	*wo**	book, article, news paper
*yomu*2	*ga*	<person>
	wo	talk, opinion, brutality
	de*	news paper, book, textbook
*yomu*3	*ga*	<person>
	wo*	future
⋮	⋮	⋮
*tadasu*1	*ga*	member, assemblyman
'examine'	*wo**	opinion, intention, policy
	ni tsuite	problem, <clause>, bill
*tadasu*2	*ga*	chairman, oneself
'improve'	*wo**	position, form
⋮	⋮	⋮
*kokuchi*1	*ga*	doctor
'inform'	*ni**	the said person
*kokuchi*2	*ga*	colleague
	wo*	infection, cancer
	ni*	patient, family
*sanseida*1	*ga*	<person>
'agree'	*ni**	opinion, idea, argument
*sanseida*2	*ga*	<person>
	ni*	<clause>

As shown in Table1, example case frames of noun+copulas such as *sanseida* 'positiveness+copula (agree)', and compound case markers such as *ni-tsuite* 'in terms of' of *tadasu* 'examine' are acquired.

7. EXPERIMENTS AND DISCUSSION

Since it is hard to evaluate the dictionary statically, we use the dictionary in case structure analysis and evaluate the analysis result. We used 200 sentences of Mainichi Newspaper Corpus as a test set. We analyzed case structures of the sentences using the method proposed by [4]. As the evaluation of the case structure analysis, we checked whether cases of ambiguous case components (topic markers and clausal modifiers) are correctly detected or not. The evaluation result is presented in Table 2. The baseline is the result by assigning a vacant case in order of 'ga', 'wo', and 'ni'. When we do not consider parsing errors to evaluate the case detection, the accuracy of our method for topic markers was 96% and that for clausal modifiers was 76%. The baseline accuracy for topic markers was 91% and that for clausal modifiers was 62%. Thus we see our method is superior to the baseline.

209

Table 2: The accuracy of case detection.

		correct case detection	incorrect case detection	parsing error
our method	topic marker	85	4	13
	clausal modifier	48	15	2
baseline	topic marker	81	8	13
	clausal modifier	39	24	2

The following are examples of analysis results[6]:

(1) $_1$ *ookurasyo*◯*ga*   *wa*   *ginko*   *ga*
the Ministry of Finance TM bank nom-CM

   $_2$ *tsumitate-teiru* $_2$ *ryuhokin*◯*wo*   *no*
deposit   reserve fund   of

torikuzushi wo $_3$ *mitomeru*
consume   acc-CM   consent

$_3$ *houshin*×$_{ni}$† *wo* $_1$ *kimeta*.
policy   acc-CM   decide

(The Ministry of Finance decided the policy of consenting to consume the reserve fund which the banks have deposited.)

(2) *korera no* $_1$ *gyokai*×$_{wo}$‡ *wa*   *seijiteki*
these   industry   TM political

hatsugenryoku ga   *tsuyoi toiu*
voice   nom-CM   strong

tokutyo   *ga* $_1$ *aru*.
characteristic nom-CM have
(These industries have the characteristic of strong political voice.)

Analysis errors are mainly caused by two phenomena. The first is clausal modifiers which have no case relation to the modifees such as "··· *wo mitomeru houshin*" 'policy of consenting ···' († above). The Second is verbs which take two *ga* 'nominative' case markers (one is *wa* superficially) such as "*gyokai wa* ··· *toiu tokutyo ga aru*" 'industries have the characteristic of ···' (‡ above). Handling these phenomena is an area of future work.

8. CONCLUSION

We proposed an unsupervised method to construct a case frame dictionary by coupling the verb and its closest case component. We obtained a large case frame dictionary, which consists of 71,000 verbs. Using this dictionary, we can detect ambiguous case components accurately. We plan to exploit this dictionary in anaphora resolution in the future.

9. ACKNOWLEDGMENTS

The research described in this paper was supported in part by JSPS-RFTF96P00502 (The Japan Society for the Promotion of Science, Research for the Future Program).

---

[6] The underlined words with ◯ are correctly analyzed, but ones with × are not. The detected CMs are shown after the underlines.

10. REFERENCES

[1] T. Briscoe and J. Carroll. Automatic extraction of subcategorization from corpora. In *Proceedings of the 5th Conference on Applied Natural Language Processing*, pages 356–363, 1997.

[2] S. Ikehara, M. Miyazaki, S. Shirai, A. Yokoo, H. Nakaiwa, K. Ogura, and Y. O. Y. Hayashi, editors. *Japanese Lexicon*. Iwanami Publishing, 1997.

[3] Information-Technology Promotion Agency, Japan. *Japanese Verbs : A Guide to the IPA Lexicon of Basic Japanese Verbs*. 1987.

[4] S. Kurohashi and M. Nagao. A method of case structure analysis for japanese sentences based on examples in case frame dictionary. In *IEICE Transactions on Information and Systems*, volume E77-D No.2, 1994.

[5] S. Kurohashi and M. Nagao. A syntactic analysis method of long japanese sentences based on the detection of conjunctive structures. *Computational Linguistics*, 20(4), 1994.

[6] S. Kurohashi and M. Nagao. Building a japanese parsed corpus while improving the parsing system. In *Proceedings of The First International Conference on Language Resources & Evaluation*, pages 719–724, 1998.

[7] C. D. Manning. Automatic acquisition of a large subcategorization dictionary from corpora. In *Proceedings of the 31th Annual Meeting of ACL*, pages 235–242, 1993.

[8] T. Utsuro, T. Miyata, and Y. Matsumoto. Maximum entropy model learning of subcategorization preference. In *Proceedings of the 5th Workshop on Very Large Corpora*, pages 246–260, 1997.

Japanese Text Input System With Digits
—Can Japanese text be estimated only from consonants ?—

Kumiko TANAKA-Ishii   Yusuke INUTSUKA   Masato TAKEICHI

University of Tokyo

7-3-1 Hongo Bunkyoku Tokyo

+81-5841-7412, Japan

{kumiko, inu, takeichi}@ipl.t.u-tokyo.ac.jp

ABSTRACT

We discuss a Japanese text input method for mobile phones. Different from the current methods that are based on kana kanji conversion system, our system asks user only to input the sequence of digits that in fact corresponds to the sequence of consonants, and then convert it directly into the final kanji form.

After the examination on the number of candidates for a sequence of digits, we explain our method of word estimation based on Hidden Markov Model and describe our implementation. Then we report the results of evaluation by comparing the number of needed keystrokes to input various kinds of actual texts.

1 INTRODUCTION

As the mobile phones have come into wide use, various internet services are now becoming available on these phones. For example, we may look up train timetables, or we may ask for the best Italian restaurant around the place. This is usually done not by calling up somebody, but by accessing a given home page on the phone, and by typing in the needed text.

The problem here is that mobile phones are only equipped with a small keypad of about 12 small buttons. Therefore, people are now making great efforts to minimize the number of keystrokes to input text. This is done not only from the services side (such as to use pop up menu for selection), but also from the users' side (such as to register the frequently used keywords as shortcuts). Additionally, there is another trend that appeared recently, that is, to adopt the new input method, *single-stroke-per-character* method [9][10].

Proceedings of HLT 2001, First International Conference on Human Language Technology Research, J. Allan, ed., Morgan Kaufmann, San Francisco, 2001.

With the past text input method, users have to press the keys multiple times to obtain a suitable character (*multiple-strokes-per-character* method). For example, to input "box", user taps the sequence of "2266699". Here, 'b' corresponds to the No.2 key assigned three characters of "ABC", so, "22" means the *second* character "B". Similarly, tapping No.6 three times indicates the third character of "MNO" and twice No.9 is the second character of "WXYZ". Rather, single-stroke-per-character method proposes only to press "269" for "box", the first digits of the same successive numbers. Off course this sequence does not only correspond to the word "box" but also to, "any", "cow", "boy" etc. So, the system picks all these possibilities, show them to the user and the user chooses his target word. In essence, single-stroke-per-character method tries to decrease keystrokes by increasing the ambiguity of input and resolving it interactively.

In Japanese, single-stroke-per-character method corresponds to input digits that actually are consonants. In the early 80's, when the current kana kanji conversion system was still not that established, the discussion of Japanese input system only by consonants existed in the context of desk-top computer applications [3][4]. Shortly after, the research extinguished without being able to find any application. However, the recent spread of mobile phones has once again brought this topic to the fore.

In general, single-stroke-per-character method needs less number of key strokes for input, but it should handle far larger number of candidates compared with multiple-strokes-per-character. Additionally, this problem of explosion of candidates is greater in Japanese, first because the Japanese language contains more homonyms and second because the kana alphabet has twice as many characters as the European alphabet.

Therefore, we first need to verify whether such system could be put to use. After over-viewing the current Japanese input method with digits, we will explore the possibilities for the containment of this explosion of candidates.

2 INPUT WITH DIGITS

Before we go into our topic, let us briefly explain the kana-kanji conversion system, that is used nowadays to input Japanese text on desktop computers.

The final form of Japanese could be the mixture of two sort of characters; *kanji*, the Chinese character, *kana*, the phonetic alphabet character. We input such a language as follows. First, the user inputs his target word by the sequence of phonemes, using *kana*. Then, the input system looks for the possible final forms that correspond to the user input and show them to the user. The input finishes when user selects his choice.

Currently, there are two major methods to do the same with digits. In both methods, users input the sequence of kana by digits. It is the user's responsibility to convert kana into digits. Because a kana is composed of a consonant and a vowel, each of them is attached a digit as is shown in Table 1. The user may convert any kana sequence into a unique sequence of digits with this table. For example, "は" (ha) corresponds to "61" and "こ"(ko) to "25" .

The two input methods differ in how users input the vowel (see Table 2[1]). The first method is called *Pocket-Bell method*[2] (written as PB method in the followings). The user inputs the digit sequence exactly as was obtained from the Table 1. For example, to input "はこ" (reads *hako*, means *box*), user presses "6125" successively. This method has the priority that the user needs only to input two digits per kana just as with the ordinary keyboard on desktop computers. However, the user needs to move his fingers more than the following second method.

The second method is called *Kana method*(with capital 'K'), the most popular input method among the mobile phone users at the moment. Users tap consonant digit *the vowel digit times*, just as in the multiple-strokes-per-character method for European language. In the case of "はこ", users tap once No.6 key, then five times of No.2 key. This method has a priority that the user could keep his finger at one place to input one kana. However, he needs to make many key strokes, especially when the word contains kana with the vowel of "e"(four times) or "o" (five times). Because of this, the biggest problem of users in this method is that they tend to

---
[1]Here "*" is used to transfer "k" to "g", that is similarly written in kana alphabet. For example, with the vowel "o", "こ"(ko) is transformed into "ご" (go). For PB method, 1 is needed after "*" because there are several transformation of kana of this kind. Also, "ん"(n), the unique character in Japanese without vowel is input by "03".

[2]Pocket Bell is NTT's trademark for pager.

Table 1: Digits corresponding to consonants and vowels

Consonants

0	1	2	3	4
わ (w)	あ (φ)	か (k)	さ (s)	た (t)
5	6	7	8	9
な (n)	は (h)	ま (m)	や (y)	ら (r)

Vowels

1	2	3	4	5
a	i	u	e	o

Table 2: How "にほんご"(reads *nihongo*, means *Japanese*) is input with digits

	に	ほ	ん	ご
PB method	52	65	03	25*1
Kana method	55	66666	000	22222*
Our method	5	6	0	2*

mistype by pressing the same button too many times than expected. Additional problem is that there is an ambiguity of man-machine interaction when users want to input the kana of the same consonant successively. For example, "hihi" (6262), 6 twice and then 6 twice again is exactly the same as four times of 6 (64) that corresponds to "he".

We could observe that what users want is a method that allows text input with:

- less number of replacement of fingers, and
- less total number of keystrokes.

Our method asks user to input one stroke of the digit that corresponds to the consonant of kana. In the case of "はこ", the user only needs to input the sequence of "62" (corresponding to "hk"). This method has a priority that user needs only one stroke per kana, and he neither needs to move fingers for a kana. The number of strokes by the user decreases to the half that of PB method.

Instead, because such input sequence is more ambiguous compared with the kana-based method, the system needs to guess the actual user input among candidates that have the same sequence of consonants. For example, "62" not only corresponds to "はこ", but also to other completely different kana sequences such as "ふく"(reads *huku*), "はか"(reads *haka*). Further, for each of these kana sequences, there are several final forms. For example, "ふく" corresponds to, "服" (means *dress*), "吹く"(means *to blow*), "拭く"(means *to wipe*), "福" (means *blessing*), "副"(means *vice*) etc. Therefore, the number of candidates is expected to be very numerous compared with kana-based method. In the next section, we examine some statistics and discuss whether our input method could be put to use.

212

Table 3: Number of candidates for a digit sequence

	statistics	Our method	Kana or PB method
Base line	Average	2.41	1.39
	Max	167	43
	Average by frequency	31.61	4.76
Words with POS tag	Average	1.69	1.19
	Max	74	37
	Average frequency	5.47	1.65
Words of frequency more than 100	Average	1.82	1.15
	Max	32	10
	Average by frequency	6.29	1.75

3 PROBLEM

Japanese corpus of Mainichi newspaper articles of general news page ('94, 1.3 million word occurrences, 28Mbytes) contains 90 thousand different words. The average length of words when transliterated in kana alphabet is 4.81. Because kana has 50 different characters, $50^{4.81}$ = about 143 million different kana sequences can be represented with the length of 4.81. Among 143 million, only 90 thousand are used for the vocabulary of Mainichi newspaper. Therefore, one kana sequence per one word can be easily realized if we do not think about homonyms.

On the other hand, our method only has 10 digits (consonants). This can represent only $10^{4.81}$ = about 60 thousand different digit sequences. In this space, we should assign 90 thousand words, that is larger than the space size. Therefore, large number of words need to share a digit sequence even if all different digit sequences are used. Here already we have a hunch that the number of word candidates for a sequence becomes very large.

To measure the number of candidates more precisely, we took the statistics of the number of candidates given a sequence of kana or digits that corresponds to a word. The first line of Table 3 shows the average number of candidates for an input in the case of our method and by PB or Kana. We could already see that in our case, the number of candidates amounts to more than 2 taking any word at random. The second line shows the maximum number of candidates; our case is four times as much as kana's case. Additionally, we also calculated the average number of candidates taking a word according to the word frequency distribution[3]. Looking at this

---

[3]This is done by the following formula.

$$\frac{\sum (number\ of\ candidates) \times (freqency)}{\sum frequency}$$

Note that sum is calculated for all possible kana/digit sequences.

---

line, we nearly feel that we should give up this problem.

One solution to handle this explosion of candidates is to make the selection process into two stages rather than one. After input, the user is first shown to choose among possible kana sequences. For example, when he inputs "62", then the system first shows "はか", "はき" (reads haki), "はく",..., " ほこ"(reads hoko) and user chooses his target as kana alphabet sequence. Then, the user's choice is passed to the second selection process, the kana-kanji conversion system. Such solution is taken by T9[8], or ZI[10].

However, we have a strong impression that such selection process had better be unified if possible. The largest reason for this is that twice of selection process makes the man-machine interaction rather complex. Additionally, the action of interactive candidate selection is slow because the user should look for his target by scrolling the candidates back and forth[4]. Therefore, the number of selection process had better be eliminated as much as possible.

Consequently, we seek to implement our input method within single stage of selection as is in the kana-kanji conversion system. User inputs digit and our system converts it into the final form directly. In this case, we should do something with the number of candidates. There are only two solutions: 1.decrease the whole number of candidates and 2. sort them in a preferred order.

In order to decrease the number of candidates, we may use the part of speech tag in order to discriminate words better. The 4th to 6th lines in Table 3 show the same statistics for the whole words but discriminated with part of speech tag. We could see that the values decrease.

The naive criteria to sort candidates in a better order is the frequency. Suppose that there are 32 candidates, 2 of them are frequently used but the rest 30 are hardly used. Then if the system sorts the candidates in the frequency order and shows that two as the best, then the user need not handle the useless 30 candidates.

In order to see whether frequency could be used or not, 7th to 9th rows in the Table 3 shows the same statistics calculated only for the words that occurred more frequently than 100. We could see that the number of candidates decreases to better values. Therefore, we could say that frequency information helps to show the candidates in right order.

To conclude, we try to implement our Japanese input

---

[4]In Japanese, we also had character based input method named T-code system, that is proved to be the far faster method to input Japanese, compared with any kana-kanji conversion systems. A T-code is two successive keys that corresponds to one character. T-code users first memorize codes for all Japanese characters that amounts to more than 5000. Although proved to be the fastest input method, the load of memorizing T-code was too tough to be accepted by most of the end-users.

Table 4: Various text input options

Name	Input	Unit	Completion	Selection Stage	Current System
DW1	digit	word	no	one	-
DW2	digit	word	no	two	T9[9], ZI[10]
DWC1	digit	word	yes	one	ours
DP1	digit	phrase	no	one	ours
KWC1-PB	kana(PB)	word	yes	one	-
KP1-PB	kana(PB)	phrase	no	one	any mobile phone input system
KWC1-Kana	kana(Kana)	word	yes	one	PO-Box[5] (for Palms)
KP1-Kana	kana(Kana)	phrase	no	one	any mobile phone input system

system that allows user to select the final target within the **single selection stage**. In order to do this, we make much use of the **part of speech tag** and **word frequency**.

4 LANGUAGE MODEL

The input system needs to estimate the corresponding word sequence from the input sequence of digits. We adopt language model based on Hidden Markov Model for this task.

Suppose that C denotes the user input sequence of digits. Then the best sequence of words is defined as:

$$\hat{W} = \arg\max_{W} P(W|C) \qquad (1)$$

Because C is the same to all candidates, right hand side of equation is:

$$\hat{W} = \arg\max_{W} P(W). \qquad (2)$$

If we denote T as the sequence of part of speech tags, then $P(W)$ can be rewritten as:

$$P(W) = \sum_{T} P(W,T) \qquad (3)$$

without loosing any generality. We introduce two approximations:

$$P(w_n|w_{1,n-1}, t_{1,n}) = P(w_n|t_n) \qquad (4)$$

$$P(t_n|w_{1,n-1}, t_{1,n-1}) = P(t_n|t_{n-1}). \qquad (5)$$

Here w_i means the ith word of W, $w_{i,j}$ denotes word sequence from ith to jth of W. Then the right hand side of the equation (3) is transformed into

$$P(W) = \sum_{T} \prod_{i=1}^{n} p(w_i|t_i) P(t_{i+1}|t_i). \qquad (6)$$

Such a word model for English is resumed by Charniak[2] , and also in Japanese by Nagata [7] especially for morphological analyzer.

Overall, given a digit sequence, the system calculates the above probability for all the possible candidates, and then sorted shown to the user in that order.

5 IMPLEMENTATION

5.1 Input Options

There are other various options to input text other than input by digit vs. kana (second column of Table 4). One is the language unit. The choice are among a word, a phrase or phrases (third column)[5]. Here, the longer the unit is, the larger the system load because it should look for the best target among combinatorially many candidates.

We could also think of whether to adopt the completion (fourth column). When using the completion, the system estimates and shows the best candidate not waiting until the input to be as long as the unit. For example, with DWC1, "箱"(reads *hako*, means *box* corresponds to "65") is estimated and shown to the user even when the user only taps "6". This method is very ambiguous at input. Such a input is proposed for Palm text input systems and it is distributed as free-ware [5] for kana-based input(7th row of Table 4).

Completion by phrase means to estimate the best next word as well as completing the current word. Therefore, the system might estimate " 箱は" (*a box is*) or "箱入り娘は" (*a girl from a good familiy is*, Japanese idiomatic expression using the word *box*) after a single input of "6". In this case, the load on the system will become very high because the search area for candidates is very vast.

The fourth column of the table shows how many selection stages are used until user to end the input. Our choice is one, as is explained §3.

Here, our input system is mainly to input text with the methods of DWC1 and DP1. However, we also implemented other variations as in the list, so that all could be compared against each other.

5.2 System

In general, given a digit sequence, the system looks up all possible candidates using the dictionary (see §5.3)

---

[5]Character based input means no ambiguity at input.

that is initialized at boot time. Then it calculates the probability (explained in §4) for candidates, sorts them and shows them to the user.

If the user's target word is contained in the system results, then the user may choose the word using one of the following commands:

- **| n** Select the first word of n-th candidate.
- **m** Show the next candidates.

When the input method is phrase-based, then the system cut the input sequence and convert each piece into words. For example, " 421430316 " could be words such as " 武市 (4214, takeiti, *name*) 先生 (3031, sensei, *professor*) は "(6, ha), or "竹内 (4214, takeuti, *another name*) 新政府 "(30316, sinseihu, *new government*). In this case, the system should estimate two parameters: word border and the word itself.

The number of candidates in phrase based method is large because of combinations. So, in order to decrease the calculation complexity, we adopted Nagata's Viterbi-like algorithm[7] to approximately obtain the best candidate. From this best candidate, its first word is replaced with the other possible words of the same digit length. The resulting set is shown in the order of the probability.

We could have chosen to form candidates out of the second best, or the third best according to the formula (6) and Nagata's method. However, the second and the third best could contain words of different border. This forces users to make selection among words of different length, that is rather confusing from user interface point of view. Therefore, we took the above method to form candidates, so that users may decide one parameter at a time, first by adjusting word border and then choosing the target word.

In order to allow users to adjust the word borders, some more commands are prepared:

- **s** Shorten the word border of the first word
- **l** Extend the word border of the first word

These commands are to be implemented using the direction key and special keys that is also equipped on mobile phones.

Another problem that might occur is when the user's target was not found in the dictionary that is *unknown words*. In this case, the user might need to input character by character (see §5.3). If the user's target is written by kana or kata-kana, then user may do this by:

- **h** Transliterate first word with kana
- **k** Transliterate first word with kata-kana

Unknown words will be registered automatically into the user dictionary. (However, for the evaluation section, registration is not performed to measure the system performance in the identical environment.)

For all input methods, human user can be replaced by a routine that automatically inputs any given Japanese text and counts how many keystrokes are needed for the task. Candidates are formed and shown to the routine using exactly the same statistical method of frequency and part of speech tag based on HMM. All methods use the same dictionary (described in the next section). Therefore, the number of key strokes can be compared fairly.

As for methods of completion, the timing to select the candidates are not unique. For example, user might find his target as the third best after the input of 2 digits, or find his target as the best after the input of 3 digits. For the automatic input, we decided that the target word is chosen when it appears as the best candidate. Otherwise, the next digit of the current word is tapped in to filter out the irrelevant candidates. When input for the word ends and the target does not appear as the best, then the target is chosen from the non best.

5.3 Dictionary

The dictionary is constructed from Mainichi newspaper corpus (described in the §3). First, we analyzed corpus morphologically[6], then all words that occurred in the corpus were shaped into a dictionary. One entry of the dictionary contains the following elements:

- word transliterated in kana
- corresponding sequence in digits (only of consonants)
- word
- part of speech tag
- frequency

The dictionary is added all characters in Japanese to cope with the unknown words. In order to minimize the size of the whole dictionary, we implemented the dictionary using trie-based method [1].

6 EVALUATION

6.1 Output Example

We first show two small input examples each by DP1 and DWC1 in Figure 5. The example phrase is described at the top four rows.

We see that a user inputs a digit by digit when using DWC1, and a phrase by digit when using DP1. Then system estimates candidates (five candidates are shown at a time in the example case. Some part of DWC1 is omitted for the sake of space). Then, the user interactively chooses his target. The results could be seen accumulated in front of the prompt ' >' as the input proceeds. For DWC1, the effect of completion could be seen for the words of "busy", that the target appears even when the input is not completed.

Table 5: Output example

Japanese target text	武市先生はいつも忙しい。
Translation	Prof. Takeichi is always busy.
Transliteration in roma-ji	takeichisensei ha itsumo isogashii.
Digit sequence (only consonants)	42143031 6 147 132*31

DWC1

```
> 4
1. とう (トウ)
2. っぽく (ッポク)
...
> 2
1. 的 (テキ)
2. 突き (ツキ)
...
> 1
1. 高い (タカイ)
2. 近い (チカイ)
...
> 4
1. 竹内 (タケウチ)
2. 付き合っ (ツキアッ)
3. 逐一 (チクイチ)
4. 武内 (タケウチ)
5. 突き落とさ (ツキオトサ)
> m
(more command filters out
words longer than
length 4. )
1. 竹内 (タケウチ)
2. 付き合っ (ツキアッ)
3. 逐一 (チクイチ)
4. 武内 (タケウチ)
5. 武市 (タケイチ)
> +5
武市> 3
1. さん (サン)
2. 者 (シャ)
...
武市> 0
1. さん (サン)
2. 信 (シン)
...
武市> 3
1. 信二 (シンジ)
2. 濡手 (センシュ)
...
武市> 1
1. 先生 (センセイ)
2. 申請 (シンセイ)
...
武市> +1
武市先生> 6
1. は (ハ)
2. へ (ヘ)
...
武市先生> +1
武市先生は> 1
1. 一 (イチ)
2. 大阪 (オオサカ)
...
武市先生は> 4
1. 一 (イチ)
2. あっ (アッ)
...
武市先生は> 7
1. いつも (イツモ)
2. 一万 (イチマン)
...
武市先生は> +1
武市先生はいつも> 1
1. いう (イウ)
2. ある (アル)
...
武市先生はいつも> 3
1. 異常 (イジョウ)
2. いずれ (イズレ)
...
武市先生はいつも> 2
1. 意識 (イシキ)
2. 遅く (オソク)
...
武市先生はいつも> *
(system estimated the
target as No.2 candidate
when the input of the
word is not completed yet.)
1. 急ぐ (イソグ)
2. 忙しい (イソガシイ)
3. 忙しく (イソガシク)
4. 忙しかっ (イソガシカッ)
5. 薄暗い (ウスグライ)
武市先生はいつも> +2
武市先生はいつも忙しい> *
1. 。 (。)
2. 、 (、)
...
武市先生はいつも忙しい> +1
武市先生はいつも忙しい。> quit
```

DP1

```
> 421430316
1. 竹内 (タケウチ) 先生 (センセイ) は (ハ)
2. 武内 (タケウチ) 先生 (センセイ) は (ハ)
3. 徳一 (トクイチ) 先生 (センセイ) は (ハ)
4. 高市 (タカイチ) 先生 (センセイ) は (ハ)
5. 武市 (タケイチ) 先生 (センセイ) は (ハ)
> +5
1. 先生 (センセイ) は (ハ)
2. 真相 (シンソウ) は (ハ)
3. 申請 (シンセイ) は (ハ)
4. 醒性 (リンセイ) は (ハ)
5. 戦争 (センソウ) は (ハ)
武市先生> +1
1. は (ハ)
2. へ (ヘ)
3. 府 (フ)
4. 貫 (ヒ)
5. 課 (ハ)
武市先生> +1
武市先生> 147
1. いつも (イツモ)
2. 集め (アツメ)
3. 伊丹 (イタミ)
4. 頭 (アタマ)
5. 意見 (イツミ)
武市先生> +1
武市先生はいつも> 132*31
1. 忙しい (イソガシイ)
武市先生はいつも> +1
武市先生はいつも忙しい> *
1. 。 (。)
2. 、 (、)
3. Ｊ (Ｊ)
4. 「 (「)
武市先生はいつも忙しい> +2
武市先生はいつも忙しい。> quit
```

6.2 Test Data for Automated Input

We prepared two kinds of texts for evaluation (Table 6). The first kind is the Mainichi newspaper articles. For

Table 6: Test data

	Newspaper		Personal text	
	general	economics	e-mail	book
No. of words	1752	1675	1744	1577
No.of diff. words	771	652	528	330
No. sentences	61	53	72	59
No.unknown words	1	24	22	67
No.unknown diff. words	1	23	21	28
Avr.len. of words(digits)	2.431	2.866	2.326	2.246

this first kind, two corpus is prepared, the one used for building the dictionary, and the other articles of economics domain not used to build the dictionary.

The second kind is from the completely different domain, that is user's personal texts. Here also, we prepared two texts, the third author's e-mail corpus (of 1 year, about 150 thousand words) and his article of text book of functional programming (about 90 thousand words).

In order to eliminate the local bias of context, we took a certain number of sentences randomly from all over the place of each corpus, until the total number of words amounts to more than 1500 words. Here, stops (periods, commas) are also regarded as a kind of word.

The number of unknown words that occurred at input are also shown in the table. This is not included in the number of words(first line), nor to compute average number of keystrokes in the following. Note that unknown words occur not only because it is not registered in the dictionary, but also because of the approximation of search for candidates (see §5.2).

6.3 Kana vs. Digit

Table 7 shows the results for 6 methods for the test data of economics articles. The table contains average number of keystrokes needed for each action of input, adjust word border (only for phrase based method) and selection. For the selection, we assume that it needs n strokes if the correct answer is shown as nth candidate[6].

---

[6]Readers might indicate that a stroke is not needed to choose the best candidate, because the user could go on to tap the next word directly without any explicit selection action.

As for the methods with completion, this is not true. Target is estimated at every user action, therefore the user should explicitly choose the target even when choosing the best candidate.

As for the methods without completion, the assumption is true. However, without completion, user should indicate the timing to

Table 7: Average number of keystrokes per word needed for each action to input newspaper articles of economics

	input	adjust wrd border	select
DWC1	2.476	-	1.802
KWC1-Kana	6.204	-	1.106
KWC1-PB	4.952	-	1.106
DP1	2.866	0.116	1.903
KP1-Kana	8.088	0.013	1.088
KP1-PB	5.731	0.013	1.088

Table 8: Average number of keystrokes per word for various test data

	Newspaper		Personal text	
	general	economics	e-mail	book
DWC1	4.446	4.278	4.060	4.731
KWC1-Kana	6.683	7.310	6.442	6.802
KWC1-PB	5.414	6.058	5.260	5.355
DP1	4.864	4.885	4.521	5.268
KP1-Kana	7.993	9.189	7.618	7.735
KP1-PB	5.991	6.832	5.748	5.765

The average total keystrokes needed per word is listed in the second column (of economics) in Table 8.

First of all, we see that PB and Kana methods have the same number of strokes for adjusting word border and selection. This is always true because user ultimately input kana both with PB and Kana methods Also, the number of keystrokes needed for PB method is double that of our method. We could also see that DWC1 needs less number of keystrokes for a word than DP1, that is the effect of the completion.

With DWC1 and DP1 less keystrokes are needed for input, but more for selection compared with KWC1 and KP1 methods. However, as a whole, less keystrokes are needed(Table 8, second column). We see here that our approach is successful for this test document. We also see that DWC1 is the most efficient method.

6.4 Difference among Text Kinds

Next, we compare the efficiency to input text of different kinds. This time, we only show the total average keystrokes per word in Table 8, because the breakups of keystrokes have the same trend as were discussed in the previous section.

---

invoke the digit/kana kanji conversion, therefore one extra stroke is always needed per language unit which is not counted in our evaluation. Therefore, balancing these two, for DW1, the count is equal to the minimal number of keystrokes. For DP1 and KP1, the counts are slightly larger than the minimal.

For all four texts, we see the same trends as we have seen with economics article, that is:
- Input by digits is more efficient than that by kana.
- DWC1 is the most efficient.

Therefore, we could probably say that, in general, the input by digit is more efficient than that by kana independent of the text kind.

The text that needed least keystrokes turned up to be the user e-mail text by digits, not the newspaper article used to construct the dictionary. The reason for this is that e-mail text was quite characteristic that it contains many stops (periods and commas) than other texts (see Table 6). Note that the average keystrokes that we show also measures text style as well as the efficiency of input.

The worst text by digit input was the user's book data of technical domain. For this text, DWC1 has least difference with keystrokes by KWC1-PB method. Therefore, how efficient the input by digit depends on text kind, although the fact that input by digit is the most efficient method stays with our four test data.

As a whole, for all data, DWC1 is 37.76% more efficient than KWC1-Kana, 21.82% than KWC1-PB, DP1 is 40.05% more efficient than KP1-Kana, 19.87% than KP1-PB in average.

6.5 One Stage vs. Two Stages

We also compared our method with that of T9[9] or ZI[10]. As T9 and ZI methods are word based, we also implemented a simple word based method (not using completion) DW1 and then compared it with DW2. Because our system is based on HMM, conversions of DW1 and DW2 are both estimated by HMM.

As is discussed, DW2 has two stages of selection, first to select kana and then to select the final kanji form of the word. As T9 and ZI methods both are not open to public, we guessed the minimal input method using two stages and implemented it as follows. First, user types in a word by digits of consonants, then presses a key to invoke digit to kana conversion. User selects his target then presses another key to invoke kana to kanji conversion and then selects the final form.

Because there are words of final form that only consists of kana, we made the system not to pass these words to the second selection process of kana-kanji conversion. We could sum up the number of keystrokes by addition of that needed for input, selection of kana sequence (at least 1 needed to invoke digit kana conversion for all words)[7] and selection of target (at least 1 *only* for words that contain kanji).

---

[7]When the target appears as the best, user can directly go onto the second selection process. Therefore the number of keystrokes needed to choose nth target will be n, containing the key stroke to *invoke* the conversion process.

Table 9: Number of keystrokes per word for DW1 and DW2

	action	Newspaper		Personal text	
		general	economics	e-mail	book
D W 1	select	2.298	1.783	1.959	2.599
	total	4.729	4.649	4.285	4.845
D W 2	select1	1.644	1.445	1.567	1.717
	select2	0.555	0.621	0.385	0.510
	total	4.630	4.933	4.278	4.473

The results are shown in Table 9. Here, keystrokes for input action is not indicated, because it is in common to DW1 and DW2. The result of second selection is total number of keystrokes divided by *whole* number of words (also words that does not contain any kanji.) so that values could be summed for select1 and select2.

For DW2, we could see that the number of keystrokes for selection is small at each stage. As a result, DW1 is quite defeated by DW2 for the test data of user's book. Having that the user's book was also a hard task for DP1 and DWC1 (see Table 8, first row), we should look for some other method to specialize the system to the text.

For the other three, DW1 and DW2 competes well. Having these results, we think that DW1 is better because man-machine interaction is far simpler. Also, if we compare DWC1 and DW2, then DWC1 is better (except for the user book). Therefore, we could say that DWC1 is the better choice with its simplicity of man-machine interface and also from the efficiency point of view.

7 CONCLUSION

We have discussed an alternative Japanese text input method for mobile phones. The user inputs the sequence of digits that corresponds to the sequence of consonants so that the number of key strokes decreases to at least half. The system then needs to estimate the most probable word sequence from digits. We first verified whether such input system could be put to practical use, then argued that the word frequency and part of speech tag could be the key to solving the problem. Then we implemented our system using Hidden Markov language model. With this study we verified that our system decreases more than 35% of the key strokes of the most popular text input method used on current mobile phones.

The most important future work is to examine the potential of a personalized dictionary. Mobile phones are, by nature, for personal use. Therefore if the dictionary could be personalized based on recent context

or the user's own corpus, the text input would be more efficient by eliminating the uncommon word candidates. We are currently applying a statistical learning method by extending input system described in this paper.

References

[1] J. Aoe. An efficient implementation of static string pattern matching machines. In *IEEE Transactions on Software Engineering*, 1989.

[2] E. Charniak. *Statistical Language Learning*. MIT Press, 1993.

[3] NEC Co.Ltd. Japanese text input system. In *Japanese Patent No.10-124506*, 1996.

[4] Toshiba Co.Ltd. Japanese text input system. In *Japanese Patent No.57-185528*, 1982.

[5] T. Masui. PO-BOX an efficient text input method for handheld and ubiquitous computers. In *the ACM Symposium on User Interfface Software and Technology*, pages pp.113–119, 1999.

[6] Y. Matsumoto and et. al. Manual of Japanese morphological analyzer *chasen*, 1997. Naist Technical Report.

[7] M. Nagata. *Research on Japanese with Stochastic Models*. ph.D. thesis, 1998.

[8] ASCII-24 (online news service). Tegic9 announces japanese input software for mobile phones, 2000. http://www.ascii24.com/24/news/tech /article/2000/12/26/621457-000.html.

[9] Tegic9. Tegic9 home page, 2000. Available from http://www.t9.com.

[10] ZI-Corp. Zi home page, 2000. Available from http://207.229.18.241/.

Large scale testing of a descriptive phrase finder

Hideo Joho
Department of Information Studies
University of Sheffield, Western Bank
Sheffield, S10 2TN, UK
+44 (0)114 222 2675

h.joho@sheffield.ac.uk

Ying Ki Liu
Department of Information Studies
University of Sheffield, Western Bank
Sheffield, S10 2TN, UK

Mark Sanderson
Department of Information Studies
University of Sheffield, Western Bank
Sheffield, S10 2TN, UK
+44 (0)114 222 2648

m.sanderson@sheffield.ac.uk

ABSTRACT

This paper describes an evaluation of an existing technique that locates sentences containing descriptions of a query word or phrase. The experiments expand on previous tests by exploring the effectiveness of the system when searching from a much larger document collection. The results showed the system working significantly better than when searching over smaller collections. The improvement was such, that a more stringent definition of what constituted a correct description was devised to better measure effectiveness. The results also pointed to potentially new forms of evidence that might be used in improving the location process.

Keywords

Information retrieval, descriptive phrases, WWW.

1. INTRODUCTION

Retrieving descriptions of the words and phrases, which are not often found in dictionaries, has potential benefits for a number of fields. The Descriptive Phrase Finder (DPF) is a system that retrieves descriptions of a query term from free text. The system only uses simple pattern matching to detect a description, and ranks the sentences that hold the descriptive phrases based on within document and cross document term occurrence information. The system does not attempt to extract descriptions from text, it simply locates sentences that are hopefully relevant to a user. It is assumed that users are able to read a sentence and locate any description within it. The advantage of using such an approach is that the DPF is much simplified and does not require parsing to find the exact location of the phrase. Due to its simplicity, it achieves a level of domain independence.

The DPF was implemented and succeeded in The DPF was implemented and succeeded in retrieving sentences holding descriptive phrases (DPs) of a wide range of proper nouns. Initial testing on a collection of LA Times articles from the TREC Collection showed that 90% of the queries had at least one correct DP in the top 5 ranked sentences and 94% in the top 10 ([3]). It

was shown that the effectiveness of the system was in part due to the large amount of free text being searched. What was not shown by the experiment was if performance could be further improved by searching an even larger text. Consequently, a larger scale experiment was conducted, searching for phrases from the World Wide Web (WWW) using the output of a commercial Web search engine to locate candidate documents that were then processed locally by the DPF.

In addition to increasing the number of documents searched, more queries were tested and different definitions of relevance were tried. The rest of this short paper explains the system and shows the results of the expanded experiment, followed by pointers to future work.

2. THE SYSTEM

The Web-based DPF was composed of two parts: a front-end to an existing Web search engine, which fetched documents; and the system that located sentences holding descriptive phrases.

The Web front end simply routed queries to a Web search engine (Google), and the text of the top 600 documents returned by the engine was fetched, split into sentences (using a locally developed sentence splitter), and those sentences holding the query term were passed onto the DPF.

It ranked sentences on a score calculated from multiple sources of evidence. A detailed description of the DPF is found in [3]. The primary clue to there being a descriptive phrase in a sentence was the presence of a *key phrase* within it. An example key phrase was "such as", which may be found in the sentence: "He used several search engines *such as* AltaVista, HotBot and WebTop to compare the performance". If such a sentence were returned to a user who entered the query "WebTop", they would determine it was a search engine. Specifically, the DPF is searching for the key phrase in proximity to a query noun (qn) to locate a descriptive phrase (dp) e.g.

- ... *dp* such as *qn* ...

other key phrases used, some suggested by [2], were

- ... such *dp* as *qn* ...

- ... *qn* (and | or) other *dp* ...

- ... *dp* (especially | including) *qn* ...

- ... *qn* (*dp*) ...

- ... *qn* is a *dp* ...

Proceedings of HLT 2001, First International Conference on Human Language Technology Research, J. Allan, ed., Morgan Kaufmann, San Francisco, 2001.

219

- .. *qn*, (a | the) *dp*, ...

The phrases form the key part of the DPF as they identify well sentences likely to contain descriptions of *qn*. While the number of times a particular *qn* appears in a sentence with a key phrase are small, by searching a large corpus, like the Web, the chances of finding a few (accurately identified) descriptions of *qn* in the form required are high.

Based on results from a testing phase, certain key phrases were found more accurate at locating a descriptive phrase than others. Consequently, when ranking matching sentences, different scores were assigned depending on the accuracy of the key phrase found within. Since unfamiliar words tend to be explained or rephrased at the early part of a document, sentence position was also a factor in the rank score, with earlier sentences given preference. Finally, cross-document information was taken into account. Across all the matching sentences for a particular query, the occurrence of all the terms within the sentences was noted. It was anticipated that terms occurring more frequently within the set of sentences were likely to belong to descriptions.

Consequently, sentences holding a high number of commonly occurring words were given further preference in the ranking. The last two pieces of information not only improved the accuracy of ranking, but also enabled the system to produce reasonable results when no key phrases were matched. A training phase where the optimum balance between the sources of information was run on existing training data created from the LA Time corpus described in [3].

It may be reasonable to question why such a simple approach to extracting information from free-text sources be taken when more principled NLP-based techniques are well-established (e.g. [4], [5]). There are a number of reasons:

- Any simple approach is likely to be much faster than one that requires operations such as parsing.

- We believe that the use of simple but accurate methods searching over very large corpora provides a new means of determining lexical relations from corpora that are worthy of further exploration.

3. INITIAL STUDY

A pilot study was conducted, searching ten queries using the top hundred documents returned by Google. Of the ten queries, six had the best description located in the top two ranked sentences, two more queries had a good description in the top two. For all queries, a sentence holding a descriptive phrase was returned in the top five ranked sentences.

4. DEFINING RELEVANCE

In this and the previous evaluation described in [3], relevance was defined as a sentence that told the user anything about the query term: a liberal view of relevance (described here as *binary relevance*). The results from the pilot, under this interpretation, showed the system performed well. Consequently a more stringent form of relevance was devised. A sample answer for each query was solicited from users: for example, "the Prime Minister of Great Britain" for Tony Blair. Those *key answers* were taken as an acceptable criterion of highly relevant descriptive phrases. Sentences ranked by the system were then compared to the key answer. Correctness of DPs is not enough for this aim. Only a DP that described a query as well as a key answer was regarded as relevant. To illustrate, the sentence "Tony Blair is the current Prime Minister of the United Kingdom." was regarded as relevant, but "Tony Blair is a political leader" was not.

5. THE MAIN EXPERIMENT

A total of 146 queries were tested in the main experiment: 50 of which were evaluated based on key answers; 96 using binary evaluation. In the binary test, the DPF returned a relevant (descriptive) sentence in the top twenty sentences for all 96 queries. On average sixteen of the sentences returned were relevant to each query. The minimum number of relevant was six and maximum was twenty. Across the 96 queries, at least one relevant sentence was found in the top five for every tested query. This is a significant improvement over the previously reported experimental results where 90% of queries were answered in the top five.

Using more stringent key answer based relevance, the system succeeded in retrieving at least one relevant sentence in the top five for 66% of the queries, at least one in the top ten for 82%, and one in the top twenty for 88%.

These results show that the DPF searching the Web (1 billion documents) works dramatically better than the previous experiment using LA Times (100,000 documents). As was shown in previous work, the size of the collection impacts on the effectiveness of the system. This is because by searching a larger collection, there is a better chance of locating a relevant descriptive phrase in the format of one of the searched for key phrases. However in the previous work, there appeared to be an upper bound on the accuracy of the descriptive phrases alone. By searching a much larger collection it is speculated that the cross document term occurrence statistics used contributed significantly to improving the effectiveness of the system.

6. CONCLUSION

An existing descriptive phrase system was adapted to work with a Web search engine to locate phrases describing query words. The system was found to be highly effective at locating good descriptions: finding at least one high quality descriptive phrase in the top 10 returned sentences for 82% of test queries.

7. FUTURE WORK

We plan to undertake a number of further experiments, examining through tests, the ability of people to locate descriptions within the retrieved sentences. In addition, it was notable that the results of the full experiment were not as good as those from the pilot study. One difference between the two tests was the number of web documents examined: 100 top-ranked documents in the pilot; 600 for the expanded experiment. Given that a search engine generally retrieves more relevant documents in the higher ranks, there is likely to be more noise lower down. It is also significant that the search engine used was Google, which uses the *page rank* authority measure ([1]) to enhance its ranking. Therefore, we speculate that use of an authority measure can be used to further improve the quality of our DPF. This will be investigated in future work.

8. REFERENCES

[1] Brin, S., Page, L. The Anatomy of a Large-Scale Hypertextual Web Search Engine, in Proceedings of the 7th International WWW Conference, April 1998, Brisbane, Australia.

[2] Hearst, M.A. Automated Discovery of WordNet Relations, in WordNet: an electronic lexical database, C. Fellbaum (ed.), MIT Press, 131-151, 1998.

[3] Joho, H., Sanderson, M. Retrieving Descriptive Phrases from Large Amounts of Free Text, in Proceedings of the 9th ACM CIKM Conference, November 2000, McLean, VA, 180-186.

[4] Radev, D.R., McKeown, K.R. Building a Generation Knowledge Source using Internet-Accessible Newswire, in Proceedings of the 5th ANLP Conference, March 1997, Washington, D.C., 221-228.

[5] Srihari, R & Li, W. A Question Answering System Supported by Information Extraction, in Proceedings of the 8th ANLP Conference, April-May 2000, Seattle, Washington.

LaTaT: Language and Text Analysis Tools

Dekang Lin
University of Alberta
Department of Computing Science
Edmonton, Alberta T6H 2E1 Canada

lindek@cs.ualberta.ca

ABSTRACT

LaTaT is a Language and Text Analysis Toolset. This paper gives a brief description of the components comprising LaTaT, including a Minimalist parser and language and concept learning programs.

1. INTRODUCTION

In natural language processing, syntactic and semantic knowledge are deeply intertwined with each other, both in their acquisition and usage. The goal of our research is to build a syntactic and semantic knowledge base through an iterative process that involves both language processing and language acquisition. We start the process by parsing a large corpus with a manually constructed parser that has only syntactic knowledge. We then extract lexical semantic and statistical knowledge from the parsed corpus, such as similar words and phrases, collocations and idiomatic expressions, and selectional preferences. In the second cycle, the text corpus is parsed again with the assistance of the newly acquired semantic and statistical knowledge, which allows the parser to better resolve systematic syntactic ambiguities, removing unlikely parts of speech. Our hypothesis is that this will result in higher quality parse trees, which in turn allows extraction of higher quality semantic and statistical knowledge in the second and later cycles.

LaTaT is a Language and Text Analysis Toolset that demonstrates this iterative learning process. The main components in the toolset consist of the following:

- A broad coverage English parser, called Minipar. The grammar is constructed manually, based on the Minimalist Program (Chomsky 1995). Instead of using a large number of CFG rules, Minipar achieves its broad coverage by using a small set of principles to constrain the overgerating X-bar schema;

- A collocation extractor that extracts frequency counts of grammatical dependency relationships from a corpus parsed with Minipar. The frequency counts are then injected into Minipar to help it rank candidate parse trees;

Proceedings of HLT 2001, First International Conference on Human Language Technology Research, J. Allan, ed., Morgan Kaufmann, San Francisco, 2001.

- A thesaurus constructor (Lin, 1998) that automatically computes the word similarities based on the distributional characteristics of words in the parsed corpus. The resulting word similarity database can then be used to smooth the probability distribution in statistical language models (Dagan *et al*, 1997);

- A clustering algorithm that constructs Roget-like semantic categories in an unsupervised fashion (Lin and Pantel, 2001a); and

- An unsupervised learner to identify similar expressions from a parsed corpus (Lin and Pantel, 2001b).

2. Minipar

Minipar is a principle-based English parser (Berwick *et al*, 1991). Like Principar (Lin, 1993), Minipar represents its grammar as a network where nodes represent grammatical categories and links represent types of syntactic (dependency) relationships. The grammar network consists of 35 nodes and 59 links. Additional nodes and links are created dynamically to represent subcategories of verbs.

Minipar employs a message passing algorithm that essentially implements distributed chart parsing. Instead of maintaining a single chart, each node in the grammar network maintains a chart containing partially built structures belonging to the grammatical category represented by the node. The grammatical principles are implemented as constraints associated with the nodes and links.

The lexicon in Minipar is derived from WordNet (Miller, 1990). With additional proper names, the lexicon contains about 130,000 entries (in base form). The lexicon entry of a word lists all possible parts of speech of the word and its subcategorization frames (if any). The lexical ambiguities are handled by the parser instead of a tagger.

Minipar works with a constituency grammar internally. However, the output of Minipar is a dependency tree. A dependency relationship is an asymmetric binary relationship between a word called **head**, and another word called **modifier** (Mel'čuk, 1987). The structure of a sentence can be represented by a set of dependency relationships that form a tree. A word in the sentence may have several modifiers, but each word may modify at most one word. The root of the dependency tree does not modify any word. It is also called the head of the sentence.

Figure 1 shows an example dependency tree for the sentence "*John found a solution to the problem.*" The links in the diagram represent dependency relationships. The direction of a link is from the head to the modifier in the relationship. Labels

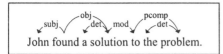
John found a solution to the problem.

Figure 1. Example dependency tree.

Table 1. A subset of dependency relations in Minipar outputs.

RELATION	DESCRIPTION	EXAMPLE
appo	appositive of a noun	the CEO, **John**
det	determiner of a noun	**the** dog
gen	genitive modifier of a noun	**John's** dog
mod	adjunct modifier of any head	**tiny** hole
nn	prenominal modifier of a noun	**station** manager
pcomp	complement of a preposition	in the **garden**
subj	subject of a verb	**John** loves Mary.

associated with the links represent types of dependency relations. Table 1 lists a subset of the dependency relations in Minipar outputs.

Minipar constructs all possible parses of an input sentence. However, only the highest ranking parse tree is outputted. Although the grammar is manually constructed, the selection of the best parse tree is guided by the statistical information obtained by parsing a 1GB corpus with Minipar. The statistical ranking of parse trees is based on the following probabilistic model. The probability of a dependency tree is defined as the product of the probabilities of the dependency relationships in the tree. Formally, given a tree T with root $root$ consisting of D dependency relationships ($head_i$, $relationship_i$, $modifier_i$), the probability of T is given by:

$$P(T) = P(root) \prod_{i=1}^{D} P(relationship_i, modifier_i \mid head_i)$$

where $P(relationship_i, modifier_i \mid head_i)$ is obtained using Maximum Likelihood Estimation.

Minipar parses newspaper text at about 500 words per second on a Pentium-III 700Mhz with 500MB memory. Evaluation with the manually parsed SUSANNE corpus (Sampson, 1995) shows that about 89% of the dependency relationships in Minipar outputs are correct.

3. Collocation and Word Similarity

We define a collocation to be a dependency relationship that occurs more frequently than predicted by assuming the two words in the relationship are independent of each other. Lin (1998) presented a method to create a collocation database by parsing a large corpus. Given a word w, the database can be used to retrieve all the dependency relationships involving w and the frequency counts of the dependency relationships. Table 2 shows excerpts of the entries in the collocation database for the words *duty* and *responsibility*. For example, in the corpus from which the collocation database is constructed, *fiduciary duty* occurs 319 times and *assume [the] responsibility* occurs 390 times.

The collocation database entry of a given word can be viewed as a feature vector for that word. Similarity between words can be computed using the feature vectors. Intuitively, the more features that are shared between two words, the higher the similarity between the two words will be. This intuition is captured by the Distributional Hypothesis (Harris, 1985).

Features of words are of varying degree of importance. For example, while almost any noun can be used as object of *include*, very few nouns can be modified by *fiduciary*. Two words sharing the feature *object-of-include* is less indicative of their similarity

Table 2. Excerpts of entries in the collocation database for *duty* and *responsibility*.

	DUTY		RESPONSIBILITY	
modified-by adjectives	fiduciary 319, active 251, other 82, official 76, additional 47, administrative 44, military 44, constitutional 41, reserve 24, high 23, moral 21, double 16, day-to-day 15, normal 15, specific 15, assigned 14, extra 13, operating 13, temporary 13, corporate 12, peacekeeping 12, possible 12, regular 12, retaliatory 12, heavy 11, routine 11, sacred 11, stiff 11, congressional 10, fundamental 10, hazardous 10, main 10, patriotic 10, punitive 10, special 10, ...		modified-by adjectives	more 107, full 92, fiduciary 89, primary 88, personal 79, great 69, financial 64, fiscal 59, social 59, moral 48, additional 46, ultimate 39, day-to-day 37, special 37, individual 36, legal 35, other 35, corporate 30, direct 30, constitutional 29, given 29, overall 29, added 28, sole 25, operating 23, broad 22, political 22, heavy 20, main 18, shared 18, professional 17, current 15, federal 14, joint 14, enormous 13, executive 13, operational 13, similar 13, administrative 10, fundamental 10, specific 10, ...
object-of verbs	have 253, assume 190, perform 153, do 131, impose 118, breach 112, carry out 79, violate 54, return to 50, fulfill 44, handle 42, resume 41, take over 35, pay 26, see 26, avoid 19, neglect 18, shirk 18, include 17, share 17, discharge 16, double 16, relinquish 16, slap 16, divide 14, split 13, take up 13, continue 11, levy 11, owe 10, ...		object-of verbs	have 747, claim 741, take 643, assume 390, accept 220, bear 187, share 103, deny 86, fulfill 53, meet 48, feel 47, retain 47, shift 47, carry out 45, take over 41, shoulder 29, escape 28, transfer 28, delegate 26, give 25, admit 23, do 21, acknowledge 20, exercise 20, shirk 20, divide 19, get 19, include 19, assign 18, avoid 17, put 17, recognize 17, hold 16, understand 16, evade 15, disclaim 12, handle 12, turn over 12, become 11, expand 11, relinquish 11, show 11, violate 11, discharge 10, duck 10, increase 10, ...

223

than if they shared the feature *modified-by-fiduciary*. The similarity measure proposed in (Lin, 1998) takes this into account by computing the mutual information between two words involved in a dependency relationship.

Using the collocation database, (Lin, 1998) presented an unsupervised method to construct a similarity matrix. Given a word *w*, the matrix returns a set of similar words of *w* along with their similarity to *w*. For example, the 35 most similar words of *duty, Beethoven*, and *eat* are shown in Table 3. The similarity matrix consists of about 20,000 nouns, 4,000 verbs and 6,000 adjectives and adverbs.

4. Unsupervised Induction of Semantic Classes

Consider the similar words of *Beethoven*. The quality of similar words obviously decreases as the similarity value decreases. Some of the words have non-zero similarity simply because they share common features with *Beethoven* by accident. For example, *tough guy* is similar to *Beethoven* because both *Beethoven* and *tough guy* can be used as the object of the verb *play*.

The similar words of *duty* exemplify another problem: The top similar words of a given word may be similar to different senses of the word. However, this is not made explicit by the similarity matrix.

LaTaT includes an algorithm called UNICON (UNsupervised Induction of CONcepts) that clusters similar words to create semantic classes (Lin and Pantel, 2001a). UNICON uses a heuristic maximal-clique algorithm, called CLIMAX, to find clusters in the similar words of a given word. The purpose of CLIMAX is to find small, tight clusters. For example, two of the clusters returned by CLIMAX are:

```
(Nq34
    "Harvard University"            0.610996
    Harvard                        0.482834
    "Stanford University"          0.469302
    "University of Chicago"        0.454686
    "Columbia University"          0.44262
    "New York University"          0.436737
    "University of Michigan"       0.43055
    "Yale university"              0.416731
    MIT                            0.414907
    "University of Pennsylvania"   0.384016
    "Cornell University"           0.333958
)

(Nq184
    "University of Rochester"      0.525389
    "University of Miami"          0.466607
    "University of Colorado"       0.46347
    "Ohio State University"        0.430326
    "University of Florida"        0.398765
    "Harvard Medical School"       0.39485
    "University of North Carolina" 0.394256
    "University of Houston"        0.371618
)
```

Nq34 and *Nq184* are automatically generated names for the clusters. The number after each word in the clusters is the similarity between the word and the centroid of that cluster.

The UNICON algorithm computes the centroids of a cluster by averaging the collocational features of the words in the cluster. The CLIMAX algorithm is then recursively used to construct clusters of centroids and the clusters whose centroids are clustered together are merged. This process continues until no more clusters

Table 3. The top 35 most similar words of *duty, Beethoven* and *eat* as given by (Lin, 1998).

WORD	SIMILAR WORDS (WITH SIMILARITY SCORE)
DUTY	responsibility 0.182, obligation 0.138, job 0.127, function 0.121, post 0.121, task 0.119, role 0.116, assignment 0.114, mission 0.109, requirement 0.109, tariff 0.109, position 0.108, restriction 0.103, procedure 0.101, tax 0.101, salary 0.1, fee 0.099, training 0.097, commitment 0.096, penalty 0.095, burden 0.094, quota 0.094, work 0.093, staff 0.093, regulation 0.093, sanction 0.093, liability 0.092, personnel 0.092, service 0.091, action 0.09, activity 0.09, rule 0.089, practice 0.089, authority 0.088
BEETHOVEN	Mozart 0.193, Brahms 0.178, Schubert 0.148, Mahler 0.143, Bach 0.142, Tchaikovsky 0.128, Prokofiev 0.118, Wagner 0.089, chamber music 0.087, Handel 0.073, cello 0.069, classical music 0.067, Strauss 0.066, Shakespeare 0.063, concerto 0.062, Cole Porter 0.062, Verdi 0.06, Sonata 0.057, violin 0.056, Elvis 0.053, Berg 0.053, composer 0.053, Lenin 0.052, flute 0.049, Bernstein 0.047, jazz 0.047, Beatles 0.046, Frank Sinatra 0.045, Warhol 0.043, Bob Dylan 0.043, Napoleon 0.043, symphony 0.042, solo 0.042, tough guy 0.042, Bruce Springsteen 0.041, grandparent 0.041
EAT	drink 0.204, cook 0.193, smoke 0.164, sleep 0.162, consume 0.156, love 0.153, enjoy 0.152, pick up 0.142, look at 0.141, feed 0.141, wear 0.14, talk about 0.139, watch 0.138, forget 0.136, like 0.136, taste 0.134, go out 0.133, sit 0.133, pack 0.133, wash 0.132, stay 0.131, burn 0.13, serve 0.129, ride 0.128, pick 0.128, grab 0.128, freeze 0.126, go through 0.126, throw 0.126, remember 0.124, get in 0.123, feel 0.123, learn 0.123, live 0.123

are merged. The details of the UNICON and CLIMAX algorithms are presented in (Lin and Pantel, 2001a). Table 4 shows 10 sample semantic classes identified by the UNICON algorithm, using a 1GB newspaper text corpus.

5. Automatic Discovery of Inference Rules

In many natural language processing and information retrieval applications, it is very useful to know the paraphrase relationships between natural language expressions. LaTaT includes an unsupervised method for discovering paraphrase inference rules from text, such as "*X is author of Y* ≈ *X wrote Y*", "*X solved Y* ≈ *X found a solution to Y*", and "*X caused Y* ≈ *Y is triggered by X*" (Lin and Pantel, 2001b). Our algorithm is based on an extended version of Harris' Distributional Hypothesis. Instead of using this hypothesis on words, we apply it to paths in the dependency trees of a parsed corpus.

Table 4. Ten concepts discovered by UNICON.

CONCEPT	SIZE	MEMBERS
Nq1	210	"Max von Sydow", "Paul Newman", "Jeremy Irons", "Lynn Redgrave", "Lloyd Bridges", "Jack Lemmon", "Jaclyn Smith", "Judd Nelson", "Beau Bridges", "Raymond Burr", "Gerald McRaney", "Robert de Niro", "Tim Matheson", "Kevin Costner", "Kurt Russell", "Arnold Schwarzenegger", "Michael J. Fox", "Dustin Hoffman", "Tom Hanks", "Robert Duvall", "Michael Keaton", "Edward James Olmos", "John Turturro", "Robin Williams", "Sylvester Stallone", "John Candy", "Whoopi Goldberg", "Eddie Murphy", "Rene Auberjonois", "Vanessa Redgrave", "Jeff Bridges", "Robert Mitchum", "Clint Eastwood", "James Woods", "Al Pacino", "William Hurt", "Richard Dreyfuss", "Tom Selleck", "Barry Bostwick", "Harrison Ford", "Tom Cruise", "Jon Cryer", "Pierce Brosnan", "Donald Sutherland", "Anthony Quinn", "Farrah Fawcett", "Louis Gossett Jr.", "Mark Harmon", "Steven Bauer", "William Shatner", "Diane Keaton", "Billy Crystal", "Omar Sharif", "Paul Hogan", "Woody Allen", "Fred Savage", "Jodie Foster", "Chuck Norris", "Kirk Douglas", "Glenn Close", "Ed Asner", "Dan Aykroyd", "Steve Guttenberg", "Sissy Spacek", "Jonathan Pryce", "Sean Penn", "Bill Cosby", "Robert Urich", "Steve Martin", "Karl Malden", "John Lithgow", "Charles Bronson", "Danny DeVito", "Michael Douglas", "John Ritter", "Gerard Depardieu", "Val Kilmer", "Jamie Lee Curtis", "Randy Quaid", "John Cleese", "James Garner", "Albert Finney", "Richard Gere", "Jim Belushi", "Christopher Reeve", "Telly Savalas", "Chevy Chase"....
Nq178	39	Toyota, Honda, Volkswagen, Mazda, Oldsmobile, BMW, Audi, Mercedes-Benz, Cadillac, Volvo, Subaru, Chevrolet, Mercedes, Buick, Porsche, Nissan, VW, Mitsubishi, Renault, Hyundai, Isuzu, Jaguar, Suzuki, Dodge, Rolls-Royce, Pontiac, Fiat, Chevy, Saturn, Yugo, Ferrari, "Mercedes Benz", Plymouth, mustang, Beretta, Panasonic, Corvette, Nintendo, Camaro
Nq214	41	mathematics, physic, math, "political science", chemistry, "computer science", biology, sociology, "physical education", "electrical engineering", anthropology, astronomy, "social science", geology, psychology, "mechanical engineering", physiology, geography, economics, psychiatry, calculus, biochemistry, algebra, science, civics, journalism, literature, theology, "molecular biology", humanity, genetics, archaeology, nursing, anatomy, pathology, arithmetic, pharmacology, literacy, architecture, undergraduate, microbiology
Nq223	59	shirt, jacket, dress, pant, skirt, coat, sweater, T-shirt, hat, blouse, jean, trouser, sock, gown, scarf, slack, vest, boot, uniform, shoe, robe, cloth, sunglasses, clothing, outfit, glove, underwear, sneaker, blazer, jersey, costume, wig, mask, helmet, button, hair, collar, ribbon, short, belt, necktie, bra, stocking, sleeve, silk, red, pin, banner, badge, sheet, sticker, makeup, stripe, bow, logo, linen, curtain, shade, quilt
Nq292	31	barley, oat, sorghum, "feed grain", alfalfa, "soybean meal", "soybean oil", "sugar beet", maize, sunflower, "pork belly", soybean, millet, Rye, oilseed, wheat, "grain sorghum", rapeseed, canola, hay, "palm oil", durum, safflower, psyllium, "sunflower seed", flaxseed, bran, broiler, buckwheat, cantaloupe, cottonseed
Nq293	22	"Joseph Cicippio", "Terry Anderson", "Terry Waite", Cicippio, Waite, "Terry A. Anderson", "William Higgins", "John McCarthy", "Joseph James Cicippio", "Thomas Sutherland", "Brian Keenan", "Alann Steen", "Jesse Turner", "Alec Collett", "Edward Austin Tracy", "Edward Tracy", "Frank Reed", "American Terry Anderson", "Jack Mann", Buckley, westerner, "Giandomenico Picco", "Robert Polhill", "Benjamin Weir"
Nq352	8	heroin, cocaine, marijuana, narcotic, alcohol, steroid, crack, opium
Nq356	15	Saskatchewan, Alberta, Manitoba, "British Columbia", Ontario, "New Brunswick", Newfoundland, Quebec, Guangdong, "Prince Edward Island", "Nova Scotia", "Papua New Guinea", "Northwest Territories", Luzon, Mindanao
Nq396	29	sorrow, sadness, grief, anguish, remorse, indignation, insecurity, loneliness, discomfort, agony, despair, regret, heartache, dismay, shame, revulsion, angst, jubilation, humiliation, bitterness, pity, outrage, anxiety, empathy, happiness, mourning, letdown, distaste, indignity
Nq776	30	baldness, hemophilia, acne, infertility, sepsis, "cold sore", "sleeping sickness", "morning sickness", "kidney stone", "common cold", heartburn, "eye disease", "heroin addiction", osteoporosis, "pneumocystis carinii pneumonia", dwarfism, incontinence, "manic depression", atherosclerosis, "Dutch elm disease", hyperthyroidism, discoloration, "cancer death", spoilage, gonorrhea, hemorrhoid, wart, mildew, sterility, "athlete's foot"

In the dependency trees generated by Minipar, each link between two words in a dependency tree represents a direct semantic relationship. A path allows us to represent indirect semantic relationships between two content words. We name a path by concatenating dependency relationships and words along the path, excluding the words at the two ends. For the sentence in Figure 1, the path between *John* and *problem* is named: N:subj:V←find→V:obj:N→solution→N:to:N (meaning "X finds solution to Y"). The **root** of the path is *find*.

A path begins and ends with two dependency relations. We call them the two slots of the path: *SlotX* on the left-hand side and *SlotY* on the right-hand side. The words connected by the path are the fillers of the slots. For example, *John* fills the *SlotX* and *problem* fills the *SlotY* in the above example.

We extract the fillers and frequency counts of all the slots of all the paths in a parsed corpus. Table 5 shows an excerpt of the fillers of two paths. The underlying assumption of algorithm is that when the meanings of paths are similar, their corresponding sets of fillers share a large number of common words.

Richardson (1997) extracted semantic relationships (e.g., hypernym, location, material and purpose) from dictionary definitions using a parser and constructed a semantic network. He then described an algorithm that uses paths in the semantic network to compute the similarity between words. In a sense, our algorithm is a dual of Richardson's approach. While Richardson used paths as features to compute the similarity between words, we use words as features to compute the similarity of paths.

We use the notation $|p, SlotX, w|$ to denote the frequency count of word w filling in the *SlotX* of a path p, and $|p, SlotX, *|$ to denote $\sum_w |p, SlotX, w|$, and $|*, *, *|$ to denote $\sum_{p,s,w} |p, s, w|$.

Following (Lin, 1998), the mutual information between a path slot and its filler can be computed by the formula:

$$mi(p, Slot, w) = \log\left(\frac{|p, Slot, w| \times |*, Slot, *|}{|p, Slot, *| \times |*, Slot, w|}\right) \quad (1)$$

The similarity between a pair of slots: $slot_1 = (p_1, s)$ and $slot_2 = (p_2, s)$, is defined as:

$$sim(slot_1, slot_2) = \frac{\sum_{w \in T(p_1,s) \cap T(p_2,s)} mi(p_1, s, w) + mi(p_2, s, w)}{\sum_{w \in T(p_1,s)} mi(p_1, s, w) + \sum_{w \in T(p_2,s)} mi(p_2, s, w)} \quad (2)$$

where p_1 and p_2 are paths, s is a slot, $T(p_i, s)$ is the set of words that fill in the s slot of path p_i.

The similarity between a pair of paths p_1 and p_2 is defined as the geometric average of the similarities of their *SlotX* and *SlotY* slots:

$$S(p_1, p_2) = \sqrt{sim(SlotX_1, SlotX_2) \times sim(SlotY_1, SlotY_2)} \quad (3)$$

Table 6 and 7 list the top-50 most similar paths to "*X solves Y*". and "*X causes Y*" generated by our algorithm. The ones tagged with an asterisk (*) are incorrect. Most of the paths can be considered as paraphrases of the original expression.

Table 5. Sample slot fillers for two paths extracted from a newspaper corpus.

"X finds a solution to Y"		"X solves Y"	
SLOTX	SLOTY	SLOTX	SLOTY
commission	strike	committee	problem
committee	civil war	clout	crisis
committee	crisis	government	problem
government	crisis	he	mystery
government	problem	she	problem
he	problem	petition	woe
legislator	budget deficit	researcher	mystery
sheriff	dispute	sheriff	murder

Table 6. The top-50 most similar paths to "X solves Y".

Y is solved by X	X clears up Y
X resolves Y	*X creates Y
X finds a solution to Y	*Y leads to X
X tries to solve Y	*Y is eased between X
X deals with Y	X gets down to Y
Y is resolved by X	X worsens Y
X addresses Y	X ends Y
X seeks a solution to Y	*X blames something for Y
X do something about Y	X bridges Y
X solution to Y	X averts Y
Y is resolved in X	*X talks about Y
Y is solved through X	X grapples with Y
X rectifies Y	*X leads to Y
X copes with Y	X avoids Y
X overcomes Y	X solves Y problem
X eases Y	X combats Y
X tackles Y	X handles Y
X alleviates Y	X faces Y
X corrects Y	X eliminates Y
X is a solution to Y	Y is settled by X
X makes Y worse	*X thinks about Y
X irons out Y	X comes up with a solution to Y
*Y is blamed for X	X offers a solution to Y
X wrestles with Y	X helps somebody solve Y
X comes to grip with Y	*Y is put behind X

6. References

Berwick R., Abney S., and Tenny, C, editors. *Principle-Based Parsing: Computation and Psycholinguistics.* Kluwer Academic Publishers, 1991.

Chomsky N. 1995. *Minimalist Program.* MIT Press.

Dagan I, Lee L, and Pereira F., Similarity-based Methods for Word Sense Disambiguation. In *Proceedings of ACL/EACL-97,* pp.56-63. Madrid, Spain.

Harris, Z. 1985. Distributional Structure. In: Katz, J. J. (ed.) *The Philosophy of Linguistics.* New York: Oxford University Press. pp. 26-47.

Lin, D. and Pantel, P. 2001a. Induction of Semantic Classes from Natural Language Text. To appear in Proceedings of KDD-2001. San Francisco, CA.

Lin, D. and Pantel, P. 2001b. DIRT: Discovery of Inference Rules from Text. To appear in Proceedings of KDD-2001. San Francisco, CA.

Lin, D. 1998. Extracting Collocations from Text Corpora. Workshop on Computational Terminology. pp. 57-63. Montreal, Canada.

Lin, D. 1993. Parsing Without OverGeneration. In Proceedings ACL-93. pp. 112-120. Columbus, OH.

Mel'čuk, I. A. 1987. Dependency Syntax: theory and practice. State University of New York Press. Albany, NY.

Miller, G. 1990. WordNet: An Online Lexical Database. International Journal of Lexicography, 1990.

Richardson, S. D. 1997. Determining Similarity and the Inferring Relations in a Lexical Knowledge-Base. Ph.D. Thesis. The City University of New York.

Sampson, G. 1995. English for the Computer - The SUSANNE Corpus and Analytic Scheme. Clarendon Press. Oxford, England.

Table 7. The top-50 most similar paths to "*X causes Y*".

Y is caused by X	*Y contributes to X
X cause something Y	*X results from Y
X leads to Y	*X adds to Y
X triggers Y	X means Y
*X is caused by Y	*X reflects Y
*Y causes X	X creates Y
Y is blamed on X	*Y prompts X
X contributes to Y	X provoke Y
X is blamed for Y	Y reflects X
X results in Y	X touches off Y
X is the cause of Y	X poses Y
*Y leads to X	Y is sparked by X
Y results from X	*X is attributed to Y
Y is result of X	*Y is cause of X
X prompts Y	*X stems from Y
X sparks Y	*Y is blamed for X
*Y triggers X	*X is triggered by Y
X prevents Y	Y is linked to X
*X is blamed on Y	X sets off Y
Y is triggered by X	X is a factor in Y
Y is attributed to X	X exacerbates Y
X stems from Y	X eases Y
*Y results in X	Y is related to X
*X is result of Y	X is linked to Y
X fuels Y	X is responsible for Y

Linguatronic
Product-Level Speech System for Mercedes-Benz Cars

Paul Heisterkamp
DaimlerChrysler AG
Research and Technology
Speech Understanding
Wilhelm-Runge-Str. 11, D-89081 Ulm, Germany
Tel. +49 731 505 2152

Paul.Heisterkamp@DaimlerChrysler.com

1. INTRODUCTION

A recent press release (Murray 2000) indicates that many car manufacturers have announced speech recognition and voice-operated Command&Control systems for their cars, but so far have not introduced any. They are still struggling with technology, both in reliability and pricing. The article finishes by a quote from an industry person saying:

"The reality is that today's systems are still failing in a lot of different modes. [...] But the technology will get better before it reaches the market. Right now, we just don't know when that will be."

In the light of this statement, we consider it appropriate in the context of a scientific conference, to draw the attention of the speech and language community to the fact that in-car speech *is* on the market, and successfully so, since fall 1996 in Germany and since May 1999 in the USA.

2. LINGUATRONIC

In the S-Class car of 1996, Mercedes-Benz introduced the first generation of Linguatronic. Linguatronic is the brand name used in Europe of a speech dialogue system that allows completely hands-free operation of the car's mobile phone, including number dialing (with connected digit dialog), number storing, user-defined telephone directory entry name, name dialing, and directory editing. Linguatronic I has a vocabulary of about 30 speaker-independent words (digits and control words). The second version has a vocabulary of about 300 words, and, in addition, allows for operation of comfort electronics (radio, CD-player/changer, air condition etc). The system is now available for German, US English, UK English, Italian, Spanish, French and Swiss-German. Japanese and Dutch are currently under development.

Proceedings of HLT 2001, First International Conference on Human Language Technology Research, J. Allan, ed., Morgan Kaufmann, San Francisco, 2001.

3. ORGANIZATION

The basic algorithms incorporated in Linguatronic are developed by the Speech Understanding group of DaimlerChrysler Research and Technology in Ulm, Germany. These algorithms then are taken up by the Speech Processing Division of DaimlerChrysler's TEMIC business unit and put into products. These products are first marketed exclusively to the Mercedes-Benz premium brand of DaimlerChrysler, but in time, they are available to other brands and manufacturers as well. This reflects the Mercedes-Benz philosophy that safety-enhancing technology should be deployed by everybody. Thus, the speech technology from Temic is currently also available in BMW's and Audi's, with other car makers and suppliers to follow shortly with their top products..

4. TECHNOLOGY

The recognizer used in Linguatronic is speaker independent HMM-based. For the user definable telephone directory, an additional DTW recognizer is used. A key issue for speech technology in the car, noise reduction, is achieved by an integrated signal pre-processing that reduces the influence of noise and other sources of interference to improve the quality of the recognition. Furthermore, the system automatically and imperceptibly adapts itself to the characteristics of the speaker's voice or the acoustic background within vehicles. So, the key technology features are:

- Noise Robustness
- Echo Cancellation for hands-free telephone applications
- Continuous speaker independent speech recognition
- Speaker dependent recognition
- Active vocabulary of about 300 words
- Background adaptation
- Dynamically loadable vocabulary

Now, from the recognizer side, that doesn't seem too much different to what other speech companies and research groups offer. Yet, recognition accuracy is at a very high level. What is it, then, that makes the difference? Obviously, training of speech data plays a major role here, but others (e.g. the SpeechDat-Car project) have done major data gathering exercises as well. So, we'll point here to some items that are not naturally in the focus of the scientific community, *viz.* integration, co-operation and engineering.

5. INTEGRATION

All upper-level cars of the major European makers these days are equipped with a data bus system, sometimes still over copper wire, but mostly using fiber optics. The Temic system supports the most common automotive bus systems like D2B, CAN, I-Bus and in the near future MOST. This means that a multitude of devices

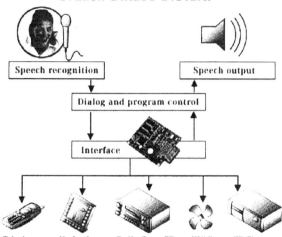

SPEECH DIALOG SYSTEM:

on the bus can be addressed and operated using a single and uniform speech dialogue module, and there is no need to put extra wiring in the car. Furthermore, the push-to-activate (PTA) button, muting of the audio and use of the car's loudspeakers are facilitated, and, very important, the same microphone can be used for both speech commands and telephone. The quality of the microphone (or an array), its characteristics and its positioning are extremely important.

6. CO-OPERATION

This kind of close integration can only be achieved in an equally close co-operation with the car manufacturer. The speech

Command&Control has to fit smoothly into the overall human-machine-interface for the driver. From the position of the PTA button or lever, via the cancellation function to the analogous behavior of speech and tactile operation of devices, everything has to be done to ensure that speech is an integrated and natural part of the interaction. Fallback modes must be made available in case speech fails. The auto maker must also be aware that even if recognition were one-hundred-percent accurate, people do not always say what they mean or know what they can say, so there will be failures.

7. ENGINEERING

And, of course, the car manufacturer also knows which price people are willing to pay. The key issue now is the engineering task to deliver a product with a certain quality standard for a certain price. Besides software solutions, Temic currently offers two harware versions of its Command&Control system for cars, one as a plug-in board the size of a credit card, the other as a self-contained box that interfaces directly to the bus and does not require any host processor. Both not only do the recognition, but also store the speech output for the dialogue. And: at a recognition rate that convinced not only Mercedes-Benz, but also others who have a reputation for quality, Linguatronic, under the label 'voice recognition' sells in the US as part of a mobile phone package for a retail price of $480.00; the majority of integrated phones in Mercedes-Benz cars in the US is ordered with this option. Up to the end of the year 2000, Temic has sold more than 170,000 units for automotive applications..

8. OUTLOOK

The scientific community is well aware that speech in cars is *the* enabling technology to interactively and selectively bring news and information to mobile environments without causing a safety hazard (cf., e.g. ElBoghdady 2000). Yet, we all have seen tides of enthusiasm and reluctance towards the real-life viability of speech technology. With telephony applications now firmly established, any discussion as to whether speech technology is a commercially viable option also for use in vehicles can be abbreviated by pointing at the Linguatronic example. Speech technology is there, and it will grow. More auto makers, but also system-providers like Bosch will soon be out with more complex applications, navigation address entry being the point in question, more cars

will have speech control as an option, and, in our area of research, we are pushing the limits of what can be done in research projects both internal and co-operative, e.g. in the DARPA Communicator.

9. REFERENCES

[1] ElBoghdady, Dina (2000): Feds fear high-tech car gear. Detnews.com, 23 January 2000.

[2] Images thanks to http://www.temic.com/speech

[3] Murray, Charles J. (2000): Automakers struggle with speech recognition technology (03 December 2000). http://www.eet.com/story/industry/systems_and_softwa re_news/OEG20001201S0109

LingWear: A Mobile Tourist Information System

Christian Fügen[1], Martin Westphal[1,3], Mike Schneider[2], Tanja Schultz[2] and Alex Waibel[2]

fuegen@ira.uka.de, westphal@de.ibm.com, {schneider, tanja, ahw}@cs.cmu.edu

[1] Interactive Systems Laboratories
University of Karlsruhe
Am Fasanengarten 5
76131 Karlsruhe, Germany
++49 721 608 4730

[2] Interactive Systems Laboratories
Carnegie Mellon University
School of Computer Science
Pittsburgh, PA 15221, USA
++1 412 268 76

ABSTRACT

In this paper, we describe LingWear, a mobile tourist information system that allows uninformed users to find their way around in foreign cities and to ask for information about sights, accommodations, and other places of interest. The user can communicate with LingWear either by means of spontaneous speech queries or via a touch screen. LingWear automatically decides whether to respond through the integrated speech synthesis or display messages. LingWear is currently available for the cities of Heidelberg and Karlsruhe. It was designed to run on wearable computer, e.g. the Xybernaut family, and is available in both Windows and Linux versions.

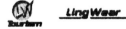 

Figure 1. Welcome Screen of LingWear for Karlsruhe.

1. INTRODUCTION

Due to the rapid development within the area of processors and memory modules, the performance of today's wearable computer is sufficient, to enable it to run processor and memory intensive applications. This makes it possible to develop user friendly multi modal user interfaces including speech recognition for wearables.

For this reason we have decided to develop LingWear, a mobile tourist information system that allows uninformed users to find their way around in foreign cities and to ask for information about sights, accommodations, and other places of interest. Hence we were able to make use of valuable information collected in the course of other projects like VODIS [9], C-STAR [3] and cooperations like DeepMap [5].

The following modules are integrated in LingWear:

- The **tour manager** presents some sights depending on the user's current location and on user's preferences (Figure 2). User preferences are handled through a user model. Sights that are currently open or closed are marked with special icons.

- The **navigation module** helps the user to find specified places in the city (Figure 3). It searches for the shortest path between the user's current and desired locations. The route segments can be retrieved step by step. In the near future a GPS-Module will be integrated to enhance this capability.

- The **information module** provides information about sights or other places of interests saved in the database (Figure 4). The information is presented to the user by images and short text descriptions.

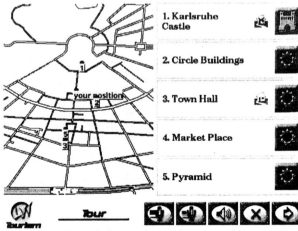

Figure 2. Screen shot of the tour mode.

Proceedings of HLT 2001, First International Conference on Human Language Technology Research, J. Allan, ed., Morgan Kaufmann, San Francisco, 2001.

[3] Now with: European Speech Research – IBM Deutschland Entwicklung GmbH

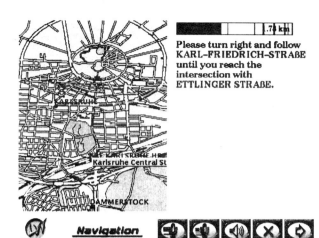

Please turn right and follow
KARL–FRIEDRICH–STRAßE
until you reach the
intersection with
ETTLINGER STRAßE.

Karlsruhe Central St

DAMMERSTOCK

Navigation

Figure 3. Screen shot of the navigation mode.

KARLSRUHE CASTLE

The Karlsruhe Palace was built in
1715 as the residence of Margrave
Karl Wilhelm of Baden–Durlach. It
served for 200 years as the seat of
government of the Baden dynasty.
In 1849 Grand Duke Leopold was
thrown out of the palace by Baden
revolutionaires. It finally left the
monarchy in November 1918.
Karlsruhe Palace was completely
destroyed by air raids, during
September 1944.

Information

Figure 4. Screen shot of the information mode.

- The **translation module** helps foreign visitors to communicate with local residents, as required when making hotel reservations, physician-visits etc. (Figure 6 and Figure 7). It accepts user queries in either English or German, and can produce translations in any of the target languages, English, German and Japanese. The translation output is both displayed and spoken.

We have currently modified our system to also support medical queries (Figure 7). Such a capability allows for example an English-speaking patient on vacation in Germany to describe his symptoms to a German-speaking doctor, and receive in return instructions and other medical advice.

2. MODULES OF LINGWEAR

The following figure shows the architecture of LingWear and the dependencies of the component modules:

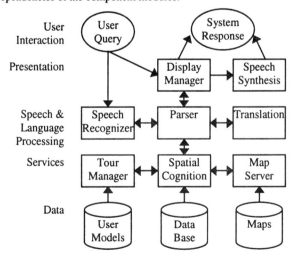

Figure 5. Module dependencies of LingWear.

2.1 User Interaction and Presentation

User queries, given by keyboard or via touch sensitive display, are processed by the display manager. Speech user queries are

processed directly by the speech recognizer. The results of both components are passed to the parser for further analysis.

The Display Manager is responsible for presenting the current status of the system to the user in suitable form. In addition it arranges pictures, texts, and icons with given layouts and depending on their size on the display. The output can take place either in HTML or directly in Tcl/Tk.

Text information is also synthesized via an integrated speech synthesis system. For English and German we are currently using the speech synthesis system Festival [1], and for Japanese the Fujitsu VoiceSeries provided by Animo Ltd.

2.2 Speech and Language Processing

2.2.1 Speech Recognizer

The speech recognition engine used in LingWear is a part of the Janus Recognition Toolkit [6]. The full continuous English and German system uses approx. 2,500 context-dependent acoustic models with 32 Gaussians per model. Cepstral Mean Normalization is used to compensate for channel variations. In addition to the mean-subtracted mel-cepstral coefficients, the first and second order derivatives are also calculated. Linear Discriminant Analysis is applied to reduce feature dimensionality to 24, followed by a speaker-based maximum likelihood signal adaptation. With all optimisations the recognizer runs in nearly real time. To reduce the waiting periods for the user, the recognizer works in run-on mode.

We are using a class-based trigram language model to cover a vocabulary of approx. 5,000 words. Classes are introduced for places, streets, hotels, and all other location-dependent and some location-independent types like numbers. This allows us to easily switch between different cities by only providing location-dependent lists for the language model classes. More work has to be done for providing dictionary entries for these lists, especially for English pronunciations of proper names, like German street names. For this purpose we are using Festival together with some post processing scripts to remove misspellings at word composita boundaries.

To support also medical user queries, a domain specific, class-based language model was built. In addition to the medical domain, information for switching between different modes, e.g.

into Japanese:

ダブルの部屋はおいくらですか？

 the meaning is:

how much is a double room

Figure 6. Screen shot of the translation mode.

 into English:

I will prescribe an antifungal spray for you.

 the meaning is:

Ich werden Ihnen ein Anti–Pilzspray verschreiben

Figure 7. Screen shot of the medical translation mode.

"Switch to Navigation", is included in the language model. Wherever a model switch occurs, the appropriate search object is selected.

2.2.2 Parser

The parser analyses the hypothesis received from the speech recognizer and, according to the content of the hypothesis, decides which further components are needed to produce the system response. In addition, clarification dialogues are generated for underspecified user queries.

We are using SOUP as a parser, which was developed at the Carnegie Mellon University. It is a stochastic, chart-based, top-down parser, which was designed for real-time analysis of spoken language with very large, multi-domain semantic grammars [8]. SOUP achieves flexibility by encoding context-free grammars, specified for example in the Java Speech Grammar Format, as probabilistic recursive transition networks. Robustness is achieved by allowing skipping of input words at any position and producing ranked interpretations that may consists of multiple parse trees.

In LingWear, modular semantic grammars are used to model system knowledge. Semantic grammars are known to be robust against ungrammaticalities in spontaneous speech and recognition errors. However, they are usually hard to expand to cover new domains. For this reason we are using modular semantic grammars. Each sub-grammar covers the dialogue acts required for one sub-domain. An additional grammar provides cross-domain dialogue acts such as common openings and closings. All grammars share one library with common concepts, such as time expressions. Also location-dependent proper names are located in a separate grammar file. This makes extensions to new locations straightforward. Each grammar is associated with a special tag that reflects the domain of that grammar. Currently we are using tags for the domains navigation (NAV), travel planning (TPL), hotel reservation (HTL), medical (MED) and mode switching (SWI).

The output of the parser is converted to typed feature structures as defined in [2], which simplifies processing and interpretation by other components of the system. The notion of a type in a feature structure refers to the fact that every feature structure is assigned to a type from a type hierarchy. Moreover, for every type, a set of appropriate features is specified so that type inference is possible. Naturally, feature structures are well-suited for representing partial information. They do not adequately represent ambiguity, however. For this reason, we are using underspecified feature structures as introduced in [4]. In addition to feature structures, they are able to leave disjunctions unresolved.

Since underspecified feature structures represent unresolved disjunctions, they provide a good point of departure for generating clarification dialogues.

2.2.3 Translation

The Translation Module was developed mainly during the C-STAR-II-Project and integrated into LingWear. Within C-STAR-II, we have been developing a translation system for the broad domain of travel planning, including hotel reservation.

We have extended our system by grammars for covering also translations in the medical domain. Currently only a small set of translations are possible, but the grammars are constantly being extended.

Both translations are based on Interlingua as an interchange format, and make use of modular semantic grammars, which allows us to easily expand our system to new languages. Such grammars have also been shown to be effective in providing accurate translation for limited domains [10]. This gives us the possibility to use once more the SOUP parser. The assignment of domain tags to different sub-grammars allows us to switch easily between navigation, global translation, and medical translation mode.

2.3 Services

The spatial cognition, together with the map server and the tour manager are used for all navigation and information queries.

The tour manager presents some sights depending on the user's location and on his preferences. When starting LingWear, the user is asked for his name, and when using LingWear for the first time, for his preferences as well. Preferences may include sites like churches, museums, bars and restaurants. Each object in the database is also assigned an importance factor. When suggesting sites, both importance and distance from the user's current location are taken into account.

The spatial cognition is responsible for all navigation queries. It is the interface to the database, which includes all objects like sights and restaurants, together with optional short descriptions, pictures, and hours of operation. The location of all objects is also saved in the database. The system's current mode determines what information is returned to the parser module.

The map server is responsible for drawing the desired portions of the map. Desired route segments within the map are shown highlighted. It is also possible to include additional text information and icons in the map, for an easy identification of specified objects by the user.

3. COMMUNICATION

As shown in Figure 8, a communication server (ComServer) is integrated into the system for the communication between the different modules. Modules can connect to this ComServer via socket with a given ID. After connection they have to specify an entry procedure, which is called every time a message is sent to a module specified by ID.

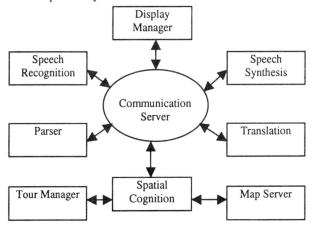

Figure 8. Communication between the modules.

Although all messages must go through the communication server, our central communication has several advantages over a distributed communication or communication via a bus:

- All connected modules are known by the ComServer, so error messages can be returned, if a module is not reachable.

- The communication between the modules is direct. So that the message is only sent to the module given by the ID. Grouping of IDs to virtual IDs is also allowed, for broadcasting one message to a group of modules. This is necessary for example when switching between different modes.

- The direct communications reduces processor load, because unaddressed modules do not have to analyze the message.

The databases and the map server are connected directly to the spatial cognition.

The communication format between the different modules is FIPA (Foundation of Intelligent Physical Agents) [7].

3.1 Communication Flow

An incoming English or German speech user query is processed by the corresponding recognizer and then transferred via the ComServer to the parser.

The parser analyses the hypothesis by producing a parse tree and, depending on the parse tree, the typed feature structure. Each user query belongs to a specific use case, which means, that two features are used to specify a user query: the grammar ID tag and the use case. In each mode besides the mode switching grammar, only the grammars belonging to the mode are active.

Depending on the grammar ID and the use case, the modules involved in producing the system response are defined.

- For navigation queries the spatial cognition is asked for the shortest way between two desired locations on the map. The path is highlighted and transferred, together with a generated description of the way, to the display manager.

- For information queries the spatial cognition is asked for information about the specified objects. All available information, e.g. text, images, etc., is collected and given to the display manager.

- If the user wants to know what there is to see around here, then the tour manager is asked for some objects depending on the user's current location and preferences defined in the user model. The objects are ordered by descendent ratings, whereby already-visited objects are left out.

- The translation becomes accessible when switching to the translation mode. Each user query, apart from queries to switch between different modes, will be treated as a query for the translation and sent to the translation module. The translation module produces the results for all available languages in parallel, which are sent directly to the display manager.

4. CONCLUSION AND FUTURE WORK

We have shown a system that allows uninformed users to find their way around in foreign cities and to ask for information about sights, accommodations, and other places of interest. The medical translation expedites a visit to a German doctor in the case of illness or injury.

The system is now in a state, where we can pass it to users, who are unfamiliar with the system, for real user studies. For this purpose two additional modules are already integrated into LingWear:

- A data collection module stores all recordings with the speaker information and the hypothesis produced by the speech recognizer.

- A history module logs all messages, which are sent through the system into one file. An integrated simulation component allows us to rerun a complete log file for error analysis and to make improvements of the system visible.

The system is continually updated and improved. New approaches in speech recognition, such as integrating new words into a running system and decoding along context free grammars will be integrated as soon as they have proven effective. We would expect to get a large gain in speed and accuracy by decoding along context free grammars, because of the more limited search space and because no additional parser is needed.

Unsupervised adaptation of the systems acoustic component in order to adapt to the current user will be integrated soon. As well as archiving the adaptation parameters together with the user preferences in the user model.

The display manger will be extended by a multimodal component, which detects user input via the touch screen; e.g., handwriting and other gestures. This would make it possible to specify new objects in the map and also allows the addition of user comments to objects, such as "This is my favourite restaurant".

For automatical output of the route segments while the user is walking, a GPS module will be integrated. This also allows us to give additional information about sights and other interesting objects along the route.

One major disadvantage of the system are the databases with the location-dependent information, because this information must be collected manually. Therefore a module should be integrated, which builds automatically the location-dependent databases, including images, sight descriptions, and new dictionary and language model entries for streets and other proper names. This could be done directly via Internet by connecting to a city's web server.

5. ACKNOWLEDGMENTS

We would like to thank Céline Morel for the graphic design of LingWear and Florian Metze and Thomas Schaaf for training the English and German recognizers. Our thanks also to Donna Gates, Chad Langley, Alon Lavie, Lori Levin, Kay Peterson, Alicia Tribble, and Dorcas Wallace for writing and integrating the medical translation modules and grammars.

6. REFERENCES

[1] A. W. Black, P. Taylor: *The Festival Speech Synthesis System: system documentation*, Technical Report HCR/TR-83, Human Communication Research Centre, University of Edinburgh, Scotland, UK, 1997. Available at http://www.cstr.ed.ac.uk/projects/festival.html.

[2] B. Carpenter: *The Logic of Typed Feature Structures*, Cambridge University Press, 1992.

[3] C-STAR: Consortium for Speech Translation Advanced Research. Homepage: http://www.c-star.org.

[4] M. Denecke: *A Programmable Multi-Blackboard Architecture for Dialogue Processing System*, in Proc. of the Workshop on Spoken Dialogue Systems, ACL/EACL-1997.

[5] DeepMap: cooperation with the European Media Lab (EML), Heidelberg. More information at http://www.eml.org/english/research/deepmap/deepmap.html

[6] M. Finke, P. Geutner, H. Hild, T. Kemp, K. Ries, M. Westphal: *The Karlsruhe-Verbmobil Speech Recognition Engine*, in Proc. of the IEEE International Conference on Acoustics, Speech and Signal Processing, ICASSP-97, Munich, Germany, 1997.

[7] FIPA (Foundation of Intelligent Physical Agents) Homepage: http://www.fipa.org

[8] M. Gavaldà: *SOUP: A Parser for Real-World Spontaneous Speech*, in Proc. of the 6th International Workshop on Parsing Technologies, IWPT-2000, Trento, Italy, February 2000.

[9] P. Geutner, M. Denecke, U. Meier, M. Westphal and A. Waibel: *Conversational Speech System For On Board Car Navigation And Assistance*, in Proc. Of ICSLP '98, Adelaide, Australia, 1998.

[10] M. Woszczyna, M. Broadhead, D. Gates, M. Gavaldà, A. Lavie, L. Levin, A. Waibel: *A Modular Approach to Spoken Language Translation for Large Domains*, in Proc. of AMTA-1998.

[11] J. Yang, W. Yang, M. Denecke, A. Waibel: *Smart Sight: A Tourist Assistant System*, 3rd Inter-national Symposium on Wearable Computers, ISWC-1999, San Francisco, California, October 1999.

Listen-Communicate-Show (LCS): Spoken Language Command of Agent-based Remote Information Access

Jody J. Daniels and Benjamin Bell
Lockheed Martin Advanced Technology Laboratories
1 Federal Street, A&E 3W
Camden, NJ 08102

{jdaniels, bbell@atl.lmco.com}

ABSTRACT

Listen-Communicate-Show (LCS) is a new paradigm for human interaction with data sources. We integrate a spoken language understanding system with intelligent mobile agents that mediate between users and information sources. We have built and will demonstrate an application of this approach called LCS-Marine. Using LCS-Marine, tactical personnel can converse with their logistics system to place a supply or information request. The request is passed to a mobile, intelligent agent for execution at the appropriate database. Requestors can also instruct the system to notify them when the status of a request changes or when a request is complete. We have demonstrated this capability in several field exercises with the Marines and are currently developing applications of this technology in new domains.

Keywords

Spoken language understanding, agents, dialogue management.

1. INTRODUCTION

An LCS system listens for information requests, communicates both with the user and networked information resources, and shows a tailored visualization to the individual user. The LCS-Marine system employs a spoken language understanding system (SLS) for assisting the user in placing a request and mobile, intelligent agents for information access to implement the LCS paradigm. The SLS converses with the user to generate a request or to check status, amend, or cancel an existing request. Once sufficient information is obtained from the user, the SLS launches an agent to accomplish the requested task. The agent accesses the appropriate databases via whatever network services are available (including existing tactical communications networks). Once the agent's tasks are complete, it returns to the SLS, which generates an appropriate response to the user. The response may be visual, verbal, or a combination, depending on the available devices.

Proceedings of HLT 2001, First International Conference on Human Language Technology Research, J. Allan, ed., Morgan Kaufmann, San Francisco, 2001.

2. SYSTEM OVERVIEW

The LCS-Marine system consists of four major components: an SLS, a collection of agents for information access, real-world operational databases, and communications networks to connect the user to the SLS and the agents to the databases. The underlying architecture for the system is the MIT Galaxy II conversational architecture [3]. It is a distributed, component-based middleware product designed to be "plug and play". Specialized servers handle specific tasks, such as translating audio data to text. All Galaxy II-compliant servers communicate with each other through a central server known as the Hub. The Hub manages flow control, handles traffic among distributed servers, and provides state maintenance.

In the SLS, speech is sent from the Audio I/O server to the Recognizer. The top *n* recognitions are then parsed, prior context added, and processed using the Natural Language (NL) servers (Frame Construction and Context Tracking) to verify the new input's validity and context. The Turn Manager (TM) determines how to proceed with the conversations and generates a response. NL (Language Generation) converts it to text and the Synthesis server generates the verbal response. The audio server then speaks the waveform file to the user. We customize the various servers to work with domain specific issues and application-specific information and training. Figure 1 shows our LCS architecture.

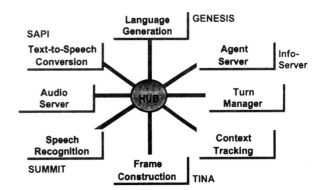

Figure 1. The LCS-Marine architecture.

We have integrated an additional server into the architecture to support information access—an Agent server. The Agent server manages a collection of agents that can be tasked to accomplish a variety of missions, including migration to distant machines with possibly different operating systems to gather information or to monitor and report events [2].

Typically, the Agent server receives its tasking from the TM and supplies the TM with information from the data source(s). For persistent tasks, the Agent server becomes the initiator of a dialogue to inform the user of specific events by passing agent reports to the TM. When a visual display is present, the Agent server will dispatch an agent to pass the updated information to the display machine.

For the LCS-Marine application our agents had to interact with a logistics database that could be between one to one hundred miles away. We later describe how our agents were able to reach this live database over the tactical communication links available.

Users interact with the LCS-Marine system using the voice capture device appropriate to their organization (telephone, cell phone, tactical radios, computer headsets, etc.).

3. MARINE COMBAT SERVICE SUPPORT PROBLEM

Marines work in a dynamic, fluid environment where requirements and priorities are constantly subject to change. Under current operations, it might take up to 72 hours before a Marine in a Combat Service Support Operations Center (CSSOC) can confirm with a requesting unit that their order is in the logistics system. This is due to a lack of resources available to the tactical units as well as a difficulty in turning logistics data into information to enable timely analysis and decision making. For Marines conducting tactical operations, these restrictions and limited visibility into the supply chain hamper logistics planning, decision, execution, and assessment. Figure 2 shows the various echelons involved in tactical Marine logistics operations. It is noteworthy that tactical units have no organic means of accessing the logistical databases other than via radio contact with personnel at the CSSOC.

The focus of the LCS-Marine project is to provide Marines in the field with this missing visibility into the supply chain. By using standard radio protocols and a common form, Marines can now converse with a system that understands their task and end goal and can assist them in getting both the information and supplies they need. Figure 3 shows a sample of the Rapid Request form, used when placing an order.

Supporting the LCS-Marine domain required understanding and using proper radio protocols to communicate. It required the system to understand call signs, military times, grid coordinates, and special ordinance nomenclature. Additionally, to fully support the dynamic environment, LCS-Marine needed the ability to understand and translate usages of the military phonetic alphabet. This alphabet is used to spell difficult or unusual words. For example, to give the point of contact for the request as Sergeant Frew, the user could say: " P O C is Sergeant I spell Foxtrot Romeo Echo Whiskey over." LCS-Marine would convert the phonetic words to the proper letter combination. This way the vocabulary is potentially much larger than that used for system training.

Supporting the dynamic aspects of the Marine environment, the system is speaker independent. This is critical in applications where the user may change and there is no additional time for training the system for a new operator.

The recognizer is trained on the domain vocabulary, but not on individual operator voices. The system also fully supports natural, conversational dialogue, i.e., the recognizer expects utterances at a normal rate of speech and the speaker does not need to enunciate each syllable.

It is important to note that the amount of time spent training personnel to use the LCS-Marine system is generally less than 10 minutes. After a short introduction, the user is shown a sample dialogue for familiarization. The user is also given information about meta-instructions – how to start over or to clear their previous statement – before they begin operation.

4. OPERATIONAL EVALUATION

To measure the effectiveness of the LCS paradigm under operational conditions—real users placing real requests, accessing a live database, and using existing communications links—we conducted a series of Integrated Feasibility Experiments (IFE). The IFEs ranged from a pilot study that featured scripted dialogue, replicated databases, and testing in the lab with prior military personnel, to field experiments where active duty Marines used the system operationally over a series of days as their sole means of interaction with the logistics system for rapid requests. We tested the system's support of placing and checking on requests for ammunition (Class V), fuels (Class III), and subsistence (Class I) supplies. More on the experimentation protocols can be found in [1] and [4].

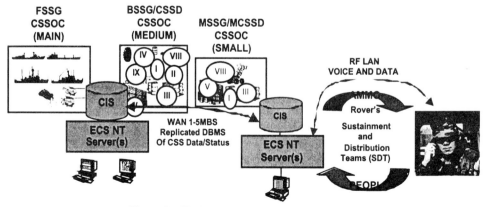

Figure 2. The Marine logistics ordering chain.

236

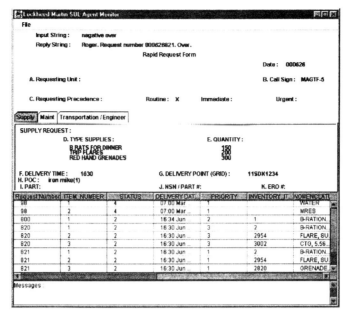

Figure 3. Partially Complete Rapid Request Form along with a portion of the database.

Over the course of the IFE process we were able to experiment with differing server configurations as well as varying communications linkages between servers. The most recent IFE (December 2000) used the server layout shown in Figure 4.

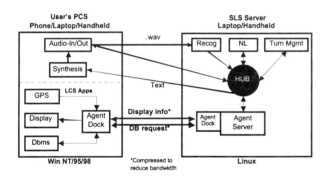

Figure 4. The physical LCS-Marine server layout.

The ideal configuration of the system would have a Marine using their organic communications system calling in to a remote location and communicating with the SLS there. This would not add any additional cost or hardware to the existing Marine infrastructure. This operational layout is depicted in Figure 5. Unfortunately, the current tactical radio, the Single Channel Ground and Airborne Radio System (SINCGARS), can create a large amount of channel noise, which alters or distorts the acoustic signal. Current recognizers can not yet compensate for this distortion, although there is active research into solving this problem.

We used a second operational layout to test the system and get operator feedback on using a spoken language understanding interface. This layout is depicted in Figure 6. In this layout, we required the user to beat the same location as the entire SLS system and the agents migrated over the SINCGARS data link

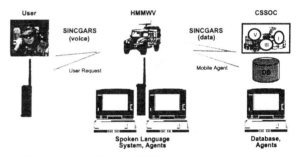

Figure 5. The ideal LCS-Marine operational layout.

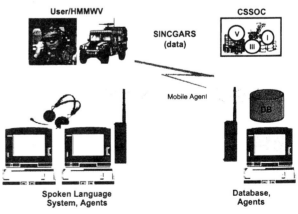

Figure 6. The LCS-Marine actual operational layout.

to reach the logistics database. The recognizer still had to contend with the issue of a noisy and dynamic background, but the acoustic distortion was eliminated.

237

5. CONCLUSION

We have built a system that integrates a spoken language understanding system with a mobile, intelligent agent system that allows users in a hostile acoustic environment to place and access data requests via a conversational interface. LCS-Marine is speaker independent and requires little training. The time to accomplish a task is significantly lower than the manual input method it seeks to enhance, but it can still be improved. Being able to rapidly access, insert, modify, and delete requests gives the users greater visibility into the supply system.

6. ACKNOWLEDGMENTS

Thanks to members of the LCS team: James Denny, Jerry Franke, Ray Hill, Bob Jones, Steve Knott, Dan Miksch, Kathy Stiller and Mike Thomas. This research was supported by DARPA contract N66001-98-D-8507 and Naval contract N47406-99-C-7033.

7. REFERENCES

[1] Daniels, J. Integrating a Spoken Language System with Agents for Operational Information Access. In *Proc.. of Innovative Applications of Artificial Intelligence (IAAI-2000)*, August, 2000, Austin, TX.

[2] McGrath, S., Chacón, D., and Whitebread, K. Intelligent Mobile Agents in the Military Domain. In *Proc.. Of Autonomous Agents 2000 Workshop on Agents in Industry*. Barcelona, Spain.

[3] Seneff, S., Lau, R., and Polifroni, J. 1999. Organization, Communication, and Control in the GALAXY-II Conversational System. In *Proc.. of Eurospeech '98*. Budapest, Hungary.

[4] Stibler, K., and Denny, J. A Three-tiered Evaluation Approach for Interactive Spoken Dialogue Systems. In *Proc.. of the Human Language Technology Conference HLT-2001*, Mar, 2001, San Diego, CA.

Mandarin-English Information (MEI):
Investigating Translingual Speech Retrieval

Helen Meng,[1] Berlin Chen,[2] Sanjeev Khudanpur,[3] Gina-Anne Levow,[4] Wai-Kit Lo,[1] Douglas Oard,[4]
Patrick Schone,[5] Karen Tang,[6] Hsin-Min Wang[2] and Jianqiang Wang[4]

The Chinese University of Hong Kong,[1] Academia Sinica,[2] Johns Hopkins University,[3]
University of Maryland at College Park,[4] US Department of Defense,[5] Princeton University[6]
Phone: +852.2609.8327
[1]hmmeng@se.cuhk.edu.hk

ABSTRACT

This paper describes the Mandarin-English Information (MEI) project, where we investigated the problem of cross-language spoken document retrieval (CL-SDR), and developed one of the first English-Chinese CL-SDR systems. Our system accepts an entire English news story (text) as query, and retrieves relevant Chinese broadcast news stories (audio) from the document collection. Hence this is a cross-language and cross-media retrieval task. We applied a multi-scale approach to our problem, which unifies the use of phrases, words and subwords in retrieval. The English queries are translated into Chinese by means of a dictionary-based approach, where we have integrated phrase-based translation with word-by-word translation. Untranslatable named entities are transliterated by a novel subword translation technique. The multi-scale approach can be divided into three subtasks – multi-scale query formulation, multi-scale audio indexing (by speech recognition) and multi-scale retrieval. Experimental results demonstrate that the use of phrase-based translation and subword translation gave performance gains, and multi-scale retrieval outperforms word-based retrieval.

Keywords

Cross-language, spoken document retrieval, English-Chinese

1. INTRODUCTION

Mandarin-English Information (MEI) is a research project conducted in the Johns Hopkins University Summer Workshop 2000. We have developed one of the first English-Chinese cross-language spoken document retrieval (CL-SDR) systems. Our objective is to develop technologies for cross-language and cross-media information retrieval. Massive quantities of audio and multimedia content are becoming increasingly available in the global information infrastructures – www.real.com in mid-March 2001 listed over 2500 Internet-accessible radio and television stations. Of these, over a third were broadcasting in languages other than English. Monolingual speech retrieval is now practical, as evidenced by services such as SpeechBot (speechbot.research.compaq.com), and it is clear that there is a potential demand for CL-SDR if effective techniques can be developed. Since English and Mandarin Chinese are projected to be the two predominant languages of the Internet user population,[1] we have selected this language pair in our investigation of cross-language spoken document retrieval techniques. As multimedia content continues to grow in the global information infrastructure, we need to develop technologies which enable the user to retrieve personally-relevant content on-demand, and across the barriers of language and media. Possible applications of this work include audio and video browsing, spoken document retrieval, automated routing of information, and automatically alerting the user when special events occur.

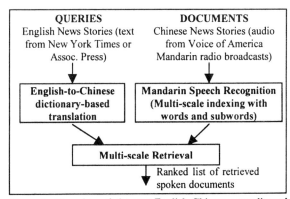

Figure 1. Overview of the our English-Chinese cross-lingual spoken document retrieval system. In this task, the query is formed from an entire English news story (text) from the New York Times or Associated Press. The spoken documents are Mandarin news stories (audio) from Voice of America news broadcasts. Multi-scale retrieval of the spoken documents is evaluated based on the relevance of the ranked list of spoken documents retrieved for each query.

The MEI task involves the use of an entire English newswire story (text) as query, to retrieve relevant Mandarin Chinese[2] radio broadcast news stories (audio) in the document collection. Such a retrieval context is termed *query-by-example*. As illustrated in Figure 1, MEI integrates speech recognition, machine translation,

Proceedings of HLT 2001, First International Conference on Human Language Technology Research, J. Allan, ed., Morgan Kaufmann, San Francisco, 2001.

---

[1] Source: Global Reach, 2000.
[2] Mandarin is the official Chinese dialect.

and information retrieval technologies for English-Chinese CL-SDR.

Our work demonstrates the use of a *multi-scale paradigm* for English-Chinese CL-SDR. The paradigm leverages off of our knowledge about the linguistic and acoustic-phonetic properties related to English and Chinese. We unify multi-scale units for retrieval, and these units include phrases, words as well as subwords (Chinese characters and syllables). Our multi-scale paradigm aims to alleviate problems related to English-Chinese CL-SDR, such as:

(i) *Multiplicity in Translation* – dictionary-based term-by-term translation may produce multiple translation alternatives, or no translations, e.g. for proper names. The use of phrases can often resolve translation ambiguity, e.g. "human rights" as a phrase has one translation; but "human" has about thirty translations, rights has about seven and together they form over two hundred translation alternatives for "human rights". The use of phonetic translation can help address the out-of-vocabulary problem in translation, e.g. Kosovo becomes /ke suo fu/ (科索沃), and its *subword translation* (pinyin transcription) can be utilized for SDR.

(ii) *Open vocabulary in recognition* – indexing spoken documents with word-based speech recognition is constrained to the recognizer's vocabulary. Out-of-vocabulary words (OOV) cannot be indexed by this method. Since Mandarin Chinese can be fully represented by about 400 base syllables or 6000 characters,[3] we can obtain full phonological / lexical coverage of the spoken documents using syllables / characters for indexing.

(iii) *Ambiguity in Chinese homophones* – each Chinese character is pronounced as a single syllable, and the mapping is many-to-many. Hence there are many Chinese homophones, which can cause word-level confusions in SDR. For example, the bi-syllable word pronounced as /fu shu/ may be 富庶 (meaning "rich"), 負數 ("negative number"), 復數 ("complex number" or "plural"), and 覆述 ("repeat"). Homophones are often confused with one another during speech recognition, and the use of syllables for retrieval offers a solution to such recognition errors.

(iv) *Ambiguity in Chinese word tokenization* – the Chinese word contains one or more characters, with no word delimiter. Word tokenization has much ambiguity, which can cause word-level mismatches between queries and documents in retrieval. Consider the following character string with at least two plausible word segmentations:

這一晚　會　如常　舉行

(Meaning: It will take place tonight as usual.)

這一　晚會　如常　舉行

(Meaning: The evening banquet will take place as usual.)

This problem can be addressed by retrieval based on overlapping character n-grams.

---

[3] According to the GB-2312 character set.

(v) *Speech recognition errors* – speech recognition output is imperfect. Errors may be caused by OOV words or acoustic confusions among in-vocabulary words (especially with respect to homophones). SDR based on syllables can improve robustness with respect to recognition errors in retrieval.

As can be seen, our multi-scale paradigm involves the use of variable-sized units. Query translation involves the translation of English *phrases* to reduce the translation ambiguity. Subsequent retrieval is based on the translated words. In addition, we also use *overlapping character n-grams*, where the overlap aims to handle tokenization ambiguity, and the n-gram serves to capture some sequential (lexical) constraints. Since each character is pronounced as a syllable in Chinese, overlapping character n-grams can be converted to *overlapping syllable n-grams* for retrieval. As mentioned above, the use of syllables can handle the OOV problem in recognition, as well as ambiguity due to Chinese homophones. Characters and syllables are subword units for the Chinese language. Hence our multi-scale approach unifies phrases, words and subwords for English-Chinese cross-language spoken document retrieval problem.

2. THE TDT COLLECTION

We used the Topic Detection and Tracking (TDT) Collection for this work. TDT is a DARPA-sponsored program where participating sites tackle tasks such as identifying the first time a story is reported on a given topic; or grouping similar topics from audio and textual streams of newswire data. In recent years, TDT has focused primarily on performing such tasks in both English and Mandarin Chinese. The task that we tackle in the MEI project is not part of TDT, because we are performing retrospective retrieval, which permits knowledge of the statistics for the entire document collection. Nevertheless, the TDT collection serves as a valuable resource for our work. The TDT multi-lingual collection includes English and Mandarin news text as well as (audio) broadcast news. Most of the Mandarin audio data are furnished with word transcriptions produced by the Dragon automatic speech recognition system. All news stories are exhaustively tagged with event-based topic labels, which serves as the relevance judgements for performance evaluation of our CL-SDR work. We used the TDT-2 corpus as our development test set, and TDT-3 as our evaluation test. Table 1 describes the content in these collections.

	TDT-2 (Dev set)	TDT-3 (Eval set)
English news (New York Times or Associated Press)	17 topics, variable # of exemplars	56 topics, variable # of exemplars
Mandarin audio news (Voice of America)	2265 stories, 46.0 hours	3371 stories, 98.4 hours

Table 1. Statistics of TDT-2 and TDT-3: our development and evaluation data sets. (The Mandarin audio documents are accompanied by recognized words from the Dragon system).

3. THE MULTI-SCALE PARADIGM

This section describes our multi-scale paradigm in detail. It is divided into several sub-tasks – query formulation, audio indexing and retrieval. As described earlier, we make use of phrases, words, overlapping character n-grams and overlapping syllable n-grams in retrieval. We mainly use subword bigrams since previous work (Kwok and Grunfeld, 1996) (Wang 2000) (Meng et al., 2000) indicated that bigrams are most effective (among the different n-grams) for retrieval.

3.1 Multi-scale Query Formulation

3.1.1 Query Term Selection

In the MEI task, the query consists of an *entire* English news story. Such queries tend to be long, and not all query terms are important for retrieval. The first step in query formulation is to select terms from the query exemplar.[4] First we excluded all stopwords, based on the English default stopword list used by the InQuery retrieval engine (Callan et al. 1992). Then we ranked all of the terms in the exemplar and all the single word components of multi-word units according to how well they distinguish the exemplar from a background model. This model is formed from the terms of approximately one thousand temporally earlier documents in the English collection from which the exemplars were drawn. We used a χ^2 test in a manner similar to that used in (Schuetze et al., 1995) to select these terms. The pure χ^2 statistic is symmetric, assigning equal value to terms that help to recognize known relevant stories and those that help to reject the other contemporaneous stories. We limited our choice to terms that were positively associated with the known relevant training stories.

3.1.2 Query Translation

Named entities have been tagged by the BBN Identifinder (Bikel et al. 1997) system in our English query exemplars. Examples of named entities include "U.N. Security Council," and "partners of Goldman, Sachs and Co." Additional multi-word expressions (e.g. "human rights", "guiding principles", and "best interests") are identified in our bilingual term list (BTL), which we formed by combining LDC's English-Chinese bilingual term list with translated extracted from the CETA (Chinese-English Translation Assistance) dictionaries. Our BTL has nearly 200,000 total English terms corresponding to 400,000 translation pairs. The multi-word expressions (from Identifinder or our BTL) are treated as a "single term" in our term selection and query formulation procedures.

We traverse the tagged English text exemplar and, for each identified term, if it is on the list of selected terms, we translate it. This approach preserves term frequency information in the query. Translation proceeds on the phrasal scale, word scale, as well as the subword scale. For tagged named entities, we first attempt to translate the entity as a single unit by lookup in our BTL. If the named entity is not found, we translate the individual words one by one. For example, "security council" is present in the bilingual term list and can be translated directly; "First Bank of Siam", however, is not present and is translated word by word. All other terms are translated directly by searching the bilingual term list. We also incorporated a stemming backoff translation procedure to maximize matching with the translation dictionary (Oard et al., 2001).

3.1.3 Named Entity Transliteration

Despite the use of an extensive BTL for phrasal and word-based translation, there will inevitably be untranslatable terms. These are often named entities (names of people, places, locations and organizations), since we are dealing with a topically diverse domain. These untranslatable named entities need to be salvaged since they tend to be important for retrieval. Chinese translations of foreign names often strive to attain phonetic similarity, though the mapping may be inconsistent. For example, consider the translation of "Kosovo" – sampling Chinese newspapers in China, Taiwan, Hong Kong and Singapore produces the following translations:

科索沃 /ke-suo-wo/, 科索佛 /ke-suo-fo/,

科索夫 /ke-suo-fu/, 科索伏 /ke-suo-fu/, or

柯索佛 /ke-suo-fo/.

To this end, we have developed a technique for *subword translation*. This is another research contribution in the MEI project. In designing the subword translation procedure, we applied our knowledge in acoustic-phonetics and phonology related to both English and Chinese, we also applied machine learning techniques and other techniques used in speech recognition. The aim of subword translation is to transliterate named entities in the queries and represent them in the phonetic space, and if the document collection is also indexed in the phonetic space, we can perform matching in the phonetic space for retrieval. In this way, we salvage the use of named entities which are otherwise untranslatable and cannot be used for retrieval. Details of this technique are described in (Meng et al., 2001). We provide a succinct description in the following.

Figure 2 presents an overview of the named entity transliteration process. We examine units in our query exemplar that are tagged by the BBN Identifinder system, and those absent from our translation dictionary (the BTL) are processed by our transliteration system. As shown in Figure 2, subword translation begins by discriminating between Chinese names and non-Chinese names. Chinese names are often represented in English by means of their syllable pinyin transcription, e.g. Diaoyutai consists of the three syllables *diao, yu and tai*. As mentioned, there is a finite set of pinyin syllables, so identification of Chinese names is accomplished by string matching, with reference to the syllable inventory. Non-Chinese names are modeled as a single category, which is an over-generalization, as we will see later. We attempt to look up the English pronunciation of the non-Chinese names.[5] Failing that, we generate the English pronunciation automatically from the spelling, by the application of letter-to-sound rules acquired by the transformation-based error-driving learning technique (Brill, 1994). For example, we can generate the English phoneme pronunciation /kk rr ih ss tt aa ff er/ from the spelling "Christopher" (see Figure 2).

---

[4] These may be multi-word units which are tagged or found in our term list, as will be explained later.

[5] We used the pronunciation lexicon PRONLEX provided by the LDC.

Since Chinese is a monosyllabic language, transliteration of names to Chinese syllables should abide by a set of phonological rules. We have hand-designed a set of cross-lingual phonological rules that partially transforms an English pronunciation into a Chinese pronunciation. The transformation involves such processes as syllable nuclei insertion to separate consonant clusters. This is followed by an automatic mapping of English phonemes to Chinese "phonemes", a procedure we termed cross-lingual phonetic mapping (CLPM). This is also an automatic procedure in which we have applied the transformation-based error-driven learning technique. By this time, our process has transformed the English phonemes into Chinese phonemes, e.g. /kk rr ih ss tt aa ff er/ is transformed into /k e l i s i t uo f u/ (see Figure 2). This is essentially a phoneme translation procedure. The technique of subword translation based on pronunciation lexicons has previously been applied to English/Japanese and English/Arabic translation (Knight and Graehl, 1997), (Stalls and Knight, 1998). Ours is one of the first attempts in phoneme translation for English and Chinese and incorporating the automatic letter/phoneme generation technique.

In order to obtain names transliteration alternatives from this Chinese phoneme sequence, we borrow ideas from lexical access in speech recognition. By expanding each Chinese phoneme into its list of acoustically confusable counterparts, we obtain a Chinese phoneme lattice. Applying the Chinese syllable constraints to the Chinese phoneme lattice produces a Chinese syllable lattice, and searching the syllable lattice with a syllable bigram language model can produce N-best hypotheses of Chinese syllable sequences.[6] These form the output of our names transliteration procedure, e.g. /ji li si te fu/ (see Figure 2). It is interesting to note that when we use a character bigram in place of a syllable bigram, our transliteration algorithm can produce subword translations in terms of character sequences, e.g. 基里斯特弗.

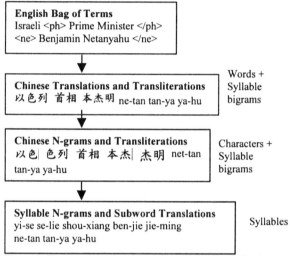

Figure 3. The process of multi-scale query construction in our system. The query representations at various stages of processing may be used. The representations seek to integrate information from phrase-based translation, word-based translation, subword translation and overlapping character/syllable n-grams which alleviates the problem of word tokenization ambiguities. Transformation from characters to syllables references a Chinese pronunciation lexicon.[7]

3.1.4 Multi-Scale Query Construction

The input to our query construction process is a bag of English query terms. Multi-scale query construction integrates the translated phrases, named entities, individual translated words as well as translated syllables. Hence the output of our query construction process is a representation which includes Chinese words, subwords, or a mixture of both. Subwords refer to character n-grams (to capture sequential constraints) or syllable n-grams. This process is depicted in Figure 3.

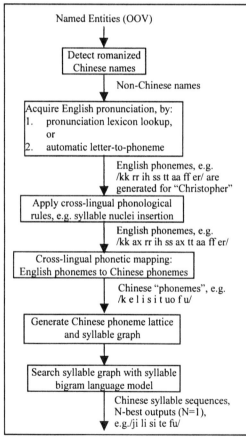

Figure 2. Overview of our subword translation process for handling untranslatable named entities in the query exemplars.

---

[6] We set N=1 for simplicity.
[7] This is the LDC CALLHOME lexicon.

3.2 Multi-Scale Audio Indexing

The Dragon large-vocabulary continuous speech recognizer (Zhan et al., 1999) provided Chinese word transcriptions for our Mandarin audio collections (TDT2 and TDT3). Based on these word transcriptions, we can use the same procedures as in query formulation to obtain overlapping character bigrams and overlapping syllable bigrams from the word transcriptions. Hence we can index our audio on the word, character and syllable scales. To assess the performance level of the recognizer, we spot-checked a fraction of the TDT-2 test set (~23 hours) by comparing the Dragon recognition hypotheses with the anchor scripts (treated as ground truth), and obtained error rates of 18.0% (word); 12.1% (character) and 7.9% (syllable). Spot-checking approximately 27 hours of the TDT-3 test set gave error rates of 19.1% (word); 13.0% (character) and 8.6% (syllable). We feel that the Dragon recognizer has a respectable performance level.

We have also developed our own recognizer (the MEI recognizer) to provide a syllable hypothesis as an alternative to Dragon's. Both recognition outputs have been combined in retrieval, in an attempt to achieve robustness against speech recognition errors. However, using two speech recognizers instead of one did not bring obvious gains in CL-SDR performance. Possible reasons may be that Dragon's performance is quite good to begin with, and we have to further investigate methods to effectively combine multiple recognizer outputs for audio indexing. Details regarding to this investigation is reported in (Wang et al., 2001).

3.3 Multi-Scale Retrieval

We use InQuery as our retrieval engine, developed by the University of Massachusetts (Callan et al., 1992).[8] InQuery uses a probabilistic belief network as the main data structure behind its query language.

A key feature that we have employed is the "balanced query" mechanism (Leek et al., 2000) (Levow and Oard, 2000). Suppose that we had a query given by E_1, E_2, ... E_n, where E_i represent the English query terms, and that E_1 has three possible Chinese translations, C_{11}, C_{12}, C_{13}. With balanced translation, the belief value for E_1 in the Chinese document will be computed as the mean of the belief values for C_{11}, C_{12}, C_{13}. in that document. Repeating the same process for additional terms produces a set of belief values for each English query term with respect to every Chinese document. The InQuery #sum operator implements this computation, so a balanced translation of the query would be represented as #sum(#sum(C_{11}, C_{12}, C_{13})#sum(C_{21}, C_{22})...#sum(C_{n1}, C_{n2}, C_{n3})) in InQuery, with the outer #sum operators being the typical way of combining belief values across query terms in Inquery and the inner #sum operators implementing balanced translation. Balanced translation prevents query term that have a disproportionate number of translations from dominating the computing of the scores by which the ranked list of documents are sorted.

Our main strategy for multi-scale retrieval is as follows: retrieval proceeds for each scale (word, characters and syllables) individually, and each scale produces its own retrieved list of

documents, ranked in decreasing order of scores. We can then combine these ranked lists into a *single* ranked list by a linear combination of their respective scores. The weights used in linear combination are obtained by optimization experiments based on training data. This is termed *loose coupling*. An alternative strategy, *tight coupling*, integrates different unit types into a hybrid query / document representation, and then produces a single ranked list in retrieval.

4. EXPERIMENTS

4.1 Evaluation Criterion

In order to evaluate our retrieval performance, we use a variant of the non-interpolated mean average precision as our evaluation metric.

We compute the non-interpolated mean average precision for a ranked list of retrieved documents. We proceed from the top downwards and calculate the precision for every relevant document retrieved. The average of all the precision values is the average precision for that particular query. An average is then made across all queries in the batches for each of the topics. Taking another average over all queries produce a single value as our evaluation metric. Equation (1) summarizes the process:

$$metric = \frac{1}{L} \sum_{i=1}^{L} \left\{ \frac{1}{M_i} \sum_{j=1}^{M_i} \left\{ \frac{1}{N_i} \sum_{k=1}^{N_i} P_{ijk} \right\} \right\} \quad ... \quad (1)$$

where *metric* is the non-interpolated mean average precision, L is the number of topics; M_i is a sample of the exemplars for topic i; N_i is number of relevant documents for topic i; and P_{ijk} is the precision after the kth relevant document is retrieved for exemplar j of topic i.

In order to achieve statistical significance, we used up to twelve exemplars (i.e., $M_i = 12$) for each of the 17 topics whenever available.

4.2 Tuning with the Development Test Set

The TDT2 collection was our development test set, which forms our basis for tuning free parameters, e.g. the number of query terms to include, the number of translation alternative to use, the linear combination weights used in our multi-scale retrieval strategy, etc. In addition, the TDT2 audio collection was also used in training the MEI recognizer to optimize its recognition performance.

We found that in query term selection, it is beneficial to include all query terms (after stopword removal), and translate them. We also tuned the experimental configuration based on the number of translation alternatives to use, and results suggest that we include up to fifty translation alternatives, and combine them with a #sum operator for balanced queries. In applying our subword translation technique, we took the 200 most frequent names (tagged named entities) from the TDT2 collection and translated them at the subword level. This is used to augment the queries in both the TDT2 and TDT3 runs. Hence the development test set should have greater leverage based on subword translation.

---

[8] We used InQuery with a trivial modification to handle two-byte characters.

4.3 Experimental Results

In the MEI project, we have investigated a variety of issues related to English-Chinese CL-SDR. This paper focuses on the use of phrases in query translation, the merits of multi-scale retrieval in comparison with word-based retrieval, and the use of subword translation to salvage untranslatable named entities. We provide the key results in this section.

4.3.1 Phrase-based Translation

Our investigation of phrase-based translation took place in an early phase on our project. At the time, word-based translation gave a performance of mean average precision (mAP)=0.35. The addition of phrase-based translation raised it to 0.392. The 12% relative improvement was statistically significant, based on a paired two tailed t-test on the means across exemplars of each topic, with $p<0.05$. These results are tabulated in Table 2. Thereafter, we have always included phrase-based translation in our experiments.

Query Translation Method	Retrieval Performance (mAP)	Relative Improve-ment
Word-by-Word Translation	0.350	--
Augmented with Phrase-based Translation	0.392	12% (statistically significant)

Table 2. Effect of phrase-based translation in CL-SDR retrieval performance.

4.3.2 Multi-scale Retrieval

Overlapping character bigrams gave the best retrieval performance overall, and even outperforming words. The trend is consistent across our development and evaluation test sets. Results are shown in Table 3.

	Word-based Retrieval (mAP)	Character Bigrams (mAP)
TDT2 (dev test)	0.471	0.522
TDT3 (eval test)	0.462	0.477

Table 3. English-Chinese CL-SDR results for word-based retrieval, in comparison with retrieval based on overlapping character bigrams.

The relative difference of 3.2% (w.r.t. TDT3) is also statistically significant, based on a paired two-tailed t-test with $p<0.05$. This suggests that the character bigrams may be effective in ameliorating the problem of word tokenization ambiguities. We also tried loosely coupling of the retrieval lists based on words and character bigrams, using weights optimized from TDT2, and tested on TDT3. This gave a performance of mAP=0.482 on TDT3, which is better than retrieval on each scale alone. Overlapping syllable bigrams performed below words. TDT2 and TDT3 results were at 0.468 and 0.422 respectively.

4.3.3 Subword Translation

Subword translation improved retrieval performance across multiple unit types. We reference the named entities that were tagged by Identifinder but cannot be translated with our BTL, and we extracted the 200 most frequent ones to be processed by subword translation. Results based on the words and character bigrams (the two units giving the highest retrieval performance) are shown in Table 4.

	TDT2 Performance (mAP)	TDT3 Performance (mAP)
Words only	0.464	0.462
Words with subword translation	0.471	0.462
Character bigrams only	0.514	0.475
Character bigrams with subword translation	0.522	0.477

Table 4. Investigation into the use of subword translation to salvage untranslatable named entities for CL-SDR. The procedure brought some performance gains.

While such improvements were not statistically significant, they were consistent across the units. We expect that the benefits of subword translation will be greater if the technique is used for a greater number of (untranslatable) terms, or if we need to retrieve collections for which our bilingual term list has lower coverage.

5. CONCLUSIONS

In this paper, we have described the Mandarin-English Information (MEI) project, where we developed one of the first English-Chinese cross-language spoken document retrieval systems. Our system accepts an entire English news story (text) as query, and retrieves relevant Chinese broadcast news stories (audio) from the document collection. Hence this is a cross-language and cross-media retrieval task. We applied a multi-scale approach to our problem, which unifies the use of phrases, words as well as subword in retrieval. The English queries are translated into Chinese by means of a dictionary-based approach, where we have integrated phrase-based translation with word-by-word translation. Untranslatable named entities are transliterated by a novel subword translation technique. This can automatically generate a Chinese pinyin representation that sounds similar to the name's original pronunciation. The multi-scale approach can be divided into three subtasks of multi-scale query formulation, multi-scale audio indexing and multi-scale retrieval. We experimented with the TDT collections, which have English newswire from New York Times and Associated Press, and Mandarin Chinese radio news broadcasts from Voice of America. The radio news is transcribed by Dragon's large-vocabulary continuous speech recognizer.

Experimental results show that augmenting word-by-word query translation with phrase-based translation brought statistically significant improvements in retrieval performance. Overlapping character bigrams gave the best retrieval results overall, and outperformed words, which, in turn, performed better than overlapping syllable bigrams. Using both words and character bigrams together (by loose coupling) gave better retrieval performance than each alone. In addition, both word-based retrieval and character-based retrieval benefit from the use of subword translation to salvage untranslatable named entities. These results suggest that our multi-scale approach is promising and applicable to the English-Chinese CL-SDR task. It should also be possible to leverage off of our experience in a translingual setting, which involves SDR across any language pair.

6. ACKNOWLEDGMENTS

We acknowledge the contributions of all MEI team members. The MEI project is conducted during the Johns Hopkins University Summer Workshop 2000 (an NSF Workshop). www.clsp.jhu.edu/ws2000/groups/mei/welcome.html. This work is supported by the NSF grant no. IIS-00712125, Gina's work was supported by the DARPA cooperative agreement N660010028910, and Berlin's participation was supported by Academia Sinica (Taiwan), as well as the research grant (88-S-0128) from Professor Lin-Shan Lee of National Taiwan University. We thank the Linguistic Data Consortium for providing the TDT Corpora. We also thank Charles Wayne, George Doddington, James Allan, John Garafolo, Hsin-Hsi Chen, Richard Schwartz and Ralph Weischedel for their help. We are grateful to Fred Jelinek and his staff at CLSP for organizing the workshop.

7. REFERENCES

D. Bikel, S. Miller, R. Schwartz, and R. Weischedel, "Nymble: a High-Performance Learning Name-finder," *Proceedings of the Fifth Conference on Applied Natural Language Processing,* pp. 194-201 (1997).

E. Brill, "Transformation-Based Error-Driven Learning and Natural Language Processing: A Case Study in Part of Speech Tagging," *Computational Linguistics*, December 1995.

J. P. Callan, W. B. Croft, and S. M. Harding, "The INQUERY Retrieval System," *Proceedings of the 3rd International Conference on Database and Expert Systems Applications*, pp. 78-83, 1992.

K. Knight and J. Graehl, "Machine Transliteration," *Proceedings of the Conference of the Association for Computation Linguistics* (ACL), 1997.

K. L. Kwok and L. Grunfeld, "TREC-5 English and Chinese Experiments using PIRCS, " *Proceedings of the Fifth Annual Text Retrieval Conference (TREC-5)*, 1996.

T. Leek, H. Jin, S. Sista and R. Schwartz, "The BBN Crosslingual Topic Detection and Tracking System," *Proceedings of the 1999 Topic Detection and Tracking Workshop*, 2000.

G. Levow and D. Oard, "Translingual Topic Tracking with PRISE," *Proceedings of the 1999 Topic Detection and Tracking Workshop*, 2000.

H. Meng, B. Chen, W. K. Lo and K. Tang, "Automatic Named Entity Transliteration for English-Chinese Cross-Language Spoken Document Retrieval," working paper, 2001.

H. Meng, W. K. Lo, Y. C. Li, and P. C. Ching, "Multi-Scale Audio Indexing for Chinese Spoken Document Retrieval," *Proceedings of ICSLP2000*, Vol. IV, pp. 101-4, 2000.

D. Oard, G. Levow and C. Cabezas, "CLEF Experiemnts at Maryland: Statistical Stemming and Backoff Translation," *Lecture Notes in Computer Science*, forthcoming (2001).

H. Schuetze, D. Hull and J. O. Pedersen, "A Comparison of Classifiers and Document Representations for the Routing Problem," *Proceedings of the 18th Annual International ACM SIGIR Conference on Research and Development in Information Retrieval*, 1995, pp. 229-237.

B. Stalls and K. Knight, "Translating Names and Technical Terms in Arabic Text," *Proceedings of the COLING/ACL Workshop on Computational Approaches to Semitic Languages*, 1998.

H. M. Wang, "Experiments in Syllable-based Retrieval of Broadcast News Speech in Mandarin Chinese," *Speech Communication*, Vol. 32, pp. 49-60, 2000.

H. M. Wang, H. Meng, P. Schone, B. Chen and W. K. Lo, "Multi-scale Audio Indexing for Translingual Spoken Document Retrieval," *Proceedings of the IEEE Conference on Acoustics Speech and Signal Processing* (ICASSP), 2001.

P. Zhan, S. Wegmann, and L. Gillick, "Dragon Systems' 1998 Broadcast News Transcription System for Mandarin," *Proceedings of the DARPA Broadcast News Workshop*, 1999.

The Meeting Project at ICSI

Nelson Morgan[1,4]   Don Baron[1,4]   Jane Edwards[1,4]   Dan Ellis[1,2]   David Gelbart[1,4]
Adam Janin[1,4]   Thilo Pfau[1]   Elizabeth Shriberg[1,3]   Andreas Stolcke[1,3]

[1]International Computer Science Institute, Berkeley, CA
[2]Columbia University, New York, NY
[3]SRI International, Menlo Park, CA
[4]University of California at Berkeley, Berkeley, CA

{morgan,dbaron,edwards,dpwe,gelbart,janin,tpfau,ees,stolcke}@icsi.berkeley.edu

ABSTRACT

In collaboration with colleagues at UW, OGI, IBM, and SRI, we are developing technology to process spoken language from informal meetings. The work includes a substantial data collection and transcription effort, and has required a nontrivial degree of infrastructure development. We are undertaking this because the new task area provides a significant challenge to current HLT capabilities, while offering the promise of a wide range of potential applications. In this paper, we give our vision of the task, the challenges it represents, and the current state of our development, with particular attention to automatic transcription.

1. THE TASK

We are primarily interested in the processing (transcription, query, search, and structural representation) of audio recorded from informal, natural, and even impromptu meetings. By "informal" we mean conversations between friends and acquaintances that do not have a strict protocol for the exchanges. By "natural" we mean meetings that would have taken place regardless of the recording process, and in acoustic circumstances that are typical for such meetings. By "impromptu" we mean that the conversation may take place without any preparation, so that we cannot require special instrumentation to facilitate later speech processing (such as close-talking or array microphones). A plausible image for such situations is a handheld device (PDA, cell phone, digital recorder) that is used when conversational partners agree that their discussion should be recorded for later reference.

Given these interests, we have been recording and transcribing a series of meetings at ICSI. The recording room is one of ICSI's standard meeting rooms, and is instrumented with both close-talking and distant microphones. Close-mic'd recordings will support research on acoustic modeling, language modeling, dialog modeling, etc., without having to immediately solve the difficulties of far-field microphone speech recognition. The distant microphones are included to facilitate the study of these deep acoustic problems, and to provide a closer match to the operating conditions ultimately envisaged. These ambient signals are collected by 4 omnidirectional PZM table-mount microphones, plus a "dummy" PDA that has two inexpensive microphone elements. In addition to these 6 distant microphones, the audio setup permits a maximum of 9 close-talking microphones to be simultaneously recorded. A meeting recording infrastructure is also being put in place at Columbia University, at SRI International, and by our colleagues at the University of Washington. Recordings from all sites will be transcribed using standards evolved in discussions that also involved IBM (who also have committed to assist in the transcription task). Colleagues at NIST have been in contact with us to further standardize these choices, since they intend to conduct related collection efforts.

A segment from a typical discussion recorded at ICSI is included below in order to give the reader a more concrete sense of the task. Utterances on the same line separated by a slash indicate some degree of overlapped speech.

> **A:** Ok. So that means that for each utterance, .. we'll need the time marks.
> **E:** Right. / **A:** the start and end of each utterance.
> [a few turns omitted]
> **E:** So we - maybe we should look at the um .. the tools that Mississippi State has.
> **D:** Yeah.
> **E:** Because, I - I - I know that they published .. um .. annotation tools.
> **A:** Well, X-waves have some as well, .. but they're pretty low level .. They're designed for uh - / **D:** phoneme / **A:** for phoneme-level / **D:** transcriptions. Yeah.
> **J:** I should -
> **A:** Although, they also have a nice tool for - .. that could be used for speaker change marking.
> **D:** There's a - there are - there's a whole bunch of tools
> **J:** Yes. / **D:** web page, where they have a listing. **D:** like 10 of them or something.
> **J:** Are you speaking about Mississippi State per se? or
> **D:** No no no, there's some .. I mean, there just - there are - there are a lot of / **J:** Yeah.
> **J:** Actually, I wanted to mention - / **D:** (??)
> **J:** There are two projects, which are .. international .. huge projects focused on this kind of thing, actually .. one of them's MATE, one of them's EAGLES .. and um.
> **D:** Oh, EAGLES.
> **D:** (??) / **J:** And both of them have
> **J:** You know, I shou-, I know you know about the big book.
> **E:** Yeah.
> **J:** I think you got it as a prize or something.
> **E:** Yeah. / **D:** Mhm.
> **J:** Got a surprise. {laugh} {J. thought "as a prize" sounded like "surprise"}

Note that interruptions are quite frequent; this is, in our experience, quite common in informal meetings, as is acoustic overlap

Proceedings of HLT 2001, First International Conference on Human Language Technology Research, J. Allan, ed., Morgan Kaufmann, San Francisco, 2001.

between speakers (see the section on error rates in overlap regions).

2. THE CHALLENGES

While having a searchable, annotatable record of impromptu meetings would open a wide range of applications, there are significant technical challenges to be met; it would not be far from the truth to say that the problem of generating a full representation of a meeting is "AI complete", as well as "ASR complete". We believe, however, that our community can make useful progress on a range of associated problems, including:

- ASR for very informal conversational speech, including the common overlap problem.

- ASR from far-field microphones - handling the reverberation and background noise that typically bedevil distant mics, as well as the acoustic overlap that is more of a problem for microphones that pick up several speakers at approximately the same level.

- Segmentation and turn detection - recovering the different speakers and turns, which also is more difficult with overlaps and with distant microphones (although inter-microphone timing cues can help here).

- Extracting nonlexical information such as speaker identification and characterization, voice quality variation, prosody, laughter, etc.

- Dialog abstraction - making high-level models of meeting 'state'; identifying roles among participants, classifying meeting types, etc. [2].

- Dialog analysis - identification and characterization of fine-scale linguistic and discourse phenomena [3][10].

- Information retrieval from errorful meeting transcriptions - topic change detection, topic classification, and query matching.

- Summarization of meeting content [14] - representation of the meeting structure from various perspectives and at various scales, and issues of navigation in thes representations.

- Energy and memory resource limitation issues that arise in the robust processing of speech using portable devices [7].

Clearly we and others working in this area (e.g., [15]) are at an early stage in this research. However, the remainder of this paper will show that even a preliminary effort in recording, manually transcribing, and recognizing data from natural meetings has provided some insight into at least a few of these problems.

3. DATA COLLECTION AND HUMAN TRANSCRIPTION

Using the data collection setup described previously, we have been recording technical meetings at ICSI. As of this writing we have recorded 38 meetings for a total of 39 hours. Note that there are separate microphones for each participant in addition to the 6 far-field microphones, and there can be as many as 15 open channels. Consequently the sound files comprise hundreds of hours of recorded audio. The total number of participants in all meetings is 237, and there were 49 unique speakers. The majority of the meetings recorded so far have either had a focus on "Meeting Recorder"

(that is, meetings by the group working on this technology) or "Robustness" (primarily concerned with ASR robustness to acoustic effects such as additive noise). A smaller number of other meeting types at ICSI were also included.

In addition to the spontaneous recordings, we asked meeting participants to read digit strings taken from a TI digits test set. This was done to facilitate research in far-field microphone ASR, since we expect this to be quite challenging for the more unconstrained case. At the start or end of each meeting, each participant read 20 digit strings.

Once the data collection was in progress, we developed a set of procedures for our initial transcription. The transcripts are word-level transcripts, with speaker identifier, and some additional information: overlaps, interrupted words, restarts, vocalized pauses, backchannels, and contextual comments, and nonverbal events (which are further subdivided into vocal types such as cough and laugh, and nonvocal types such as door slams and clicks). Each event is tied to the time line through use of a modified version of the "Transcriber" interface (described below). This Transcriber window provides an editing space at the top of the screen (for adding utterances, etc), and the wave form at the bottom, with mechanisms for flexibly navigating through the audio recording, and listening and re-listening to chunks of virtually any size the user wishes.

The typical process involves listening to a stretch of speech until a natural break is found (e.g., a long pause when no one is speaking). The transcriber separates that chunk from what precedes and follows it by pressing the Return key. Then he or she enters the speaker identifier and utterance in the top section of the screen. The interface is efficient and easy to use, and results in an XML representation of utterances (and other events) tied to time tags for further processing.

The "Transcriber" interface [13] is a well-known tool for transcription, which enables the user to link acoustic events to the wave form. However, the official version is designed only for single-channel audio. As noted previously, our application records up to 15 parallel sound tracks generated by as many as 9 speakers, and we wanted to capture the start and end times of events on each channel as precisely as possible and independently of one another across channels. The need to switch between multiple audio channels to clarify overlaps, and the need to display the time course of events on independent channels required extending the "Transcriber" interface in two ways. First, we added a menu that allows the user to switch the playback between a number of audio files (which are all assumed to be time synchronized). Secondly, we split the time-linked display band into as many independent display bands as there are channels (and/or independent layers of time-synchronized annotation). Speech and other events on each of the bands can now be time-linked to the wave form with complete freedom and totally independently of the other bands. This enables much more precise start and end times for acoustic events.

See [8] for links to screenshots of these extensions to Transcriber (as well as to other updates about our project).

In the interests of maximal speed, accuracy and consistency, the transcription conventions were chosen so as to be: quick to type, related to standard literary conventions where possible (e.g., - for interrupted word or thought, .. for pause, using standard orthography rather than IPA), and minimalist (requiring no more decisions by transcribers than absolutely necessary).

After practice with the conventions and the interface, transcribers achieved a 12:1 ratio of transcription time to speech time. The amount of time required for transcription of spoken language is known to vary widely as a function of properties of the discourse (amount of overlap, etc.), and amount of detailed encoding (prosodics, etc.), with estimates ranging from 10:1 for word-level with minimal added information to 20:1, for highly detailed discourse transcriptions (see [4] for details).

In our case, transcribers encoded minimal added detail, but had two additional demands: marking boundaries of time bins, and switching between audio channels to clarify the many instances of overlapping speech in our data. We speeded the marking of time bins by providing them with an automatically segmented version (described below) in which the segmenter provided a preliminary set of speech/nonspeech labels. Transcribers indicated that the pre-segmentation was correct sufficiently often that it saved them time.

After the transcribers finished, their work was edited for consistency and completeness by a senior researcher. Editing involved checking exhaustive listings of forms in the data, spell checking, and use of scripts to identify and automatically encode certain distinctions (e.g., the distinction between vocalized nonverbal events, such as cough, and nonvocalized nonverbal events, like door slams). This step requires on average about 1:1 - one minute of editing for each minute of speech.

Using these methods and tools, we have currently transcribed about 12 hours out of our 39 hours of data. Other data have been sent to IBM for a rough transcription using commercial transcribers, to be followed by a more detailed process at ICSI. Once this becomes a routine component of our process, we expect it to significantly reduce the time requirements for transcription at ICSI.

4. AUTOMATIC TRANSCRIPTION

As a preliminary report on automatic word transcription, we present results for six example meetings, totalling nearly 7 hours of speech, 36 total speakers, and 15 unique speakers (since many speakers participated in multiple meetings). Note that these results are preliminary only; we have not yet had a chance to address the many obvious approaches that could improve performance. In particular, in order to facilitate efforts in alignment, pronunciation modeling, language modeling, etc., we worked only with the close-mic'd data. In most common applications of meeting transcription (including those that are our chief targets in this research) such a microphone arrangement may not be practical. Nevertheless we hope the results using the close microphone data will illustrate some basic observations we have made about meeting data and its automatic transcription.

4.1 Recognition system

The recognizer was a stripped-down version of the large-vocabulary conversational speech recognition system fielded by SRI in the March 2000 Hub-5 evaluation [11]. The system performs vocal-tract length normalization, feature normalization, and speaker adaptation using all the speech collected on each channel (i.e., from one speaker, modulo cross-talk). The acoustic model consisted of gender-dependent, bottom-up clustered (genonic) Gaussian mixtures. The Gaussian means are adapted by a linear transform so as to maximize the likelihood of a phone-loop model, an approach that is fast and does not require recognition prior to adaptation. The adapted models are combined with a bigram language model for decoding. We omitted more elaborate adaptation, cross-word triphone modeling, and higher-order language and duration models from the full SRI recognition system as an expedient in our initial recognition experiments (the omitted steps yield about a 20% relative error rate reduction on Hub-5 data).

It should be noted that both the acoustic models and the language model of the recognizer were identical to those used in the Hub-5 domain. In particular, the acoustic front-end assumes a telephone channel, requiring us to downsample the wide-band signals

of the meeting recordings. The language model contained about 30,000 words and was trained on a combination of Switchboard, CallHome English and Broadcast News data, but was not tuned for or augmented by meeting data.

4.2 Speech segmentation

As noted above, we are initially focusing on recognition of the individual channel data. Such data provide an upper bound on recognition accuracy if speaker segmentation were perfect, and constitute a logical first step for obtaining high quality forced alignments against which to evaluate performance for both near- and far-field microphones. Individual channel recordings were partitioned into "segments" of speech, based on a "mixed" signal (addition of the individual channel data, after an overall energy equalization factor per channel). Segment boundary times were determined either by an automatic segmentation of the mixed signal followed by hand-correction, or by hand-correction alone. For the automatic case, the data was segmented with a speech/nonspeech detector consisting of an extension of an approach using an ergodic hidden Markov model (HMM) [1]. In this approach, the HMM consists of two main states, one representing "speech" and one representing "nonspeech" and a number of intermediate states that are used to model the time constraints of the transitions between the two main states. In our extension, we are incorporating mixture densities rather than single Gaussians. This appears to be useful for the separation of foreground from background speech, which is a serious problem in these data.

The algorithm described above was trained on the speech/nonspeech segmentation provided manually for the first meeting that was transcribed. It was used to provide segments of speech for the manual transcribers, and later for the recognition experiments. Currently, for simplicity and to debug the various processing steps, these segments are synchronous across channels. However, we plan to move to segments based on separate speech/nonspeech detection in each individual channel. The latter approach should provide better recognition performance, since it will eliminate cross-talk in segments in which one speaker may say only a backchannel (e.g. "uhhuh") while another speaker is talking continuously.

Performance was scored for the spontaneous conversational portions of the meetings only (i.e., the read digit strings referred to earlier were excluded). Also, for this study we ran recognition only on those segments during which a transcription was produced for the particular speaker. This overestimates the accuracy of word recognition, since any speech recognized in the "empty" segments would constitute an error not counted here. However, adding the empty regions would increase data load by a factor of about ten—which was impractical for us at this stage. Note that the current NIST Hub-5 (Switchboard) task is similar in this respect: data are recorded on separated channels and only the speech regions of a speaker are run, not the regions in which they are essentially silent. We plan to run all speech (including these "empty" segments) in future experiments, to better assess actual performance in a real meeting task.

4.3 Recognition results and discussion

Overall error rates. Table 1 lists word error rates for the six meetings, by speaker. The data are organized into two groups: native speakers and nonnative speakers. Since our recognition system is not trained on nonnative speakers, we provide results only for the native speakers; however the word counts are listed for all partici-

Table 1: Recognition performance by speaker and meeting (MRM = "Meeting Recorder meeting"; ROB = "Robustness meeting"). Speaker gender is indicated by "M" or "F" in the speaker labels. "* ... *" marks speakers using a lapel microphone; all other cases used close-talking head-mounted microphones. "—" indicates speakers with severely degraded or missing signals due to incorrect microphone usage. Word error rates are in boldface, total number of words in Roman, and out-of-vocabulary (OOV) rates in *italics*. OOV rate is by token, relative to a Hub-5 language model. WER is for conversational speech sections of meetings only, and are not reported for nonnative speakers.

Meeting	MRM002	MRM003	MRM004	MRM005	ROB005	ROB004
Duration (minutes)	45	78	60	68	81	70
Native speakers						
M_004		**42.4**	**48.1**	**44.3**	**48.4**	**45.1**
		4550	3087	3432	4912	5512
		2.07	*2.75*	*1.60*	*2.12*	*1.61*
M_001	**42.4**	**50.6**	**37.6**	**38.6**		
	2311	2488	1904	3400		
	1.82	*2.09*	*2.78*	*1.56*		
F_001	**45.2**	**43.2**	**42.9**	**41.9**		
	3008	3360	2714	2705		
	2.59	*3.18*	*4.05*	*2.14*		
M_009		***100.1***	***115.8***	**38.2**		***68.7***
		1122	367	1066		696
		1.59	*2.45*	*1.88*		*2.01*
F_002		**45.2**	**43.7**	***46.0***		
		1549	1481	2480		
		2.26	*2.64*	*1.63*		
M_002	***55.6***					
	990					
	2.12					
Speakers with low word counts						
M_007					**55.6**	**—**
					198	69
					2.97	*2.90*
M_008					**72.7**	**59.5**
					55	121
					5.45	*5.79*
M_015						**—**
						59
						6.56
Non-native speakers (total words only)						
M_003 (British)	2189					
M_011 (Spanish)		2653	1239	663		
F_003 (Spanish)					620	220
M_010 (German)			28			
M_012 (German)			639			
M_006 (French)					3524	2648

pants for completeness.[1]

The main result to note from Table 1 is that overall word error rates are not dramatically worse than for Switchboard-style data. This is particularly impressive since, as described earlier, no meeting data were used in training, and no modifications of the acoustic or language models were made. The overall WER for native speakers was 46.5%, or only about a 7% relative increase over a comparable recognition system on Hub-5 telephone conversations. This suggests that from the point of view of pronunciation and language (as opposed to acoustic robustness, e.g., for distant microphones), Switchboard may also be "ASR-complete". That is, talkers may not really speak in a more "sloppy" manner in meetings than they do in casual phone conversation. We further investigate this claim in the next section, by breaking down results by overlap versus nonoverlap regions, by microphone type and by speaker.

Note that in some cases there were very few contributions from a speaker (e.g., speakers M_007, M_008, and M_015), and such speakers also tended to have higher word error rates. We initially suspected the problem was a lack of sufficient data for speaker adaptation; indeed the improvement from adaptation was less than for other speakers. Thus for such speakers it would make sense to pool data across meetings for repeat participants. However, in looking at their word transcripts we noted that their utterances, while few, tended to be dense with information content. That is, these were not the speakers uttering "uhhuh" or short common phrases (which are generally well modeled in the Switchboard recognizer) but rather high-perplexity utterances that are generally harder to recognize. Such speakers also tend to have a generally higher overall OOV rate than other speakers.

Error rates in overlap versus nonoverlap regions. As noted in the previous section, the overall word error rate in our sample meetings was slightly higher than in Switchboard. An obvious question to ask here is: what is the effect on recognition of overlapping speech? To address this question, we defined a crude measure of overlap. Since segments were channel-synchronous in these meetings, a segment was either non-overlapping (only one speaker was talking during that time segment), or overlapping (two or more speakers were talking during the segment). Note that this does not measure amount of overlap or number of overlapping speakers; more sophisticated measures based on the phone backtrace from forced alignment would provide a better measure for more detailed analyses. Nevertheless, the crude measure provides a clear first answer to our question. Since we were also interested in the interaction if any between overlap and microphone type, we computed results separately for the head-mounted and lapel microphones. Results were also computed by speaker, since as shown earlier in Table 1, speakers varied in word error rates, total words, and words by microphone type. Note that speakers M_009 and F_002 have data from both conditions.

As shown, our measure of overlap (albeit crude), clearly shows that overlapping speech is a major problem for the recognition of speech from meetings. If overlap regions are removed, the recognition accuracy overall is actually better than that for Switchboard. It is premature to make absolute comparisons here, but the fact that the same pattern is observed for all speakers and across microphone

---

[1]Given the limitations of these pilot experiments (e.g., no on-task training material and general pronunciation models), recognition on nonnative speakers is essentially not working at present. In the case of one nonnative speaker, we achieved a 200% word error rate, surpassing a previous ICSI record. Word error results presented here are based on meeting transcripts as of March 7, 2000, and are subject to small changes as a result of ongoing transcription error checking.

Table 2: Word error rates broken down by whether or not segment is in a region of overlapping speech.

Speaker	No overlap		With overlap	
	Headset	Lapel	Headset	Lapel
M_004	41.0	-	50.3	-
M_001	34.2	-	47.6	-
F_001	40.5	-	45.8	-
M_009	30.7	41.0	40.7	117.8
F_002	37.7	29.8	50.5	56.3
M_002	-	48.6	-	71.3
M_007	52.2	-	81.3	-
M_008	50.9	-	69.9	
Overall	39.9	38.5	48.7	85.2

conditions suggests that it is not the inherent speech properties of participants that makes meetings difficult to recognize, but rather the presence of overlapping speech.

Furthermore, one can note from Table 2 that there is a large interaction between microphone type and the effect of overlap. Overlap is certainly a problem even for the close-talking head-mounted microphones. However, the degradation due to overlap is far greater for the lapel microphone, which picks up a greater degree of background speech. As demonstrated by speaker F_002, it is possible to have a comparatively good word error rate (29.8%) on the lapel microphone in regions of no overlap (in this case 964/2480 words were in nonoverlapping segments). Nevertheless, since the rate of overlaps is so high in the data overall, we are avoiding the use of the lapel microphone where possible in the future, preferring head-mounted microphones for obtaining ground truth for research purposes. We further note that for tests of acoustic robustness for distant microphones, we tend to prefer microphones mounted on the meeting table (or on a mock PDA frame), since they provide a more realistic representation of the ultimate target application that is a central interest to us - recognition via portable devices. In other words, we are finding lapel mics to be too "bad" for near-field microphone tests, and too "good" for far-field tests.

Error rates by error type. The effect of overlapping speech on error rates is due almost entirely to insertion errors, as shown in Figure 1. Rates of other error types are nearly identical to those observed for Switchboard (modulo a a slight increase in substitutions associated with the lapel condition). This result is not surprising, since background speech obviously adds false words in the hypothesis. However, it is interesting that there is little increase in the other error types, suggesting that a closer segmentation based on individual channel data (as noted earlier) could greatly improve recognition accuracy (by removing the surrounding background speech).

Error rates by meeting type. Different types of meetings should give rise to differences in speaking style and social interaction, and we may be interested in whether such effects are realized as differences in word error rates. The best way to measure such effects is within speaker. The collection of regular, ongoing meetings at ICSI offers the possibility of such within-speaker comparisons, since multiple speakers participate in more than one type of regular meeting. Of the speakers shown in the data set used for this study, speaker M_004 is a good case in point, since he has data from three "Meeting Recorder" meetings and two "Robustness" meetings. These two meeting types differ in social interaction; in the first, there is a fairly open exchange between many of the partici-

250

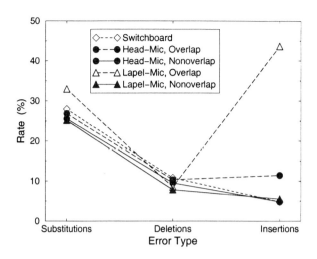

Figure 1: Word error rates by error type and microphone/overlap condition. Switchboard scores refer to an internal SRI development testset that is a representative subset of the development data for the 2001 hub-5 evals. It contains 41 speakers (5-minute conversation sides), from Switchboard-1, Switchboard-2 and Cellular Switchboard in roughly equal proportions, and is also balanced for gender and ASR difficulty. The other scores are evaluated for the data described in the text.

pants, while in the second, speaker ML004 directs the flow of the meeting. It can also be seen from the table that speaker ML004 contributes a much higher rate of words relative to overall words in the latter meeting type. Interestingly however, his recognition rate and OOV rates are quite similar across the meeting types. Study of additional speakers across meetings will allow us to further examine this issue.

5. FUTURE WORK

The areas mentioned in the earlier section on "Challenges" will require much more work in the future. We and our colleagues at collaborating institutions will be working in all of these. Here, we briefly mention some of the work in our current plans for the study of speech from meetings.

Far-field microphone ASR. Starting with the read digits and proceeding to spontaneous speech, we will have a major focus on improving recognition on the far-field channels. In earlier work we have had some success in recognizing artificially degraded speech [6][5], and will be adapting and more fully developing these approaches for the new data and task. Our current focus in these methods is on the designing of multiple acoustic representations and the combination of the resulting probability streams, but we will also compare these to methods that are more standard (but impractical for the general case) such as echo cancellation using both the close and distant microphones.

Overlap type modeling. One of the distinctive characteristics of naturalistic conversation (in contrast to monolog situations) is the presence of overlapping speech. Overlapping speech may be of several types, and affects the flow of discourse in various ways. An overlap may help to usurp the floor from another speaker (e.g., interruptions), or to encourage a speaker to continue (e.g., back channels). Also, some overlaps may be accidental, or a part of joint

action (as when a group tries to help a speaker to recall a person's name when he is in mid-sentence). In addition, different speakers may differ in the amount and kinds of overlap in which they engage (speaker style). In future work we will explore types of overlaps and their physical parameters, including prosodic aspects.

Language modeling. Meetings are also especially challenging for the language model, since they tend to comprise a diverse range of topics and styles, and matched training data is hard to come by (at least in this initial phase of the project). Therefore, we expect meeting recognition to necessitate investigation into novel language model adaptation and robustness techniques.

Prosodic modeling. Finally, we plan to study the potential contribution of prosodic (temporal and intonational) features to automatic processing of meeting data. A project just underway is constructing a database of prosodic features for meeting data, extending earlier work [10, 9]. Goals include using prosody combined with language model information to help segment speech into coherent semantic units, to classify dialog acts [12], and to aid speaker segmentation.

6. ACKNOWLEDGMENTS

The current work has been funded under the DARPA Communicator project (in a subcontract from the University of Washington), supplemented by an award from IBM. In addition to the authors of this abstract, the project involves colleagues at a number of other institutions, most notably: Mari Ostendorf, Jeff Bilmes, and Katrin Kirchhoff from the University of Washington; and Hynek Hermansky from the Oregon Graduate Institute.

7. REFERENCES

[1] M. Beham and G. Ruske, Adaptiver stochastischer Sprache/Pause-Detektor. *Proc. DAGM Symposium Mustererkennung*, pp. 60–67, Bielefeld, May 1995, Springer.

[2] D. Biber, *Variation across speech and writing.* 1st pbk. ed. Cambridge [England]; New York: Cambridge University Press, 1991.

[3] W. Chafe, Cognitive constraints on information flow. In R. S. Tomlin (ed.) *Coherence and grounding in discourse.* Philadelphia: John Benjamins, pp. 21–51, 1987.

[4] J. Edwards, The transcription of Discourse. In D. Tannen, D. Schiffrin, and H. Hamilton (eds). *The Handbook of Discourse Analysis.* NY: Blackwell (in press).

[5] H. Hermansky, D. Ellis, and S. Sharma, Tandem connectionist feature stream extraction for conventional HMM systems, Proc. ICASSP, pp. III-1635–1638, Istanbul, 2000.

[6] H. Hermansky and N. Morgan, RASTA Processing of Speech, *IEEE Trans. Speech and Audio Processing* 2(4), 578–589, 1994.

[7] A. Janin and N. Morgan, SpeechCorder, the Portable Meeting Recorder, *Workshop on hands-free speech communication*, Kyoto, April 9-11, 2001.

[8] http://www.icsi.berkeley.edu/speech/mtgrcdr.html

[9] E. Shriberg, R. Bates, A. Stolcke, P. Taylor, D. Jurafsky, K. Ries, N. Coccaro, R. Martin, M. Meteer, and C. Van Ess-Dykema. Can prosody aid the automatic classification of dialog acts in conversational speech? *Language and Speech*, 41(3-4):439–487, 1998.

[10] E. Shriberg, A. Stolcke, D. Hakkani-Tür, and G. Tür. Prosody-based automatic segmentation of speech into sentences and topics. *Speech Communication*, 32(1-2):127–154, 2000.

[11] A. Stolcke, H. Bratt, J. Butzberger, H. Franco, V. R. Rao Gadde, M. Plauché, C. Richey, E. Shriberg, K. Sönmez, F. Weng, and J. Zheng. The SRI March 2000 Hub-5 conversational speech transcription system. *Proc. NIST Speech Transcription Workshop*, College Park, MD, May 2000.

[12] A. Stolcke, K. Ries, N. Coccaro, E. Shriberg, R. Bates, D. Jurafsky, P. Taylor, R. Martin, C. Van Ess-Dykema, and M. Meteer, Dialogue Act Modeling for Automatic Tagging and Recognition of Conversational Speech, *Computational Linguistics* 26(3), 339–373, 2000.

[13] http://www.etca.fr/CTA/gip/Projets/Transcriber/

[14] A. Waibel, M. Bett, M. Finke, and R. Stiefelhagen, Meeting Browser: Tracking and Summarizing Meetings, *Proc. DARPA Broadcast News Transcription and Understanding Workshop*, Lansdowne, VA, 1998.

[15] H. Yu, C. Clark, R. Malkin, and A. Waibel, Experiments in Automatic Meeting Transcription Using JRTK, *Proc. ICASSP*, pp. 921–924, Seattle, 1998.

Mitigating the Paucity-of-Data Problem: Exploring the Effect of Training Corpus Size on Classifier Performance for Natural Language Processing

Michele Banko and Eric Brill

Microsoft Research

1 Microsoft Way

Redmond, WA 98052 USA

{mbanko, brill}@microsoft.com

ABSTRACT

In this paper, we discuss experiments applying machine learning techniques to the task of confusion set disambiguation, using three orders of magnitude more training data than has previously been used for any disambiguation-in-string-context problem. In an attempt to determine when current learning methods will cease to benefit from additional training data, we analyze residual errors made by learners when issues of sparse data have been significantly mitigated. Finally, in the context of our results, we discuss possible directions for the empirical natural language research community.

Keywords

Learning curves, data scaling, very large corpora, natural language disambiguation.

1. INTRODUCTION

A significant amount of work in empirical natural language processing involves developing and refining machine learning techniques to automatically extract linguistic knowledge from on-line text corpora. While the number of learning variants for various problems has been increasing, the size of training sets such learning algorithms use has remained essentially unchanged. For instance, for the much-studied problems of part of speech tagging, base noun phrase labeling and parsing, the Penn Treebank, first released in 1992, remains the de facto training corpus. The average training corpus size reported in papers published in the ACL-sponsored *Workshop on Very Large Corpora* was essentially unchanged from the 1995 proceedings to the 2000 proceedings. While the amount of available on-line text has been growing at an amazing rate over the last five years (by some estimations, there are currently over 500 billion readily accessible words on the web), the size of training corpora used by

our field has remained static.

Confusable word set disambiguation, the problem of choosing the correct use of a word given a set of words with which it is commonly confused, (e.g. {to, too, two}, {your, you're}), is a prototypical problem in NLP. At some level, this task is identical to many other natural language problems, including word sense disambiguation, determining lexical features such as pronoun case and determiner number for machine translation, part of speech tagging, named entity labeling, spelling correction, and some formulations of skeletal parsing. All of these problems involve disambiguating from a relatively small set of tokens based upon a string context. Of these disambiguation problems, lexical confusables possess the fortunate property that supervised training data is free, since the differences between members of a confusion set are surface-apparent within a set of well-written text.

To date, all of the papers published on the topic of confusion set disambiguation have used training sets for supervised learning of less than one million words. The same is true for most if not all of the other disambiguation-in-string-context problems. In this paper we explore what happens when significantly larger training corpora are used. Our results suggest that it may make sense for the field to concentrate considerably more effort into enlarging our training corpora and addressing scalability issues, rather than continuing to explore different learning methods applied to the relatively small extant training corpora.

2. PREVIOUS WORK

2.1 Confusion Set Disambiguation

Several methods have been presented for confusion set disambiguation. The more recent set of techniques includes multiplicative weight-update algorithms [4], latent semantic analysis [7], transformation-based learning [8], differential grammars [10], decision lists [12], and a variety of Bayesian classifiers [2,3,5]. In all of these papers, the problem is formulated as follows: Given a specific confusion set (e.g. {to, two, too}), all occurrences of confusion set members in the test set are replaced by some marker. Then everywhere the system sees this marker, it must decide which member of the confusion set to choose. Most learners that have been applied to this problem use as features the words and part of speech tags

Proceedings of HLT 2001, First International Conference on Human Language Technology Research, J. Allan, ed., Morgan Kaufmann, San Francisco, 2001.

appearing within a fixed window, as well as collocations surrounding the ambiguity site; these are essentially the same features as those used for the other disambiguation-in-string-context problems.

2.2 Learning Curves for NLP

A number of learning curve studies have been carried out for different natural language tasks. Ratnaparkhi [12] shows a learning curve for maximum-entropy parsing, for up to roughly one million words of training data; performance appears to be asymptoting when most of the training set is used. Henderson [6] showed similar results across a collection of parsers.

Figure 1 shows a learning curve we generated for our task of word-confusable disambiguation, in which we plot test classification accuracy as a function of training corpus size using a version of winnow, the best-performing learner reported to date for this well-studied task [4]. This curve was generated by training on successive portions of the 1-million word Brown corpus and then testing on 1-million words of Wall Street Journal text for performance averaged over 10 confusion sets. The curve might lead one to believe that only minor gains are to be had by increasing the size of training corpora past 1 million words.

While all of these studies indicate that there is likely some (but perhaps limited) performance benefit to be obtained from increasing training set size, they have been carried out only on relatively small training corpora. The potential impact to be felt by increasing the amount of training data by any signifcant order has yet to be studied.

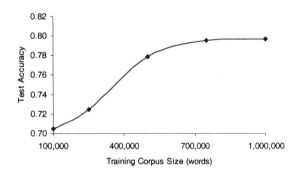

Figure 1: An Initial Learning Curve for Confusable Disambiguation

3. EXPERIMENTS

This work attempts to address two questions – at what point will learners cease to benefit from additional data, and what is the nature of the errors which remain at that point. The first question impacts how best to devote resources in order to improve natural language technology. If there is still much to be gained from additional data, we should think hard about ways to effectively increase the available training data for problems of interest. The second question allows us to study failures due to inherent weaknesses in learning methods and features rather than failures due to insufficient data.

Since annotated training data is essentially free for the problem of confusion set disambiguation, we decided to explore learning curves for this problem for various machine learning algorithms, and then analyze residual errors when the learners are trained on all available data. The learners we used were memory-based learning, winnow, perceptron,[1] transformation-based learning, and decision trees. All learners used identical features[2] and were used out-of-the-box, with no parameter tuning. Since our point is not to compare learners we have refrained from identifying the learners in the results below.

We collected a 1-billion-word training corpus from a variety of English texts, including news articles, scientific abstracts, government transcripts, literature and other varied forms of prose. Using this collection, which is three orders of magnitude greater than the largest training corpus previously used for this task, we trained the five learners and tested on a set of 1 million words of Wall Street Journal text.[3]

In Figure 2 we show learning curves for each learner, for up to one billion words of training data.[4] Each point in the graph reflects the average performance of a learner over ten different confusion sets which are listed in Table 1. Interestingly, even out to a billion words, the curves appear to be log-linear. Note that the worst learner trained on approximately 20 million words outperforms the best learner trained on 1 million words. We see that for the problem of confusable disambiguation, none of our learners is close to asymptoting in performance when trained on the one million word training corpus commonly employed within the field.

Table 1: Confusion Sets

{accept, except}	{principal, principle}
{affect, effect}	{then, than}
{among, between}	{their, there}
{its, it's}	{weather, whether}
{peace, piece}	{your, you're}

The graph in Figure 2 demonstrates that for word confusables, we can build a system that considerably outperforms the current best results using an incredibly simplistic learner with just slightly more training data. In the graph, Learner 1 corresponds to a trivial memory-based learner. This learner simply keeps track of all $<w_{i-1}, w_{i+1}>$, $<w_{i-1}>$ and $<w_{i+1}>$ counts for all occurrences of the confusables in the training set. Given a test set instance, the learner will first check if it has seen $<w_{i-1}, w_{i+1}>$ in the training set. If so, it chooses the confusable word most frequently observed with this tuple. Otherwise, the learner backs off to check for the frequency of $<w_{i-1}>$; if this also was not seen then it will back off to $<w_{i+1}>$, and lastly, to the most frequently observed confusion-

---

[1] Thanks to Dan Roth for making both Winnow and Perceptron available.

[2] We used the standard feature set for this problem. For details see [4].

[3] The training set contained no text from WSJ.

[4] Learner 5 could not be run on more than 100 million words of training data.

Test Accuracy

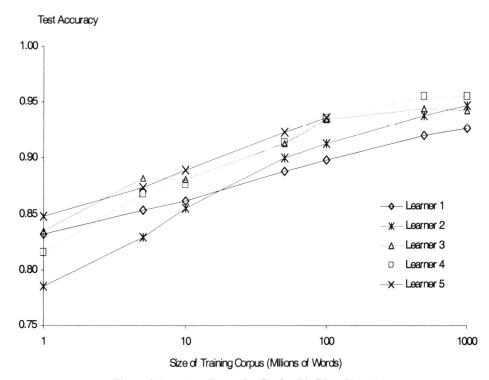

Figure 2. Learning Curves for Confusable Disambiguation

set member as computed from the training corpus. Note that with 10 million words of training data, this simple learner outperforms all other learners trained on 1 million words.

Many papers in empirical natural language processing involve showing that a particular system (only slightly) outperforms others on one of the popular standard tasks. These comparisons are made from very small training corpora, typically less than a million words. We have no reason to believe that any comparative conclusions drawn on one million words will hold when we finally scale up to larger training corpora. For instance, our simple memory based learner, which appears to be among the best performers at a million words, is the worst performer at a billion. The learner that performs the worst on a million words of training data significantly improves with more data.

Of course, we are fortunate in that labeled training data is easy to locate for confusion set disambiguation. For many natural language tasks, clearly this will not be the case. This reality has sparked interest in methods for combining supervised and unsupervised learning as a way to utilize the relatively small amount of available annotated data along with much larger collections of unannotated data [1,9]. However, it is as yet unclear whether these methods are effective other than in cases where we have relatively small amounts of annotated data available.

4. RESIDUAL ERRORS
After eliminating errors arising from sparse data and examining the residual errors the learners make when trained on a billion

words, we can begin to understand inherent weaknesses in ourlearning algorithms and feature sets. Sparse data problems can always be reduced by buying additional data; the remaining problems truly require technological advances to resolve them.

We manually examined a sample of errors classifiers made when trained on one billion words and classified them into one of four categories: strongly misleading features, ambiguous context, sparse context and corpus error. In the paragraphs that follow, we define the various error types, and discuss what problems remain even after a substantial decrease in the number of errors attributed to the problem of sparse data.

Strongly Misleading Features
Errors arising from *strongly misleading features* occur when features which are strongly associated with one class appear in the context of another. For instance, in attempting to characterize the feature set of *weather* (vs. its commonly-confused set member *whether*), according to the canonical feature space used for this problem we typically expect terms associated with atmospheric conditions, temperature or natural phenomena to favor use of *weather* as opposed to *whether*. Below is an example which illustrates that such strong cues are not always sufficient to accurately disambiguate between these confusables. In such cases, a method for better weighing features based upon their syntactic context, as opposed to using a simple bag-of-words model, may be needed.

Example: *On a sunny day whether she swims or not depends on the temperature of the water.*

Ambiguous Context

Errors can also arise from *ambiguous contexts*. Such errors are made when feature sets derived from shallow local contexts are not sufficient to disambiguate among members of a confusable set. Long-range, complex dependencies, deep semantic understanding or pragmatics may be required in order to draw a distinction among classes. Included in this class of problems are so-called "garden-path" sentences, in which ambiguity causes an incorrect parse of the sentence to be internally constructed by the reader until a certain indicator forces a revision of the sentence structure.

Example 1: *It's like you're king of the hill.*

Example 2: *The transportation and distribution departments evaluate weather reports at least four times a day to determine if delivery schedules should be modified.*

Sparse Context

Errors can also be a result of *sparse contexts*. In such cases, an informative term appears, but the term was not seen in the training corpus. Sparse contexts differ from ambiguous contexts in that with more data, such cases are potentially solvable using the current feature set. Sparse context problems may also be lessened by attributing informative lexical features to a word via clustering or other analysis.

Example: *It's baseball's only team-owned spring training site.*

Corpus Error

Corpus errors are attributed to cases in which the test corpus contains an incorrect use of a confusable word, resulting in incorrectly evaluating the classification made by a learner. In a well-edited test corpus such as the Wall Street Journal, errors of this nature will be minimal.

Example: *If they don't find oil, its going to be quite a letdown.*

Table 2 shows the distribution of error types found after learning with a 1-billion-word corpus. Specifically, the sample of errors studied included instances that one particular learner, winnow, incorrectly classified when trained on one billion words. It is interesting that more than half of the errors were attributed to sparse context. Such errors could potentially be corrected were the learner to be trained on an even larger training corpus, or if other methods such as clustering were used.

The ambiguous context errors are cases in which the feature space currently utilized by the learners is not sufficient for disambiguation; hence, simply adding more data will not help.

Table 2: Distribution of Error Types

Error Type	Percent Observed
Ambiguous Context	42%
Sparse Context	57%
Misleading Features	0%
Corpus Error	1%

5. A BILLION-WORD TREEBANK?

Our experiments demonstrate that for confusion set disambiguation, system performance improves with more data, up to at least one billion words. Is it feasible to think of ever having a billion-word Treebank to use as training material for tagging, parsing, named entity recognition, and other applications? Perhaps not, but let us run through some numbers.

To be concrete, assume we want a billion words annotated with part of speech tags at the same level of accuracy as the original million word corpus.[5] If we train a tagger on the existing corpus, the naïve approach would be to have a person look at every single tag in the corpus, decide whether it is correct, and make a change if it is not. In the extreme, this means somebody has to look at one billion tags. Assume our automatic tagger has an accuracy of 95% and that with reasonable tools, a person can verify at the rate of 5 seconds per tag and correct at the rate of 15 seconds per tag. This works out to an average of 5*.95 + 15*.05 = 5.5 seconds spent per tag, for a total of 1.5 million hours to tag a billion words. Assuming the human tagger incurs a cost of $10/hour, and assuming the annotation takes place after startup costs due to development of an annotation system have been accounted for, we are faced with $15 million in labor costs. Given the cost and labor requirements, this clearly is not feasible. But now assume that we could do perfect error identification, using sample selection techniques. In other words, we could first run a tagger over the billion-word corpus and using sample selection, identify all and only the errors made by the tagger. If the tagger is 95% accurate, we now only have to examine 5% of the corpus, at a correction cost of 15 seconds per tag. This would reduce the labor cost to $2 million for tagging a billion words. Next, assume we had a way of clustering errors such that correcting one tag on average had the effect of correcting 10. This reduces the total labor cost to $200k to annotate a billion words, or $20k to annotate 100 million. Suppose we are off by an order of magnitude; then with the proper technology in place it might cost $200k in labor to annotate 100 million additional words.

As a result of the hypothetical analysis above, it is not absolutely infeasible to think about manually annotating significantly larger corpora. Given the clear benefit of additional annotated data, we should think seriously about developing tools and algorithms that would allow us to efficiently annotate orders of magnitude more data than what is currently available.

6. CONCLUSIONS

We have presented learning curves for a particular natural language disambiguation problem, confusion set disambiguation, training with more than a thousand times more data than had previously been used for this problem. We were able significantly reduce the error rate, compared to the best system trained on the standard training set size, simply by adding more training data.

---

[5] We assume an annotated corpus such as the Penn Treebank already exists, and our task is to significantly grow it. Therefore, we are only taking into account the marginal cost of additional annotated data, not start-up costs such as style manual design.

We see that even out to a billion words the learners continue to benefit from additional training data.

It is worth exploring next whether emphasizing the acquisition of larger training corpora might be the easiest route to improved performance for other natural language problems as well.

7. REFERENCES

[1] Brill, E. Unsupervised Learning of Disambiguation Rules for Part of Speech Tagging. In Natural Language Processing Using Very Large Corpora, 1999.

[2] Gale, W. A., Church, K. W., and Yarowsky, D. (1993). A method for disambiguating word senses in a large corpus. Computers and the Humanities, 26:415--439.

[3] Golding, A. R. (1995). A Bayesian hybrid method for context-sensitive spelling correction. In Proc. 3rd Workshop on Very Large Corpora, Boston, MA.

[4] Golding, A. R. and Roth, D. (1999), A Winnow-Based Approach to Context-Sensitive Spelling Correction. Machine Learning, 34:107--130.

[5] Golding, A. R. and Schabes, Y. (1996). Combining trigram-based and feature-based methods for context-sensitive spelling correction. In Proc. 34th Annual Meeting of the Association for Computational Linguistics, Santa Cruz, CA.

[6] Henderson, J. Exploiting Diversity for Natural Language Parsing. PhD thesis, Johns Hopkins University, August 1999.

[7] Jones, M. P. and Martin, J. H. (1997). Contextual spelling correction using latent semantic analysis. In Proc. 5th Conference on Applied Natural Language Processing, Washington, DC.

[8] Mangu, L. and Brill, E. (1997). Automatic rule acquisition for spelling correction. In Proc. 14th International Conference on Machine Learning. Morgan Kaufmann.

[9] Nigam, K, McCallum, A, Thrun, S and Mitchell, T. Text Classification from Labeled and Unlabeled Documents using EM. Machine Learning. 39(2/3). pp. 103-134. 2000.

[10] Powers, D. (1997). Learning and application of differential grammars. In Proc. Meeting of the ACL Special Interest Group in Natural Language Learning, Madrid.

[11] Ratnaparkhi, Adwait. (1999) Learning to Parse Natural Language with Maximum Entropy Models. Machine Learning, 34, 151-175.

[12] Yarowsky, D. (1994). Decision lists for lexical ambiguity resolution: Application to accent restoration in Spanish and French. In Proc. 32nd Annual Meeting of the Association for Computational Linguistics, Las Cruces, NM.

Monitoring the News: a TDT demonstration system

David Frey, Rahul Gupta, Vikas Khandelwal,
Victor Lavrenko, Anton Leuski, and James Allan
Center for Intelligent Information Retrieval
Department of Computer Science
University of Massachusetts
Amherst, MA 01003

ABSTRACT

We describe a demonstration system built upon Topic Detection and Tracking (TDT) technology. The demonstration system monitors a stream of news stories, organizes them into clusters that represent topics, presents the clusters to a user, and visually describes the changes that occur in those clusters over time. A user may also mark certain clusters as interesting, so that they can be "tracked" more easily.

1. TDT BACKGROUND

The Topic Detection and Tracking (TDT) research program investigates methods for organizing an arriving stream of news stories by the topics the stories discuss.[1, 4, 7, 8] Topics are defined to be the set of stories that follow from some seminal event in the world—this is in contrast to a broader subject-based notion of topic. That is, stories about a particular airline crash fall into one topic, and stories from other airline crashes will be in their own topics.

All organization is done as stories arrive, though variations of the task allow final organizational decisions to be postponed for minutes, hours, or even days. The formal TDT evaluation program includes the following research tasks:

1. Segmentation is used to separate a television or radio program into distinct news stories. This process is not needed for newswire services, since those stories arrive pre-segmented.

2. Detection is the task of putting all arriving news stories into bins that represent broad news topics. If a new topic appears in the news, the system must create a new bin. Neither the set of bins nor the total number of them is known in advance. This task is carried out without any supervision—i.e., the system never knows whether or not the stories it is putting together actually belong together.

3. Tracking is the task of finding all stories that follow are on the same topic as an initial small set. This task is different from detection in that the starting stories are *known* to be on the same topic. Typically tracking is evaluated with 2-4 on-topic stories.

Proceedings of HLT 2001, First International Conference on Human Language Technology Research, J. Allan, ed., Morgan Kaufmann, San Francisco, 2001.

The TDT research workshops also include a few other tasks (first story detection, and story link detection). TDT has also inspired other event-based organization methods, including automatic time-line generation to visualize the temporal locality of topics[10], and the identification of new information within a topic's discussion[3].

This demonstration system illustrates event-based news organization by visualizing the creation of, changes within, and relationships between clusters created by the detection task. It leverages the segmentation results so that audio stories are distinct stories, but does not directly visualize the detection. Tracking is implicitly presented by allowing clusters to be marked so that they receive special attention by the user.

2. ARCHITECTURE

The TDT demonstration system is based upon Lighthouse, an interactive information retrieval system developed by Leuski.[6] Lighthouse provides not only a typical ranked list search result, but a visualization of inter-document similarities in 2- or 3-dimensions. The user interface is a Java client that can run as an application or an applet. Lighthouse uses http protocols to send queries to a server and receive the ranked list, summary information about the documents, and the visualization data.

The TDTLighthouse system requires a TDT system running in the background. In this version of the demonstration, the TDT system is only running the segmentation and detection tasks described above. Stories arrive and are put into clusters (bins).

The TDTLighthouse client can query its server to receive up-to-date information about the clusters that the TDT system has found. The server in turn queries the TDT system to get that information and maintains state information so that changes (cluster growth, additional clusters, etc.) can be highlighted.

3. DEMONSTRATION DATA

The data for this demonstration was taken from the our TDT 2000 evaluation output on the TDT cluster detection task [8]. The sytem is running on the TDT-3 evaluation collection of news articles, approximately 40,000 news stories spanning October 1 through December 31, 1998.

We simulated incremental arrival of the data as follows. At the end of each day in the collection, we looked at the incremental output of the TDT detection system. At this point, every story has been classified into a cluster. Every story seen to date is in one of the clusters for that day, even if the cluster has the same contents as it did yesterday.

The demonstration is designed to support text summarization tools that could help a user understand the content of the cluster. For our purposes, each cluster was analyzed to construct the following information:

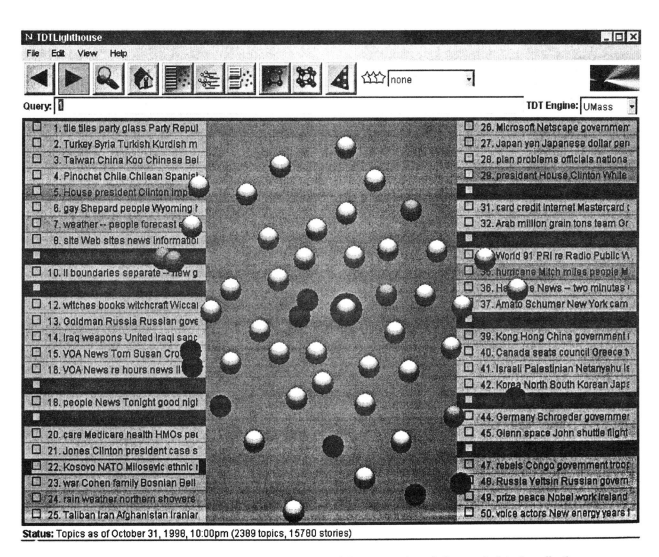

Figure 1: TDT demonstration system running on TDT-3 data, approximately four weeks into the collection.

1. The *title* was generated by selecting the 10 most commonly occurring non-stopwords throughout the cluster. A better title would probably be the headline of the most "representative" news story, though this is an open research question.

2. The *summary* was generated by selecting the £ve sentences that were most representative of the entire cluster. Better approaches might generate a summary from the multiple documents [9] or summarize the changes from the previous day [5, 2].

3. The *contents* of the cluster is just a list of every story in the cluster, presented in reverse chronological order. Various alternative presentations are possible, including leveraging the multimedia (radio and television) that is the basis for the TDT data.

The demonstration system was setup so that it could move from between the days. All of the input to the client was generated automatically, but we saved the information so that it could be shown more quickly. It typically takes a few minutes to generate all of the presentation information for a single day's clusters.

4. DEMONSTRATION SYSTEM

Figure 1 shows the client window. This snapshot shows the system on October 31 at 10:00pm, approximately four weeks into the data. The status line on the lower-left shows that at this point the system has already encountered almost 16,000 stories and has broken them into about 2400 topic clusters.

The system is showing the 50 topics with the largest number of stories. The ranked list (by size) starts on the upper-left, shows the £rst 25, and the continues in the upper-right. The "title" for each of those topics is generated in this case by the most common words within the cluster. Any system that does a better job of building a title for a large cluster of stories could be used to improve this capability.

In addition to the ranked list of topics, the system computes intertopic similarities and depicts that using the spheres in the middle. If two topics are highly similar, their spheres will appear near each other in the visualization. This allows related topics to be detected quickly. Because the 50 largest topics are shown, the topics are more unalike than they would be with a wider range, but it is still possible to see, for example, that topics about the Clinton presidency are near each other (the cyan pair of spheres overlapping rank number 9, topic rank numbers 5 and 29). The spheres and the ranked list are tightly integrated, so selecting one causes the other to be highlighted.

Topics can be assigned colors to make them easier to pick out in future sessions. In this case, the user has chosen to use the same color for a range of related topics—e.g., red for sports topics, green for weather topics, etc. The color selection is in the control of the user and is not done automatically. However, once a color is assigned to a topic, the color is "sticky" for future sessions. A user might choose to color a critical topic bright red so that changes to it stand out in the future.

Figure 2 shows the same visualization, but here a summary of a selected topic is shown in a pop-up balloon. This summary was generated by selecting sentences that contained large numbers of key concepts from the topic. Any summarization of a cluster could be used here if it provided more useful information.

To illustrate how the demonstration system shows changes in TDT clusters over time, Figure 3 shows an updated visualization for two weeks later (November 14, 1998). The topic colors are

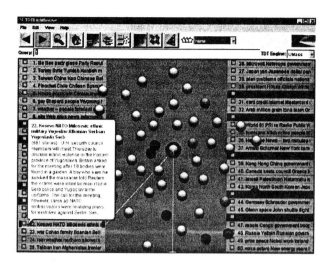

Figure 2: Similar to Figure 1, but showing a pop-up balloon.

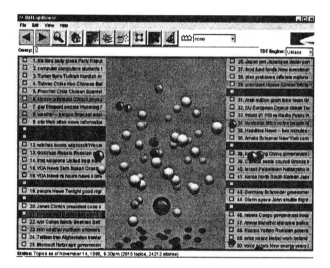

Figure 4: A 3-dimensional version of Figure 3.

persistent from Figure 1, though one of the marked topics ("Strawberry cancer colon Yankee") is no longer in the largest 50 so does not appear.

Most of the spheres include a small "wedge" of yellow in them. That indicates the proportion of the topic that is new stories (since Figure 1). Some topics have large numbers of new stories, so have a large yellow slice, whereas a few have a very small number of new stories, so have only a thin wedge. The yellow wedge can be as much as 50% of the sphere (which would represent an entirely new topic), and only covers the top of the sphere. This restriction ensures that the topic color is still visible.

The controls at the top of the screen are for moving between queries, issuing a query, and returning the visualization to a "home" point. The next £ve controls affect the layout of the display, including allowing a 3-D display: a 3-D version of Figure 3 is shown in Figure 4. The £nal control enables a browsing wizard that can be used to £nd additional topics that are very similar to a selected topic color (that set is chosen using the pull-down menu that has "none" in it).

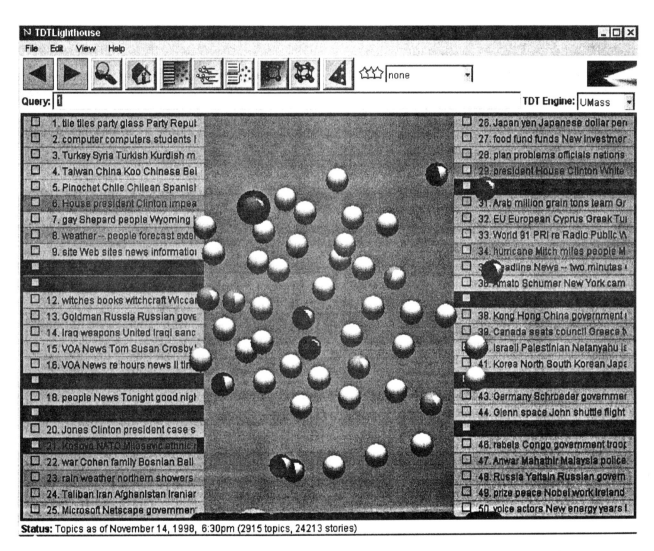

Within the figure, the following interface text is visible:

N TDTLighthouse

File   Edit   View   Help

Query: 1   TDT Engine: UMass

□ 1. tile tiles party glass Party Repul
□ 2. computer computers students l
□ 3. Turkey Syria Turkish Kurdish m
□ 4. Taiwan China Koo Chinese Bel
□ 5. Pinochet Chile Chilean Spanist
□ 6. House president Clinton impea
□ 7. gay Shepard people Wyoming
□ 8. weather -- people forecast exte
□ 9. site Web sites news informatior
□
□
□ 12. witches books witchcraft Wicca
□ 13. Goldman Russia Russian gove
□ 14. Iraq weapons United Iraqi sanc
□ 15. VOA News Tom Susan Crosby
□ 16. VOA News re hours news ll tir
□
□ 18. people News Tonight good nigl
□
□ 20. Jones Clinton president case s
□ 21. Kosovo NATO Milosevic ethnici
□ 22. war Cohen family Bosnian Bell
□ 23. rain weather northern showers
□ 24. Taliban Iran Afghanistan Iraniar
□ 25. Microsoft Netscape governmen

□ 26. Japan yen Japanese dollar pen
□ 27. food fund funds New investmer
□ 28. plan problems officials nations
□ 29. president House Clinton White
■
□ 31. Arab million grain tons team Gr
□ 32. EU European Cyprus Greek Tu
□ 33. World 91 PRI re Radio Public W
□ 34. hurricane Mitch miles people M
□ 35. adline News -- two minutes
□ 36. Amato Schumer New York cam
■
□ 38. Kong Hong China government
□ 39. Canada seats council Greece
□ 40. Israeli Palestinian Netanyahu Is
□ 41. Korea North South Korean Japa
■
□ 43. Germany Schroeder governmer
□ 44. Glenn space John shuttle flight
■
□ 46. rebels Congo government troop
□ 47. Anwar Mahathir Malaysia police
□ 48. Russia Yeltsin Russian govern
□ 49. prize peace Nobel work Ireland
□ 50. voice actors New energy years l

Status: Topics as of November 14, 1998, 6:30pm (2915 topics, 24213 stories)

Figure 3: TDT demonstration system running on TDT-3 data, approximately six weeks into the collection.

261

5. CONCLUSION AND FUTURE WORK

The demonstration system described above illustrates the effect of TDT technology. It is also interesting in its own right, allowing a user to track news topics of interest and to see how changes occur over time. There is no reason that the same system could not be used for non-TDT environments: any setting that clusters documents might be appropriate for this system.

We are working to extend the demonstration system to include some additional features.

- Considering the large number of topics (almost 3,000 in Figure 3), it is unlikely that all "interesting" topics will be £ndable. The query box at the top of the display will be used to allow the user to £nd topics that match a request. The ranked list will display the top 50 topics that match the query.

- Related to querying, we hope to include an "alert" feature that will ¤ag newly-created topics that match a query. For example, an analyst interested in the Middle East might develop a query that would identify topics in that region. When such a topic appeared, it would be ¤agged for the user (probably with a "hot topic" color).

- We hope to allow user "correction" of the topic breakdown provided by the TDT system. The state-of-the-art in TDT still makes mistakes, sometimes pulling two similar topics together, and sometimes breaking a single topic into multiple clusters. We intend that a user who sees such a mistake be able to indicate it to the system. That information will, in turn, to be relayed back to the TDT system to affect future processing.

- We will be implementing an "explode this topic" feature that will show the stories within a topic analogously to the way the current system shows the topics within the news. If the topic is small enough, for example, the spheres would represent stories within the topic. If the topic is larger, the spheres might represnt sub-clusters within the topic.

Acknowledgments

This material is based on work supported in part by the Library of Congress and Department of Commerce under cooperative agreement number EEC-9209623, and in part by SPAWARSYSCEN-SD contract number N66001-99-1-8912. Any opinions, £ndings and conclusions or recommendations expressed in this material are the authors' and do not necessarily re¤ect those of the sponsor.

6. REFERENCES

[1] J. Allan, J. Carbonell, G. Doddington, J. Yamron, and Y. Yang. Topic detection and tracking pilot study: Final report. In *Proceedings of the DARPA Broadcast News Transcription and Understanding Workshop*, pages 194–218, 1998.

[2] J. Allan, R. Gupta, and K. Khandelwal. Temporal summaries of news topics. Technical Report IR-226, University of Massachusetts, CIIR, 2001.

[3] J. Allan, H. Jin, M. Rajman, C. Wayne, D. Gildea, V. Lavrenko, R. Hoberman, and D. Caputo. Topic-based novelty detection: 1999 summer workshop at CLSP, £nal report. Available at http://www.clsp.jhu.edu/ws99/tdt, 1999.

[4] DARPA, editor. *Proceedings of the DARPA Broadcast news Workshop*, Herndon, Virginia, February 1999.

[5] V. Khandelwal, R. Gupta, and J. Allan. An evaluation scheme for summarizing topic shifts in news streams. In *Notebook proceedings of HLT 2001*, 2001.

[6] A. Leuski and J. Allan. Lighthouse: Showing the way to relevant information. In *Proceedings of the IEEE Symposium on Information Visualization (InfoVis)*, pages 125–130, 2000.

[7] NIST. Proceedings of the TDT 1999 workshop. Notebook publication for participants only, March 2000.

[8] NIST. Proceedings of the TDT 2000 workshop. Notebook publication for participants only, November 2000.

[9] D. R. Radev, H. Jing, and M. Budzikowska. Summarization of multiple documents: clustering, sentence extraction, an d evaluation. *ANLP/NAACL Workshop on Summarization, Seattle, WA*, 2000.

[10] Russell Swan and James Allan. Automatic generation of overview timelines. In *Proceedings of SIGIR*, pages 49–56, Athens, Greece, 2000. ACM.

Multidocument Summarization via Information Extraction

Michael White and Tanya Korelsky
CoGenTex, Inc.
Ithaca, NY
mike,tanya@cogentex.com

Claire Cardie, Vincent Ng, David Pierce, and
Kiri Wagstaff
Department of Computer Science
Cornell University, Ithaca, NY
cardie,yung,pierce,wkiri@cs.cornell.edu

ABSTRACT

We present and evaluate the initial version of RIPTIDES, a system that combines information extraction, extraction-based summarization, and natural language generation to support user-directed multidocument summarization.

1. INTRODUCTION

Although recent years has seen increased and successful research efforts in the areas of single-document summarization, multidocument summarization, and information extraction, very few investigations have explored the potential of merging summarization and information extraction techniques. This paper presents and evaluates the initial version of RIPTIDES, a system that combines information extraction (IE), extraction-based summarization, and natural language generation to support user-directed multidocument summarization. (RIPTIDES stands for RapIdly Portable Translingual Information extraction and interactive multiDocumEnt Summarization.) Following [10], we hypothesize that IE-supported summarization will enable the generation of more accurate and targeted summaries in specific domains than is possible with current domain-independent techniques.

In the sections below, we describe the initial implementation and evaluation of the RIPTIDES IE-supported summarization system. We conclude with a brief discussion of related and ongoing work.

2. SYSTEM DESIGN

Figure 1 depicts the IE-supported summarization system. The system first requires that the user select (1) a set of documents in which to search for information, and (2) one or more scenario templates (extraction domains) to activate. The user optionally provides filters and preferences on the scenario template slots, specifying what information s/he wants to be reported in the summary. RIPTIDES next applies its Information Extraction subsystem to generate a database of extracted events for the selected domain and then invokes the Summarizer to generate a natural language summary of the extracted information subject to the user's constraints. In the subsections below, we describe the

Proceedings of HLT 2001, First International Conference on Human Language Technology Research, J. Allan, ed., Morgan Kaufmann, San Francisco, 2001.

IE system and the Summarizer in turn.

2.1 IE System

The domain for the initial IE-supported summarization system and its evaluation is natural disasters. Very briefly, a top-level natural disasters scenario template contains: document-level information (e.g. *docno*, *date-time*); zero or more *agent* elements denoting each *person*, *group*, and *organization* in the text; and zero or more *disaster* elements. *Agent* elements encode standard information for named entities (e.g. *name*, *position*, *geo-political unit*). For the most part, *disaster* elements also contain standard event-related fields (e.g. *type*, *number*, *date*, *time*, *location*, *damage* sub-elements).

The final product of the RIPTIDES system, however, is not a set of scenario templates, but a user-directed multidocument summary. This difference in goals influences a number of template design issues. First, disaster elements must distinguish different reports or views of the same event from multiple sources. As a result, the system creates a separate *disaster* event for each such account. Disaster elements should also include the *reporting agent*, *date*, *time*, and *location* whenever possible. In addition, *damage* elements (i.e. *human* and *physical effects*) are best grouped according to the reporting event. Finally, a slight broadening of the IE task was necessary in that extracted text was not constrained to noun phrases. In particular, adjectival and adverbial phrases that encode *reporter confidence*, and sentences and clauses denoting *relief effort* progress appear beneficial for creating informed summaries. Figure 2 shows the scenario template for one of 25 texts tracking the 1998 earthquake in Afghanistan (TDT2 Topic 89). The texts were also manually annotated for noun phrase coreference; any phrase involved in a coreference relation appears underlined in the running text.

The RIPTIDES system for the most part employs a traditional IE architecture [4]. In addition, we use an in-house implementation of the TIPSTER architecture [8] to manage all linguistic annotations. A preprocessor first finds *sentences* and *tokens*. For syntactic analysis, we currently use the Charniak [5] parser, which creates Penn Treebank-style parses [9] rather than the partial parses used in most IE systems. Output from the parser is converted automatically into TIPSTER *parse* and *part-of-speech* annotations, which are added to the set of linguistic annotations for the document. The extraction phase of the system identifies domain-specific relations among relevant entities in the text. It relies on Autoslog-XML, an XSLT implementation of the Autoslog-TS system [12], to acquire extraction patterns. Autoslog-XML is a weakly supervised learning system that requires two sets of texts for training — one set comprises texts relevant to the domain of interest and the other, texts not relevant

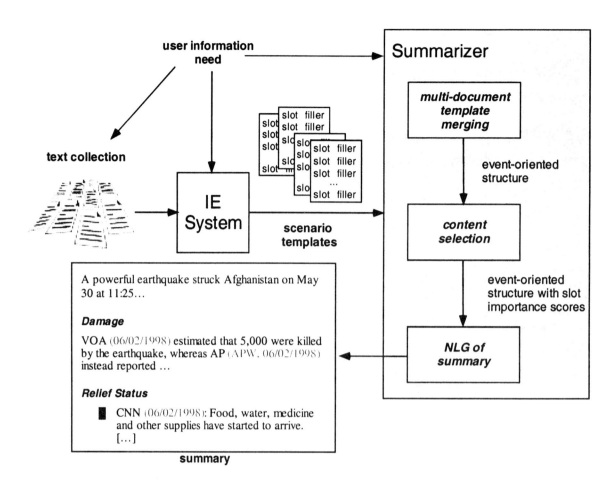

Figure 1. RIPTIDES System Design

to the domain. Based on these and a small set of extraction pattern templates, the system finds a ranked list of possible extraction patterns, which a user then annotates with the appropriate extraction label (e.g. victim). Once acquired, the patterns are applied to new documents to extract slot fillers for the domain. Selectional restrictions on allowable slot fillers are implemented using WordNet [6] and BBN's Identifinder [3] named entity component. In the current version of the system, no coreference resolution is attempted; instead, we rely on a very simple set of heuristics to guide the creation of output templates. The disaster scenario templates extracted for each text are provided as input to the summarization component along with all linguistic annotations accrued in the IE phase. No relief slots are included in the output at present, since there was insufficient annotated data to train a reliable sentence categorizer.

2.2 The Summarizer

In order to include relief and other potentially relevant information not currently found in the scenario templates, the Summarizer extracts selected sentences from the input articles and adds them to the summaries generated from the scenario templates. The extracted sentences are listed under the heading

Selected News Excerpts, as shown in the two sample summaries appearing in Figures 3 and 4, and discussed further in Section 2.2.5 below.

2.2.1 Summarization Stages

The Summarizer produces each summary in three main stages. In the first stage, the output templates are merged into an event-oriented structure, while keeping track of source information. The merge operation currently relies on simple heuristics to group extracted facts that are comparable; for example, during this phase damage reports are grouped according to whether they pertain to the event as a whole, or instead to damage in the same particular location. Heuristics are also used in this stage to determine the most relevant damage reports, taking into account specificity, recency and news source. Towards the same objective but using a more surface-oriented means, simple word-overlap clustering is used to group sentences from different documents into clusters that are likely to report similar content. In the second stage, a base importance score is first assigned to each slot/sentence based on a combination of document position, document recency and group/cluster membership. The base importance scores are then adjusted according to user-specified preferences and matching

Document no.: ABC19980530.1830.0342
Date/time: 05/30/1998 18:35:42.49
Disaster Type: earthquake
•location: *Afghanistan*
•date: *today*
•magnitude: *6.9*
•magnitude-confidence: high
•epicenter: *a remote part of the country*
•damage:

        human-effect:
            victim: *Thousands of people*
            number: *Thousands*
            outcome: dead
            confidence: medium
            confidence-marker: *feared*
        physical-effect:
            object: *entire villages*
            outcome: damaged
            confidence: medium
            confidence-marker: *Details now hard to*
                    come by / reports say

PAKISTAN MAY BE PREPARING FOR ANOTHER TEST

Thousands of people are feared dead following... (voice-over) ...a powerful earthquake that hit Afghanistan today. The quake registered 6.9 on the Richter scale, centered in a remote part of the country. (on camera) Details now hard to come by, but reports say entire villages were buried by the quake.

Figure 2. Example scenario template for the natural disasters domain

criteria. The adjusted scores are used to select the most important slots/sentences to include in the summary, subject to the user-specified word limit. In the third and final stage, the summary is generated from the resulting content pool using a combination of top-down, schema-like text building rules and surface-oriented revisions. The extracted sentences are simply listed in document order, grouped into blocks of adjacent sentences.

2.2.2 Specificity of Numeric Estimates

In order to intelligently merge and summarize scenario templates, we found it necessary to explicitly handle numeric estimates of varying specificity. While we did find specific numbers (such as *3,000*) in some damage estimates, we also found cases with no number phrase at all (e.g. *entire villages*). In between these extremes, we found vague estimates (*thousands*) and ranges of numbers (*anywhere from 2,000 to 5,000*). We also found phrases that cannot be easily compared (*more than half the region's residents*).

To merge related damage information, we first calculate the numeric specificity of the estimate as one of the values NONE, VAGUE, RANGE, SPECIFIC, or INCOMPARABLE, based on the presence of a small set of trigger words and phrases (e.g. *several, as many as, from ... to*). Next, we identify the most specific current estimates by news source, where a later estimate is considered to update an earlier estimate if it is at least as specific. Finally, we determine two types of derived information units, namely (1) the minimum and maximum estimates across the news sources, and

(2) any intermediate estimates that are lower than the maximum estimate.[1]

In the content determination stage, scores are assigned to the derived information units based on the maximum score of the underlying units. In the summary generation stage, a handful of text planning rules are used to organize the text for these derived units, highlighting agreement and disagreement across sources.

2.2.3 Improving the Coherence of Extracted Sentences

In our initial attempt to include extracted sentences, we simply chose the top ranking sentences that would fit within the word limit, subject to the constraint that no more than one sentence per cluster could be chosen, in order to help avoid redundancy. We found that this approach often yielded summaries with very poor coherence, as many of the included sentences were difficult to make sense of in isolation.

To improve the coherence of the extracted sentences, we have experimented with trying to boost coherence by favoring sentences in the context of the highest-ranking sentences over those with lower ranking scores, following the hypothesis that it is better to cover fewer topics in more depth than to change topics excessively. In particular, we assign a score to a set of sentences by summing the base scores plus increasing coherence boosts for adjacent sentences, sentences that precede ones with an initial

---

[1] Less specific estimates such as "hundreds" are considered lower than more specific numbers such as "5000" when they are lower by more than a factor of 10.

Earthquake strikes Afghanistan

A powerful earthquake struck Afghanistan last Saturday at 11:25. The earthquake was centered in a remote part of the country and had a magnitude of 6.9 on the Richter scale.

Damage

Estimates of the death toll varied. VOA (06/02/1998) provided the highest estimate of 5,000 dead. CNN (05/31/1998) and CNN (06/02/1998) supplied lower estimates of 3,000 and up to 4,000 dead, whereas APW (06/02/1998) gave the lowest estimate of anywhere from 2,000 to 5,000 dead. People were injured, while thousands more were missing. Thousands were homeless.

Quake-devastated villages were damaged. Estimates of the number of villages destroyed varied. CNN (05/31/1998) provided the highest estimate of 50 destroyed, whereas VOA (06/04/1998) gave the lowest estimate of at least 25 destroyed.

In Afghanistan, thousands of people were killed.

Further Details

Heavy after shocks shook northern afghanistan. More homes were destroyed. More villages were damaged.

Landslides or mud slides hit the area.

Another massive quake struck the same region three months earlier. Some 2,300 victims were injured.

Selected News Excerpts

ABC (05/30/98):
PAKISTAN MAY BE PREPARING FOR ANOTHER TEST
Thousands of people are feared dead following...

ABC (06/01/98):
RESCUE WORKERS CHALLENGED IN AFGHANISTAN
There has been serious death and devastation overseas. In Afghanistan...

CNN (06/02/98):
Food, water, medicine and other supplies have started to arrive. But a U.N. relief coordinator says it's a "scenario from hell".

Figure 3. 200 word summary of simulated IE output, with emphasis on damage

---

Earthquake strikes quake-devastated villages in northern Afghanistan

A earthquake struck quake-devastated villages in northern Afghanistan Saturday. The earthquake had a magnitude of 6.9 on the Richter scale on the Richter scale.

Damage

Estimates of the death toll varied. CNN (06/02/1998) provided the highest estimate of 4,000 dead, whereas ABC (06/01/1998) gave the lowest estimate of 140 dead.

In capital: Estimates of the number injured varied.

Selected News Excerpts

CNN (06/01/98):
Thousands are dead and thousands more are still missing. Red cross officials say the first priority is the injured. Getting medicine to them is difficult due to the remoteness of the villages affected by the quake.

PRI (06/01/98):
We spoke to the head of the international red cross there, Bob McCaro on a satellite phone link. He says it's difficult to know the full extent of the damage because the region is so remote. There's very little infrastructure.

PRI (06/01/98):
Bob McCaro is the head of the international red cross in the neighboring country of Pakistan. He's been speaking to us from there on the line.

APW (06/02/98):
The United Nations, the Red Cross and other agencies have three borrowed helicopters to deliver medical aid.

Figure 4. 200 word summary of actual IE output, with emphasis on Red Cross

---

cases. We then perform a randomized local search for a good set of sentences according to these scoring criteria.

2.2.4 Implementation

The Summarizer is implemented using the Apache implementation of XSLT [1] and CoGenTex's Exemplars Framework [13]. The Apache XSLT implementation has provided a convenient way to rapidly develop a prototype implementation of the first two processing stages using a series of XML transformations. In the first step of the third summary generation stage, the text building component of the Exemplars Framework constructs a "rough draft" of the summary text. In this rough draft version, XML markup is used to partially encode the rhetorical, referential, semantic and morpho-syntactic structure of the text. In the second generation step, the Exemplars text polishing component makes use of this markup to trigger surface-

pronoun, and sentences that preceded ones with strongly connecting discourse markers such as *however, nevertheless,* etc. We have also softened the constraint on multiple sampling from the same cluster, making use of a redundancy penalty in such

oriented revision rules that smooth the text into a more polished form. A distinguishing feature of our text polishing approach is the use of a bootstrapping tool to partially automate the acquisition of application-specific revision rules from examples.

2.2.5 Sample Summaries

Figures 3 and 4 show two sample summaries that were included in our evaluation (see Section 3 for details). The summary in Figure 3 was generated from simulated output of the IE system, with preference given to damage information; the summary in Figure 4 was generated from the actual output of the current IE system, with preference given to information including the words *Red Cross*.

While the summary in Figure 3 does a reasonable job of reporting the various current estimates of the death toll, the estimates of the death toll shown in Figure 4 are less accurate, because the IE system failed to extract some reports, and the Summarizer failed to correctly merge others. In particular, note that the lowest estimate of 140 dead attributed to ABC is actually a report about the number of school children killed in a particular town. Since no location was given for this estimate by the IE system, the Summarizer's simple heuristic for localized damaged reports — namely, to consider a damage report to be localized if a location is given that is not in the same sentence as the initial disaster description — did not work here. The summary in Figure 3 also suffered from some problems with merging: the inclusion of a paragraph about thousands killed in Afghanistan is due to an incorrect classification of this report as a localized one (owing to an error in sentence boundary detection), and the discussion of the number of villages damaged should have included a report of *at least 80 towns or villages* damaged.

Besides the problems related to slot extraction and merging mentioned above, the summaries shown in Figures 3 and 4 suffer from relatively poor fluency. In particular, the summaries could benefit from better use of descriptive terms from the original articles, as well as better methods of sentence combination and rhetorical structuring. Nevertheless, as will be discussed further in Section 4, we suggest that the summaries show the potential for our techniques to intelligently combine information from many articles on the same natural disaster.

3. EVALUATION AND INITIAL RESULTS

To evaluate the initial version of the IE-supported summarization system, we used Topic 89 from the TDT2 collection — 25 texts on the 1998 Afghanistan earthquake. Each document was annotated manually with the natural disaster scenario templates that comprise the desired output of the IE system. In addition, treebank-style syntactic structure annotations were added automatically using the Charniak parser. Finally, MUC-style noun phrase coreference annotations were supplied manually. All annotations are in XML. The manual and automatic annotations were automatically merged, leading to inaccurate annotation extents in some cases.

Next, the Topic 89 texts were split into a development corpus and a test corpus. The development corpus was used to build the summarization system; the evaluation summaries were generated from the test corpus. We report on three different variants of the RIPTIDES system here: in the first variant (RIPTIDES-SIM1), an

earlier version of the Summarizer uses the simulated output of the IE system as its input, including the relief annotations; in the second variant (RIPTIDES-SIM2), the current version of the Summarizer uses the simulated output of the IE system, without the relief annotations; and in the third variant (RIPTIDES-IE), the Summarizer uses the actual output of the IE system as its input.[2]

Summaries generated by the RIPTIDES variants were compared to a Baseline system consisting of a simple, sentence-extraction multidocument summarizer relying only on document position, recency, and word overlap clustering. (As explained in the previous section, we have found that word overlap clustering provides a bare bones way to help determine what information is repeated in multiple articles, thereby indicating importance to the document set as a whole, as well as to help reduce redundancy in the resulting summaries.) In addition, the RIPTIDES and Baseline system summaries were compared against the summaries of two human authors. All of the summaries were graded with respect to content, organization, and readability on an A-F scale by three graduate students, all of whom were unfamiliar with this project. Note that the grades for RIPTIDES-SIM1, the Baseline system, and the two human authors were assigned during a first evaluation in October, 2000, whereas the grades for RIPTIDES-SIM2 and RIPTIDES-IE were assigned by the same graders in an update to this evaluation in April, 2001.

Each system and author was asked to generate four summaries of different lengths and emphases: (1) a 100-word summary of the May 30 and May 31 articles; (2) a 400-word summary of all test articles, emphasizing specific, factual information; (3) a 200-word summary of all test articles, focusing on the damage caused by the quake, and excluding information about relief efforts, and (4) a 200-word summary of all test articles, focusing on the relief efforts, and highlighting the Red Cross's role in these efforts.

The results are shown in Tables 1 and 2. Table 1 provides the overall grade for each system or author averaged across all graders and summaries, where each assigned grade has first been converted to a number (with A=4.0 and F=0.0) and the average converted back to a letter grade. Table 2 shows the mean and standard deviations of the overall, content, organization, and readability scores for the RIPTIDES and the Baseline systems averaged across all graders and summaries. Where the differences vs. the Baseline system are significant according to the t-test, the p-values are shown.

Given the amount of development effort that has gone into the system to date, we were not surprised that the RIPTIDES variants fared poorly when compared against the manually written summaries, with RIPTIDES-SIM2 receiving an average grade of C, vs. A- and B+ for the human authors. Nevertheless, we were pleased to find that RIPTIDES-SIM2 scored a full grade ahead of the Baseline summarizer, which received a D, and that

---

[2] Note that since the summarizers for the second and third variants did not have access to the relief sentence categorizations, we decided to exclude from their input the two articles (one training, one test) classified by TDT2 Topic 89 as only containing brief mentions of the event of interest, as otherwise they would have no means of excluding the largely irrelevant material in these documents.

Table 1

Baseline	RIPTIDES-SIM1	RIPTIDES-SIM2	RIPTIDES-IE	Person 1	Person 2
D	C/C-	C	D+	A-	B+

Table 2

	Baseline	RIPTIDES-SIM1	RIPTIDES-SIM2	RIPTIDES-IE
Overall	0.96 +/- 0.37	1.86 +/- 0.56 (p=.005)	2.1 +/- 0.59 (p=.005)	1.21 +/- 0.46 (p=.05)
Content	1.44 +/- 1.0	1.78 +/- 0.68	2.2 +/- 0.65 (p=.005)	1.18 +/- 0.6
Organization	0.64 +/- 0.46	2.48 +/- 0.56 (p=.005)	2.08 +/- 0.77 (p=.005)	1.08 +/- 0.65 (p=.05)
Readability	0.75 +/- 0.6	1.58 +/- 0.61 (p=.005)	2.05 +/- 0.65 (p=.005)	1.18 +/- 0.62 (p=.05)

RIPTIDES-IE managed a slightly higher grade of D+, despite the immature state of the IE system. As Table 2 shows, the differences in the overall scores were significant for all three RIPTIDES variants, as were the scores for organization and readability, though not for content in the cases of RIPTIDES-SIM1 and RIPTIDES-IE.

4. RELATED AND ONGOING WORK

The RIPTIDES system is most similar to the SUMMONS system of Radev and McKeown [10], which summarized the results of MUC-4 IE systems in the terrorism domain. As a pioneering effort, the SUMMONS system was the first to suggest the potential of combining IE with NLG in a summarization system, though no evaluation was performed. In comparison to SUMMONS, RIPTIDES appears to be designed to more completely summarize larger input document sets, since it focuses more on finding the most relevant current information, and since it includes extracted sentences to round out the summaries. Another important difference is that SUMMONS sidestepped the problem of comparing reported numbers of varying specificity (e.g. *several thousand* vs. *anywhere from 2000 to 5000* vs. *up to 4000* vs. *5000*), whereas we have implemented rules for doing so. Finally, we have begun to address some of the difficult issues that arise in merging information from multiple documents into a coherent event-oriented view, though considerable challenges remain to be addressed in this area.

The sentence extraction part of the RIPTIDES system is similar to the domain-independent multidocument summarizers of Goldstein et al. [7] and Radev et al. [11] in the way it clusters sentences across documents to help determine which sentences are central to the collection, as well as to reduce redundancy amongst sentences included in the summary. It is simpler than these systems insofar as it does not make use of comparisons to the centroid of the document set. As pointed out in [2], it is difficult in general for multidocument summarizers to produce coherent summaries, since it is less straightforward to rely on the order of sentences in the underlying documents than in the case of single-document summarization. Having also noted this problem, we have focused our efforts in this area on attempting to balance coherence and informativeness in selecting sets of sentences to include in the summary.

In ongoing work, we are investigating techniques for improving merging accuracy and summary fluency in the context of summarizing the more than 150 news articles we have collected from the web about each of the recent earthquakes in Central America and India (January, 2001). We also plan to investigate using tables and hypertext drill-down as a means to help the user verify the accuracy of the summarized information.

By perusing the web collections mentioned above, we can see that trying to manually extricate the latest damage estimates from 150+ news articles from multiple sources on the same natural disaster would be very tedious. Although estimates do usually converge, they often change rapidly at first, and then are gradually dropped from later articles, and thus simply looking at the latest article is not satisfactory. While significant challenges remain, we suggest that our initial system development and evaluation shows that our approach has the potential to accurately summarize damage estimates, as well as identify other key story items using shallower techniques, and thereby help alleviate information overload in specific domains.

5. ACKNOWLEDGMENTS

We thank Daryl McCullough for implementing the coherence boosting randomized local search, and we thank Ted Caldwell, Daryl McCullough, Corien Bakermans, Elizabeth Conrey, Purnima Menon and Betsy Vick for their participation as authors and graders. This work has been partially supported by DARPA TIDES contract no. N66001-00-C-8009.

6. REFERENCES

[1] The Apache XML Project. 2001. "Xalan Java." http://xml.apache.org/.

[2] Barzilay, R., Elhadad, N. and McKeown, K. 2001. "Sentence Ordering in Multidocument Summarization." In *Proceedings of HLT 2001*.

[3] Bikel, D., Schwartz, R. and Weischedel, R. 1999. "An Algorithm that Learns What's in a Name." *Machine Learning* 34:1-3, 211-231.

[4] Cardie, C. 1997. "Empirical Methods in Information Extraction." *AI Magazine* 18(4): 65-79.

[5] Charniak, E. 1999. "A maximum-entropy-inspired parser." Brown University Technical Report CS99-12.

[6] Fellbaum, C. 1998. *WordNet: An Electronic Lexical Database.* MIT Press, Cambridge, MA.

[7] Goldstein, J., Mittal, V., Carbonell, J. and Kantrowitz, M. 2000. "Multi-document summarization by sentence extraction." In *Proceedings of the ANLP/NAACL Workshop on Automatic Summarization,* Seattle, WA.

[8] Grishman, R. 1996. "TIPSTER Architecture Design Document Version 2.2." DARPA, available at http://www.tipster.org/.

[9] Marcus, M., Marcinkiewicz, M. and Santorini, B. 1993. "Building a Large, Annotated Corpus of English: The Penn Treebank." *Computational Linguistics* 19:2, 313-330.

[10] Radev, D. R. and McKeown, K. R. 1998. "Generating natural language summaries from multiple on-line sources." *Computational Linguistics* 24(3):469-500.

[11] Radev, D. R., Jing, H. and Budzikowska, M. 2000. "Summarization of multiple documents: clustering, sentence extraction, and evaluation." In *Proceedings of the ANLP/NAACL Workshop on Summarization,* Seattle, WA.

[12] Riloff, E. 1996. "Automatically Generating Extraction Patterns from Untagged Text." In *Proceedings of the Thirteenth National Conference on Artificial Intelligence,* Portland, OR, 1044-1049. AAAI Press / MIT Press.

[13] White, M. and Caldwell, T. 1998. "EXEMPLARS: A Practical, Extensible Framework for Dynamic Text Generation." In *Proceedings of the Ninth International Workshop on Natural Language Generation*, Niagara-on-the-Lake, Canada, 266-275.

Natural Language Generation in Dialog Systems

Owen Rambow   Srinivas Bangalore   Marilyn Walker

AT&T Labs – Research
Florham Park, NJ, USA
rambow@research.att.com

ABSTRACT

Recent advances in Automatic Speech Recognition technology have put the goal of naturally sounding dialog systems within reach. However, the improved speech recognition has brought to light a new problem: as dialog systems understand more of what the user tells them, they need to be more sophisticated at responding to the user. The issue of system response to users has been extensively studied by the natural language generation community, though rarely in the context of dialog systems. We show how research in generation can be adapted to dialog systems, and how the high cost of hand-crafting knowledge-based generation systems can be overcome by employing machine learning techniques.

1. DIALOG SYSTEMS AND GENERATION

Recent advances in Automatic Speech Recognition (ASR) technology have put the goal of naturally sounding dialog systems within reach.[1] However, the improved ASR has brought to light a new problem: as dialog systems understand more of what the user tells them, they need to be more sophisticated at responding to the user. If ASR is limited in quality, dialog systems typically employ a **system-initiative dialog strategy** in which the dialog system prompts the user for specific information and then presents some information to the user. In this paradigm, the range of user input at any time is limited (thus facilitating ASR), and the range of system output at any time is also limited. However, such interactions are not very natural. In a more natural interaction, the user can supply more and different information at any time in the dialog. The dialog system must then support a **mixed-initiative dialog strategy**. While this strategy places greater requirements on ASR, it also increases the range of system responses and the requirements on their quality in terms of informativeness and of adaptation to the context.

For a long time, the issue of system response to users has been studied by the Natural Language Generation (NLG) community, though rarely in the context of dialog systems. What have emerged from this work are a "consensus architecture" [17] which modularizes the large number of tasks performed during NLG in a par-

[1]The work reported in this paper was partially funded by DARPA contract MDA972-99-3-0003.

Proceedings of HLT 2001, First International Conference on Human Language Technology Research, J. Allan, ed., Morgan Kaufmann, San Francisco, 2001.

ticular way, and a range of linguistic representations which can be used in accomplishing these tasks. Many systems have been built using NLG technology, including report generators [8, 7], system description generators [10], and systems that attempt to convince the user of a particular view through argumentation [20, 4].

In this paper, we claim that the work in NLG is relevant to dialog systems as well. We show how the results can be incorporated, and report on some initial work in adapting NLG approaches to dialog systems and their special needs. The dialog system we use is the AT&T Communicator travel planning system. We use machine learning and stochastic approaches where hand-crafting appears to be too complex an option, but we also use insight gained during previous work on NLG in order to develop models of what should be learned. In this respect, the work reported in this paper differs from other recent work on generation in the context of dialog systems [12, 16], which does not modularize the generation process and proposes a single stochastic model for the entire process. We start out by reviewing the generation architecture (Section 2). In Section 3, we discuss the issue of text planning for Communicator. In Section 4, we summarize some initial work in using machine learning for sentence planning [19]. Finally, in Section 5 we summarize work using stochastic tree models in generation [2].

2. TEXT GENERATION ARCHITECTURE

NLG is conceptualized as a process leading from a high-level communicative goal to a sequence of communicative acts which accomplish this communicative goal. A communicative goal is a goal to affect the user's cognitive state, e.g., his or her beliefs about the world, desires with respect to the world, or intentions about his or her actions in the world. Following (at least) [13], it has been customary to divide the generation process into three phases, the first two of which are planning phases. Reiter [17] calls this architecture a "consensus architecture" in NLG.

- During **text planning**, a high-level communicative goal is broken down into a structured representation of atomic communicative goals, i.e., goals that can be attained with a single communicative act (in language, by uttering a single clause). The atomic communicative goals may be linked by rhetorical relations which show how attaining the atomic goals contributes to attaining the high-level goal.

- During **sentence planning**, abstract linguistic resources are chosen to achieve the atomic communicative goals. This includes choosing meaning-bearing lexemes, and how the meaning-bearing lexemes are connected through abstract grammatical constructions (basically, lexical predicate-argument

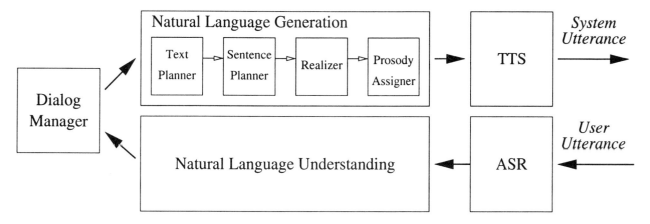

Figure 1: Architecture of a dialog system with natural language generation

structure and modification). As a side-effect, sentence planning also determines sentence boundaries: there need not be a one-to-one relation between elementary communicative goals and sentences in the final text.

- During **realization**, the abstract linguistic resources chosen during sentence planning are transformed into a surface linguistic utterance by adding function words (such as auxiliaries and determiners), inflecting words, and determining word order. This phase is not a planning phase in that it only executes decisions made previously, by using grammatical information about the target language. (Prosody assignment can be treated as a separate module which follows realization and which draws on all previous levels of representation. We do not discuss prosody further in this paper.)

Note that sentence planning and realization use resources specific to the target-language, while text planning is language-independent (though presumably it is culture-dependent).

In integrating this approach into a dialog system, we see that the dialog manager (DM) no longer determines surface strings to send to the TTS system, as is often the case in current dialog systems. Instead, the DM determines high-level communicative goals which are sent to the NLG component. Figure 1 shows a complete architecture. An advantage of such an architecture is the possibility for extended plug-and-play: not only can the entire NLG system be replaced, but also modules within the NLG system, thus allowing researchers to optimize the system incrementally.

The main objection to the use of NLG techniques in dialog systems is that they require extensive hand-tuning of existing systems and approaches for new domains. Furthermore, because of the relative sophistication of NLG techniques as compared to simpler techniques such as templates, the hand-tuning requires specialized knowledge of linguistic representations; hand-tuning templates only requires software engineering skills. An approach based on machine learning can provide a solution to this problem: it draws on previous research in NLG and uses the same sophisticated linguistic representations, but it learns the domain-specific rules that use these representation automatically from data. It is the goal of our research to show that for dialog systems, approaches based on machine learning can do as well as or outperform hand-crafted approaches (be they NLG- or template-based), while requiring far less time for tuning. In the following sections, we summarize the current state of our research on an NLG system for the Communicator dialog system.

3. TEXT PLANNER

Based on observations from the travel domain of the Communicator system, we have categorized system responses into two types. The first type occurs during the initial phase when the system is gathering information from the user. During this phase, the high-level communicative goals that the system is trying to achieve are fairly complex: the goals include getting the hearer to supply information, and to explicitly or implicitly confirm information that the hearer has just supplied. (These latter goals are often motivated by the still not perfect quality of ASR.) The second type occurs when the system has obtained information that matches the user's requirements and the options (flights, hotel, or car rentals) need to be presented to the user. Here, the communicative goal is mainly to make the hearer believe a certain set of facts (perhaps in conjunction with a request for a choice among these options).

In the past, NLG systems typically have generated reports or summaries, for which the high-level communicative goal is of the type "make the hearer/reader believe a given set of facts", as it is in the second type of system response discussed above. We believe that NLG work in text planning can be successfully adapted to better plan these system responses, taking into account not only the information to be conveyed but also the dialog context and knowledge about user preferences. We leave this to ongoing work.

In the first type of system response, the high-level communicative goal typically is an unordered list of high-level goals, all of which need to be achieved with the next turn of the system. An example is shown in Figure 2. NLG work in text planning has not addressed such complex communicative goals in the past. However, we have found that for the Communicator domain, no text planning is needed, and that the sentence planner can act directly on a representation of the type shown in Figure 2, because the number of goals is limited (to five, in our studies). We expect that further work in other dialog domains will require an extension of existing work in text planning to account better for communicative goals other than those that simply aim to affect the user's (hearer's) beliefs.

```
implicit-confirm(orig-city:NEWARK)
implicit-confirm(dest-city:DALLAS)
implicit-confirm(month:9)
implicit-confirm(day-number:1)
request(depart-time)
```

Figure 2: Sample text plan (communicative goals)

Realization	Score
What time would you like to travel on September the 1st to Dallas from Newark?	5
Leaving on September the 1st. What time would you like to travel from Newark to Dallas?	4.5
Leaving in September. Leaving on the 1st. What time would you, traveling from Newark to Dallas, like to leave?	2

Figure 3: Sample alternate realizations of the set of communicative goals shown in Figure 2 suggested by our sentence planner, with human scores

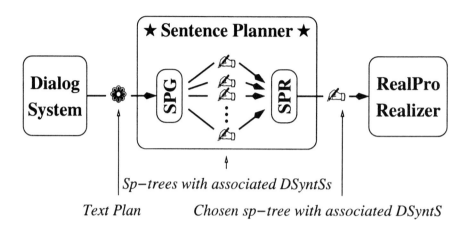

Figure 4: Architecture of our sentence planner

4. SENTENCE PLANNER

The principal challenge facing sentence planning for dialog systems is that there is no good corpus of naturally occurring interactions of the type that need to occur between a dialog system and human users. This is because of the not-yet perfect ASR and the need for implicitly or explicitly confirming most or all of the information provided by the user. In conversations between two humans, communicative goals such as implicit or explicit confirmations are rare, and thus transcripts of human-human interactions in the same domain cannot be used for the purpose of learning good strategies to attain communicative goals. And of course we do not want to use transcripts of existing systems, as we want to improve on their performance, not mirror it.

We have therefore taken the approach of randomly generating a set of solutions and having human judges score each of the options. Each turn of the system is, as described in Section 3, characterized by a set of high-level goals such as that shown in Figure 2. In the turns we consider, no text planning is needed. To date, we have concentrated on the issue of choosing abstract syntactic constructions (rather than lexical choice), so we map each elementary communicative goal to a canonical lexico-syntactic structure (called a **DSyntS** [11]). We then randomly combine these DSyntSs into larger DSyntSs using a set of clause-combining operations identified previously in the literature [14, 18, 5], such as RELATIVE-CLAUSE, CONJUNCTION, and MERGE.[2] The way in which the elementary DSyntSs are combined is represented in a structure called the **sp-tree**. Each sp-tree is then realized using an off-the-shelf realizer, RealPro [9]. Some sample realizations for the same text plan are shown in Figure 3, along with the average of the scores assigned by two human judges.

Using the human scores on each of the up to twenty variants per turn, we use RankBoost [6] to learn a scoring function which uses a large set of syntactic and lexical features. The resulting sentence planner consists of two components: the sentence plan generator (SPG) which generates candidate sentence plans and the sentence plan ranker (SPR) which scores each one of them using the rules learned by RankBoost and which then chooses the best sentence plan. This architecture is shown in Figure 4.

We compared the performance of our sentence planner to a random choice of sentence plans, and to the sentence plans chosen as top-ranked by the human judges. The mean score of the turns judged best by the human judges is 4.82 as compared with the mean of 4.56 for the turns generated by our sentence planner, for a mean difference of 0.26 (5%) on a scale of 1 to 5. The mean of the scores of the turns picked randomly is 2.76, for a mean difference of 1.8 (36%). We validated these results in an independent experiment in which 60 subjects evaluated different realizations for a given turn [15]. (Recall that our trainable sentence planner was trained on the scores of only two human judges.) This evaluation revealed that the choices made by our trainable sentence planner were not statistically distinguishable from the choices ranked at the top by the two human judges. More importantly, they were also not distinguishable statistically from the current hand-crafted template-based output of the AT&T Communicator system, which has been developed and fine-tuned over an extended period of time (the trainable sentence planner is based on judgments that took about three person-days to make).

5. REALIZER

At the level of the surface language, the difference in communicative intention between human-human travel advisory dialogs and the intended dialogs is not as relevant: we can try and mimic the human-human transcripts as closely as possible. To show this, we have performed some initial experiments using FERGUS (Flex-

---

[2] MERGE identifies the verbs and arguments of two lexico-syntactic structures which differ only in adjuncts. For example, *you are flying from Newark* and *you are flying on Monday* are merged to *you are flying from Newark on Monday*.

ible Empiricist-Rationalist Generation Using Syntax), a stochastic surface realizer which incorporates a tree model and a linear language model [2]. We have developed a metric which can be computed automatically from the syntactic dependency structure of the sentence and the linear order chosen by the realizer, and we have shown that this metric correlates with human judgments of the felicity of the sentence [3]. Using this metric, we have shown that the use of both the tree model and the linear language model improves the quality of the output of FERGUS over the use of only one or the other of these resources.

FERGUS was originally trained on the Penn Tree Bank corpus consisting of Wall Street Journal text (WSJ). The results on an initial set of Communicator sentences were not encouraging, presumably because there are few questions in the WSJ corpus, and furthermore, specific constructions (including *what* as determiner) appear to be completely absent (perhaps due to a newspaper style file). In an initial experiment, we replaced the linear language model (LM) trained on 1 million words of WSJ by an LM trained on 10,000 words of human-human travel planning dialogs collected at CMU. This resulted in a dramatic improvement, with almost all questions being generated correctly. Since the CMU corpus is relatively small for a LM, we intend to experiment with finding the ideal combination of WSJ and CMU corpora. Furthermore, we are currently in the process of syntactically annotating the CMU corpus so that we can derive a tree model as well. We expect further improvements in quality of the output, and we expect to be able to exploit the kind of limited lexical variation allowed by the tree model [1].

6. CONCLUSION

We have discussed how work in NLG can be applied in the development of dialog systems, and we have presented two approaches to using stochastic models and machine learning in NLG. Of course, the final justification for using a more sophisticated NLG architecture must come from user trials of an integrated system. However, we suspect that, as in the case of non-dialog NLG systems, the strongest arguments in favor of NLG often come from software engineering issues of maintainability and extensibility, which can be difficult to quantify in research systems.

7. REFERENCES

[1] S. Bangalore and O. Rambow. Corpus-based lexical choice in natural language generation. In *38th Meeting of the Association for Computational Linguistics (ACL'00)*, Hong Kong, China, 2000.

[2] S. Bangalore and O. Rambow. Exploiting a probabilistic hierarchical model for generation. In *Proceedings of the 18th International Conference on Computational Linguistics (COLING 2000)*, Saarbrücken, Germany, 2000.

[3] S. Bangalore, O. Rambow, and S. Whittaker. Evaluation metrics for generation. In *Proceedings of the First International Natural Language Generation Conference (INLG2000)*, Mitzpe Ramon, Israel, 2000.

[4] G. Carenini and J. Moore. A strategy for generating evaluative arguments. In *Proceedings of the First International Natural Language Generation Conference (INLG2000)*, Mitzpe Ramon, Israel, 2000.

[5] L. Danlos. G-TAG: A lexicalized formalism for text generation inspired by tree adjoining grammar. In A. Abeillé and O. Rambow, editors, *Tree Adjoining Grammars: Formalisms, Linguistic Analysis, and Processing*. CSLI Publications, 2000.

[6] Y. Freund, R. Iyer, R. E. Schapire, and Y. Singer. An efficient boosting algorithm for combining preferences. In *Machine Learning: Proceedings of the Fifteenth International Conference*, 1998. Extended version available from http://www.research.att.com/ schapire.

[7] E. Goldberg, N. Driedger, and R. Kittredge. Using natural-language processing to produce weather forecasts. *IEEE Expert*, pages 45–53, 1994.

[8] K. Kukich. *Knowledge-Based Report Generation: A Knowledge Engineering Approach to Natural Language Report Generation*. PhD thesis, University of Pittsuburgh, 1983.

[9] B. Lavoie and O. Rambow. RealPro – a fast, portable sentence realizer. In *Proceedings of the Conference on Applied Natural Language Processing (ANLP'97)*, Washington, DC, 1997.

[10] B. Lavoie, O. Rambow, and E. Reiter. Customizable descriptions of object-oriented models. In *Proceedings of the Conference on Applied Natural Language Processing (ANLP'97)*, Washington, DC, 1997.

[11] I. A. Mel'čuk. *Dependency Syntax: Theory and Practice*. State University of New York Press, New York, 1988.

[12] A. H. Oh and A. I. Rudnicky. Stochastic language generation for spoken dialog systems. In *Proceedings of the ANL/NAACL 2000 Workshop on Conversational Systems*, pages 27–32, Seattle, 2000. ACL.

[13] O. Rambow and T. Korelsky. Applied text generation. In *Third Conference on Applied Natural Language Processing*, pages 40–47, Trento, Italy, 1992.

[14] O. Rambow and T. Korelsky. Applied text generation. In *Proceedings of the Third Conference on Applied Natural Language Processing, ANLP92*, pages 40–47, 1992.

[15] O. Rambow, M. Rogati, and M. Walker. A trainable sentence planner for spoken dialogue systems. In *39th Meeting of the Association for Computational Linguistics (ACL'01)*, Toulouse, France, 2001.

[16] A. Ratnaparkhi. Trainable methods for surface natural language generation. In *Proceedings of First North American ACL*, Seattle, USA, May 2000.

[17] E. Reiter. Has a consensus NL generation architecture appeared, and is it psycholinguistically plausible? In *Proceedings of the 7th International Workshop on Natural Language Generation*, pages 163–170, Maine, 1994.

[18] J. Shaw. Clause aggregation using linguistic knowledge. In *Proceedings of the 8th International Workshop on Natural Language Generation*, Niagara-on-the-Lake, Ontario, 1998.

[19] M. Walker, O. Rambow, and M. Rogati. A trainable sentence planner for spoken dialogue systems. In *2nd Meeting of the North American Chapter of the Association for Computational Linguistics (NAACL'01)*, Pittsburgh, PA, 2001.

[20] I. Zukerman, R. McConachy, and K. Korb. Bayesian reasoning in an abductive mechanism for argument generation and analysis. In *AAAI98 Proceedings – the Fifteenth National Conference on Artificial Intelligence*, pages 833–838, Madison, Wisconsin, 1998.

NewsInEssence: A System For Domain-Independent, Real-Time News Clustering and Multi-Document Summarization

Dragomir R. Radev*†, Sasha Blair-Goldensohn*, Zhu Zhang*, Revathi Sundara Raghavan†
*School of Information
†Department of EECS
University of Michigan
Ann Arbor, MI 48109
{radev,sashabg,zhuzhang,rsundara}@umich.edu

1. INTRODUCTION

NEWSINESSENCE is a system for finding, visualizing and summarizing a topic-based cluster of news stories. In the generic scenario for NEWSINESSENCE, a user selects a single news story from a news Web site. Our system then searches other live sources of news for other stories related to the same event and produces summaries of a subset of the stories that it finds, according to parameters specified by the user.

2. THE NEWSINESSENCE SYSTEM

NewsInEssence's search agent, NewsTroll, runs in two phases. First, it looks for related articles by traversing links from the page containing the seed article. Using the seed article and any related articles it finds in this way, the agent then decides on a set of keywords for further search. In the second phase, it attempts to add to the cluster of related articles by going to the search engines of various news websites and using the keywords which it found in the first phase as search terms.

In both phases, NewsTroll selectively follows hyperlinks with the aim of reaching pages which contain related stories and/or further hyperlinks to related stories pages.

Both general and site-specific rules help NewsTroll determine which URLs are likely to be useful. Only if NewsTroll determines that a URL is "interesting", will it go to the Internet to fetch the new page. A more stringent set of rules are applied to determine whether the URL is likely to be a news story itself. If so, the similarity of its text to that of the original seed page is computed using an IDF-weighted vector measure. If the similarity is above a certain threshold, the page is considered to contain a related article and added to the cluster. The user may use our web interface (Figure 2) to adjust the similarity threshold used in a given search.

Using several levels of filtering, NewsTroll is able to screen out large numbers web pages quite efficiently. The expensive operation of testing lexical similarity is reserved for the small number of pages which NewsTroll finds interesting. Consequently, the agent can return useful results in real time.

3. ANNOTATED SAMPLE RUN

The example begins when we find a news article we would like to read more about. In this case we pick a story is about a breaking story regarding one of President-Elect Bush's cabinet nominees (see Figure 1).

We input the URL using the web interface of the NEWSINESSENCE system, then select our search options, click 'Proceed' and wait for our results (see Figure 2).

In response to the user query, NewsTroll begins looking for related articles linked from the chosen start page. In a selection from the agent's output log in Figure 3, we can see that it extracts and tests links from the page, and decides to test one which looks like a news article. We then see that it tests this article and determines it to be related. This article is added to the initial cluster, from which the list of top keywords is drawn.

In its secondary phase, NewsTroll inputs its keywords to the search engines of news sites and lets them do the work of finding stories. Since we have selected good keywords, most of the links seen by NewsTroll in this part of the search are indeed related articles (see Figure 4). Upon exiting, NewsTroll reports the number of links it has considered, followed, tested, and retrieved (see Figure 4).

The system's web interface reports its progress to the user in real time and provides a link to the visualization GUI once the cluster is complete (Figure 5). Using the GUI, the user can select which of the articles to summarize (see Figures 6 and 7). Figure 8 shows the output of the cluster summarizer.

4. FUTURE WORK

We are currently working on the integration of Cross-Document structure theory (CST) [1] with NEWSINESSENCE. CST is used to describe relations between textual units in multi-document clusters. It is used for example to identify which portions of a cluster contain background information, which sections are redundant, and which ones contain additional information about an event.

5. REFERENCES

[1] Dragomir Radev. A common theory of information fusion from multiple text sources, step one: Cross-document structure. In *Proceedings, 1st ACL SIGDIAL Workshop on Discourse and Dialogue*, Hong Kong, October 2000.

Proceedings of HLT 2001, First International Conference on Human Language Technology Research, J. Allan, ed., Morgan Kaufmann, San Francisco, 2001.

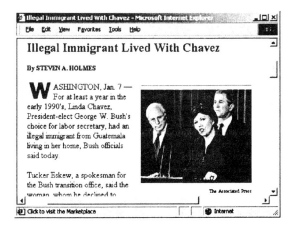

Figure 1: Seed article.

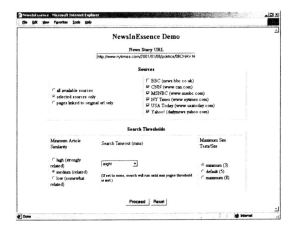

Figure 2: User interface.

Figure 3: Run-time log (part I).

275

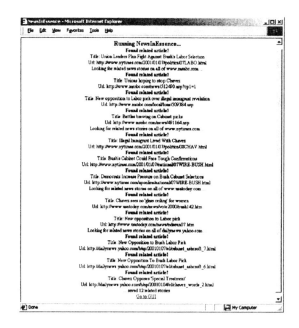

```
sashabgmsvuroq.scumith.edu                              _|□| x|
NewsTroll Starting secondary run...
Extract links from http://search.msn.com/vresults.asp?q=chavez%20eskew%20sweeneys
---
Visiting page... title: Unions hoping to stop Chavez
        running lexsim comparison... Passed! (score = 0.73)
---
Visiting page... title: New opposition to Labor pick over illegal immigrant revel
ation
        running lexsim comparison... Passed! (score = 0.83)
---
Visiting page... title: Battles brewing on Cabinet picks
        running lexsim comparison... Passed! (score = 0.67)
---
Visiting page... title: Security expert suggests passenger skills list
        running lexsim comparison... Failed! (score = 0.004)
---
Extract links from http://search.news.yahoo.com/search/news?p=chavez%20eskew%20sw
eeneys
---
Visiting page... title: Bush's Cabinet Could Face Tough Confirmations
        running lexsim comparison... Passed! (score = 0.84)
---
Visiting page... title: Democrats Increase Pressure on Bush Cabinet Selections
        running lexsim comparison... Passed! (score = 0.74)
---
NewsTroll Completely Finished... Exiting
        Total Considered:       70
        Total Visited:          24
        Total Tested:           13
        Total Retrieved:        12
```

Figure 4: Run-time log (part II).

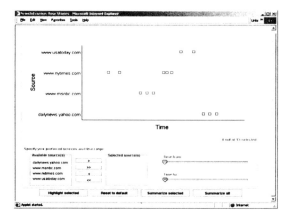

Figure 5: System progress.

Figure 6: Cluster visualization.

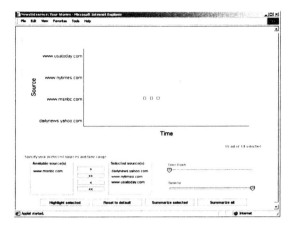

Figure 7: Selected articles.

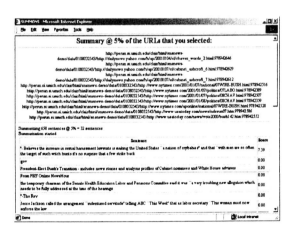

Figure 8: Summarization interface.

Non-Dictionary-Based Thai Word Segmentation Using Decision Trees

Thanaruk Theeramunkong[1]
Information Technology Program
Sirindhorn International Institute of Technology
Thammasat University, Pathumthani 12121, Thailand
+66-2-986-9103(-8) Ext. 2004

ping@siit.tu.ac.th

Sasiporn Usanavasin
Information Technology Program
Sinrindhorn International Institute of Technology
Thammasat University, Pathumthani 12121, Thailand
+66-2986-9103(-8) Ext. 2002

sasiporn@kind.siit.tu.ac.th

ABSTRACT

For languages without word boundary delimiters, dictionaries are needed for segmenting running texts. This figure makes segmentation accuracy depend significantly on the quality of the dictionary used for analysis. If the dictionary is not sufficiently good, it will lead to a great number of unknown or unrecognized words. These unrecognized words certainly reduce segmentation accuracy. To solve such problem, we propose a method based on decision tree models. Without use of a dictionary, specific information, called syntactic attribute, is applied to identify the structure of Thai words. C4.5 is used as a tool for this purpose. Using a Thai corpus, experiment results show that our method outperforms some well-known dictionary-dependent techniques, maximum and longest matching methods, in case of no dictionary.

Keywords

Decision trees, Word segmentation without a dictionary

1. INTRODUCTION

Word segmentation is a crucial topic in analysis of languages without word boundary markers. Many researchers have been trying to develop and implement in order to gain higher accuracy. Unlike in English, word segmentation in Thai, as well as in many other Asian languages, is more complex because the language does not have any explicit word boundary delimiters, such as a space, to separate between each word. It is even more complicated to precisely segment and identify the word boundary in Thai language because there are several levels and several roles in Thai characters that may lead to ambiguity in segmenting the words. In the past, most researchers had implemented Thai word segmentation systems based on using a dictionary ([2], [3], [4], [6], [7]). When using a dictionary, word segmentation has to cope with an unknown word problem. Up to present, it is clear that

most researches on Thai word segmentation with a dictionary suffer from this problem and then introduce some particular process to handle such problem. In our preliminary experiment, we extracted words from a pre-segmented corpus to form a dictionary, randomly deleted some words from the dictionary and used the modified dictionary in segmentation process based two well-known techniques; Maximum and Longest Matching methods. The result is shown in Figure 1. The percentages of accuracy with different percentages of unknown words are explored. We found out that in case of no unknown words, the accuracy is around 97% in both maximum matching and longest matching but the accuracy drops to 54% and 48% respectively, in case that 50% of words are unknown words. As the percentage of unknown words rises, the percentage of accuracy drops continuously. This result reflects seriousness of unknown word problem in word segmentation.

Unknown word (%)	Accuracy (%)	
	Maximum Matching	Longest Matching
0	97.24	97.03
5	95.92	95.63
10	93.12	92.23
15	89.99	87.97
20	86.21	82.60
25	78.40	74.41
30	68.07	64.52
35	69.23	62.21
40	61.53	57.21
45	57.33	54.84
50	54.01	48.67

Figure 1. The accuracy of two dictionary-based systems vs. percentage of unknown words

In this paper, to take care of both known and unknown words, we propose the implementation of a non-dictionary-based system with the knowledge based on the decision tree model ([5]). This model attempts to identify word boundaries of a Thai text. To do

Proceedings of HLT 2001, First International Conference on Human Language Technology Research, J. Allan, ed., Morgan Kaufmann, San Francisco, 2001.

[1] National Electronics and Computer Technology Center (NECTEC), 539/2 Sriyudhya Rd., Rajthevi Bangkok 10400, Thailand

this, the specific information about the structure of Thai words is needed. We called such information in our method as syntactic attributes of Thai words. As the learning stage, a training corpus is utilized to construct a decision tree based on C4.5 algorithm. In the segmentation process, a Thai text is segmented according to the rules produced by the obtained decision tree. The rest shows the proposed method, experimental results, discussion and conclusion.

2. PREVIOUS APPROACHES
2.1 Longest Matching
Most of Thai early works in Thai word segmentation are based on longest matching method ([4]). The method scans an input sentence from left to right, and select the longest match with a dictionary entry at each point. In case that the selected match cannot lead the algorithm to find the rest of the words in the sentence, the algorithm will backtrack to find the next longest one and continue finding the rest and so on. It is obvious that this algorithm will fail to find the correct the segmentation in many cases because of its greedy characteristic. For example:ไปหามเหสี (go to see the queen) will be incorrectly segmented as: ไป(go) หาม (carry) เท(deviate) สี (color), while the correct one that cannot be found by the algorithm is: ไป(go) หา(see) มเหสี (Queen).

2.2 Maximum Matching
The maximum matching algorithm was proposed to solve the problem of the longest matching algorithm describes above ([7]). This algorithm first generates all possible segmentations for a sentence and then select the one that contain the fewest words, which can be done efficiently by using dynamic programming technique. Because the algorithm actually finds real maximum matching instead of using local greedy heuristics to guess, it always outperforms the longest matching method. Nevertheless, when the alternatives have the same number of words, the algorithm cannot determine the best candidate and some other heuristics have to be applied. The heuristic often used is again the greedy one: to prefer the longest matching at each point. For the example, ตาก(expose) ลม(wind) is preferred to ตา(eye) กลม(round).

2.3 Feature-based Approach
A number of feature-based methods have been developed in ([3]) for solving ambiguity in word segmentation. In this approach, the system generates multiple possible segmentation for a string, which has segmentation ambiguity. The problem is that how to select the best segmentation from the set of candidates. At this point, this research applies and compares two learning techniques, called RIPPER and Winnow. RIPPER algorithm is a propositional learning algorithm that constructs a set of rules while Winnow algorithm is a weighted-majority learning algorithm that learns a network, where each node in the network is called a specialist. Each specialist looks at a particular value of an attribute of the target concept, and will vote for a value of the target concept based on its specialty; i.e., based on a value of the attribute it examines. The global algorithm combines the votes from all specialists and makes decision. This approach is a dictionary-based approach. It can acquire up to 91-99% of the number of correct segmented sentences to the total number of sentences.

2.4 Thai Character Chuster
In Thai language, some contiguous characters tend to be an inseparable unit, called Thai character cluster (TCC). Unlike word segmentation that is a very difficult task, segmenting a text into TCCs is easily realized by applying a set of rules. The method to segment a text into TCCs was proposed in ([8]). This method needs no dictionary and can always correctly segment a text at every word boundaries.

3. WORD SEGMENTATION WITH DECISION TREE MODELS
In this paper, we propose a word segmentation method that (1) uses a set of rules to combine contiguous characters to an inseparable unit (syllable-like unit) and (2) then applies a learned decision tree to combine these contiguous units to words. This section briefly shows the concept of TCC and the proposed method based on decision trees.

3.1 Segmenting a Text into TCCs
In Thai language, some contiguous characters tend to be an inseparable unit, called Thai character cluster (TCC). Unlike word segmentation that is a very difficult task, segmenting a text into TCCs is easily recognized by applying a set of rules (in our system, 42 BNF rules). The method to segment a text into TCCs was proposed in [8]. This method needs no dictionary and can always correctly segment a text at every word boundaries. As the first step of our word segmentation approach, a set of rules is applied to group contiguous characters in a text together to form TCCs. The accuracy of this process is 100% in the sense that there is no possibility that these units are divided to two or more units, which are substrings in two or more different words. This process can be implemented without a dictionary, but uses a set of simple linguistic rules based on the types of characters. Figure 2 displays the types of Thai characters. As an example rule, a front vowel and its next consonant must exist in the same unit. Figure 3 shows a fragment of a text segmented into TCCs by the proposed method and its correct word segmentation. Here, a character '|' indicates a segmentation point. The corpus where characters are grouped into TCCs is called a TCC corpus.

Types of Thai Characters	Members
Consonant	กขฃคฅฆงจฉชซฌญฎฏฐฑฒณดตถ ทธนบปผฝพฟภมยรฤลฦวศษสหฬอฮ
Upper vowel	◌ ◌ ◌ ◌ ◌ ◌
Lower vowel	◌ ◌
Front vowel	เแโใไ
Rear vowel	ำๅๆะฯๆ

Figure 2. Types of Thai characters

279

TCCs	ก|า|ร| เก็บ|ภา|ษี|ป|ระ|เท|ศ|ไท|ย|และ|ป|ระ|เท|ศ|
CORRECT	การ| เก็บ|ภาษี|ประเทศ|ไทย|และ|ประเทศ|

Figure 3. An example of TCCs vs. correct segmentation

3.2 Learning a Decision Tree for Word Segmentation

To learn a decision tree for this task, some attributes are defined for classifying whether two contiguous TCCs are combined to one unit or not. In this paper, eight types of attributes (in Figure 4 are proposed to identify possible word boundaries in the text. The answers (or classes) in the decision tree for this task are of two types: combine and not combine. Moreover, to decide whether two contiguous TCCs should be combined or not, the TCC in front of the current two TCCs and the TCC behind them are taken into account. That is, there are four sets of attributes concerned: two for current two TCCs and two for TCCs in front of and behind the current TCCs. Therefore, the total number of attributes is 32 (that is, 8x4) and there is one dependent variable indicating whether the current two contiguous TCCs should be combined or not.

Attribute Name	Attribute Detail
Front_vowel	0(don't have), 1(don't have rear vowel), 2(may be followed by rear vowel)
Front_consonant	0(don't have), 1(don't lead with hohip or oang), 2(lead with hohip or oang)
Middle_vowel	0(don't have), 1(upper vowel), 2(lower vowel)
Middle_consonant	0(don't have), 1 (have)
Rear_vowel	0(don't have), 1 (sara_a), 2 (sara_aa, sara_am)
Rear_consonant	0-9 are (don't have), (kok_tone), (kod_tone), (kong_tone), (kom_tone), (kob_tone), (kon_tone), (wowaen_tone), (yoyak_tone), (others)
Length	Length of the block (the number of characters)
Space & Enter	0 (don't have), 1 (have)

Figure 4. Types of TCC Attributes

Figure 5 illustrates an example of the process to extract attributes from the TCC corpus and use them as a training corpus. The process is done by investigating the current TCCs in the buffer and recording their attribute values. The dependent variable is set by comparing the combination of the second and the third blocks of characters in the buffer to the same string in the correct word-segmented corpus, the corpus that is segmented by human. The result of this comparison will output whether the second and the third blocks in the buffer should be merged to each other or not. This output is then kept as a training set with the dependent variable, "Combine (1)" or "NotCombine (0)". Repetitively, the start of the buffer is shifted by one block. This process executes until the buffer reaches the end of the corpus. The obtained training set then is used as the input to the C4.5 application ([5]) for learning a decision tree.

The C4.5 program will examine and construct the decision tree using the statistical values calculated from the events occurred. After the decision tree is created, the certainty factor is calculated and assigned to each leaf as a final decision-making factor. This certainty factor is the number that identifies how certain the answer at each terminal node is. It is calculated according to the number of terminal class answers at each leaf of the tree. For example, at leaf node i, if there are ten terminal class answers; six of them are "Combine" and the rest are "Not Combine". The answer at this node would be "Combine" with the certainty factor equals to 0.6 (6/10). On the other hand, leaf node j has 5 elements; two are "Combine" and three are "Not Combine", then the answer at this node would be "Not Combine" with the certainty factor equals to 0.6 (3/5). The general formula for the certainty factor (CF) is shown as follow:

$$CFi = \frac{\text{Total number of the answer elements at leaf node } i}{\text{Total number of all elements at leaf node } i}$$

We also calculate the recall, precision, and accuracy as defined below:

$$\text{Precision} = \frac{\text{number of correct '|'s in the system answer}}{\text{number of '|'s in the system answer}}$$

$$\text{Recall} = \frac{\text{number of correct '|'s in the system answer}}{\text{number of '|'s in the correct answer}}$$

$$\text{Accuracy} = \frac{\text{number of correct segmented units in system answer}}{\text{total number of segmented units in correct answer}}$$

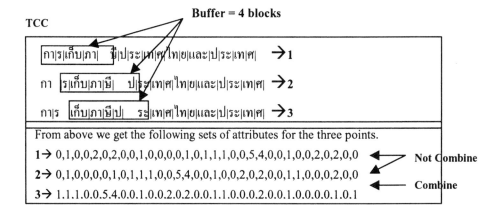

Figure 5. Attributes taken from the corpus

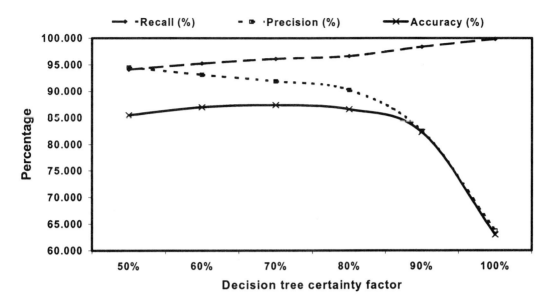

Figure 4. Recall, precision, and accuracy

4. EXPERIMENT RESULTS

In our experiments, the TCC corpus is divided into five sets, four for training and one for testing. Based on this, five times cross validation are performed. To test the accuracy, we trained the decision trees and tested them several times for six different levels of merging permission according to certainty factor(CF). Each level is the starting level of merging permission of the strings in the second and the third blocks in the buffer. Recall, precision, and accuracy where the certainty factor ranges between 50% and 100% are shown in Figure 6.

From the result, we observed that our method presented the satisfactory in the percentage of accuracy and both in precision and recall compared to those numbers of the original TCC performance. The TCC corpus has 100% recall but has 52.12% precision, and 44.93% accuracy. Using the decision tree learned from a Thai corpus, the precision improves up to 94.11-99.85% and the accuracy increases up to 85.51-87.41%. However, the recall drops to 63.72-94.52%. For a high CF, say 100 %, recall drops a little because there are few cases to merge two TCCs but precision and accuracy improve dominantly to 63.72% and 62.97, respectively. For a lower CF, say 50%, recall drops dominantly but precision and accuracy dramatically improve to 94.52% and 85.51% respectively.

However, from 50 to 100% CF, at approximately 80% CF, the accuracy had declined. The reason to this declination is that with a very high level of merging permission, there are a few chances for removing '|' because of the %CF at those leaves are lower than this permission level. Therefore, there are more chances for wrong word segmentation, which lead to decrease accuracy. In conclusion, the appropriate level of merging permission has to be used in order to achieve high accuracy. From our experiment, the best permission level is approximately equal to 70%, which gives

the recall equals to 96.13%, precision equals to 91.92% and the accuracy equals to 87.41%.

5. DISCUSSION AND CONCLUSION

Due to the problem of the unknown words that most of the existing Thai word segmentation systems have to cope with, this paper has introduced an alternative method for avoiding such problem. Our approach is based on using the decision tree as the decision support model with no need of dictionary at all. The experimental results clearly show that our method gives some promises on achieving high accuracy when suitable and appropriate merging permission factor is used. In our experiments, the best level of permission that leads to the highest accuracy is approximately equals to 70%, which gives the accuracy equal to 87.41%, as shown in Figure 6.

The dictionary-based method so-called the feature-based system with context independence gives the highest accuracy equals to 99.74% and with context dependence, which has the highest accuracy equals to 95.33% ([3]). In [1], the Japanese word segmentation is explored based on decision tree. However, it focuses on the part-of-speech for word segmentation. Another two well known dictionary-based methods, Maximum and Longest Matching methods, have the accuracy equal to 86.21% and 82.60% respectively when there are 20% of unknown words, which are lower than our system accuracy, and their accuracy drops as percentage of unknown words increases. By comparing these percentages of accuracy, we can conclude that our method can achieve satisfied accuracy even without dictionary. Therefore, our method is useful for solving an unknown word problem and it will be even more useful to apply our method to the dictionary-based system in order to improve the system accuracy. In addition, our results seem to suggest that our method is efficient not only for Thai texts but also for any language when suitable and appropriate syntactic attributes are used.

Our plan for further research is to apply our method to the dictionary based system in order to take care of the unknown word parts. This would improve the accuracy of the system regardless of the level of the unknown words found in the context.

6. ACKNOWLEDGEMENT

This work has been supported by National Electronics and Computer Technology Center (NECTEC) under the project number NT-B-06-4F-13-311.

7. REFERENCES

[1] Kasioka, H., Eubank, S. G., and Black, E. W., Decision-Tree Morphological Analysis without a Dictionary for Japanese, Proceedings of the Natural Language Processing Pacific Rim Symposium, pp. 541-544, Phuket, Thailand, 1997.

[2] Kawtrakul, A., Thumkanon, C., Poovorawan, Y., Varasrai, P. and Suktarachan, M., Automatic Thai Unknown Word Recognition, Proceedings of the Natural Language Processing Pacific Rim Symposium, pp. 341-348, Phuket, Thailand, 1997.

[3] Mekanavin, S., Charenpornsawat, P., and Kijsirikul, B., Feature-based Thai Words Segmentation, Proceedings of the Natural Language Processing Pacific Rim Symposium, pp. 41-48, Phuket, Thailand, 1997.

[4] Poowarawan, Y., Dictionary-based Thai Syllable Separation, Proceedings of the Ninth Electronics Engineering Conference, 1986.

[5] Quinlan, J.R., Induction of Decision Trees, Machine Learning, 1, pp. 81-106, 1986.

[6] Rarunrom, S. Dictionary-based Thai Word Separation, Thesis, Thailand.

[7] Sornlertlamvanich, V., Word Segmentation for Thai in a Machine Translation system (in Thai), Papers on Natural Language processing, NECTEC, Thailand, 1995.

[8] Theeramunkong, T., Sornlertlamvanich, V., Tanhermhong, T., Chinnan, W., Character-Cluster Based Thai Information Retrieval, Proceedings of the Fifth International Workshop on Information Retrieval with Asian Languages, September 30 - October 20, 2000, Hong Kong, pp.75-80.

On Combining Language Models : Oracle Approach*

Kadri Hacioglu and Wayne Ward
Center for Spoken Language Research
University of Colorado at Boulder
{hacioglu,whw}@cslr.colorado.edu

ABSTRACT

In this paper, we address the problem of combining several language models (LMs). We find that simple interpolation methods, like log-linear and linear interpolation, improve the performance but fall short of the performance of an oracle. The oracle knows the reference word string and selects the word string with the best performance (typically, word or semantic error rate) from a list of word strings, where each word string has been obtained by using a different LM. Actually, the oracle acts like a dynamic combiner with hard decisions using the reference. We provide experimental results that clearly show the need for a dynamic language model combination to improve the performance further. We suggest a method that mimics the behavior of the oracle using a neural network or a decision tree. The method amounts to tagging LMs with confidence measures and picking the best hypothesis corresponding to the LM with the best confidence.

1. INTRODUCTION

Statistical language models (LMs) are essential in speech recognition and understanding systems for high word and semantic accuracy, not to mention robustness and portability. Several language models have been proposed and studied during the past two decades [8]. Although it has turned out to be a rather difficult task to beat the (almost) standard class/word n-grams (typically $n = 2$ or 3), there has been a great deal of interest in grammar based language models [1]. A promising approach for limited domain applications is the use of semantically motivated phrase level stochastic context free grammars (SCFGs) to parse a sentence into a sequence of semantic tags which are further modeled using n-grams [2, 9, 10, 3]. The main motivation behind the grammar based LMs is the inability of n-grams to model longer-distance constraints in a language. With the advent of fairly fast computers and efficient parsing and search schemes several researchers have focused on incorporating relatively complex language models into speech recognition and understanding systems at different levels. For example, in [3], we

*The work is supported by DARPA through SPAWAR under grant #N66001-00-2-8906.

Proceedings of HLT 2001, First International Conference on Human Language Technology Research, J. Allan, ed., Morgan Kaufmann, San Francisco, 2001.

report a significant perplexity improvement with a moderate increase in word/semantic accuracy, at N-best list (rescoring) level, using a dialog-context dependent, semantically motivated grammar based language model.

Statistical language modeling is a "learning from data" problem. The generic steps to be followed for language modeling are

- preparation of training data
- selection of a model type
- specification of the model structure
- estimation of model parameters

The training data should consist of large amounts of text, which is hardly satisfied in new applications. In those cases, complex models fit to the training data. On the other hand, simple models can not capture the actual structure. In the Bayes' (sequence) decision framework of speech recognition/understanding we heavily constrain the model structure to come up with a tractable and practical LM. For instance, in a class/word n-gram LM the dependency of a word is often restricted to the class that it belongs and the dependency of a class is limited to n-1 previous classes. The estimation of the model parameters, which are commonly the probabilities, is another important issue in language modeling. Besides data sparseness, the estimation algorithms (e.g. EM algorithm) might be responsible for the estimated probabilities to be far from optimal.

The aforementioned problems of learning have different effects on different LM types. Therefore, it is wise to design LMs based on different paradigms and combine them in some optimal sense. The simplest combination method is the so called linear interpolation [4]. Recently, the linear interpolation in the logarithmic domain has been investigated in [6]. Perplexity results on a couple of tasks have shown that the log-linear interpolation is better than the linear interpolation. Theoretically, a far more powerful method for LM combination is the maximum entropy approach [7]. However, it has not been widely used in practice, since it is computationally demanding.

In this research, we consider two LMs:

- class-based 3-gram LM (baseline).
- dialog dependent semantic grammar based 3-gram LM [3].

After N-best list rescoring experiments with linear and log-linear interpolation, we realized that the performance in terms of word and semantic accuracies fall considerably short of the performance of an oracle. We explain the set-up for the oracle experiment and point out that the oracle is a dynamic LM combiner. To fill the performance gap, we suggest a method that can mimic the oracle.

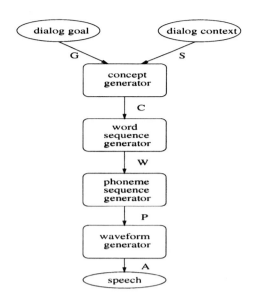

Figure 1: A speech production model

The paper is organized as follows. Section 2 presents the language models considered in this study. In Section 3, we briefly explain combining of LMs using linear and log-linear interpolation. Section 4 explains the set up for the oracle experiment. Experimental results are reported in Section 5. The future work and conclusions are given in the last section.

2. LANGUAGE MODELS

In language modeling, the goal is to find the probability distribution of word sequences, i.e. $P(W)$, where $W = w_1, w_2 \cdots, w_L$. We first describe a model for sentence generation in a dialog [5] on which our grammar LM is based. The model is illustrated in Figure 1. Here, the user has a specific goal that does not change throughout the dialog. According to the goal and the dialog context the user first picks a set of concepts with respective values and then use phrase generators associated with concepts to generate the word sequence. The word sequence is next mapped into a sequence of phones and converted into a speech signal by the user's vocal apparatus which we finally observe as a sequence of acoustic feature vectors.

Assuming that

- the dialog context S is given,

- W is independent of S but the concept sequence C, i.e. $P(W/C, S) = P(W/C)$,

- (W,C) pair is unique (possible with either Viterbi approximation or unambiguous association between C and W),

one can easily show that $P(W)$ is given by

$$P(W) = P(W/C)P(C/S) \qquad (1)$$

In (1) we identify two models:

- Concept model: $P(C/S)$

- Syntactic model : $P(W/C)$

<s> I WANT TO FLY FROM MIAMI FLORIDA TO SYDNEY AUSTRALIA ON OCTOBER FIFTH </s>
<s> [i_want] [depart_loc] [arrive_loc] [date] </s>

<s> I DON'T TO FLY FROM MIAMI FLORIDA TO SYDNEY AFTER AREA ON OCTOBER FIFTH </s>
<s> [Pronoun] [Contraction] [depart_loc] [arrive_loc] [after] [Noun] [date] </s>

Figure 2: Examples of parsing into concepts and filler classes

The concept model is conditioned on the dialog context. Although there are several ways to define a dialog context, we select the last question prompted by the system as the dialog context. It is simple and yet strongly predictive and constraining.

The concepts are classes of phrases with the same meaning. Put differently, a concept class is a set of all phrases that may be used to express that concept (e.g. [i_want], [arrive_loc]). Those concept classes are augmented with single word, multiple word and a small number of broad (and unambigious) part of speech (POS) classes. In cases where the parser fails, we break the phrase into a sequence of words and tag them using this set of "filler" classes. Two examples in Figure 2 clearly illustrate the scheme.

The structure of the concept sequences is captured by an n-gram LM. We train a seperate language model for each dialog context. Given the context S and $C = c_0 c_1 \cdots c_K, c_{K+1}$, the concept sequence probabilities are calculated as (for $n = 3$)

$$P(C/S) = P(c_1/<s>, S)P(c_2/<s>, c_1, S)$$

$$\prod_{k=3}^{K+1} P(c_k/c_{k-2}, c_{k-1}, S)$$

where c_0 and c_{K+1} are for the sentence-begin and sentence-end symbols, respectively.

Each concept class is written as a CFG and compiled into a stochastic recursive transition network (SRTN). The production rules define complete paths beginning from the start-node through the end-node in these nets. The probability of a complete path traversed through one or more SRTNs initiated by the top-level SRTN associated with the concept is the probability of the phrase given that concept. This probability is calculated as the multiplication of all arc probabilities that defines the path. That is,

$$P(W/C) = \prod_{i=1}^{K} P(s_i/c_i)$$
$$= \prod_{i=1}^{K} \prod_{j=1}^{M_i} P(r_j/c_i)$$

where s_i is a substring in $W = w_1, w_2..w_L = s_1,..s_2, s_K$ ($K \leq L$) and $r_1, r_2, ...r_{M_i}$ are the production rules that construct s_i. The concept and rule sequences are assumed to be unique in the above equations. The parser uses heuristics to comply with this assumption.

SCFG and n-gram probabilities are learned from a text corpus by simple counting and smoothing. Our semantic grammars have a low degree of ambiguity and therefore do not require computationally intensive stochastic training and parsing techniques.

The class based LM can be considered as a very special case of our grammar based model. Concepts (or classes) are restricted to those that represent a list of semantically similar words, like [city_name] , [day_of_week], [month_day] and so forth. So, instead of rule probabilities we have given the class the word probabilities, $P(w_i/c_j)$. For simplicity, each word belongs to at most one class.

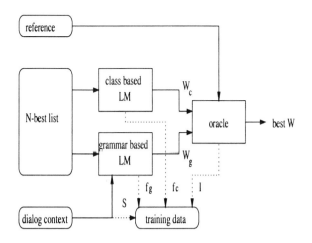

Figure 3: The set up for oracle experiments

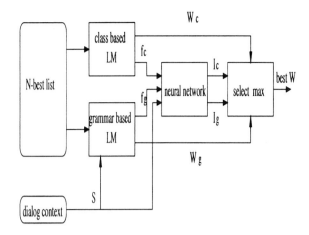

Figure 4: The LM combining system based on the oracle approach.

3. LINEAR AND LOG-LINEAR INTERPOLATION

Assuming that we have M language models, $P_i(W), i = 1, 2, \cdots, M$, the combined LM obtained using the linear interpolation (at sentence level) is given by

$$P(W) = \sum_{i=1}^{M} \lambda_i P_i(W) \qquad (2)$$

where λ_i are positive interpolation weights that sum up to unity.

The log-linear interpolation suggests an LM, again at sentence level, given by

$$P(W) = \frac{1}{Z(\lambda)} \prod_{i=1}^{M} P_i(W)^{\lambda_i} \qquad (3)$$

where $Z(\lambda)$ is the normalization factor and it is a function of the interpolation weights. The linearity in logarithmic domain is obvious if we take the logarithm of both sides. In the sequel, we omit the normalization term, as its computation is very expensive. We hope that its impact on the performance is not significant. Yet, it prevents us from reporting perplexity results.

4. THE ORACLE APPROACH

The set-up for oracle experiments is illustrated in Figure 3. The purpose of this set-up is twofold. First, we use it to evaluate the oracle performance. Second, we use it to prepare data for the training of a stochastic decision model. For the sake of simplicity, we show the set-up for two LMs and do experiments accordingly. Nonetheless, the set-up can be extended to an arbitrary number of LMs.

The language models are used for N-best list rescoring. The N-best list is generated by a speech recognizer using a relatively simpler LM (here, a class-based trigram LM). The framework for N-best list rescoring is the following MAP decision:

$$W^* = \underset{W \in L_N}{\operatorname{argmax}} \ p_A P(W/C_W) P(C_W/S) \qquad (4)$$

where p_A is the acoustic probability from the first pass, C_W is the unique concept sequence associated with W, and L_N denotes the N-best list. Each rescoring module supplies the oracle with their best hypothesis after rescoring. The oracle compares each hypothesis to the reference and pick the one with the best word (or semantic) accuracy.

For training purposes, we create the input feature vector by augmenting features from each rescoring module (f_g, f_c) and the dialog context (S). The output vector is the LM indicator I from the oracle. The element that corresponds to the LM with the best final hypothesis is unity and the rest are zeros. After training the oracle combiner (here, we assume a neural network), we set our system as shown in Figure 4. The input to the neural network (NN) is the augmented feature vector. The output of the NN is the LM indicator probably with fuzzy values. So, we first pick the max output, and then, we select and output the respective word string.

5. EXPERIMENTAL RESULTS

The models were developed and tested in the context of the CU Communicator dialog system which is used for telephone-based flight, hotel and rental car reservations [11]. The text corpus was divided into two parts as training and test sets with 15220 and 1220 sentences, respectively. The test set was further divided into two parts. Each part, in turn, was used to optimize language and interpolation weights to be used for the other part in a "jacknife paradigm". The results were reported as the average of the two results. The average sentence length of the corpus was 4 words (end-of-sentence was treated as a word). We identified 20 dialog contexts and labeled each sentence with the associated dialog context.

We trained a dialog independent (DI) class based LM and dialog dependent (DD) grammar based LM. In all LMs n is set to 3. It must be noted that the DI class-based LM served as the LM of the baseline system with 921 unigrams including 19 classes. The total number of the distinct words in the lexicon was 1681. The grammar-based LM had 199 concept and filler classes that completely cover the lexicon. In rescoring experiments we set the N-best list size to 10. We think that the choice of $N = 10$ is a resonable tradeoff between performance and complexity.

The perplexity results are presented in Table 1. The perplexity of the grammar-based LM is 36.8% better than the baseline class-based LM.

We did experiments using 10-best lists from the baseline recognizer. We first determined the best possible performance in WER

Table 1: Perplexity results

LM	Perplexity
DI class 3-gram	22.0
DD SCFG 3-gram	13.9

offered by 10-best lists. This is done by picking the hypothesis with the lowest WER from each list. This gives an upperbound for the performance gain possible from rescoring 10-best lists . The rescoring results in terms of absolute and relative improvements in WER and semantic error rate (SER) along with the best possible improvement are reported in Table 2. It should be noted that the optimizations are made using WER. The slight drop in SER with interpolation might be due to that. Actually this is good for text transcription but not for a dialog system. We believe that the results will reverse if we replace the optimization using WER with the optimization using SER.

Table 2: The WER and SER results of the 10-best list rescoring with different LMs: the baseline WER is 25.9% and SER is 23.7%

Method	WER	SER
Class based LM alone	0.0%	0.0%
Grammar based LM alone	1.4(5.4)%	1.4(5.9)%
Linear interpolation	1.6(6.2)%	1.3(5.5)%
Log-linear interpolation	1.7(6.6)%	1.2(5.1)%
Oracle	3.0(11.6)%	2.7(11.4) %
Best	6.4(24.1)%	5.5(23.2)%

The performance gap between the oracle and interpolation methods promotes the system in Figure 4. We expect that, based on the universal approximation theory, a neural network with consistent features, sufficiently large training data and proper training would approximate fairly well the behavior of the oracle. On the other hand, the performance gap between the oracle and the best possible performance from 10-best lists suggests the use of more than two language models and dynamic combination with the acoustic model.

6. CONCLUSIONS

We have presented our recent work on language model combining. We have shown that although a simple interpolation of LMs improves the performance, it fails to reach the performance of an oracle. We have proposed a method for LM combination that mimics the behavior of the oracle. Although our work is not complete without a neural network that mimics the oracle, we argue that the universal approximation theory ensures the success of such a method. However, extensive experiments are required to reach the

goal with the main focus on the selection of features. At the moment, the number of concepts, the number of filler classes and the number of 3-gram hits in a sentence (all normalized by the length of the sentence) and the behavior of n-grams in a context are the features that we consider to use. Also, it has been observed that the performance of the oracle is still far from the best possible performance. This is partly due to the very small number of LMs used in the rescoring, partly due to the oracle's hard decision combining strategy and partly due to the static combination with the acoustic model. The work is in progress towards the goal of filling the performance gap.

7. REFERENCES

[1] J. K. Baker. Trainable grammars for speech recognition. In *Speech Communications for th 97th Meeting of the Acoustical Society of America*, pages 31–35, June 1979.

[2] J. Gillett and W. Ward. A language model combining trigrams and stochastic context-free grammars. In *5-th International Conference on Spoken Language Processing*, pages 2319–2322, Sydney, Australia, 1998.

[3] K. Hacioglu and W. Ward. Dialog-context dependent language models combining n-grams and stochastic context-free grammars. In *submitted toInternational Conference of Acoustics, Speech, and Signal Processing*, Salt-Lake, Utah,, 2001.

[4] F. Jelinek and R. Mercer. Interpolated estimation of markov source parameters from sparse data. *Pattern Recognition in Practice*, 23:381, 1980.

[5] A. Keller, B. Rueber, F. Seide, and B. Tran. PADIS - an automatic telephone switchboard and directory information system. *Speech Communication*, 23:95–111, 1997.

[6] D. Klakow. Log-linear interpolation of language models. In *5-th International Conference on Spoken Language Processing*, pages 1695–1699, Sydney, Australia, 1998.

[7] R. Rosenfeld. A maximum entropy approach to adaptive language modeling. *Computer Speech and Language*, (10):187–228, 1996.

[8] R. Rosenfeld. Two decades of statistical language modeling: Where do we go from here? *Proceedings of the IEEE*, 88(8):1270–1278, August 2000.

[9] B. Souvignier, A. Keller, B. Rueber, H.Schramm, and F. Seide. The thoughtful elephant: Strategies for spoken dialog systems. *IEEE Transactions on Speech and Audio Processing*, 8(1):51–62, January 2000.

[10] Y. Wang, M. Mahajan, and X.Huang. A unified context-free grammar and n-gram model for spoken language processing. In *International Conference of Acoustics, Speech, and Signal Processing*, pages 1639–1642, Istanbul, Turkey, 2000.

[11] W. Ward and B. Pellom. The CU communicator system. In *IEEE Workshop on Automatic Speech Recognition and Understanding*, Keystone, Colorado, 1999.

Portability Issues for Speech Recognition Technologies·

Lori Lamel, Fabrice Lefevre, Jean-Luc Gauvain and Gilles Adda

Spoken Language Processing Group,
CNRS-LIMSI, 91403 Orsay, France
{lamel,lefevre,gauvain,gadda}@limsi.fr

ABSTRACT

Although there has been regular improvement in speech recognition technology over the past decade, speech recognition is far from being a solved problem. Most recognition systems are tuned to a particular task and porting the system to a new task (or language) still requires substantial investment of time and money, as well as expertise. Todays state-of-the-art systems rely on the availability of large amounts of manually transcribed data for acoustic model training and large normalized text corpora for language model training. Obtaining such data is both time-consuming and expensive, requiring trained human annotators with substantial amounts of supervision.

In this paper we address issues in speech recognizer portability and activities aimed at developing generic core speech recognition technology, in order to reduce the manual effort required for system development. Three main axes are pursued: assessing the genericity of wide domain models by evaluating performance under several tasks; investigating techniques for lightly supervised acoustic model training; and exploring transparent methods for adapting generic models to a specific task so as to achieve a higher degree of genericity.

1. INTRODUCTION

The last decade has seen impressive advances in the capability and performance of speech recognizers. Todays state-of-the-art systems are able to transcribe unrestricted continuous speech from broadcast data with acceptable performance. The advances arise from the increased accuracy and complexity of the models, which are closely related to the availability of large spoken and text corpora for training, and the wide availability of faster and cheaper computational means which have enabled the development and implementation of better training and decoding algorithms. Despite the extent of progress over the recent years, recognition accuracy is still extremely sensitive to the environmental conditions and speaking style: channel quality, speaker characteristics, and background

*This work was partially financed by the European Commission under the IST-1999 Human Language Technologies project 11876 Coretex.

Proceedings of HLT 2001, First International Conference on Human Language Technology Research, J. Allan, ed., Morgan Kaufmann, San Francisco, 2001.

noise have an important impact on the acoustic component of the speech recognizer, whereas the speaking style and the discourse domain have a large impact on the linguistic component.

In the context of the EC IST-1999 11876 project CORETEX we are investigating methods for fast system development, as well as development of systems with high genericity and adaptability. By fast system development we refer to: language support, i.e., the capability of porting technology to different languages at a reasonable cost; and task portability, i.e. the capability to easily adapt a technology to a new task by exploiting limited amounts of domain-specific knowledge. Genericity and adaptability refer to the capacity of the technology to work properly on a wide range of tasks and to dynamically keep models up to date using contemporary data. The more robust the initial generic system is, the less there is a need for adaptation. Concerning the acoustic modeling component, genericity implies that it is robust to the type and bandwidth of the channel, the acoustic environment, the speaker type and the speaking style. Unsupervised normalization and adaptation techniques evidently should be used to enhance performance further when the system is exposed to data of a particular type.

With today's technology, the adaptation of a recognition system to a new task or new language requires the availability of sufficient amount of transcribed training data. When changing to new domains, usually no exact transcriptions of acoustic data are available, and the generation of such transcribed data is an expensive process in terms of manpower and time. On the other hand, there often exist incomplete information such as approximate transcriptions, summaries or at least key words, which can be used to provide supervision in what can be referred to as "informed speech recognition". Depending on the level of completeness, this information can be used to develop confidence measures with adapted or trigger language models or by approximate alignments to automatic transcriptions. Another approach is to use existing recognizer components (developed for other tasks or languages) to automatically transcribe task-specific training data. Although in the beginning the error rate on new data is likely to be rather high, this speech data can be used to re-train a recognition system. If carried out in an iterative manner, the speech data base for the new domain can be cumulatively extended over time *without* direct manual transcription.

The overall objective of the work presented here is to reduce the speech recognition development cost. One aspect is to develop "generic" core speech recognition technology, where by "generic" we mean a transcription engine that will work reasonably well on a wide range of speech transcription tasks, ranging from digit recognition to large vocabulary conversational telephony speech, without the need for costly task-specific training data. To start with we assess the genericity of wide domain models under cross-task con-

Table 1: Brief descriptions and best reported error rates for the corpora used in this work.

Corpus	Test Year	Task	Train (#spkr)	Test (#spkr)	Textual Resources	Best WER
BN	98	TV & Radio News	200h	3h	Closed-captions, commercial transcripts, manual transcripts of audio data	13.5
TI-digits	93	Small Vocabulary	3.5h (112)	4h (113)	-	0.2
ATIS	93	H-M Dialog	40h (137)	5h (24)	Transcriptions	2.5
WSJ	95	News Dictation	100h (355)	45mn (20)	Newspaper, newswire	6.6
S9_WSJ	93	Spontaneous Dictation		43mn (10)	Newspaper, newswire	19.1

ditions, i.e., by recognizing task-specific data with a recognizer developed for a different task. We chose to evaluate the performance of broadcast news acoustic and language models, on three commonly used tasks: small vocabulary recognition (TI-digits), read and spontaneous text dictation (WSJ), and goal-oriented spoken dialog (ATIS). The broadcast news task is quite general, covering a wide variety of linguistic and acoustic events in the language, ensuring reasonable coverage of the target task. In addition, there are sufficient acoustic and linguistic training data available for this task that accurate models covering a wide range of speaker and language characteristics can be estimated.

Another research area is the investigation of lightly supervised techniques for acoustic model training. The strategy taken is to use a speech recognizer to transcribe unannotated data, which are then used to estimate more accurate acoustic models. The light supervision is applied to the broadcast news task, where unlimited amounts of acoustic training data are potentially available. Finally we apply the lightly supervised training idea as a transparent method for adapting the generic models to a specific task, thus achieving a higher degree of genericity. In this work we focus on reducing training costs and task portability, and do not address language transfer.

We selected the LIMSI broadcast news (BN) transcription system as the generic reference system. The BN task covers a large number of different acoustic and linguistic situations: planned to spontaneous speech; native and non-native speakers with different accents; close-talking microphones and telephone channels; quiet studio, on-site reports in noisy places to musical background; and a variety of topics. In addition, a lot of training resources are available including a large corpus of annotated audio data and a huge amount of raw audio data for the acoustic modeling; and large collections of closed-captions, commercial transcripts, newspapers and newswires texts for linguistic modeling. The next section provides an overview of the LIMSI broadcast news transcription system used as our generic system.

2. SYSTEM DESCRIPTION

The LIMSI broadcast news transcription system has two main components, the audio partitioner and the word recognizer. Data partitioning [6] serves to divide the continuous audio stream into homogeneous segments, associating appropriate labels for cluster, gender and bandwidth with the segments. The speech recognizer uses continuous density HMMs with Gaussian mixture for acoustic modeling and *n*-gram statistics estimated on large text corpora for language modeling. Each context-dependent phone model is a tied-state left-to-right CD-HMM with Gaussian mixture observation densities where the tied states are obtained by means of a decision tree. Word recognition is performed in three steps: 1) initial hypothesis generation, 2) word graph generation, 3) final hypothesis generation. The initial hypotheses are used for cluster-based acoustic model adaptation using the MLLR technique [13] prior to

word graph generation. A 3-gram LM is used in the first two decoding steps. The final hypotheses are generated with a 4-gram LM and acoustic models adapted with the hypotheses of step 2.

In the baseline system used in DARPA evaluation tests, the acoustic models were trained on about 150 hours of audio data from the DARPA Hub4 Broadcast News corpus (the LDC 1996 and 1997 Broadcast News Speech collections) [9]. Gender-dependent acoustic models were built using MAP adaptation of SI seed models for wide-band and telephone band speech [7]. The models contain 28000 position-dependent, cross-word triphone models with 11700 tied states and approximately 360k Gaussians [8].

The baseline language models are obtained by interpolation of models trained on 3 different data sets (excluding the test epochs): about 790M words of newspaper and newswire texts; 240M word of commercial broadcast news transcripts; and the transcriptions of the Hub4 acoustic data. The recognition vocabulary contains 65120 words and has a lexical coverage of over 99% on all evaluation test sets from the years 1996-1999. A pronunciation graph is associated with each word so as to allow for alternate pronunciations. The pronunciations make use of a set of 48 phones set, where 3 phone units represent silence, filler words, and breath noises. The lexicon contains compound words for about 300 frequent word sequences, as well as word entries for common acronyms, providing an easy way to allow for reduced pronunciations [6].

The LIMSI 10x system obtained a word error of 17.1% on the 1999 DARPA/NIST evaluation set and can transcribe unrestricted broadcast data with a word error of about 20% [8].

3. TASK INDEPENDENCE

Our first step in developing a "generic" speech transcription engine is to assess the most generic system we have under cross-task conditions, i.e., by recognizing task-specific data with a recognizer developed for a different task. Three representative tasks have been retained as target tasks: small vocabulary recognition (TI-digits), goal-oriented human-machine spoken dialog (ATIS), and dictation of texts (WSJ). The broadcast news transcription task (Hub4E) serves as the baseline. The main criteria for the task selection were that they are realistic enough and task-specific data should be available. The characteristics of these four tasks and the available corpora are summarized in Table 1.

For the small vocabulary recognition task, experiments are carried out on the adult speaker portion of the TI-digits corpus [14], containing over 17k utterances from a total of 225 speakers. The vocabulary contains 11 words, the digits '1' to '9', plus 'zero' and 'oh'. Each speaker uttered two versions of each digit in isolation and 55 digit strings. The database is divided into training and test sets (roughly 3.5 hours each, corresponding to 9k strings). The speech is of high quality, having been collected in a quiet environment. The best reported WERs on this task are around 0.2-0.3%. The digit phonemic coverage being very low, only 108 context-dependent models are used in our recognition system. The task-

Table 2: Word error rates (%) for BN98, TI-digits, ATIS94, WSJ95 and S9_WSJ93 test sets after recognition with three different configurations: (left) BN acoustic and language models; (center) BN acoustic models combined with task-specific lexica and LMs and (right) task-dependent acoustic and language models.

Test Set	BN models	Task LMs	Task models
BN98	13.6	13.6	13.6
TI-digits	17.5	1.7	0.4
ATIS94	22.7	4.7	4.4
WSJ95	11.6	9.0	7.6
S9_WSJ93	12.1	13.6	15.3

specific LM for the TI-digits is a simple grammar allowing any sequence of up to 7 digits. Our task-dependent system performance is 0.4% WER.

The *DARPA Air Travel Information System* (ATIS) task is chosen as being representative of a goal-oriented human-machine dialog task, and the ARPA 1994 Spontaneous Speech Recognition (SPREC) ATIS-3 data (*ATIS94*) [4] is used for testing purposes. The test data amounts for nearly 5 hours of speech from 24 speakers recorded with a close-talking microphone. Around 40h of speech data are available for training. The word error rates for this task in the 1994 evaluation were mainly in the range of 2.5% to 5%, which we take as state-of-the-art for this task. The acoustic models used in our task-specific system include 1641 context-dependent phones with 4k independent HMM states. A back-off trigram language model has been estimated on the transcriptions of the training utterances. The lexicon contains 1300 words, with compounds words for multi-word entities in the air-travel database (city and airport names, services etc.). The WER obtained with our task-dependent system is 4.4%.

For the dictation task, the *Wall Street Journal* continuous speech recognition corpus [17] is used, abiding by the ARPA 1995 Hub3 test (*WSJ95*) conditions. The acoustic training data consist of 100 hours of speech from a total of 355 speakers taken from the WSJ0 and WSJ1 corpora. The Hub3 baseline test data consist of studio quality read speech from 20 speakers with a total duration of 45 minutes. The best result reported at the time of the evaluation was 6.6%. A contrastive experiment is carried out with the WSJ93 Spoke 9 data comprised of 200 spontaneous sentences spoken by journalists [11]. The best performance reported in the 1993 evaluation on the spontaneous data was 19.1% [18], however lower word error rates have since been reported on comparable test sets (14.1% on the WSJ94 Spoke 9 test data). 21000 context and position-dependent models have been trained for the WSJ system, with 9k independent HMM states. A 65k-word vocabulary was selected and a back-off trigram model obtained by interpolating models trained on different data sets (training utterance transcriptions and newspapers data). The task-dependent WSJ system has a WER of 7.6% on the read speech test data and 15.3% on the spontaneous data.

For the BN transcription task, we follow the conditions of the 1998 ARPA Hub4E evaluation (*BN98*) [15]. The acoustic training data is comprised of 150 hours of North-American TV and radio shows. The best overall result on the 1998 baseline test was 13.5%.

Three sets of experiments are reported. The first are cross-task recognition experiments carried out using the BN acoustic and language models to decode the test data for the other tasks. The second set of experiments made use of mixed models, that is the BN acoustic models and task-specific LMs. Due to the different evaluation

paradigms, some minor modifications were made in the transcription procedure. First of all, in contrast with the BN data, the data for the 3 tasks is already segmented into individual utterances so the partitioning step was eliminated. With this exception, the decoding process for the WSJ task is exactly the same as described in the previous section. For the TI-digits and ATIS tasks, word decoding is carried out in a single trigram pass, and no speaker adaptation was performed.

The WERs obtained for the three recognition experiments are reported in Table 2. A comparison with Table 1 shows that the performances of the task dependent models are close to the best reported results even though we did not devote too much effort in optimizing these models. We can also observe by comparing the task-dependent (Table 2, right) and mixed (Table 2, middle) conditions, that the BN acoustic models are relatively generic. These models seem to be a good start towards truly task-independent acoustic models. By using task-specific language models For the TI-digits and ATIS we can see that the gap in performance is mainly due a linguistic mismatch. For WSJ the language models are more closely matched to BN and only a small 1.6% WER reduction is obtained. On the spontaneous journalist dictation (WSJ S9 spoke) test data there is even an increase in WER using the WSJ LMs, which can be attributed to a better modelization of spontaneous speech effects (such as breath and filler words) in the BN models.

Prior to introducing our approach for lightly supervised acoustic model training, we describe our standard training procedure in the next section.

4. ACOUSTIC MODEL TRAINING

HMM training requires an alignment between the audio signal and the phone models, which usually relies on a perfect orthographic transcription of the speech data and a good phonetic lexicon. In general it is easier to deal with relatively short speech segments so that transcription errors will not propagate and jeopardize the alignment. The orthographic transcription is usually considered as ground truth and training is done in a closely supervised manner. For each speech segment the training algorithm is provided with the exact orthographic transcription of what was spoken, i.e., the word sequence that the speech recognizer should hypothesize when confronted with the same speech segment.

Training acoustic models for a new corpus (which could also reflect a change of task and/or language), usually entails the following sequence of operations once the audio data and transcription files have been loaded:

1. Normalize the transcriptions to a common format (some adjustment is always needed as different text sources make use of different conventions).

2. Produce a word list from the transcriptions and correct blatant errors (these include typographical errors and inconsistencies).

3. Produce a phonemic transcription for all words not in our master lexicon (these are manually verified).

4. Align the orthographic transcriptions with the signal using existing models and the pronunciation lexicon (or bootstrap models from another task or language). This procedure often rejects a substantial portion of the data, particularly for long segments.

5. Eventually correct transcription errors and realign (or just ignore these if enough audio data is available)

6. Run the standard EM training procedure.

This sequence of operations is usually iterated several times to refine the acoustic models. In general each iteration recovers a portion of the rejected data.

5. LIGHTLY SUPERVISED ACOUSTIC MODEL TRAINING

One can imagine training acoustic models in a less supervised manner, by using an iterative procedure where instead of using manual transcriptions for alignment, at each iteration the most likely word transcription given the current models and all the information available about the audio sample is used. This approach still fits within the EM training framework, which is well-suited for missing data training problems. A completely unsupervised training procedure is to use the current best models to produce an orthographic transcription of the training data, keeping only words that have a high confidence measure. Such an approach, while very enticing, is limited since the only supervision is provided by the confidence measure estimator. This estimator must in turn be trained on development data, which needs to be small to keep the approach interesting.

Between using carefully annotated data such as the detailed transcriptions provided by the LDC and no transcription at all, there is a wide spectrum of possibilities. What is really important is the cost of producing the associated annotations. Detailed annotation requires on the order of 20-40 times real-time of manual effort, and even after manual verification the final transcriptions are not exempt from errors [2]. Orthographic transcriptions such as closed-captions can be done in a few times real-time, and therefore are quite a bit less costly. These transcriptions have the advantage that they are already available for some television channels, and therefore do not have to be produced specifically for training speech recognizers. However, closed-captions are a close, but not exact transcription of what is being spoken, and are only coarsely time-aligned with the audio signal. Hesitations and repetitions are not marked and there may be word insertions, deletions and changes in the word order. They also are missing some of the additional information provided in the detailed speech transcriptions such as the indication of acoustic conditions, speaker turns, speaker identities and gender and the annotation of non-speech segments such as music. NIST found the disagreement between the closed-captions and manual transcripts on a 10 hour subset of the TDT-2 data used for the SDR evaluation to be on the order of 12% [5].

Another approach is to make use of other possible sources of contemporaneous texts from newspapers, newswires, summaries and the Internet. However, since these sources have only an indirect correspondence with the audio data, they provide less supervision.

The basic idea is of light supervision is to use a speech recognizer to automatically transcribe unannotated data, thus generating "approximate" labeled training data. By iteratively increasing the amount of training data, more accurate acoustic models are obtained, which can then be used to transcribe another set of unannotated data. The modified training procedure used in this work is:

1. Train a language model on all texts and closed captions after normalization
2. Partition each show into homogeneous segments and label the acoustic attributes (speaker, gender, bandwidth) [6]
3. Train acoustic models on a very small amount of manually annotated data (1h)
4. Automatically transcribe a large amount of training data
5. (Optional) Align the closed-captions and the automatic transcriptions (using a standard dynamic programming algorithm)
6. Run the standard acoustic model training procedure on the speech segments (in the case of alignment with the closed captions only keep segments where the two transcripts are in agreement)
7. Reiterate from step 4.

It is easy to see that the manual work is considerably reduced, not only in generating the annotated corpus but also during the training procedure, since we no longer need to extend the pronunciation lexicon to cover all words and word fragments occurring in the training data and we do not need to correct transcription errors. This basic idea was used to train acoustic models using the automatically generated word transcriptions of the 500 hours of audio broadcasts used in the spoken document retrieval task (part of the DARPA TDT-2 corpus used in the SDR'99 and SDR'00 evaluations) [3]. This corpus is comprised of 902 shows from 6 sources broadcast between January and June 1998: CNN Headline News (550 30-minute shows), ABC World News Tonight (139 30-minute shows), Public Radio International The World (122 1-hour shows), Voice of America VOA Today and World Report (111 1-hour shows). These shows contain about 22k stories with time-codes identifying the beginning and end of each story.

First, the recognition performance as a function of the available acoustic and language model training data was assessed. Then we investigated the accuracy of the acoustic models obtained after recognizing the audio data using different levels of supervision via the language model. With the exception of the baseline Hub4 language models, none of the language models include a component estimated on the transcriptions of the Hub4 acoustic training data. The language model training texts come from contemporaneous sources such as newspapers and newswires, and commercial summaries and transcripts, and closed-captions. The former sources have only an indirect correspondence with the audio data and provide less supervision than the closed captions. For each set of LM training texts, a new word list was selected based on the word frequencies in the training data. All language models are formed by interpolating individual LMs built on each text source. The interpolation coefficients were chosen in order to minimize the perplexity on a development set composed of the second set of the Nov98 evaluation data (3h) and a 2h portion of the TDT2 data from Jun98 (not included in the LM training data). The following combinations were investigated:

- **LMa** (baseline Hub4 LM): newspaper+newswire (NEWS), commercial transcripts (COM) predating Jun98, acoustic transcripts
- **LMn_t_c:** NEWS, COM, closed-captions through May98
- **LMn_t:** NEWS, COM through May98
- **LMn_c:** NEWS, closed-captions through May98
- **LMn:** NEWS through May98
- **LMn_to:** NEWS through May98, COM through Dec97
- **LMno:** NEWS through Dec97

Table 3: Word error rate for various conditions using acoustic models trained on the HUB4 training data with detailed manual transcriptions. All runs were done in less than 10xRT, except the last row. "1S" designates one set of gender-independent acoustic models, whereas "4S" designates four sets of gender and bandwidth dependent acoustic models.

Training	Conditions	bn99_1	bn99_2	Average
1h	1S, LMn_t_c	35.2	31.9	33.3
69h	1S, LMn_t_c	20.2	18.0	18.9
123h	1S, LMn_t_c	19.3	17.1	18.0
123h	4S, LMn_t_c	18.5	16.1	17.1
123h	4S, LMa	18.3	16.3	17.1
123h	4S, LMa, 50x	17.1	14.5	15.6

Table 4: Word error rate for different language models and increasing quantities of automatically labeled training data on the 1999 evaluation test sets using gender and bandwidth independent acoustic models. LMn_t_c: NEWS, COM, closed-captions through May98 LMn_t: NEWS, COM through May98 LMn_c: NEWS, closed-captions through May98 LMn: NEWS through May98 LMn_to: NEWS through May98, COM through Dec97 LMno: NEWS through Dec97.

Amount of training data		%WER					
raw	unfiltered	LMn_t_c	LMn_t	LMn_c	LMn	LMn_to	LMno
150h	123h	18.0	18.6	19.1	20.6	18.7	20.9
1h	1h	33.3	33.7	34.4	35.9	33.9	36.1
14h	8h	26.4	27.6	27.4	29.0	27.6	30.6
28h	17h	25.2	25.7	25.6	28.1	25.7	28.9
58h	28h	24.3	25.2	25.7	27.4	25.1	27.9

It should be noted that all of the conditions include newspaper and newswire texts from the same epoch as the audio data. These provide an important source of knowledge particularly with respect to the vocabulary items. Conditions which include the closed captions in the LM training data provide additional supervision in the decoding process when transcribing audio data from the same epoch.

For testing purposes we use the 1999 Hub4 evaluation data, which is comprised of two 90 minute data sets selected by NIST. The first set was extracted from 10 hours of data broadcast in June 1998, and the second set from a set of broadcasts recorded in August-September 1998 [16]. All recognition runs were carried out in under 10xRT unless stated otherwise. The LIMSI 10x system obtained a word error of 17.1% on the evaluation set (the combined scores in the penultimate row in Table 3 4S, LMa) [8]. The word error can be reduced to 15.6% for a system running at 50xRT (last entry in Table 3).

As can be seen in Table 3, the word error rates with our original Hub4 language model (LMa) and the one without the transcriptions of the acoustic data (LMn_t_c) give comparable results using the 1999 acoustic models trained on 123 hours of manually annotated data (123h, 4S). The quality of the different language models listed above are compared in the first row of Table 3 using speaker-independent (1S) acoustic models trained on the same Hub4 data (123h). As can be observed, removing any text source leads to a degradation in recognition performance. It appears it is more important to include commercial transcripts (LMn_t), even if they are old (LMn_to) than the closed captions (LMn_c). This suggests that the commercial transcripts more accurately represent spoken language than closed-captioning. Even if only newspaper and newswire texts are available (LMn), the word error increases by only 14% over the best configuration (LMn_t_c), and even using older newspaper and newswire texts (LMno) does not substantially increase the word error rate. The second row of Table 3 gives the word error rates with acoustic models trained on only 1 hour of manually transcribed data. These are the models used to initialize the process of automatically transcribing large quantities of data. These word error rates range from 33% to 36% across the language models.

We compared a straightforward approach of training on all the automatically annotated data with one in which the closed-captions are used to filter the hypothesized transcriptions, removing words that are "incorrect". In the filtered case, the hypothesized transcriptions are aligned with the closed captions story by story, and only regions where the automatic transcripts agreed with the closed captions were kept for training purposes. To our surprise, somewhat comparable recognition results were obtained both with and without filtering, suggesting that inclusion of the closed-captions in the

language model training material provided sufficient supervision (see Table 5).[1] It should be noted that in both cases the closed-caption story boundaries are used to delimit the audio segments after automatic transcription.

To investigate this further we are assessing the effects of reducing the amount of supervision provided by the language model training texts on the acoustic model accuracy (see Table 4). With 14 hours (raw) of approximately labeled training data, the word error is reduced by about 20% for all LMs compared with training on 1h of data which has carefully manual transcriptions. Using larger amounts of data transcribed with the same initial acoustic models gives smaller improvements, as seen by the entries for 28h and 58h. The commercial transcripts (LMn+t and LMn+to), even if predating the data epoch, are seen to be more important than the closed-captions (LMn+c), supporting the earlier observation that they are closer to spoken language. Even if only news texts from the same period (LMn) are available, these provide adequate supervision for lightly supervised acoustic model training.

Table 5: Word error rates for increasing quantities of automatically label training data on the 1999 evaluation test sets using gender and bandwidth independent acoustic models with the language model LMn_t_c (trained on NEWS, COM, closed-captions through May98).

Amount of training data			%WER	
raw	unfiltered	filtered	unfiltered	filtered
14h	8h	6h	26.4	25.7
28h	17h	13h	25.2	23.7
58h	28h	21h	24.3	22.5
140h	76h	57h	22.4	21.1
287h	140h	108h	21.0	19.9
503h	238h	188h	20.2	19.4

6. TASK ADAPTATION

The experiments reported in the section 3 show that while direct recognition with the reference BN acoustic models gives relatively

---

[1] The difference in the amounts of data transcribed and actually used for training is due to three factors. The first is that the total duration includes non-speech segments which are eliminated prior to recognition during partitioning. Secondly, the story boundaries in the closed captions are used to eliminate irrelevant portions, such as commercials. Thirdly, since there are many remaining silence frames, only a portion of these are retained for training.

Table 6: Word error rates (%) for TI-digits, ATIS94, WSJ95 and S9_WSJ93 test sets after recognition with three different configurations, all including task-specific lexica and LMs: (left) BN acoustic models, (middle left) unsupervised adaptation of the BN acoustic models, (middle right) supervised adaptation of the BN acoustic models and (right) task-dependent acoustic models.

Test Set	BN models	Unsupervised Adaptation BN models	Supervised Adaptation BN models	Task-dep. models
TI-digits	1.7	0.8	0.5	0.4
ATIS94	4.7	4.7	3.2	4.4
WSJ95	9.0	6.9	6.7	7.6
S9_WSJ93	13.6	12.6	11.4	15.3

competitive results, the WER on the targeted tasks can still be improved. Since we want to minimize the cost and effort involved in tuning to a target task, we are investigating methods to transparently adapt the reference acoustic models. By transparent we mean that the procedure is automatic and can be carried out without any human expertise. We therefore apply the approach presented in the previous section, that is the reference BN system is used to transcribe the training data of the destination task. This supposes of course that audio data have been collected. However, this can be carried out with an operational system and the cost of collecting task-specific training data is greatly reduced since no manual transcriptions are needed. The performance of the BN models under cross task conditions is well within the range for which the approximate transcriptions can be used for acoustic model adaptation.

The reference acoustic models are then adapted by means of a conventional adaptation technique such as MLLR and MAP. Thus there is no need to design a new set of models based on the training data characteristics. Adaptation is also preferred to the training of new models as it is likely that the new training data will have a lower phonemic contextual coverage than the original reference models.

The cross-task unsupervised adaptation is evaluated for the tasks: TI-digits, ATIS and WSJ. The 100 hours of the WSJ data were transcribed using the BN acoustic and language models. For ATIS, only 26 of the 40 hours of training data from 276 speakers were transcribed, due to time constraints. For TI-digits, the training data was transcribed using a mixed configuration, combining the BN acoustic models with the simple digit loop grammar.[2] For completeness we also used the task-specific audio data and the associated transcriptions to carry out supervised adaptation of the BN models.

Gender-dependent acoustic models were estimated using the corresponding gender-dependent BN models as seeds and the gender-specific training utterances as adaptation data. For WSJ and ATIS, the speaker ids were directly used for gender identification since in previous experiments with this test set there were no gender classification errors. Only the acoustic models used in the second and third word decoding passes have been adapted. For the TI-digits, the gender of each training utterance was automatically classified by decoding each utterance twice, once with each set of gender-dependent models. Then, the utterance gender was determined based on the best global score between the male and female models (99.0% correct classification).

Both the MLLR and MAP adaptation techniques were applied. The recognition tests were carried out under mixed conditions (i.e., with the adapted acoustic models and the task-dependent LM). The

BN models are first adapted using MLLR with a global transformation, followed by MAP adaptation.

The word error rates obtained with the task-adapted BN models are given in Table 6 for the four test sets. Using unsupervised adaptation the performance is improved for TIdigits (53% relative), WSJ (19% relative) and S9 (7% relative).

The manual transcriptions for the targeted tasks were used to carry out supervised model adaptation. The results (see the 4th column of Table 6) show a clear improvement over unsupervised adaptation for both the TI-digits (60% relative) and ATIS (47% relative) tasks. A smaller gain of about 10% relative is obtained for the spontaneous dictation task, and only 3% relative for read WSJ data. The gain appears to be correlated with the WER of the transcribed data: the difference between BN and task specific models is smaller for WSJ than ATIS and TI-digits. The TI-digit task is the only task for which the best performance is obtained using task-dependent models rather than BN models adapted with supervised. For the other tasks, the lowest WER is obtained when the supervised adapted BN acoustic models are used: 3.2% for ATIS, 6.7% for WSJ and 11.4% for S9. This result confirms our hypothesis that better performance can be achieved by adapting generic models with task-specific data than by directly training task-specific models.

7. CONCLUSIONS

This paper has explored methods to reduce the cost of developing models for speech recognizers. Two main axes have been explored: developing generic acoustic models and the use of low cost data for acoustic model training.

We have explored the genericity of state-of-the-art speech recognition systems, by testing a relatively wide-domain system on data from three tasks ranging in complexity. The generic models were taken from the broadcast news task which covers a wide range of acoustic and linguistic conditions. These acoustic models are relatively task-independent as there is only a small increase in word error relative to the word error obtained with task-dependent acoustic models, when a task-dependent language model is used. There remains a large difference in performance on the digit recognition task which can be attributed to the limited phonetic coverage of this task. On a spontaneous WSJ dictation task, the broadcast news acoustic and language are more robust to deviations in speaking style than the read-speech WSJ models. We also have shown that unsupervised acoustic model adaptation can reduce the performance gap between task-independent and task-dependent acoustic models, and that supervised adaptation of generic models can lead to better performance than that achieved with task-specific models. Both supervised and unsupervised adaptation are less effective for the digits task indicating that these may be a special case.

We have investigated the use of low cost data to train acoustic models for broadcast news transcription, with supervision provided

---

[2] In order to assess the quality of the automatic transcription, we compared the system hypotheses to the manually provided training transcriptions. For resulting word error rates on the training data are 11.8% for WSJ, 29.1% for ATIS and 1.2% for TI-digits.

the language models. Recognition results obtained with acoustic models trained on large quantities of automatically annotated data are comparable (under a 10% relative increase in word error) to results obtained with acoustic models trained on large quantities of manually annotated data. Given the significantly higher cost of detailed manual transcription (substantially more time consuming than producing commercial transcripts, and more expensive since closed captions and commercial transcripts are produced for other purposes), such approaches are very promising as they require substantial computation time, but little manual effort. Another advantage offered by this approach is that there is no need to extend the pronunciation lexicon to cover all words and word fragments occurring in the training data. By eliminating the need for manual transcription, automated training can be applied to essentially unlimited quantities of task-specific training data. While the focus of our work has been on reducing training costs and task portability, we have been exploring these in a multi-lingual context.

REFERENCES

[1] G. Adda, M. Jardino, J.L. Gauvain, "Language Modeling for Broadcast News Transcription," *ESCA Eurospeech'99*, Budapest, **4**, pp. 1759-1760, Sept. 1999.

[2] C. Barras, E. Geoffrois et al.,"Transcriber: development and use of a tool for assisting speech corpora production," *Speech Communication*, **33**(1-2), pp. 5-22, Jan. 2001.

[3] C. Cieri, D. Graff, M. Liberman, "The TDT-2 Text and Speech Corpus," *DARPA Broadcast News Workshop*, Herndon. (see also http://morph.ldc.upenn.edu/TDT).

[4] D. Dahl, M. Bates *et al.*, "Expanding the Scope of the ATIS Task : The ATIS-3 Corpus," *Proc. ARPA Spoken Language Systems Technology Workshop*, Plainsboro, NJ, pp. 3-8, 1994.

[5] J. Garofolo, C. Auzanne, E. Voorhees, W. Fisher, "1999 TREC-8 Spoken Document Retrieval Track Overview and Results," *8th Text Retrieval Conference TREC-8*, Nov. 1999.

[6] J.L. Gauvain, G. Adda, *et al.*, "Transcribing Broadcast News: The LIMSI Nov96 Hub4 System," *Proc. ARPA Speech Recognition Workshop*, pp. 56-63, Chantilly, Feb. 1997.

[7] J.L. Gauvain, C.H. Lee, "Maximum *a Posteriori* Estimation for Multivariate Gaussian Mixture Observation of Markov Chains," *IEEE Trans. on SAP*, **2**(2), pp. 291-298, April 1994.

[8] J.L. Gauvain, L. Lamel, "Fast Decoding for Indexation of Broadcast Data," *ICSLP'2000*, **3**, pp. 794-798, Beijing, Oct. 2000.

[9] D. Graff, "The 1996 Broadcast News Speech and Language-Model Corpus," *Proc. DARPA Speech Recognition Workshop*, Chantilly, VA, pp. 11-14, Feb. 1999.

[10] T. Kemp, A. Waibel, "Unsupervised Training of a Speech Recognizer: Recent Experiments," *Eurospeech'99*, **6**, Budapest, pp. 2725-2728, Sept. 1999.

[11] F. Kubala, J. Cohen *et al.*, "The Hub and Spoke Paradigm for CSR Evaluation," *Proc. ARPA Spoken Language Systems Technology Workshop*, Plainsboro, NJ, pp. 9-14, 1994.

[12] L. Lamel, J.L. Gauvain, G. Adda, "Lightly Supervised Acoustic Model Training," *Proc. ISCA ITRW ASR2000*, pp. 150-154, Paris, Sept. 2000.

[13] C.J. Leggetter, P.C. Woodland, "Maximum likelihood linear regression for speaker adaptation of continuous density hidden Markov models," *Computer Speech & Language*, **9**(2), pp. 171-185, 1995.

[14] R.G. Leonard, "A Database for speaker-independent digit recognition," *Proc. ICASSP*, 1984.

[15] D.S. Pallett, J.G. Fiscus, *et al.* "1998 Broadcast News Benchmark Test Results," *Proc. DARPA Broadcast News Workshop*, pp. 5-12, Herndon, VA, Feb. 1999.

[16] D. Pallett, J. Fiscus, M. Przybocki, "Broadcast News 1999 Test Results," *NIST/NSA Speech Transcription Workshop*, College Park, May 2000.

[17] D.B. Paul, J.M. Baker, "The Design for the Wall Street Journal-based CSR Corpus," *Proc. ICSLP*, Kobe, Nov. 1992.

[18] G. Zavaliagkos, T. Anastsakos *et al.*, "Improved Search, Acoustic, and Language Modeling in the BBN BYBLOS Large Vocabulary CSR Systems," *Proc. ARPA Spoken Language Systems Technology Workshop*, Plainsboro, NJ, pp. 81-88, 1994.

[19] G. Zavaliagkos, T. Colthurst, "Utilizing Untranscribed Training Data to Improve Performance," *DARPA Broadcast News Transcription and Understanding Workshop*, Landsdowne, pp. 301-305, Feb. 1998.

293

Rapidly Retargetable Interactive Translingual Retrieval

Gina-Anne Levow
Institute for Advanced
Computer Studies
University of Maryland,
College Park, MD 20742

gina@umiacs.umd.edu

Douglas W. Oard
College of Information Studies
Institute for Advanced
Computer Studies
University of Maryland,
College Park, MD 20742

oard@glue.umd.edu

Philip Resnik
Department of Linguistics
Institute for Advanced
Computer Studies
University of Maryland,
College Park, MD 20742

resnik@umiacs.umd.edu

ABSTRACT

This paper describes a system for rapidly retargetable interactive translingual retrieval. Basic functionality can be achieved for a new document language in a single day, and further improvements require only a relatively modest additional investment. We applied the techniques first to search Chinese collections using English queries, and have successfully added French, German, and Italian document collections. We achieve this capability through separation of language-dependent and language-independent components and through the application of asymmetric techniques that leverage an extensive English retrieval infrastructure.

Keywords

Cross-language information retrieval

1. INTRODUCTION

Our goal is to produce systems that allow interactive users to present English queries and retrieve documents in languages that they cannot read. In this paper we focus on what we call "rapid retargetability": extending interactive translingual retrieval functionality for a new document language rapidly with few language-specific resources. Our current system can be retargeted to a new language in one day with only one language-dependent resource: a bilingual term list.[1] Our language-independent architecture consists of two main components:

1. Document translation and indexing

2. Interactive retrieval

We describe each of these components, demonstrate their effectiveness for information retrieval tasks, and then conclude by describing our experience with adding French, German and Italian document collections to a system that was originally developed for Chinese.

---

[1] For Asian languages we also use a language-specific segmentation system.

Proceedings of HLT 2001, First International Conference on Human Language Technology Research, J. Allan, ed., Morgan Kaufmann, San Francisco, 2001.

2. DOCUMENT TRANSLATION AND INDEXING

We have adopted a document translation architecture for two reasons. First, we support a single query language (English) but multiple document languages, so indexing English terms simplifies query processing (where interactive response time can be a concern). Second, a document translation architecture simplifies the display of translated documents by decoupling the translation and display processes. Gigabyte collections require machine translation that is orders of magnitude faster than present commercial systems. We accomplish this using term-by-term translation, in which the basic data structure is a simple hash table lookup. Any translation requires some source of translation knowledge—we use a bilingual term list containing English translation(s) for each foreign language term. We typically construct these term lists by harvesting Internet-available translation resources, so the foreign language terms for which translations are known are typically an eclectic mix of root and inflected forms. We accommodate this limitation using a four-stage backoff statistical stemming approach to enhance translation coverage.

2.1 Preprocessing.

Differences in use of diacritic-s, case, and punctuation can inhibit matching between term list entries and document terms, so normalization is important. In order to maximize the probability of matching document words with term list entries, we normalize the bilingual term list and the documents by:

- converting characters in Western languages to lowercase,

- removing all accents and diacritics, and

- segmentation, which for Western languages merely involves separating punctuation from other text by the addition of white space.

Our preprocessing also includes conversion of the bilingual term list and the document collection into standard formats. The preprocessing typically requires about half a day of programmer time.

2.2 Four-Stage Backoff Translation.

Bilingual term lists found on the Web often contain an eclectic mix of root forms and morphological variants. We thus developed a four-stage backoff strategy to maximize coverage while limiting spurious translations:

1. Match the **surface form** of a document term to **surface forms** of source language terms in the bilingual term list.

2. Match the **stem** of a document term to **surface forms** of source language terms in the bilingual term list.

3. Match the **surface form** of a document term to **stems** of source language terms in the bilingual term list.

4. Match the **stem** of a document term to **stems** of source language terms in the bilingual term list.

The process terminates as soon as a match is found at any stage, and the known translations for that match are generated. Although this may produce an inappropriate morphological variant for a correct English translation, use of English stemming at indexing time minimizes the effect of that factor on retrieval effectiveness. Because we are ultimately interested in processing documents in any language, we may not have a hand-crafted stemmer available for the document language. We have thus explored the application of rule induction to learn stemming rules in an unsupervised fashion from the collection that is being indexed [2].

2.3 Balanced Top-2 Translation.

We produce exactly two English terms for each foreign-language term. For terms with no known translation, the untranslated term is generated twice (often appropriate for proper names in the Latin-1 character set). For terms with one translation, that translation is generated twice. For terms with two or more known translations, we generate the "best" two translations. In prior experiments we have found that this balanced translation strategy significantly outperforms the usual (unbalanced) technique of including all known translations [1]. We establish the "best" translations by sorting the bilingual term list in advance using only English resources. All single-word translations are ordered by decreasing unigram frequency in the Brown corpus, followed by all multi-word translations, and finally by any single word entries not found in the Brown corpus. This ordering has the effect of minimizing the effect of infrequent words in non-standard usages or of misspellings that sometimes appear in bilingual term lists. This translation strategy allows balancing of translations in a modular fashion, even when one does not have access to the internal parameters of the information retrieval system. We translate ~ 100 MB per hour using Perl on a SPARC Ultra 5.

2.4 Post-translation Document Expansion.

We implement post-translation document expansion for the foreign language stories after translation into English in order to enrich the indexing vocabulary beyond that which was available after term-by-term translation. This is analogous to the process that Singhal et al. applied to monolingual speech retrieval [4].

Term-by-term translation produces a set of English terms that serve as a noisy representation of the original source language document. These terms are then treated as a query to a comparable English collection, typically contemporaneous newswire text, from which we retrieve the five highest ranked documents. From those five documents, we extract the most selective terms and use them to enrich the original translations of the documents. For this expansion process we select one instance of every term with an IDF value above an *ad hoc* threshold that was tuned to yield approximately 50 new terms. This optional step is the slowest processing stage, with a throughput of about 20 MB per hour.

2.5 Indexing

The resulting collection is then indexed using Inquery (version 3.1p1), with the kstem stemmer and default English stopword list. Indexing is the fastest stage in the process, with throughput exceeding one gigabyte per hour.

3. INTERACTIVE RETRIEVAL

Interactive searches are performed using a Web interface. Summary information for the top-ranked documents is displayed in groups of ten per page. Document summaries consist of the date and a gloss translation of the document title. Users can inspect a gloss translation of the full text of any document if the title is not sufficiently informative. For both title and full text, the gloss translations are generated in advance using the same process as translation for indexing, with the following differences in detail:

- Terms added as a result of document expansion are not displayed.

- The number of retained translations is separately selectable for the title and for full text indexing.

- Translations are not duplicated when fewer than the maximum allowable number of translations are known.

Our goal is to support the process of *finding* documents, with the realization that the process of *using* documents may need to be supported in some other way (e.g., by forwarding relevant documents to someone who is able to read that language). We have therefore designed our interface to highlight the query terms in translated documents and to facilitate skimming by emphasizing the most common translation when multiple translations are displayed. We have found that such displays can support a classification task, even when the translation is not easy to read [3]. Documents must be classified by the user as relevant or not relevant, so our classification results suggest that this can be an effective user interface design.

4. RESULTS

We present results both for component-level performance of our language-independent retargeting modules and an assessment of the overall retargeting process.

4.1 Component-level Evaluation

We applied our retargeting approach and retrieval enhancement techniques described above in the context of the first Cross-Language Evaluation Forum's (CLEF) multilingual task. We used the English language forms of the queries to retrieve English, French, German, and Italian documents. Below we present comparative performance measures for two of the main processing components described above - statistical stemming backoff translation - applied to the English-French cross-language segment of the CLEF task. The post-translation document expansion component was applied to the smaller Topic Detection and Tracking (TDT-3) collection to improve retrieval of Mandarin documents using English.

4.1.1 Baseline CLEF System Configuration

Our baseline run was conducted as follows. We translated the $\sim 44,000$ documents from the 1994 issues of *Le Monde*. We used the English-French bilingual term list downloaded from the Web at http://www.freedict.com. We then inverted the term list to form a 35,000 term French-English translation resource. We performed the necessary document and term list normalization; in this case, removing accents from document surface forms to enable matching with the un-accented term list entries, converting case, and splitting clitic contractions, such as *l'horlage*, on punctuation. We trained the statistical stemming rules on a sample of the bilingual term list and document collection and applied these rules in stemming backoff. Our default condition was run with top-2 balanced translation using the Brown corpus as a source of target language unigram frequency information. Translated documents were then indexed with

	Stage 1	Stage 2	Stage 3	Stage 4
Match	70%	3%	0.5%	1%

Table 1: Percentage of document terms translated at each stage of 4-stage backoff translation with statistical stemming.

the InQuery (version 3.1p1) system, using the kstem stemmer for English stemming and InQuery's default English stopword list. Long queries were formed by concatenating the title, description, and narrative fields of the original query specification. The resulting word sequence was enclosed in an InQuery $\#sum$ operator, indicating unweighted sum.

Our figure of merit for the evaluations below is mean (uninterpolated) average precision computed using trec_eval [2] across the 34 topics in the CLEF evaluation for which relevant French documents are known.

4.1.2 Backoff Translation with Statistical Stemming

We first contrast the above baseline system with the effectiveness of an otherwise identical run *without* the stemming backoff component. Terms in the documents are thus only translated if there is an exact match between the surface form in the document and a surface form in the bilingual term list. We find that mean average precision for unstemmed translation is 0.19 as compared with 0.2919 for our baseline system including stemming backoff based on trained rules. This difference is significant at $p < 0.05$, by paired t-test, two-tailed. The per-query effectiveness is illustrated in Figure 1. Backoff translation improves translation coverage while retaining relatively high precision of matching in contrast to unstemmed effectiveness.

Backoff translation improves cross-language information retrieval effectiveness by improving translation coverage of the terms in the document collection. Using the statistical stemmer, by-token coverage of document terms increased by 7coverage. The different stages of the four-stage backoff process contributed as illustrated in 1. The majority of terms match in the Stage 1 exact match, accounting for 70% of the term instances in the documents. The remaining stages each account for between 0.5% and 3% of the document terms, while 20% of document term instances remain untranslatable. However, this relatively small increase in coverage results in the highly significant improvement in retrieval effectiveness above.

4.1.3 Top-2 Balanced Translation

Here we contrast top-2 balanced translation with top-1 translation. We retain statistical stemming backoff for the top-1 translation. We replace each French document term with the highest ranked English translation by target language unigram frequency in the Brown Corpus as detailed above, retaining the original French term when no translation is found in the bilingual term list. We achieve a mean average precision of 0.2532 in contrast with the baseline condition. This difference is significant at $p < 0.01$ by paired t-test, two-tailed. We can effectively incorporate additional translations using top-2 balanced translation without degrading performance by introducing significant additional noise. A query-by-query contrast is presented in Figure 2.

4.1.4 Document Expansion

We evaluated post-translation document expansion using the Topic Detection and Tracking (TDT-3) collection. For this evaluation, we used the TDT-1999 topic detection task evaluation framework, but

because out focus in this paper is on ranked retrieval effectiveness we report mean uninterpolated average precision rather than the topic-weighted detection cost measure typically reported in TDT. In the topic detection task, the system is presented with one or more exemplar stories from the training epoch—a form of query-by-example—and must determine whether each story in the evaluation epoch addresses either the same seminal event or activity or some directly related event or activity. This is generally thought to be a somewhat narrower formulation than the more widely used notion of topical relevance, but it seems to be well suited to query-by-example evaluations. The TDT-1999 tracking task was multilingual, searching stories in both English and Mandarin Chinese, and multi-modal, involving both newswire text and broadcast news audio. We focus on the cross-language spoken document retrieval component of the tracking task, using English exemplars to identify on-topic stories in Mandarin Chinese broadcast news audio. We compare top-1 translation of the Mandarin Chinese stories with and without post-translation document expansion.[3] We used the earlier TDT-2 English newswire text collection as our side collection for expansion. We perform topic tracking on 60 topics with 4 exemplars each. Here, we report the mean average precision on the 55 topics for which there are on-topic Mandarin audio stories. The mean uninterpolated average precision for retrieval of unexpanded documents is 0.36 while post-translation document expansion raises this figure to 0.41. This difference is significant at $p < 0.01$ by paired t-test, two-tailed. The contrast is illustrated in Figure 3. Interestingly, when we tried this with French, we noted that expansion tended to select terms from the few foreign-language documents that happened to be present in our expansion collection. We have not yet explored that effect in detail, but this observation suggests that the document expansion may be sensitive to the characteristics of the expansion collection that are not immediately apparent.

4.2 The Learning Curve

We have found that retargeting can be accomplished quite quickly (a day without document expansion, three days for TREC-sized collections with document expansion), but only if the required infrastructure is in place. Adapting a system that was developed initially for Chinese to handle French documents required several weeks, with most of that effort invested in development of four-stage backoff translation and statistical stemming. Further adapting the system to handle German documents revealed the importance of compound splitting, a problem that we will ultimately need to address by incorporating a more general segmentation strategy than we used initially for Chinese. In extending the system to Italian we have found that although our statistical stemmer presently performs poorly in that language, we can achieve quite credible results even with a fairly small (17,313 term) bilingual term list using a freely available Muscat stemmer (which exist for ten languages). So although it is possible in concept to retarget to a new language in just a few days, extending the system typically takes us between one and three weeks because we are still climbing the learning curve.

5. CONCLUSION

By building on the lessons learned using the TREC, CLEF, NT-CIR, and TDT collections, we have sought to build an infrastructure that can be applied to a broad array of languages. Arabic and Korean collections are expected to become available in the next year, and we are now evolving our interface to support user studies. Our approach is distinguished by support for interactive retrieval even

[2] Available at ftp://ftp.cs.cornell.edu/pub/smart/.

[3] Since Mandarin Chinese has little surface morphology, we omit backoff translation in this case.

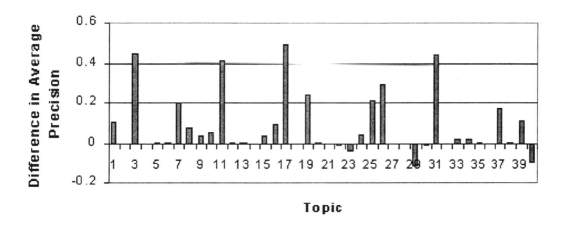

Figure 1: Comparison of effectiveness of backoff versus unstemmed translation of French documents: Bars above x-axis indicate backoff transltion outperforms unstemmed translation.

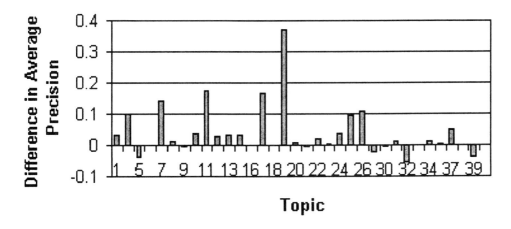

Figure 2: Comparison of effectiveness of top-2 balanced versus top-1 translation of French documents: Bars above x-axis indicate "Top-2" outperforms "Top-1"

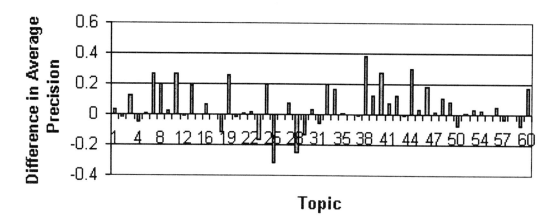

Figure 3: Comparison of effectiveness of top-1 post-translation document expansion versus bare top-1 translation of Chinese documents: Bars above x-axis indicate document expansion outperforms bare translation

in languages for which machine translation is presently unavailable, and our ultimate goal is to characterize how closely we can approximate the retrieval effectiveness users would obtain if they had the best available machine translations for the retrieved documents.

Acknowledgements

This work was supported in part by DARPA contract N6600197C8540 and DARPA cooperative agreement N660010028910.

6. ADDITIONAL AUTHORS

Clara I. Cabezas (Department of Linguistics, top University of Maryland, College Park, email: clarac@umiacs.umd.edu)

7. REFERENCES

[1] G.-A. Levow and D. W. Oard. Translingual topic tracking with PRISE. In *Working Notes of the Third Topic Detection and Tracking Worksho p*, Feb. 2000. http://www.glue.umd.edu/~oard/research.html.

[2] D. W. Oard, G.-A. Levow, and C. I. Cabezas. CLEF experiments at Maryland: Statistical stemming and backof f translation. In C. Peters, editor, *Proceedings of the First Cross-Language Evaluation Forum*. 2001. To appear. http://www.glue.umd.edu/~oard/research .html.

[3] D. W. Oard and P. Resnik. Support for interactive document selection in cross-language information retrieval. *Information Processing and Management*, 35(3):363–379, July 1999.

[4] A. Singhal, J. Choi, D. Hindle, J. Hirschberg, F. Pereira, and S. Whittaker. AT&T at TREC-7 SDR Track. In *Proceedings of the DARPA Broadcast News Workshop*, 1999.

Robust Knowledge Discovery from Parallel Speech and Text Sources

F. Jelinek, W. Byrne, S. Khudanpur, B. Hladká. CLSP, Johns Hopkins University, Baltimore, MD.
H. Ney, F. J. Och. RWTH Aachen University, Aachen, Germany
J. Curín. Charles University, Prague, Czech Rep.
J. Psutka. University of West Bohemia, Pilsen, Czech Rep.

1. INTRODUCTION

As a by-product of the recent information explosion, the same basic facts are often available from multiple sources such as the Internet, television, radio and newspapers. We present here a project currently in its early stages that aims to take advantage of the redundancies in parallel sources to achieve robustness in automatic knowledge extraction.

Consider, for instance, the following sampling of actual news from various sources on a particular day:

CNN: James McDougal, President Bill Clinton's former business partner in Arkansas and a cooperating witness in the Whitewater investigation, died Sunday while serving a federal prison term. He was 57.

MSNBC: Fort Worth, Texas, March 8. Whitewater figure James McDougal died of an apparent heart attack in a private community hospital in Fort Worth, Texas, Sunday. He was 57.

ABC News: Washington, March 8. James McDougal, a key figure in Independent Counsel Kenneth Starr's Whitewater investigation, is dead.

The Detroit News: Fort Worth. James McDougal, a key witness in Kenneth Starr's Whitewater investigation of President Clinton and First Lady Hillary Rodham Clinton, died of a heart attack in a prison hospital Sunday. He was 57.

San Jose Mercury News: James McDougal, the wily Arkansas banking rogue who drew Bill Clinton and Hillary Rodham Clinton into real estate deals that have come to haunt them, died Sunday of cardiac arrest just months before he hoped to be released from prison. He was 57.

The Miami Herald: Washington. James McDougal, the wily Arkansas financier and land speculator at the center of the original Whitewater probe against President Clinton, died Sunday.

Proceedings of HLT 2001, First International Conference on Human Language Technology Research, J. Allan, ed., Morgan Kaufmann, San Francisco, 2001.

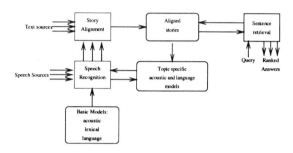

Figure 1: Information Flow in Alignment and Extraction

We propose to align collections of stories, much like the example above, from multiple text and speech sources and then develop methods that exploit the resulting parallelism both as a tool to improve recognition accuracy and to enable the development of systems that can reliably extract information from parallel sources.

Our goal is to develop systems that align text sources and recognize parallel speech streams simultaneously in several languages by making use of all related text and speech. The initial systems we intend to develop will process each language independently. However, our ultimate and most ambitious objective is to align text sources and recognize speech using a single, integrated multilingual ASR system. Of course, if sufficiently accurate automatic machine translation (MT) techniques ([1]) were available, we could address multilingual processing and single language systems in the same way. However MT techniques are not yet reliable enough that we expect all words and phrases recognized *within* languages to contribute to recognition *across* languages. We intend to develop methods that identify the particular words and phrases that both can be translated reliably and also used to improve story recognition.

As MT technology improves it can be incorporated more extensively within the processing paradigm we propose. We consider this proposal a framework within which successful MT techniques can eventually be used for multilingual acoustic processing.

2. PROJECT OBJECTIVES

The first objective is to enhance multi-lingual information systems by exploiting the processing capabilities for resource-rich languages to enhance the capabilities for resource-impoverished language. The second objective is to advance information retrieval and knowledge information systems by providing them with considerably improved multi-lingual speech recognition capabilities. Our research plan proceeds in several steps to (i) collect and (ii) align multi-lingual parallel speech and text sources, (iii) exploit parallelism for improving ASR within a language, and to (iv) exploit

299

parallelism for improving ASR across languages. The main information flows involved in aligning and exploiting parallel sources are illustrated in Figure 1. We will initially focus on German, English and Czech language sources. This section summarizes the major components of our project.

2.1 Parallel Speech and Text Sources

The monolingual speech and text collections that we will use to develop techniques to exploit parallelism for improving ASR within a language are readily available. For instance, the North American News Text corpus of parallel news streams from 16 US newspapers and newswire is available from LDC. A 3-year period yields over 350 million words of multi-source news text.

In addition to data developed within the TIDES and other HLT programs, we are in the process of identifying and creating our own multilingual parallel speech and text sources.

FBIS TIDES Multilingual Newstext Collection
For the purposes of developing multilingual alignment techniques, we intend to use the 240 day, contemporaneous, multilingual news text collection made available for use to TIDES projects by FBIS. This corpus contains news in our initial target languages of English, German, and Czech. The collections are highly parallel, in that much of the stories are direct translations.

Radio Prague Multilingual Speech and Text Corpus
Speech and news text from Radio Prague was collected under the direction of J. Psutka with the consent of Radio Prague. The collection contains speech and text in 5 languages: Czech, English, German, French, and Spanish. The collection began June 1, 2000 and continued for approximately 3 months. The text collection contains the news scripts used for the broadcast; the broadcasts more or less follow the scripts. The speech is about 3 minutes per day in each language, which should yield a total of about 5 hours of speech per language.

Our initial analysis of the Radio Prague corpus suggest that only approximately 5% of the stories coincide in topic, and that there is little, if any, direct translation of stories. We anticipate that this sparseness will make this corpus significantly hard to analyze than another, highly-parallel corpus. However, we expect this is the sort of difficulty that will likely be encountered in processing 'real-world' multilingual news sources.

2.2 Story-level Alignment

Once we have the multiple streams of information we must be able to align them according to story. A story is the description of one or more events that happened in a single day and that are reported in a single article by a daily news source the next day. We expect that we will use the same techniques used in the Topic Detection (TDT) field ([5]). Independently of the specific details of the alignment procedure, there is now substantial evidence that related stories from parallel streams can be identified using standard statistical Information Retrieval (IR) techniques.

Sentence Alignment As part of the infrastructure needed to incorporate cross-lingual information into language models, we are employing statistical MT systems to generate English/German and English/Czech alignments of sentences in the FBIS Newstext Collection. For the English/German sentence and single-word based alignments, we plan to use statistical models ([4]) [3] which generate both sentence and word alignments. For English/Czech sentence alignment, we will employ the statistical models trained as part of the Czech-English MT system developed during the 1999 Johns Hopkins Summer Workshop ([2]).

2.3 Multi-Source Automatic Speech Recognition

The scenario we propose is extraction of information from parallel text followed by repeated recognition of parallel broadcasts, resulting in a gradual lowering the WER. The first pass is performed in order to find the likely topics discussed in the story and to identify the topics relevant to the query. In this process, the acoustic model will be improved by deriving pronunciation specifications for out-of-vocabulary words and fixed phrases extracted from the parallel stories. The language model will be improved by extending the coverage of the underlying word and phrase vocabulary, and by specializing the model's statistics to the narrow topic at hand. As long as a round of recognition yields new information, the corresponding improvement is incorporated into the recognizer modules and bootstrapping of the system continues.

Story-specific Language Models from Parallel Speech and Text
Our goal is to create language models combining specific but sparse statistics, derived from relevant parallel material, with reliable but unspecific statistics obtainable from large general corpora. We will create special *n-gram* language models from the available text, related or parallel to the spoken stories. We can then interpolate this special model with a larger pre-existing model, possibly derived from training text associated to the topic of the story. Our recent STIMULATE work demonstrated success in construction of topic-specific language models on the basis of hierarchically topic-organized corpora [8].

Unlike building models from parallel texts, the training of story specific language models from recognized speech is also affected by recognition errors in the data which will be used for language modeling. Confidence measures can be used to estimate the correctness of individual words or phrases on the recognizer output. Using this information, *n-gram* statistics can be extracted from the recognizer output by selecting those events which are likely to be correct and which can therefore be used to adjust the original language model without introducing new errors to the recognition system.

Language Models with Cross-Lingual Lexical Triggers
A trigger language model ([6], [7]) will be constructed for the target language from the text corpus, where the lexical triggers are not from the word-history in the target language, but from the aligned recognized stories in the source language. The trigger information becomes most important in those cases in which the baseline *n-gram* model in the target language does not supply sufficient information to predict a word. We expect that content words in the source language are good predictors for content words in the target language and that these words are difficult to predict using the target language alone, and the mutual information techniques used to identify trigger pairs will be useful here.

Once a spoken source-language story has been recognized, the words found here there will be used as triggers in the language model for the recognition of the target-language news broadcasts.

3. SUMMARY

Our goal is to align collections of stories from multiple text and speech sources in more than one language and then develop methods that exploit the resulting parallelism both as a tool to improve recognition accuracy and to enable the development of systems that can reliably extract information from parallel sources. Much like a teacher rephrases a concept in a variety of ways to help a class understand it, the multiple sources, we expect, will increase the potential of success in knowledge extraction. We envision techniques that will operate repeatedly on multilingual sources by incorporating newly discovered information in one language into the models used for all the other languages. Applications of these methods extend beyond news sources to other multiple-source domains such as office email and voice-mail, or classroom materials such as lectures, notes and texts.

4. REFERENCES

[1] P. F. Brown, S. A. DellaPietra, V. J. D. Pietra, and R. L. Mercer. The mathematics of statistical translation. *Computational Linguistics*, 19(2), 1993.

[2] K. K. et al. Statistical machine translation, WS'99 Final Report, Johns Hopkins University, 1999. http://www.clsp.jhu.edu/ws99/projects/mt.

[3] F. J. Och and H. Ney. Improved statistical alignment models. In *ACL'00*, pages 440–447, 2000.

[4] F. J. Och, C. Tillmann, and H. Ney. Improved alignment models for statistical machine translation. In *EMNLP/VLC'99*, pages 20–28, 1999.

[5] Proceedings of the Topic Detection and Tracking workshop. University of Maryland, College Park, MD, October 1997.

[6] C. Tillmann and H. Ney. Selection criteria for word trigger pairs in language modelling. In *ICGI'96*, pages 95–106, 1996.

[7] C. Tillmann and H. Ney. Statistical language modeling and word triggers. In *SPECOM'96*, pages 22–27, 1996.

[8] D. Yarowsky. Exploiting nonlocal and syntactic word relationships in language models for conversational speech recognition, a NSF STIMULATE Project IRI9618874, 1997. Johns Hopkins University.

The RWTH System for Statistical Translation of Spoken Dialogues

H. Ney, F. J. Och, S. Vogel
Lehrstuhl für Informatik VI, Computer Science Department
RWTH Aachen, University of Technology
D-52056 Aachen, Germany

ABSTRACT

This paper gives an overview of our work on statistical machine translation of spoken dialogues, in particular in the framework of the VERBMOBIL project. The goal of the VERBMOBIL project is the translation of spoken dialogues in the domains of appointment scheduling and travel planning. Starting with the Bayes decision rule as in speech recognition, we show how the required probability distributions can be structured into three parts: the language model, the alignment model and the lexicon model. We describe the components of the system and report results on the VERBMOBIL task. The experience obtained in the VERBMOBIL project, in particular a large-scale end-to-end evaluation, showed that the statistical approach resulted in significantly lower error rates than three competing translation approaches: the sentence error rate was 29% in comparison with 52% to 62% for the other translation approaches.

1. INTRODUCTION

In comparison with written language, speech and especially spontaneous speech poses additional difficulties for the task of automatic translation. Typically, these difficulties are caused by errors of the recognition process, which is carried out before the translation process. As a result, the sentence to be translated is not necessarily well-formed from a syntactic point-of-view. Even without recognition errors, speech translation has to cope with a lack of conventional syntactic structures because the structures of spontaneous speech differ from that of written language.

The statistical approach shows the potential to tackle these problems for the following reasons. First, the statistical approach is able to avoid hard decisions at any level of the translation process. Second, for any source sentence, a translated sentence in the target language is guaranteed to be generated. In most cases, this will be hopefully a syntactically perfect sentence in the target language; but even if this is not the case, in most cases, the translated sentence will convey the meaning of the spoken sentence.

Whereas statistical modelling is widely used in speech recognition, there are so far only a few research groups that apply statistical modelling to language translation. The presentation here is based on work carried out in the framework of the EuTRANS project [8] and the VERBMOBIL project [25].

2. STATISTICAL DECISION THEORY AND LINGUISTICS

2.1 The Statistical Approach

The use of statistics in computational linguistics has been extremely controversial for more than three decades. The controversy is very well summarized by the statement of Chomsky in 1969 [6]:

> "It must be recognized that the notion of a 'probability of a sentence' is an entirely useless one, under any interpretation of this term".

This statement was considered to be true by the majority of experts from artificial intelligence and computational linguistics, and the concept of statistics was banned from computational linguistics for many years.

What is overlooked in this statement is the fact that, in an automatic system for speech recognition or text translation, we are faced with the problem of taking decisions. It is exactly here where statistical decision theory comes in. In speech recognition, the success of the statistical approach is based on the equation:

Speech Recognition = Acoustic–Linguistic Modelling
+ Statistical Decision Theory

Similarly, for machine translation, the statistical approach is expressed by the equation:

Machine Translation = Linguistic Modelling
+ Statistical Decision Theory

For the 'low-level' description of speech and image signals, it is widely accepted that the statistical framework allows an efficient coupling between the observations and the models, which is often described by the buzz word 'subsymbolic processing'. But there is another advantage in using probability distributions in that they offer an explicit formalism for expressing and combining hypothesis scores:

- The probabilities are directly used as scores: These scores are normalized, which is a desirable property: when increasing the score for a certain element in the

Proceedings of HLT 2001, First International Conference on Human Language Technology Research, J. Allan, ed., Morgan Kaufmann, San Francisco, 2001.

set of all hypotheses, there must be one or several other elements whose scores are reduced at the same time.

- It is straightforward to combine scores: depending on the task, the probabilities are either multiplied or added.

- Weak and vague dependencies can be modelled easily. Especially in spoken and written natural language, there are nuances and shades that require 'grey levels' between 0 and 1.

2.2 Bayes Decision Rule and System Architecture

In machine translation, the goal is the translation of a text given in a source language into a target language. We are given a source string $f_1^J = f_1...f_j...f_J$, which is to be translated into a target string $e_1^I = e_1...e_i...e_I$. In this article, the term *word* always refers to a *full-form* word. Among all possible target strings, we will choose the string with the highest probability which is given by Bayes decision rule [5]:

$$\hat{e}_1^I = \arg\max_{e_1^I} \{Pr(e_1^I|f_1^J)\}$$
$$= \arg\max_{e_1^I} \{Pr(e_1^I) \cdot Pr(f_1^J|e_1^I)\} \quad.$$

Here, $Pr(e_1^I)$ is the language model of the target language, and $Pr(f_1^J|e_1^I)$ is the string translation model which will be decomposed into lexicon and alignment models. The argmax operation denotes the search problem, i.e. the generation of the output sentence in the target language. The overall architecture of the statistical translation approach is summarized in Figure 1.

In general, as shown in this figure, there may be additional transformations to make the translation task simpler for the algorithm. The transformations may range from the categorization of single words and word groups to more complex preprocessing steps that require some parsing of the source string. We have to keep in mind that in the search procedure both the language and the translation model are applied *after* the text transformation steps. However, to keep the notation simple, we will not make this explicit distinction in the subsequent exposition.

3. ALIGNMENT MODELLING

3.1 Concept

A key issue in modelling the string translation probability $Pr(f_1^J|e_1^I)$ is the question of how we define the correspondence between the words of the target sentence and the words of the source sentence. In typical cases, we can assume a sort of pairwise dependence by considering all word pairs (f_j, e_i) for a given sentence pair $(f_1^J; e_1^I)$. Here, we will further constrain this model by assigning each source word to *exactly one* target word. Later, this requirement will be relaxed. Models describing these types of dependencies are referred to as *alignment models* [5, 24].

When aligning the words in parallel texts, we typically observe a strong localization effect. Figure 2 illustrates this effect for the language pair German–English. In many cases, although not always, there is an additional property: over large portions of the source string, the alignment is monotone.

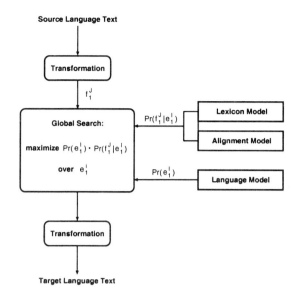

Figure 1: Architecture of the translation approach based on Bayes decision rule.

3.2 Basic Models

To arrive at a quantitative specification, we define the alignment mapping: $j \rightarrow i = a_j$, which assigns a word f_j in position j to a word e_i in position $i = a_j$. We rewrite the probability for the translation model by introducing the 'hidden' alignments $a_1^J := a_1...a_j...a_J$ for each sentence pair $(f_1^J; e_1^I)$. To structure this probability distribution, we factorize it over the positions in the source sentence and limit the alignment dependencies to a first-order dependence:

$$Pr(f_1^J|e_1^I) = p(J|I) \cdot \sum_{a_1^J} \prod_{j=1}^{J} [p(a_j|a_{j-1}, I, J) \cdot p(f_j|e_{a_j})] \quad.$$

Here, we have the following probability distributions:

- the sentence length probability: $p(J|I)$, which is included here for completeness, but can be omitted without loss of performance;

- the lexicon probability: $p(f|e)$;

- the alignment probability: $p(a_j|a_{j-1}, I, J)$.

By making the alignment probability $p(a_j|a_{j-1}, I, J)$ dependent on the jump width $a_j - a_{j-1}$ instead of the absolute positions a_j, we obtain the so-called homogeneous hidden Markov model, for short HMM [24].

We can also use a *zero-order* model $p(a_j|j, I, J)$, where there is only a dependence on the *absolute* position index j of the source string. This is the so-called model IBM-2 [5]. Assuming a uniform alignment probability $p(a_j|j, I, J) = 1/I$, we arrive at the so-called model IBM-1.

These models can be extended to allow for source words having no counterpart in the translation. Formally, this is incorporated into the alignment models by adding a so-called 'empty word' at position $i = 0$ to the target sentence and aligning all source words without a direct translation to this empty word.

303

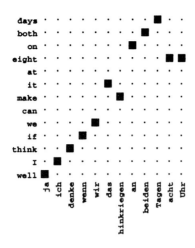

Figure 2: Word-to-word alignment.

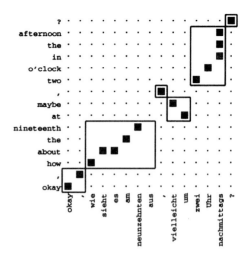

Figure 3: Example of a word alignment and of extracted alignment templates.

In [5], more refined alignment models are introduced by using the concept of fertility. The idea is that often a word in the target language may be aligned to several words in the source language. This is the so-called model IBM-3. Using, in addition, first-order alignment probabilities along the positions of the source string leads us to model IBM-4. Although these models take one-to-many alignments explicitly into account, the lexicon probabilities $p(f|e)$ are still based on single words in each of the two languages.

In systematic experiments, it was found that the quality of the alignments determined from the bilingual training corpus has a direct effect on the translation quality [14].

3.3 Alignment Template Approach

A general shortcoming of the baseline alignment models is that they are mainly designed to model the lexicon dependences between single words. Therefore, we extend the approach to handle word groups or phrases rather than single words as the basis for the alignment models [15]. In other words, a whole group of adjacent words in the source sentence may be aligned with a whole group of adjacent words in the target language. As a result, the context of words tends to be explicitly taken into account, and the differences in local word orders between source and target languages can be learned explicitly. Figure 3 shows some of the extracted alignment templates for a sentence pair from the VERBMOBIL training corpus. The training algorithm for the alignment templates extracts all phrase pairs which are aligned in the training corpus up to a maximum length of 7 words. To improve the generalization capability of the alignment templates, the templates are determined for bilingual word classes rather than words directly. These word classes are determined by an automatic clustering procedure [13].

4. SEARCH

The task of the search algorithm is to generate the most likely target sentence e_1^I of unknown length I for an observed source sentence f_1^J. The search must make use of all three knowledge sources as illustrated by Figure 4: the alignment model, the lexicon model and the language model. All three

of them must contribute in the final decision about the words in the target language.

To illustrate the specific details of the search problem, we slightly change the definitions of the alignments:

- we use *inverted* alignments as in the model IBM-4 [5] which define a mapping from *target* to *source* positions rather the other way round.

- we allow *several* positions in the source language to be covered, i.e. we consider mappings B of the form:

$$B : i \rightarrow B_i \subset \{1, ...j, ...J\}$$

We replace the sum over all alignments by the best alignment, which is referred to as maximum approximation in speech recognition. Using a trigram language model $p(e_i|, e_{i-2}, e_{i-1})$, we obtain the following search criterion:

$$\max_{B_1^I, e_1^I} \prod_{i=1}^{I} \left[[p(e_i|e_{i-2}^{i-1}) \cdot p(B_i|B_{i-1}, I, J) \cdot \prod_{j \in B_i} p(f_j|e_i)] \right]$$

Considering this criterion, we can see that we can build up hypotheses of partial target sentences in a *bottom-to-top* strategy over the positions i of the target sentence e_1^i as illustrated in Figure 5. An important constraint for the alignment is that *all* positions of the source sentence should be covered exactly *once*. This constraint is similar to that of the travelling salesman problem where each city has to be visited exactly once. Details on various search strategies can be found in [4, 9, 12, 21].

In order to take long context dependences into account, we use a class-based five-gram language model with backing-off. Beam-search is used to handle the huge search space. To normalize the costs of partial hypotheses covering different parts of the input sentence, an (optimistic) estimation of the remaining cost is added to the current accumulated cost as follows. For each word in the source sentence, a lower bound on its translation cost is determined beforehand. Using this

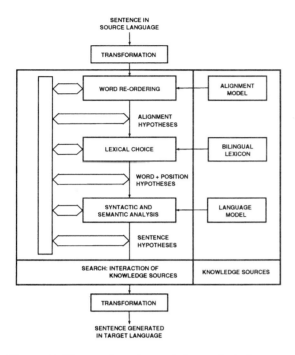

SENTENCE IN
SOURCE LANGUAGE

TRANSFORMATION

WORD RE-ORDERING — ALIGNMENT MODEL

ALIGNMENT HYPOTHESES

LEXICAL CHOICE — BILINGUAL LEXICON

WORD + POSITION HYPOTHESES

SYNTACTIC AND SEMANTIC ANALYSIS — LANGUAGE MODEL

SENTENCE HYPOTHESES

SEARCH: INTERACTION OF KNOWLEDGE SOURCES   KNOWLEDGE SOURCES

TRANSFORMATION

SENTENCE GENERATED
IN TARGET LANGUAGE

Figure 4: Illustration of search in statistical translation.

lower bound, it is possible to achieve an efficient estimation of the remaining cost.

5. EXPERIMENTAL RESULTS

5.1 The Task and the Corpus

Within the VERBMOBIL project, spoken dialogues were recorded. These dialogues were manually transcribed and later manually translated by VERBMOBIL partners (Hildesheim for Phase I and Tübingen for Phase II). Since different human translators were involved, there is great variability in the translations.

Each of these so-called dialogues turns may consist of several sentences spoken by the same speaker and is sometimes

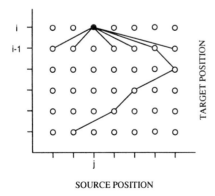

SOURCE POSITION

Figure 5: Illustration of bottom-to-top search.

rather long. As a result, there is no one-to-one correspondence between source and target sentences. To achieve a one-to-one correspondence, the dialogue turns are split into shorter segments using punctuation marks as potential split points. Since the punctuation marks in source and target sentences are not necessarily identical, a dynamic programming approach is used to find the optimal segmentation points. The number of segments in the source sentence and in the test sentence can be different. The segmentation is scored using a word-based alignment model, and the segmentation with the best score is selected. This segmented corpus is the starting point for the training of translation and language models. Alignment models of increasing complexity are trained on this bilingual corpus [14].

A standard vocabulary had been defined for the various speech recognizers used in VERBMOBIL. However, not all words of this vocabulary were observed in the training corpus. Therefore, the translation vocabulary was extended semi-automatically by adding about 13 000 German–English word pairs from an online bilingual lexicon available on the web. The resulting lexicon contained not only word-word entries, but also multi-word translations, especially for the large number of German compound words. To counteract the sparseness of the training data, a couple of straightforward rule-based preprocessing steps were applied *before* any other type of processing:

- categorization of proper names for persons and cities,
- normalization of:
  - numbers,
  - time and date phrases,
  - spelling: don't → do not,...
- splitting of
  German compound words.

Table 1 gives the characteristics of the training corpus and the lexicon. The 58 000 sentence pairs comprise about half a million running words for each language of the bilingual training corpus. The vocabulary size is the number of distinct full-form words seen in the training corpus. Punctuation marks are treated as regular words in the translation approach. Notice the large number of word singletons, i. e. words seen only once. The extended vocabulary is the vocabulary after adding the manual bilingual lexicon.

5.2 Offline Results

During the progress of the VERBMOBIL project, different variants of statistical translation were implemented, and ex-

Table 1: Bilingual training corpus, recognition lexicon and translation lexicon (PM = punctuation mark).

		German	English
Training Text	Sentences	58 332	
	Words (+PMs)	519 523	549 921
	Vocabulary	7 940	4 673
	Singletons	44.8%	37.6%
Recognition	Vocabulary	10 157	6 871
Translation	Manual Pairs	12 779	
	Ext. Vocab.	11 501	6 867

perimental tests were performed for both text and speech input. To summarize these experimental tests, we briefly report experimental offline results for the following translation approaches:

- single-word based approach [20];
- alignment template approach [15];
- cascaded transducer approach [23]:
  unlike the other two-approaches, this approach requires a semi-automatic training procedure, in which the structure of the finite state transducers is designed manually. For more details, see [23].

The offline tests were performed on text input for the translation direction from German to English. The test set consisted of 251 sentences, which comprised 2197 words and 430 punctuation marks. The results are shown in Table 2. To judge and compare the quality of different translation approaches in offline tests, we typically use the following error measures [11]:

- mWER (multi-reference word error rate):
  For each test sentence s_k in the source language, there are *several* reference translations $\mathcal{R}_k = \{r_{k1}, \dots, r_{kn_k}\}$ in the target language. For each translation of the test sentence s_k, the edit distances (number of substitutions, deletions and insertions as in speech recognition) to all sentences in $\mathcal{R}_k$ are calculated, and the smallest distance is selected and used as error measure.
- SSER (subjective sentence error rate):
  Each translated sentence is judged by a human examiner according to an error scale from 0.0 (semantically and syntactically correct) to 1.0 (completely wrong).

Both error measures are reported in Table 2. Although the experiments with the cascaded transducers [23] were not fully optimized yet, the preliminary results indicated that this semi-automatic approach does not generalize as well as the other two fully automatic approaches. Among these two, the alignment template approach was found to work consistently better across different test sets (and also tasks different from VERBMOBIL). Therefore, the alignment template approach was used in the final VERBMOBIL prototype system.

5.3 Disambiguation Examples

In the statistical translation approach as we have presented it, no explicit word sense disambiguation is performed. However, a kind of implicit disambiguation is possible due to the context information of the alignment templates and the language model as shown by the examples in Table 3. The first two groups of sentences contain the

Table 2: Comparison of three statistical translation approaches (test on text input: 251 sentences = 2197 words + 430 punctuation marks).

Translation Approach	mWER [%]	SSER [%]
Single-Word Based	38.2	35.7
Alignment Template	36.0	29.0
Cascaded Transducers	>40.0	>40.0

verbs 'gehen' and 'annehmen' which have different translations, some of which are rather collocational. The correct translation is only possible by taking the whole sentence into account. Some improvement can be achieved by applying morpho-syntactic analysis, e.g handling of the separated verb prefixes in German [10]. The last two sentences show the implicit disambiguation of the temporal and spatial sense for the German preposition 'vor'. Although the system has not been tailored to handle such types of disambiguation, the translated sentences are all acceptable, apart from the sentence: The meeting is to five.

5.4 Integration into the VERBMOBIL Prototype System

The statistical approach to machine translation is embodied in the *stattrans* module which is integrated into the VERBMOBIL prototype system. We briefly review those aspects of it that are relevant for the statistical translation approach. The implementation supports the translation directions from German to English and from English to German. In regular processing mode, the *stattrans* module receives its input from the *repair* module [18]. At that time, the word lattices and best hypotheses from the speech recognition systems have already been prosodically annotated, i.e. information about prosodic segment boundaries, sentence mode and accentuated syllables are added to each edge in the word lattice [2]. The translation is performed on the single best sentence hypothesis of the recognizer.

The prosodic boundaries and the sentence mode information are utilized by the *stattrans* module as follows. If there is a major phrase boundary, a full stop or question mark is inserted into the word sequence, depending on the sentence mode as indicated by the *prosody* module. Additional commas are inserted for other types of segment boundaries. The *prosody* module calculates probabilities for segment boundaries, and thresholds are used to decide if the sentence marks are to be inserted. These thresholds have been selected in such a way that, on the average, for each dialogue turn, a good segmentation is obtained. The segment boundaries restrict possible word reordering between source and target language. This not only improves translation quality, but also restricts the search space and thereby speeds up the translation process.

5.5 Large-Scale End-to-End Evaluation

Whereas the offline tests reported above were important for the optimization and tuning of the system, the most important evaluation was the final evaluation of the VERBMOBIL prototype in spring 2000. This end-to-end evaluation of the VERBMOBIL system was performed at the University of Hamburg [19]. In each session of this evaluation, two native speakers conducted a dialogue. They did not have any direct contact and could only interact by speaking and listening to the VERBMOBIL system.

Three other translation approaches had been integrated into the VERBMOBIL prototype system:

- a classical transfer approach [3, 7, 22], which is based on a manually designed analysis grammar, a set of transfer rules, and a generation grammar,

- a dialogue act based approach [16], which amounts to a sort of *slot filling* by classifying

Table 3: Disambiguation examples (*: using morpho-syntactic analysis).

Ambiguous Word	Text Input	Translation
gehen	Wir gehen ins Theater.	We will go to the theater.
	Mir geht es gut.	I am fine.
	Es geht um Geld.	It is about money.
	Geht es bei Ihnen am Montag?	Is it possible for you on Monday?
	Das Treffen geht bis 5 Uhr.	The meeting is to five.
annehmen	Wir sollten das Angebot annehmen.	We should accept that offer.
	Ich nehme das Schlimmste an.	I will assume the worst.*
vor	Wir treffen uns vor dem Frühstück.	We meet before the breakfast.
	Wir treffen uns vor dem Hotel.	We will meet in front of the hotel.

each sentence into one out of a small number of possible sentence patterns and filling in the slot values,

- an example-based approach [1],
  where a sort of nearest neighbour concept is applied to the set of bilingual training sentence pairs after suitable preprocessing.

In the final end-to-end evaluation, human evaluators judged the translation quality for each of the four translation results using the following criterion:

Is the sentence approximatively correct: yes/no?

The evaluators were asked to pay particular attention to the semantic information (e.g. date and place of meeting, participants etc) contained in the translation. A missing translation as it may happen for the transfer approach or other approaches was counted as wrong translation. The evaluation was based on 5069 dialogue turns for the translation from German to English and on 4136 dialogue turns for the translation from English to German. The speech recognizers used had a word error rate of about 25%. The overall sentence error rates, i.e. resulting from recognition *and* translation, are summarized in Table 4. As we can see, the error rates for the statistical approach are smaller by a factor of about 2 in comparison with the other approaches.

In agreement with other evaluation experiments, these experiments show that the statistical modelling approach may be comparable to or better than the conventional rule-based approach. In particular, the statistical approach seems to have the advantage if robustness is important, e.g. when the input string is not grammatically correct or when it is corrupted by recognition errors.

Although both text and speech input are translated with good quality on the average by the statistical approach,

there are examples where the syntactic structure of the produced sentence is not correct. Some of these syntactic errors are related to long range dependencies and syntactic structures that are not captured by the m-gram language model used. To cope with these problems, morpho-syntactic analysis [10] and grammar-based language models [17] are currently being studied.

6. SUMMARY

In this paper, we have given an overview of the statistical approach to machine translation and especially its implementation in the VERBMOBIL prototype system. The statistical system has been trained on about 500 000 running words from a bilingual German–English corpus. Translations are performed for both directions, i.e. from German to English and from English to German. Comparative evaluations with other translation approaches of the VERBMOBIL prototype system show that the statistical translation is superior, especially in the presence of speech input and ungrammatical input.

Acknowledgment

The work reported here was supported partly by the VERBMOBIL project (contract number 01 IV 701 T4) by the German Federal Ministry of Education, Science, Research and Technology and as part of the EuTRANS project (ESPRIT project number 30268) by the European Community.

Training Toolkit

In a follow-up project of the statistical machine translation project during the 1999 Johns Hopkins University workshop, we have developed a publically available toolkit for the training of different alignment models, including the models IBM-1 to IBM-5 [5] and an HMM alignment model [14, 24]. The software can be downloaded at

```
http://www-i6.Informatik.RWTH-Aachen.DE/
        ~och/software/GIZA++.html.
```

Table 4: Sentence error rates of end-to-end evaluation (speech recognizer with WER=25%; corpus of 5069 and 4136 dialogue turns for translation German to English and English to German, respectively).

Translation Method	Error [%]
Semantic Transfer	62
Dialogue Act Based	60
Example Based	52
Statistical	29

7. REFERENCES

[1] M. Auerswald: Example-based machine translation with templates. In [25], pp. 418–427.

[2] A. Batliner, J. Buckow, H. Niemann, E. Nöth, V. Warnke: The prosody module. In [25], pp. 106–121.

[3] T. Becker, A. Kilger, P. Lopez, P. Poller: The Verbmobil generation component VM-GECO. In [25], pp. 481–496.

[4] A. L. Berger, P. F. Brown, J. Cocke, S. A. Della Pietra, V. J. Della Pietra, J. R. Gillett, J. D. Lafferty, R. L. Mercer, H. Printz,L. Ures: The Candide System for Machine Translation. *ARPA Human Language Technology Workshop*, Plainsboro, NJ, Morgan Kaufmann Publishers, pp. 152-157, San Mateo, CA, March 1994.

[5] P. F. Brown, S. A. Della Pietra, V. J. Della Pietra, R. L. Mercer: The mathematics of statistical machine translation: Parameter estimation. *Computational Linguistics*, Vol. 19, No. 2, pp. 263–311, 1993.

[6] N. Chomsky: "Quine's Empirical Assumptions", in D. Davidson, J. Hintikka (eds.): *Words and objections. Essays on the work of W. V. Quine*, Reidel, Dordrecht, The Netherlands, 1969.

[7] M. C. Emele, M. Dorna, A. Lüdeling, H. Zinsmeister, C. Rohrer: Semantic-based transfer. In [25], pp. 359–376.

[8] EuTrans Project; Instituto Tecnológico de Informática (ITI, Spain), Fondazione Ugo Bordoni (FUB, Italy), RWTH Aachen, Lehrstuhl f. Informatik VI (Germany), Zeres GmbH Bochum (Germany): Example-Based Language Translation Systems. *Final report of the EuTrans project* (EU project number 30268), July 2000.

[9] H. Ney, S. Nießen, F. J. Och, H. Sawaf, C. Tillmann, S. Vogel: Algorithms for statistical translation of spoken language. *IEEE Trans. on Speech and Audio Processing* Vol. 8, No. 1, pp. 24–36, Jan. 2000.

[10] S. Nießen, H. Ney: Improving SMT quality with morpho-syntactic analysis. *18th Int. Conf. on Computational Linguistics*, pp. 1081-1085, Saarbrücken, Germany, July 2000.

[11] S. Nießen, F.-J. Och, G. Leusch, H. Ney: An evaluation tool for machine translation: Fast evaluation for MT research. *2nd Int. Conf. on Language Resources and Evaluation*, pp.39–45, Athens, Greece, May 2000.

[12] S. Nießen, S. Vogel, H. Ney, C. Tillmann: A DP based search algorithm for statistical machine translation. *COLING–ACL '98: 36th Annual Meeting of the Association for Computational Linguistics and 17th Int. Conf. on Computational Linguistics*, pp. 960–967, Montreal, Canada, Aug. 1998.

[13] F. J. Och: An efficient method to determine bilingual word classes. *9th Conf. of the European Chapter of the Association for Computational Linguistics*, pp. 71–76, Bergen, Norway, June 1999.

[14] F. J. Och, H. Ney: A comparison of alignment models for statistical machine translation. *18th Int. Conf. on Computational Linguistics*, pp. 1086-1090, Saarbrücken, Germany, July 2000.

[15] F. J. Och, C. Tillmann, H. Ney: Improved alignment models for statistical machine translation. *Joint SIG-DAT Conf. on Empirical Methods in Natural Language Processing and Very Large Corpora*, 20–28, University of Maryland, College Park, MD, June 1999.

[16] N. Reithinger, R. Engel: Robust content extraction for translation and dialog processing. In [25], pp. 428–437.

[17] H. Sawaf, K. Schütz, H. Ney: On the use of grammar based language models for statistical machine translation. *6th Int. Workshop on Parsing Technologies*, pp. 231–241, Trento, Italy, Feb. 2000.

[18] J. Spilker, M. Klarner, G. Görz: Processing self-corrections in a speech-to-speech system. In [25], pp. 131–140.

[19] L. Tessiore, W. v. Hahn: Functional validation of a machine translation system: Verbmobil. In [25], pp. 611–631.

[20] C. Tillmann, H. Ney: Word re-ordering in a DP-based approach to statistical MT. *18th Int. Conf. on Computational Linguistics 2000*, Saarbrücken, Germany, pp. 850-856, Aug. 2000.

[21] C. Tillmann, S. Vogel, H. Ney, A. Zubiaga: A DP-based search using monotone alignments in statistical translation. *35th Annual Conf. of the Association for Computational Linguistics*, pp. 289–296, Madrid, Spain, July 1997.

[22] H. Uszkoreit, D. Flickinger, W. Kasper, I. A. Sag: Deep linguistic analysis with HPSG. In [25], pp. 216–263.

[23] S. Vogel, H. Ney: Translation with Cascaded Finite-State Transducers. *ACL Conf. (Assoc. for Comput. Linguistics), Hongkong*, pp. 23-30, Oct. 2000.

[24] S. Vogel, H. Ney, C. Tillmann: HMM-based word alignment in statistical translation. *16th Int. Conf. on Computational Linguistics*, pp. 836–841, Copenhagen, Denmark, August 1996.

[25] W. Wahlster (Ed.): *Verbmobil: Foundations of speech-to-speech translations*. Springer-Verlag, Berlin, Germany, 2000.

Scalability and Portability of a Belief Network-based Dialog Model for Different Application Domains

Carmen Wai
The Chinese University of Hong Kong
Shatin, N.T., Hong Kong
SAR, China
Tel: +852 2609 8327

cmwai@se.cuhk.edu.hk

Helen M. Meng
The Chinese University of Hong Kong
Shatin, N.T., Hong Kong
SAR, China
Tel: +852 2609 8327

hmmeng@se.cuhk.edu.hk

Roberto Pieraccini
SpeechWorks International Ltd
17 State Street
New York, NY 1004
Tel: +1.212.425.7200

roberto.pieraccini@speechworks.com

ABSTRACT

This paper describes the scalability and portability of a Belief Network (BN)-based mixed initiative dialog model across application domains. The Belief Networks (BNs) are used to automatically govern the transitions between a system-initiative and a user-initiative dialog model, in order to produce mixed-initiative interactions. We have migrated our dialog model from a simpler domain of foreign exchange to a more complex domain of air travel information service. The adapted processes include: (i) automatic selection of specified concepts in the user's query, for the purpose of informational goal inference; (ii) automatic detection of missing / spurious concepts based on backward inference using the BN. We have also enhanced our dialog model with the capability of discourse context inheritance. To ease portability across domains, which often implies the lack of training data for the new domain, we have developed a set of principles for hand-assigning BN probabilities, based on the "degree of belief" in the relationships between concepts and goals. Application of our model to the ATIS data gave promising results.

1. INTRODUCTION

Spoken dialog systems demonstrate a high degree of usability in many restricted domains, and dialog modeling in such systems plays an important role in assisting users to achieve their goals. The system-initiative dialog model assumes complete control in guiding the user through an interaction towards task completion. This model often attains high task completion rates, but the user is bound by many constraints throughout the interaction. Conversely, the user-initiative model offers maximum flexibility to the user in determining the preferred course of interaction. However this model often has lower task completion rates relative to the system-initiative model, especially when the user's request falls beyond the system's competence level. To strike a balance between these two models, the mixed-initiative dialog model allows both the user and the system to influence the course of interaction. It is possible to *handcraft* a sophisticated mixed-initiative dialog flow, but the task is expensive, and may become intractable for complex application domains.

We strive to reduce handcrafting in the design of mixed-initiative dialogs. We propose to use Belief Networks (BN) to automatically govern the transitions between a system-initiative and a user-initiative dialog model, in order to produce mixed-initiative interactions. Previous work includes the use of semantic interpretation rules for natural language understanding, where the rules are learnt by decision trees known as Semantic Classification Trees (SCTs) [6]. Moreover, there is also previous effort that explores the use of machine learning techniques to automatically determine the optimal dialog strategy. A dialog system can be described as a sequential decision process that has states and actions. An optimal strategy can be obtained by reinforcement learning [7, 8]. While the system is interacting with users, it can explore the state space and thus learn different actions.

Our BN framework was previously used for natural language understanding [1,2]. We have extended this model for dialog modeling, and demonstrated feasibility in the CU FOREX (foreign exchange) [3,4] system, whose domain has low complexity. This work explores the scalability and portability of our BN-based dialog model to a more complex application. We have chosen the ATIS (Air Travel Information Service) domain due to data availability.[1]

2. BELIEF NETWORKS FOR MIXED-INITIATIVE DIALOG MODELING – THE CU FOREX DOAMIN

We have devised an approach that utilizes BNs for mixed-initiative dialog modeling, and demonstrated its feasibility in the CU FOREX domain. Details can be found in [4]. We provide a brief description here for the sake of continuity.

CU FOREX is a bilingual (English and Cantonese) conversational hotline that supports inquiries regarding foreign exchange. The domain is relatively simple, and can be characterized by two query types (or informational goals – Exchange Rate or Interest Rate); and five domain-specific concepts (a CURRENCY pair, TIME DURATION, EXCHANGE RATE and INTEREST RATE). Our approach involves two processes:

2.1 Informational Goal Inference

A BN is trained for each informational goal. Each BN receives as input the concepts that are related to its corresponding goal. In CU FOREX, there are two BNs, each with five input concepts. The pre-defined BN topology shown in Figure 1 (without dotted arrow) incorporates the simplifying assumption that all concepts are dependent only on the goal, but are independent of one another. This topology can be enhanced by

---

[1] The ATIS data can be licensed from the Linguistic Data Consortium (www.ldc.upenn.edu).

Proceedings of HLT 2001, First International Conference on Human Language Technology Research, J. Allan, ed., Morgan Kaufmann, San Francisco, 2001.

309

learning the inter-concept dependencies from training data according to the Minimum Description Length (MDL) principle [2]. The resultant topology is illustrated in Figure 1.

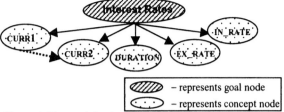

Figure 1. The predefined topology of our BNs is enhanced by the linkage (dotted arrow) learnt to capture dependencies among concepts. The arrows of the acyclic graph are drawn from cause to effect.

Given an input query, each trained BN will make a binary decision (using pre-set threshold of 0.5)[2] regarding the presence or absence of its corresponding informational goal, based on the presence or absence of its input concepts in the query. The decisions across all BNs are combined to identify the informational goal of the input query. We labeled the query to a goal if the corresponding BN votes positive with the maximum *aposteriori* probability. Alternatively, we may label the query with all goals for which the BNs vote positive. Should all BNs vote negative, the query is rejected as out-of-domain (OOD).

2.2 Detection of Missing / Spurious Concepts

Automatic detection of missing or spurious concepts is achieved by *backward inference* in the BN. Given an identified goal from the previous process, the goal node of the corresponding BN is instantiated (i.e. $P(G_j)$ set to *1*), and backward inference updates the probability of each concept $P(C_i)$. Comparison between $P(C_i)$ and a pre-set threshold θ *(=0.5)* determines whether the concept should be present or absent; and further comparison with the actual occurrence(s) determines whether the concept is missing or spurious. In this way, domain-specific constraints for database access is captured and enforced in the BN, i.e. an Exchange Rate inquiry requires a currency pair, and an Interest Rate inquiry requires specifications of the currency and the duration. A missing concept will cause the dialog model to automatically trigger a system prompt. A spurious concept will cause automatically trigger a request for clarification.

Table 1 provides an illustrative example from the CU FOREX domain. The first process infers that the query "Can I have the interest rate of the yen?" has the informational goal of Interest Rate. The second process of backward inference indicates that the concept <DURATION> should be present, but is absent from the query. Hence <DURATION> is a missing concept and the dialog model prompts for the information.

Table 1. This table steps through our dialog modeling process. The input query is "Can I have the interest rate of the yen". Process 1 (informational goal inference) identifies that this is an interest rate inquiry. Process 2 performs backward inference to compute the concept probabilities. Thresholding with θ=0.5 indicates whether the concept should be present or absent. Comparison between this binary decision and the actual occurrence detects that the concept <DURATION> is missing. Hence the dialog model prompts for the missing information.

Query: *Can I have the interest rate of the yen?*			
Process 1: Informational Goal Inference			
BN for Interest Rate P(Goal = Interest Rate | Query) = 0.801 → goal present			
BN for Exchange Rate P(Goal = Exchange Rate | Query) = 0.156 → goal absent			
Hence, inferred goal is Interest Rate.			

Process 2: Detection of Missing / Spurious Concepts			
Concept C_i	$P(C_i)$	Binary Decision for C_i	Actual Occurrence of C_i
CURRENCY1	0.91	present	present
CURRENCY2	0.058	absent	absent
DURATION	**0.77**	**present**	**absent**
EXCHANGE_RATE	0.011	absent	absent
INTEREST RATE	0.867	present	present
Response: *How long would you like to deposit?*			

3. MIGRATION TO THE ATIS DOMAIN

Our experiments are based on the training and test sets of the Air Travel Information Service (ATIS) domain. ATIS is a common task in the ARPA (Advanced Research Projects Agency) Speech and Language Program in the US. We used the Class A (context-independent) as well as Class D (context-dependent) queries of the ATIS-3 corpus. The disjoint training and test sets consist of 2820, 773 (1993 test), 732 (1994 test) transcribed utterances respectively. Each utterance is accompanied with its corresponding SQL query for retrieving the relevant information.

We derive the informational goal for each utterance from the main attribute label of its SQL query. Inspection of the Class A training data reveals that out of the 32 query types (or informational goals, e.g. flight identification, fare identification, etc.), only 11 have ten or more occurrences. These 11 goals cover over 95% of the training set, and 94.7% of the testing set (1993 test). Consequently, we have developed 11 BNs to capture the domain-specific constraints for each informational goal. Also, with the reference to the attribute labels identified as key semantic concepts from the SQL query, we have designed our semantic tags for labeling the input utterance. We have a total of 60 hand-designed semantic tags, where both syntactic (e.g. <PREPOSITION> <SUPERLATIVE>) and semantic concepts (e.g. <DAY_NAME>, <FLIGHT_NUMBER>) are present. Hence, ATIS presents increased domain complexity, which is characterized by 11 query types and total 60 domain-specific concepts.

---

[2] We choose threshold at 0.5 since $P(G=1/C)+P(G=0/C)=1$

4. SCALABILITY OF A BN-BASED DIALOG MODEL

4.1 Informational Goal Inference

There is a total of 60 hand-designed[3] semantic concepts in the ATIS domain. In order to constrain computation time for goal inference, we have limited the number of semantic concepts (N) that are indicative of each goal G_j. The parameter N (=20) has been selected using the Information Gain criterion to optimize on overall goal identification accuracy on the Class A training utterances [1].

We have also refined the pre-defined topology using Minimum Description Length (MDL) principle to model concept dependencies. Example of the BN is shown in Figure 2. Their inclusion brought performance improvements in goal identification [2].

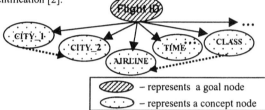

Figure 2. Topology of the BNs for the informational goal Flight_ID.

Consequently, each BN has a classification-based network topology – there are N (=20) input concept nodes (e.g. airline, flight_number, etc.) and a single output node. To avoid the use of sparsely trained BNs, we have developed 11 BNs to capture the domain-specific constraints for each informational goal using Class A training data. The remaining goals are then treated as out-of-domain.

A trained BN is then used to infer the presence / absence of its corresponding informational goal, based on the input concepts. According to the topology shown in Figure 1, the learnt network is divided into sub-networks: {Flight_ID, CITY_1, CITY_2}, {Flight_ID, AIRLINE, CLASS}, {Flight_ID, TIME}, etc. The updated joint probabilities are iteratively computed according to the Equation (1) by each sub-network, the aposteriori probability $P^*(G_i)$ is computed by the marginalization of the updated joint probability $P^*(G_i, C)$. $P^*(G_i)$ is then compared to a threshold (θ) to make the binary decision.

$$P^*(G_i, \bar{C}) = P(G_i \mid \bar{C}) P^*(\bar{C}) \to P^*(G_i, \bar{C}) = \frac{P(G_i, \bar{C})}{P(\bar{C})} P^*(\bar{C}) \quad (1)$$

where $P^*(C)$ is instantiated according the presence or absence of the concepts; $P(G_i, C)$ is the joint probability obtained from training and $P^*(G_i, C)$ is the updated joint probability

The binary decisions across all BNs are combined to identify the informational goal of the input query. We may label the query to a goal if the corresponding BN votes positive with the highest *aposteriori* probability. Alternatively, we may label the query with all the goals for which the BNs votes positive. Should all BNs vote negative, the input query is rejected as out-of-domain (OOD).

---

[3] We have included the concepts/attributes needed for database access, as well as others that play a syntactic role for natural language understanding.

4.2 Detection of Missing / Spurious Concepts

Having inferred the informational goal of the query, the corresponding node (goal node) is instantiated, and we perform backward inference to test the networks' confidence in each input concept. In this way, we can test for cases of *spurious* and *missing* concepts, and generate the appropriate systems response.

When the goal node is instantiated for backward inference, the joint probability of $P(C, G_i)$ will be updated for each sub-network by Equation 2:

$$P^*(\bar{C}, G_i) = P(\bar{C} \mid G_i) P^*(G_i) \quad (2)$$

where $P^*(G)$ is updated and instantiated to 1, $P(C|G_i)$ is the conditional probability obtained from training data and $P^*(C, G_i)$ is the updated joint probability

By marginalization, we can get $P(C_j)$. We have pre-set threshold 0.5 for the CU FOREX domain to determine whether the concept should be present or absent. However, when the dialog modeling using single threshold scheme is applied to the ATIS domain, we often obtained *several* missing / spurious concepts for an input query. For example, consider the query.

Query:	What type of aircraft is used in American airlines flight number seventeen twenty three?
Concepts:	\<WHAT\> \<TYPE\> \<AIRCRAFT\> \<AIRLINE_NAME\> \<FLIGHT_NUMBER\>
Goal:	Aircraft_Code

Our BN for AIRCRAFT_CODE performed backward inference and the results in Table 2 using single threshold scheme indicated that the concepts \<ORIGIN\> and \<DESTINATION\> are missing, while \<FLIGHT_NUMBER\> is spurious. One reason is because in the training data, most queries with the goal Aircraft_Code provided the city pair instead of the flight number, but *both* serve equally well as an additional specification for database access. If our dialog model followed through with these detected missing and spurious concepts, it would prompt the user for the city of origin, then the city of destination; and then clarify that the flight number is spurious. In order to avoid such redundancies, we defined two thresholds for backward inferencing, as follows:

$$P(C_j) \begin{cases} >= \theta_{upper} \to C_j \text{ should be } present \text{ in the given } G_i \text{ query} \\ < \theta_{upper} \text{ and } >= \theta_{lower} \to C_j \text{ is } optional \text{ in the given } G_i \text{ query} \\ < \theta_{lower} \to C_j \text{ should be } absent \text{ in the given } G_i \text{ query} \end{cases}$$

Hence concepts whose probabilities (from backward inference) scores between θ_{upper} and θ_{lower} will not take effect in response generation (i.e. prompting / clarification). Concepts whose scores exceed θ_{upper}, and also correspond to an SQL attribute will be prompted if missing; and concepts whose scores scant θ_{lower}, and correspond to an SQL attribute will be clarified if spurious. By minimizing number of dialog turns interacting with the users in the training data, we have empirically adopted 0.7 and 0.2 for θ_{upper} and θ_{lower} respectively. The double threshold scheme enables the dialog model to prompt for missing concepts that are truly needed, and clarify for spurious concepts that may confuse the query's interpretation.

Table 2. Aposteriori probabilities obtained from backward inferencing using *0.5* as threshold for the query "*What type of aircraft is used in american airlines flight number seventeen twenty three?*"

Concept$_j$ (C_j) (Part of concepts)	P(C_j)	Binary Decision For C_i	Actual Occurrence for C_i
AIRCRAFT	1.000	present	present
CITY_NAME1	0.645	present	absent
CITY_NAME2	0.615	present	absent
DAY_NAME	0.077	absent	absent
FLIGHT_NUMBER	0.420	absent	present

4.3 Context Inheritance

We attempt to test our framework using ATIS-3 Class A and D queries. As the Class D queries involve referencing discourse context derived from previous dialog turns, we have enhanced our BN-based dialog model with the capability of context inheritance. Since the additional concepts may affect our goal inference, we choose to invoke goal inference *again* (after context inheritance) *only if* query was previously (prior to context inheritance) classified as OOD. Otherwise, the original inferred goal of the query is maintained. This is illustrated in Table 3. Context inheritance serves to fill in the concepts detected missing from the original query. This is illustrated in Tables 4 and 5.

Table 3. Examples of ATIS dialogs produced by the BN-based dialog model. It indicates that the OOD query is inferred again as Flight_ID query after the inheritance of discourse context.

System	What kind of flight information are you interested in?
User	I'd like to fly from miami to chicago on american airlines. (Class A query)
System	*Goal Inference: Flight_ID (Concepts pass the domain constraints)*
User	**Which ones arrive around five p.m.? (Class D)**
System	*Goal Inference: Flight_ID. (System first infers this query as OOD, but it retrieves the concepts from the discourse context and infers again to get Flight _ ID.)*

Table 4. Examples of ATIS dialogs produced by the BN-based dialog model with the capability of inheritance for the missing concepts.

System	What kind of flight information are you interested in?
User	Please list all the flights from Chicago to Kansas city on June seventeenth. (Class A query)
System	*Goal Inference: Flight_ID (Concepts pass the domain constraints)*
User	**For this flight how much would a first class fare cost. (Class D)**
System	*Goal Inference: Fare_ID. (The missing concepts <CITY_NAME1> <CITY_NAME2> are automatically retrieved from the discourse context.)*

Table 5. Aposteriori probabilities obtained from backward inferencing using double threshold scheme for the Class D query "*For this flight how much would a first class fare cost.*" in Table 4. It indicates that the cities of origin and destination are missing.

Concept$_j$ (C_j) (Part of concepts)	P(C_j)	Decision for C_i	Actual Occurrence for C_i
AIRPORT_NAME	0.0000	absent	absent
CITY_NAME1	0.9629	present	absent
CITY_NAME2	0.9629	present	absent
CLASS_NAME	0.2716	optional	present
FARE	0.8765	present	present

We inherit discourse context for all the Class D queries. Based on the training data, we have designed a few context refresh rules to "undo" context inheritance for several query types. For example, if the goal of the Class D query is <Airline_Code>, it is obviously asking about an airline, hence the concept <AIRLINE_NAME> will not be inherited.

5. PORTABILITY OF A BN-BASED DIALOG MODEL

In addition to scalability, this work conducts a preliminary examination of the portability of our BN-based dialog models across different application domains. Migration to a new application often implies the lack of domain-specific data to train our BN probabilities. At this stage, BN probabilities can be hand-assigned to reflect the "degree of belief" of the knowledge domain expert.

5.1 General Principles for Probability Assignment

For each informational goal, we have to identify the concepts that are related to the goal. For example, the informational goal Ground_Transportation is usually associated with the key concepts of <AIRPORT_NAME> <CITY_NAME> and <TRANSPORT_TYPE>. After the identification of all concepts for the 11 goals, 23 key concepts (more details below) are extracted from the total 60 concepts. Each of the 11 handcrafted BNs hence receives as input of the identical set of 23 concepts.

13 semantic concepts (out of 23) (e.g. <CITY_NAME>, <AIRPORT_NAME>, <AIRLINE_NAME>) correspond to the SQL attributes for database access, while the reminding 10 correspond to syntactic/semantic concepts (e.g. <AIRCRAFT>, <FARE>, <FROM>). For the sake of simplicity, we assumed independence among concepts in the BN (pre-defined topology), and we then hand-assigned the four probabilities for each of the 11 BNs, namely $P(C_j=1/G_i=1)$, $P(C_j=0/G_i=1)$, $P(C_j=1/G_i=0)$, $P(C_j=0/G_i=0)$. We avoid assigning the probabilities of 1 or 0 since they are not supportive of probabilistic inference. In the following we describe the general principles for assigning $P(C_j=1/G_i=1)$ and $P(C_j=1/G_i=0)$. The remaining $P(C_j=0/G_i=1)$ and $P(C_j=0/G_i=0)$ can be derived by the complement of the former two probabilities.

5.1.1 Probability Assignment for $P(C_j=1/G_i=1)$

We assign the probabilities of $P(C_j=1/G_i=1)$ based on the occurrence of the concept C_j with the corresponding G_i query as shown in Table 6.

Case 1. C_j must occur given G_i

If we identify a concept that is mandatory for a query of goal G_i, we will hand-assign a high probability (0.95-0.99) for $P(C_j=1/G_i=1)$. For example, concept <FARE> (for words e.g. *fare*, *price*, etc.) must occur in Fare_ID query. ("what is the first class **fare** from detroit to las vegas" and "show me the first class and coach **price**").

Case 2. C_j often occurs given G_i

If the concept often occurs with the G_i query, then we will lower the probabilities of $P(C_j=1/G_i=1)$ to the range of 0.7-0.8. For example, the Fare_ID query often comes with the concepts of <CITY_ORIGIN> and <CITY_DESTINATION>.

Case 3. C_j may occur given G_i

This applies to the concepts that act as additional constraints for database access. Examples are <TIME_VALUE>, <DAY_NAME>, <PERIOD>specified in the user query.

Case 4. C_j seldom occurs given G_i

The occurrence of this kind of concepts in the user query is infrequent. Example includes the concept <STOPS> which specify the nonstop flight for the Fare_ID query.

Case 5. C_j never occurs given G_i

This kind of concepts usually provides negative evidence for goal inference. Examples include the concept <FLIGHT_NUMBER> in the Flight_ID query. The presence of <FLIGHT_NUMBER> in the input query implies that the goal Flight_ID is unlikely, because the aposteriori probability for the BN Flight_ID is lowered.

Table 6. Conditions for assigning the probabilities $P(C_j=1/G_i=1)$.

Condition	Probability of $P(C_j=1/G_i=1)$
1. C_i must occur given G_i	0.95 – 0.99
2. C_i often occur given G_i	0.7 – 0.8
3. C_i may occur given G_i	0.4 – 0.6
4. C_i seldom occur given G_i	0.2 – 0.3
5. C_i must not occur given G_i	0.01 – 0.1

5.1.2 Probability Assignment for $P(C_j=1/G_i=0)$

For assignment the probabilities of $P(C_j=1/G_i=0)$ for BN_i, we have to consider the occurrence of the concepts for goals other than G_i, i.e. for goal G_m (where m ranges between 1 and 11 but is not equal to i). The scheme for assigning $P(C_j=1/G_i=0)$, i.e. probability of concept C_j being present while goal G_i is absent, is shown in Table 7.

Case 1. C_j always occurs for goals other than G_i

Consider the relationship between the concept <CITY> and the goal Aircraft_Code. Since <CITY> always occur for *other* informational goals, (e.g. Flight_ID, Fare_ID, etc.), we assign $P(C<CITY>=1/G<Aircraft\_Code>=0)$ in the range of 0.7-0.9.

Case 2. C_j sometimes occurs for goals other than G_i

Consider the relationship between the concept <CLASS> and the goal Aircraft_Code. Since <CLASS> sometimes occurs in the informational goals other than Aircraft_Code, and acts as the additional constraints for database access, we assign $P(C<CLASS>=1/G<Aircraft\_Code>=0)$ in the range of 0.2-0.5.

Case 3. C_j seldom occurs for goals other than G_i

This applies to the concepts that are strongly dependent on a specific goal and hence seldom appear for other goals. For example, the concept <TRANSPORTATION> usually accompanies the goal Ground_Transportation only. Hence $P(C<TRANSPORTATION>=1/G<Ground\_Transportation>=0)$ is set closed to 0.

Table 7 Conditions for assigning the probabilities $P(C_j=1/G_i=0)$

Condition	Probability of $P(C_j=1/G_i=0)$
1. C_j always occurs for goals other than G_i	0.7 – 0.9
2. C_j sometimes occurs for goals other than G_i	0.2 – 0.5
3. C_j seldom occurs for goals other than G_i	0.01 – 0.1

5.2 Evaluation

BNs with hand-assigned probabilities achieved a goal identification accuracy of 80.9% for the ATIS-3 1993 test set (Class A and D sentences included). This compares to 84.6% when they have been automatically trained on the training data. The availability of training data for the BNs enhances performance in goal identification. Queries whose goals are not covered by our 11 BNs are treated as OOD, and are considered to be identified correctly if there are classified as such.

We have compared the handcrafted probabilities with the trained probabilities based on natural language understanding, where the evaluation metric is the sentence error rate. A sentence is considered correct only if the inferred goal and extracted concepts in the generated semantic frame agrees with those in the reference semantic frame (derived from the SQL in the ATIS corpora). The goal identification accuracies and the sentence error rates for the ATIS-3 1993 test set are summarized in Table 8. When we compare the our results with the NL understanding results from the 10 ATIS evaluation sites shown in Table 9, our performance falls within a reasonable range.

Table 8 Goal identification accuracies and the sentence error rates of Class A and D queries of ATIS test 93 data for the handcrafted probabilities and automatically trained probabilities respectively.

	Class	BNs (handcrafted probabilities)	BNs (trained probabilities)
Goal ID Accuracy	A (448)	90.18%	91.74%
	D (325)	68.31%	74.78%
	A+D	80.98%	84.61%
Sentence Error Rate	A (448)	12.05%	9.15%
	D (325)	40.92%	33.85%
	A+D	24.19%	19.53%

Table 9 Benchmark NL results from the 10 ATIS evaluation sites [6].

Class	Sentence Error Rate
A (448)	6.0 – 28.6%
D (325)	13.8 – 63.1%
A+D (773)	9.3 – 43.1%

We observed that our strategy for context inheritance may be too aggressive, which leads to concept insertion errors in the generated semantic frame. This is illustrated in the example in Table 10.

Table 10 The case frame for query 3 indicates our context inheritance strategy may be too aggressive which leads to a concept insertion error in the generated semantic frame.

Query 1:	List flights from oakland to salt lake city before six a m Thursday morning *(Our system generates a correct semantic frame.)*	
Query 2:	List delta flights before six a m (Class D) *(Our system generates a correct semantic frame.)*	
Query 3:	List all flights from twelve oh one a m until six a m (Class D) *(Our system detects missing concepts of <CITY_NAME>, which are inherited from discourse)*	
	Case Frame	**SQL Reference**
Goal:	Flight_ID	Flight_ID
Concepts:	CITY_NAME = oakland CITY_NAME = salt lake city DEPARTURE_TIME = twelve oh one a m until six a m AIRLINE_NAME = delta *(a concept insertion error)*	CITY_NAME = oakland CITY_NAME = salt lake city DEPARTURE_TIME = >=1 && <= 600

6. SUMMARY AND CONCLUSIONS

This paper describes the scalability and portability of the BN-based dialog model as we migrate from the foreign exchange domain (CU FOREX) to the relatively more complex air travel domain (ATIS). The complexity of an application domain is characterized by the number of in-domain informational goals and concepts. The presence / absence of concepts are used to infer the presence/absence of each goal, by means of the BN. When a large number of in-domain concepts are available, we used an information-theoretic criterion (Information Gain) to automatically select the small set of concepts most indicative of a goal, and do so for every in-domain goal. Automatic detection of missing / spurious concepts is achieved by backward inference using the BN corresponding to the inferred goal. This detection procedure drives our mixed-initiative dialog model – the system prompts the user for missing concepts, and asks for clarification if spurious concepts are detected. For the simpler CU FOREX domain, detection of missing / spurious concepts was based on a single probability threshold. However, scaling up to ATIS (which has many more concepts) shows that some concepts need to be present, others should be absent, but still others should be optional. Hence we need to use two levels of thresholding to decide if a concept should be present, optional or absent in the query. We have also enhanced our BN-based dialog model with the capability of context-inheritance, in order to handle the context-dependent user queries in the ATIS domain. Discourse context is inherited for the Class D queries, and we invoke goal inference again after context inheritance if a query was previously classified as OOD.

As regards portability, migration to a new application domain often implies the lack of domain-specific training data. Hence we have proposed a set of general principles for probability assignment to the BNs, as a reflection of our "degree of belief" in the relationships between concepts and goals. We compared the goal identification performance, as well as concept error rates between the use of hand-assigned probabilities, and the probabilities trained from the ATIS training set. Results show that the hand-assigned probabilities offer a decent starting performance to ease portability to a new domain. The system performance can be further improved if data is available to train the probabilities.

7. REFERENCES

[1] Meng, H., W. Lam and C. Wai, "To Believe is to Understand," Proceedings of Eurospeech, 1999.

[2] Meng, H., W. Lam and K. F. Low, "Learning Belief Networks for Language Understanding," Proceedings of ASRU, 1999.

[3] Meng, H., S. Lee and C. Wai, "CU FOREX: A Bilingual Spoken Dialog System for the Foreign Exchange Domain," Proceedings of ICASSP, 2000.

[4] Meng, H., C. Wai, R. Pieraccini, "The Use of Belief Networks for Mixed-Initiative Dialog Modeling," Proceeding of ICSLP, 2000.

[5] Kuhn, R., and R. De Mori, "The Application of Semantic Classification Trees for Natural Language Understanding," IEEE Trans. PAMI, Vol. 17, No. 5, pp. 449-460, May 1995.

[6] Pallet, D., J. Fiscus, W. Fisher, J. Garofolo, B. Lund, and M. Przybocki, "1993 Benchmark Tests for the ARPA Spoken Language Program," Proceedings of the Spoken Language Technology Workshop, 1994.

[7] Levin, E., Pieraccini, R., and Eckert, W., "A Stochastic Model of Human-Machine Interaction for Learning Dialogue Strategies", Speech and Audio Processing, IEEE Transactions, Vol 8, pp. 11-23, Jan 2000.

[8] Walker, M., Fromer, J., Narayanan, S., "Learning Optimal Dialogue Strategies: A Case Study of a Spoken Dialogue Agent for Email", in Proceedings of ACL/COLING 98 , 1998.

SCANMail: Audio Navigation in the Voicemail Domain

Michiel Bacchiani   Julia Hirschberg   Aaron Rosenberg   Steve Whittaker

Donald Hindle   Phil Isenhour   Mark Jones   Litza Stark

Gary Zamchick

{michiel,julia,aer,stevew}@research.att.com, dhindle@answerlogic.com, isenhour@vt.edu,

jones@research.att.com, litza@udel.edu, zamchick@attlabs.att.com

AT&T Labs – Research

180 Park Avenue

Florham Park, NJ 07932-0971, USA

ABSTRACT

This paper describes SCANMail, a system that allows users to browse and search their voicemail messages by content through a GUI. Content based navigation is realized by use of automatic speech recognition, information retrieval, information extraction and human computer interaction technology. In addition to the browsing and querying functionalities, acoustics-based caller ID technology is used to proposes caller names from existing caller acoustic models trained from user feedback. The GUI browser also provides a note-taking capability. Comparing SCANMail to a regular voicemail interface in a user study, SCANMail performed better both in terms of objective (time to and quality of solutions) as well as subjective objectives.

1. INTRODUCTION

Increasing amounts of public, corporate, and private audio present a major challenge to speech, information retrieval, and human-computer interaction research: how can we help people to take advantage of these resources when current techniques for navigating them fall far short of text-based search methods? In this paper, we describe SCANMail, a system that employs automatic speech recognition (ASR), information retrieval (IR), information extraction (IE), and human computer interaction (HCI) technology to permit users to browse and search their voicemail messages by content through a GUI interface. A CallerId server also proposes caller names from existing caller acoustic models and is trained from user feedback. An Email server sends the original message plus its ASR transcription to a mailing address specified in the user's profile. The SCANMail GUI also provides note-taking capabilities as well as browsing and querying features. Access to messages and information about them is presented to the user via a Java applet running under Netscape. Figure 1 shows the SCANMail GUI.

Proceedings of HLT 2001, First International Conference on Human Language Technology Research, J. Allan, ed., Morgan Kaufmann, San Francisco, 2001.

2. SYSTEM DESCRIPTION

In SCANMail, messages are first retrieved from a voicemail server, then processed by the ASR server that provides a transcription. The message audio and/or transcription are then passed to the IE, IR, Email, and CallerId servers. The acoustic and language model of the recognizer, and the IE and IR servers are trained on 60 hours of a 100 hour voicemail corpus, transcribed and hand labeled for telephone numbers, caller names, times, dates, greetings and closings. The corpus includes approximately 10,000 messages from approximately 2500 speakers. About 90% of the messages were recorded from regular handsets, the rest from cellular and speaker-phones. The corpus is approximately gender balanced and approximately 12% of the messages were from non-native speakers. The mean duration of the messages was 36.4 seconds; the median was 30.0 seconds.

2.1 Automatic Speech Recognition

The baseline ASR system is a decision-tree based state-clustered triphone system with 8k tied states. The emission probabilities of the states are modeled by 12 component Gaussian mixture distributions. The system uses a 14k vocabulary, automatically generated by the AT&T Labs NextGen Text To Speech system. The language model is a Katz-style backoff trigram trained on 700k words from the transcriptions of the 60 hour training set. The word-error rate of this system on a 40 hour test set is 34.9%.

Since the messages come from a highly variable source both in terms of speaker as well as channel characteristics, transcription accuracy is significantly improved by application of various normalization techniques, developed for Switchboard evaluations [9]. The ASR server uses Vocal Tract Length Normalization (VTLN) [5], Constrained Modelspace Adaptation (CMA) [3], Maximum Likelihood Linear Regression (MLLR) [6] and Semi-Tied Covariances (STC) [4] to obtain progressively more accurate acoustic models and uses these in a rescoring framework. In contrast to Switchboard, voicemail messages are generally too short too allow direct application of the normalization techniques. A novel message clustering algorithm based on MLLR likelihood [1] is used to guarantee sufficient data for normalization. The final transcripts, obtained after 6 recognition passes, have a word error rate of 28.7% – a 6.2% accuracy improvement. Gender dependency provides 1.6% of this gain. VTLN then additively improves accuracy with 1.0% when applied only on the test data and an additional 0.3% when subsequently applied with a VTLN trained model. The use of STC further improves accuracy with 1.2%. Finally CMA and MLLR provide additive gains of 1.5% and 0.6% respectively. The ASR

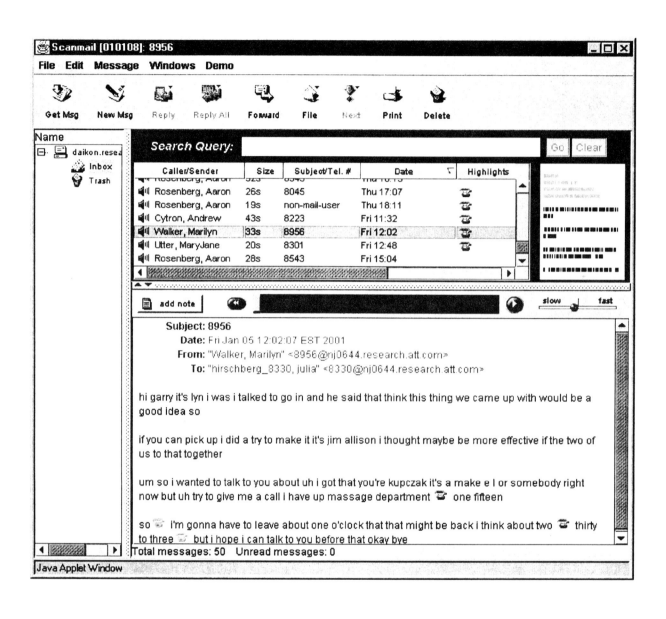

Figure 1: The SCANMail User Interface

316

server, running on a 667 MHz 21264 Alpha processor, produces the final transcripts in approximately 20 times real-time.

2.2 Information Retrieval

Messages transcripts are indexed by the IR server using the SMART IR [8, 2] engine. SMART is based on the vector space model of information retrieval. It generates weighted term (word) vectors for the automatic transcriptions of the messages. SMART preprocesses the automatic transcriptions of each new message by tokenizing the text into words, removing common words that appear on its stop-list, and performing stemming on the remaining words to derive a set of terms, against which later user queries can be compared. When the IR server is used to execute a user query, the query terms are also converted into weighted term vectors. Vector inner-product similarity computation is then used to rank messages in decreasing order of their similarity to the user query.

2.3 Information Extraction

Key information is extracted from the ASR transcription by the IE server, which currently extracts any phone numbers identified in the message. Currently, this is done by recognizing digit strings and scoring them based on the sequence length. An improved extraction algorithm, trained on our hand-labeled voicemail corpus, employs a digit string recognizer combined with a trigram language model, to recognize strings in their lexical contexts, e.g. <word> <digit string> <word>.

2.4 Caller Identification

The CallerID server proposes caller names by matching messages against existing caller models; this module is trained from user feedback. The caller identification capability is based on text independent speaker recognition techniques applied to the processed speech in the voicemail messages. A user may elect to label a message he/she has reviewed with a caller name for the purpose of creating a speaker model for that caller. When the cumulative duration of such user-labeled messages is sufficient, a caller model is constructed. Subsequent messages will be processed and scored against this caller model and models for other callers the user may have designated. If the best matching model score for an incoming message exceeds a decision threshold, a caller name hypothesis is sent to the GUI client; if there is no PBX-supplied identification (i.e. caller name supplied from the owner of the extension for calls internal to the PBX), the CallerId hypothesis is presented in the message header, for either accepting or editing by the user; if there is a PBX identification, the CallerId hypothesis appears as the first item in a user 'contact menu', together with all previously id'd callers for that user. To optimize the use of the available speech data, and to speed model-building, caller models are shared among users. Details and a performance evaluation of the CallerId process are described in [7].

2.5 Graphical User Interface

In the SCANMail GUI, users see message headers (callerid, time and date, length in seconds, first line of any attached note, and presence of extracted phone numbers) as well as a thumbnail and the ASR transcription of the current message. Any note attached to the current message is also displayed. A search panel permits users to search the contents of their mailbox by inputting any text query. Results are presented in a new search window, with keywords color-coded in the query, transcript, and thumbnail.

2.6 User Studies

User studies compared SCANMail with a standard over-the-phone voicemail access. Eight subjects performed a series of fact-finding, relevance ranking, and summarization tasks on artificial mailboxes of twenty messages each, using either SCANMail or phone access. SCANMail showed advantages for fact-finding and relevance ranking tasks in quality of solution normalized by time to solution, for fact-finding in time to solution and in overall user preference. Normalized performance scores are higher when subjects employ IR searches that are successful (i.e. the queries they choose contain words correctly recognized by the recognizer) and for subjects who listen to less audio and rely more upon the transcripts. However, we also found that SCANMail's search capability can be misleading, causing subjects to assume that they have found all relevant documents when in fact some are NOT retrieved, and that when subjects rely upon the accuracy of the ASR transcript, they can miss crucial but unrecognized information. A trial of 10 friendly users is currently underway, with modifications to access functionality suggested by our subject users. A larger trial of the system is being prepared, for more extensive testing of user behavior with their own mailboxes over time.

Acknowledgements

The authors would like to thank Andrej Ljolje, S. Parthasarathy, Fernando Pereira, and Amit Singhal for their help in developing this application.

3. REFERENCES

[1] M. Bacchiani. Using maximum likelihood linear regression for segment clustering and speaker identification. In *Proceedings of the Sixth International Conference on Spoken Language Processing*, volume 4, pages 536–539, Beijing, 2000.

[2] C. Buckley. Implementation of the SMART information retrieval system. Technical Report TR85-686, Department of Computer Science, Cornell University, Ithaca, NY 14853, May 1985.

[3] M. J. F. Gales. Maximum likelihood linear transformations for hmm-based speech recognition. *Computer Speech and Language*, pages 75–90, 1998.

[4] M. J. F. Gales. Semi-tied covariance matrices for hidden markov models. *IEEE Transactions on Acoustics, Speech, and Signal Processing*, 7(3), 1999.

[5] T. Kamm, G. Andreou, and J. Cohen. Vocal tract normalization in speech recognition: Compensating for systematic speaker variability. In *Proceedings of the 15th Annual Speech Research Symposium*, pages 161–167, Johns Hopkins University, Baltimore, MD, 1995.

[6] C. J. Legetter and P. C. Woodland. Maximum likelihood linear regression for speaker adaptation of continuous density hidden markov models. *Computer Speech and Language*, pages 171–185, 1995.

[7] A. Rosenberg, S. Parthasarathy, J. Hirschberg, and S. Whittaker. Foldering voicemail messages by caller using text independent speaker recognition. In *Proceedings of the Sixth International Conference on Spoken Language Processing*, Beijing, 2000.

[8] G. Salton, editor. *The SMART Retrieval System—Experiments in Automatic Document Retrieval*. Prentice Hall Inc., Englewood Cliffs, NJ, 1971.

[9] *Proceedings of the Speech Transcription Workshop*, University of Maryland, May 2000.

Sentence Ordering in Multidocument Summarization

Regina Barzilay
Computer Science
Department
1214 Amsterdam Ave
New York, 10027, NY, USA
regina@cs.columbia.edu

Noemie Elhadad
Computer Science
Department
1214 Amsterdam Ave
New York, 10027, NY, USA
noemie@cs.columbia.edu

Kathleen R. McKeown
Computer Science
Department
1214 Amsterdam Ave
New York, 10027, NY, USA
kathy@cs.columbia.edu

ABSTRACT

The problem of organizing information for multidocument summarization so that the generated summary is coherent has received relatively little attention. In this paper, we describe two naive ordering techniques and show that they do not perform well. We present an integrated strategy for ordering information, combining constraints from chronological order of events and cohesion. This strategy was derived from empirical observations based on experiments asking humans to order information. Evaluation of our augmented algorithm shows a significant improvement of the ordering over the two naive techniques we used as baseline.

1. INTRODUCTION

Multidocument summarization poses a number of new challenges over single document summarization. Researchers have already investigated issues such as identifying repetitions or contradictions across input documents and determining which information is salient enough to include in the summary [1, 3, 6, 11, 15, 19]. One issue that has received little attention is how to organize the selected information so that the output summary is coherent. Once all the relevant pieces of information have been selected across the input documents, the summarizer has to decide in which order to present them so that the whole text makes sense. In single document summarization, one possible ordering of the extracted information is provided by the input document itself. However, [10] observed that, in single document summaries written by professional summarizers, extracted sentences do not retain their precedence orders in the summary. Moreover, in the case of multiple input documents, this does not provide a useful solution: information may be drawn from different documents and therefore, no one document can provide an ordering. Furthermore, the order between two pieces of information can change significantly from one document to another.

We investigate constraints on ordering in the context of multidocument summarization. We first describe two naive ordering algorithms, used in several systems and show that they do not yield satisfactory results. The first, Majority Ordering, is critically linked to the level of similarity of the information ordering across the input texts. But many times input texts have different structure, and therefore, this algorithm is not acceptable. The second, Chronological Ordering, can produce good results when the information is event-based and can, therefore, be ordered based on temporal occurence. However, texts do not always refer to events. We have conducted experiments to identify additional constraints using a manually built collection of multiple orderings of texts. These experiments show that cohesion as an important constraint. While it is recognized in the generation community that cohesion is a necessary feature for a generated text, we provide an operational way to automatically ensure cohesion when ordering sentences in an output summary. We augment the Chronological Ordering algorithm with a cohesion constraint, and compare it to the naive algorithms.

Our framework is the MultiGen system [15], a domain independent multidocument summarizer which has been trained and tested on news articles. In the following sections, we first give an overview of MultiGen. We then describe the two naive ordering algorithms and evaluate them. We follow this with a study of multiple orderings produced by humans. This allows us to determine how to improve the Chronological Ordering algorithm using cohesion as an additional constraint. The last section describes the augmented algorithm along with its evaluation.

2. MULTIGEN OVERVIEW

MultiGen operates on a set of news articles describing the same event. It creates a summary which synthesizes common information across documents. In the case of multidocument summarization of articles about the same event, source articles can contain both repetitions and contradictions. Extracting all the similar sentences would produce a verbose and repetitive summary, while extracting only some of the similar sentences would produce a summary biased towards some sources. MultiGen uses a comparison of extracted similar sentences to select the appropriate phrases to include in the summary and reformulates them as a new text.

MultiGen consists of an analysis and a generation component. The analysis component [7] identifies units of text which convey similar information across the input documents using statistical techniques and shallow text analysis. Once similar text units are identified, we cluster them

Proceedings of HLT 2001, First International Conference on Human Language Technology Research, J. Allan, ed., Morgan Kaufmann, San Francisco, 2001.

into *themes*. Themes are sets of sentences from different documents that contain repeated information and do not necessarily contain sentences from all the documents. For each theme, the generation component [1] identifies phrases which are in the intersection of the theme sentences, and selects them as part of the summary. The intersection sentences are then ordered to produce a coherent text.

3. NAIVE ORDERING ALGORITHMS ARE NOT SUFFICIENT

When producing a summary, any multidocument summarization system has to choose in which order to present the output sentences. In this section, we describe two algorithms for ordering sentences suitable for domain independent multidocument summarization. The first algorithm, Majority Ordering (MO), relies only on the original orders of sentences in the input documents. It is the first solution one can think of when addressing the ordering problem. The second one, Chronological Ordering (CO) uses time related features to order sentences. We analyze this strategy because it was originally implemented in MultiGen and followed by other summarization systems [18]. In the MultiGen framework, ordering sentences is equivalent to ordering themes and we describe the algorithms in terms of themes, but the concepts can be adapted to other summarization systems such as [3]. Our evaluation shows that these methods alone do not provide an adequate strategy for ordering.

3.1 Majority Ordering

3.1.1 The Algorithm

Typically, in single document summarization, the order of sentences in the output summary is determined by their order in the input text. This strategy can be adapted to multidocument summarization. Consider two themes, Th_1 and Th_2; if sentences from Th_1 preceed sentences from Th_2 in all input texts, then presenting Th_1 before Th_2 is an acceptable order. But, when the order between sentences from Th_1 and Th_2 varies from one text to another, this strategy is not valid anymore. One way to define the order between Th_1 and Th_2 is to adopt the order occuring in the majority of the texts where Th_1 and Th_2 occur. This strategy defines a pairwise order between themes. However, this pairwise relation is not transitive; for example, given the themes Th_1 and Th_2 occuring in a text, Th_2 and Th_3 occuring in another text, and Th_3 and Th_1 occuring in a third text, there is a conflict between the orders (Th_1, Th_2, Th_3) and (Th_3, Th_1). Since transitivity is a necessary condition for a relation to be called an order, this relation does not form a global order.

We, therefore, have to expand this pairwise relation to a global order. In other words, we have to find a linear order between themes which maximizes the agreement between the orderings imposed by the input texts. For each pair of themes, Th_i and Th_j, we keep two counts, $C_{i,j}$ and $C_{j,i}$ — $C_{i,j}$ is the number of input texts in which sentences from Th_i occur before sentences from Th_j and $C_{j,i}$ is the same for the opposite order. The weight of a linear order $(Th_{i_1}, \ldots, Th_{i_k})$ is defined as the sum of the counts for every pair C_{i_l, i_m}, such that $i_l \leq i_m$ and $l, m \in \{1 \ldots k\}$. Stating this problem in terms of a directed graph where nodes are themes, and a vertex from Th_i to Th_j has for weight $C_{i,j}$, we are looking for a path with maximal weight which traverses each node exactly once. Unfortunately this problem

is NP-complete; this can be shown by reducing the *traveling salesman problem* to this problem. Despite this fact, we still can apply this ordering, because typically the length of the output summary is limited to a small number of sentences. For longer summaries, the approximation algorithm described in [4] can be applied. Figures 1 and 2 show examples of produced summaries.

The main problem with this strategy is that it can produce several orderings with the same weight. This happens when there is a tie between two opposite orderings. In this situation, this strategy does not provide enough constraints to determine one optimal ordering; one order is chosen randomly among the orders with maximal weight.

> The man accused of firebombing two Manhattan subways in 1994 was convicted Thursday after the jury rejected the notion that the drug Prozac led him to commit the crimes. He was found guilty of two counts of attempted murder, 14 counts of first-degree assault and two counts of criminal possession of a weapon.
> In December 1994, Leary ignited firebombs on two Manhattan subway trains. The second blast injured 50 people – 16 seriously, including Leary.
> Leary wanted to extort money from the Transit Authority.
> The defense argued that Leary was not responsible for his actions because of "toxic psychosis" caused by the Prozac.

Figure 1: A summary produced using the Majority Ordering algorithm, graded as Good.

> A man armed with a handgun has surrendered to Spanish authorities, peacefully ending a hijacking of a Moroccan jet. Officials in Spain say a person commandeered the plane. After the plane was directed to Spain, the hijacker said he wanted to be taken to Germany.
> After several hours of negotiations, authorities convinced the person to surrender early today.
> Police said the man had a pistol, but a Moroccan security source in Rabat said the gun was likely a "toy".
> There were no reported injuries.
> Officials in Spain say the Boeing 737 left Casablanca, Morocco, Wednesday night with 83 passengers and a nine-person crew headed for Tunis, Tunisia.
> Spanish authorities directed the plane to an isolated section of El Prat Airport and officials began negotiations.

Figure 2: A summary produced using the Majority Ordering algorithm, graded as Poor.

3.1.2 Evaluation

We asked three human judges to evaluate the order of information in 20 summaries produced using the MO algorithm into three categories— Poor, Fair and Good. We define a Poor summary, in an operational way, as a text whose readability would be significantly improved by reordering its sentences. A Fair summary is a text which makes sense but reordering of some sentences can yield a better readability. Finally, a summary which cannot be further improved by any sentence reordering is considered a Good summary.

The judges were asked to grade the summaries taking only into account the order in which the information is presented. To help them focus on this aspect of the texts, we resolved dangling references beforehand. Figure 8 shows the grades assigned to the summaries using majority to combine the judges grades. In our experiments, judges had strong agreement; they never gave three different grades to a summary.

The MO algorithm produces a small number of Good summaries, but most of the summaries were graded as Fair. For instance, the summary graded Good shown in Figure 1 orders the information in a natural way; the text starts with a sentence summary of the event, then the outcome of the trial is given, a reminder of the facts that caused the trial and a possible explanation of the facts. Looking at the Good summaries produced by MO, we found that it performs well when the input articles follow the same order when presenting the information. In other words, the algorithm produces a good ordering if the input articles orderings have high agreement.

On the other hand, when analyzing Poor summaries, as in Figure 2, we observe that the input texts have very different orderings. By trying to maximize the agreement of the input texts orderings, MO produces a new ordering that doesn't occur in any input text. The ordering is, therefore, not guaranteed anymore to be acceptable. An example of a new produced ordering is given in Figure 2. The summary would be more readable if several sentences were moved around (the last sentence would be better placed before the fourth sentence because they both talk about the Spanish authorities handling the hijacking).

This algorithm can be used to order sentences accurately if we are certain that the input texts follow similar organizations. This assumption may hold in limited domains. However, in our case, the input texts we are processing do not have such regularities. MO's performance critically depends on the quality of the input texts, therefore, we should design an ordering strategy which better fits our input data. From here on, we will focus only on the Chronological Ordering algorithm and ways to improve it.

3.2 Chronological Ordering

3.2.1 The Algorithm

Multidocument summarization of news typically deals with articles published on different dates, and articles themselves cover events occurring over a wide range in time. Using chronological order in the summary to describe the main events helps the user understand what has happened. It seems like a natural and appropriate strategy. As mentioned earlier, in our framework, we are ordering themes; in this strategy, we therefore need to assign a date to themes. To identify the date an event occured requires a detailed interpretation of temporal references in articles. While there have been recent developments in disambiguating temporal expressions and event ordering [12], correlating events with the date on which they occurred is a hard task. In our case, we approximate the theme time by its first publication date; that is, the first time the theme has been reported in our set of input articles. It is an acceptable approximation for news events; the first publication date of an event usually corresponds to its occurrence in real life. For instance, in a terrorist attack story, the theme conveying the attack itself will have a date previous to the date of the theme describing a trial following the attack.

Articles released by news agencies are marked with a publication date, consisting of a date and a time with three fields (hour, minutes and seconds). Articles from the same news agency are, then, guaranteed to have different publication

dates. This also holds for articles coming from different news agencies. We never encountered two articles with the same publication date during the development of MultiGen. Thus, the publication date serves as a unique identifier over articles. As a result, when two themes have the same publication date, it means that they both are reported for the first time in the same article.

Our Chronological Ordering (CO) algorithm takes as input a set of themes and orders them chronologically whenever possible. Each theme is assigned a date corresponding to its first publication. This establishes a partial order over the themes. When two themes have the same date (that is, they are reported for the first time in the same article) we sort them according to their order of presentation in this article. We have now a complete order over the input themes.

To implement this algorithm in MultiGen, we select for each theme the sentence that has the earliest publication date. We call it the time stamp sentence and assign its publication date as the time stamp of the theme. Figures 3 and 4 show examples of produced summaries using CO.

One of four people accused along with former Pakistani Prime Minister Nawaz Sharif has agreed to testify against him in a case involving possible hijacking and kidnapping charges, a prosecutor said Wednesday.
Raja Quereshi, the attorney general, said that the former Civil Aviation Authority chairman has already given a statement to police.
Sharif's lawyer dismissed the news when speaking to reporters after Sharif made an appearance before a judicial magistrate to hear witnesses give statements against him.
Sharif has said he is innocent.
The allegations stem from an alleged attempt to divert a plane bringing army chief General Pervez Musharraf to Karachi from Sri Lanka on October 12.

Figure 3: A summary produced using the Chronological Ordering algorithm graded as Good.

Thousands of people have attended a ceremony in Nairobi commemorating the first anniversary of the deadly bombings attacks against U.S. Embassies in Kenya and Tanzania.
Saudi dissident Osama bin Laden, accused of masterminding the attacks, and nine others are still at large.
President Clinton said, "The intended victims of this vicious crime stood for everything that is right about our country and the world".
U.S. federal prosecutors have charged 17 people in the bombings.
Albright said that the mourning continues.
Kenyans are observing a national day of mourning in honor of the 215 people who died there.

Figure 4: A summary produced using the Chronological Ordering algorithm graded as Poor.

3.2.2 Evaluation

Following the same methodology we used for the MO algorithm evaluation, we asked three human judges to grade 20 summaries generated by the system using the CO algorithm applied to the same collection of input texts. The results are shown in Figure 8.

Our first suspicion was that our approximation deviates too much from the real chronological order of events, and,

320

therefore, lowers the quality of sentence ordering. To verify this hypothesis, we identified sentences that broke the original chronological order and restored the ordering manually. Interestingly, the displaced sentences were mainly background information. The evaluation of the modified summaries shows a slight but not visible improvement.

When comparing Good (Figure 3) and Poor (Figure 4) summaries, we notice two phenomena: first, many of the badly placed sentences cannot be ordered based on their temporal occurence. For instance, in Figure 4, the sentence quoting Clinton is not one event in the sequence of events being described, but rather a reaction to the main events. This is also true for the sentence reporting Albright's reaction. Assigning a date to a reaction, or more generally to any sentence conveying background information, and placing it into the chronological stream of the main events does not produce a logical ordering. The ordering of these themes is therefore not covered by the CO algorithm.

The second phenomenon we observed is that Poor summaries typically contain abrupt switches of topics and general incoherences. For instance, in Figure 4, quotes from US officials (third and fifth sentences) are split and sentences about the mourning (first and sixth sentences) appear too far apart in the summary. Grouping them together would increase the readability of the summary. At this point, we need to find additional constraints to improve the ordering.

4. IMPROVING THE ORDERING: EXPERIMENTS AND ANALYSIS

In the previous section, we showed that using naive ordering algorithms does not produce satisfactory orderings. In this section, we investigate through experiments with humans, how to identify patterns of orderings that can improve the algorithm.

Sentences in a text can be ordered in a number of ways, and the text as a whole will still convey the same meaning. But undoubtedly, some orders are definitely unacceptable because they break conventions of information presentation. One way to identify these conventions is to find commonalities between different acceptable orderings of the same information. Extracting regularities in several acceptable orderings can help us specify the main ordering constraints for a given input type. Since a collection of multiple summaries over the same set of articles doesn't exist, we created our own collection of multiple orderings produced by different humans. Using this collection, we studied common behaviors and mapped them to strategies for ordering.

Our collection of multiple orderings is available at `http://www.cs.columbia.edu/~noemie/ordering/`. It was built in the following way. We collected ten sets of articles. Each set consisted of two to three news articles reporting the same event. For each set, we manually selected the intersection sentences, simulating MultiGen[1]. On average, each set contained 8.8 intersection sentences. The sentences were cleaned of explicit references (for instance, occurrences of "the President" were resolved to "President Clinton") and connectives, so that participants wouldn't use them as clues for ordering. Ten subjects participated in the experiment and they each built one ordering per set of intersection sentences. Each subject was asked to order the intersection

---

[1]We performed a manual simulation to ensure that ideal data was provided to the subjects of the experiments

sentences of a set so that they form a readable text. Overall, we obtained 100 orderings, ten alternative orderings per set. Figure 5 shows the ten alternative orderings collected for one set.

We first observe that a surprising majority of orderings are different. Out of the ten sets, only two sets had some identical orderings (in one set, one pair of orderings were identical while in the other set, two pairs of orderings were identical). In other words, there are many acceptable orderings given one set of sentences. This confirms the intuition that we do not need to look for a single ideal global ordering but rather construct an acceptable one.

We also notice that, within the multiple orderings of a set, some sentences always appear together. They do not appear in the same order from one ordering to another, but they share an adjacency relation. From now on, we refer to them as blocks. For each set, we identify blocks by clustering sentences. We use as a distance metric between two sentences the average number of sentences that separate them over all orderings. In Figure 5, for instance, the distance between the sentences D and G is 2. The blocks identified by clustering are: sentences B, D, G and I; sentences A and J; sentences C and F; and sentences E and H.

Participant 1	D B G I H F C J A E
Participant 2	D G B I C F A J E H
Participant 3	D B I G F J A E H C
Participant 4	D C F G I B J A H E
Participant 5	D G B I H F J A C E
Participant 6	D G I B F C E H J A
Participant 7	D B G I F C H E J A
Participant 8	D B C F G I E H A J
Participant 9	D G I B E H F A J C
Participant 10	D B G I C F A J E H

Figure 5: Multiple orderings for one set in our collection.

We observed that all the blocks in the experiment correspond to clusters of topically related sentences. These blocks form units of text dealing with the same subject, and exhibit cohesive properties. For ordering, we can use this to opportunistically group sentences together that all refer to the same topic.

Collecting a set of multiple orderings is an expensive task; it is difficult and time consuming for a human to order sentences from scratch. Furthermore, to discover significant commonalities across orderings, many multiple orderings of the same set are necessary. We plan to extend our collection and we are confident that it will provide more insights on ordering. Still, the existing collection enables us to identify cohesion as an important factor for ordering. We describe next how we integrate the cohesion constraint in the CO algorithm.

5. THE AUGMENTED ALGORITHM

In the output of the CO algorithm, disfluencies arise when topics are distributed over the whole text, violating cohesion properties [13]. A typical scenario is illustrated in Figure 6. The inputs are texts T_1, T_2, T_3 (in order of publication). A_1, A_2 and A_3 belong to the same theme whose intersection sentence is A and similarly for B and C. The themes A and

B are topically related, but C is not related. Summary S_1, based only on chronological clues, contains two topical shifts; from A to C and back from C to B. A better summary would be S_2 which keeps A and B together.

T_1	T_2	T_3	S_1	S_2
A_1	C_2	A_3	A	A
...	...	B_3		
	A_2	...	C	B
C_1	B_2	C_3	B	C

Figure 6: Input texts $T_1 T_2 T_3$ are summarized by the Chronological Ordering (S_1) or by the Augmented algorithm (S_2).

5.1 The Algorithm

Our goal is to remove disfluencies from the summary by grouping together topically related themes. This can be achieved by integrating cohesion as an additional constraint to the CO algorithm. The main technical difficulty in incorporating cohesion in our ordering algorithm is to identify and to group topically related themes across multiple documents. In other words, given two themes, we need to determine if they belong to the same cohesion block. For a single document, segmentation [8] could be used to identify blocks, but we cannot use such a technique to identify cohesion between sentences across multiple documents. The main reason is that segmentation algorithms exploit the linear structure of an input text; in our case, we want to group together sentences belonging to different texts.

Our solution consists of the following steps. In a preprocessing stage, we segment each input text, so that given two sentences within the same text, we can determine if they are topically related. Assume the themes A and B, where A contains sentences $(A_1 \ldots A_n)$, and B contains sentences $(B_1 \ldots B_m)$. Recall that a theme is a set of sentences conveying similar information drawn from different input texts. We denote $\#AB$ to be the number of pairs of sentences (A_i, B_j) which appear in the same text, and $\#AB^+$ to be the number of sentence pairs which appear in the same text and are in the same segment.

In a first stage, for each pair of themes A and B, we compute the ratio $\#AB^+/\#AB$ to measure the relatedness of two themes. This measure takes into account both positive and negative evidence. If most of the sentences in A and B that appear together in the same texts are also in the same segments, it means that A and B are highly topically related. In this case, the ratio is close to 1. On the other hand, if among the texts containing sentences from A and B, only a few pairs are in the same segments, then A and B are not topically related. Accordingly the ratio is close to 0. A and B are considered related if this ratio is higher than a predetermined threshold. In our experiments, we set it to 0.6.

This strategy defines pairwise relations between themes. A transitive closure of this relation builds groups of related themes and as a result ensures that themes that do not appear together in any article but are both related to a third theme will still be linked. This creates an even higher degree of relatedness among themes. Because we use a threshold to establish pairwise relations, the transitive closure does

not produce elongated chains that could link together unrelated themes. We are now able to identify topically related themes. At the end of the first stage, they are grouped into blocks.

In a second stage, we assign a time stamp to each block of related themes, as the earliest time stamp of the themes it contains. We adapt the CO algorithm described in *3.2.1* to work at the level of the blocks. The blocks and the themes correspond to, respectively, themes and sentences in the CO algorithm. By analogy, we can easily show that the adapted algorithm produces a complete order of the blocks. This yields a macro-ordering of the summary. We still need to order the themes inside each block.

In the last stage of the augmented algorithm, for each block, we order the themes it contains by applying the CO algorithm to them. Figure 7 shows an example of a summary produced by the augmented algorithm.

This algorithm ensures that cohesively related themes will not be spread over the text, and decreases the number of abrupt switches of topics. Figure 7 shows how the Augmented algorithm improves the sentence order compared with the order in the summary produced by the CO algorithm in Figure 4; sentences quoting US officials are now grouped together and so are descriptions of the mourning.

> Thousands of people have attended a ceremony in Nairobi commemorating the first anniversary of the deadly bombings attacks against U.S. Embassies in Kenya and Tanzania. Kenyans are observing a national day of mourning in honor of the 215 people who died there.
>
> Saudi dissident Osama bin Laden, accused of masterminding the attacks, and nine others are still at large. U.S. federal prosecutors have charged 17 people in the bombings.
>
> President Clinton said, "The intended victims of this vicious crime stood for everything that is right about our country and the world". Albright said that the mourning continues.

Figure 7: A Summary produced using the Augmented algorithm. Related sentences are grouped into paragraphs.

5.2 Evaluation

Following the same methodology used to evaluate the MO and the CO algorithms, we asked the judges to grade 20 summaries produced by the Augmented algorithm. Results are shown in Figure 8.

The manual effort needed to compare and judge system output is extensive; consider that each human judge had to read three summaries for each input set as well as skim the input texts to verify that no misleading order was introduced in the summaries. Consequently, the evaluation that we performed to date is limited. Still, this evaluation shows a significant improvement in the quality of the orderings from the CO algorithm to the augmented algorithm. To assess the significance of the improvement, we used the Fisher exact test, conflating Poor and Fair summaries into one category. This test is adapted to our case because of the reduced size of our test set. We obtained a p value of 0.014 [20].

6. RELATED WORK

Finding an acceptable ordering has not been studied before in summarization. In single document summarization,

	Poor	Fair	Good
Majority Ordering	2	12	6
Chronological Ordering	7	7	6
Augmented Ordering	2	7	11

Figure 8: Evaluation of the the Majority Ordering, the Chronological Ordering and the Augmented Ordering.

summary sentences are typically arranged in the same order that they were found in the full document (although [10] reports that human summarizers do sometimes change the original order). In multidocument summarization, the summary consists of fragments of text or sentences that were selected from different texts. Thus, there is no complete ordering of summary sentences that can be found in the original documents.

The ordering task has been extensively investigated in the generation community [14, 17, 9, 2, 16]. One approach is top-down, using schemas [14] or plans [5] to determine the organizational structure of the text. This appproach postulates a rhetorical structure which can be used to select information from an underlying knowledge base. Because the domain is limited, an encoding can be developed of the kinds of propositional content that match rhetorical elements of the schema or plan, thereby allowing content to be selected and ordered. Rhetorical Structure Theory (RST) allows for more flexibility in ordering content. The relations occur between pairs of propositions. Constraints based on intention (e.g., [17]), plan-like conventions [9], or stylistic constraints [2] are used as preconditions on the plan operators containing RST relations to determine when a relation is used and how it is ordered with respect to other relations.

MultiGen generates summaries of news on any topic. In an unconstrained domain like this, it would be impossible to enumerate the semantics for all possible types of sentences which could match the elements of a schema, a plan or rhetorical relations. Furthermore, it would be difficult to specify a generic rhetorical plan for a summary of news. Instead, content determination in MultiGen is opportunistic, depending on the kinds of similarities that happen to exist between a set of news documents. Similarly, we describe here an ordering scheme that is opportunistic and bottom-up, depending on the coherence and temporal connections that happen to exist between selected text. Our approach is similar to the use of basic blocks [16] where a bottom-up technique is used to group together stretches of text in a long, generated document by finding propositions that are related by a common focus. Since this approach was developed for a generation system, it finds related propositions by comparisons of proposition arguments at the semantic level. In our case, we are dealing with a surface representation, so we find alternative methods for grouping text fragments.

7. CONCLUSION AND FUTURE WORK

In this paper we investigated information ordering constraints in multidocument summarization. We analyzed two naive ordering algorithms, the Majority Ordering (MO) and the Chronological Ordering (CO). We show that the MO algorithm performs well only when all input texts follow similar presentation of the information. The CO algorithm can provide an acceptable solution for many cases, but is not sufficient when summaries contain information that is not

event based. We report on the experiments we conducted to identify other constraints contributing to ordering. We show that cohesion is an important factor, and describe an operational way to incorporate it in the CO algorithm. This results in a definite improvement of the overall quality of automatically generated summaries.

In future work, we first plan to extend our collection of multiple orderings, so that we can extract more regularities and understand better how human order information to produce a readable and fluent text. Even though we did not encounter any misleading inferences introduced by reordering MultiGen output, we plan to do an extended study of the side effects caused by reorderings. We also plan to investigate whether the MO algorithm can be improved by applying it on cohesive blocks of themes, rather than themes.

8. ACKNOWLEDGMENT

This work was partially supported by DARPA grant N66001-00-1-8919, a Louis Morin scholarship and a Viros scholarship. We thank Eli Barzilay for providing help with the experiments interface, Michael Elhadad for the useful discussions and comments, and all the voluntary participants in the experiments.

9. REFERENCES

[1] R. Barzilay, K. McKeown, and M. Elhadad. Information fusion in the context of multi-document summarization. In *Proc. of the 37th Annual Meeting of the Assoc. of Computational Linguistics*, 1999.

[2] N. Bouayad-Agha, R. Power, and D. Scott. Can text structure be incompatible with rhetorical structure? In *Proceedings of the First International Conference on Natural Language Generation (INLG'2000)*, Mitzpe Ramon, Israel, 2000.

[3] J. Carbonell and J. Goldstein. The use of MMR, diversity-based reranking for reordering documents and producing summaries. In *Proceedings of the 21st Annual International ACM SIGIR Conference on Research and Development in Information Retrieval*, 1998.

[4] T. Cormen, C. Leiserson, and R. Rivest. *Introduction to Algorithms*. The MIT Press, 1990.

[5] R. Dale. *Generating Referring Expressions: Constructing Descriptions in a Domain of Objects and Processes*. MIT Press, Cambridge, MA, 1992.

[6] N. Elhadad and K. McKeown. Generating patient specific summaries of medical articles. Submitted, 2001.

[7] V. Hatzivassiloglou, J. Klavans, and E. Eskin. Detecting text similarity over short passages: Exploring linguistic feature combinations via machine learning. In *Proceedings of the Joint SIGDAT Conference on Empirical Methods in Natural Language Processing and Very Large Corpora*, 1999.

[8] M. Hearst. Multi-paragraph segmentation of expository text. In *Proceedings of the 32th Annual Meeting of the Association for Computational Linguistics*, 1994.

[9] E. Hovy. Automated discourse generation using discourse structure relations. *Artificial Intelligence*, 63, 1993. Special Issue on NLP.

[10] H. Jing. Summary generation through intelligent cutting and pasting of the input document. Technical report, Columbia University, 1998.

[11] I. Mani and E. Bloedorn. Multi-document summarization by graph search and matching. In *Proceedings of the Fifteenth National Conference on Artificial Intelligence*, 1997.

[12] I. Mani and G. Wilson. Robust temporal processing of news. In *Proceedings of the 38th Annual Meeting of the Association for Computational Linguistics*, 2000.

[13] K. McCoy and J. Cheng. Focus of attention: Constraining what can be said next. In C. Paris, W. Swartout, and W. Mann, editors, *Natural Language Generation in Artificial Intelligence and Computational Linguistics*. Kluwer Academic Publishers, 1991.

[14] K. McKeown. *Text Generation: Using Discourse Strategies and Focus Constraints to Generate Natural Language Text*. Cambridge University Press, England, 1985.

[15] K. McKeown, J. Klavans, V. Hatzivassiloglou, R. Barzilay, and E. Eskin. Towards multidocument summarization by reformulatin: Progress and prospects. In *Proceedings of the Seventeenth National Conference on Artificial Intelligence*, 1999.

[16] D. Mooney, S. Carberry, and K. McCoy. The generation of high-level structure for extended explanations. In *Proceedings of the International Conference on Computational Linguistics (COLING-90)*, pages 276–281, Helsinki, 1990.

[17] J. Moore and C. Paris. Planning text for advisory dialogues: Capturing intentional and rhetorical information. *Journal of Computational Linguistics*, 19(4), 1993.

[18] D. Radev, H. Jing, and M. Budzikowska. Centroid-based summarization of multiple documents: sentence extraction, utility-based evaluation, and user studies. In *Proceedings of the ANLP/NAACL 2000 Workshop on Automatic Summarization*, 2000.

[19] D. Radev and K. McKeown. Generating natural language summaries from multiple on-line sources. *Computational Linguistics*, 24(3):469–500, September 1998.

[20] S. Siegal and N. J. Castellan. *Non-Parametric statistics for the behavioural sciences*. McGraw Hill, 1988.

A Server for Real-Time Event Tracking in News

Ralf D. Brown
Language Technologies Institute
Carnegie Mellon University
5000 Forbes Avenue
Pittsburgh, PA 15213-3890 USA
ralf@cs.cmu.edu

1. INTRODUCTION

As the flood of information continues to grow, it becomes ever more necessary to extract just the portion of the flow which is of interest to each user. The Topic Detection and Tracking (TDT) project [1, 3, 6, 5] addressed and continues to address this need, but has been of necessity applied in a batch-processing context on a static collection. What is required for topic detection and tracking to be of utility to end-users is a real-time system which operates on a live stream of information. This paper describes the extension and modification of a batch-oriented tracking system into a real-time server for event detection, event tracking, document summarization, and translation.

2. ARCHITECTURE

To allow sharing of resources such as the collection of news stories between multiple users, a client-server architecture is used. For added flexibility, not all functionality need be implemented in the central server; in addition to user-interface clients, several types of service-provider clients are supported. Service-provider clients initially connect to the server and authenticate themselves in the same manner as a user would, but then send additional commands to identify themselves as service providers and which service(s) they provide. It is also possible for a service-provider client to act as an interface to a news source such as a modem-based newswire service, extracting stories from the news source and adding them to a specified collection on the server. Such external interface programs will likely be the primary source of live data; the current prototype server by itself is only capable of retrieving specified web pages, either once on demand or at regular intervals.

For a multilingual context with high-volume news streams, one needs more than simple alerting – the system must also translate stories which are not in the user's language and generate summaries of sets of relevant stories. Since the language(s) of the news streams that will be used is not fixed before-hand, translation and summarization are handled by external processes. The server can load and/or establish network connections to one or more instances of our multi-engine machine translation system[1] [2, 4] and will invoke the proper instance when a client requests a translation from one language into another. Similarly, service-provider clients provide summarization services for specified languages, with the server routing the summarization request to the appropriate summarizer (or a very rudimentary language-independent summarizer built into the server if there is no service provider available for a particular language). Tracking requests are processed not only by the internal tracking engines, but are also passed to any external clients which have registered as trackers.

Since having a network interface implies that the server can be accessed from anywhere in the world, each user has an account with an associated set of privileges that can, for example, restrict a guest account to minimal read-only access without the ability to view the list of users currently logged in to the server.

Although the primary interaction between clients and the server consists of synchronous request-response pairs, notification of newly detected or tracked events occurs asynchronously on a separate network connection. Using a separate connection permits the notification to be broadcast to all interested clients even if a request-response interaction is currently in progress with a particular client, and allows a dedicated thread or process on the client side to monitor the real-time notifications. The main notifications are NEWEVENT, which indicates that some (unspecified) event differing from all other current news stories has occurred, and TRACKED, which indicates that the story discusses an event which was previously defined using one or more example instances and optionally some counterexamples. Secondary notifications are SHUTDOWN and passed-through requests for tracking, summarization, or document clustering.

Because the live data stream continues 24 hours per day but the client may not be logged in all the time, all notifications are permanently stored in a file, and clients may later request retrieval of the notifications that were missed while the client was not active. Thus, for example, a user can get a listing of all "interesting" stories received overnight when (s)he logs in each morning.

Figure 1 summarizes the various components of this distributed system. It shows the server communicating with

Proceedings of HLT 2001, First International Conference on Human Language Technology Research, J. Allan, ed., Morgan Kaufmann, San Francisco, 2001.

---

[1]The multi-engine translator currently supports translation between English and French, Spanish, German, Mandarin Chinese, Croatian, and Haitian Creole, with "toy" versions of Korean and Slovenian also available.

multiple tracking, detection, summarization, clustering, and translation servers (some on the same computer, some remote), as well as a web crawler and newswire retrieval engine for adding news stories to the server. Multiple users, each with a separate client program, access the server simultaneously.

3. IMPLEMENTATION

The first hurdle in implementing the TDT server was to create a real-time version of the topic tracking system. The pre-existing system had been batch-oriented because the definition of the TDT tracking task requires each event to be processed as though it were the only event, generating a separate output file for each event. For efficiency, the entire collection was loaded into memory and then multiple tracking passes (one per event) made over the collection. Fortunately, the individual tracking engines were structured with separate decision procedures and control structures to allow multi-engine combination, so only the control structure needed to be modified to create a tracking system which operates incrementally as news stories are loaded into the in-memory collection. To handle a live data stream – which, unlike a static collection, is potentially unbounded – stories which are too old to further affect the training phase of the tracking engines are removed from the in-memory collection after each addition of new stories.

Because the removal of documents from the in-memory collection would make older stories inaccessible to clients fairly quickly in a high-volume application, the documents which are removed from memory are stored on disk to allow retrieval by their document ID (which is provided in each notification message). At this time, the permanent repository is not indexed for retrieval by document content or metadata such as timestamp and language, but there is no inherent obstacle to adding such indexing.

Once the incremental version of the tracker was operational, a network interface was added. The network protocol for the server uses plain-text commands and result codes to facilitate debugging – one can simply "telnet" to the server and start entering commands (a simple command-line client which prompts for a command's arguments was also written). Commands to the server include user authentication, enabling/disabling asynchronous alerts, adding and removing documents from a collection, management of multiple collections, requests to track a particular event, lookup of documents by date/time or boolean query, translation, summarization, fetching of web pages, server statistics, and registration as a tracker, summarizer, new-event detector, or clustering engine.

The final step in producing the full system is the implementation and integration of various clients, which is currently in progress. A summarizer for English, Spanish, Mandarin, and Japanese has been adapted into a service-provider client for the TDT Server, as has a document-clustering program. A user-interface client is near completion, and a new-event detection client is planned. The central server is written in C++, and the various clients are implemented in C, C++, and Java.

4. REFERENCES

[1] J. Allan, J. G. Carbonell, G. Doddington, J. Yamron, and Y. Yang. Topic Detection and Tracking Pilot Study Final Report. In *Proceedings of the DARPA Broadcast News Transcription and Understranding Workshop*, Feb 1998.

[2] R. D. Brown. Example-Based Machine Translation in the PANGLOSS System. In *Proceedings of the Sixteenth International Conference on Computational Linguistics*, pages 169–174, Copenhagen, Denmark, 1996. http://www.cs.cmu.edu/~ralf/papers.html.

[3] J. Carbonell, Y. Yang, J. Lafferty, R. D.Brown, T. Pierce, and X. Liu. CMU report on TDT-2: Segmentation, Detection and Tracking. In *Proceedings of the DARPA Broadcast News Workshop*, pages 117–120, San Francisco, CA, 1999. Morgan Kaufmann Publishers, Inc.

[4] C. Hogan and R. E. Frederking. An Evaluation of the Multi-engine MT Architecture. In *Machine Translation and the Information Soup: Proceedings of the Third Conference of the Association for Machine Translation in the Americas (AMTA '98)*, volume 1529 of *Lecture Notes in Artificial Intelligence*, pages 113–123. Springer-Verlag, Berlin, October 1998.

[5] Y. Yang, T. Ault, T. Pierce, and C. W. Lattimer. Improving Text Categorization Methods for Event Tracking. In *Proceedings of ACM SIGIR Conference on Research and Development in Information Retrieval*, 2000.

[6] Y. Yang, J. Carbonell, R. D. Brown, T. Pierce, B. T. Archibald, and X. Liu. Learning Approaches for Detecting and Tracking News Events. *IEEE Intelligent Systems*, 14(4):32–43, July/August 1999. Special Issue on Applications of Intelligent Information Retrieval.

Back–End Service Providers

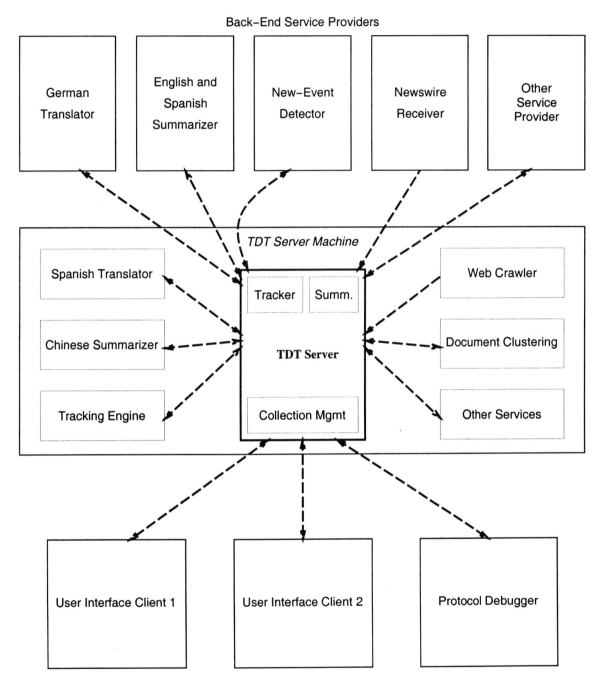

Figure 1: The Distributed TDT-Server Architecture

327

The SYNDIKATE Text Knowledge Base Generator

Udo Hahn

Text Knowledge Engineering Lab
Albert-Ludwigs-Universität Freiburg
D-79085 Freiburg, Germany

hahn@coling.uni-freiburg.de

Martin Romacker

Text Knowledge Engineering Lab
Albert-Ludwigs-Universität Freiburg
D-79085 Freiburg, Germany

romacker@coling.uni-freiburg.de

ABSTRACT

SYNDIKATE comprises a family of text understanding systems for automatically acquiring knowledge from real-world texts, viz. information technology test reports and medical finding reports. Their content is transformed to formal representation structures which constitute corresponding text knowledge bases. SYNDIKATE's architecture integrates requirements from the analysis of single sentences, as well as those of referentially linked sentences forming cohesive texts. Besides centering-based discourse analysis mechanisms for pronominal, nominal and bridging anaphora, SYNDIKATE is supplied with a learning module for automatically bootstrapping its domain knowledge as text analysis proceeds.

1. INTRODUCTION

The SYNDIKATE system belongs to the broad family of information extraction (IE) systems [1]. Significant progress has been made already, as current IE systems provide robust shallow text processing such that frame-style templates are filled with factual information about particular entities (locations, persons, event types, etc.) from the analyzed documents. Nevertheless, typical MUC-style systems are also limited in several ways. They provide no inferencing capabilities which allow substantial reasoning about the template fillers (hence, their understanding depth is low), and their potential to deal with textual phenomena is highly constrained, if it is available at all. Also novel and unexpected though potentially relevant information which does not match given template structures is hard to account for, since system designers commit to a fixed collection of domain knowledge templates (i.e., they have no concept learning facilities).

With SYNDIKATE, we are addressing these shortcomings and aim at a more sophisticated level of knowledge acquisition from real-world texts. The documents we deal with are technical narratives in German language taken from two domains, viz. test reports from the information technology (IT) domain as processed by the ITSYNDIKATE system [8],

Proceedings of HLT 2001, First International Conference on Human Language Technology Research, J. Allan, ed., Morgan Kaufmann, San Francisco, 2001.

and finding reports from a medical subdomain (MED), the framework of the MEDSYNDIKATE system [10, 9]. Our first goal is to extract conceptually and inferentially richer forms of knowledge than those captured by standard IE systems such as evaluative assertions and comparisons [25, 24], temporal [26] and spatial information [22]. Second, we also want to dynamically enhance the set of knowledge templates through incremental taxonomy learning devices [12] so that the information extraction capability of the system is increased in a bootstrapping manner. Third, SYNDIKATE is particularly sensitive to the treatment of textual reference relations [27, 6, 14]. The capability to properly deal with various forms of anaphora is a prerequisite for the soundness and validity of the knowledge bases we create as a result of the text understanding process and likewise for the feasibility of sophisticated retrieval and question answering applications based on the acquired text knowledge.

2. SYSTEM ARCHITECTURE

The overall architecture of SYNDIKATE, an acronym which stands for "SYNthesis of DIstributed Knowledge Acquired from TExts", is summarized in Figure 1. Incoming texts, T_i, are mapped into corresponding *text knowledge bases*, TKB_i, which contain a representation of T_i's content. This knowledge base platform may feed various information services, such as inferentially supported question answering (fact retrieval), text passage retrieval or text summarization [7].

2.1 Sentence-Level Understanding

Grammatical knowledge for syntactic analysis is based on a fully lexicalized dependency grammar [11], we refer to as *Lexicon* in Figure 1. Basic word forms (lexemes) constitute the leaf nodes of the lexicon tree, which are further abstracted in terms of a hierarchy of lexeme class specifications at different levels of generality. The *Generic Lexicon* in Figure 1 contains lexical material which is domain-independent (lexemes such as *move, with,* or *month*), while domain-specific extensions are kept in specialized lexicons serving the needs of particular subdomains, e.g., IT (*hard disk, color printer,* etc.) or MED (*gastritis, surface mucus,* etc.). Dependency grammars capture binary valency constraints between a syntactic head (e.g., a noun) and possible modifiers (e.g., a determiner or an adjective). To establish a dependency relation between a head and a modifier, all the lexicalized constraints on word order, compatibility of morphosyntactic features, and semantic criteria must be fulfilled. This leads to a strictly local computation scheme which inherently lends itself to robust partial parsing [5].

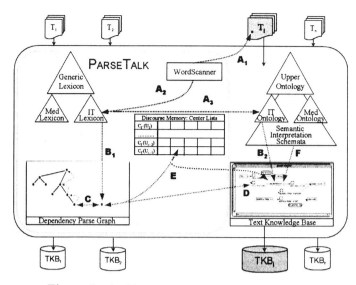

Figure 1: Architecture of a SYNDIKATE System

Conceptual knowledge about the different domains is expressed in a KL-ONE-like description logic language [28]. Corresponding to the division at the lexical level, the ontologies we provide are split up between one that is used by all applications, the *Upper Ontology*, while several dedicated ontologies account for the conceptual requirements of particular domains, e.g., IT (HARDDISK, COLORPRINTER, etc.) or MED (GASTRITIS, SURFACEMUCUS, etc.).

Semantic knowledge accounts for emerging conceptual relations between conceptual items according to those dependency relations that are established between their corresponding lexical items. Semantic interpretation schemata mediate between both levels in a way as abstract and general as possible [20]. These schemata are applied to *semantically interpretable subgraphs* which are, from a semantic point of view, "minimal" subgraphs of the incrementally built dependency graph. Their bounding nodes contain content words (i.e., nouns, verbs, and adjectives, all of which have a conceptual correlate in the domain ontologies), while all possibly intervening nodes (zero up to four) contain only noncontent words (such as prepositions, articles, auxiliaries, etc., all of which have no conceptual correlates). Semantic interpretation schemata are fully embedded in the knowledge representation model and system (cf. Figure 1).

The PARSETALK system, which comprises the lexicalized grammar and associated dependency parser, is embedded in an object-oriented computation model. So, the dependency relations are computed by lexical objects, so-called *word actors*, through strictly local message passing, only involving the lexical items they represent. To illustrate how a dependency relation is established computationally, we give a sketch of the basic protocol for incremental **parsing** [5]:

- After a word has been read from textual input by the *WordScanner* (step A_1 in Figure 1), its associated lexeme (specified in the *Lexicon*) is identified (step A_2) and a corresponding word actor gets initialized (step B_1). As all content words are directly linked to the conceptual system, each lexical item w that has a conceptual correlate C in the domain knowledge base (step A_3) gets instantiated in the text knowledge base (step B_2). The lexical item Festplatte (*hard disk*) with the conceptual correlate HARD-DISK is instanti-

ated, e.g., by HARD-DISK.3, the particular item being talked about in a given text.[1]

- For integration in the parse tree, the newly created word actor searches its head (alternatively, its modifier) by sending parallel requests for dependential government to its left context (step C). The search space is restricted, since these requests are propagated upwards only along the 'right shoulder' of the dependency graph constructed so far. All word actors addressed this way check, in parallel, whether their valency restrictions, i.e., grammatical and conceptual constraints, are met by the requesting word actor. Step D simulates a conceptual check in the text knowledge base, step E illustrates a test in the discourse memory.

- If all required constraints are fulfilled by one of the targeted word actors, an immediate semantic interpretation is performed. This usually alters the conceptual representation structures by way of slot filling (step F).

Semantic interpretation consists of finding a relational link between the conceptual correlates of the two content words bounding the associated semantically interpretable subgraph. The linkage may either be constrained by dependency relations (e.g., the *subject:* relation of a transitive verb such as *"sell"* may only be interpreted conceptually in terms of AGENT or PATIENT roles), by intervening lexical material (e.g., some prepositions impose special role constraints, such as mit (*with*) does in terms of HAS-PART or INSTRUMENT roles), or it may be constrained by conceptual criteria only (as with the *genitive:* dependency relation, which unlike *subject:* imposes no additional selective conceptual constraints for interpretation). The corresponding knowledge about these language-specific constraints is densely encoded in the *Lexicon* class hierarchy, an approach which heavily relies on the property inheritance mechanisms inherent to the object-oriented paradigm.

2.2 Text-Level Understanding

2.2.1 Referential Text Phenomena

The textual phenomena we deal with in SYNDIKATE establish referential links between consecutive utterances in a coherent text such as illustrated by three possible continuations of sentence (1), with three different forms of extrasentential anaphora:

(1) Compaq verkauft *ein Notebook* mit einer Festplatte, die von Seagate hergestellt wird.
(Compaq sells *a notebook* with a hard disk that is manufactured by Seagate.)

(2) **Pronominal Anaphora:**
Es ist mit einer Pentium-III-CPU ausgestattet.
(*It* comes with a Pentium-III CPU.)

(3) **Nominal Anaphora:**
Der Rechner ist mit einer Pentium-III-CPU ausgestattet.
(*The machine* comes with a Pentium-III CPU.)

(4) **Functional Anaphora:**
Der Arbeitsspeicher kann auf 96 MB erweitert werden.
(*The main memory* can be expanded up to 96MB.)

---

[1]Due to the recognition of referential relations at the text level of analysis this instantiation might be readjusted by subsequent coreference declarations (cf. Section 2.2).

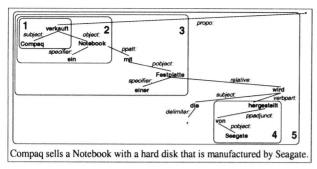

Compaq sells a Notebook with a hard disk that is manufactured by Seagate.

Figure 2: Dependency Parse for Sentence (1)

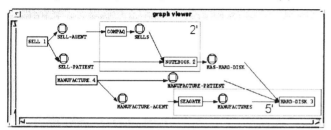

Figure 3: Conceptual Interpretation for Sentence (1)

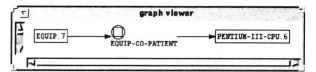

Figure 4: Unresolved Pronominal Anaphor, Sentence (2)

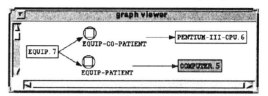

Figure 5: Unresolved Nominal Anaphor, Sentence (3)

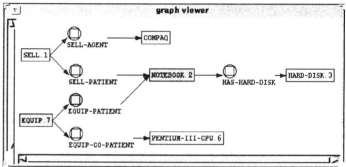

Figure 6: Resolved Anaphors, Sentences (1) and (2)/(3)

The results of sentence-level analysis for sentence (1) are given in Figure 2, which contains a syntactic dependency graph (together with five configurations of semantically interpretable subgraphs), and Figure 3, which displays its conceptual representation. For text-level analysis, pronominal anaphora still heavily depend on grammatical conditions – the agreement of the antecedent (*"Notebook"*) and the pronoun (*"Es" (it)*) in gender and number; also conceptual criteria apply insofar as a potential antecedent must fit the conceptual role (or case frame) restrictions when it is integrated in governing structures, say, the head verb of the clause. In general, however, the influence of grammatical criteria gradually diminishes for other types of text phenomena, while the influence of conceptual criteria increases. For nominal anaphora, number constraints are still valid, while a generalization relation between the anaphoric noun (*"Rechner" (machine)*) and its proper antecedent (*"Notebook"*) must hold, in addition. In the case of functional anaphora, no grammar constraints at all apply, while quite sophisticated conceptual role path conditions come into play, e.g., *"Arbeitsspeicher" (main memory)* being a constituent physical part of *"Notebook"*.

The problems text phenomena cause are of vital importance for the adequacy of the representation structures resulting from text processing, and are centered around the notions of incomplete, invalid and incoherent knowledge bases.

Incomplete knowledge bases emerge when references to already established discourse entities are simply not recognized, as in the case of *pronominal anaphora*. Consider the reference relationship between the pronoun *"Es" (it)* in sentence (2) which refers to the noun phrase *"ein Notebook" (a notebook)* in sentence (1). The occurrence of the pronoun is not reflected at the conceptual level, since pronouns (as noncontent words) do not have conceptual correlates. Hence, an incomplete concept graph emerges as shown in Figure 4 — the referent for the pronoun *"Es" (it)*, NOTEBOOK.2, is not linked to PENTIUM-III-CPU.6. An adequate treatment with a properly resolved anaphor is shown in Figure 6, where the representation of the relevant portions of sentence (1) is linked to the one of sentence (2), in particu-

lar by determining the EQUIP-PATIENT role between EQUIP.7 and the proper referent, NOTEBOOK.2.

Invalid knowledge bases emerge when each entity which has a different denotation at the text surface is treated as a formally distinct conceptual item at the symbol level of knowledge representation, although all different denotations refer literally to the same conceptual entity. This is the case for *nominal anaphora*, an example of which is given by the reference relation between the noun phrase *"Der Rechner" (the machine)* in sentence (3) and the noun phrase *"ein Notebook" (a notebook)* in sentence (1). An invalid referential description appears in Figure 5, where COMPUTER.5 is introduced as a new entity in the discourse, whereas Figure 6 shows the valid conceptual representation capturing the intended meaning at the representation level, *viz.* maintaining NOTEBOOK.2 as the proper referent (note that pronominal as well as nominal anaphora are two equivalent ways to *co*refer to the discourse entity denoted by NOTEBOOK.2).

Finally, *incoherent* knowledge bases emerge when entities which are linked by nontaxonomic conceptual relations at the knowledge level occur in a text such that an implicit reference to these relations can be made in the text source. Unlike the previously discussed cases of coference, these relations have to be made explicit at the symbol level of the targeted text knowledge base by a search for connecting paths between the concepts involved [6]. This is the basic scenario for *functional (or bridging) anaphora*. Consider, e.g., the relationship holding between the noun phrase *"Der Arbeitsspeicher" (the main memory)* in sentence (4), which refers to the noun phrase *"ein Notebook" (a notebook)* in sentence (1). In Figure 8 the relational link missing in Figure 7 between MAIN-MEMORY.8 and NOTEBOOK.2 is established (via a HAS-PART-type relation, *viz.* HAS-MAIN-MEMORY), and, hence, representational coherence at the symbol level of knowledge representation is preserved.

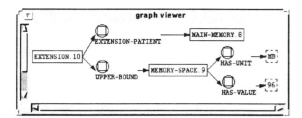

Figure 7: Unresolved Functional Anaphor, Sentence (4)

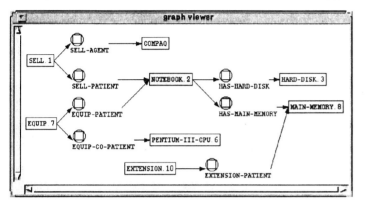

Figure 8: Resolved Functional Anaphor, Sentences (1) and (4)

Disregarding textual phenomena will cause dysfunctional system behavior. A query Q such as

```
Q : (retrieve ?x (Computer ?x))
A-: (|I| Notebook.2, |I| Computer.5)
A+: (|I| Notebook.2)
```

triggers a search for all instances of COMPUTER in the text knowledge base. Given an invalid knowledge base (cf. Figures 3 and 5), the incorrect answer (A-) contains two entities, *viz.* NOTEBOOK.2 and COMPUTER.5 — both are in the extension of the concept COMPUTER. If, however, a valid text knowledge base such as the one in Figure 6 or 8 is given, only the correct answer, NOTEBOOK.2, is inferred (A+).

Rendering also quantitative substance to our claims, we analyzed a randomly chosen sample of 100 reports on histological findings with approximately 14,000 text tokens [9]. In IT texts, (pro)nominal anaphora and functional anaphora occur at an almost balanced rate [27]. In the medical texts, however, functional anaphora turn out to be the major glue for establishing local coherence, while anaphora, pronominal anaphora in particular, play a far less important role than in other text genres. The high proportion of functional anaphora (45%) [42%-48%][2] and the remarkable rate of nominal (34%) [31%-37%] compared to extrasentential pronominal anaphora (2%) [1%-3%] is clearly an indication of the primary orientation in medical texts to convey facts in a very compact manner. Two consequences can be drawn from this observation. First, resolution procedures for functional anaphora – supplementing well-researched procedures for (pro)nominal anaphora – have to be provided urgently (cf. [6] for a fully worked out approach). Second, functional anaphora presuppose a considerable amount of deep background knowledge, with emphasis on partonomic reasoning [13], supplementing well-known principles of taxonomic reasoning for text understanding.

---

[2]For all percentage numbers 95% confidence intervals are supplied in square brackets.

2.2.2 Centering Model for Anaphora Resolution

In order to avoid the emergence of incomplete, invalid and incoherent text knowledge bases we consider discourse entities for establishing reference relations with upcoming items from the textual input at a local [27] and at a global level [14] of cohesion. To preserve adequate text representation structures a *centering* mechanism is used. The discourse entities which occur in an utterance U_i constitute its set of *forward-looking centers*, $C_f(U_i)$. The elements in $C_f(U_i)$ are ordered to reflect relative prominence in U_i in the sense that the most highly ranked element of $C_f(U_i)$ is the most likely antecedent of an anaphoric expression in U_{i+1}, while the remaining elements are ordered according to decreasing preference for establishing referential links.

While it is usually assumed (for the English language, in particular) that *grammatical* roles are the major determinant for the ranking on the C_f [4], we claim that for German – a language with relatively free word order – it is the *functional* information structure of the sentence [27]. Accordingly, the constraints on the ordering of entries in $C_f(U_i)$ prefer *hearer-old* (either evoked or unused) elements in an utterance (i.e., those that can be related to previously introduced discourse elements or generally accessible world knowledge) over *mediated* (inferrable) ones, while these are preferred over *hearer-new* (brand-new) elements for anaphora resolution. If two elements belong to the same category, then preference is defined in terms of linear precedence of the discourse units in the source text.

When we apply these criteria to sentence (1), Table 1 depicts the resulting order of forward-looking centers in $C_f(S_1)$. Since we have no discourse-bound elements in the first sentence, textual precedence applies exclusively to the ordering of the center list items. Only nouns and their conceptual correlates are taken into consideration. The tuple notation takes the conceptual correlate of the lexical item in the text knowledge base in the first place, while the lexical surface form appears in the second place.

(1)	**Cf:**	[COMPAQ: Compaq, NOTEBOOK.2: Notebook, HARD-DISK.3: Festplatte, SEAGATE: Seagate]

Table 1: Centering Data for Sentence (1)

Processing of the centering list $C_f(S_1)$ for sentence (3) until the generalization constraint is fulfilled, finally, results in a query whether NOTEBOOK is subsumed by COMPUTER, the conceptual correlate of the lexical item *"Rechner"*. As this relationship obviously holds, in the conceptual representation structure of sentence (3) (cf. Figure 5) COMPUTER.5, the literal instance identifier, is declared coreferent to NOTEBOOK.2, the referentially valid identifier. Instead of having two unlinked sentence graphs, Figures 3 and 5, the reference resolution for (pro)nominal anaphora leads to joining them in a common valid text graph (Figure 6). In particular, NOTEBOOK.2 links to the relation EQUIP-PATIENT, formerly occupied by COMPUTER.5. The corresponding centering list at the end of the analysis of sentence (3) is provided in Table 2 ($C_f(S_1)$ has been updated to reflect the consumption of the antecedent, NOTEBOOK.2, in the processing of $C_f(S_3)$).

(1)	**Cf:**	[COMPAQ: Compaq, ~~NOTEBOOK.2: Notebook,~~ HARD-DISK.3: Festplatte, SEAGATE: Seagate]
(3)	**Cf:**	[NOTEBOOK.2: Rechner, PENTIUM-III-CPU.6: Pentium-III-CPU]

Table 2: Centering Data for Sentences (1) and (3)

2.3 Textual Learning

The approach to learning new concepts as a result of text understanding builds on two different sources of evidence — the prior knowledge of the domain the texts are about, and grammatical constructions in which unknown lexical items occur in the texts. The architecture of SynDiKATe's concept learning component is depicted in Figure 9.

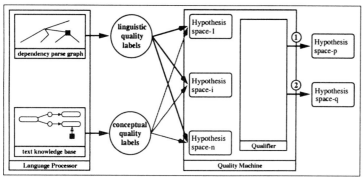

Figure 9: SynDiKATe's **Learning Component**

The ParseTalk system generates *dependency parse graphs*. The kinds of syntactic constructions (e.g., genitive, appositive, comparative), in which unknown lexical items appear, are recorded and later assessed relative to the credit they lend to a particular concept hypothesis, e.g., high for appositives (*"the notebook X"*), lower for genitives (*"Compaq's X"*). The conceptual interpretation of parse trees involving unknown lexical items in the *text knowledge base* leads to the deduction of *concept hypotheses*. These are further enriched by conceptual annotations which reflect structural patterns of consistency, mutual justification, analogy, etc. relative to already available concept descriptions in the text knowledge base or other hypothesis spaces. Both kinds of evidence, in particular their predictive 'goodness' for the learning task, are represented by corresponding sets of *linguistic* and *conceptual quality labels*.

Alternative concept hypotheses for each unknown lexical item are organized in terms of corresponding *hypothesis spaces*, each of which holds a different conceptual reading. An inference engine embedded in the terminological system, the so-called *quality machine*, determines the overall credibility of single concept hypotheses by taking the available set of quality labels for each hypothesis into account. The *qualifier*, a terminological classifier extended by an evaluation metric for quality classes, computes a preference ranking of those hypotheses which remain valid after the text has been processed completely (cf. [12] for details).

3. COVERAGE AND EVALUATION

SynDiKATe's coverage varies considerably depending on the target domain. The generic lexicon currently includes 3,000 entries, the IT lexicon adds 5,000, while the MED lexicon contributes 70,000 entries each. The Upper Ontology contains 1,200 concepts and roles, to which the IT ontology adds 3,000 and the MED ontology contributes 240,000 items.

The IT domain was chosen as a testbed that can be extended on demand. The MED domain, however, is subject to ontology engineering efforts on a larger scale. In order to cope with the enormous knowledge engineering requirements, we semi-automatically transformed large portions of

a semantically weak, yet high-volume medical terminology (UMLS) to a very large terminological knowledge base [21].

Admittedly, SynDiKATe has not yet undergone a thorough empirical evaluation in one of the envisaged application dimensions. We have, however, carefully evaluated its subcomponents. The results can be summarized as follows:

Sentence Parsing. We compared a standard active chart parser with full backtracking capabilities with the parser of SynDiKATe, which is characterized by limited memoization and restricted backtracking capabilities, using the same grammar specifications. On average, SynDiKATe's parser exhibits a linear time complexity the factor of which is dependent on ambiguity rates of input sentences. The active chart parser runs into exponential time complexity whenever it encounters extragrammatical or ungrammatical input, since then it conducts an exhaustive search of the entire parse space. The loss of structural descriptions due to the parser's incompleteness amounts to 10% compared with the complete, though intractable parser [5].

Text Parsing. While with respect to resolution capacity (effectiveness) no significant differences could be determined, the functional centering model we propose outperforms the best-known centering algorithms by a rate of 50% with respect to a measure of computation costs which considers "cheap" and "expensive" transitional moves between utterances to assess a text's coherency. Hence, the procedure we propose is more efficient [27].

Semantic Interpretation. Our group has been pioneering work on the empirical evaluation of meaning representations. We assessed the quality and coverage of semantic interpretation for randomly sampled texts in the two domains we consider. While recall was rather low (57% for MED, 31% for IT), precision peaked at 97% and 94%, respectively [19].

"Heavy" Semantics. We can deal with intricate semantic phenomena for which we have provided the first empirical evaluation data available at all. This relates to the resolution of metonymies, where we have determined a gain in effectiveness that amounts to 16% compared with the best procedures known so far [16], as well as it relates to comparatives and evaluative assertions, where gains in effectiveness were almost tripled [25].

Concept Learning. The performance of the concept learning component has been compared to standard learning mechanisms based on the terminological classifier available in any sort of description logics systems. Our data indicate an increase of performance of 8% (87% accuracy, while that of standard classifiers is on the order of 79%) [12].

Evaluating a text knowledge acquisition rather than an IE system poses hard methodological problems [2]. The main reason being that a gold standard for comparison — what constitutes a canonical, commonly agreed upon interpretation of the content of a text? — is hard to establish, even for technical texts. A follow-up problem is constituted by the lack of a significant amount of annotated text knowledge bases on which comparative analyses might be assessed. MUC-style evaluation metrics, e.g., have already been qualified not to adequately reflect the functionality of less constrained text understanders [29].

4. CONCLUSIONS

A major hypothesis underlying the design of SynDiKATe is that ignoring the referential relations between adjacent utterances will lead to referentially incomplete, invalid, or incoherent text knowledge bases. We determine plausible discourse units for reference resolution using the centering model. This allows us to deal with various forms of pronominal, nominal and functional anaphora in a uniform way.

In order to establish local coherence at the text representation level, single discourse entities related by anaphoric expressions have to be conceptually linked. We claim that only sophisticated knowledge representation languages with powerful terminological reasoning capabilities, such as those from the KL-ONE family, are able to deal with the full range of challenges of referentially adequate text understanding, in particular considering nominal and functional anaphora.

These two types of anaphora pose an enormous burden on the availability of rich domain knowledge. We respond to this challenge in two ways. In a large-scale knowledge engineering effort, we semi-automatically transform a semantically weak though huge thesaurus-style medical knowledge source into a terminological knowledge base. If such a human-made resource is missing, we turn to a purely automatic approach of bootstrapping a given domain knowledge base as part of on-going text understanding processes.

The depth of understanding we provide comes closest to systems such as SCISOR [18], TACITUS [15] or PUNDIT/KERNEL [17], but SYNDIKATE's knowledge acquisition strategies or learning capabilities have no counterpart there. Text understanders which incorporate learning components are even rarer but systems such as SNOWY [3] or WRAP-UP [23] either have a very narrow domain theory and lack robustness for dealing with unseen input effectively, or fail to account for a wide range of referential text phenomena, respectively.

5. ACKNOWLEDGMENTS

The development of the SYNDIKATE system has been supported by various grants from *Deutsche Forschungsgemeinschaft* under Ha 2097/*. SYNDIKATE would not have come to existence without the exciting contributions and enthusiasm of current and former members of the ⒸⒾⒻ group, in particular, Steffen Staab, Katja Markert, Michael Strube, Martin Romacker, Stefan Schulz, Klemens Schnattinger, Norbert Bröker, Peter Neuhaus, Susanne Schacht, Manfred Klenner, and Holger Schauer.

6. REFERENCES

[1] Jim Cowie and Wendy Lehnert. Information extraction. *Communications of the ACM*, 39(1):80–91, 1996.

[2] Carol Friedman and George Hripcsak. Evaluating natural language processors in the clinical domain. *Methods of Information in Medicine*, 37(4/5):334–344, 1998.

[3] Fernando Gomez and Carlos Segami. The recognition and classification of concepts in understanding scientific texts. *Journal of Experimental and Theoretical Artificial Intelligence*, 1(1):51–77, 1989.

[4] Barbara J. Grosz, Aravind K. Joshi, and Scott Weinstein. Centering: A framework for modeling the local coherence of discourse. *Computational Linguistics*, 21(2):203–225, 1995.

[5] Udo Hahn, Norbert Bröker, and Peter Neuhaus. Let's PARSETALK: Message-passing protocols for object-oriented parsing. In H. Bunt and A. Nijholt, editors, *Advances in Probabilistic and other Parsing Technologies*, pages 177–201. Kluwer, 2000.

[6] Udo Hahn, Katja Markert, and Michael Strube. A conceptual reasoning approach to textual ellipsis. In *Proceedings of the ECAI'96*, pages 572–576, 1996.

[7] Udo Hahn and Ulrich Reimer. Knowledge-based text summarization: Salience and generalization operators for knowledge base abstraction. In I. Mani and M. Maybury, editors, *Advances in Automatic Text Summarization*, pages 215–232. MIT Press, 1999.

[8] Udo Hahn and Martin Romacker. Content management in the SYNDIKATE system: How technical documents are automatically transformed to text knowledge bases. *Data & Knowledge Engineering*, 35(2):137–159, 2000.

[9] Udo Hahn, Martin Romacker, and Stefan Schulz. Discourse structures in medical reports – watch out! The generation of referentially coherent and valid text knowledge bases in the MEDSYNDIKATE system. *International Journal of Medical Informatics*, 53(1):1–28, 1999.

[10] Udo Hahn, Martin Romacker, and Stefan Schulz. How knowledge drives understanding: Matching medical ontologies with the needs of medical language processing. *Artificial Intelligence in Medicine*, 15(1):25–51, 1999.

[11] Udo Hahn, Susanne Schacht, and Norbert Bröker. Concurrent, object-oriented natural language parsing: The PARSETALK model. *International Journal of Human-Computer Studies*, 41(1/2):179–222, 1994.

[12] Udo Hahn and Klemens Schnattinger. Towards text knowledge engineering. In *Proceedings of the AAAI'98*, pages 524–531, 1998.

[13] Udo Hahn, Stefan Schulz, and Martin Romacker. Partonomic reasoning as taxonomic reasoning in medicine. In *Proceedings of the AAAI'99*, pages 271–276, 1999.

[14] Udo Hahn and Michael Strube. Centering in-the-large: Computing referential discourse segments. In *Proceedings of the ACL'97/EACL'97*, pages 104–111, 1997.

[15] Jerry R. Hobbs, Mark E. Stickel, Douglas E. Appelt, and Paul Martin. Interpretation as abduction. *Artificial Intelligence*, 63(1/2):69–142, 1993.

[16] Katja Markert and Udo Hahn. On the interaction of metonymies and anaphora. In *Proceedings of the IJCAI'97*, pages 1010–1015, 1997.

[17] Martha S. Palmer, Rebecca J. Passonneau, Carl Weir, and Tim Finin. The KERNEL text understanding system. *Artificial Intelligence*, 63(1/2):17–68, 1993.

[18] Lisa F. Rau, Paul S. Jacobs, and Uri Zernik. Information extraction and text summarization using linguistic knowledge acquisition. *Information Processing & Management*, 25(4):419–428, 1989.

[19] Martin Romacker and Udo Hahn. An empirical assessment of semantic interpretation. In *Proceedings of the NAACL 2000*, pages 327–334, 2000.

[20] Martin Romacker, Katja Markert, and Udo Hahn. Lean semantic interpretation. In *Proceedings of the IJCAI'99*, pages 868–875, 1999.

[21] Stefan Schulz and Udo Hahn. Knowledge engineering by large-scale knowledge reuse: Experience from the medical domain. In *Proceedings of KR 2000*, pages 601–610, 2000.

[22] Stefan Schulz, Udo Hahn, and Martin Romacker. Modeling anatomical spatial relations with description logics. In *Proceedings of the AMIA 2000*, pages 779–783, 2000.

[23] Stephen Soderland and Wendy Lehnert. Wrap-up: A trainable discourse module for information extraction. *Journal of Artificial Intelligence Research*, 2:131–158, 1994.

[24] Steffen Staab and Udo Hahn. Comparatives in context. In *Proceedings of the AAAI'97*, pages 616–621, 1997.

[25] Steffen Staab and Udo Hahn. "Tall", "good", "high" – compared to what? In *Proceedings of the IJCAI'97*, pages 996–1001, 1997.

[26] Steffen Staab and Udo Hahn. Scalable temporal reasoning. In *Proceedings of the IJCAI'99*, pages 1247–1252, 1999.

[27] Michael Strube and Udo Hahn. Functional centering: Grounding referential coherence in information structure. *Computational Linguistics*, 25(3):309–344, 1999.

[28] William A. Woods and James G. Schmolze. The KL-ONE family. *Computers & Mathematics with Applications*, 23(2/5):133–177, 1992.

[29] P. Zweigenbaum, J. Bouaud, B. Bachimont, J. Charlet, and J.-F. Boisvieux. Evaluating a normalized conceptual representation produced from natural language patient discharge summaries. In *Proceedings of the AMIA'97*, pages 590–594.

A Three-Tiered Evaluation Approach for Interactive Spoken Dialogue Systems

Kathleen Stibler and James Denny
Lockheed Martin Advanced Technology Laboratories
1 Federal Street, A&E 3W
Camden NJ 08102
{kcomegno, jdenny}@atl.lmco.com

ABSTRACT

We describe a three-tiered approach for evaluation of spoken dialogue systems. The three tiers measure user satisfaction, system support of mission success and component performance. We describe our use of this approach in numerous fielded user studies conducted with the U.S. military.

Keywords

Evaluation, spoken language system, spoken dialogue system

1. INTRODUCTION

Evaluation of spoken language systems is complicated by the need to balance distinct goals. For collaboration with others in the speech technology community, metrics must be generic enough for comparison to analogous systems. For project management and business purposes, metrics must be specific enough to demonstrate end-user utility and improvement over other approaches to a problem.

Since 1998, we have developed a spoken language dialogue technology called Listen-Communicate-Show (LCS) and applied it to demonstration systems for U.S. Marines logistics, U.S. Army test data collection, and commercial travel reservations. Our focus is the transition of spoken dialogue technology to military operations. We support military users in a wide range of tasks under diverse conditions. Therefore, our definition of success for LCS is operational success. It must reflect the real world success of our military users in performing their tasks. In addition, for our systems to be considered successful, they must be widely usable and easy for all users to operate with minimal training. Our evaluation methodology must model these objectives.

With these goals in mind, we have developed a three-tier metric system for evaluating spoken language system effectiveness. The three tiers measure (1) user satisfaction, (2) system support of mission success and (3) component performance.

Proceedings of HLT 2001, First International Conference on Human Language Technology Research, J. Allan, ed., Morgan Kaufmann, San Francisco, 2001.

2. THE THREE-TIERED APPROACH

Our three-tier metric scheme evaluates multiple aspects of LCS system effectiveness. *User satisfaction* is a set of subjective measures that introduces user perceptions into the assessment of the system. *System support of mission success* measures overall system performance with respect to our definition of success. *Component performance* scores the individual system component's role in overall system success.

Collection of user input is essential in evaluation for two reasons. First, it is necessary to consider user perspective during evaluation to achieve a better understanding of user needs. Second, user preference can influence interpretation of success measurements of mission success and component performance. Mission success and component performance are often tradeoffs, with inefficient systems producing higher scores of success. Since some users are willing to overlook efficiency for guaranteed performance while others opt for efficiency, our collection of user input helps determine the relative importance of these aspects.

Mission success is difficult to quantify because it is defined differently by users with different needs. Therefore, it is essential to establish a definition of mission success early in the evaluation process. For our applications, we derive this definition from domain knowledge acquisition with potential users.

It is important to evaluate components individually since component evaluations reveal distinctive component flaws. These flaws can negatively impact mission success because catastrophic failure of a component can prevent the completion of tasks. For example, in the Marine logistics domain, if the system fails to recognize the user signing onto the radio network, it will ignore all subsequent utterances until the user successfully logs on. If the recognition of sign-on completely fails, then no tasks can be completed. In addition, periodic evaluation of component performance focuses attention on difficult problems and possible solutions to these problems [1].

3. EVALUATION METRICS

At the top level of our approach, measurements of overall user satisfaction are derived from a collection of user reactions on a Likert-scaled questionnaire. The questions are associated with eight user satisfaction metrics: ease of use, system response, system understanding, user expertise, task ease, response time, expected behavior and future use. We have categorized our user satisfaction questions in terms of specific metrics as per the PARADISE methodology [5, 2]. These metrics are detailed in Table 1.

Table 1. User Satisfaction metrics

Metric	Description	Example Likert Survey Questions
Ease of Use	User perception of ease of interaction with overall system	The system was easy to use
System Response	Clarity of system response	System responses were clear and easy to understand
System Understanding	System comprehension of the user	The system understood what you said
User Expertise	Shows us how prepared the user felt due to our training	You knew how to interact with the system based on previous experience or training
Task Ease	User ease in performing a given task	It was easy to make a request
Response Time	User's impression of the speed of system's reply	The system responded to you in a timely manner
Expected Behavior	Connection between the user's experience and preconceived notions	The system worked the way that you expected it to
Future Use	Determination of overall acceptance of this type of system in the future	You would use a mature system of this type in the future

The middle tier metrics measure the ability of users to successfully complete their domain tasks in a timely manner. Success, in this case, is defined as completion of a task and segments of the task utilizing the information supplied by the user. A task is considered successful if the system was able to comprehend and process the user's request correctly. It is important to determine if success was achieved and at what cost. The user's ability to make a request in a reasonable amount of time with little repetition is also significant. The mission success metrics fall under nine categories: task completion, task complexity, dialogue complexity, task efficiency, dialogue efficiency, task pace, dialogue pace, user frustration and intervention rate.

For these metrics, we consider the tasks the user is trying to accomplish and the dialogue in which the user has with the system to accomplish those tasks. A session is a continuous period of user interaction with the spoken dialogue system. A session can be examined from two perspectives, task and dialogue, as shown in Figure 1. Segments are atomic operations performed within a task. The success rate of each segment is an important part of the analysis of the system, while the success rate of each task is essential for the comprehensive evaluation of the system. For example, a task of ordering supplies in the Marine logistics domain includes segments of signing onto the radio network, starting the request form, filling in items a through h, submitting the form and signing off the network. Each segment receives an individual score of successfully completion. The Task Completion metric consists of success scores for the overall task and the segments of the task.

Dialogue is the collection of utterances spoken to accomplish the given task. It is necessary to evaluate Dialogue Efficiency to achieve an understanding of how complex the user's dialogue is for the associated task. A turn is one user utterance, a step in accomplishing the task through dialogue. Concepts are atomic bits of information conveyed in a dialogue. For example, if the user's utterance consists of delivery time and delivery location for a particular Marine logistic request, the time and location are the concepts of that turn. These metrics are described in greater detail in Table 2.

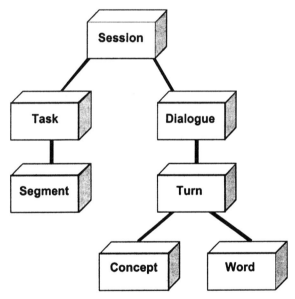

Figure 1. Structural Hierarchy of a Spoken Dialogue System Session

The lowest level tier measures the effectiveness of individual system components along specific dimensions, including component error rates. Overall system level success is determined by how well each component accomplishes its responsibility. This concerns measurements such as word accuracy, utterance accuracy, concept accuracy, component speed, processing errors, and language errors. These measurements aid system developers by emphasizing component weakness. Component Performance metrics also offer explanations for others metrics. For example, bottlenecks within a component may be responsible for slow system response time. Another example is concerned with recognition accuracy. Poor word accuracy may account for low scores of task completion and user satisfaction with the system.

Table 2. Mission metrics

Metric	Description	Measurement
Task Completion	Success rate of a given task	$\dfrac{\sum \text{correct segments}}{\sum \text{items}}$
Task Complexity	Ideal minimal information required to accomplish a task	$\dfrac{\sum \text{ideal concepts}}{\text{task}}$
Dialogue Complexity	Ideal amount of interaction with the system necessary to complete a task	$\dfrac{\sum \text{ideal turns}}{\text{task}}$
Task Efficiency	Amount of extraneous information in dialogue	$\dfrac{\sum \text{ideal concepts}}{\sum \text{actual concepts}}$
Dialogue Efficiency	Number of extraneous turns in dialogue	$\dfrac{\sum \text{ideal turns}}{\sum \text{actual turns}}$
Task Pace	Real world time spent entering information into the system to accomplish the task	$\dfrac{\sum \text{elapsed time}}{\text{task complexity}}$
Dialogue Pace	Actual amount of system interaction spent entering segments of a task	$\dfrac{\sum \text{turns}}{\text{task complexity}}$
User Frustration	Ratio of repairs and repeats to useful turns	$\dfrac{\sum (\text{rephrases} + \text{repeats})}{\sum \text{relevant turns}}$
Intervention Rate	How often the user needs help to use the system	$\sum (\text{user questions} + \text{moderator corrections} + \text{system crashes})$

Some component performance metrics rely upon measurements from multiple components. For example, Processing Errors combines data transfer errors, logic errors, and agent errors. Those measurements map to the Turn Manager which controls the system's dialogue logic, the Mobile Agents which interface with data sources, and the Hub which coordinates component communication. The metrics are discussed in Table 3.

4. EVALUATION PROCESS

Our LCS systems are built upon MIT's Galaxy II architecture [3]. Galaxy II is a distributed, plug and play component-based architecture in which specialized servers handle specific tasks, such as translating audio data to text, that communicate through a central server (Hub). The LCS system shown in Figure 2 includes servers for speech recording and playback (Audio I/O), speech synthesis (Synthesis), speech recognition (Recognizer), natural language processing (NL), discourse/

response logic (Turn Manager), and an agent server (Mobile Agents) for application/database interaction.

We implement a number of diverse applications and serve a user population that has varying expertise. The combination of these two factors result in a wide range of expectations of system performance by users. We have found that the three-tier system and related evaluation process not only capture those expectations, but also aid in furthering our development.

Our evaluation process begins with conducting a user study, typically in the field. We refer to these studies as Integrated Feasibility Experiments (IFE). Participants involved in the IFEs are trained to use their particular LCS application by a member of our development team. The training usually takes 15 to 30 minutes. The training specifies the purpose of the LCS application in aiding their work, includes a brief description of the LCS architecture, and details the speech commands and

Table 3. Component metrics

Metric	Description	Measurement
Word Accuracy	System recognition per word	NIST String Alignment and Scoring Program
Utterance Accuracy	System recognition per user utterance	$\dfrac{\sum \text{recognized turns}}{\sum \text{turns}}$
Concept Accuracy*	Semantic understanding of the system	$\dfrac{\sum \text{recognized concepts}}{\sum \text{concepts}}$
Component Speed	Speed of various components	time per turn
Processing Errors	Percent of turns with low level system error measurements	$\dfrac{\sum (\text{agent errors} + \text{frame construction errors} + \text{logic errors})}{\sum \text{system turns}}$
Language Errors	Percent of turns with errors in sentence construction, word parsing and spoken output of the system	$\dfrac{\sum (\text{parse errors} + \text{synthesis errors})}{\sum \text{system turns}}$

*Our use of concept accuracy was inspired by the concept accuracy metric of the PARADISE methodology [5].

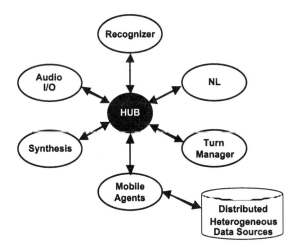

Figure 2. LCS architecture

expected responses through demonstration. After the introductory instruction and demonstration, participants practice interacting with the system.

For each study, we develop a set of scenarios based upon our knowledge of the domain and ask each participant to complete the scenarios as quickly as they can with maximal accuracy and minimal moderator assistance. The study usually consists of approximately five task scenarios of varying difficulty. The scenarios are carried out in fixed order and are given a time limit, generally no longer than 30 minutes. The system logs key events at the Hub, including times and values for the user's speech recording, recognition hypotheses, grammatical parse, resultant query, component speeds, any internal errors, and the system's response. In addition, the moderator notes any assistance or intervention, such as reminding the user of proper usage or fixing an application error. Once the tasks are completed, the user fills out a web-based survey and participates in a brief interview. These determine user satisfaction with the system.

Upon conclusion of a user study, we extract the log files and code the users' recordings through manual transcription. We add diagnostic tags to the log files, noting such events as rephrased utterances and causes of errors and then audit all of the logs for accuracy and consistency. Some of the diagnostic tags that we annotate are number of items and concepts within an utterance, frame construction errors, repeated or rephrased utterances and deficiencies of the training sentence corpus. This is a very time consuming process. Therefore, it is necessary to involve multiple people in this phase of the evaluation. However, one individual is tasked with the final responsibility of examining the annotations for consistency.

A series of scripts and spreadsheets calculate our metrics from the log files. These scripts take the log files as parameters and produce various metric values. While interpreting the metrics values, we may re-examine the log files for an exploration of detail related to particular tasks or events in order to understand any significant and surprising results or trends.

Finally, through a mixture of automated formatting and manual commentary, we create a summary presentation of the user study results. Web pages are generated that contain some of the metrics collected throughout the study.

5. APPROACH VERIFICATION

We have applied our approach in four separate IFEs to date. In each case, our metrics revealed areas for improvement. As these improvements were made, the problems discovered in the next IFE were more subtle and deeply ingrained within the system. Mission success and component metrics aided in the interpretation of user perception and drove future system development. A top-level summary of IFEs, metrics and system improvements is described.

The first IFE was our pilot study, which took place in-house in September 1999. Five subjects with varying military experience were asked to complete three tasks, which were scripted for them. The tier one metrics revealed the users' dissatisfaction with the system responses and the time required in receiving them. These perceptions led to system changes within our Agent and Turn Manager structures that improved the speed of our database agents and more appropriate responses from the LCS system.

The second IFE took place during the Desert Knight 1999 Marine exercise at Twentynine Palms, CA in December 1999. Ten subjects, each an active duty Marine with varying radio operator experience, were given five tasks. This user study offered the subjects the option of following scripts in their tasks. The metrics of tier one showed an increase in overall user satisfaction and revealed the users' difficulty using the system and anticipating its behavior. These concerns influenced future user training and the development of more explicit system responses.

The third IFE occurred during the Marine CAX 6 (Combined Arms Exercise) at Twentynine Palms, CA in April 2000. The seven subjects were active duty Marines, some with minimal radio training. They were required to complete five tasks that had scenario-based, non-scripted dialogues. A combination of tier one, tier two and tier three metrics exposed a deficiency in the speech recognition server, prompting us to increase recognizer training for subsequent IFEs. A recognizer training corpus builder was developed to boost recognition scores.

The most recent IFE was conducted in Gulfport, MS during the August 2000 Millennium Dragon Marine exercise. Six active duty Marines with varied radio experience completed five scenario-based tasks. This time the users expressed concern with system understanding and ease of use through the tier one metrics. The tier three metrics revealed an error in our natural language module, which sometimes had been selecting the incorrect user utterance from recognizer output. This error has since been removed from the system.

The three-tiered approach organizes analysis of the interdependence among metrics. It is useful to study the impact of a metric in one tier against metrics in another tier through principal component analysis. These statistics do not necessarily evidence causality, of course, but they do suggest insightful correlation. This insight exposes the relative significance of various factors' contribution to particular assessments of mission success or user satisfaction.

6. FUTURE ENHANCEMENTS

Although this three-tier evaluation process provides useful metrics, we have identified three improvements that we plan to incorporate into our process: (1) an annotation aide, (2) community standardization, and (3) increased automation. The annotation aide would allow multiple annotators to review and edit logs independently. With this tool, we could automatically measure and control cross-annotator consistency, currently a labor-intensive chore. Community standardization entails a logging format, an annotation standard, and calculation tools common to the DARPA Communicator project [4], several of which have been developed, but we are still working to incorporate them. The advantage of community standardization is the benefit from tools developed by peer organizations and the ability to compare results. Accomplishing the first two improvements largely leads to the third improvement, increased automation, because most (if not all) aspects from measurement through annotation to calculation then have a controlled format and assistive tools. These planned improvements will make our evaluation process more reliable and less time-consuming while simultaneously making it more controlled and more comparable.

7. CONCLUSION

We have found that structuring evaluation according to the three tiers described above improves the selection of metrics and interpretation of results. While the essence of our approach is domain independent, it does guide the adaptation of metrics to specific applications. First, the three tiers impose a structure that selects certain metrics to constitute a broad pragmatic assessment with minimal data, refining the subject of evaluation. Second, the three tiers organize metrics so that user satisfaction and mission metrics have clear normative semantics (results interpreted as good/bad) and they reveal the impact of low-level metrics (results tied to particular components which may be faulted/lauded). Finally, improvements in selection and interpretation balance satisfaction, effectiveness, and perform-ance, thus imbuing the evaluation process with focus toward utility for practical applications of spoken language dialogue.

8. ACKNOWLEDGEMENT

Thanks to members of the LCS team: Ben Bell, Jody Daniels, Jerry Franke, Ray Hill, Bob Jones, Steve Knott, Dan Miksch, Mike Orr, and Mike Thomas. This research was supported by DARPA contract N66001-98-D-8507 and Naval contract N47406-99-C-7033.

9. REFERENCES

[1] Hirschman, L. and Thompson, H. Survey of the State of the Art in Human Language Technology. Edited by J. Mariani. Chapter 13.1, Overview of Evaluation in Speech and Natural Language Processing. Cambridge University Press ISBN 0-521-592777-1, 1996.

[2] Kamm, C., Walker, M. and Litman, D. Evaluating Spoken Language Systems, American Voice Input/Output Society, AVIOS, 1999.

[3] Seneff, S., Lau, R., and Polifroni, J. Organization, Communication, and Control in the Galaxy-ii Conversational System. Proc. Eurospeech, 1999.

[4] Walker, M. Hirschman, L. and Aberdeen, J. Evaluation for DARPA Communicator Spoken Dialogue Systems. Language Resources and Evaluation Conference, LREC, 2000.

[5] Walker, M. Litman, Kamm, D.C. and Abella, A. PARADISE: A Framework for Evaluating Spoken Dialogue Agents. 35th Annual Meeting of the Association of Computational Linguistics, ACL 97, 1997.

Toward Semantics-Based Answer Pinpointing

Eduard Hovy, Laurie Gerber, Ulf Hermjakob, Chin-Yew Lin, Deepak Ravichandran

Information Sciences Institute
University of Southern California
4676 Admiralty Way
Marina del Rey, CA 90292-6695
USA
tel: +1-310-448-8731

{hovy,gerber,ulf,cyl,ravichan}@isi.edu

ABSTRACT

We describe the treatment of questions (Question-Answer Typology, question parsing, and results) in the Weblcopedia question answering system.

1. INTRODUCTION

Several research projects have recently investigated the problem of automatically answering simple questions that have brief phrasal answers ('factoids'), by identifying and extracting the answer from a large collection of text.

The systems built in these projects exhibit a fairly standard structure: they create a query from the user's question, perform IR with the query to locate (segments of) documents likely to contain an answer, and then pinpoint the most likely answer passage within the candidate documents. The most common difference lies in the pinpointing. Many projects employ a window-based word scoring method that rewards desirable words in the window. They move the window across the candidate answers texts/segments and return the window at the position giving the highest total score. A word is desirable if it is a content word and it is either contained in the question, or is a variant of a word contained in the question, or if it matches the words of the expected answer. Many variations of this method are possible—of the scores, of the treatment of multi-word phrases and gaps between desirable words, of the range of variations allowed, and of the computation of the expected answer words.

Although it works to some degree (giving results of up to 30% in independent evaluations), the window-based method has several quite serious limitations:

- it cannot pinpoint answer boundaries precisely (e.g., an exact name or noun phrase),
- it relies solely on information at the word level, and hence cannot recognize information of the desired type (such as Person or Location),
- it cannot locate and compose parts of answers that are distributed over areas wider than the window.

Window-based pinpointing is therefore not satisfactory in the long run, even for factoid QA. In this paper we describe work in our Webclopedia project on semantics-based answer pinpointing. Initially, though, recognizing the simplicity and power of the window-based technique for getting started, we implemented a version of it as a fallback method. We then implemented two more sophisticated methods: syntactic-semantic question analysis and QA pattern matching. This involves classification of QA types to facilitate recognition of desired answer types, a robust syntactic-semantic parser to analyze the question and candidate answers, and a matcher that combines word- and parse-tree-level information to identify answer passages more precisely. We expect that the two methods will really show their power when more complex non-factoid answers are sought. In this paper we describe how well the three methods did relative to each other. Section 2 outlines the Webclopedia system. Sections 3, 4, and 5 describe the semantics-based components: a QA Typology, question and answer parsing, and matching. Finally, we outline current work on automatically learning QA patterns using the Noisy Channel Model.

2. WEBCLOPEDIA

Webclopedia's architecture (Figure 1) follows the pattern outlined above:

Question parsing: Using BBN's IdentiFinder [1], our parser CONTEX (Section 4) produces a syntactic-semantic analysis of the question and determines the QA type (Section 3).

Query formation: Single- and multi-word units (content words) are extracted from the analysis, and WordNet synsets are used for query expansion. A Boolean query is formed. See [9].

IR: The IR engine MG [12] returns the top-ranked 1000 documents.

Proceedings of HLT 2001, First International Conference on Human Language Technology Research, J. Allan, ed., Morgan Kaufmann, San Francisco, 2001.

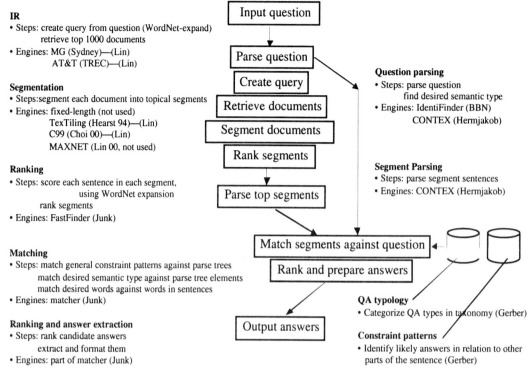

IR
- Steps: create query from question (WordNet-expand)
  retrieve top 1000 documents
- Engines: MG (Sydney)—(Lin)
  AT&T (TREC)—(Lin)

Segmentation
- Steps: segment each document into topical segments
- Engines: fixed-length (not used)
  TexTiling (Hearst 94)—(Lin)
  C99 (Choi 00)—(Lin)
  MAXNET (Lin 00, not used)

Ranking
- Steps: score each sentence in each segment,
  using WordNet expansion
  rank segments
- Engines: FastFinder (Junk)

Matching
- Steps: match general constraint patterns against parse trees
  match desired semantic type against parse tree elements
  match desired words against words in sentences
- Engines: matcher (Junk)

Ranking and answer extraction
- Steps: rank candidate answers
  extract and format them
- Engines: part of matcher (Junk)

Input question

Parse question

Create query

Retrieve documents

Segment documents

Rank segments

Parse top segments

Match segments against question

Rank and prepare answers

Output answers

Question parsing
- Steps: parse question
  find desired semantic type
- Engines: IdentiFinder (BBN)
  CONTEX (Hermjakob)

Segment Parsing
- Steps: parse segment sentences
- Engines: CONTEX (Hermjakob)

QA typology
- Categorize QA types in taxonomy (Gerber)

Constraint patterns
- Identify likely answers in relation to other
  parts of the sentence (Gerber)

Figure 1. Webclopedia architecture.

Segmentation: To decrease the amount of text to be processed, the documents are broken into semantically coherent segments. Two text segmenter—TexTiling [5] and C99 [2]—were tried; the first is used; see [9].

Ranking segments: For each segment, each sentence is scored using a formula that rewards word and phrase overlap with the question and its expanded query words. Segments are ranked. See [9]

Parsing segments: CONTEX parses each sentence of the top-ranked 100 segments (Section 4).

Pinpointing: For each sentence, three steps of matching are performed (Section 5); two compare the analyses of the question and the sentence; the third uses the window method to compute a goodness score.

Ranking of answers: The candidate answers' scores are compared and the winner(s) are output.

3. THE QA TYPOLOGY

In order to perform pinpointing deeper than the word level, the system has to produce a representation of what the user is asking. Some previous work in automated question answering has categorized questions by question word or by a mixture of question word and the semantic class of the answer [11, 10]. To ensure full coverage of all forms of simple question and answer, and to be able to factor in deviations and special requirements, we are developing a QA Typology.

We motivate the Typology (a taxonomy of QA types) as follows.

There are many ways to ask the same thing: *What is the age of the Queen of Holland? How old is the Netherlands' queen? How long has the ruler of Holland been alive?* Likewise, there are many ways of delivering the same answer: *about 60; 63 years old; since January 1938*. Such variations form a sort of semantic equivalence class of both questions and answers. Since the user may employ any version of his or her question, and the source documents may contain any version(s) of the answer, an efficient system should group together equivalent question types and answer types. Any specific question can then be indexed into its type, from which all equivalent forms of the answer can be ascertained. These QA equivalence types can help with both query expansion and answer pinpointing.

However, the equivalence is fuzzy; even slight variations introduce exceptions: *who invented the gas laser?* can be answered by both *Ali Javan* and *a scientist at MIT*, while *what is the name of the person who invented the gas laser?* requires the former only. This inexactness suggests that the QA types be organized in an inheritance hierarchy, allowing the answer requirements satisfying more general questions to be overridden by more specific ones 'lower down'.

These considerations help structure the Webclopedia QA Typology. Instead of focusing on question word or semantic type of the answer, our classes attempt to represent the user's intention, including for example the classes Why-Famous (for *Who was Christopher Columbus?* but not *Who discovered*

America?, which is the QA type Proper-Person) and Abbreviation-Expansion (for *What does HLT stand for?*). In addition, the QA Typology becomes increasingly specific as one moves from the root downward.

To create the QA Typology, we analyzed 17,384 questions and their answers (downloaded from answers.com); see (Gerber, in prep.). The Typology (Figure 2) contains 72 nodes, whose leaf nodes capture QA variations that can in many cases be further differentiated.

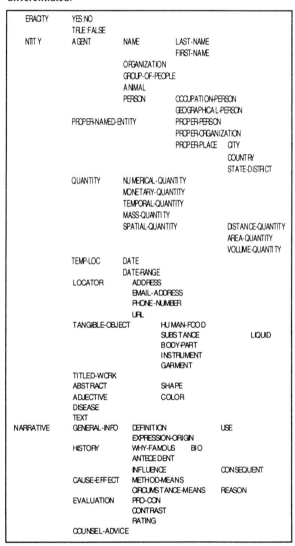

Figure 2. Portion of Webclopedia QA Typology.

Each Typology node has been annotated with examples and typical patterns of expression of both Question and Answer, using a simple template notation that expressed configurations of words and parse tree annotations (Figure 3). Question pattern information (specifically, the semantic type of the answer required, which we call a Qtarget) is produced by the CONTEX parser (Section 4) when analyzing the question, enabling it to output its guess(s) for the QA type. Answer

pattern information is used by the Matcher (Section 5) to pinpoint likely answer(s) in the parse trees of candidate answer sentences.

Question examples and question templates

Who was Johnny Mathis' high school track coach?
Who was Lincoln's Secretary of State?
        who be <entity>'s <role>

Who was President of Turkmenistan in 1994?
Who is the composer of Eugene Onegin?
Who is the chairman of GE?
        who be <role> of <entity>

Answer templates and actual answers

<person>, <role> of <entity>
        Lou Vasquez, track coach of…and Johnny Mathis

<person> <role-title*> of <entity>
        Signed Saparmurad Turkmenbachy [Niyazov],
        president of Turkmenistan

<entity>'s <role> <person>
        …Turkmenistan's President Saparmurad Niyazov

<person>'s <entity>
        …in Tchaikovsky's Eugene Onegin…

<role-title> <person> … <entity> <role>
        Mr. Jack Welch, GE chairman…

<subject>|<psv object> of related role-verb
        …Chairman John Welch said …GE's

Figure 3. Some QA Typology node annotations for Proper-Person.

At the time of the TREC-9 Q&A evaluation, we had produced approx. 500 patterns by simply cross-combining approx. 20 Question patterns with approx. 25 Answer patterns. To our disappointment (Section 6), these patterns were both too specific and too few to identify answers frequently—when they applied, they were quite accurate, but they applied too seldom. We therefore started work on automatically learning QA patterns in parse trees (Section 7). On the other hand, the semantic class of the answer (the Qtarget) is used to good effect (Sections 4 and 6).

4. PARSING

CONTEX is a deterministic machine-learning based grammar learner/parser that was originally built for MT [6]. For English, parses of unseen sentences measured 87.6% labeled precision and 88.4% labeled recall, trained on 2048 sentences from the Penn Treebank. Over the past few years it has been extended to Japanese and Korean [7].

4.1 Parsing Questions

Accuracy is particularly important for question parsing, because for only one question there may be several answers in a large document collection. In particular, it is important to identify as specific a Qtarget as possible. But grammar rules

341

for declarative sentences do not apply well to questions, which although typically shorter than declaratives, exhibit markedly different word order, preposition stranding ("What university was Woodrow Wilson President of?"), etc.

Unfortunately for CONTEX, questions to train on were not initially easily available; the Wall Street Journal sentences contain a few questions, often from quotes, but not enough and not representative enough to result in an acceptable level of question parse accuracy. By collecting and treebanking, however, we increased the number of questions in the training data from 250 (for our TREC-9 evaluation version of Webclopedia) to 400 on Oct 16 to 975 on Dec 9. The effect is shown in Table 1. In the first test run ("[trained] without [additional questions]"), CONTEX was trained mostly on declarative sentences (2000 Wall Street Journal sentences, namely the enriched Penn Treebank, plus a few other non-question sentences such as imperatives and short phrases). In later runs ("[trained] with [add. questions]"), the system was trained on the same examples plus a subset of the 1153 questions we have treebanked at ISI (38 questions from the pre-TREC-8 test set, all 200 from TREC-8 and 693 TREC-9, and 222 others).

The TREC-8 and TREC-9 questions were divided into 5 subsets, used in a five-fold cross validation test in which the system was trained on all but the test questions, and then evaluated on the test questions.

Reasons for the improvement include (1) significantly more training data; (2) a few additional features, some more treebank cleaning, a bit more background knowledge etc.; and (3) the 251 test questions on Oct. 16 were probably a little bit harder on average, because a few of the TREC-9 questions initially treebanked (and included in the October figures) were selected for early treebanking because they represented particular challenges, hurting subsequent Qtarget processing.

4.2 Parsing Potential Answers

The semantic type ontology in CONTEX was extended to include 115 Qtarget types, plus some combined types; more details in [8]. Beside the Qtargets that refer to concepts in CONTEX's concept ontology (see first example below), Qtargets can also refer to part of speech labels (first example), to constituent roles or slots of parse trees (second and third examples), and to more abstract nodes in the QA Typology (later examples). For questions with the Qtargets Q-WHY-FAMOUS, Q-WHY-FAMOUS-PERSON, Q-SYNONYM, and others, the parser also provides Qargs—information helpful for matching (final examples).

Semantic ontology types (I-EN-CITY) **and part of speech labels** (S-PROPER-NAME):
> What is the capital of Uganda?
> QTARGET: ((((I-EN-CITY S-PROPER-NAME))
> ((EQ I-EN-PROPER-PLACE)))

Parse tree roles:
> Why can't ostriches fly?
> QTARGET: (((ROLE REASON)))
> Name a film in which Jude Law acted.
> QTARGET: (((SLOT TITLE-P TRUE)))

QA Typology nodes:
> What are the Black Hills known for?
> Q-WHY-FAMOUS
> What is Occam's Razor?
> Q-DEFINITION
> What is another name for nearsightedness?
> Q-SYNONYM
> Should you exercise when you're sick?
> Q-YES-NO-QUESTION

Qargs for additional information:
> Who was Betsy Ross?
> QTARGET: (((Q-WHY-FAMOUS-PERSON)))
> QARGS: (("Betsy Ross"))
> How is "Pacific Bell" abbreviated?
> QTARGET: (((Q-ABBREVIATION)))
> QARGS: (("Pacific Bell"))
> What are geckos?
> QTARGET: (((Q-DEFINITION)))
> QARGS: (("geckos" "gecko") ("animal"))

These Qtargets are determined during parsing using 276 hand-written rules. Still, for approx. 10% of the TREC-8&9 questions there is no easily determinable Qtarget ("What does the Peugeot company manufacture?"; "What is caliente in English?"). Strategies for dealing with this are under investigation. More details appear in (Hermjakob, 2001). The current accuracy of the parser on questions and resulting Qtargets sentences is shown in Table 2.

5. ANSWER MATCHING

The Matcher performs three independent matches, in order:
- match QA patterns in the parse tree,
- match Qtargets and Qwords in the parse tree,
- match over the answer text using a word window.
Details appear in [9].

Table 1. Improvement in parsing of questions.

	Precision	Recall	Labeled Precision	Labeled Recall	Tagging Accuracy	Crossing Brackets
Without, Oct 16	90.74%	90.72%	84.62%	83.48%	94.95%	0.6
With, Oct 16	94.19%	94.86%	91.63%	91.91%	98.00%	0.48
With, Dec 9	97.33%	97.13%	95.40%	95.13%	98.64%	0.19

Table 2. Question parse tree and Qtarget accuracies.

# Penn Treebank sentences	# Question sentences added	Labeled Precision	Labeled Recall	Tagging Accuracy	Crossing brackets (/ sent)	Qtarget accuracy (strict)	Qtarget accuracy (lenient)
2000	0	83.47%	82.49%	94.65%	0.34	63.00%	65.50%
3000	0	84.74%	84.16%	94.51%	0.35	65.30%	67.40%
2000	38	91.20%	89.37%	97.63%	0.26	85.90%	87.20%
3000	38	91.52%	90.09%	97.29%	0.26	86.40%	87.80%
2000	975	95.71%	95.45%	98.83%	0.17	96.10%	97.30%

Table 3. Relative performance of Webclopedia modules on training corpus.

Date	Number Qs	IR hits	Ranker hits	QA pattern	Qtgt match	Qword fallback	Window fallback	Total
2-Jul	52	1.00	0.61	0.12	0.49	0.15	0.19	0.62
8-Jul	38	0.89	0.40	0.28	0.40	0.12	n/a	0.53
13-Jul	52	1.00	0.61	0.04	0.48	0.15	0.22	0.53
3-Aug	55	n/a	n/a	0.04	0.32	0.15	0.19	0.41

6. RESULTS

We entered the TREC-9 short form QA track, and received an overall Mean Reciprocal Rank score of 0.318, which put Webclopedia in essentially tied second place with two others. (The best system far outperformed those in second place.)

In order to determine the relative performance of the modules, we counted how many correct answers their output contained, working on our training corpus. Table 3 shows the evolution of the system over a sample one-month period, reflecting the amount of work put into different modules. The modules QA pattern, Qtarget, Qword, and Window were all run in parallel from the same Ranker output.

The same pattern, albeit with lower scores, occurred in the TREC test (Table 4). The QA patterns made only a small contribution, the Qtarget made by far the largest contribution, and, interestingly, the word-level window match lay somewhere in between.

Table 4. TREC-9 test: correct answers attributable to each module.

IR hits	QA pattern	Qtarget	Window	Total
78.1	5.5	26.2	10.4	30.3

We are pleased with the performance of the Qtarget match. This shows that CONTEX is able to identify to some degree the semantic type of the desired answer, and able to pinpoint these types also in candidate answers. The fact that it outperforms the window match indicates the desirability of looking deeper than the surface level. As discussed in Section 4, we are strengthening the parser's ability to identify Qtargets.

We are disappointed in the performance of the 500 QA patterns. Analysis suggests that we had too few patterns, and the ones we

had were too specific. When patterns matched, they were rather accurate, both in finding correct answers and more precisely pinpointing the boundaries of answers. However, they were too sensitive to variations in phrasing. Furthermore, it was difficult to construct robust and accurate question and answer phraseology patterns manually, for several reasons. First, manual construction relies on the inventiveness of the pattern builder to foresee variations of phrasing, for both question and answer. It is however nearly impossible to think of all possible variations when building patterns.

Second, it is not always clear at what level of representation to formulate the pattern: when should one specify using words? Parts of speech? Other parse tree nodes? Semantic classes? The patterns in Figure 3 include only a few of these alternatives. Specifying the wrong elements can result in non-optimal coverage. Third, the work is simply tedious. We therefore decided to try to learn QA patterns automatically.

7. TOWARD LEARNING QA PATTERNS AUTOMATICALLY

To learn corresponding question and answer expressions, we pair up the parse trees of a question and (each one of) its answer(s). We then apply a set of matching criteria to identify potential corresponding portions of the trees. We then use the EM algorithm to learn the strengths of correspondence combinations at various levels of representation. This work is still in progress.

In order to learn this information we observe the truism that there are many more answers than questions. This holds for the two QA corpora we have access to—TREC and an FAQ website (since discontinued). We therefore use the familiar version of the Noisy Channel Model and Bayes' Rule. For each basic QA type (Location, Why-Famous, etc.):

$$P(A|Q) = \text{argmax } P(Q|A) \cdot P(A)$$

$$P(A) = \sum\nolimits_{\text{all trees}} (\text{\# nodes that may express a true A})$$
$$/ \text{ (number of nodes in tree)}$$

$$P(Q|A) = \sum\nolimits_{\text{all QA tree pairs}} (\text{number of covarying nodes}$$
$$\text{in Q and A trees)}$$
$$/ \text{ (number of nodes in A tree)}$$

As usual, many variations are possible, including how to determine likelihood of expressing a true answer; whether to consider all nodes or just certain major syntactic ones (N, NP, VP, etc.); which information within each node to consider (syntactic? semantic? lexical?); how to define 'covarying information'—node identity? individual slot value equality?; what to do about the actual answer node in the A trees; if (and how) to represent the relationships among A nodes that have been found to be important; etc. Figure 4 provides an answer parse tree that indicates likely Location nodes, determined by appropriate syntactic class, semantic type, and syntactic role in the sentence.

Our initial model focuses on bags of corresponding QA parse tree nodes, and will help to indicate for a given question what type of node(s) will contain the answer. We plan to extend this model to capture structured configurations of nodes that, when matched to a question, will help indicate where in the parse tree of a potential answer sentence the answer actually lies. Such bags or structures of nodes correspond, at the surface level, to important phrases or words. However, by using CONTEX output we abstract away from the surface level, and learn to include whatever syntactic and/or semantic information is best suited for predicting likely answers.

8. REFERENCES

[1] Bikel, D., R. Schwartz, and R. Weischedel. 1999. An Algorithm that Learns What s in a Name. *Machine Learning Special Issue on NL Learning*, 34, 1—3.

[2] Choi, F.Y.Y. 2000. Advances in independent linear text segmentation. *Proceedings of the 1ˢᵗ Conference of the North American Chapter of the Association for Computational Linguistics* (NAACL-00), 26—33.

[3] Fellbaum, Ch. (ed). 1998. *WordNet: An Electronic Lexical Database*. Cambridge: MIT Press.

[4] Gerber, L. 2001. A QA Typology for Webclopedia. In prep.

[5] Hearst, M.A. 1994. Multi-Paragraph Segmentation of Expository Text. *Proceedings of the Annual Conference of the Association for Computational Linguistics* (ACL-94).

[6] Hermjakob, U. 1997. *Learning Parse and Translation Decisions from Examples with Rich Context*. Ph.D. dissertation, University of Texas at Austin. file://ftp.cs.utexas.edu/pub/ mooney/papers/hermjakob-dissertation-97.ps.gz.

[7] Hermjakob, U. 2000. Rapid Parser Development: A Machine Learning Approach for Korean. *Proceedings of the 1ˢᵗ Conference of the North American Chapter of the Association for Computational Linguistics* (ANLP-NAACL-2000). http://www.isi.edu/~ulf/papers/kor_naacl00.ps.gz.

[8] Hermjakob, U. 2001. Parsing and Question Classification for Question Answering. In prep.

[9] Hovy, E.H., L. Gerber, U. Hermjakob, M. Junk, and C.-Y. Lin. 2000. Question Answering in Webclopedia. *Proceedings of the TREC-9 Conference*. NIST. Gaithersburg, MD.

[10] Moldovan, D., S. Harabagiu, M. Pasca, R. Mihalcea,, R. Girju, R. Goodrum, and V. Rus. 2000. The Structure and Performance of an Open-Domain Question Answering System. *Proceedings of the Conference of the Association for Computational Linguistics* (ACL-2000), 563—570.

[11] Srihari, R. and W. Li. 2000. A Question Answering System Supported by Information Extraction. In *Proceedings of the 1ˢᵗ Conference of the North American Chapter of the Association for Computational Linguistics* (ANLP-NAACL-00), 166—172.

[12] Witten, I.H., A. Moffat, and T.C. Bell. 1994. *Managing Gigabytes: Compressing and Indexing Documents and Images*. New York: Van Nostrand Reinhold.

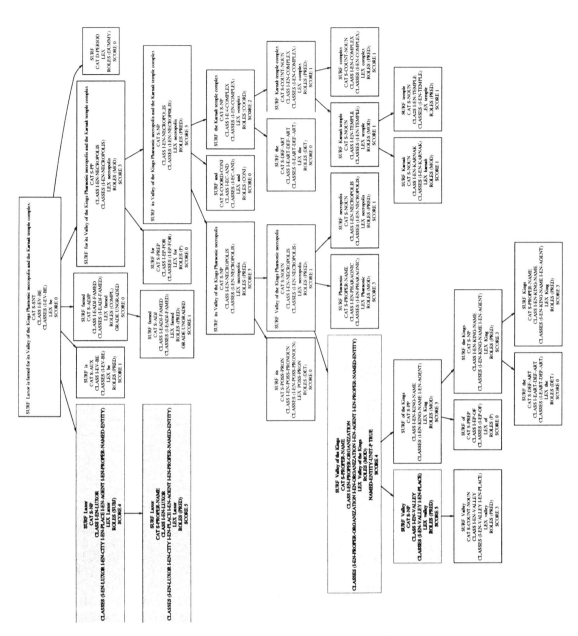

Figure 4. Candidate answer tree showing likely Location answers.

Towards an Intelligent Multilingual Keyboard System

Tanapong Potipiti, Virach Sornlertlamvanich, Kanokwut Thanadkran

National Electronics and Computer Technology Center,
National Science and Technology Development Agency,
Ministry of Science and Technology Environment,
22nd Floor Gypsum Metropolitan Tower 539/2 Sriayudhya Rd. Rajthevi Bangkok 10400 Thailand
Email: tanapong@nectec.or.th, virach@nectec.or.th, kanokwutt@notes.nectec.or.th

ABSTRACT

This paper proposes a practical approach employing n-gram models and error-correction rules for Thai key prediction and Thai-English language identification. The paper also proposes rule-reduction algorithm applying mutual information to reduce the error-correction rules. Our algorithm reported more than 99% accuracy in both language identification and key prediction.

1 INTRODUCTION

For Thai users, there are always two annoyances while typing Thai-English bilingual documents, which are usual for Thais. The first is when the users want to switch from typing Thai to English, they have to input a special key to tell the operating system to change the language mode. Further, if the language-switching key is ignored, they have to delete the token just typed and re-type that token after language switching. The second is that Thai has more than 100 alphabets, to input about half of all Thai characters, the user has to use combinations of two keys (shift key + another key) to input them. Some of the other Asian users also have the same problem.

It will be wonderful, if there is a intelligent keyboard system that is able to perform these two tasks –switching language and shifting key– automatically. This paper proposes a practical solution for these disturbances by applying trigram character probabilistic model and error-correction rules. To optimize number of the generated error-correction rules, we propose a rule reduction approach using mutual information. More than 99 percent of key prediction accuracy results are reported.

2 RELATED WORKS

There is only one related work on inputting Chinese words through 0-9 numpad keys. [8] applied lexical trees and Chinese word n-grams to word prediction for inputting Chinese sentences by using digit keys. They reported 94.4% prediction accuracy. However, they did not deal with automatic language identification process. The lexical trees they employed required a large amount of space. Their algorithm is required some improvement for a practical use.

3 THE APPROACH
3.1 Overview

In the traditional Thai keyboard input system, a key button with the help of language-switching key and the shift key can output 4 different characters. For example, in the Thai keyboard the 'a'-key button can represent 4 different characters in different modes as shown in Table 1.

Table 1: A key button can represent different characters in different modes.

English Mode without Shift	English Mode with Shift	Thai Mode without Shift	Thai Mode with Shift
'a'	'A'	'ฟ'	'ฤ'

However, using NLP technique, the Thai-English keyboard system which can predict the key users intend to type without the language-selection key and the shift key, should be efficiently implemented. We propose an intelligent keyboard system to solve this problem and have implemented with successful result.

To solve this problem, there are basically two steps: language identification and Thai key prediction. Figure 1 shows how the system works.

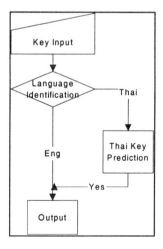

Figure 1: How the System Works

3.2 Language Identification

The following example illustrates the disturbance of language switching. In the Thai input mode, typing a word "language" will result "ลฟืพ฿ฟ". It is certain that the user has to delete sequence "ลฟืพ฿ฟ" and then switches to the English mode before retyping the key sequence to get the correct result of "language".

Proceedings of HLT 2001, First International Conference on Human Language Technology Research, J. Allan, ed., Morgan Kaufmann, San Francisco, 2001.

Therefore an intelligent system to perform language switching automatically is helpful in eliminating the annoyance.

In general, different languages are not typed connectedly without spaces between them. The language-identification process starts when a non-space character is typed after a space. Many works in language identification, [3] and [5], have claimed that the n-gram model gives a high accuracy on language identification. After trying both trigrams and bigrams, we found that bigrams were superior. We then compare the following bigram probability of each language.

$$Tprob = \prod_{i=1}^{m-1} p_T(K_i K_{i+1})$$

$$Eprob = \prod_{i=1}^{m-1} p_E(K_i K_{i+1})$$

where

$p_T(\,)$ is the probability of the bi-gram key buttons considered in Thai texts.
K is the key button considered.
$p_E(\,)$ is the probability of the bi-gram key buttons considered in English texts.
$Tprob$ is the probability of the considered key-button sequence to be Thai.
$Eprob$ is the probability of the considered key-button sequence to be English.
m is the number of the leftmost characters of the token considered. (See more details in the experiment.)

The language being inputted is identified by comparing the key sequence probability. The language will be identified as Thai if $Tprob > Eprob$ and vice versa.

3.3 Key Prediction without Using Shift Key for Thai Input

3.3.1 Trigram Key Prediction

The trigram model is selected to apply for the Thai key prediction. The problem of the Thai key prediction can be defined as:

$$\tau = \arg\max_{c_1, c_2, ..., c_n} \prod_{i=1}^{n} p(c_i \mid c_{i-1}, c_{i-2}) . p(K_i \mid c_i)$$

where

τ is the sequence of characters that maximizes the character string sequence probability,
c is the possible input character for the key button K,
K is the key button,
n is the length of the token considered.

3.3.2 Error Correction for Thai Key Prediction

In some cases of Thai character sequence, the trigram model fails to predict the correct key. To correct these errors, the error-correction rules proposed by [1] and [2] is employed.

3.3.2.1 Error-correction Rule Extraction

After applying trigram prediction to the training corpus are considered to prepare the error correction rule. The left and right

three keys input around each error character and the correct pattern corresponding with the error will be collected as an error-correction pattern. For example, if the input key sequence "glik[lkl9in" is predicted as "เศรษฐศาตรี", where the correct prediction is "เศรษฐศาสตร์". The string "ik[lkl9" is then collected as an error sequence and "ษฐศาสต" is collected as the correct pattern to amend the error.

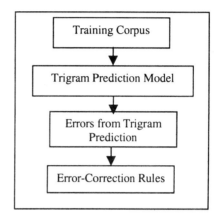

Figure 2: Error-Correction Rule Extraction

3.3.2.2 Rule Reduction

In the process of collecting the patterns, there are a lot of redundant patterns collected. For example, patterns no.1-3 in Table 2 should be reduced to pattern 4. To reduce the number of rules, left mutual information and right mutual information ([7]) are employed. When all patterns are shortened, the duplicate patterns are then eliminated in the final.

Table 2: Error-Correction Rule Reduction

Pattern No.	Error Key Sequences	Correct Patterns
1.	k[lkl9	ษฐศาสต
2.	mpklkl9	ทยาศาสต
3.	kkklkl9	ฬาศาสต
4.	lkl9	ศาสต

Left mutual information (Lm) and right mutual information (Rm) are the statistics used to shorten the patterns. Lm and right Rm are defined as follows.

$$Lm(xyz) = \frac{p(xyz)}{p(x)p(yz)},$$

$$Rm(xyz) = \frac{p(xyz)}{p(xy)p(z)},$$

where

xyz is the pattern being considered,
x is the leftmost character of xyz,
y is the middle substring of xyz,
z is the rightmost character of xyz,
$p(\,)$ is the probability function.

347

The pattern-shortening rules are as follows.
1) If the $Rm(xyz)$ is less than 1.20 then pattern xyz is reduced to xy.
2) Similarly, If the $Lm(xyz)$ is less than 1.20 then pattern xyz is reduced to yz.
3) Rules 1 and 2 are applied recursively until the considered pattern cannot be shortened anymore.

After all patterns are shortened, the following rules are applied to eliminate the redundant patterns.
1) All duplicate rules are unified.
2) The rules that contribute less 0.2 per cent of error corrections are eliminated.

3.3.3 Applying Error-correction Rules
There are three steps in applying the error-correction rules:
1) Search the error patterns in the text being typed.
2) Replace the error patterns with the correct patterns.
3) If there are more than one pattern matched, the longest pattern will be selected.

In order to optimize the speed of error-correction processing and correct the error in the real time, the finite-automata pattern matching ([4] and [6]) is applied to search error sequences. We constructed an automaton for each pattern, then merge these automata into one as illustrated in Figure 3.

4. EXPERIMENTS
4.1 Language Identification
To create an artificial corpus to test the automatic language switching, 10,000 random words from an English dictionary and 10,000 random words from a Thai dictionary are selected to build a corpus for language identification experiment. All characters in the test corpus are converted to their mapping characters of the same key button in normal mode (no shift key applied) without applying the language-switching key. For example, character 'ห', 'ๆ' and 'a' will be converted to 'a'. For the language identification, we employ the key-button bi-grams extracted As a conclusion the first 6 characters of the token are enough to yield a high accuracy on English-Thai language identification.

Table 3: The Accuracy of Thai-English Language Identification

m (the number of the first characters to be considered)	Identification Accuracy (%)
3	94.27
4	97.06
5	98.16
6	99.10
7	99.11

4.2 Thai Key Prediction
4.2.1 Corpus Information
The sizes of training and test sets applied to our key prediction algorithm are 25 MB and 5 MB respectively. The table below shows the percentage of shift and unshift alphabets used in the corpora.

Table 4: Information on Alphabets Used in Corpus

	Training Corpus (%)	Test Corpus (%)
Unshift Alphabets	88.63	88.95
Shift Alphabets	11.37	11.05

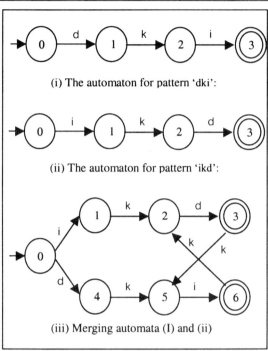

(i) The automaton for pattern 'dki':

(ii) The automaton for pattern 'ikd':

(iii) Merging automata (I) and (ii)

Figure 3: The Example of Constructing and Merging Automata

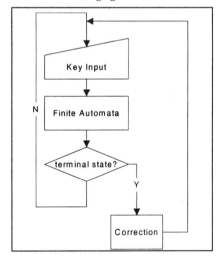

Figure 4: The Error-Correction Process

348

4.2.2 Thai Key Prediction with Trigram

Because the Thai language has no word boundary, we trained the trigram model from a 25-MB Thai corpus instead of a word list from a dictionary as in the language identification. The trigram model was tested on another 5-MB corpus (the test set). Similarly, a typing situation without applying shift key was simulated for the test. The result is shown in Table 4.

Table 5: Thai Key Prediction Using Trigram Model

Training Corpus	Test Corpus
93.11	92.21

4.2.3 Error-correction Rules

From the errors of trigram key prediction when applied to the training corpus, about 12,000 error-correction rules are extracted and then reduced to 1,500. These error-correction rules are applied to the result of key prediction. The results are shown in the table below.

Table 6: The Accuracy of Key Prediction Using Trigram Model and Applying Error-correction Rules

	Prediction Accuracy from Training Corpus (%)	Prediction Accuracy from Test Corpus (%)
Trigram Prediction	93.11	92.21
Trigram Prediction + Error Correction	99.53	99.42

5 CONCLUSION

In this paper, we have applied trigram model and error-correction rules for intelligent Thai key prediction and English-Thai language identification. The result of the experiment shows the high accuracy of more than 99 percent accuracy, which is very impressive. Through this system typing is much more easier and enjoyable for Thais. This technique is expected to be able to apply to other Asian languages. Our future work is to apply the algorithm to mobile phones, handheld devices and multilingual input systems.

REFERENCES

[1] Brill, E. (1997) Automatic Rule Acquisition for Spelling Correction. *ICML.*

[2] Brill, E. (1993) A Corpus-Based Approach to Language Learning. *Ph.D. Dissertation*, University of Pennsylvania.

[3] Cavnar, W. (1994) N-gram Based Text Categorization. *Proceedings of the Third Annual Symposium on Document Analysis and Information Retrieval*, pp.161-169.

[4] Cormen, T., Leiserson, C. and Rivest, R. (1990) *Introduction to Algorithms*, MIT Press

[5] Kikui, G. (1998) Identifying the Coding System and Language of On-line Documents on the Internet. *Proceedings of the 16th International Conference on Computational Linguistics*, pp. 652-657.

[6] Knuth, D., Morris J., and Pratt V. (1977) Fast pattern matching in strings. *SIAM Journal on Computing.* 6(2), pp.323-350.

[7] Sornlertlamvanich, V., Potipiti, T., and Charoenporn, T. (2000) Automatic Corpus-Based Thai Word Extraction with the C4.5 Machine Learning Algorithm. *The Proceedings of the 18th International Conference on Computational Linguistics*, pp. 802-807.

[8] Zheng, F., Wu, J. and Wu, W. (2000) Input Chinese Sentences Using Digits. *The Proceedings of the 6th International Conference on Spoken Language Processing*, vol. 3, pp. 127-130.

Towards Automatic Sign Translation

Jie Yang, Jiang Gao, Ying Zhang, Alex Waibel

Interactive Systems Laboratory
Carnegie Mellon University
Pittsburgh, PA 15213 USA

{yang+,jgao,joy,waibel}@cs.cmu.edu

ABSTRACT

Signs are everywhere in our lives. They make our lives easier when we are familiar with them. But sometimes they also pose problems. For example, a tourist might not be able to understand signs in a foreign country. In this paper, we present our efforts towards automatic sign translation. We discuss methods for automatic sign detection. We describe sign translation using example based machine translation technology. We use a user-centered approach in developing an automatic sign translation system. The approach takes advantage of human intelligence in selecting an area of interest and domain for translation if needed. A user can determine which sign is to be translated if multiple signs have been detected within the image. The selected part of the image is then processed, recognized, and translated. We have developed a prototype system that can recognize Chinese signs input from a video camera which is a common gadget for a tourist, and translate them into English text or voice stream.

Keywords

Sign, sign detection, sign recognition, sign translation.

1. INTRODUCTION

Languages play an important role in human communication. We communicate with people and information systems through diverse media in increasingly varied environments. One of those media is a sign. A sign is something that suggests the presence of a fact, condition, or quality. Signs are everywhere in our lives. They make our lives easier when we are familiar with them. But sometimes they also pose problems. For example, a tourist might not be able to understand signs in a foreign country. Unfamiliar language and environment make it difficult for international tourists to read signs, take a taxi, order food, and understand the comments of passersby.

At the Interactive Systems Lab of Carnegie Mellon University, we are developing technologies for tourist

Proceedings of HLT 2001, First International Conference on Human Language Technology Research, J. Allan, ed., Morgan Kaufmann, San Francisco, 2001.

applications [12]. The systems are equipped with a unique combination of sensors and software. The hardware includes computers, GPS receivers, lapel microphones and earphones, video cameras and head-mounted displays. This combination enables a multimodal interface to take advantage of speech and gesture inputs to provide assistance for tourists. The software supports natural language processing, speech recognition, machine translation, handwriting recognition and multimodal fusion. A vision module is trained to locate and read written language, is able to adapt to new environments, and is able to interpret intentions offered by the user, such as a spoken clarification or pointing gesture.

In this paper, we present our efforts towards automatic sign translation. A system capable of sign detection and translation would benefit three types of individuals: tourists, the visually handicapped and military intelligence. Sign translation, in conjunction with spoken language translation, can help international tourists to overcome these barriers. Automatic sign recognition can help us to increase environmental awareness by effectively increasing our field of vision. It can also help blind people to extract information. A successful sign translation system relies on three key technologies: sign extraction, optical character recognition (OCR), and language translation. Although much research has been directed to automatic speech recognition, handwriting recognition, OCR, speech and text translation, little attention has been paid to automatic sign recognition and translation in the past. Our current research is focused on automatic sign detection and translation while taking advantage of OCR technology available. We have developed robust automatic sign detection algorithms. We have applied Example Based Machine Translation (EBMT) technology [1] in sign translation.

Fully automatic extraction of signs from the environment is a challenging problem because signs are usually embedded in the environment. Sign translation has some special problems compared to a traditional language translation task. They can be location dependent. The same text on different signs can be treated differently. For example, it is not necessary to translate the meanings for names, such as street names or company names, in most cases. In the system development, we use a user-centered approach. The approach takes advantage of human intelligence in selecting an area of interest and domain for translation if needed. For example, a user can determine which sign is to be translated if multiple signs have been detected within the image. The selected part of the image is then processed, recognized, and translated, with the translation displayed on a hand-held wearable display, or a head mounted display, or synthesized as a voice output message over the earphones. By focusing only on the information of interest and providing domain knowledge, the approach provides a flexible method for sign translation. It can enhance the robustness of sign recognition and translation, and speed up the recognition and translation process. We have developed a prototype system that can recognize Chinese sign input from a video camera which is a common gadget for a tourist, and translate the signs into English text or voice stream.

The organization of this paper is as follows: Section 2 describes challenges in sign recognition and translation. Section 3 discusses methods for sign detection. Section 4 addresses the application of EBMT technology into sign translation. Section 5 introduces a prototype system for Chinese sign translation. Section 6 gives experimental results. Section 7concludes the paper.

2. PROBLEM DESCRIPTION

A sign can be a displayed structure bearing letters or symbols, used to identify or advertise a place of business. It can also be a posted notice bearing a designation, direction, or command. Figure 1 and Figure 2 illustrate two examples of signs. Figure 1 shows a Russian sign completely embedded in the background. Figure 2 is a sign that contains German text with no verb and article. In this research, we are interested in translating signs that have direct influence upon a tourist from a different country or culture. These signs, at least, include the following categories:

- Names: street, building, company, etc.
- Information: designation, direction, safety advisory, warning, notice, etc.
- Commercial: announcement, advertisement, etc.
- Traffic: warning, limitation, etc.
- Conventional symbol: especially those are confusable to a foreign tourist, e.g., some symbols are not international.

Fully automatic extraction of signs from the environment is a challenging problem because signs are usually embedded in the environment. The related work includes video OCR and automatic text detection. Video OCR is used to capture text in the video images and recognize the text. Many video images contain text contents. Such text can come from computer-generated text that is overlaid on the imagery (e.g., captions in broadcast news programs) or text that appears as a part of the video scene itself (e.g., a sign outside a place of business, or a post). Location and

recognition of text in video imagery is challenging due to low resolution of characters and complexity of background. Research in video OCR has mainly focused on locating the text in the image and preprocessing the text area for OCR [4][6][7][9][10]. Applications of the research include automatically identifying the contents of video imagery for video index [7][9], and capturing documents from paper source during reading and writing [10]. Compared to other video OCR tasks, sign extraction takes place in a more dynamic environment. The user's movement can cause unstable input images. Non-professional equipment can make the video input poorer than that of other video OCR tasks, such as detecting captions in broadcast news programs. In addition, sign extraction has to be implemented in real time using limited resources.

Figure 1 A sign embedded in the background

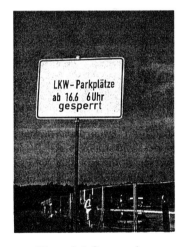

Figure 2 A German sign

Sign translation requires sign recognition. A straightforward idea is to use advanced OCR technology. Although OCR technology works well in many applications, it requires some improvements before it can be applied to sign recognition. At current stage of the research, we will focus our research on sign detection and translation while taking advantage of state-of-the-art OCR technologies.

Sign translation has some special problems compared to a traditional language translation task. The function of signs lead to the characteristic of the text used in the sign: it has to be short and concise. The lexical mismatch and structural mismatch problems become more severe in sign translation because shorter words/phrases are more likely to be ambiguous and insufficient information from the text to resolve the ambiguities which are related to the environment of the sign.

We assume that a tourist has a video camera to capture signs into a wearable or portable computer. The procedure of sign translation is as follows: capturing the image with signs, detecting signs in the image, recognizing signs, and translating results of sign recognition into target language.

3. AUTOMATIC SIGN DETECTION

Fully automatic extraction of signs from the environment is very difficult, because signs are usually embedded in the environment. There are many challenges in sign detection, such as variation, motion and occlusion. We have no control in font, size, orientation, and position of sign texts. Originating in 3-D space, text on signs in scene images can be distorted by slant, tilt, and shape of objects on which they are found [8]. In addition to the horizontal left-to-right orientation, other orientations include vertical, circularly wrapped around another object, slanted, sometimes with the characters tapering (as in a sign angled away from the camera), and even mixed orientations within the same text area (as would be found on text on a T-shirt or wrinkled sign). Unlike other text detection and video OCR tasks, sign extraction is in a more dynamic environment. The user's movement can cause unstable input images. Furthermore, the quality of the video input is poorer than that of other video OCR tasks, such as detecting captions in broadcast news programs, because of low quality of equipment. Moreover, sign detection has to be real-time using a limited resource. Though automatic sign detection is a difficult task, it is crucial for a sign translation system.

We use a hierarchical approach to address these challenges. We detect signs at three different levels. At the first level, the system performs coarse detection by extracting features from edges, textures, colors/intensities. The system emphasizes robust detection at this level and tries to effectively deal with the different conditions such as lighting, noise, and low resolution. A multi-resolution detection algorithm is used to compensate different lighting and low contrasts. The algorithm provides hypotheses of sign regions for a variety of scenes with large variations in both lighting condition and contrast. At the second level, the system refines the initial detection by employing various adaptive algorithms. The system focuses on each detected area and makes elaborate analysis to guarantee reliable and complete detection. In most cases, the adaptive algorithms can lead to finding the regions without missing any sign

region. At the third level, the system performs layout analysis based on the outcome from the previous levels. The design and layout of signs are language and culture dependent. For example, many Asia languages, such as Chinese and Japanese, have two types of layout: the horizontal and the vertical. The system provides considerable flexibility to allow the detection of slanted signs and signs with non-uniform character sizes.

4. SIGN TRANSLATION

Sign translation has some special problems compared to a traditional language translation task. Sign translation depends not only on domain but also on functionality of the sign. The same text on different signs can be treated differently. In general, the text used in the sign is short and concise. For example, the average length of each sign in our Chinese sign database is 6.02 Chinese characters. The lexical mismatch and structural mismatch problems become more severe for sign translation because shorter words/phrases are more likely to be ambiguous and there isn't sufficient information from the text to resolve the ambiguities which are related to the environment of the sign. For example, in order to make signs short, abbreviations are widely used in signs, e.g., 寄研所 (/ji yan suo/) is the abbreviation for 寄生虫研究所 , (/ji sheng chong yan jiu suo/ institute of parasites), such abbreviations are difficult, if not impossible, even for a human to understand without knowledge of the context of the sign. Since designers of signs always assume that readers can use the information from other sources to understand the meaning of the sign, they tend to use short words. e.g. in sign 慢行 (/man xing/, drive slowly), the word 行 (/xing/, walk, drive) is ambiguous, it can mean 行走 (/xing zou/ "move of human," walk) or 行驶 "move of a car," drive). The human reader can understand the meaning if he knows it is a traffic sign for cars, but without this information, MT system cannot select the correct translation for this word. Another problem in sign is structural mismatch. Although this is one of the basic problems for all MT systems, it is more serious in sign translation: some grammatical functions are omitted to make signs concise. Examples include: (1) the subject "we" is omitted in 礼貌待客 (/li mao dai ke/, treat customers politely); (2) the sentence is reordered to emphasize the topic: rather than saying 请将包装纸投入垃圾箱 (/qing jiang bao zhuang zhi tou ru la ji xiang/, please throw wrapping paper into the garbage can), using 包装纸请投入垃圾箱 (/bao zhuang zhi qing tou ru la ji xiang/, wrapping paper, please throw it into the garbage can) to highlight the "wrapping paper." With these special features, sign translation is not a trivial problem of just using existing MT technologies to translate the text recognized by OCR module.

Although a knowledge-based MT system works well with grammatical sentences, it requires a great amount of human effort to construct its knowledge base, and it is difficult for such a system to handle ungrammatical text that appears frequently in signs.

We can use a database search method to deal with names, phrases, and symbols related to tourists. Names are usually location dependent, but they can be easily obtained from many information sources such as maps and phone books. Phrases and symbols related to tourists are relative fixed for a certain country. The database of phrases and symbols is relatively stable once it is built

We propose to apply Generalized Example Based Machine Translation (GEBMT) [1][2] enhanced with domain detection to a sign translation task. This is a data-driven approach. What EBMT needs are a set of bilingual corpora each for one domain and a bilingual dictionary where the latter can be constructed statistically from the corpora. Matched from the corpus, EBMT can give the same style of translations as the corpus. The domain detection can be achieved from other sources. For example, shape/color of the sign and semantics of the text can be used to choose the domain of the sign.

We will start with the EBMT software [1]. The system will be used as a shallow system that can function using nothing more than sentence-aligned plain text and a bilingual dictionary; and given sufficient parallel text, the dictionary can be extracted statistically from the corpus. In a translation process, the system looks up all matching phrases in the source-language half of the parallel corpus and performs a word-level alignment on the entries containing matches to determine a (usually partial) translation. Portions of the input for which there are no matches in the corpus do not generate a translation. Because the EBMT system does not generate translations for 100% of its input text, a bilingual dictionary and phrasal glossary are used to fill any gaps. Selection of the "best" translation is guided by a trigram model of the target language and a chart table [3].

5. A PROTOTYPE SYSTEM

We have developed a prototype system for Chinese sign recognition and translation. Figure 3 shows the architecture of the prototype system. A user can interactively involve sign recognition and translation process when needed. For example, a user can select the area of interest, or indicate that the sign is a street name. The system works as follows. The system captures the sign in a natural background using a video camera. The system then automatically detects or interactively selects the sign region. The system performs

sign recognition and translation within the detected/selected region. It first preprocesses the selected region, binarizes the image to get text or symbol, and feeds the binary image into the sign recognizer. OCR software from a third party is used for text recognition. The recognized text is then translated into English. The output of the translation is fed to the user by display on screen or synthesized speech. Festival, a general purpose multi-lingual text-to-speech (TTS) system is used for speech synthesis.

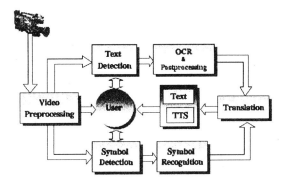

Figure 3 Architecture of the prototype system

Figure 4 The interface of the prototype system

An efficient user interface is important to a user-centered system. Use of interaction is not only necessary for an interactive system, but also useful for an automatic system. A user can select a sign from multiple detected signs for translation, and get involved when automatic sign detection is wrong. Figure 4 is the interface of the system. The window of the interface displays the image from a video camera. The translation result is overlaid on the location of the sign. A user can select the sign text using pen or mouse anywhere in the window.

6. EXPERIMENTAL RESULTS

We have evaluated the prototype system for automatic sign detection and translation. We have built a Chinese sign database with about 800 images taken from China and Singapore. We have tested the automatic detection module using 50 images randomly selected from the database. Table 1 shows the test result of automatic sign detection. Figure 5 and Figure 6 show examples of automatic sign detection with white rectangles indicating the sign regions. Figure 5 shows correct detection after layout analysis. Figure 6 illustrates a result with a false detection (Note the small detection box below and to the left of the larger detection).

Table 1 Test Results of Automatic Detection on 50 Chinese Signs

Detection without missing characters	Detection with false alarm	Detection with missing characters
43	12	5

Figure 5 An example of automatic sign detection

Figure 6 An example of false detection

Figure 7 illustrates two difficult examples of sign detection. The text in Figure 7(a) is easily confused with the reflective background. The sign in Figure 7(b) is embedded in the background

(a)   (b)

Figure 7 Difficult examples of sign detection

We have also tested the EBMT based method. We assume perfect sign recognition in our test. We randomly selected 50 signs from our database. We first tested the system includes a Chinese-English dictionary from the Linguistic Data Consortium, and a statistical dictionary built from the HKLC (Hong Kong Legal Code) corpus. As a result, we only got about 30% reasonable translations. We then trained with a small corpus of 670 pairs of bilingual sentences [7], The accuracy is improved from 30% to 52% on 50 test signs. Some examples of errors are illustrated below:

Mis-segmentaion:

Chinese with wrong segmentation:
[各种] [车辆] [请] [绕] [行]
/ge zhong che liang qing rao xing/
Translation from MT:
All vehicles are please wind profession
Correct segmentation:
[各种] [车辆] [请] [绕行]

Translation if segmentation is correct:
All vehicles please use detour

Lack-domain information:
Chinese with segmentation:
[请勿] [动手]

/qing wu dong shou/
Please don't touch it
Translation from MT:
Please do not get to work

Domain knowledge needed to translate 动手: "start to work" in domain such as work plan and "don't touch" in domains like tourism, exhibition etc.

Proper Name:

Chinese with segmentation:
[北京] [同仁] [医院]

/bei jing tong ren yi yuan/

Beijing Tongren Hospital
Translation from MT:
Beijing similar humane hospital

同仁 is translated to the meaning of each character because it is not identified as a proper name which then should only be represented by its pronunciation.

Figure 8 illustrates error analysis of the translation module. It is interesting to note that 40% of errors come from mis-segmentation of words. There is a big room for improvement in proper word segmentation. In addition, we can take advantage of the contextual information provided by the OCR module to further improve the translation quality.

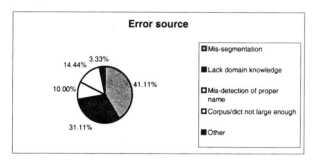

Figure 8 Error analysis of the translation module

7. CONCLUSION

We have reported progress on automatic sign translation in this paper. Sign translation, in conjunction with spoken language translation, can help international tourists to overcome language barriers. A successful sign translation system relies on three key technologies: sign extraction, OCR, and language translation. We have developed algorithms for robust sign detection. We have applied EBMT technology for sign translation. We have employed a user-centered approach in developing an automatic sign translation system. The approach takes advantage of human intelligence in selecting an area of interest and domain for translation if needed. We have developed a prototype system that can recognize Chinese signs input from a video camera which is a common gadget for a tourist, and translate them into English text or voice stream.

ACKNOWLEDGMENTS

We would like to thank Dr. Ralf Brown and Dr. Robert Frederking for providing initial EBMT software and William Kunz for developing the interface for the prototype system. We would also like to thank other members in the Interactive Systems Labs for their inspiring discussions and support. This research is partially supported by DARPA under TIDES project.

REFERENCES

[1] R.D. Brown. Example-based machine translation in the pangloss system. Proceedings of the 16th International Conference on Computational Linguistics, pp. 169-174, 1996.

[2] R.D. Brown. Automated generalization of translation examples". In Proceedings of the Eighteenth International Conference on Computational Linguistics (COLING-2000), p. 125-131. Saarbrücken, Germany, August 2000.

[3] C. Hogan and R.E. Frederking. An evaluation of the multi-engine MT architecture. Machine Translation and the Information Soup: *Proceedings of the Third Conference of the Association for Machine Translation in the Americas (AMTA '98)*, vol. 1529 of Lecture Notes in Artificial Intelligence, pp. 113-123. Springer-Verlag, Berlin, October.

[4] A.K. Jain and B. Yu. Automatic text location in images and video frames. Pattern Recognition, vol. 31, no. 12, pp. 2055--2076, 1998.

[5] C. C. Kubler. "Read Chinese Signs". Published by Chheng & Tsui Company, 1993.

[6] H. Li and D. Doermann, Automatic Identification of Text in Digital Video Key Frames, *Proceedings of IEEE International Conference of Pattern Recognition*, pp. 129-132, 1998.

[7] R. Lienhart, Automatic Text Recognition for Video Indexing, *Proceedings of ACM Multimedia 96*, pp. 11-20, 1996.

[8] J. Ohya, A. Shio, and S. Akamatsu. Recognition characters in scene images. IEEE Transactions on Pattern Analysis and Machine Intelligence, vol. 16, no. 2, pp. 214--220, 1994.

[9] T. Sato, T. Kanade, E.K. Hughes, and M.A. Smith. Video ocr for digital news archives. IEEE Int. Workshop on Content-Based Access of Image and Video Database, 1998.

[10] M.J. Taylor, A. Zappala, W.M. Newman, and C.R. Dance, Documents through cameras, *Image and Vision Computing*, vol. 17, no. 11, pp. 831-844, 1999.

[11] V. Wu, R. Manmatha, and E.M. Riseman, Textfinder: an automatic system to detect and recognize text in images. IEEE Transactions on Pattern Analysis and Machine Intelligence, vol. 21, no. 11, pp. 1224-1229, 1999.

[12] J. Yang, W. Yang, M. Denecke, and A. Waibel. Smart sight: a tourist assistant system. Proceedings of Third International Symposium on Wearable Computers, pp. 73--78. 1999.

TüSBL: A Similarity-Based Chunk Parser for Robust Syntactic Processing

Sandra Kübler
Seminar für Sprachwissenschaft
University of Tübingen
Wilhelmstr. 113
D-72074 Tübingen, Germany
kuebler@sfs.nphil.uni-tuebingen.de

Erhard W. Hinrichs
Seminar für Sprachwissenschaft
University of Tübingen
Wilhelmstr. 113
D-72074 Tübingen, Germany
eh@sfs.nphil.uni-tuebingen.de

ABSTRACT

Chunk parsing has focused on the recognition of partial constituent structures at the level of individual chunks. Little attention has been paid to the question of how such partial analyses can be combined into larger structures for complete utterances.

The TüSBL parser extends current chunk parsing techniques by a tree-construction component that extends partial chunk parses to complete tree structures including recursive phrase structure as well as function-argument structure. TüSBL's tree construction algorithm relies on techniques from memory-based learning that allow similarity-based classification of a given input structure relative to a pre-stored set of tree instances from a fully annotated treebank.

A quantitative evaluation of TüSBL has been conducted using a semi-automatically constructed treebank of German that consists of appr. 67,000 fully annotated sentences. The basic PARSEVAL measures were used although they were developed for parsers that have as their main goal a complete analysis that spans the entire input. This runs counter to the basic philosophy underlying TüSBL, which has as its main goal robustness of partially analyzed structures.

Keywords

robust parsing, chunk parsing, similarity-based learning

1. INTRODUCTION

Current research on natural language parsing tends to gravitate toward one of two extremes: robust, partial parsing with the goal of broad data coverage versus more traditional parsers that aim at complete analysis for a narrowly defined set of data. Chunk parsing [1, 2] offers a particularly promising and by now widely used example of the former kind. The main insight that underlies the chunk parsing strategy is to isolate the (finite-state) analysis of non-recursive, syntactic structure, i.e. chunks, from larger, recursive structures. This results in a highly-efficient parsing architecture that is realized as a cascade of finite-state transducers and that pur-

sues a longest-match, right-most pattern-matching strategy at each level of analysis.

Despite the popularity of the chunk parsing approach, there seem to be two apparent gaps in current research:

1. Chunk parsing research has focused on the recognition of partial constituent structures at the level of individual chunks. By comparison, little or no attention has been paid to the question of how such partial analyses can be combined into larger structures for complete utterances.

2. Relatively little has been reported on quantitative evaluations of chunk parsers that measure the correctness of the output structures obtained by a chunk parser.

The main goal of the present paper is help close those two research gaps.

2. THE TÜSBL ARCHITECTURE

In order to ensure a robust and efficient architecture, TüSBL, a similarity-based chunk parser, is organized in a three-level architecture, with the output of each level serving as input for the next higher level. The first level is part-of-speech (POS) tagging of the input string with the help of the bigram tagger LIKELY [10].[1] The parts of speech serve as pre-terminal elements for the next step, i.e. the chunk analysis. Chunk parsing is carried out by an adapted version of Abney's [2] scol parser, which is realized as a cascade of finite-state transducers. The chunks, which extend if possible to the simplex clause level, are then remodeled into complete trees in the tree construction level.

The tree construction is similar to the DOP approach [3, 4] in that it uses complete tree structures instead of rules. Contrary to Bod, we do not make use of probabilities and do not allow tree cuts, instead we only use the complete trees and minimal tree modifications. Thus the number of possible combinations of partial trees is strictly controlled. The resulting parser is highly efficient (3770 English sentences took 106.5 seconds to parse on an Ultra Sparc 10).

3. CHUNK PARSING AND TREE CONSTRUCTION

The division of labor between the chunking and tree construction modules can best be illustrated by an example.

Proceedings of HLT 2001, First International Conference on Human Language Technology Research, J. Allan, ed., Morgan Kaufmann, San Francisco, 2001.

---

[1]The inventory of POS tags is based on the Stuttgart-Tübingen Tagset (STTS) [11].

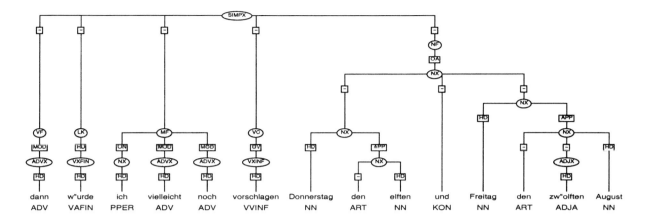

Figure 2: Sample tree construction output

Input:
dann w"urde ich vielleicht noch vorschlagen Donnerstag den elften und Freitag den zw"olften August
(then I would suggest maybe Thursday eleventh and Friday twelfth of August)

Chunk parser output:

```
[simpx  [advx    [adv      dann]]
        [vxfin   [vafin    w"urde]]
        [nx2     [pper     ich]]
        [advx    [adv      vielleicht]]
        [advx    [advmd    noch]]
        [vvinf   vorschlagen]]

[nx3    [day      Donnerstag]
        [art      den]
        [adja     elften]]

[kon    und]

[nx3    [day      Freitag]
        [art      den]
        [adja     zw"olften]
        [month    August]]
```

Figure 1: Chunk parser output

For complex sentences such as the German input *dann w"urde ich vielleicht noch vorschlagen Donnerstag den elften und Freitag den zw"olften August* (then I would suggest maybe Thursday eleventh and Friday twelfth of August), the chunker produces a structure in which some constituents remain unattached or partially annotated in keeping with the chunk-parsing strategy to factor out recursion and to resolve only unambiguous attachments, as shown in Fig. 1.

In the case at hand, the subconstituents of the extraposed co-ordinated noun phrase are not attached to the simplex clause that ends with the non-finite verb that is typically in clause-final position in declarative main clauses of German. Moreover, each conjunct of the coordinated noun phrase forms a completely flat structure. TüSBL's tree construction module enriches the chunk output

as shown in Fig. 2[2]. Here the internally recursive NP conjuncts have been coordinated and integrated correctly into the clause as a whole. In addition, function labels such as *mod* (for: modifier), *hd* (for: head), *on* (for: subject), *oa* (for: direct object), and *ov* (for: verbal object) have been added that encode the function-argument structure of the sentence.

4. SIMILARITY-BASED TREE CONSTRUCTION

The tree construction algorithm is based on the machine learning paradigm of *memory-based learning* [12].[3] Memory-based learning assumes that the classification of a given input should be based on the similarity to previously seen instances of the same type that have been stored in memory. This paradigm is an instance of *lazy learning* in the sense that these previously encountered instances are stored "as is" and are crucially not abstracted over, as is typically the case in rule-based systems or other learning approaches. Past applications of memory-based learning to NLP tasks consist of classification problems in which the set of classes to be learnt is simple in the sense that the class items do not have any internal structure and the number of distinct items is small.

The use of a memory-based approach for parsing implies that parsing needs to be redefined as a classification task. There are two fundamentally different, possible approaches: the one is to split parsing up into different subtasks, that is, one needs separate classifiers for each functional category and for each level in a recursive structure. Since the classifiers for the functional categories as well as the individual decisions of the classifiers are independent, multiple or no candidates for a specific grammatical function or constituents with several possible functions may be found so that an additional classifier is needed for selecting the most appropriate assignment (cf. [6]).

The second approach, which we have chosen, is to regard the complete parse trees as classes so that the task is defined as the selection of the most similar tree from the instance base. Since in

---

[2]All trees in this contribution follow the data format for trees defined by the NEGRA project of the Sonderforschungsbereich 378 at the University of the Saarland, Saarbrücken. They were printed by the NEGRA annotation tool [5].

[3]Memory-based learning has recently been applied to a variety of NLP classification tasks, including part-of-speech tagging, noun phrase chunking, grapheme-phoneme conversion, word sense disambiguation, and pp attachment (see [9], [14], [15] for details).

```
construct_tree(chunk_list, treebank):
    while (chunk_list is not empty) do
        remove first chunk from chunk_list
        process_chunk(chunk, treebank)
```

Figure 3: Pseudo-code for tree construction, main routine.

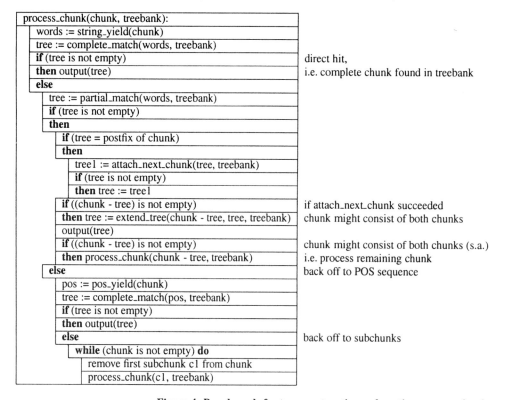

```
process_chunk(chunk, treebank):
    words := string_yield(chunk)
    tree := complete_match(words, treebank)
    if (tree is not empty)                              direct hit,
    then output(tree)                                   i.e. complete chunk found in treebank
    else
        tree := partial_match(words, treebank)
        if (tree is not empty)
        then
            if (tree = postfix of chunk)
            then
                tree1 := attach_next_chunk(tree, treebank)
                if (tree is not empty)
                then tree := tree1
            if ((chunk - tree) is not empty)            if attach_next_chunk succeeded
            then tree := extend_tree(chunk - tree, tree, treebank)   chunk might consist of both chunks
            output(tree)
            if ((chunk - tree) is not empty)            chunk might consist of both chunks (s.a.)
            then process_chunk(chunk - tree, treebank)  i.e. process remaining chunk
        else                                            back off to POS sequence
            pos := pos_yield(chunk)
            tree := complete_match(pos, treebank)
            if (tree is not empty)
            then output(tree)
            else                                        back off to subchunks
                while (chunk is not empty) do
                    remove first subchunk c1 from chunk
                    process_chunk(c1, treebank)
```

Figure 4: Pseudo-code for tree construction, subroutine process_chunk.

this case, the internal structure of the item to be classified (i.e. the input sentence) and of the class item (i.e. the most similar tree in the instance base) need to be considered, the classification task is much more complex, and the standard memory-based approach needs to be adapted to the requirements of the parsing task.

The features TüSBL uses for classification are the sequence of words in the input sentence, their respective POS tags and (to a lesser degree) the labels in the chunk parse. Rather than choosing a bag-of-words approach, since word order is important for choosing the most similar tree, the algorithm needed to be modified in order to rely more on sequential information.

Another modification was necessitated by the need to generalize from the limited number of trees in the instance base. The classification is simple only in those cases where a direct hit is found, i.e. where a complete match of the input with a stored instance exists. In all other cases, the most similar tree from the instance base needs to be modified to match the chunked input.

If these strategies for matching complete trees fail, TüSBL attempts to match smaller subchunks in order to preserve the quality of the annotations rather than attempt to pursue only complete parses.

The algorithm used for tree construction is presented in a slightly simplified form in Figs. 3-6. For readability's sake, we assume here that chunks and complete trees share the same data structure

so that subroutines like *string_yield* can operate on both of them indiscriminately.

The main routine *construct_tree* in Fig. 3 separates the list of input chunks and passes each one to the subroutine *process_chunk* in Fig. 4 where the chunk is then turned into one or more (partial) trees. *process_chunk* first checks if a complete match with an instance from the instance base is possible.[4] If this is not the case, a partial match on the lexical level is attempted. If a partial tree is found, *attach_next_chunk* in Fig. 5 and *extend_tree* in Fig. 6 are used to extend the tree by either attaching one more chunk or by resorting to a comparison of the missing parts of the chunk with tree extensions on the POS level. *attach_next_chunk* is necessary to ensure that the best possible tree is found even in the rare case that the original segmentation into chunks contains mistakes. If no partial tree is found, the tree construction backs off to finding a complete match in the POS level or to starting the subroutine for processing a chunk recursively with all the subchunks of the present chunk.

The application of memory-based techniques is implemented in the two subroutines *complete_match* and *partial_match*. The presentation of the two cases as two separate subroutines is for expository purposes only. In the actual implementation, the search is carried out only once. The two subroutines exist because of

---

[4] *string_yield* returns the sequence of words included in the input structure, *pos_yield* the sequence of POS tags.

```
attach_next_chunk(tree, treebank):            attempts to attach the next chunk to the tree
    take first chunk chunk2 from chunk_list
    words2 := string_yield(tree, chunk2)
    tree2 := complete_match(words2, treebank)
    if (tree2 is not empty)
    then
        remove chunk2 from chunk_list
        return tree2
    else return empty
```

Figure 5: Pseudo-code for tree construction, subroutine attach_next_chunk.

```
extend_tree(rest_chunk, tree, treebank):       extends the tree on basis of POS comparison
    words := string_yield(tree)
    rest_pos := pos_yield(rest_chunk)
    tree2 := partial_match(words + rest_pos, treebank)
    if ((tree2 is not empty) and (subtree(tree, tree2)))
    then return tree2
    else return empty
```

Figure 6: Pseudo-code for tree construction, subroutine extend_tree.

the postprocessing of the chosen tree which is necessary for partial matches and which also deviates from standard memory-based applications. Postprocessing mainly consists of shortening the tree from the instance base so that it covers only those parts of the chunk that could be matched. However, if the match is done on the lexical level, a correction of tagging errors is possible if there is enough evidence in the instance base. TüSBL currently uses an *overlap metric*, the most basic metric for instances with symbolic features, as its similarity metric. This overlap metric is based on either lexical or POS features. Instead of applying a more sophisticated metric like the weighted overlap metric, TüSBL uses a backing-off approach that heavily favors similarity of the input with pre-stored instances on the basis of substring identity. Splitting up the classification and adaptation process into different stages allows TüSBL to prefer analyses with a higher likelihood of being correct. This strategy enables corrections of tagging and segmentation errors that may occur in the chunked input.

4.1 Example

Input:
dann w"urde ich sagen ist das vereinbart

(then I would say this is arranged)
Chunk parser output:

```
[simpx  [advx    [adv dann]]
        [vxfin   [vafin w"urde]]
        [nx2     [pper ich]]
        [vvinf   sagen]]

[simpx  [vafin   ist]
        [nx2     [pds das]]
        [vvpp    vereinbart]]
```

Figure 7: Chunk parser output

For the input sentence *dann w"urde ich sagen ist das vereinbart* (then I would say this is arranged), the chunked output is shown in Fig. 7. The chunk parser correctly splits the input into two clauses

Table 1: Quantitative evaluation

	minimum	maximum	average
precision	76.82%	77.87%	77.23%
recall	66.90%	67.65%	67.28%
crossing accuracy	93.44%	93.95%	93.70%

dann w"urde ich sagen and *ist das vereinbart*. A look-up in the instance base finds a direct hit for the first clause. Therefore, the correct tree can be output directly. For the second clause, only a partial match on the level of words can be found. The system finds the tree for the subsequence of words *ist das*, as shown in Fig. 8. By backing off to a comparison on the POS level, it finds a tree for the sentence *hatten die gesagt* (they had said) with the same POS sequence and the same structure for the first two words. Thus the original tree that covers only two words is extended via the newly found tree. TüSBL's output for the complete sentence is shown in Fig. 9.

5. QUANTITATIVE EVALUATION

A quantitative evaluation of TüSBL has been conducted using a semi-automatically constructed treebank of German that consists of appr. 67,000 fully annotated sentences or sentence fragments.[5] The evaluation consisted of a ten-fold cross-validation test, where the training data provide an instance base of already seen cases for TüSBL's tree construction module.

The evaluation focused on three PARSEVAL measures: labeled precision, labeled recall and crossing accuracy, with the results shown in Table 1.

While these results do not reach the performance reported for other parsers (cf. [7], [8]), it is important to note that the task carried out here is more difficult in a number of respects:

1. The set of labels does not only include phrasal categories, but also functional labels marking grammatical relations such as subject, direct object, indirect object and modifier. Thus, the evaluation carried out here is not subject to the justified criticism levelled against the gold standards that are typically

---

[5]See [13] for further details.

359

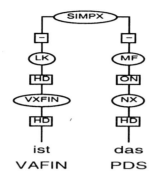

Figure 8: A partial tree found be the system

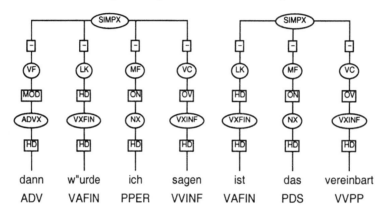

Figure 9: TüSBL's output for the complete sentence

in conjunction with the PARSEVAL measures, namely that the gold standards used typically do not include annotations of syntactic-semantic dependencies between bracketed constituents.

2. The German treebank consists of transliterated spontaneous speech data. The fragmentary and partially ill-formed nature of such spoken data makes them harder to analyze than written data such as the Penn treebank typically used as gold standard.

It should also be kept in mind that the basic PARSEVAL measures were developed for parsers that have as their main goal a complete analysis that spans the entire input. This runs counter to the basic philosophy underlying an amended chunk parser such as TüSBL, which has as its main goal robustness of partially analyzed structures: Precision and recall measure the percentage of brackets, i.e. constituents with the same yield or bracketing scope, which are identical in the parse tree and the gold standard. If TüSBL finds only a partial grouping on one level, both measures consider this grouping wrong, as a consequence of the different bracket scopes. In most cases, the error 'percolates' up to the highest level. Fig. 10 gives an example of a partially matched tree structure for the sentence "bei mir ginge es im Februar ab Mittwoch den vierten" (for me it would work in February after Wednesday the fourth). The only missing branch is the branch connecting the second noun phrase (NX) above "Mittwoch" to the NX "den vierten". This results in precision and recall values of 10 out of 15 because of the

altered bracketing scopes of the noun phrase, the two prepositional phrases (PX), the field level (MF) and the sentence level (SIMPX).

In order to capture this specific aspect of the parser, a second evaluation was performed that focused on the quality of the structures produced by the parser. This evaluation consisted of manually judging the TüSBL output and scoring the accuracy of the recognized constituents. The scoring was performed by the human annotator who constructed the treebank and was thus in a privileged position to judge constituent accuracy with respect to the treebank annotation standards. This manual evaluation resulted in a score of 92.4% constituent accuracy; that is: of all constituents that were recognized by the parser, 92.4% were judged correct by the human annotator. This seems to indicate that approximately 20% of the precision errors are due to partial constituents whose yield is shorter than in the corresponding gold standard. Such discrepancies typically arise when TüSBL outputs only partial trees. This occurs when no complete tree structures can be constructed that span the entire input.

6. CONCLUSION AND FUTURE RESEARCH

In this paper we have described how the TüSBL parser extends current chunk parsing techniques by a tree-construction component that completes partial chunk parses to tree structures including function-argument structure.

As noted in section 4, TüSBL currently uses an *overlap metric*, i. e. the most basic metric for instances with symbolic features, as its

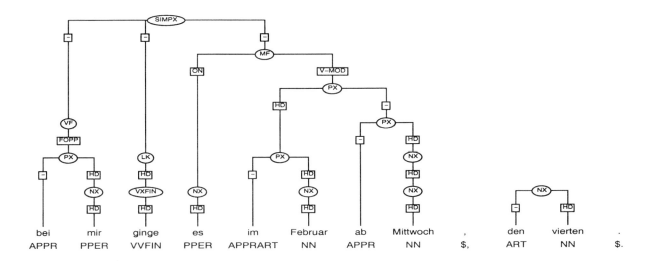

Figure 10: A partially grouped tree output of the TÜSBL system

similarity metric. We anticipate that the results reported in Fig. 1 can be further improved by experimenting with more sophisticated similarity metrics. However, we will have to leave this matter to future research.[6]

7. ACKNOWLEDGMENTS

The research reported here was funded both by the German Federal Ministry of Education, Science, Research, and Technology (BMBF) in the framework of the VERBMOBIL Project under Grant 01 IV 101 N 0 and by the Deutsche Forschungsgemeinschaft (DFG) in the framework of the Sonderforschungsbereich 441.

8. REFERENCES

[1] S. Abney. Parsing by chunks. In R. Berwick, S. Abney, and C. Tenney, editors, *Principle-Based Parsing*. Kluwer Academic Publishers, 1991.

[2] S. Abney. Partial parsing via finite-state cascades. In J. Carroll, editor, *Workshop on Robust Parsing (ESSLLI '96)*, 1996.

[3] R. Bod. *Beyond Grammar: An Experience-Based Theory of Language*. CSLI Publications, Stanford, California, 1998.

[4] R. Bod. Parsing with the shortest derivation. In *Proceedings of COLING 2000*, 2000.

[5] T. Brants and W. Skut. Automation of treebank annotation. In *Proceedings of NeMLaP-3/CoNLL98, Sydney, Australia*, 1998.

[6] S. Buchholz, J. Veenstra, and W. Daelemans. Cascaded grammatical relation assignment. In *Proceedings of EMNLP/VLC-99, University of Maryland, USA, June 21-22, 1999*, pages 239 – 246, 1999.

[7] E. Charniak. Statistical parsing with a context-free grammar and word statistics. In *Proceedings of the Fourteenth National Conference on Artifical Intelligence, Menlo Park*, 1997.

[8] M. Collins. *Head-Driven Statistical Models for Natural Language Parsing*. PhD thesis, University of Pennsylvania, 1999.

[9] W. Daelemans, J. Zavrel, and A. van den Bosch. Forgetting exceptions is harmful in language learning. *Machine Learning: Special Issue on Natural Language Learning*, 34, 1999.

[10] H. Feldweg. Stochastische Wortartendisambiguierung für das Deutsche: Untersuchungen mit dem robusten System LIKELY. Technical report, Universität Tübingen, 1993. SfS-Report-08-93.

[11] A. Schiller, S. Teufel, and C. Thielen. Guidelines für das Tagging deutscher Textkorpora mit STTS. Technical report, Universität Stuttgart and Universität Tübingen, 1995. (URL: http://www.sfs.nphil.uni-tuebingen.de/Elwis/stts/stts.html).

[12] C. Stanfill and D. Waltz. Towards memory-based reasoning. *Communications of the ACM*, 29(12), 1986.

[13] R. Stegmann, H. Schulz, and E. W. Hinrichs. Stylebook for the German Treebank in VERBMOBIL. Technical Report 239, Verbmobil, 2000.

[14] J. Veenstra, A. van den Bosch, S. Buchholz, W. Daelemans, and J. Zavrel. Memory-based word sense disambiguation. *Computers and the Humanities, Special Issue on Senseval, Word Sense Disambiguations*, 34, 2000.

[15] J. Zavrel, W. Daelemans, and J. Veenstra. Resolving PP attachment ambiguities with memory-based learning. In M. Ellison, editor, *Proceedings of the Workshop on Computational Natural Language Learning (CoNLL'97), Madrid*, 1997.

---

[6][9] reports that the *gain ratio* similarity metric has yielded excellent results for the NLP applications considered by these investigators.

University of Colorado Dialog Systems for Travel and Navigation

B. Pellom, W. Ward, J. Hansen, R. Cole, K. Hacioglu, J. Zhang, X. Yu, S. Pradhan

Center for Spoken Language Research, University of Colorado
Boulder, Colorado 80303, USA
{pellom, whw, jhlh, cole, hacioglu, zjp, xiu, spradhan}@cslr.colorado.edu

ABSTRACT

This paper presents recent improvements in the development of the University of Colorado "CU Communicator" and "CU-Move" spoken dialog systems. First, we describe the CU Communicator system that integrates speech recognition, synthesis and natural language understanding technologies using the DARPA Hub Architecture. Users are able to converse with an automated travel agent over the phone to retrieve up-to-date travel information such as flight schedules, pricing, along with hotel and rental car availability. The CU Communicator has been under development since April of 1999 and represents our test-bed system for developing robust human-computer interactions where reusability and dialogue system portability serve as two main goals of our work. Next, we describe our more recent work on the CU Move dialog system for in-vehicle route planning and guidance. This work is in joint collaboration with HRL and is sponsored as part of the DARPA Communicator program. Specifically, we will provide an overview of the task, describe the data collection environment for in-vehicle systems development, and describe our initial dialog system constructed for route planning.

1. CU COMMUNICATOR

1.1 Overview

The Travel Planning Task

The CU Communicator system [1,2] is a Hub compliant implementation of the DARPA Communicator task [3]. The system combines continuous speech recognition, natural language understanding and flexible dialogue control to enable natural conversational interaction by telephone callers to access information from the Internet pertaining to airline flights, hotels and rental cars. Specifically, users can describe a desired airline flight itinerary to the Communicator and use natural dialog to negotiate a flight plan. Users can also inquire about hotel availability and pricing as well as obtain rental car reservation information.

System Overview

The dialog system is composed of a Hub and several servers as shown in Fig. 1. The Hub is used as a centralized message router through which servers can communicate with one another [4]. Frames containing keys and values are emitted by each server, routed by the hub, and received by a secondary server based on rules defined in a "Hub script".

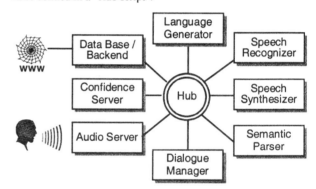

Figure 1. **Block diagram of the functional components that comprise the CU Communicator system[1].**

1.2 Audio Server

The audio server is responsible for answering the incoming call, playing prompts and recording user input. Currently, our system uses the MIT/MITRE audio server that was provided to DARPA Communicator program participants. The telephony hardware consists of an external serial modem device that connects to the microphone input and speaker output terminals on the host computer. The record process is pipelined to the speech recognition server and the play process is pipelined the text-to-speech server. This audio server does not support barge-in.

Recently we have developed a new audio server that supports barge-in using the Dialogic hardware platform. The new audio server implements a Fast Normalized Least-Mean-Square (LMS) algorithm for software-based echo cancellation. During operation, the echo from the system speech is actively cancelled from the recorded audio to allow the user to cut through while

Proceedings of HLT 2001, First International Conference on Human Language Technology Research, J. Allan, ed., Morgan Kaufmann, San Francisco, 2001.

[1] This work was supported by DARPA through SPAWAR under Grant No. N66001-002-8906. The "CU Move" system is supported in part through a joint collaboration with HRL Laboratories.

the system is speaking. The new audio server operates in the Linux environment and is currently being field-tested at CSLR. Because the server implements software-based echo cancellation, it can work on virtually any low-cost Dialogic hardware platform. This server will be made available to the research community as a resource in the near future.

1.3 Speech Recognizer

We are currently using the Carnegie Mellon University Sphinx-II system [5] in our speech recognition server. This is a semi-continuous Hidden Markov Model recognizer with a class trigram language model. The recognition server receives the input vectors from the audio server. The recognition server produces a word lattice from which a single best hypothesis is picked and sent to the hub for processing by the dialog manager.

Acoustic Modeling

During dialog interaction with the user, the audio server sends the acoustic samples to three Sphinx-II speech recognizers. While the language model is the same for each decoder, the acoustic models consist of (i) speaker independent analog telephone, (ii) female adapted analog telephone, and (iii) cellular telephone adapted acoustic model sets. Each decoder outputs a word string hypothesis along with a word-sequence probability for the best path. An intermediate server is used to examine each hypothesis and pass the most likely word string onto the natural language understanding module.

Language Modeling

The Communicator system is designed for end users to get up-to-date worldwide air travel, hotel and rental car information via the telephone. In the task there are word lists for countries, cities, states, airlines, etc. To train a robust language model, names are clustered into different classes. An utterance with class tagging is shown in Fig.2. In this example, *city*, *hour_number*, and *am_pm* are class names.

Original Utterance

I want to go from Boston to Portland around nine a_m

Class-Tagged Utterance

I want to go from [city:Boston] to [city:Portland] around [hour_number:nine] [am_pm:a_m]

Concept-Tagged Utterance

[I_want: I want to go] [depart_loc: from Boston] [arrive_loc: to Portland] [time:around nine a_m]

Figure 2. Examples of class-based and grammar-based language modeling

Each commonly used word takes one class. The probability of word W_i given class C_i is estimated from training corpora. After the corpora are correctly tagged, a back-off class-based trigram language model can be computed from the tagged corpora. We use the CMU-Cambridge Statistical Language Modeling Toolkit to compute our language models.

More recently, we have developed a dialog context dependent language model (LM) combining stochastic context free grammars (SCFGs) and n-grams [6,7]. Based on a spoken language production model in which a user picks a set of concepts with respective values and constructs word sequences using phrase generators associated with each concept in accordance with the dialog context, this LM computes the probability of a word, P(W), as

$$P(W) = P(W/C) \, P(C/S) \qquad (1)$$

where W is the sequence of words, C is the sequence of concepts and S is the dialog context. Here, the assumptions are (i) S is given, (ii) W is independent of S but C, and (iii) W and C associations are unambiguous. This formulation can be considered as a general extension of the standard class word based statistical language model as seen in Fig. 2.

The first term in (1) is modeled by SCFGs, one for each concept. The concepts are classes of phrases with the same meaning. Each SCFG is compiled into a stochastic recursive transition network (STRN). Our grammar is a semantic grammar since the nonterminals correspond to semantic concepts instead of syntactic constituents. The set of task specific concepts is augmented with a single word, multiple word and a small number of broad but unambigious part of speech (POS) classes to account for the phrases that are not covered by the grammar. These classes are considered as "filler" concepts within a unified framework. The second term in (1) is modeled as a pool of concept n-gram LMs. That is, we have a separate LM for each dialog context. At the moment, the dialog context is selected as the last question prompted by the system, as it is very simple and yet strongly predictive and constraining. SCFG and n-gram probabilities are learned by simple counting and smoothing. Our semantic grammars have a low degree of ambiguity and therefore do not require computationally intensive stochastic training and parsing techniques.

Experimental results with N-best list rescoring were found promising (5-6% relative improvement in WER). In addition, we have shown that a dynamic combining of our new LM and the standard class word n-gram (the LM currently in use in our system) should result in further improvements. At the present, we are interfacing the grammar LM to the speech recognizer using a word graph.

1.4 Confidence Server

Our prior work on confidence assessment has considered detection and rejection of word-level speech recognition errors and out-of-domain phrases using language model features [8]. More recently [9], we have considered detection and rejection of misrecognized units at the concept level. Because concepts are used to update the state of the dialog system, we believe that concept level confidence is vitally important to ensuring a graceful human-computer interaction. Our current work on concept error detection has considered language model features (e.g., LM back-off behavior, language model score) as well as acoustic features from the speech recognizer (e.g., normalized acoustic score, lattice density, phone perplexity). Confidence features are combined to compute word-level, concept-level, and utterance-level confidence scores.

1.5 Language Understanding

We use a modified version of the Phoenix [10] parser to map the speech recognizer output onto a sequence of semantic frames. A Phoenix frame is a named set of slots, where the slots represent related pieces of information. Each slot has an associated context-free semantic grammar that specifies word string patterns that can fill the slot. The grammars are compiled into Recursive Transition Networks, which are matched against the recognizer output to fill slots. Each filled slot contains a semantic parse tree with the slot name as root.

Phoenix has been modified to also produce an extracted representation of the parse that maps directly onto the task concept structures. For example, the utterance

"I want to go from Boston to Denver Tuesday morning"

would produce the extracted parse:

Flight_Constraint: Depart_Location.City.Boston
Flight_Constraint: Arrive_Location.City.Denver
Flight Constraints:[Date_Time].[Date].[Day_Name].tuesday
              [Time_Range].[Period_Of_Day].morning

1.6 Dialog Management

The Dialogue Manager controls the system's interaction with the user and the application server. It is responsible for deciding what action the system will take at each step in the interaction. The Dialogue Manager has several functions. It resolves ambiguities in the current interpretation; Estimates confidence in the extracted information; Clarifies the interpretation with the user if required; Integrates new input with the dialogue context; Builds database queries (SQL); Sends information to NL generation for presentation to user; and prompts the user for missing information.

We have developed a flexible, event driven dialogue manager in which the current context of the system is used to decide what to do next. The system does not use a dialogue network or a dialogue script, rather a general engine operates on the semantic representations and the current context to control the interaction flow. The Dialogue Manager receives the extracted parse. It then integrates the parse into the current context. Context consists of a set of frames and a set of global variables. As new extracted information arrives, it is put into the context frames and sometimes used to set global variables. The system provides a general-purpose library of routines for manipulating frames.

This "event driven" architecture functions similar to a production system. An incoming parse causes a set of actions to fire which modify the current context. After the parse has been integrated into the current context, the DM examines the context to decide what action to take next. The DM attempts the following actions in the order listed:

- Clarify if necessary
- Sign off if all done
- Retrieve data and present to user
- Prompt user for required information

The rules for deciding what to prompt for next are very straightforward. The frame in focus is set to be the frame produced in response to the user, or to the last system prompt.

- If there are unfilled required slots in the focus frame, then prompt for the highest priority unfilled slot in the frame.

- If there are no unfilled required slots in the focus frame, then prompt for the highest priority missing piece of information in the context.

Our mechanism does not have separate "user initiative" and "system initiative" modes. If the system has enough information to act on, then it does it. If it needs information, then it asks for it. The system does not require that the user respond to the prompt. The user can respond with anything and the system will parse the utterance and set the focus to the resulting frame. This allows the user to drive the dialog, but doesn't require it. The system prompts are organized locally, at the frame level. The dialog manager or user puts a frame in focus, and the system tries to fill it. This representation is easy to author, there is no separate dialog control specification required. It is also robust in that it has a simple control that has no state to lose track of.

An additional benefit of Dialog Manager mechanism is that it is very largely declarative. Most of the work done by a developer will be the creation of frames, forms and grammars. The system developer creates a task file that specifies the system ontology and templates for communicating about nodes in the hierarchy. The templates are filled in from the values in the frames to generate output in the desired language. This is the way we currently generate SQL queries and user prompts. An example task frame specification is:

Frame:Air
[Depart_Loc]+
  Prompt: "where are you departing from"
  [City_Name]*
        Confirm: "You are departing from $([City_Name]).
              Is that correct?"
        Sql: "dep_$[leg_num] in (select airport_code from
        airport_codes where city like '!%' $(and state_province
        like '[Depart_Loc].[State]'))"
  [Airport_Code]*

This example defines a frame with name Air and slot [Depart_Loc]. The child nodes of Depart_Loc are are [City_Name] and [Airport_Code]. The "+" after [Depart_Loc] indicates that it is a mandatory field. The Prompt string is the template for prompting for the node information. The "*" after [City_Name] and [Airport_Code] indicate that if either of them is filled, the parent node [Depart_Loc] is filled. The Confirm string is a template to prompt the user to confirm the values. The SQL string is the template to use the value in an SQL query to the database.

The system will prompt for all mandatory nodes that have prompts. Users may specify information in any order, but the system will prompt for whatever information is missing until the frame is complete.

1.7 Database & Internet Interface

The back-end interface consists of an SQL database and domain-specific Perl scripts for accessing information from the Internet. During operation, database requests are transmitted by the Dialog Manager to the database server via a formatted frame.

The back-end consists of a static and dynamic information component. Static tables contain data such as conversions between 3-letter airport codes and the city, state, and country of the airport (e.g., BOS for Boston Massachusetts). There are over 8000 airports in our database, 200 hotel chains, and 50 car rental companies. The dynamic information content consists of database tables for car, hotel, and airline flights.

When a database request is received, the Dialog Manager's SQL command is used to select records in local memory. If no records are found to match, the back-end can submit an HTTP-based request for the information via the Internet. Records returned from the Internet are then inserted as rows into the local SQL database and the SQL statement is once again applied.

1.8 Language Generation

The language generation module uses templates to generate text based on dialog speech acts. Example dialog acts include "prompt" for prompting the user for needed information, "summarize" for summarization of flights, hotels, and rental cars, and "clarify" for clarifying information such as departure and arrival cities that share the same name.

1.9 Text-to-Speech Synthesis

For audio output, we have developed a domain-dependent concatenative speech synthesizer. Our concatenative synthesizer can adjoin units ranging from phonemes, to words, to phrases and sentences. For domain modeling, we use a voice talent to record entire task-dependent utterances (e.g., "What are your travel plans?") as well as short phrases with carefully determined break points (e.g., "United flight", "ten", "thirty two", "departs Anchorage at"). Each utterance is orthographically transcribed and phonetically aligned using a HMM-based recognizer. Our research efforts for data collection are currently focused on methods for reducing the audible distortion at segment boundaries, optimization schemes for prompt generation, as well as tools for rapidly correcting boundary misalignments. In general, we find that some degree of hand-correction is always required in order to reduce distortions at concatenation points.

During synthesis, the text is automatically divided into individual sentences that are then synthesized and pipelined to the audio server. A text-to-phoneme conversion is applied using a phonetic dictionary. Words that do not appear in the phonetic dictionary are automatically pronounced using a multi-layer perceptron based pronunciation module. Here, a 5-letter context is extracted from the word to be pronounced. The letter input is fed through the MLP and a phonetic symbol (or possibly epsilon) is output by the network. By sliding the context window, we can extract the phonetic pronunciation of the word. The MLP is trained using letter-context and symbol output pairs from a large phonetic dictionary.

The selection of units to concatenate is determined using a hybrid search algorithm that operates at the word or phoneme level.

During synthesis, sections of word-level text that have been recorded are automatically concatenated. Unrecorded words or word sequences are synthesized using a Viterbi beam search across all available phonetic units. The cost function includes information regarding phonetic context, pitch, duration, and signal amplitude. Audio segments making up the best-path are then concatenated to generate the final sentence waveform.

2. DATA COLLECTION & EVALUATION

2.1 Data Collection Efforts

Local Collection Effort

The Center for Spoken Language Research maintains a dialup Communicator system for data collection[1]. Users wishing to use the dialogue system can register at our web site [1] and receive a PIN code and system telephone number. To date, our system has fielded over 1750 calls totaling over 25,000 utterances from nearly 400 registered users.

NIST Multi-Site Data Collection

During the months of June and July of 2000, The National Institute of Standards (NIST) conducted a multi-site data collection effort for the nine DARPA Communicator participants. Participating sites included: AT&T, IBM, BBN, SRI, CMU, Colorado, MIT, Lucent, and MITRE. In this data collection, a pool of potential users was selected from various parts of the United States by a market research firm. The selected subjects were native speakers of American English who were possible frequent travelers. Users were asked to perform nine tasks. The first seven tasks consisted of fixed scenarios for one-way and round-trip flights both within and outside of the United States. The final two tasks consisted of users making open-ended business or vacation.

2.2 System Evaluation

Task Completion

A total of 72 calls from NIST participants were received by the CU Communicator system. Of these, 44 callers were female and 28 were male. Each scenario was inspected by hand and compared against the scenario provided by NIST to the subject. For the two open-ended tasks, judgment was made based on what the user asked for with that of the data provided to the user. In total, 53/72 (73.6%) of the tasks were completed successfully. A detailed error analysis can be found in [11].

Word Error Rate Analysis

A total of 1327 utterances were recorded from the 72 NIST calls. Of these, 1264 contained user speech. At the time of the June 2000 NIST evaluation, the CU Communicator system did not implement voice-based barge-in. We noticed that one source of error was due to users who spoke before the recording process was started. Even though a tone was presented to the user to signify the time to speak, 6.9% of the utterances contained instances in which the user spoke before the tone. Since all users were exposed to several other Communicator systems that

---

[2] The system can be accessed toll-free at 1-866-735-5189

365

employed voice barge-in, there may be some effect from exposure to those systems. Table 3 summarizes the word error rates for the system utilizing the June 2000 NIST data as the test set. Overall, the system had a word error rate (WER) of 26.0% when parallel gender-dependent decoders were utilized. Since June of 2000, we have collected an additional 15,000 task-dependent utterances. With the extra data, we were able to remove our dependence on the CMU Communicator training data [12]. When the language model was reestimated and language model weights reoptimized using only CU Communicator data, the WER dropped from 26.0% to 22.5%. This amounts to a 13.5% relative reduction in WER.

Table 1: CU Communicator Word Error Rates for (A) Speaker Independent acoustic models and June 2000 language model, (B) Gender-dependent parallel recognizers with June 2000 Language Model, and (C) Language Model retrained in December 2000.

June 2000 NIST Evaluation Data, 1264 utterances, 72 speakers	Word Error Rate
(A) Speaker Indep. HMMs (LM#1)	29.8%
(B) Gender Dependent HMMs (LM#1)	26.0%
(C) Gender Dependent HMMs (LM#2)	22.5%

Core Metrics

Sites in the DARPA Communicator program agreed to log a common set of metrics for their systems. The proposed set of metrics was: Task Completion, Time to Completion, Turns to Completion, User Words/Turn, System Words/Turn, User Concepts/Turn, Concept Efficiency, State of Itinerary, Error Messages, Help Messages, Response Latency, User Words to Completion, System Words to Completion, User Repeats, System Repeats/Reprompts, Word Error, Mean Length of System Utterance, and Mean Length of System Turn.

Table 2: Dialogue system evaluation metrics

Item	Min	Mean	Max
Time to Completion (secs)	120.9	260.3	537.2
Total Turns to Completion	23	37.6	61
Response Latency (secs)	1.5	1.9	2.4
User Words to Task End	19	39.4	105
System Words to End	173	331.9	914
Number of Reprompts	0	2.4	15

Table 2 summarizes results obtained from metrics derived automatically from the logged timing markers for the calls in which the user completed the task assigned to them. The average time to task completion is 260. During this period there are an average of 19 user turns and 19 computer turns (37.6 average total turns). The average response latency was 1.86 seconds. The response latency also includes the time required to access the data live from the Internet travel information provider.

3. CU MOVE

3.1 Task Overview

The "CU Move" system represents our work towards achieving graceful human-computer interaction in automobile environments. Initially, we have considered the task of vehicle route planning and navigation. As our work progresses, we will expand our dialog system to new tasks such as information retrieval and summarization and multimedia access.

The problem of voice dialog within vehicle environments offers some important speech research challenges. Speech recognition in car environments is in general fragile, with word-error-rates (WER) ranging from 30-65% depending on driving conditions. These changing environmental conditions include speaker changes (task stress, emotion, Lombard effect, etc.) as well as the acoustic environment (road/wind noise from windows, air conditioning, engine noise, exterior traffic, etc.).

In developing the CU-Move system [13,14], there are a number of research challenges that must be overcome to achieve reliable and natural voice interaction within the car environment. Since the speaker is performing a task (driving the vehicle), the driver will experience a measured level of user task stress and therefore this should be included in the speaker-modeling phase. Previous studies have clearly shown that the effects of speaker stress and Lombard effect can cause speech recognition systems to fail rapidly. In addition, microphone type and placement for in-vehicle speech collection can impact the level of acoustic background noise and speech recognition performance.

3.2 Signal Processing

Our research for robust recognition in automobile environments is concentrated on development of an intelligent microphone array. Here, we employ a Gaussian Mixture Model (GMM) based environmental classification scheme to characterize the noise conditions in the automobile. By integrating an environmental classification system into the microphone array design, decisions can be made as to how best to utilize a noise-adaptive frequency-partitioned iterative enhancement algorithm [15,16] or model-based adaptation algorithms [17,18] during decoding to optimize speech recognition accuracy on the beam-formed signal.

3.3 Data Collection

A five-channel microphone array was constructed using Knowles microphones and a multi-channel data recorder housing built (Fostex) for in-vehicle data collection. An additional reference microphone is situated behind the driver's seat. Fig. 3 shows the constructed microphone array and data recorder housing.

Figure 3: Microphone array and reference microphone (left), Fostex multi-channel data recorder (right).

As part of the CU-Move system formulation, a two phase data collection plan has been initiated. Phase I focuses on collecting acoustic noise and probe speech from a variety of cars and driving conditions. Phase II focuses on a extensive speaker collection across multiple U.S. sites. A total of eight vehicles have been selected for acoustic noise analysis. These include the following: a compact car, minivan, cargo van, sport utility vehicle (SUV), compact and full size trucks, sports car, full size luxury car. A fixed 10 mile route through Boulder, CO was used for Phase I data collection. The route consisted of city (25 & 45mph) and highway driving (45 & 65mph). The route included stop-and-go traffic, and prescribed locations where driver/passenger windows, turn signals, wiper blades, air conditioning were operated. Each data collection run per car lasted approximately 35-45 minutes. A detailed acoustic analysis of Phase I data can be found in [13]. Our plan is to begin Phase II speech/dialogue data collection during spring 2001, which will include (i) phonetically balanced utterances, (ii) task-specific vocabularies, (iii) natural extemporaneous speech, and (iv) human-to-human and Wizard-of-Oz (WOZ) interaction with CU-Communicator and CU-Move dialog systems.

3.4 Prototype Dialog System

Finally, we have developed a prototype dialog system for data collection in the car environment. The dialog system is based on the MIT Galaxy-II Hub architecture with base system components derived from the CU Communicator system [1]. Users interacting with the dialog system can enter their origin and destination address by voice. Currently, 1107 street names for Boulder, CO area are modeled. The system can resolve street addresses by business name via interaction with an Internet telephone book. This allows users to ask more natural route queries (e.g., "I need an auto repair shop", or "I need to get to the Boulder Marriott"). The dialog system automatically retrieves the driving instructions from the Internet using an online WWW route direction provider. Once downloaded, the driving directions are queried locally from an SQL database. During interaction, users mark their location on the route by providing spoken odometer readings. Odometer readings are needed since GPS information has not yet been integrated into the prototype dialog system. Given the odometer reading of the vehicle as an estimate of position, route information such as turn descriptions, distances, and summaries can be queried during travel (e.g., "What's my next turn", "How far is it", etc.).

The prototype system uses the CMU Sphinx-II speech recognizer with cellular telephone acoustic models along with the Phoenix Parser [10] for semantic parsing. The dialog manager is mixed-initiative and event driven. For route guidance, the natural language generator formats the driving instructions before presentation to the user by the text-to-speech server. For example, the direction, "Park Ave W. becomes 22nd St." is reformatted to, "Park Avenue West becomes Twenty Second Street". Here, knowledge of the task-domain can be used to significantly improve the quality of the output text. For speech synthesis, we have developed a Hub-compliant server that interfaces to the AT&T NextGen speech synthesizer.

3.5 Future Work

We have developed a Hub compliant server that interfaces a Garmin GPS-III global positioning device to a mobile computer via a serial port link. The GPS server reports vehicle velocity in the X,Y,Z directions as well as real-time updates of vehicle position in latitude and longitude. HRL Laboratories has developed a route server that interfaces to a major navigation content provider. The HRL route server can take GPS

coordinates as inputs and can describe route maneuvers in terms of GPS coordinates. In the near-term, we will interface our GPS server to the HRL route server in order to provide real-time updating of vehicle position. This will eliminate the need for periodic location update by the user and also will allow for more interesting dialogs to be established (e.g., the computer might proactively tell the user about upcoming points of interest, etc.).

4. REFERENCES

[1] http://communicator.colorado.edu

[2] W. Ward, B. Pellom, "The CU Communicator System," *IEEE Workshop on Automatic Speech Recognition and Understanding*, Keystone Colorado, December, 1999.

[3] http://fofoca.mitre.org

[4] Seneff, S., Hurley, E., Lau, R., Pao, C., Schmid, P., Zue, V., "Galaxy-II: A Reference Architecture for Conversational System Development," *Proc. ICSLP*, Sydney Australia, Vol. 3, pp. 931-934, 1998.

[5] Ravishankar, M.K., "Efficient Algorithms for Speech Recognition". Unpublished Dissertation CMU-CS-96-138, Carnegie Mellon University, 1996

[6] K. Hacioglu, W. Ward, "Dialog-Context Dependent Language Modeling Using N-Grams and Stochastic Context-Free Grammars", *Proc. IEEE ICASSP*, Salt Lake City, May 2001.

[7] K. Hacioglu, W. Ward, "Combining Language Models : Oracle Approach", *Proc. Human Language Technology Conference*, San Diego, March 2001.

[8] R. San-Segundo, B. Pellom, W. Ward, J. M. Pardo, "Confidence Measures for Dialogue Management in the CU Communicator System," *Proc. IEEE ICASSP*, Istanbul Turkey, June 2000.

[9] R. San-Segundo, B. Pellom, K. Hacioglu, W. Ward, J.M. Pardo, "Confidence Measures for Dialogue Systems," *Proc. IEEE ICASSP*, Salt Lake City, May 2001.

[10] Ward, W., "Extracting Information From Spontaneous Speech", *Proc. ICSLP*, September 1994.

[11] B. Pellom, W. Ward, S. Pradhan, "The CU Communicator: An Architecture for Dialogue Systems", *Proc. ICSLP*, Beijing China, November 2000.

[12] Eskenazi, M., Rudnicky, A., Gregory, K., Constantinides, P., Brennan, R., Bennett, K., Allen, J., "Data Collection and Processing in the Carnegie Mellon Communicator," *Proc. Eurospeech-99*, Budapest, Hungary.

[13] J.H.L. Hansen, J. Plucienkowski, S. Gallant, B.L. Pellom, W. Ward, "CU-Move: Robust Speech Processing for In-Vehicle Speech Systems," *Proc. ICSLP*, vol. 1, pp. 524-527, Beijing, China, Oct. 2000.

[14] http://cumove.colorado.edu/

[15] J.H.L. Hansen, M.A. Clements, "Constrained Iterative Speech Enhancement with Application to Speech Recognition," *IEEE Trans. Signal Proc.*, 39(4):795-805, 1991.

[16] B. Pellom, J.H.L. Hansen, "An Improved Constrained Iterative Speech Enhancement Algorithm for Colored Noise Environments," IEEE Trans. Speech & Audio Proc., 6(6):573-79, 1998.

[17] R. Sarikaya, J.H.L. Hansen, "Improved Jacobian Adaptation for Fast Acoustic Model Adaptation in Noisy Speech Recognition," *Proc. ICSLP*, vol. 3, pp. 702-705, Beijing, China, Oct. 2000.

[18] R. Sarikaya, J.H.L. Hansen, "PCA-PMC: A novel use of a priori knowledge for fast model combination," *Proc. ICASSP*, vol. II, pp. 1113-1116, Istanbul, Turkey, June 2000.

The Use of Dynamic Segment Scoring for Language-Independent Question Answering[*]

Daniel Pack[†] and Clifford Weinstein
MIT Lincoln Laboratory
244 Wood Street
Lexington, Massachusettes
dpack@ll.mit.edu
cjw@ll.mit.edu

ABSTRACT

This paper presents a novel language-independent question/answering (Q/A) system based on natural language processing techniques, shallow query understanding, dynamic sliding window techniques, and statistical proximity distribution matching techniques. The performance of the proposed system using the latest Text REtrieval Conference (TREC-8) data was comparable to results reported by the top TREC-8 contenders.

Keywords

Question/Answer, Natural Language Processing, Query Understanding, Dynamic Sliding Window, Proximity Distribution

1. INTRODUCTION

Over the past decade, the TREC community has invested its efforts on and advanced technologies of automatic information retrieval systems. Recently, the same community decided to divide the traditional information retrieval task to several so called tracks: the cross-language information retrieval track, the filtering track, the interactive track, the question and answering track, the query track, the spoken document retrieval track, and the web track[6]. The decision is mainly due to the mature technologies in the traditional information retrieval field and the desire to expand the technologies to additional areas of interest. The goal of the question and answering track is the development of systems that generate concise answers to user queries. This goal is similar in nature to the goal of a traditional information retrieval system where relevant

[*]This work was funded by DARPA under Air Force Contract F19628-00-c-0002. Opinions, interpretations, conclusions, and recommendations are those of the authors and do not necessarily represent the views of the agency or the US Air Force.

[†]Daniel Pack is an associate professor of Electrical Engineering from the Air Force Academy on his sabbatical leave.

Proceedings of HLT 2001, First International Conference on Human Language Technology Research, J. Allan, ed., Morgan Kaufmann, San Francisco, 2001.

documents are extracted for user queries; users are then required to read through the selected documents to find answers. In a question answering system, it is the system's responsibility to find the answers to queries.

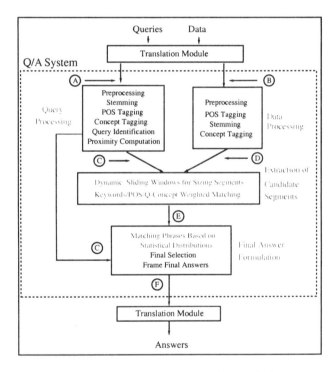

Figure 1: The Question and Answering System Architecture

In this paper, we present a Q/A system that combines (1) natural language processing techniques, (2) query understanding, (3) dynamic sliding window techniques, and (4) keyword distance proximity distribution matching techniques for a language-independent question/answering system. The system architecture is shown in Figure 1. We call the system language-independent since the system architecture remains the same regardless of any particular language used. The only requirement is to have a translation module at the front end and the back end of our system. Developing such systems is becoming increasingly important as the diverse communities across national boundaries are brought together through the internet. The effectiveness of the proposed system architecture is validated with experimental results.

<P>
"I always knew they wanted," he said. "They wanted something about Joe."
<\P>
<P>
One day, though, someone ran a different notion by DOM: A book about 1941.
<\P>
<P>
If ever the major leagues had a magical, almost mythic year, it was 1941. There was Joe DiMaggio's 56-game hitting streak. There was Ted Williams' .406 batting average. There was the anticipated, but nonetheless gripping, death of Lou Gehrig. There was Mickey Owen's dropped third strike in the World Series.
<\P>
<P>
And beyond the outfield walls, there was a worried America, waiting and watching as World War II headed its way. Two months after the 1941 world Series, the Japanese planes attacked Pearl Harbor.
<\P>

(a) input

i/PRONOUN always/GENERALITY know/KNOWLEDGE what/WHAT
they/PRONOUN want/DESIRE he/PRONOUN say/AFFIRMATION they/PRONOUN
want/DESIRE something/SUBSTANTIALITY about/ABOUT joe/PERSON one/NUMBER
day/PERIOD though/COMPENSATION someone/PRONOUN run/CONTINUANCE a /DT
different/DIFFERENCE notion/IDEA by/BY dom/PERSON a/DT book/BOOK about/ABOUT
1941/TIME if/CIRCUMSTANCE ever/PERPETUITY the/DT major/SIGNIFICANT league/PARTY
had/POSSESSION a/DT magical/SORCERY almost/IMPERFECTION mythic/IMAGINATION
year/PERIOD it/PRONOUN was/EXISTENCE   DATE/TIME   there/PRESENCE was/EXISTENCE
joe/PERSON dimaggio/PERSON 's/POS 56-game/TIME hit/IMPULSE streak/SEQUENCE
there/PRESENCE was/EXISTENCE t/PERSON william/PERSON 406/NUMBER bat/AMUSEMENT
average/MEAN there/PRESENCE was/EXISTENCE the/DT anticipated/PERSON but/BUT
nonetheless/COMPENSATION grip/TENACITY death/DEATH of/OF lou/PERSON gehrig/PERSON
there/PRESENCE was/EXISTENCE mickey/PERSON owen/PERSON 's/POS drop/DESCENT
third/NUMBER strike/ATTACK in/IN the/DT world/WORLD series/SEQUENCE and/AND
watch/ATTENTION as/AS world/WORLD war/WARFARE ii/NUMBER head/DIRECTOR its/PRONOUN
way/DEGREE two/NUMBER month/PERIOD after/POSTERIORITY the/DT 1941/TIME world/WORLD
series/SEQUENCE the/DT japanese/COUNTRY plane/AIRCRAFT attack/ATTACK peral/ORNAMENT
harbor/STORE

(b) output

Figure 2: A sample input and output of the Data Processing module

2. SYSTEM DESCRIPTION

In this section we present the system architecture of the proposed Q/A system and describe its components in detail. The system contains five different modules as shown in Figure 1. The top module is responsible for translating input queries and a set of documents to a common language. The common coalition language system developed at MIT Lincoln Laboratory (CCLINC)[8] performs the translation tasks. For the work reported here, we assume that queries are in English, documents are in either English or Korean, and answers are returned in English. Our focus in this paper is on the four modules between the two translation modules (modules contained in the box with a dotted line) in Figure 1.

The Query Processing module and the Data Processing module use natural language processing techniques such as parsing, morphological stemming and part of speech and concept tagging for word sense disambiguation to extract critical query and document information. In addition, the Query Processing module categorizes queries and assigns appropriate answer concepts associated with each query. In the next two modules, candidate segments with optimal matching scores of keywords and answer concepts are extracted using dynamic sliding windowing techniques. The candidate segments are then further analyzed based on the similarities of proximity distributions of search keywords and rank ordered.

A case example, a query and a document segment from the TREC-8 official data, is used throughout this section to illustrate functions of the four processing modules. Our illustration starts with the following query entering the Query Processing module.

Query: *In what year did Joe DiMaggio compile his 56-game hitting streak?*

Several processes take place within the Query Processing module: a preprocessing unit removes punctuation marks and extra spaces; a trained Brill tagger[1] tags each word with corresponding part of speech tags; a set of morphological rules and a concept trained Brill tagger convert words into their root forms and determine answer concepts; a proximity indexing unit records the keyword positions in queries; and a query identification/post processing unit removes stop words and formats the output, as shown below.

Output of the Query Processing module: *Question Special 101 NNT year TIME 2 NNP joe PERSON 4 NNP dimaggio PERSON 5 VB compile ASSEMBLAGE 6 NN 56-game TIME 8 VB hit IMPULSE 9 NN streak SEQUENCE 10*

The output contains critical query information including answer concepts which are identified by categorizing queries using a method similar in spirit to extracting named entities[5, 4], named focuses[2], and question-answer tokens[3]. Each stemmed keyword is tagged with a POS tag, a concept tag, and an index number. The POS tags are used to discriminate search terms by assigning different weights, the concept tags are used to identify answer concepts, and the index numbers are used to compute proximity values between terms for matching.

Documents, represented with symbol B in Figure 1, go through a similar procedure in the Data Processing Module as did a query in the Query Processing Module. Due to the large data size of the document collection, the documents are processed off line. The input and the output of the module for an example document segment is shown in Figure 2. The output of the data processing module is processed documents with stemmed words and their associated concepts, represented with symbol D in Figure 1.

The Extraction of Candidate Segments module selects candidate segments that contain answers. The size of each candidate segment is determined by a dynamic sliding window, which uses an iterative procedure to maximize the score of a segment as its size changes. To ensure the optimal segmentation of a document, adjacent segments are overlapped while the size of the window can vary from one sentence to tens of sentences, as shown in Figure 3. To determine the optimal size for a current sliding window, the score for an initial window with one sentence is compared to scores corre-

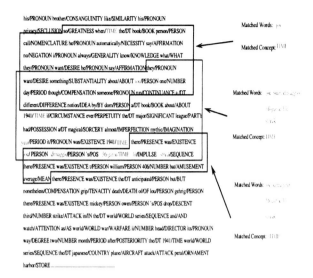

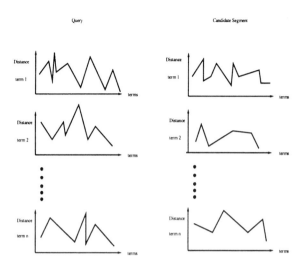

Figure 4: Matching distance distributions of keywords between a query and a candidate segment

Figure 3: An example of applying dynamic sliding window techniques: Three adjacent optimally formulated windows are shown. The top window segment with four sentences contains the query concept "TIME" and matching word "joe." The second window with five sentences contains the query concept and six keywords. The last window with two sentences contains the query concept and five keywords.

keywords.

Recall the format of the output from the query processing module. Using the differences between index numbers to specify physical distance relationships among query keywords, we can compute the corresponding proximity distributions of keywords in candidate segments. We create a list of distributions by computing proximity distances from a keyword to the rest of keywords.

sponding to windows with increasing number of sentences. The scoring criteria is based on appearances of answer concepts and query keywords in candidate segments. Weighted scores are assigned to keywords in segments; the contribution of a match varies according to the query keyword's part of speech tag. Specifically, the score for a match decreases according to the following priority list in the order shown: (1) answer concept, (2) quoted keyword, (3) proper noun keyword, (4) noun keyword, and (5) all other keyword.

Figure 3 shows an example case of using the dynamic sliding window technique. In this figure, the darkened window contains the answer to the example query, *1941*. Optimally sized windows form candidate segments that are rank ordered based on their scores. Currently, we select and send top 200 segments per query (symbol E in Figure 1) to the Final Answer Formulation module.

The Final Answer Formulation module takes an advantage of the keyword proximity distributions in queries and the corresponding statistical keyword distributions in candidate segments to further distinguish segments with high likelihoods of containing answers from those that merely contain search terms and query concepts. The module creates a list of proximity distributions from a keyword to the rest of keywords as shown in Figure 4. In this figure, the left hand column shows the distance distributions from a query keyword to the rest of query keywords. The index numbers for query keywords are used here to compute the distributions. The right column shows the corresponding distance distributions in a candidate segment. Once the distributions are available, the job of the Final Answer Formulation module is to search for candidate segments with similar keyword proximity distributions to those appeared in queries. By distance, we mean the word counts that separate two

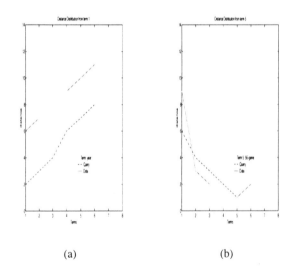

(a)   (b)

Figure 5: Proximity distribution examples

Figure 5 shows two actual distribution graphs of our example. Frame (a) shows that the distances from keyword *year* in query (dashed line) to other keywords. The vertical axis represents physical word distance while the horizontal axis denotes query terms.

370

	I	II	III	IV	V	VI	VII
I	(0,0)	(2,6)	(3,7)	(4,)	(6,9)	(7,10)	(8,11)
II	(2,6)	(0,0)	(1,1)	(2,)	(4,3)	(5,4)	(6,5)
III	(3,7)	(1,1)	(0,0)	(1,)	(3,2)	(4,3)	(5,4)
IV	(4,)	(2,)	(1,)	(0,)	(2,)	(3,)	(4,)
V	(6,9)	(4,3)	(3,2)	(2,)	(0,0)	(1,1)	(2,2)
VI	(7,10)	(5,4)	(4,3)	(3,)	(1,1)	(0,0)	(1,1)
VII	(8,11)	(6,5)	(5,4)	(4,)	(2,2),	(1,1)	(0,0)

Table 1: Distance pairs separating query keywords

The distance values grow from 2 for keyword *joe* to 8 for keyword *streak*. The solid line shows the distance distribution of the same keywords appearing in a candidate segment. The numbers vary from 6 for keyword *joe* to 11 for keyword *streak*. The pattern of gradual increase, however, in both lines indicates a similarity between the two distributions. The break in the solid line is caused by the missing term, *compile*, in the candidate segment. Frame (b) again shows the proximity distributions from keyword *56-game* to the rest of keywords in the query and the candidate segment. The distance values for the candidate segment are 9, 3, 2, 1, and 2 while the corresponding distances in the query are 6, 4, 3, 1, and 2. Note that the last two data points are identical for both distributions. Again, we find a similar distribution pattern in both the query and the candidate segment. The similarities between the variances of the distributions in both a query and a candidate segment determine the likelihood of the particular segment containing an answer to the query. Table 1 shows the actual distance differences between keywords in the query and the candidate segment. Keywords year, joe, dimaggio, compile, 56-game, hit, and streak are represented by I, II, III, IV, V, VI, and VII, respectively. For each pair in the table, the first number represents the distance between the corresponding keywords (row/column) in the query while the second number shows the distance between the same keywords in the candidate segment. Blanks represent that distances can not be computed because the particular keyword pair could not be found in the candidate segment.

The similarities between the variances of the distributions in both a query and a candidate segment determine the likelihood of the particular segment containing an answer to the query. For the experiments, we used a simplified version of the distribution matching where only adjacent query term distances were compared.

The equation for assigning a final score for each candidate segment is as follows.

$$
\begin{aligned}
\text{Segment Score} \quad = \quad &\text{Normalized Original Score} \\
+ \quad &\text{Current Pair Proximity Score} \\
+ \quad &\text{Processed Term Score}
\end{aligned}
$$

where Normalized Original Score represents the score generated by the Extraction of the Candidate Segment module and

$$
\text{Current Pair Proximity Score} =
$$

$$
\frac{\frac{1}{|diff|+1} \times std}{max} \times \frac{1}{\text{number of term pairs in query}}
$$

$$
\text{Processed Term Score} = \text{current score} \times
$$

$$
\frac{\text{number of term pairs processed in query}}{\text{number of term pairs in query}}
$$

where symbol *max* is a normalization factor and symbol *diff* is the proximity difference between a query and a candidate segment for a given pair of keywords. Symbol *std* is the standard deviation of the distance values between two keywords in the candidate segments. The standard deviation term helps further differentiate scoring between a common pair and pairs which do not appear often.

Once all candidate segments are scored, the top five[1] segments are selected based on their final scores: a segment with the minimum length was chosen in cases when scores for multiple segments are equal. The top segment for the example candidate at this point is

They wanted something about Joe. One day, though, someone ran a different notion by Dom: A book about 1941. If ever the major leagues had a magical, almost mythic year, it was 1941. There was Joe Dimaggio's 56-game hitting streak.

The selected segments are then sent to the final answer framing stage where only the corresponding keywords matching desired question concepts are extracted. The final answer for the example query is "1941" which had associated concept tag "TIME." This answer is the output fed into the translation module, if necessary, shown as symbol F in Figure 1. Presently, our system does not perform the final answer framing process using the concept tags. The system simply applys a set of rules to remove stop words to reduce the final answer size.

3. EXPERIMENTAL RESULTS

We conducted two different experiments: monolingual and translingual experiments. The monolingual experiment used the TREC-8 questions and the documents extracted by the AT & T information retrieval engine[5]. For the translingual experiment, our preliminary experimental results are based on a set of 10 queries in English and 877 Korean newspaper articles, containing Korean equivalent word *missile*.

We adopted the same criteria used at the TREC-8 Q/A track meeting [7] for our system evaluation. For the monolingual experiment, answers to two queries didn't exist in the original data. Furthermore, we found that answers to four additional queries were not contained in the retrieved documents, making the total number of queries to 194. The system found correct answers in the top five selections for 73.2% of questions (142/194). Answers to 103 queries were found as the first selections. Table 2 shows the categorized results based on question types. The average number of words per answer was 34.68 (approximately 244 bytes/answer). The value will significantly decrease provided that the final answer framing stage in the Final Answer Formulation module is implemented.

The current overall score would have placed the system in the top third at the TREC-8 Q/A meeting[7].[2] The current research focus

---

[1] The particular number, five, is chosen to adhere the criteria of the TREC Q/A Track evaluation.

[2] We hasten to add that a fair comparison can only be made in the

Type	# Q	Score	Type	# Q	Score
Who	45/194	0.7378	How	31/194	0.4707
When	18/194	0.5185	Which	7/194	0.7857
Where	21/194	0.5754	Why	2/194	0.625
What	58/194	0.6261	Name	4/194	0.75
Others	7/194	0.1429	**Overall**	194/194	0.6019

Table 2: Experimental Results using TREC-8 Data

is to further improve the system performance using query concept term matching in addition to the current query keyword matching. We also plan to devise better tools to answer non-standard queries.

For the translingual Q/A experiment, the following 10 queries were used.

- Which country launched a missile?

- Which countries are involved in missile development?

- What is the difference between missile and satellite?

- What is the status of North Korea's missile technology?

- What did North Korea request to United States for ceasing of their missile export?

- Why did North Korea launch a missile?

- Where did the missile land?

- When was a missile launched?

- What is the South Korean government policy toward North Korea?

The overall score for the translingual experiment was 0.4833. This performance is achieved by turning off the proximity distribution process since the translation did not generate expressions similar to ones found in the queries[3]. Answers were not found in the top five selections for two queries; answers for only two queries were found as the top selections (20% versus approximately 53% for the English experiment). The performance discrepancies between the monolingual Q/A experiment and the translingual Q/A experiment are twofold. A higher percentage of translingual questions required a "deep" level understanding of the queries to identify correct answers in the database. The second, more important factor, was that the translated documents were not true equivalents of the original Korean documents. Many sentences were not fully parsed, resorting to a word by word translation without the use of contextual information. We are currently exploring ways to overcome the problem. Nevertheless, given the early stage of the system development, we are encouraged by the high translingual performance of the system.

4. CONCLUSION

In this paper, we showed a novel language-independent question and answering system. The unique features of the system are the use of the POS tags to distinguish terms appearing in queries for differential weights, dynamic sliding windows that automatically adjust the optimal size of a candidate segment containing answers, and the proximity matching techniques that award similarities between query keyword distance distributions and the corresponding distributions in data segments for best fit, which is based on statistical distributions of search terms in the data set. The system also incorporates popular methods of categorizing queries to identify desired answers using concept tags and natural language processing techniques such as the preprocessing, stemming, and POS tagging, which also contributed to the high performance results reported.

5. REFERENCES

[1] E. Brill, " A Simple Rule-Based part of Speech Tagger," *Proceedings of the Third Conference on Applied. Natural Language Processing*,pp.152-155, ACL, Trento, Italy, 31 March - 3 April, 1992.

[2] Dan Moldovan, Sanda Harabagiu, Marius Pasca, Rada Mihalcea, Richard Goodrumm, Roxana Girju, and Vasile Rus, "LASSO: A Tool for Surfing the Answer Net," *Proceedings of the Eighth Text REtrieval Conference*, pp. 175-184, November, 1999.

[3] John Prager, Dragomir Radev, Eric Brown, Anni Coden, Valerie Samn, "The Use of Predictive Annotation for Question Answering in TREC-8," *Proceedings of the Eighth Text REtrieval Conference*, pp. 399-410, November, 1999.

[4] Rohini Srihari and Wei Li, "Information Extraction Supported Question Answering," *Proceedings of the Eighth Text REtrieval Conference*, pp.185-196, November 1999.

[5] Amit Singhal, John Choi, Donald Hindle, David Lewis, Fernando Pereira, "AT & T at Trec-7," *Proceedings of the Seventh Text REtrieval Conference*, pp. 239-252, November, 1998.

[6] Ellen Voorhees and Donna Harman, "Overview of the Eighth Text REtrieval Conference(TREC-8)," *Proceedings of the Eighth Text REtrieval Conference*, November, 1999.

[7] Ellen Voorhees and Dawn Tice, "The TREC-8 Question Answering Track Evaluation," *Proceedings of the Eighth Text REtrieval Conference*, November, 1999.

[8] Clifford Weinstein, Young-Suk Lee, Stephanie Seneff, Dinesh Tummala, Beth Carlson, John Lynch, Jun-Taik Hwang, and Linda Kukolich, "Automated English-Korean Translation for Enhanced Coalition Communications," *The Lincoln Laboratory Journal*, vol. 10, no. 1, pp. 35-60, 1997.

---

next TREC meeting since our system was able to exploit the published queries while other systems did not.

[3] It was difficult to separate the translingual Q/A system performance from the performance of the translation system since the Q/A system results depended on the accurate document translation.

Using Speech and Language Technology to Coach Reading

Patti Price

Formerly BravoBrava! LLC

Now PPRICE Speech and Language

1-650-503-7053

pjp@pprice.com

Luc Julia

BravoBrava! LLC

32980 AlvaradoNiles Road, Suite 856

Union City, CA 94587

1-510-477-0493

Julia@bravobrava.com

ABSTRACT

BravoBrava! is expanding the repertoire of commercial user interfaces by incorporating multimodal techniques combining traditional point and click interfaces with speech recognition, speech synthesis, and gesture recognition. One of these applications is software to help children read. While the child reads aloud, the computer keeps the child on track and offers feedback when the child has difficulty. The feedback can be as subtle as changing the text color for a well articulated phrase or as friendly as a cartoon character that talks. The computer is infinitely patient and can keep detailed records of the child's progress. The reading software is being commercialized by BravoBrava!'s spinoff company, SUP Inc.

Keywords: Reading, pedagogy

Figure 1. Here is an example from a sample story. The system tracks the reading and intervenes when help is needed. This screen shows a sample intervention if the child stumbles on the word 'butterflies'.

Proceedings of HLT 2001, First International Conference on Human Language Technology Research, J. Allan, ed., Morgan Kaufmann, San Francisco, 2001.

1. INTRODUCTION

Our vision is to use technology to provide a high-quality, low cost reading coach that delivers voice-activated reading instruction, practice, and assessment over electronic media. Reading is fundamental; it can also be fun. However, about 40% of mainstream 4th graders cannot read at the basic level. One of our country's critical needs is to improve reading performance for *all* children since their future, both individually and together, depends on literacy. Reading level predicts economic performance for both individuals and societies.

Beyond the basics, as reviewed in the recent report of the National Reading Panel (2000), engaging children in supported oral reading is the most valuable means toward building their reading proficiency. At present, however, the only means of giving children such practice is by finding a human adult who will sit with them and help them. However, technology can provide an automated reading coach to break through this bottleneck, so that every child in every school can get the support that she or he needs. This technology will help reduce the digital divide, and provide an unprecedented level of tracking data to leverage teachers' instruction and assessment efforts and to build the next generation of intervention techniques.

2. SUP'S APPROACH

SUP targets the stage at which children have learned the letter to sound rules but are still struggling to gain vocabulary and fluency. This stage has sometimes been called the transition from 'learning to read' to 'reading to learn' and comes just after the stage requiring explicit pronunciation and vocabulary tutoring, provided by Mostow's Project Listen at CMU and other reading software. At this stage in reading development, language skills are usually too poor to make traditional dictionaries much of a help. Dictionaries disrupt the child's focus on the text being read, offer too many definitions, and usually provide definitions that are harder for the child to read than the original text. Instead, SUP provides a generalized 'dictionary', the Reading Resource, to give immediate context specific help when needed, much the way a human reading coach might intervene. "SUPplementing" text with the Reading Resource, which includes word definitions, sample sentences, graphics and multimedia can create an engaging environment for learning. However, the immediacy and context-specificity of this resource aims to maintain the child's focus on the material being read. Becoming engaged in the text itself is the real goal of reading. SUPplementation can make texts accessible to children that would otherwise be above their reading level, so that the content of the text can draw them into the desire to read. Vocabulary and grammatical knowledge grow with experience of more words in more contexts.

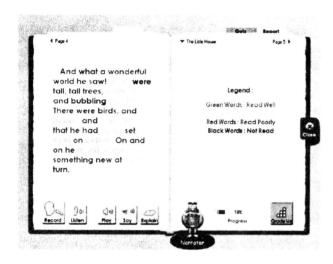

Figure 2. The screen shot above a sample after the child has asked for a display of how well the selection was read.

SUP has developed a modular architecture that allows for rapid reconfiguration:

- The current demonstration uses Microsoft speech recognition software. However, the architecture supports the use of other recognizers, and we have experimented with others for use on other platforms.

- The audio outputs can be from recorded waveforms or, for maximum flexibility, can use a text to speech synthesis system.

- Any text can flow through the system for reading practice.

Although explicit measures, such as a quiz to assess comprehension or vocabulary, can be included, several automatic measures are important by-products of use of the tool:

- Total number of words read by session, and which were fluent or not

- Words per minute as a function of time

- Level of the material read as a function of time

- Number of times intervention of the Reading Resource was used

- Number of times the child had the story read to him/her

- The actual recordings of what was read

3. FUTURE DIRECTIONS

Of course, such software will not help unless it gets into the hands of the children who need it. Therefore, an important strategy of the company is to support as many different platforms as possible to enable this goal. The modular architecture of the system facilitates transition to various platforms. Similarly, to be of maximal interest to the most children, we need as much appealing content as possible. In the area of human language technology, we hope such technology will evolve to automatically provide:

- Context-specific definitions

- Context-specific and child-specific synonyms

- Rewriting of complex phrases into simpler ones

Solving these problems completely is a major research project. However, we believe that with careful matchmaking between the technical possibilities and the real needs of beginning readers that progress can be made in the near term.

We hope that experience in the usability trials, just beginning, will also help us to plan similar products for adult language learners and learners of English as a second language. Reading is still the principal way that people learn information. In this information age, reading well is crucial to the individual and to society.

AUTHOR INDEX